O9-BUB-328

Network Protocol Handbook

McGraw-Hill Series on Computer Communications

BLACK • *Network Management Standards*

BLACK • *The V Series Recommendations: Protocols for Data Communications Over the Telephone Network*

BLACK • *The X Series Recommendations: Protocols for Data Communications Networks*

BLACK • *TCP/IP and Related Protocols*

FEIT • *TCP/IP: Architecture, Protocols, and Implementation*

HUGHES • *Data Communications*

KIMBERLY • *Electronic Data Interchange*

MINOLI • *1st, 2nd, and Next Generation LANs*

NAUGLE • *Local Area Networking*

RADICATI • *Electronic Mail: An Introduction to the X.400 Message Handling Standards*

WHITE • *Internetworking and Addressing*

Network Protocol Handbook

Matthew G. Naugle

McGraw-Hill, Inc.

New York San Francisco Washington, D.C. Auckland Bogotá
Caracas Lisbon London Madrid Mexico City Milan
Montreal New Delhi San Juan Singapore
Sydney Tokyo Toronto

Library of Congress Cataloging-in-Publication Data

Naugle, Matthew G.
Network protocol handbook / Matthew G. Naugle.
p. cm. — (McGraw-Hill series on computer communications)
Includes index.
ISBN 0-07-046461-8
1. Computer network protocols. I. Title. II. Series.
TK5105.55.N38 1994
004.6'2—dc20 93-2013
CIP

3 4 5 6 7 8 9 0 DOC/DOC 9 9 8 7 6 5 4

ISBN 0-07-046461-8

The sponsoring editors for this book were Neil Levine and Jeanne Glasser, and the production supervisor was Pamela Pelton. It was set in Century Schoolbook by North Market Street Graphics.

Printed and bound by R. R. Donnelley & Sons Company.

This book is dedicated to my wife, Regina. Her constant reassurance and most of all her unrelenting patience made it possible to write this book. Also many thanks to my three children: Bryan, Courtney, and Lauren, who have proven that life is most enjoyable when looking at it through simplistic, innocent, and trusting eyes.

Contents

Preface

Today, there are an incredible amount of protocols that make up an internet. This includes local area networks, wide area networks, and the software that runs them. Although most of them go unnoticed, protocols range from the electrical specifications of the connectors to the protocols that run the internetwork. Just to mention a few:

Local Area Networks

Ethernet

Token Ring

Fiber Data Distributed Interface (FDDI)

Asynchronous Transfer Mode (ATM)

WAN Protocols

Proprietary (usually a derivative of HDLC)

Point-to-Point Protocol (PPP)

Switched Multimegabit Data Service (SMDS)

Frame relay

Synchronous Optical Network (SONET)

High-Speed Serial Interface (HSSI)

X.25

High-level Data Link Control (HDLC)

Telecommunications (phone systems, clocking, CSU/DSU)

LAN/WAN Protocols

Transport Control Protocol/Internet Protocol (TCP/IP)

Xerox Network Standard (XNS) and any derivative thereof

Internet Packet eXchange (IPX; i.e., Novell NetWare)

DECnet

IEEE 802.2

Local Area Transport (LAT)

AppleTalk

SNA and SNA Gateways

Open System Interconnect (OSI)

Bridging (Source Route, Transparent with Spanning Tree, Translation, Source Route Transparent)

Miscellaneous

Network Management Systems
- Simple Network Management Protocol (SNMP)
- Common Management Interface Protocol (CMIP)
- Common Management Interface Specification (CMIS)
- CMIP over TCP/IP (CMOT)
- Proprietary
- Protocol analyzers
- NetView

Operating systems (too many to mention)

Wiring hubs

Hardware platforms (personal computers, workstations, mini's and mainframes)

Network Applications

Novell NetWare

IBM LAN Server

TCP applications (and the applications for other protocols)
- Telnet
- File Transfer Protocol (FTP)
- Simple Mail Transfer Protocol (SMTP)
- Domain Name Server (DNS)

There are more that should be on the list, but from the foregoing sampling, I think the reader should have an understanding of the problems associated with the many intricacies of networking. All the preceding protocols are less than 25 years old and most are not more than 12 years old.

The real problem is that network specialists are expected to know everything there is to know about the protocols (hardware or software) that make up an internet. Besides that, a network administrator, network user, network planner, network buyer, etc., expects any vendor of any network communication equipment to understand all of the preceding protocols. It is impossible to understand all the protocols that have evolved since 1981 (the beginning of the network in the commercial workplace). Let me explain right here that it is impossible to know all the intricacies about each and every network protocol in use today.

The intent of this book is to introduce the readers to the majority of the basic functions of the aforementioned protocols. It introduces and explains the protocols so that if the reader needs to understand any protocol that is not in this book, he or she should have an easier time in comprehending that protocol.

To understand networks, it is best to *believe what you experience, not what you read.*

It is my belief that studying XNS is the fastest way to introduce any reader into the world of networks and internetworks. It is the fastest way to understand them. It was a protocol derived and meant to run on top of a LAN (Ethernet). The technical portion of the protocol is easy to understand and, by completely understanding this protocol, the reader will be able to read any of the remaining chapters with a greater comprehension at the end of the reading of that chapter. It is therefore suggested that the reader read Chaps. 1, 2, and 3 of this book before reading any other chapter. There are terms and definitions in these chapters that will be used throughout the rest of the chapters. (Chapter 3 on IEEE 802.2, although not mandatory, will provide the reader valuable information that will make the rest of the book easier to read.)

Otherwise, the reader should feel free to skip through the chapters and read them as needed. For example, if you are most interested in the operation of DECnet, it is suggested that you read the first three chapters and then move on to the DECnet chapter. There is no reason to read any other protocol chapter.

The book does not try to make the reader understand all the aspects of each and every protocol. It merely tries to introduce the reader to some fairly common protocols found on most of today's networks. The book is not meant to be used to write code or to troubleshoot a network. It is meant to introduce a reader to the protocols and to give a fairly detailed comprehension of network protocols without the theory.

Some topics are complex; some are not. The book is fairly balanced in this regard. It is not a "fluff" book that introduces only simple concepts into networks. It starts out with introduction material and then digs into the protocols fairly heavily. The reader of this book can be technical or nontechnical and the outcome will be the same: a full understanding of network protocols.

Acknowledgments

Many thanks go to four individuals:

Uyless Black who is the consulting editor for this book. He definitely fed me good information.

My editor, Neil Levine, who never seems to get into a bad mood, is incredibly patient, and has always offered genuinely good advice.

Brad Black, who is manager of the internet of the Duke Power Company in Charlotte, North Carolina. Brad accepted the invitation to review the original manuscript of this book and offered great advice to improve the book. Many of his ideas and suggestions are in this book.

Jack Maxfield, a systems engineer for Wellfleet Communications in Atlanta, Georgia, improved the book with his vast knowledge of protocols and many years of experience in the networking arena. Jack offered great advice and corrected the manuscript where needed (even if it is dry in some places!).

Also, I would like to thank all the individuals I have met throughout the years who have not held back in conveying their knowledge and ideas to me. These individuals are true tributes to their fields of expertise.

Matthew G. Naugle

Network Protocol Handbook

Chapter

1

Introduction and Wiring Concepts

Local Area Networks* (LANs) have accelerated into the commercial business place at an unprecedented rate. Most computers sold today will eventually have some type of connection to a LAN. Before 1980, the typical computing environment consisted of large mainframes with terminals attached directly to the mainframe. The mainframes resided in expensive, environmentally controlled computer rooms, along with peripheral devices such as printers and modem banks.

Referring to Fig. 1.1, you will see that the early method of computing had many advantages as well as disadvantages. The advantages were multiple users on one computer which allowed for shared file access, electronic messaging (E-mail), and equal access to the associated peripheral devices. The computer itself was managed in one room, and all external access to this machine could be controlled from there.

With advantages come disadvantages, and the centralized computing scheme had its share. The cost of running individual cables between the user's terminal and the computer room equipment was expensive. Also, the cost of maintaining a centralized computer was high and sometimes beyond a small business's reach. If the mainframe went down, all attached users and devices were also down with it. This environment is known as *centralized computing.*

The user's interface to the computer were dumb terminals, in the sense they possessed very little intelligence—usually just enough to

---

* This chapter is an abbreviation from the book *Local Area Networking,* McGraw-Hill, 1991. Although most concepts are fully explained, please refer to chapters 1 and 2 of that book for a detailed explanation of wiring systems, Ethernet and Token Ring access methods, bridging, and routing.

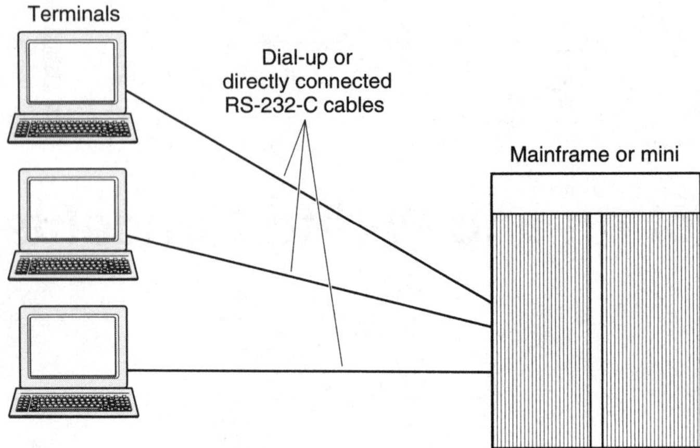

Figure 1.1 Host to terminal.

show minor word processing functions such as bold, underline, blinking, etc. If the user wanted multiple host connections, there was very little choice. A new connection (cable) could be run or a modem could be used. For those businesses that had some money, a special device known as a Digital Private Branch Exchange (DPBX) could be used to interconnect user's terminal and multiple mainframes, and the DPBX would provide the switching of terminals and mainframes for the users. This device was not inexpensive.

The centralized computing environment was effective for its time, but user demands were growing and the only alternative was to build faster and larger mainframes. In 1981, IBM introduced its version of the personal computer (PC) and the users' computing environment was forever changed.

The personal computer gave any user a lot of freedom. In effect, a PC brought the mainframe applications to the user's desk top. It eliminated some of the major disadvantages of the centralized computer. Gone were the expensive computer rooms, cable costs, etc.

PCs did allow the users to gain control over their computer environment, but stand-alone computer devices brought many disadvantages. A user could not share files simultaneously with another user. Electronic messaging, printers, and other shared devices were no longer available. One of the first applications developed for the PC (besides spreadsheets) was a terminal emulator. This allowed connection back to the mainframe via the cable originally used for the dumb terminal. Users could have access to the mainframe and were also allowed to use a desktop computer for their own use. Terminal emulation programs had file transfer capabilities between the personal computer and the mainframe. The most popular one developed was known as KERMIT and was used on VAX computer systems from Digital Equipment Corporation.

Before the connection of computers to LANs, users would make a copy of their work accomplished on the PC and place it on a diskette. This diskette would then be walked over to other users for them to use. For distant sites, the user would mail the diskette. This was affectionately known as "sneakernet."

The LAN was introduced commercially in 1980, which again eliminated some disadvantages of stand-alone PCs. A PC can connect to a LAN, thus enabling the user to communicate with other PC users connected to the same LAN. The original mainframes provided a connection to a LAN, and this created two logical connections for a user: mainframe access and the ability to communicate with other PC users directly on the LAN. Refer to Fig. 1.2. This figure shows personal computers and host computer access on a LAN. Users have the ability to communicate with both personal computer and host computers connected to the LAN.

When LANs were introduced, their first connections allowed asynchronous terminal connection to the LAN through the use of a commu-

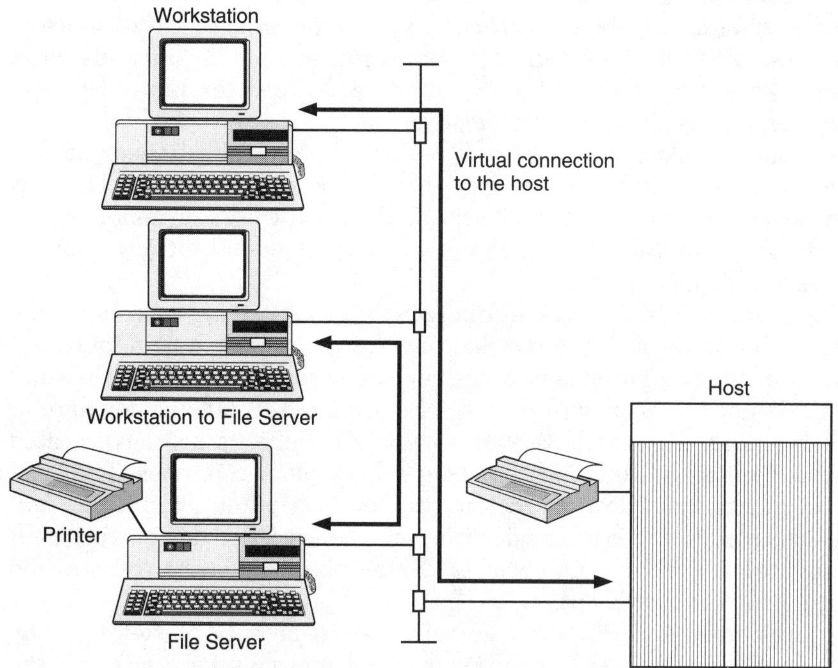

Figure 1.2 PC LAN with host connection.

nication server (also known as a terminal server). (These devices are discussed in Chap. 9.) The reason behind this is that before the LAN, most devices (with the exception of SNA) were connected to their host computer via asynchronous protocols running over RS-232 cables. In order to provide network capabilities like that promoted by SNA, asynchronous terminal servers were invented as the first device to allow this connectivity. There was no reason to discard all the asynchronous devices just because the LAN provided a new connectivity.

This device allowed multiple asynchronous terminals to connect to it, and the terminal server would connect to the LAN. The other end of the connection (before the advent of host LAN boards) was a communication server which also had a connection to the LAN and then multiple asynchronous connections to the host. This allowed a LAN to be installed into a business and the existing equipment could be used. This granted multiple host access, the distribution of printers and modems, while completely eliminating the single-cable-to-host attachment required in centralized computing.

Overview

It is difficult to define exactly what a LAN is. LANs provide many capabilities, but a one-line sentence to sum it is: *A LAN permits information and peripherals to be shared efficiently and economically*—economically in the sense that LANs can save companies money. This is truly what networks are all about: to allow information to be exchanged in any manner, efficiently and economically.

Given the vastness of LANs, it is difficult to establish clear advantages and disadvantages of one type of network over another. The particular choice of a network clearly depends on the requirements that are to placed on the LAN. Each networking scheme has its own advantages and disadvantages.

Networks have been called *distributed* or *decentralized* computing. This is good term for networks, for the processing and application power of the computer is now distributed through the LAN. The computer is not the big complex piece of equipment located somewhere in the building. The computers and their attachments are now located throughout a building and sometimes throughout countries. The LAN is the device that allows the connection for distributed computing. Centralized computing is on the decline (sometimes called downsizing), but mainframes are far from obsolete. Today, the LAN is the "centralized computing" environment.

Mainframes and PCs do peacefully coexist on a LAN. Refer to Fig. 1.3. It should be noted that the original methods for accessing the mainframe were not replaced per se; only the physical method of connection was replaced. Each user's terminal was connected to the main-

OSI Layer	Function Provided
Application	Network applications such as file transfer and terminal emulation
Presentation	Data formating and encryption
Session	Negotiation and establishment of sessions
Transport	Provision for end to end reliable delivery
Network	Routing of packets of information across multiple networks
Data Link	Transfer of units of information, framing and error checking
Physical	Transmission of binary data of a medium

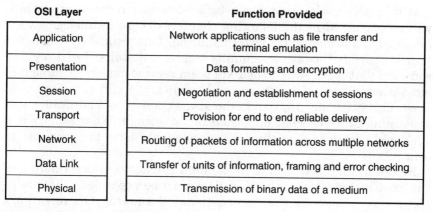

Figure 1.3 (*a*) OSI model and functions.

OSI Layer	Protocol
Application	File Server concepts
Presentation	
Session	Courier Netbios
Transport	TCP SPP
Network	IP IDP Routers
Data Link	Ethernet, Token Ring bridges
Physical	Wiring systems

Figure 1.3 (*b*) OSI model filled in.

frame with a single cable. Applications were run on the mainframe and the data was output to the terminal. Today, with LANs and PCs, the mainframe application is still run on the mainframe and the data is still output to the user's screen. Only the connection to the mainframe changed. While many of the applications still run on a mainframe computer, many of these applications have been ported to run on a personal computer. With this is a peaceful coexistence on a LAN. PC users can run their own applications on their PC, communicate with others on the LAN, and can access the mainframe as if they were still directly connected to it—all this using a standard cabling and protocol scheme for all attachments to the LAN.

With LANs came many never-before-heard-of technologies, which will be explained in the following chapters. These technologies were invented to allow decentralized computing. This technology had never been exposed to the user community before, and at first LANs and the software that is required to operate them seemed extremely foreign to most users. Today, the software and hardware is still very foreign to most users. Simply replacing the connection to a mainframe and explaining to users what happened is not enough. What exactly is a LAN and how does the software it uses enable users to communicate over it?

Before a full discussion is invoked on LANs, an understanding of the architecture that all LANs follow must be explained. This architecture is known as the International Standards Organization's Open System Interconnect model (the OSI model). You will see this model time and time again, and it provides the best introduction to this book.

The Open Systems Interconnection (OSI) Model

This model was developed in 1974 by the standards body known as the International Standards Organization. This model, known as the Open Systems Interconnection, or OSI model, divides a LAN into seven processing modules. Each layer performs specific functions as part of the overall task of allowing application programs on different systems to communicate as if they were operating on the same system.

The OSI model is an architectural model based on modularity. The model is not specific to any software or hardware. OSI defines the functions of each layer but does not provide the software or design the hardware to allow compliance to this model. The model's ultimate goal is for interoperability between multiple vendors' communication products.

Any communications equipment may be designed after this model. Although mentioned more often in terms of LANs, many data and telephone communications are designed with the OSI model in mind. All the LAN hardware and software explained in this book will relate to this model.

There are seven and only seven modules that comprise this model. (The terms *modules* and *layers* can be used interchangeably.) As shown in Fig. 1.3*a* and *b,* the modules in sequence of bottom to top are: physical, data link, network, transport, session, presentation, and application layers. Each layer has a specific purpose, and functions independently of the other layers. However, each layer is "aware" of its immediate upper and lower layers.

Layer	Function
Application	Specialized network functions such as file transfer, virtual terminal, electronic mail, and file servers
Presentation	Data formatting and character code conversion and data encryption
Session	Negotiation and establishment of a connection with another node
Transport	Provision for reliable end-to-end delivery of data
Network	Routing of packets of information across multiple networks
Data link	Transfer of addressable units of information, frames, and error checking
Physical	Transmission of binary data over a communications medium

Physical layer. This layer defines the methods used to transmit and receive data on the network. It consists of the wiring, the devices that are used to connect a station's network interface controller to the wiring, the signaling involved to transmit/receive data, and the ability to detect signaling errors on the network media (the cable plant).

Data-link layer. This layer synchronizes transmission and handles frame-level error control and recovery so that information can be transmitted over the physical layer. The frame formatting and the CRC (cyclic redundancy check, which checks for errors in the whole frame) are accomplished at this layer. This layer performs the access methods known as Ethernet and Token Ring. It also provides the physical layer addressing for transmitted frame.

Network layer. This layer controls the forwarding of messages between stations. On the basis of certain information, this layer will allow data to flow sequentially between two stations in the most economical path both logically and physically. This layer allows units of data to be transmitted to other networks though the use of special devices known as *routers.* Routers are defined at this layer.

Transport layer. This layer provides for end-to-end (origination station to destination station) transmission of data. It allows data to be transferred reliably (i.e., with a guarantee that it will be delivered in the same order that it was sent). It ensures that data is transmitted or received without error, in the correct order (received in the same order as it was sent), and in a timely manner.

Session layer. This layer establishes, maintains, and disconnects a communications link between two stations on a network. This layer is also responsible for name-to-station address translation. (This is the same as placing a call to someone on the phone knowing only their name. You must find their phone number if you want to create a connection to them.)

Presentation layer. This layer is responsible for data translation (format of the data) and data encryption (scrambling and descrambling the data as it is transmitted and received). It is not always implemented in a network protocol.

Application layer. This layer is used for those applications that were specifically written to run over the network. Applications such as file transfer, terminal emulation, electronic mail (E-mail), and NetBIOS-based applications are examples.

That is what the OSI model is and accomplishes. It is not to difficult to understand and, will become more clear as you read further into this book. Each LAN protocol discussed will be related to the OSI model and will also be identified as to the layer in which it resides.

This model will be used throughout the text of this book. Each of the protocols that will be explained has different modules that, when taken as a whole (all seven layers together), constitute a network protocol. Each of these modules fits into a certain layer of the OSI model. Since each layer of the OSI model defines a certain subset of a protocol, we will break down each protocol studied in this book to each layer. In essence, each layer of the model will be shown and explained in each chapter. It is enough now just to introduce the model and to explain each of the layer functions. As you read a protocol chapter, the sections in that chapter will take you into an implemented technology that will conform to each layer.

Topologies

Before we study the physical layer for any of the protocols of the OSI model, it is important, at least conceptually, to understand topologies. Networks are built based on topologies. Topologies are architectural drawings that represent the cable layout and methodologies used for a LAN or Wide Area Network (WAN). Topologies can be hardware dependent, i.e., when a particular LAN is chosen, a specific topology must be followed when implementing the LAN. Some LANs have the capability of representing many types of topologies.

Star topology

Refer to Fig. 1.4. The *star topology* is probably the oldest topology used for communications. It was first introduced with analog and digital switching devices known as Private Branch Exchanges (PBX).

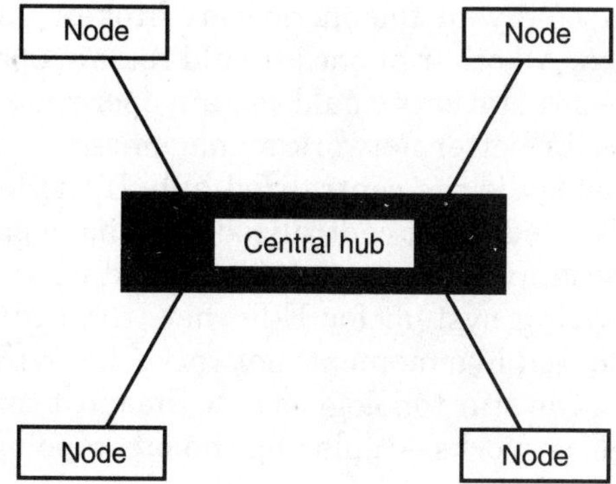

Node: Any station that can directly connect to a network

Figure 1.4 Star topology.

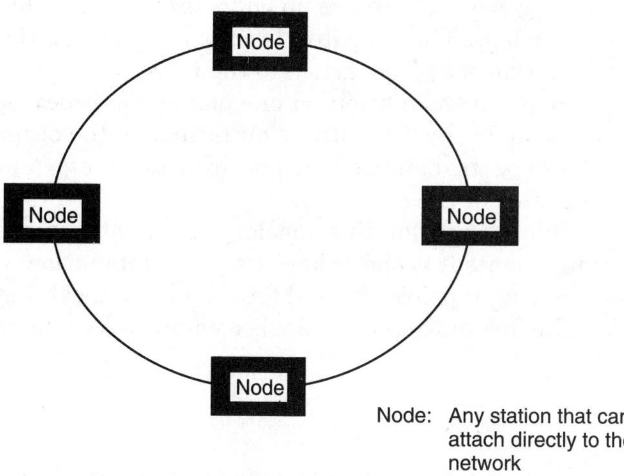

Figure 1.5 Ring topology.

In the star topology all stations are attached to one common point. As shown in Fig. 1.5, this common point is usually a wiring hub with all stations attached via cables that extend from it. Since the stations are on a point-to-point link with the central wiring hub, the cost and the amount of cable may increase. Considering the type of cable implemented, however, the overall cost is about equal to that of other topologies.

There are two primary advantages to this topology. First, there is no cabling single point of failure that would affect the whole network. If one of the cables should develop a problem, only the station directly using that cable would be effected. The example of the telephone can be used here. If the wire that connected your telephone were broken, only your telephone would be disabled. All other phones should remain operational. Similarly, all other network stations would remain operational. Second, the star topology allows for better network management.

The disadvantage to this topology is the centralized hub. If the hub fails, all connections to it are disabled. Most centralized hubs have passive backplanes and dual power supplies to enable 100 percent uptime.

With the advent of a new wiring system for Ethernet (the access method of Ethernet will be discussed in a moment) networks, known as Unshielded Twisted Pair (UTP), the star topology is now the most common topology used for Ethernet networks—replacing the bus topology.

Ring topology

Refer to Fig. 1.5. This is the general topology of the ring. In the ring topology all stations attached to the ring are considered repeaters on the LAN that is enclosed in loop. There are no endpoints to this cable topology as in the bus topology. The repeater, for our purposes, is the controller board in the station that is attached to the LAN.

Each station will receive a transmission on one end of the repeater and repeat the transmission, bit by bit, with no buffering, on the other end of the repeater. Data is transmitted in one direction only and received by the next repeater in the loop.

The most common cable design for this topology is the star-wired ring. The LAN that implements it is the Token Ring. A combination of the star topology and the ring topology is used for the physical cabling system of Token Ring. The Token Ring topology is commonly known as *the star-wired ring.*

Bus topology

The *bus topology* is sometimes known as the *linear-bus* topology. It is a simple design, as shown in Fig. 1.6. It uses a single length of cable (also known as the *medium*) with network stations attached to this cable. All stations share this single cable, and transmissions from the stations can be received by any station attached to the cable (a *broadcast medium*). There are endpoints to the cable segment commonly known as *terminating points.*

Given the simplicity of this topology, the cost of implementing it is usually low. The management costs are high. No single station on the LAN can be easily individually administered when compared to a star topology. There are no management designs in stations that are attached to a single cable. The single cable can lead to a major problem. It contains a single point of failure. If the cable breaks, then no station

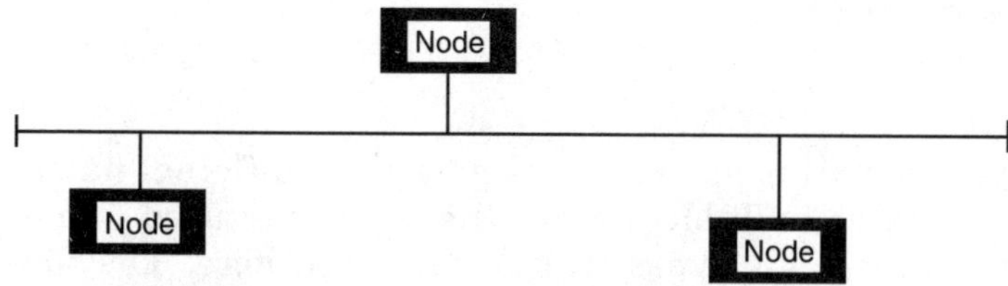

Node: Any station that can directly attach to the cable plant

Figure 1.6 Bus topology.

will have the ability to transmit. The LAN that best represents this topology is the Ethernet access method.

Wiring Systems for Ethernet and Token Ring—Physical Layer

This section provides the reader with the cabling systems used for Ethernet and Token Ring. Although the protocols (Ethernet and Token Ring) are discussed later, their terms will be used here. The reader should bear with the terms until the cabling systems are discussed. It is important to understand the cabling system of each protocol before comprehending the protocol. The access methods of Ethernet and Token Ring will be explained in detail in Chap. 2.

The physical layer of the OSI model is the bottom layer, and is represented by the wiring systems and associated physical components (connectors) used in LANs. The role of the physical layer is to allow transmission and reception of raw data (a stream of data) over the communications medium* (the cable plant). This means that all data being transmitted and received for the network will pass through this layer. For LANs, the layer is implemented fully in hardware. The first protocol to study is Ethernet. The actual Ethernet protocol will be studied in a moment. First, the wiring systems for Ethernet will be discussed.

For Ethernet networks, there are four types of wiring systems that may be used:

1. Thick coaxial cable
2. Thin coaxial cable

* Communications medium and transmission medium mean the same thing: the cable plant.

3. Unshielded Twisted Pair
4. Fiber

These four types of wiring are also known by many different names. The column headings in Table 1.1 are the commonly used names. Only the first three cable types will be discussed here. The fiber standard for Ethernet is not yet adopted by any of the standards bodies.

Throughout the changes in wiring, the access method defined for Ethernet remains unchanged—that is, the access method,* defined at layer 2 of the OSI model has not been revised. The only thing that changes is the wiring methodology (layer 1) of the OSI model. This is a perfect example of why data communications systems rely on the OSI model for architecture. We can change the physical layer of the model with something different and the remainder of the layers remain unchanged.

There can be confusion about which type of wiring system is best used for Ethernet. This will the topic for the next discussion.

A brief summary of the components used in each type of wiring system follows, and should be referenced throughout the text:

Ethernet layer physical components

1. Thick coaxial cable—standardized in 1980
   a. Thick coaxial cable
   b. Transceivers

* Access methods are the rules that govern the transmission and reception of data on a network. This will be discussed later.

TABLE 1.1 Commonly Used Names for Ethernet Wiring

Thick coaxial cable	Thin coaxial cable	Unshielded twisted pair	Fiber
RG-8*	RG-58 A/U or C/U	22–26 AWG† telephone cable	62.5/125 micron
10BASE5	10BASE2	10BASET	10BASEF (not formally adopted)
IEEE 802.3 Thicknet	IEEE 802.3a Cheapernet or Thinnet	IEEE 802.3i UTP	

* Not actually RG-8 cable but characteristic of it.
† American Wire Gauge.

   c. Transceiver cables
   d. 50-ohm terminators
   e. Coring tool
   f. Wiring concentrators (not always required—depends on the size of the network)
   g. Connectors on cables and network controllers (N-series connectors)
2. Thin coaxial cable—standardized in 1985
   a. RG-58 A/U thin coaxial cable
   b. T connectors
   c. 50-ohm terminators
   d. Wiring concentrators, repeaters (not always required—depends on the size of the network)
   e. Connectors on cables and controllers (BNC connectors)
3. Unshielded twisted pair—standardized in 1990
   a. 22-26 AWG two pair wire (telephone cable)
   b. Repeater modules and wiring concentrator (always required)
   c. RJ-45 connectors and plugs

Thick coaxial cable

This cabling scheme is representative of a bus topology. Thick coaxial cable is characteristic of type RG-8 (RG means Radio Grade) cable and was the original cabling scheme used when Ethernet was standardized in 1980. This cable is used on 10BASE5 networks. 10BASE5 is the standard term applied by the standards body of IEEE (Institute of Electrical and Electronics Engineers, pronounced "I triple E"). It represents the primary characteristics of the cabling scheme, using a kind of shorthand. The 10 represents the transmission speed in megabits per second, Mbps. The middle term represents the transmission signaling method used, and the last number is the longest cable segment used multiplied by 100 meters (notice the unit of measurement is in meters). Therefore, 10BASE5 is a LAN running at 10 Mbps, using baseband (access method) technology (as opposed to broadband) and the longest cable run is 500 meters (after 500 meters a repeater is needed, which is explained later).

This type of cable is usually colored yellow, although other colors are available. Every 2.5 meters there is a black painted mark to show the placement of a network attachment (a PC, host computer, or a repeater, etc.). Devices may not be placed any closer together than this due to a phenomenon known as *reflections.* Without going into great detail, piercing the cable (placing devices on the cable plant) causes electrical reflections on the cable which can be incorrectly interpreted by other devices as errors on the network. It is best to follow the markings on the cable.

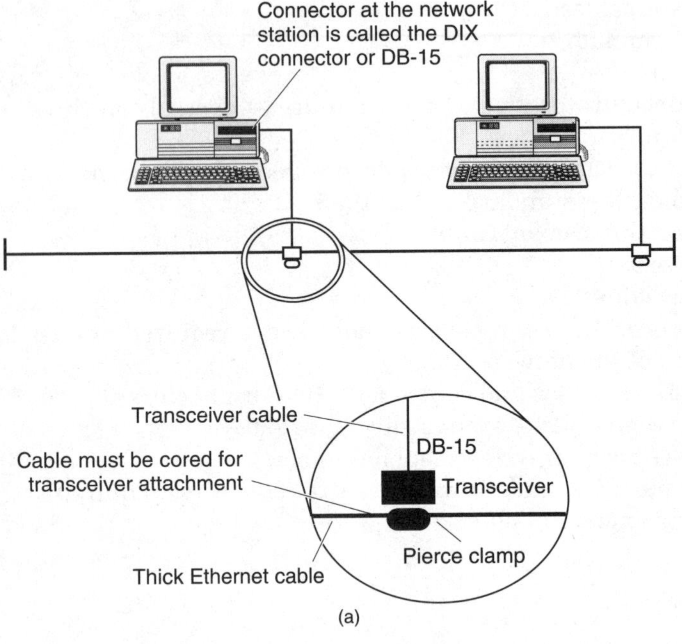
Connector at the network station is called the DIX connector or DB-15
Transceiver cable
DB-15
Cable must be cored for transceiver attachment
Transceiver
Pierce clamp
Thick Ethernet cable
(a)

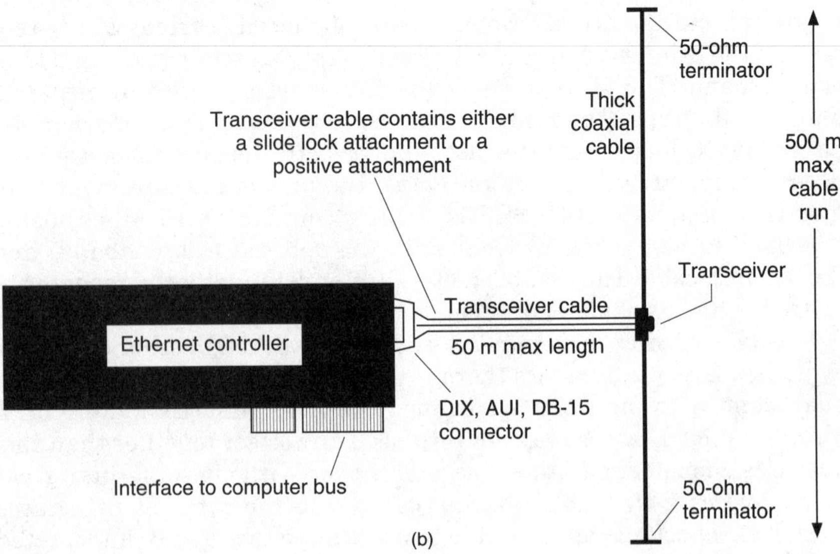
50-ohm terminator
Thick coaxial cable
Transceiver cable contains either a slide lock attachment or a positive attachment
500 m max cable run
Transceiver
Transceiver cable
Ethernet controller
50 m max length
DIX, AUI, DB-15 connector
Interface to computer bus
50-ohm terminator
(b)

Figure 1.7 Thick coaxial connection.

A network attachment is accomplished through the use of a transceiver cable and a transceiver. (See Fig. 1.7*a* and *b*.) The Ethernet controller (the controller is the integral hardware device that allows a device to attach and work on the network) cannot attach to the cable plant without the use of these devices.

A *transceiver* (transmitter-receiver) is the intermediate device that transmits and receives the data from the Ethernet controller onto or from the cable plant. The transceiver couples the network device to the coaxial cable and is the most important part of the transmission system. At the time of Ethernet's introduction, around 1980, the components that made up a transceiver were expensive. The components that allowed for a 10-Mbps transmission were not readily available. But this device allowed for the ability to transmit a signal up to 500 meters from its origination and to detect when two or more network attachments were transmitting at the same time (error detection). This device allowed for the speed to be mandated at 10 Mbps, a speed that was unheard of in the data communications industry at that time. The designers of Ethernet could have allowed for faster speeds and longer distances, but the cost would have been prohibitive. Initial costs of adding an Ethernet connection to a host computer were estimated to be $1200 to $1500 per connection.

The transceiver cable is the cable that connects transceivers to the Ethernet controller itself. It is not a coaxial cable of any type. The cable contains nine individual wires used to transmit and receive data and to relay errors in the transmission system to the controller card. This cable may be up to 50 meters long.

Before the transceiver is physically attached to the cable, the site on the thick coaxial cable must be prepared for its use. A small hole must be cored into the cable to expose the center conductor of the cable. This is accomplished with a special piercing (coring) tool. It is a drill bit in a specially designed handle that drills a hole into the cable to at a specified depth. The transceiver is then placed on the cable. The transceiver cable is attached to the transceiver and to the Ethernet controller card of the network attachment.

Each end of a single cable segment will be terminated using a device known as a 50-Ω terminator. There are only two terminators per cable segment. The terminators must be used on every cable segment.

Installing a network attachment on thick Ethernet may take up to five minutes or more to ensure a good connection. This cable type is not commonly used in today's LANs. Its primary use is for factory installations and backbone connections. Backbone connections will be shown later in the repeater section. The advantage to using this type of cable is that it is not as susceptible to noise and can run for longer distances than the other types of cables for Ethernet.

Each network segment of thick Ethernet cable may be up to 500 meters long. With this, 100 network attachments are allowed. A distinction here should be made about a network attachment. *A network attachment is any device that may attach to a cable plant.* This includes PCs, host computers, communication servers, repeaters, bridges, and routers. In other words, the network attachment is any device that can attach to a network cable plant. This is important for all cable schemes since networks have their limitation on connections. So, on a thick Ethernet cable plant, if there are 100 PCs attached to the cable, you cannot connect another attachment to that cable. You must add a repeater to extend the cable plant if more network attachments are needed. If you added a repeater to this cable plant, one attachment (one PC) must be taken off, for the repeater is included in the 100-attachment limitation. There are other ways around this limitation and these devices will be fully explained in a later section of this chapter.

For now, repeaters are devices that will extend a single cable segment beyond its maximum length. Refer to Table 1.2 for exact specifications on each cable type. For Ethernet, a maximum of four repeaters may be placed between two communicating stations. This does not mean that no more than four repeaters may exist on an Ethernet cable plant. As many repeaters as are needed may exist on any cable plant, but a data path between two communicating network stations may not have more than four repeaters separating the two. Repeaters will be covered in complete detail later.

No matter what the cable type (thick or thin coaxial, UTP), the total amount of network stations that may exist on an Ethernet cable plant is 1024. This assumes that devices such as bridges or repeaters are not in use. These devices are explained in a moment.

Remember, when using Ethernet wire systems, when a network device is attached to the Ethernet cable plant (no matter what type of cable used), it is called an *attachment.* A network attachment may be a computing device (host, personal computer, etc.), a repeater, a bridge or router, etc. For example, if you had 100 attachments to a single piece of thick coaxial cable, you could not attach a repeater to this cable to extend it. One device should be taken off the cable and then the repeater can be attached. The distinction to make is that any attachment adds up to the maximum number of attachments. Attachments are not just workstations. Attachments are all attachments for that cable.

Thin coaxial cable

This cabling scheme also represents a bus topology. Thin coaxial cabling (used on 10BASE2 networks) was standardized in 1985.

TABLE 1.2 Cable Specifications

Parameter	Value or specification
Cable type	Thick coaxial cable (impedance of 50 ohms)
Signaling techniques	Baseband (Manchester)
Data rate	10 million bits per second
Maximum cable segment length	500 meters
Maximum network length (with repeaters)	2500 meters
Attachments per segment	100
Attachment spacing	2.5 meters, minimum
Connector type	DB-15
Topology	Linear bus
Maximum number of stations per network	1024
Impedance rating of cable	50 ohms (cable ends are terminated)

Parameter	Value or specification
Cable type	Thin coaxial cable
Signaling techniques	Baseband (Manchester)
Data rate	10 million bits per second
Maximum cable segment length	185 meters
Maximum network length (with repeaters)	1000 meters
Attachments per segment	30
Attachment spacing	0.5 meter, minimum
Connector type	BNC and T connectors
Topology	Bus
Maximum number of stations per network	1024
Impedance of cable	50 ohms (cable ends are terminated)

Parameter	Value or specification
Cable type	Unshielded twisted pair
Signaling techniques	Baseband (Manchester)
Data rate	10 million bits per second
Maximum cable segment length	100 meters
Maximum network length (with repeaters)	2500 meters using thick coaxial backbone
Attachments per segment	1
Attachment spacing	N/A
Connector type	RJ-45 (8 pin connector) 1,4,5,6 straight through
Topology	Star
Maximum number of stations per network	1024
Impedance of cable	75–150 ohms

Besides being lower in cost, this cabling scheme offers many advantages over the thick coaxial cabling scheme. A major advantage is that this cable does not have to be pierced in order to place the transceiver on the cable plant. The external transceiver was moved to the Ethernet controller itself. Refer to Fig. 1.8*a* and *b*. This move represents a cost savings of more than $200.00 per connection. Also, the transceiver cable was eliminated. The cable attaches directly to the back of the Ethernet controller card. RG-58 cable is low-cost cable and has been around for a long time (used for other things besides LANs).

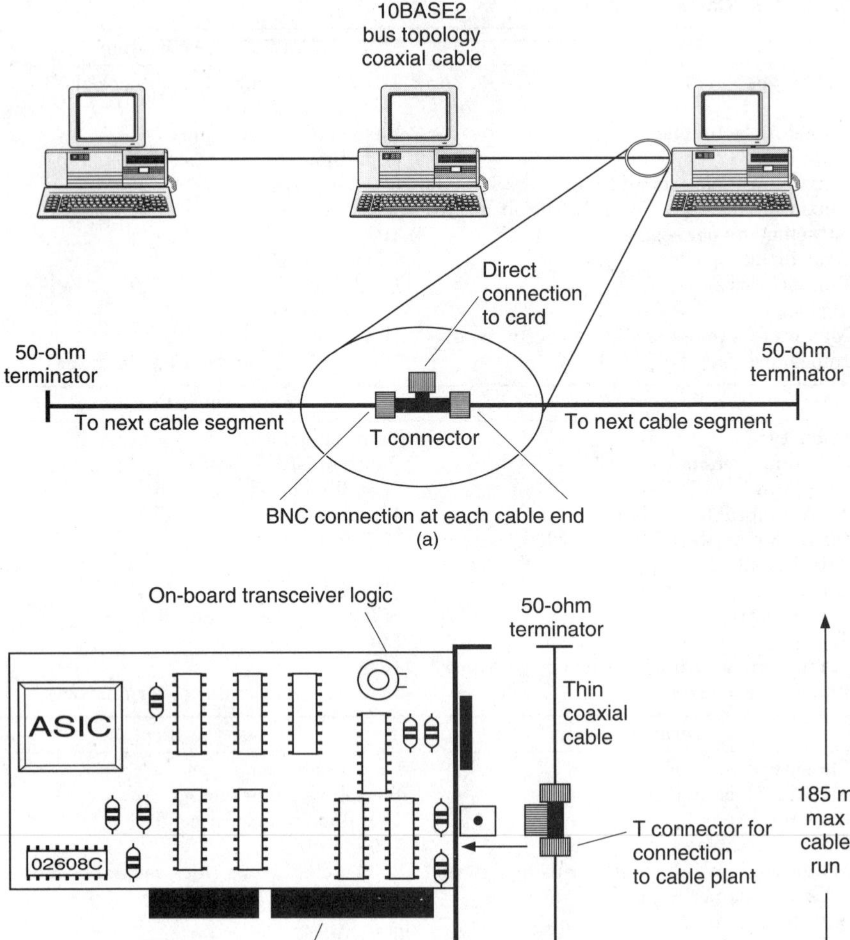

Figure 1.8 Thin coaxial connections.

Stations are attached to this cable through the use of a BNC connectors and T connectors. Refer to Fig. 1.8*a*. Each cable segment endpoint contains a male BNC connector. These connectors attach to a T connector. This T connector is placed on the Ethernet card itself. The cable is simply twisted together to form a cable plant.

Like thick coaxial cable, each end of a single cable segment will be terminated by a 50-Ω terminator. Usually, the terminator is attached to one end of the T connector on the final attachment at each end of the cable segment.

There are also limitations, not disadvantages, to this cable plant. Compared to the thick Ethernet standard, the maximum cable length is now 200 (actually 185) meters in length. Only 30 network attachments are allowed per cable plant. The amount of shielding in this cable has been reduced, although it is more than enough for most applications. Repeaters are used to extend the cable length, thereby allowing more than 30 network attachments to communicate.

Changing the cable plant does not change the repeater rule. No more than four repeaters may separate two communicating devices on an Ethernet network. Repeaters are explained in a moment along with this rule.

Unshielded twisted pair

Until this cabling scheme was devised, thin coaxial cable was the most commonly used cable type in Ethernet network environments. Unshielded twisted pair (10BASET) was standardized by the IEEE in October of 1990. (See Fig. 1.9.) The advantages of this cable scheme are many, and it has become the most popular cabling scheme for Ethernet networks. It is representative of the star topology. The term *twisted* comes from the fact that the wires are twisted together. There must be at least two twists per foot of wire. If the wire were not twisted, the signal strength would be greatly attenuated.

Unlike the coaxial cabling schemes mentioned before, UTP is a point-to-point cabling scheme, and its topology represents a star. The cable is not a coaxial cable. It consists of four strands of 22-26 AWG (American Wire Gauge) wire (standard telephone wire). Although standard telephone wire may be used for this cable scheme, there is a UTP cable standard commonly used for transmitting digital data (LAN data) over UTP. Consult a cable company for these standards.

UTP may be run for 100 meters between the Ethernet controller and the repeater hub. This type of wiring scheme requires the use of a wiring hub. Each network connection is terminated at this wiring hub (which is a repeater). See Fig. 1.10.

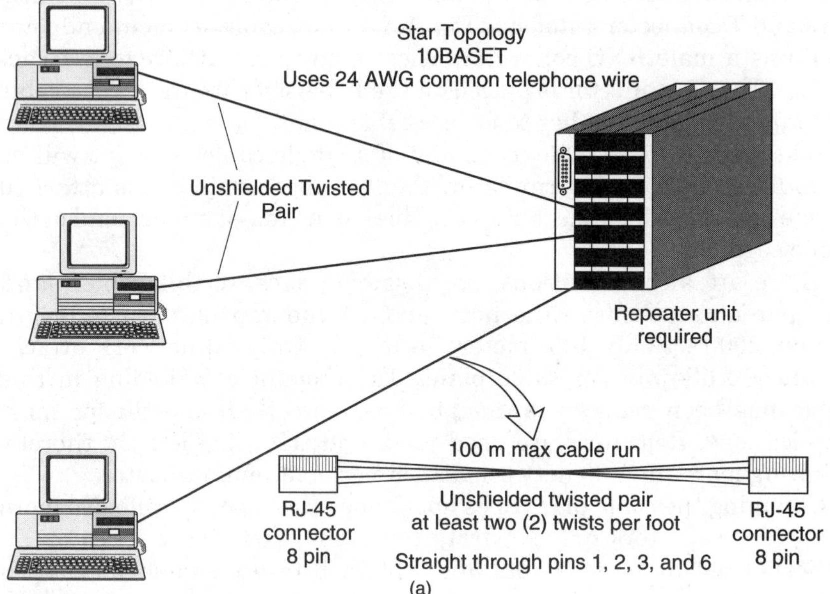

Figure 1.9 (*a*) Unshielded twisted pair.

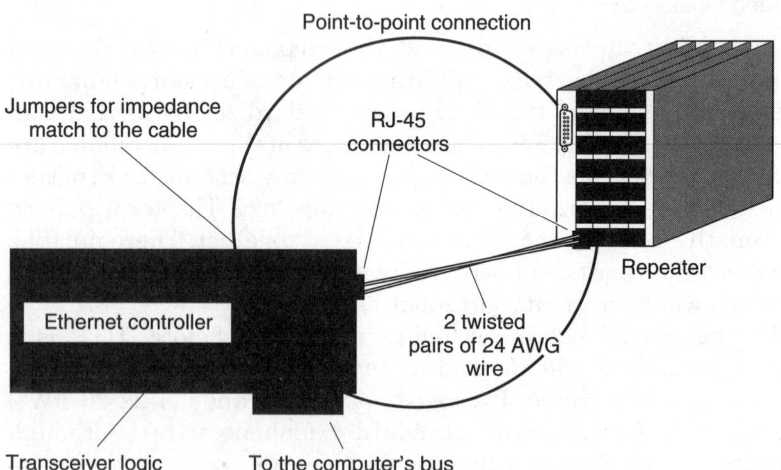

Figure 1.9 (*b*) Unshielded twisted pair controller.

With this cabling scheme, there are no external terminators. The cable is still terminated, only it is terminated on the Ethernet controller and the repeater (each end of the physical connection). This cable type follows the Ethernet specification, allowing no more than four repeaters (one 10BASET concentrator constitutes one repeater whether or not the two communicating stations are connected to the same repeater), and there may be a maximum of 1024 stations connected to a physical cable plant (all cable segments combined to form a single cable plant). Although two UTP stations may be attached back to back, each station should run through a repeater to communicate with another. If two stations are connected back to back, then no other stations can be connected. Two repeaters hubs, though, may be connected together through UTP wire. This is not generally recommended.

With this cabling scheme, the transceiver is still physically located on the Ethernet card, just as are thin coaxial controllers. The only thing that changed was the wiring, the interface, and the connector for that wire. Stations are not concatenated with each other as with the previous coaxial cabling schemes.

A network that utilizes UTP is far more manageable than the aforementioned bus methodologies. For example, if the cable that links a station with its repeater hub is damaged in any way, only that station will shut down. With the coaxial cabling schemes, if that cable is damaged, all network stations on that physical cable are down also.

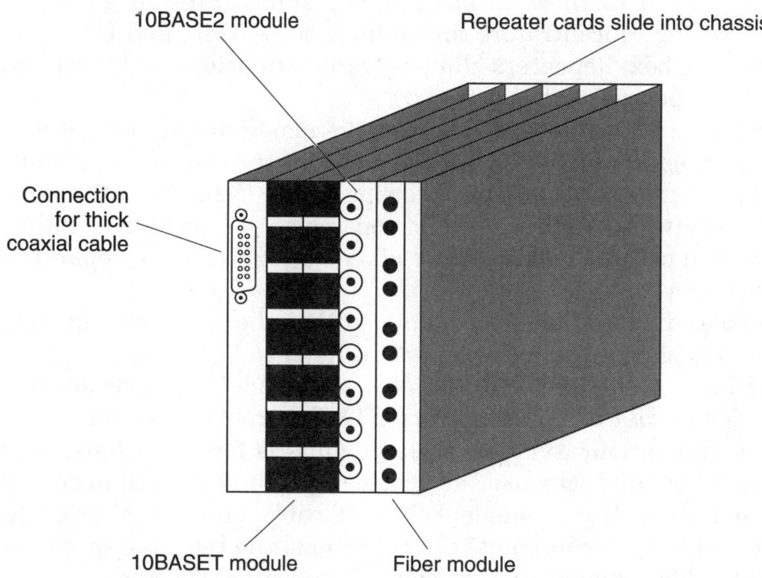

Figure 1.10 Wiring concentrators—hubs.

The purposes for developing UTP as a cable alternative for Ethernet were many. The primary reasons were the ability to use common household telephone cable as the Ethernet cable. This cable is very inexpensive. Second, in some cases it allowed the use of already installed telephone cable. In most cases this is not recommended. Third, managing a UTP network is easily accomplished through smart hubs and network management software.

Using existing telephone wire (no telephones may be attached to the same wire as the network station), the wire may be very old, probably has "noise" on it, and is probably not very well documented as the wire run in the building. Most companies have found that it is easier to install new UTP cable than it is to use the old, existing cable.

There is a new proposal the IEEE committee is working on. It is called 100BASEVG. This is going to allow Ethernet to run at 100 Mbps on UTP wire. Currently, Ethernet supports 10-Mbps transmission rate. The protocol has been coined "100-megabit Ethernet." It will be at least a year before this standard comes out of the IEEE and, most likely, new controller cards and software will be needed to run this protocol.

Repeaters

There are many different types of repeaters, but the one most commonly employed in Ethernet environments is known as a *wiring concentrator*. The wiring concentrator allows for multiple wiring types to be connected to it to allow all media types to integrate. As shown in Fig. 1.10, wiring concentrators can connect thick, thin, and UTP networks into one box. Repeaters allow for cable extensions and therefore more stations per network segments.

For example, with thin coaxial cable, the maximum number of network attachments was 30. Regulators allow for the connection of multiple cable segments, therefore allowing more than 30 stations to attach to a network. With the use of repeaters, the number is within the restriction of 1023 maximum for all cable segments not separated by a bridge or a router.

These concentrators have card slots so that the repeaters (in card form) literally slide into the concentrator. Refer to Fig. 1.11.

The wiring concentrator is absolutely needed in a UTP environment. It is this device that terminates every UTP Ethernet connection.

The original specification for repeater units is for the extension of the 10BASE5 cabling scheme. Each cable segment is allowed to be 500 meters in length. But a single Ethernet cable plant is allowed to stretch to 2500 meters in length. This is due to the repeater specification. Each cable segment may attach to a repeater. There may be no

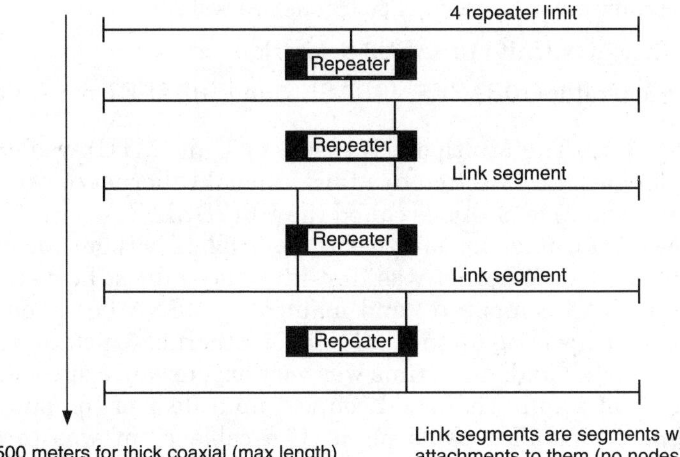

Figure 1.11 Repeater limits.

more than four repeaters in a path between two communicating stations. Refer to Fig. 1.11. This figure shows five Ethernet segments (the cable may be of 10BASE5 or 10BASE2) separated by four repeaters. In this configuration, two of the segments may only have repeater connections to it. It may not have any other attachments. This is only for extended Ethernet cable segments up to the theoretical maximum limit. Most network installations will not run into this limitation with proper design and the use of wiring hubs.

This does not mean that no more than four repeaters may be on a network. There may be many repeaters on the cable plant—just no more than four repeaters between two communicating stations. One last rule is that if there are five Ethernet Cable segments separated by four repeaters, two of the links (usually the ones in the middle) are not allowed to have any network station attachment. This means that the only connections on these two cable segments are the repeaters themselves. What this means is that in any LAN there may be more than four repeaters comprising the network. The network must be designed so that a station A, when communicating with station B, must not pass through more than four repeaters when transmitting a signal to station B. This is generally not a problem today with network designs.

Repeaters come in various sizes and shapes from a lot of vendors. The one specification that they must all conform to is the IEEE 802.3c repeater specification. Almost all do this. There are three types of repeaters:

1. Multiport Transceiver Units (10BASE5 networks)
2. Multiport Repeater Unit (10BASE2 networks)
3. Wiring Concentrator (10BASE5, 10BASE2, and 10BASET networks)

Refer to Fig. 1.12. The Multiport Transceiver Unit (MTU) was created to allow for easier connection to a thick coaxial Ethernet network. The best-known example of this is called the DEC DELNI.

It also allowed for connection of Ethernet controllers without the use of a cable plant. When Ethernet was first introduced, most hosts in a site were minis (VAX computers) and mainframes (SNA hosts, etc.). Therefore, instead of wiring up the building for Ethernet (thick coaxial cable is hard to install and at the time was very expensive), a site could install this type of a unit and could connect up a floor of computers without having to install a cable plant. If a cable plant was to be installed, it could be a backbone cable (usually run up the risers of a building and not spread throughout the floor). The MTU provided connections on the floor, and it has one port which will allow connection to an external cable plant.

Refer to Fig. 1.13. MTUs can also be cascaded. In this configuration, there is one MTU that acts as the root MTU. All other MTUs connect

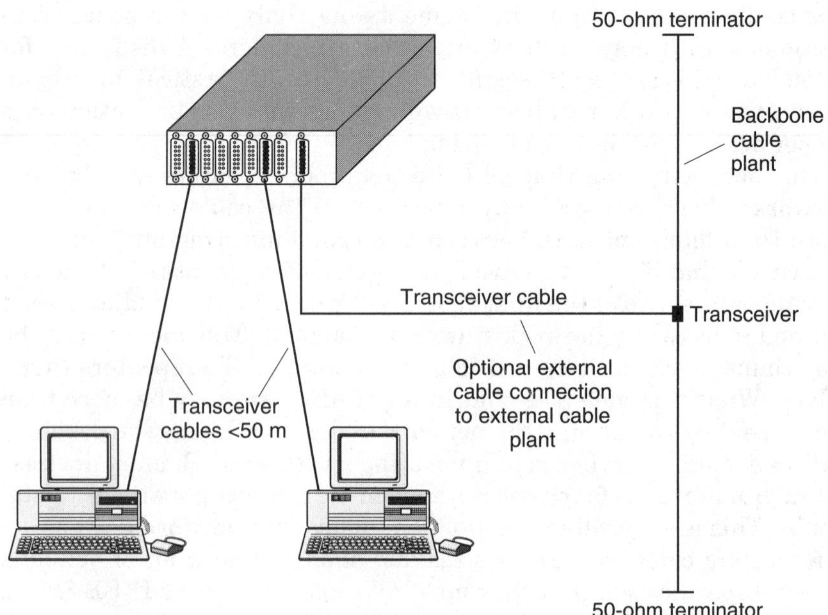

Figure 1.12 MTU connection.

their external cable connection port to this MTU. This allows up to 64 stations to be connected without the use of a cable plant.

One other purpose for this repeater is when the thick coaxial cable plant is being installed throughout a building (not just as a backbone cable). From the previous text, it was stated that thick Ethernet cable allows for only 100 attachments to a single cable segment, no matter how long that one cable is (up to 500 meters per cable segment). The MTU overcame this obstacle by allowing up to eight connections into the MTU, and the MTU is a single attachment to a cable segment. In applying the MTU this way, you could have up to 800 stations on a single cable segment. The MTU allows for up to 800 stations to attach to one cable segment.

Refer to Fig. 1.14. The Multiport Repeater (MPR) is used with 10BASE2 (thin net) cable plants. With the thin coaxial cable came the restrictions that only 30 stations may attach to one cable segment. It did not change the Ethernet maximum of 1024 stations. Therefore, this unit was developed so that up to eight thin cable segments could be attached. Each of the cable segments allowed for 29 stations to be attached (the repeater became the thirtieth attachment). There was usually one port on this unit that allowed for connection to an external cable plant. The best-known example of this is the DEC DEMPR. Refer to Fig. 1.15. Over the last few years (especially with the advent of 10BASET networks),

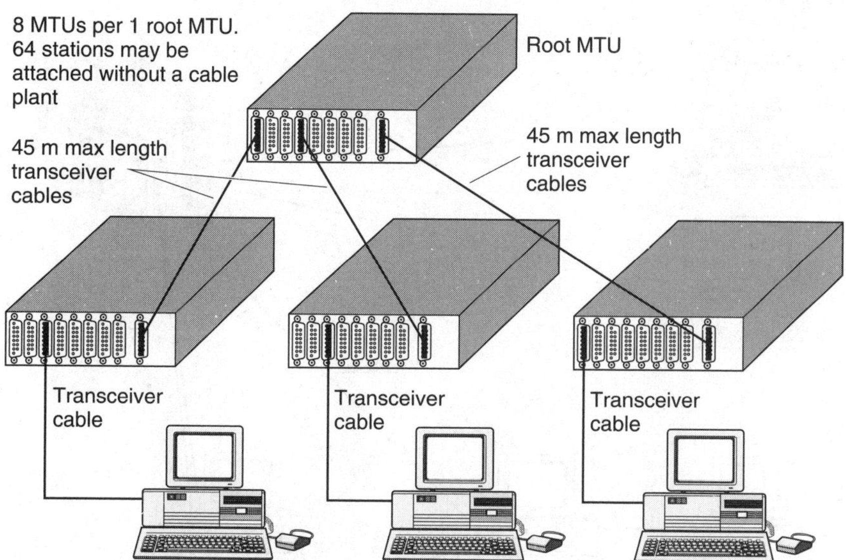

Figure 1.13 Cascaded MTU.

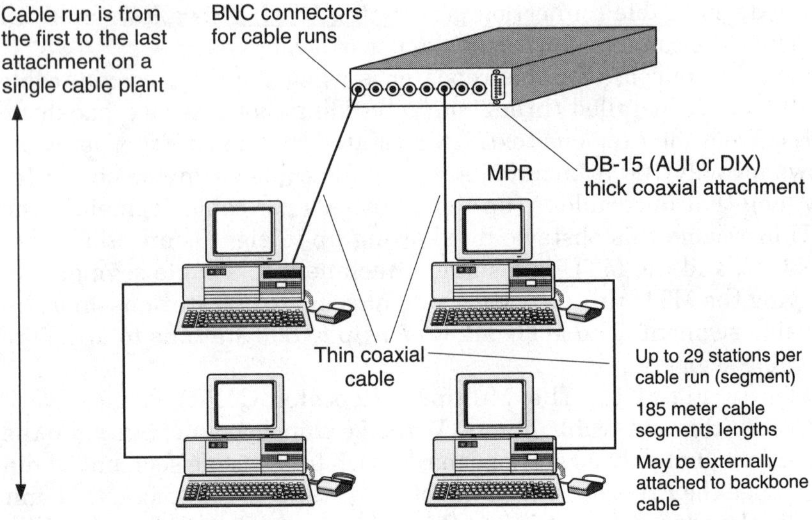

Figure 1.14 10BASE2 MPR.

wiring concentrators have become the most popular type of repeater. This is especially true for Token Ring environments. These units allow for not only 10BASET connections (a requirement for 10BASET network stations), but also allow for 10BASE2 and 10BASE5 connections, all in one unit, known as a *concentrator.*

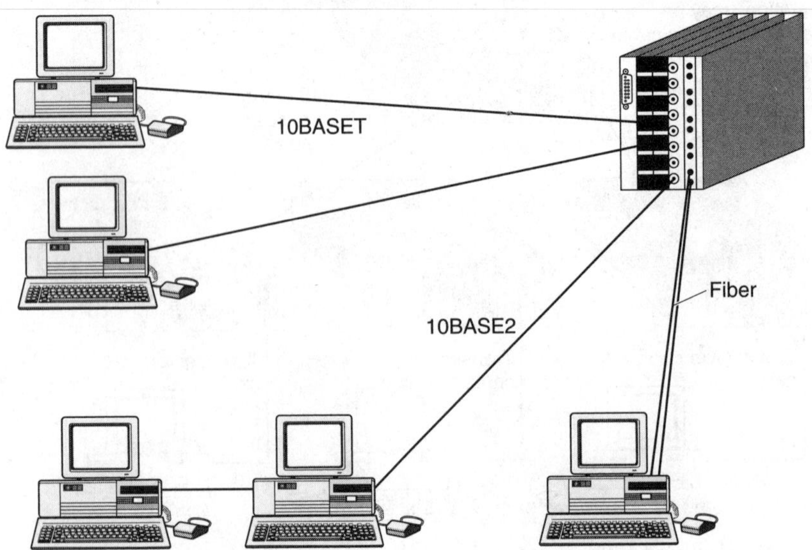

Figure 1.15 Wiring concentrator.

There really was no reason why there had to be separate repeater units for each type of cable plant, so all the repeaters types were combined into one unit. This allows the network to be more manageable, for the wiring hubs contain special hardware and software that allow them to be remotely managed over the network (called *in-band management*).

This means that a network station located somewhere on the network that contained specialized software could "talk" to the wiring concentrator. With this, the network administrator could turn on and off ports, get statistics from the unit (collisions, deinsertions, bytes transmitted and received, etc.). This allowed for a network management scheme to be brought to Ethernet.

Originally, Ethernet was implemented on a bus topology and all stations attached to it. This made it very hard to manage the individual stations on the network. The Ethernet standard did not mandate any type of management capabilities in the controller card. (In contrast, Token Ring has many management functions built into the IEEE 802.5 specification.)

The wiring hub made it a little better to manage the network. It is true that for those stations that are connected on the 10BASE2 ports, the network administrator can get statistics only for the single cable plant, or possibly turn off the part attached to the cable plant (not the individual stations on the cable plant). This is extremely useful for those who perform troubleshooting of Ethernet networks. Had it not been for this type of repeater and 10BASET cabling for Ethernet, Token Ring networks would easily be the dominant access protocol in use today.

These repeater units are shown in Fig. 1.16. All three types of repeater units may be intermixed on a LAN. This is also shown in Fig. 1.16. Examples of this type of hub are Synoptics Lattisnet Hub, Cabletron MMAC, and Ungermann-Bass Access One.

Token ring physical layer

The cabling scheme use for Token Ring networks is commonly known as the *IBM cabling scheme for Token Ring networks.* It has been designed to provide a structured wiring system that will work with all IBM communicating devices, including the IBM Token Ring.

One chief advantage of the wiring scheme for Token Ring is that it changed only slightly since its inception. The same wiring that was proposed in 1985 is the same type specified today. Token Ring is still a physical star, logical ring topology, the same as it was in 1985. The only new connector type is the RJ-45 for unshielded and shielded twisted pair. This will be fully discussed in the connector section.

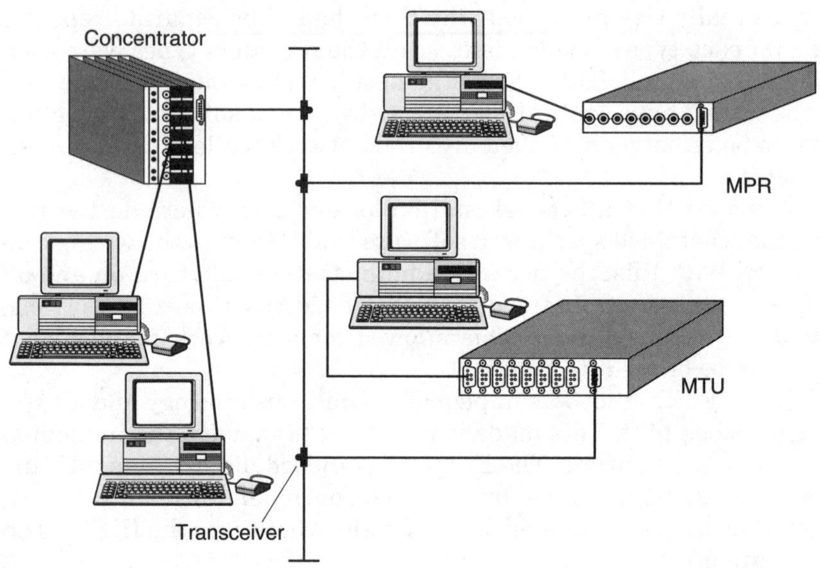

Figure 1.16 Mixing repeater types.

The types of wire used are described as follows:

Type	Description
1	An overall, shielded, data-grade cable, with two solid twisted pair 22 AWG wires. It is available as an indoor version with a braided shield or as an outdoor version with a corrugated metallic shield that is suitable for aerial installation or underground conduit. Type 1 indoor is also available in nonplenum or plenum versions for fire code regulations.
2	A type 1 indoor cable with four solid twisted pairs of telephone-grade (26 AWG) wire added around the outside of the shield. Type 2 is not available in an outdoor version. Type 1 cable is used exclusively for outdoor or indoor use.
3	This wire can be used where existing or unused phone wire is already in place. Since this is unshielded cable, a special device known as a *media filter,* must be added to the connection on the network attachment to filter out unwanted signals. This media filter is installed at the network station. Installing new wire is recommended.
5	This is a fiber cable used in repeater-to-repeater connection. It uses 100/140 micron cable.
6	This is a data-grade wire of stranded 26 AWG wire used for short runs in patch cables. This cable offers high attenuation and should not be used to connect a network attachment directly to a wiring concentrator over long runs.

8 This wire is 26 AWG twisted pair data-grade wire with a plastic ramp covering used in places where the cable must be run over the floor. It is used where cable cannot be run through the walls and floors. Older and historic buildings commonly use this.

9 This wire is 26 AWG shielded twisted pair wire in a plenum jacket, and is used in those areas where fire codes restrict the type of wire used in ceilings.

Although there are many different wiring types for Token Ring, types 1, 2, and 3 are the most commonly used. The maximum cable run for type 1 is 300 meters for connection between the wiring concentrator and the network attachment. This is for only one wiring concentrator. If there is more than one concentrator on the network, the maximum run of 100 meters is recommended. Notice that this is the same maximum cable run recommended for UTP wire for Ethernet.

There is a survey that has been provided by AT&T showing that most phones are not located more than 100 meters from the telephone closet. Usually, where there is a phone, a data jack should be placed there also. Therefore, most cable runs for UTP (Ethernet) and type 3 (Token Ring) are no more than 100 meters from their concentrators. Type 3 wire is the same wire used for UTP in Ethernet.

Refer to Fig. 1.17. The network workstations are connected to the concentrator shown, called a Multistation Access Unit (MAU). The IBM part number is 8228. All Token Ring devices must attach to the MAU. The MAU can connect up to eight type 1 wire connections. Another type of MAU used for type 3 wire can hold up to 16 connections (the maximum number of possible attachments can be vendor independent but most follow the 8 and 16 standard).

The MAU was introduced with IBM's Token Ring. Today, this MAU has evolved into wiring concentrators similar to those shown in the

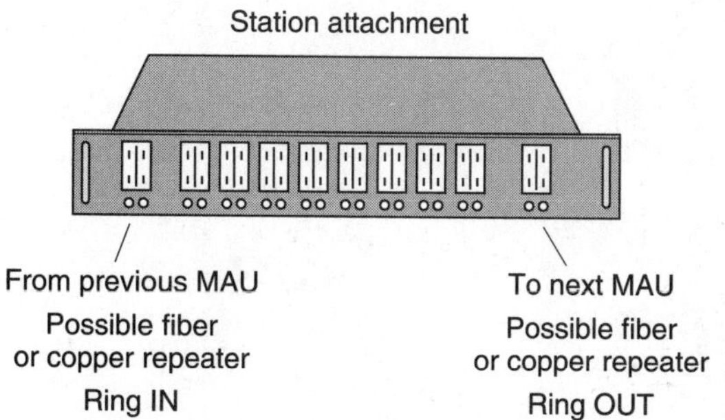

Figure 1.17 Picture of a shielded twisted pair (STP) MAU.

previous Ethernet repeater section. The concentrators can hold many connections, not just eight. The wiring concentrators also provide better network management through the use of network management stations. This is covered in the previous section on Ethernet concentrator. Although IBM still supports the 8228, IBM is now using a product known as the 8230. This concentrator allows up to four MAUs (8228's) to be connected to a fiber or copper repeater unit. This unit is then connected to another 8230 repeater unit that can attach to four more 8228's.

The topology represented here is the star-wired ring. As shown in Fig. 1.17, on either side of the MAU are the Ring In and the Ring Out ports. These ports are used to connect to other MAUs. See Fig. 1.18. This is how a single Token Ring network may expand to up to 260 stations for type 1 cable (33 eight-port MAUs) and 72 stations for type 3 cable. Allowing for more than 72 (nine eight-port MAUs) stations on an UTP cable plant is not allowed because of a phenomenon called *jitter.* This is the ability of an electrical signal to become distorted. UTP allows jitter to become more prevalent than type 1 cable.

As shown in Fig. 1.18, MAUs are connected together through the Ring In and Ring Out ports. The Ring In port is attached to another MAU's Ring Out port. That MAU's Ring In port would be connected to the next MAU's Ring Out port. As shown in Fig. 1.18, the last MAU's Ring In port is connected back to the first MAU's Ring Out port. The completes the logical ring.

Most wiring hubs (MAUs) now use a technology known as *active hub.* This turns each port on a hub into a repeater. With this, a UTP net-

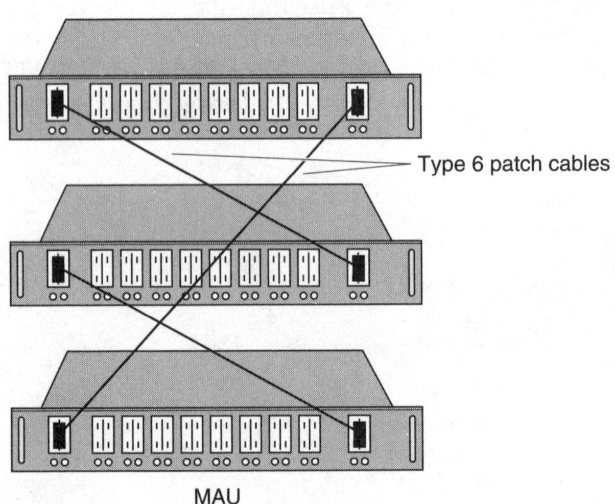

Figure 1.18 Multiple MAU connection.

work may connect up to 150 stations per UTP ring. The number varies from hub vendor to hub vendor.

To expand the station limits, a bridge or router is needed, which is explained later. The ring in port from one MAU is connected to ring out of another MAU. The last MAU should be connected to the first MAU in this method. The cable that attaches a network attachment to the MAU is called the *lobe cable.*

When the network attachment wishes to insert itself in the ring, the attached network station is responsible for providing a phantom voltage (a small, steady voltage applied to the lobe cable from the Token Ring controller card to the MAU) on the lobe cable, which will flip a relay in the MAU. This allows the network station to connect to the ring through the MAU. If the network station is power off, the phantom voltage is gone. The relay will be closed and data will not flow out to the network attachment. This will be covered in more detail later.

Data connectors

The data connector is the plug which terminates all cable in a Token Ring network. There are three types of data connectors used in a Token Ring environment. These connectors are: the hermaphroditic, the DB-9, and the RJ-11 and the RJ-45.

The hermaphroditic is a large black connector shell specifically designed to be used with type 1 and type 2 wire. It is commonly called the IBM Data Connector and is used in SNA environments as well as Token Ring. It is used on one end of a type 1 or type 2 connection and is plugged into the MAU. The other end of the cable is a DB-9 connector and is used to connect to the network station. Normally, hermaphroditic and DB-9 connectors are used only for type 1, type 2 cable, and other types of shielded cable. Hermaphroditic literally means having no gender, and this allows two hermaphroditic connectors to connect together. This is useful for providing long lengths of cable using multiple shorter cables.

The RJ-11 connector (the same type of connector used in residential phones) is used on one end of the type 3 cable. It attaches to the network station. Remember, using this type of cable, the type 3 media filter has to be used. Type 3 cable is not shielded and allows for unwanted electrical signal (noise, those signals which did not originate from the ring). The media filter is set so that only the Token Ring data signal is allowed to pass to the controller card. The media filter is typically attached to the Token Ring controller in the network workstation, and the type 3 wire is connected to the media filter. It can be an integral of the type 3 cable. Types 1 and 2 have foil shielding surrounding the data cables so that this does not happen. Therefore, media filters are not used with types 1 and 2 cable. Some Token Ring controllers have this filter built in. Check with the Token Ring controller vendor. The other end of the type 3 cable will be the RJ-45 connector, which will attach to the wiring hub.

The hermaphroditic connector may be used on unshielded twisted pair wire, but the connector is extremely expensive and the RJ-45 connector should be used. RJ-45 connector can be used on shielded or unshielded cable wire. Hub vendors are starting to use the RJ-45 (eight-pin telephone-type connector) on unshielded or shielded twisted pair—but only on the hub. Most Token Ring controller cards still have the RJ-11 or DB-9 connector. The RJ-45 connector is used by IBM. The RJ-45 connector is the same connector recommended for UTP wire in Ethernet installations. The hermaphroditic connector is used on shielded twisted pair cable to connect to IBM-type MAUs. It is not commonly used on other vendor's hubs. The RJ-45 connector is used mostly on other hubs.

Multistation access unit (MAU or MSAU)

These units are the wiring concentrators for Token Ring. These devices are the units which all network attachments connect to. Token Ring stations are not connected like a coaxial Ethernet network. This is where Token Ring follows the star topology.

Refer to Fig. 1.19.* The 8228 MAU is used to connect up to eight stations in a Token Ring LAN. (There are other MAUs that can connect up to 16 stations per MAU, but this book is following the IBM specification.) The cable that connects the station to the MAU is called a lobe cable and, for most installations, is allowed to be 100 meters in total length.† There are two other ports on the MAU: the *ring in* and *ring out* ports. These ports are used only for the connection to other MAUs.

Connecting two MAUs together does not create two distinct rings. Only when a bridge or router (explained in the next section) separate the two MAUs will there be more than one ring. Although not recommended, the maximum number of attachments allowed on one ring using shielded twisted pair cable is 260. For unshielded twisted pair,

---

* Although Token Ring sites now commonly use the same wiring concentrator (the same one as the Ethernet concentrator, except with MAU ports) as the MAU, the MAU explained in the here is the standard defined by IBM.

† This applies unless the site is using the 8230 concentrator. This concentrator allows for up to 200 meter lobe cables. This is due to the fact that every network station port in the concentrator is a repeater.

the number is reduced to 72.* Unshielded twisted pair allows for the original signal to be skewed easily on the cable (known as jitter) and the number of stations has to be reduced to 72.

Each attached device on the LAN is responsible for flipping a relay in the MAU, which allows a data path to the ring. This relay is flipped by the network attachments applying a phantom voltage onto the lobe cable, which will flip the relay into the closed stated and allow data to come off the ring and into the network attachment. When the Token Ring station is powered off or brought down for any reason, the phantom voltage is released and the relay will be flipped to the open state—in essence, taking the network station off the ring.

One important reason for the flipping of the relay is ring length. Ring length is variable in a Token Ring system. With a network that is 200 nodes large, with all stations powered on, the ring length is the total length of all cables (including all cables from the users attachments, the interconnection of the MAUs, etc.). If half of the stations are powered off, the ring length becomes smaller since the stations that are not powered on do not have their relay activated. This shortens the ring length. Signals passing through the MAU will bypass the inactive relay and move onto the next activated relay. This is supposed to be an efficient way to speed up the network. The lower the number of activated relays, the shorter the ring length.

* Other hub vendors besides IBM now allow for 120 to 150 stations to attach to one ring using UTP. This is allowed using a technology known as an *active hub*.

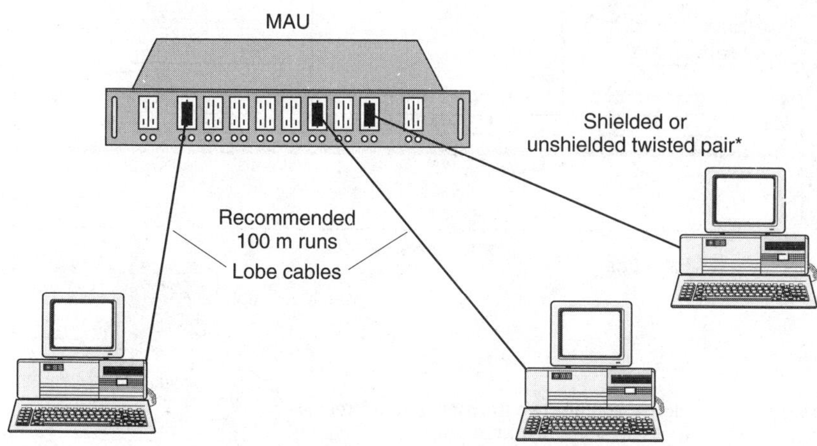

Figure 1.19 Controller attachment to a MAU.

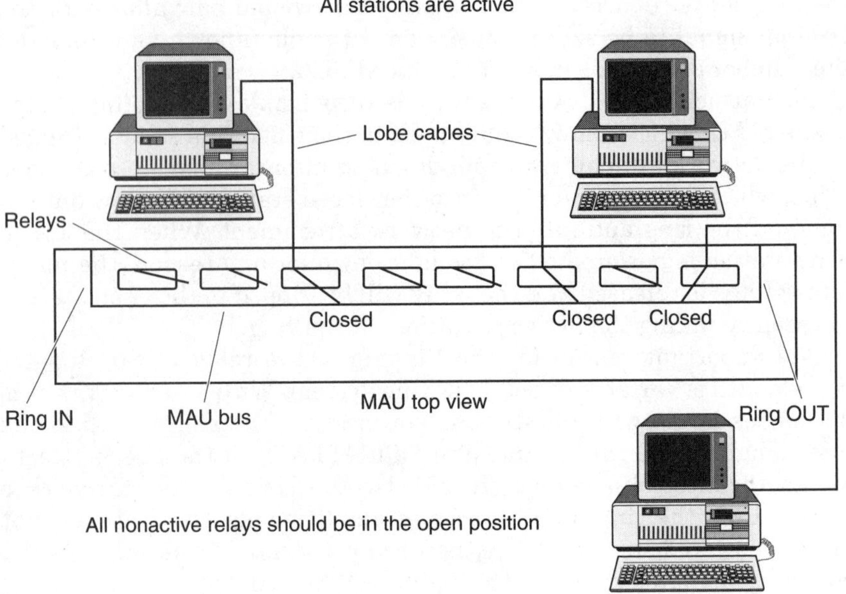

Figure 1.20 MAU operation.

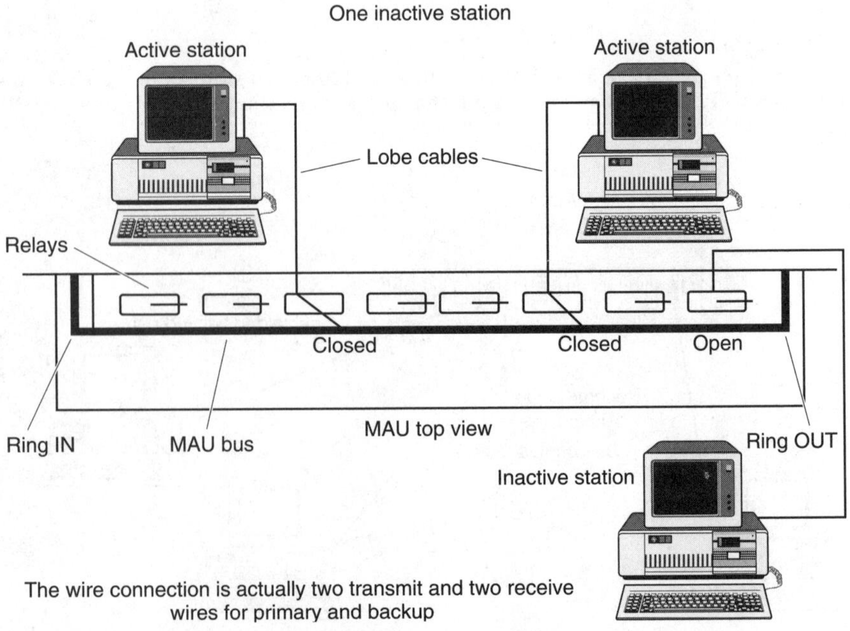

Figure 1.21 MAU operation with one inactive workstation.

Refer to Fig. 1.20. This figure shows three network stations that are active. Each of the workstations have an attachment to a MAU. Since each of the workstations are active, the relay is flipped to show attachment to the internal bus of the MAU.

Fig. 1.21 shows the same three stations, with the exception of one workstation that is not active. With this configuration, the workstation that is not active will not have its relay flipped to the closed state. In this state, the data that passes between the other two stations will not be passed to the workstation that is not active.

Chapter

2

Ethernet and Token Ring

The Data Link Layer

Ethernet

In a transmitting and receiving communication system, if there is only one cable to use and multiple stations need access to it, there must be a control mechanism in place to allow a fair system for stations to share the cable plant. In an Ethernet LAN system, the control mechanism is an access method known as Carrier Sense Multiple Access with Collision Detection (CSMA/CD). Ethernet applies the functions of the algorithm of CSMA/CD. It is easier to say Ethernet than it is to say CSMA/CD. Ethernet basically performs three functions:

1. Transmitting and receiving formatted data or packets
2. Decoding the packets and checking for valid addresses before informing upper-layer software
3. Detecting errors within the data packet (as a whole packet) or on the network

Packets. The basic unit of information that is transmitted on any LAN is structured into an envelope called the *packet.* At different levels of the OSI model, data will be encapsulated before transmission onto a LAN and will be called different things: a frame or a packet. For the purposes of this writing, data transmitted on a LAN, no matter at which level of the OSI model, will be called a packet.

All data that is transferred (for example, inside of a PC) will be transmitted as units of information on the memory bus between the

CPU and memory for processing. When this data has to be transferred between two stations that are separated by a LAN, some special formatting needs to be done on the data. This is the purpose of the packet. It is called *data encapsulation.* Each layer of the OSI model will encapsulate the data received from its higher level with its own information. There are many encapsulation techniques, and they will be discussed under each protocol. The original data is not changed, it will just have information appended to it so the network knows what to do with it.

Refer to Fig. 2.1. This figure shows the internals of two network stations: a workstation and a file server. In order for the two to transmit and receive data from each other, the data to be transmitted must be formatted for transmission over the network. This is shown in Fig. 2.1.

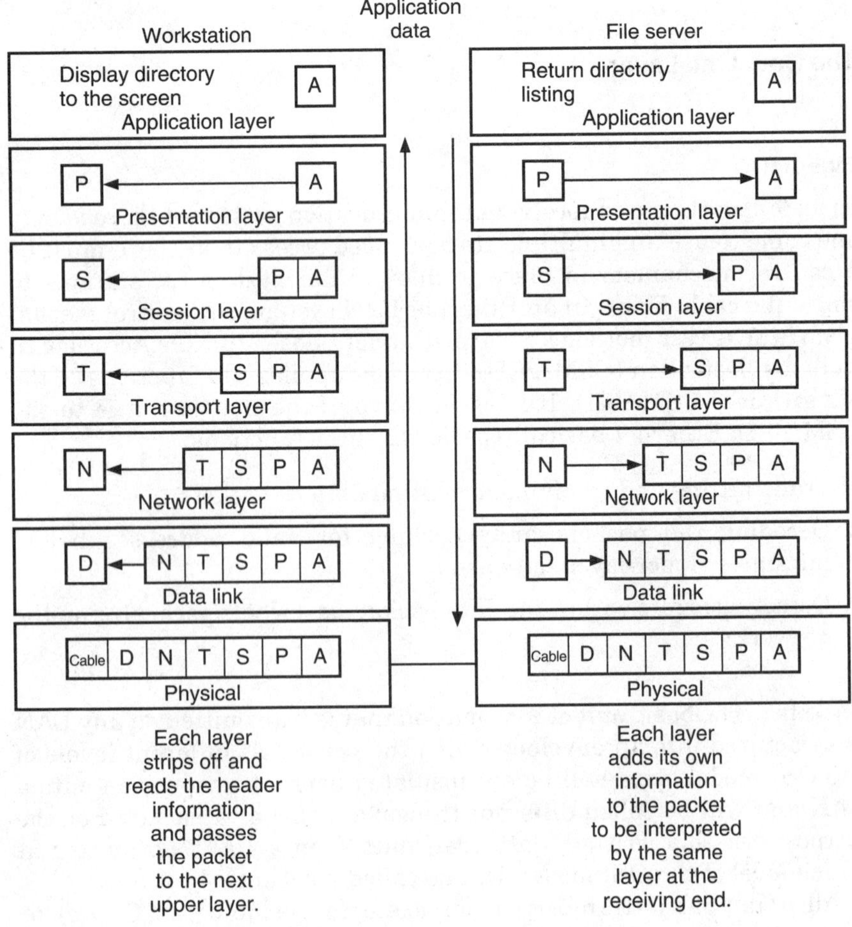

Figure 2.1 Packet terminating.

In this figure the workstation is requesting the file server to provide a directory listing from the server. As the application responds to the request, each layer of the network software will place information on the front or end of the data.

For example, the application layer passes information down to the presentation layer. This layer will add presentation layer information to the data and pass it on to the session layer. The session layer will add its information and pass it on to the transport layer. The process will be repeated down through the network stack. This is indicated by the A, P, S, T, N, and D in the figure. This stands for the application, presentation, session, transport, network, and data-link layers, respectively.

When this transmission is received by the server, each layer of the protocol stack will read the associated information in the received packet. For example, the data-link layer will read the data-link (D) information, strip off the data-link header, and then pass the rest of the packet to the network layer. The network layer will read the network-layer header, strip it off and pass the rest of the packet to the transport layer. The process will be repeated until the rest of the packet reaches the application layer. The application layer will read the data (in this case, it is a request for read of the hard disk).

When the server responds to this request, it will pass the data back down the network stack and network headers and trailers will be added to the applications data. The packet is again formatted as stated previously and sent back to the workstation.

Data that would normally be transferred between the CPU and memory inside of a PC is now encapsulated into a LAN packet for transmission and reception on a LAN. This encapsulation is called a packet and contains information that only the LAN will use to interpret what kind of data it is and where it is to be transferred. Figure 2.2 shows the packetized information being sent between a workstation and file server in a more simplistic view.

You can think of packets as sentences. When carrying on a conversation with someone, you will speak in sentences. These sentences will contain a starting and stopping point and will be directed towards someone who is listening to you. Carried in these sentences can be commands or simply information. Commands could be asking someone to sit down and retrieve something for you. Information sentences could be an idea or data that you have collected and are explaining to someone. Packets (also called *frames*) will be shown throughout the following text.

Simply stated, a packet is a special frame that contains data or commands that is formatted for transmitting these data or commands across the network. It is encapsulated data.

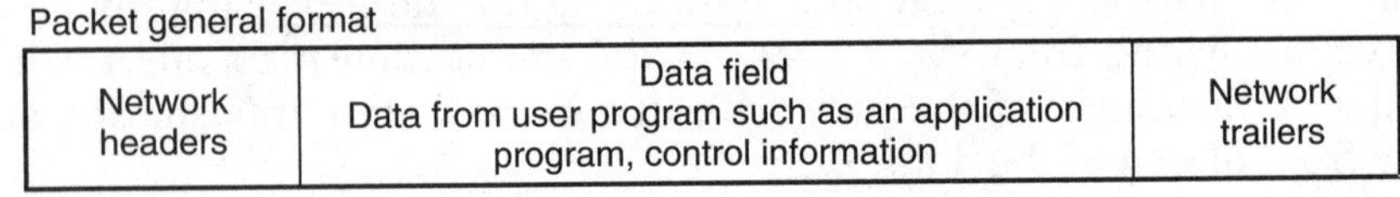

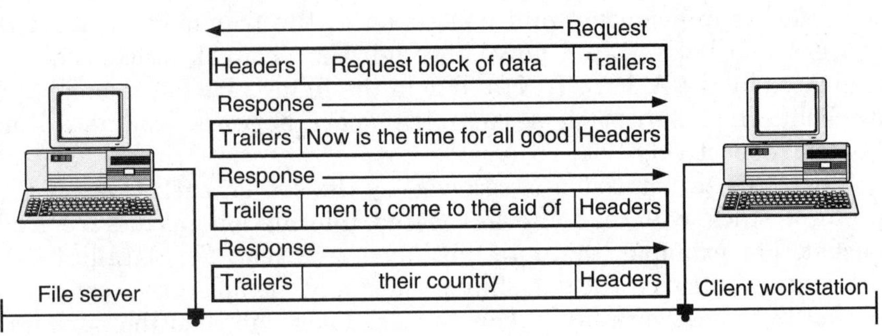

Figure 2.2 Packets.

Ethernet is also known as IEEE 802.3. With the exception of the frame format (shown later under the addressing section), the algorithm for both Ethernet and IEEE 802.3 is the same algorithm. Ethernet was invented by Bob Metcalf at Xerox Corporation and was standardized by a consortium consisting of Xerox, Intel, and Digital Equipment Corporation.

Refer to Fig. 2.3. A station wishing to transmit is said to contend for sole use of the cable plant. Once the cable is acquired, the station uses it to transmit a packet. All other stations on the cable plant listen for incoming packets or enter into defer mode (defer transmission of a packet). Only one station may transmit on the cable plant at a time.

To contend for sole use of the cable plant, any station wishing to transmit checks whether the cable plant is busy (i.e., uses carrier sense). It looks to see if any signals are on the cable. If the cable plant has not been busy for a specified amount of time, the station immediately begins to transmit its data. During the transmission, the station listens while transmitting. This process of listening while transmitting is to ensure that no other stations transmit data to the cable plant while it is transmitting.

If no other station transmits during that time and the station transmits all of its data, the station will then return to listening to the cable. The transmission is said to have been successful. If any other station transmitted during that time, a *collision* is said to have occurred. Any station transmitting will know a collision has occurred by the structure

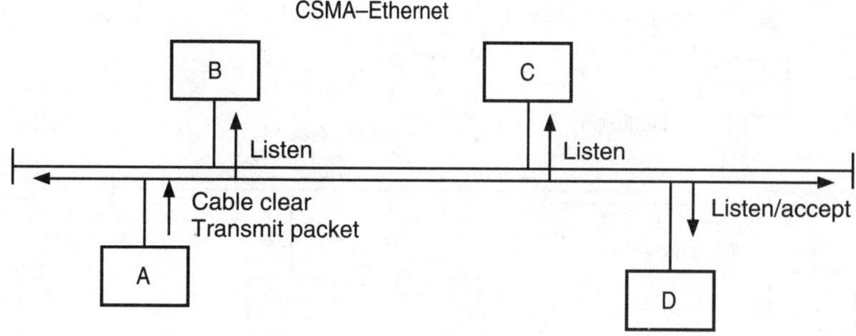

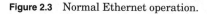

1. Node A receives data to transmit to Node D.
2. Build a packet.
3. Checks to see if the cable plant is clear (no one else is currently transmitting).
4. Transmits packet while listening to the cable.
5. If there were no collisions, return to listen mode.

Figure 2.3 Normal Ethernet operation.

of the signals on the cable plant. One example is if the strength of the signal doubles, then a station knows that another station has begun transmitting, and the algorithm known as *collision detection* is invoked to recover from this error.

When a collision occurs, each of the stations that are transmitting simultaneously (involved in the collision) will continue to transmit for a small length of time (4 to 6 bytes more). Refer to Fig. 2.4. This figure shows two stations transmitting at the same time, with a collision occuring. This is to ensure that all stations have seen the collision. All stations on the network will then invoke the collision backoff algorithm. The algorithm will then generate a random number which will be used as the amount of time to defer any further transmissions. This generated time should be different for all stations on the network. No two stations should generate the same number.* To ensure this, the algorithm also takes into account the number of previous collisions and other factors. Therefore, all stations should defer transmission for a different amount of time. This should allow no two stations to defer transmission for the same amount of time, thereby reducing the possibility of another collision.

* It is possible that two or more stations will generate the same number, but the case will be extremely rare.

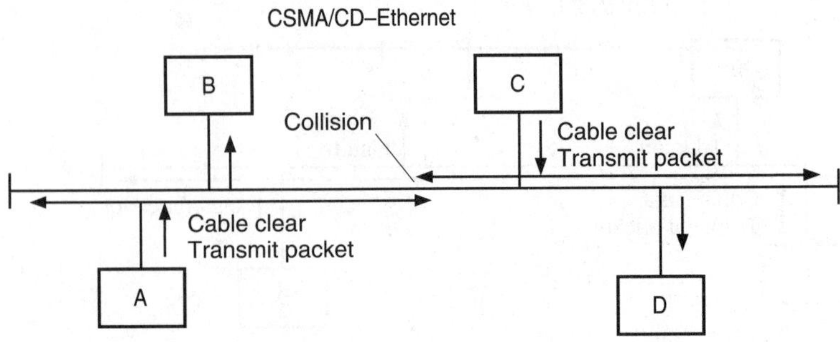

1. Node A receives data to transmit to Node D.
2. Builds a packet.
3. Checks to see if the cable plant is clear (no one else is currently transmitting).
4. Transmits packet while listening to the cable.
5. Node C accomplishes steps 1–4 and starts to transmit.
6. Collision between station A and C.
7. All station invoke the backoff algorithm.
8. All stations are free to gain control of the cable plant.

Figure 2.4 Ethernet with collision.

After the collision, all stations will back off. From there, any station may then try to gain access to the cable plant. The stations involved in the collision do not have priority. All stations have equal access to the cable plant after a collision.

Ethernet reception. Packet reception by Ethernet is just as simple. On the receiving station, the station will retrieve all the data being transmitted on the cable plant. Since Ethernet is a broadcast transmission medium, all stations on the cable plant (those not separated by a bridge or a router) will receive all packets that are transmitted on the cable. This does not mean that all stations will process each packet. The receiver will check to ensure a minimum packet size (64 bytes). It will then check to see if the address (addressing is discussed later) from the received packet is that of its controller board. If the addresses do not match, the packet will be discarded and the station will wait for the next packet. The user will not see this process.

If the address matches,* the receiver will check the packet for errors by checking the Cyclic Redundancy Check (CRC) field of the packet. This

* Every controller is assigned a unique number to identify itself on the network. Addressing will be discussed in detail later.

is a field used to check for the validity of the data packet. If there are any errors within the whole packet, the packet will be discarded. If there are no errors, the receiver will check to make sure it is not over the maximum length (1518 bytes total length, which includes the Ethernet headers). If this check is okay, the packet will be handed to its upper-layer software. Only the data portion of the packet is handed to the upper-layer protocols (network layer and above). Ethernet will strip off its headers (the addressing) and trailers (the CRC field) and submit the data portion of the packet to the upper-layer software for processing.

If any errors were detected, the packet will always be discarded. When a packet is discarded, the receiver will not notify the sender that it has discarded the packet. For that matter, the receiver will not inform the sender that the packet was received in good condition. Ethernet is known as a *connectionless* protocol. Ethernets main function is to deliver packets to the network and to retrieve packets from the network. Ethernet does not care what is in the packet. It only cares about transmitting and receiving packets. Packets sent and received are not acknowledged at the data-link layer. Ethernet is also known as best-effort delivery system or a *probabilistic network.*

The upper-layer software* has the responsibility to ensure that the data is received in good condition with error and in the same order as it was sent. These functions will be discussed fully in the following chapters.

Figures 2.5 and 2.6 show the algorithm flow for Ethernet packet transmission and reception.

Token Ring

Token Ring is probably the oldest ring access technique, and it was supposedly originally proposed by Olaf Soderblum in 1969. The IEEE version of the Token Ring access method has become the most popular ring access technique. There are proprietary ring access techniques made by different manufacturers. None of these have been adopted by the IEEE.

In Token Ring, although there is still one cable plant and multiple stations needing access to this cable plant, operation of the Token Ring access method is completely different than that of the CSMA/CD algorithm used for Ethernet (IEEE 802.3).

On a Token Ring network, a formatted 24-bit (3-byte) packet (shown in Fig. 2.7) is continuously transmitted on the ring. This packet is known as the *token.* The packet contains three 8-bit fields, Starting Delimiter (DS), Access Control (AC), and the Ending Delimiter (ED). These fields will be explained in a moment. With a few exceptions, any station that

---

* Upper layer software in this text refers to the software that runs at any of the layers 3 through 7 of the ISO model.

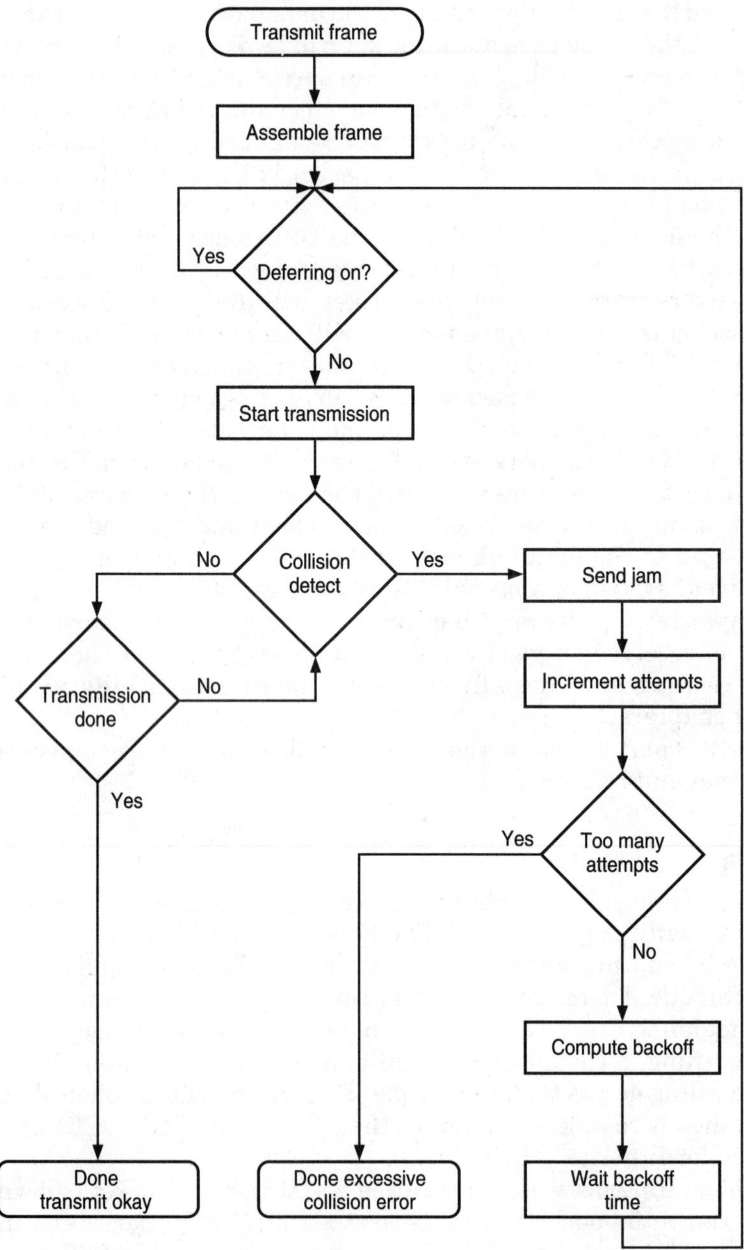

Figure 2.5 Ethernet transmission flowchart.

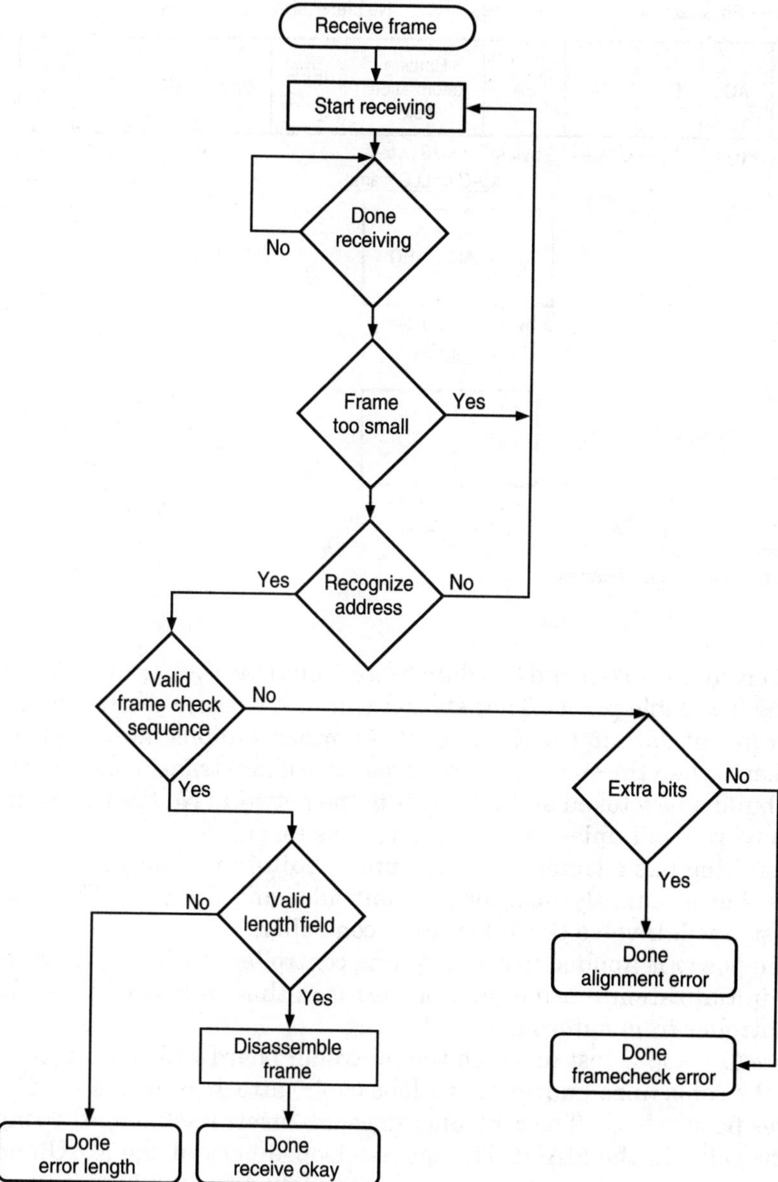

Figure 2.6 Ethernet reception flowchart.

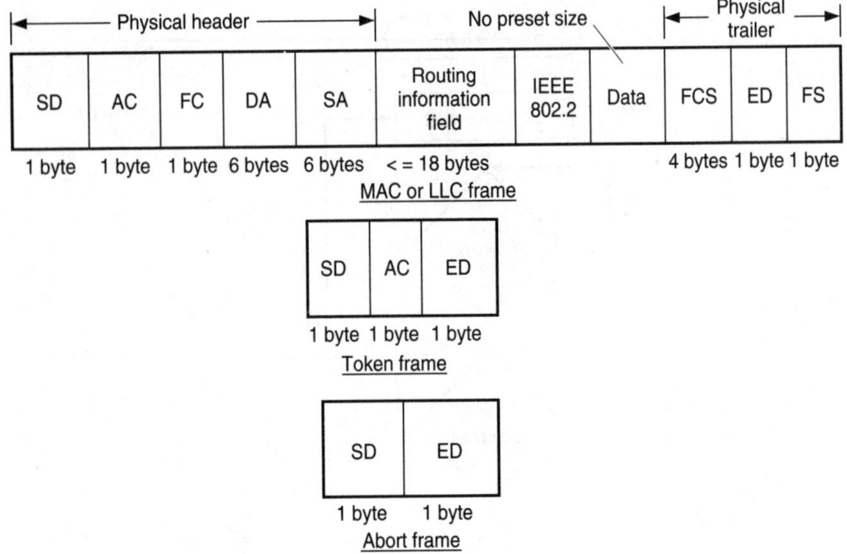

Figure 2.7 Token Ring frames.

has received this token and has data to transmit may then transmit onto the ring (the cable plant). That station will first capture the token and then transmit data to the cable plant. All other stations must wait for the token. When the station has received its original transmission back, it will build a new token and release it to the network. No station on the ring may transmit unless it has captured the token.

Token Ring has a tremendous amount of built-in management techniques that constantly monitor the controller and the ring. The next discussion will involve the Token Ring controller.

When power is applied to a Token Ring controller, it will begin a five-phase initialization routine. Any one error in this process will disable the controller from entering onto the ring.

Phase 0. A lobe test in which the controller board will submit packets to the cable (also known as the lobe cable) attached to it to see if it receives frames back. The controller does not insert itself onto the ring (flip the relay in the MAU). The cable is looped back at the MAU and any packet transmitted should be immediately returned in the same format as the transmission. If this test succeeds, the controller will enter phase 1.

Phase 1. The controller will produce the signal necessary (the phantom voltage) to flip the relay in the MAU to insert itself onto the ring. Flipping relay will cause an interruption on the ring. Flipping this relay produces electrical noise on the ring. This will cause an error on the ring in which the token or any transmitting station's data will be lost. In other words, any station that inserts itself into the ring will cause an interruption on the ring.

A special station on the ring known as the Active Monitor will recover the ring from this error and put a new token on the ring. Once this is accomplished, the controller waits for a special frame that it knows must be present on the ring. Once these frames have been found, it knows that the ring is active. In the case that none of these frames are found on the ring, the controller will assume that it is the first station on the ring and it will insert the frames itself and wait for them to return. If this test succeeds, the controller will enter phase 2.

Phase 2. The controller board will transmit one or two frames with the source and destination address set to its address. This is called the *duplicate address test* and is used to check if any other controller has its address. If the packet returns with the address-recognized bit set in the packet, the controller will deinsert itself from the ring. Addressing is discussed in a moment. If the frame returns with the address-recognized bit not set, it will enter phase 3.

Phase 3. The controller will try to find its neighbor by waiting for certain control frames to pass by. It will also identify itself to its downstream neighbor. In a ring environment, each active station will repeat signals it received to the next controller on the ring. With this, a network station can and will identify who is "downstream" of it (who passed the data to this station). Likewise, the new station will be identified to its upstream neighbor, for it will repeat data to it. Keeping track of the downstream neighbor is an important network management facility for Token Ring. As stations are added and deleted to the ring, any station can report this occurrence to the network management on the ring. If this test succeeds, the controller will enter phase 4.

Phase 4. The controller will request its initialization parameters from a station on the network known as the Ring Parameter Server* (RPS). The RPS resides on each ring. It sends initialization information to new stations that are attaching to the ring, ensures that stations on the ring have consistent values for operational parameters. In this request packet to the RPS will be registration information from the newly attached station. This information is the individual address of the ring station NAUN, the product instance ID of the attached product and the ring station's microcode level. The RPS parameters will be the ring number of the attached ring, etc. If there is not a server present, the initializing controller will use its default parameters. The servers on Token Ring are fully discussed at the end of the next chapter.

---

* Token Ring servers will be explained later.

Providing there were no errors during this initialization process, the network station is now active on the ring and may transmit and receive data as discussed in the following paragraphs. Even after initialization, the controller has the capability to take itself off of the ring, if there were too many errors.

Operation. Basically, a Token Ring controller may be one of three states: repeat mode, transmit mode, and copy mode. When a Token Ring controller does not contain any data that needs to be transmitted on the network, the controller will stay in a mode known as the *normal repeat mode.* Remembering the ring topology, this allows the controller to repeat any signals to the next active station on the network.

When the controller has data that needs to be transmitted on the network, the Token Ring controller must wait until the token frame comes around to it. Once the token is presented, the controller will make sure that the token has not been reserved by another station. If it was not reserved, the controller will capture the token (take it off the ring) and transmit its data to the ring. With no token on the ring, no other station can transmit.

Each station on the ring will receive this new transmitted information. Upon receipt of the SD field, the network station looks further into the packet to find an indicator that the receiving station either sent the packet or that it should receive the packet. If the network station did not originally send the packet but the packet is destined for it (the destination address in the packet indicates the network station is the intended recipient), the network station continues to copy the frame. If the frame is not destined for it, it will simply repeat the frame back onto the ring, unaltered, without continuing to copy.

The station that originally submitted the packet is the *only* station that may take the packet off the ring. This is called *stripping.* The destination station merely copies the frame as it repeats it back onto the ring. In case of an error in which the originating station cannot take the packet off the ring, a special monitor on the ring known as the Active Monitor will notice that this packet has traversed the ring more than once and it will take the packet off the ring.

After the originating station takes the packet off the ring, it will then submit the token back on the ring. The token frame will then circulate around the ring for the next station that has data to transmit.

Whereas the Ethernet specification states that the network will operate at 10 Mbps, there is no specification for clocking on Token Ring. Currently, IBM is supporting two speeds for its Token Ring network. These are 4 Mbps and 16 Mbps, commonly known as the 16/4 standard. The original Token Ring network ran at 4 Mbps. In 1989, IBM began to ship the 16-Mbps controllers. Some words of caution

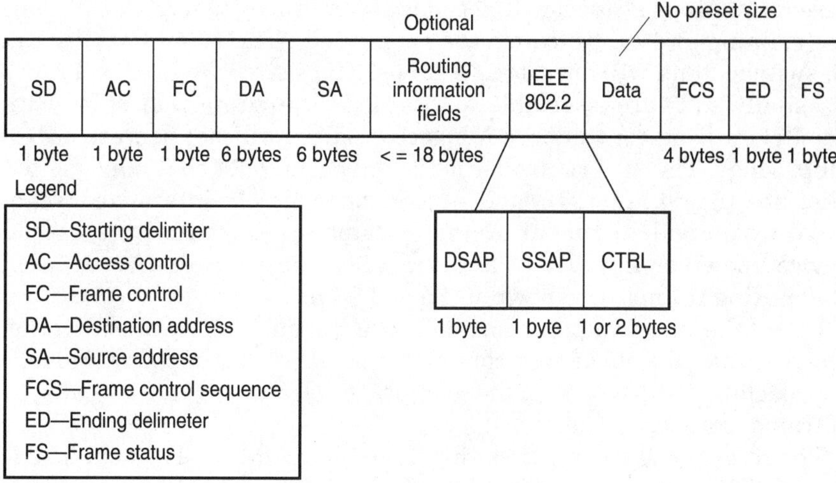

Figure 2.8 Token Ring, data frame.

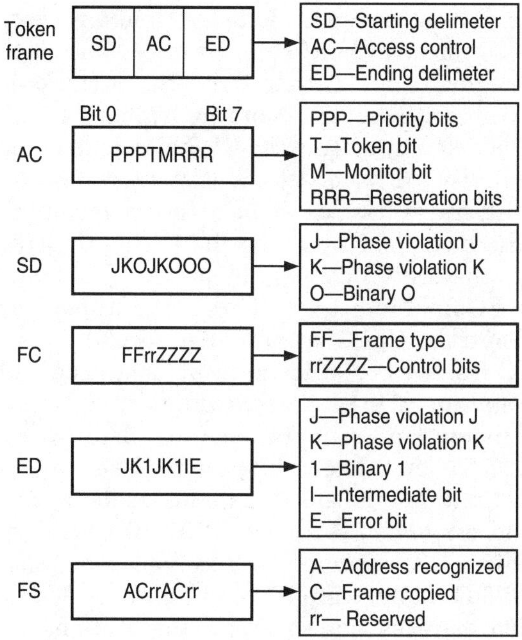

Figure 2.9 Token Ring frame fields.

here: a 16-Mbps station will not operate on a ring where the stations are running at 4 Mbps (called the ring speed). The 16/4 controller can be switched and will operate at 4 Mbps. The switch from 16 or 4 Mbps is usually software selectable with a utility program that ships with any Token Ring controller. 4-Mbps controllers will not operate on 16-Mbps rings. The 16/4 controller is the only controller that may operate at either 16 or 4 Mbps. 16- and 4-Mbps rings may be intermixed (separated by individual rings running at same speeds) through a special device known as a *bridge* or a *router*. These devices are covered later. Token Ring frames are shown in Figs. 2.8 and 2.9.

Let's take an example frame. When a Token Ring network station receives the SD field of an incoming frame, it will know that a frame is approaching. At this point, the network station has no idea what type of frame is approaching.

The receiving station will continue to read the frame, The next field is the AC field and is shown in Fig. 2.9, there are some bits that provide more information to the controller. If the T bit is set, this will indicate to the network station that the frame is a token frame (no data is associated with a token frame). Notice also in this figure are the Priority (P) and Reservation bits (R). If the network station wanted to transmit a packet, it would read the P bits. This indicates the current priority of a token frame. If the priority bits are equal to or less than the network station's priority bits, a frame may be transmitted. If the P bits are higher, the network station may "reserve" the token by setting the RRR bits, indicating that it has the next shot at it. The M bit is set the by Active Monitor (explained later) to indicate this frame has passed by an active monitor.

If the T bit was not set, the next field would be the Frame Control field. If the T bit was set, the next field would be the ED field, explained in a moment. The FC field indicates whether the frame is a data frame (Logical Link Control or LLC frame) or a special frame called a MAC frame. A MAC frame is used for network management purposes such as a network station reporting errors, duplicate address testing, active and standby monitor present frames. The MAC frame types are represented by the ZZZZ bits. The rr bits are reserved.

The next fields are the destination and source address fields, which indicate the 16- or 48-bit address of the sender and the 16- or 48-bit address of the intended recipient of the frame. The receiving controller would read the destination field to determine if the packet is intended for it. If the destination address was not the receiving stations, it would simply repeat the rest of the packet back to the ring. If the destination address was its address, it would copy the rest of the frame.

The next field is the Routing Information Field (RIF). This is used for source routing information and is explained in detail later in this chapter. The DSAP, SSAP, and Control fields are used by the data link for controlling the frames on the LAN. This is fully discussed in Chap. 3 of this book.

The data field contains user data for an LLC frame and contains management information if it is a MAC frame. To distinguish between the two types of frames, the controller reads the FC field. If the FC field indicates a MAC frame, it will read the ZZZZ bits; otherwise, those bits are ignored.

The FCS is a 32-bit Cyclic Redundancy Check and is used to maintain accuracy for the whole frame (minus the Frame Status field).

The Ending Delimiter has special symbols, J and K, to indicate to the controller that the end of the frame is arriving. It also has two other important bits: the I and the E bits. The I bit indicates to the recipient of this frame that it is an intermediate frame and more data is to come in another packet. The E bit indicates that another station has found an error in the frame and it should not be copied. This type of error is an electrical signal type of error. This frame should return to the sender to be "stripped." Being stripped means the station will take the packet off the ring and put a token back on the ring.

The Frame Status field has two bits of importance. These are the address-recognized (A) and the frame-copied (C) bits. The A bit is used to indicate that a destination station recognized its address. The destination will set this bit to indicate to the sender that the address was recognized. This bit is also used during the Token Ring controller initialization. When an initializing controller starts, it sends out a duplicate address frame. With this frame, the controller sets both the destination and source address to its physical address. If the frame returns with the A bit set, the initializing controller knows another station on the ring has the same address. The initializing controller will remove itself from the ring after notifying the ring error monitor.

If the C bit is set, a destination station has copied the frame. When the frame returns to the originator, it will know the destination has copied the frame. Therefore, it will not have to resend the frame. If the E bit is set, the A and C bits should not be set. The A bit can be set without the C bit, indicating the destination station recognizes its address but could not copy the frame for some reason. The frame may also be returned with both the A and C bits set to a 0, indicating no station is out there with that address and therefore the frame was not copied.

Notice that this field has two A bits and two C bits. The reason behind this is the FCS does not cover the Frame Status field. The FCS is set by the originator of a packet to be used by the destination station to ensure the integrity of the packet. Since the A and C bits are set by the destination station, the A and C bits are not covered (with a few exceptions, those bits should always be set to zero by the sending station).

One final note, if the C bit is set and the A bit is not set, the frame is in error. The receiving station must recognize its address before copying the frame.

There are many monitors that run on a Token Ring network. All are used for configuration and status report information. The following is a short listing and definition of the monitors.

Active Monitor. Resolves the following conditions:

Lost tokens

Frames and priority tokens the circle the ring more than once

Other active monitors on the ring (only one may be active at a time)

Short ring (a ring with such a low bit delay that it cannot hold a token

Control the master clock

Ring Error Monitor. The Ring Error Monitor observes, collects, and analyzes hard-error and soft-error reports sent by ring stations and assists in fault isolation and correction.

Configuration report server. The configuration report server accepts commands from LAN Network Manager to get station information, set station parameters, and remove station on its ring.

Ring parameter server. The ring parameter server resides on each ring in a multiple-ring environment. It sends initialization information to new stations that are attaching to the ring, ensures that stations on the ring have consistent values for operational parameters, and forwards registration information to LAN Network Manager from stations attaching to the ring.

LAN bridge server. The LAN bridge server keeps statistical information about frames forwarded through a bridge and provides bridge reconfiguration capabilities.

The IBM LAN Network Manager is a PC application that communicates optionally with NetView, IBM's host-based network management product. It allows a network administrator to manage multisegment IBM Token Ring networks. It also provides facilities for managing the LAN media and LAN adapters in the network and for managing the bridges that interconnect the networks. Figure 2.10 shows the relationship between the servers, the ring stations, LAN Network Manager and the SNA Control Point (NetView).

Addressing the Packet

Throughout the previous section, MAC or physical-layer addressing has been discussed. But what exactly are these addresses? These addresses are very important in a LAN environment.

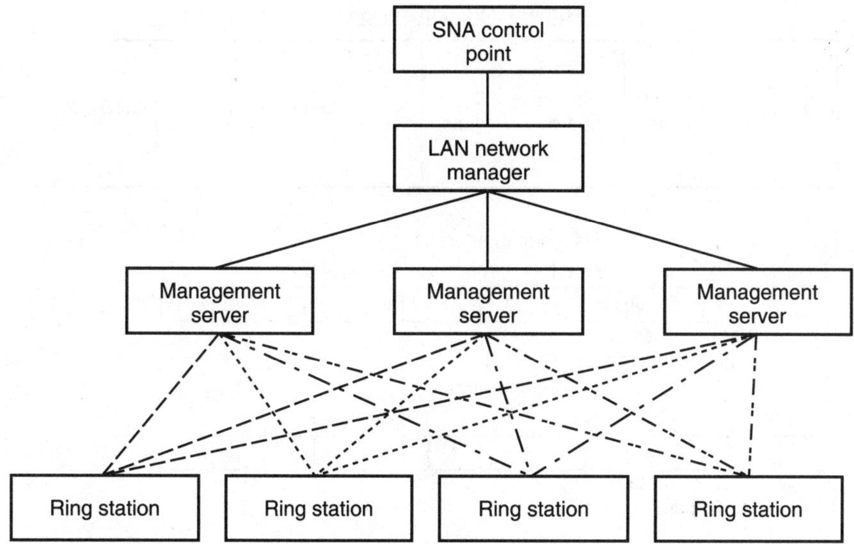

Figure 2.10 LAN reporting mechanism for Token Ring.

All stations on a LAN are identified by a special address. This is known as the MAC-layer address or the physical-layer address. This address is used to "physically" identify a station on a LAN. It is different than that address used to identify the station via the network software that it is running. These "software or protocol" addresses are discussed in the following chapters. It is called a MAC address, for it is at this sublayer (the Media Access Control, or MAC) that addressing is defined. Addressing is defined at the MAC sublayer of the data-link layer.

To identify a host by its physical address is placing its location on the network. Like the phone number in the telephone system, addressing in either Token Ring or Ethernet is the most basic way two stations will communicate with each other over a LAN. All data, once the connection is established, will be transferred between the source and destination addresses of the two stations. All numbers indicated in this section will be specified in hexadecimal unless otherwise noted.

Ethernet V2.0, IEEE 802.3, and Token Ring addressing will be discussed.

Frame identification (Ethernet). Refer to Fig. 2.11. The Ethernet frame,* reading from left to right (byte 0 to byte 5), consists of the destination

---

* The beginning of an Ethernet frame is an 8-byte preamble. This is used by the receiving network stations as a receiving clock. Receiving stations synchronize their receiving clocks to the signal of this preamble. Since it is never seen by a network administrator or a user, it will not be shown in any packets in this chapter.

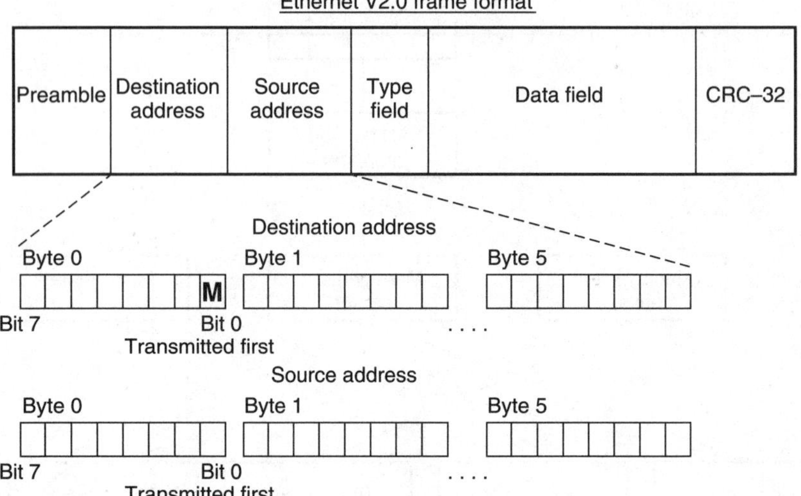

Figure 2.11 M—multicast bit.

address, the source address, the type field, the data field, and the Cyclic Redundancy Check (CRC).

1. *Destination address.* The address of the immediate recipient of the packet (does not have to be the final destination). Included in this field is the M bit, which indicates if the packet is a multicast or broadcast address, explained in a moment.
2. *Source address.* Address of the sender of the packet.
3. *Type field.* Indicates what type of data is in the packet: TCP, XNS, AppleTalk, etc.
4. *Data field.* Contains upper-layer software headers and user data.
5. *CRC-32.* An error-checking algorithm to ensure the integrity of the packet.

Each of the data encapsulation techniques is different. But each of them (Ethernet, IEEE 802.3, and Token Ring) uses something similar. This is the addressing portion of the packet. Each packet that is transmitted onto a network must have a physical address associated with it. There are destination and source addresses. These addresses are also called physical or MAC (Media Access Control, the portion of the data-link layer that controls the addressing information of the packet) addresses.

All physical addresses for Ethernet, IEEE 802.3, and Token Ring are 48 bits long.* There are two physical addresses in each packet: the source and the destination address. Each is 48 bits long, and is expressed as 6 bytes. There is a 6-byte source address and a 6-byte destination address.

For LAN interfaces, there are three types of physical addresses:

1. *Unique station address.* Much like the telephone number, there is one number assigned per machine. When a packet is transmitted onto the network, each station will receive the packet and look at the destination address field. The LAN interface card will do a comparison to the address that was loaded into its memory at start-up time. If there is a match, the adapter then passes the packet on to the upper-layer software (upper-layer software may be TCP/IP, XNS, IPX, etc.) for the software to determine the outcome. If there is not a match on the address, the LAN interface card will simply discard the packet. These are known as *unicast packets.*
2. *Multicast address.* A special type of address that is used to identify a group of network stations on the network. Each network station will have this multicast address assigned to it. In this way, a single station may transmit a packet with the destination address set to multicast and it can be received by more than one network station on the network. The easiest way to determine an Ethernet or IEEE 802.3 multicast address is by the first byte. If the first byte is an odd number, the address is a multicast address. A multicast address example is the Spanning Tree Algorithm used in bridges. With this address, all bridges may receive information by one station transmitting it in multicast mode. How a station indicates a multicast destination address is shown later. Source addresses will never be multicast.
3. *Broadcast address.* This is a special form of the multicast address. When you hear the term *broadcast,* this means that the packet is destined for all stations on the network. All stations on the network will pick up this packet and will automatically send it to its upper layer software. The physical address for broadcast is FF-FF-FF-FF-FF-FF. IBM Token Ring also includes C0-00-FF-FF-FF-FF as a broadcast address for Token Ring. This type of broadcast is usually used as an on-the-local-ring broadcast.

There is one more type of address used in Token Ring networks. It is called the *functional address.* With this if the first two bits are set to an 11 (hex C), and bit 0 of byte 2 is set to a 0, then the address

* IEEE 802.3 and IEEE 802.5 (Token Ring) frames allow for 16-bit addresses. These are hardly ever used and will not be discussed in this chapter.

is a functional address. Token Ring has no system of multicast. A packet is either addressed with a unique address or a broadcast address. This is the purpose of a functional address. The following functional addresses are reserved, except for the user-defined range. Functional addresses have a special meaning in Token Ring, as shown:

Function name	Functional address (in hex)
Active monitor	C00000000001
Ring parameter server	C00000000002
Ring error monitor	C00000000008
Configuration report server	C00000000010
NetBIOS	C00000000080
Bridge	C00000000100
LAN network manager	C00000002000
User-defined	C0000008000 through C00040000000

Table 2—functional addresses

Physical (MAC) addressing. This universal type address is placed by the controller manufacturer into a prom on the LAN card. Upon start-up of the network station software, the network controller software will read its physical address from the prom and assign this number to its software. For example, when the Ethernet drivers are loaded into a network station, the drivers will read the address from the prom and use the address in its software loading. It will use this number as the physical address for all packets that are transmitted or received by this network station. Although generally not used in Ethernet controllers, Token Ring controllers have the ability to allow the network administrator to overwrite this prom address with a private address. This is known as the Locally Assigned Address or LAA. To indicate this type of address, bit 1 of byte 0 of a Token Ring frame must be set to a 1 to indicate that it is a locally administered address. This will be more apparent when we discuss the addressing of the Token Ring frame. But for now, any address that starts out with a 4 in a Token Ring address is a locally administered unique address. Therefore, unique LAA addresses will always begin with a 4.

In looking at Figs. 2.12 and 2.13, there are distinct entities in the addressing portion of any of the frames. Figure 2.12 shows the Ethernet frame and Fig. 2.13 shows an IEEE 802.3 with IEEE 802.2 headers.

For now, pay attention to the address headers of each of the frames. The destination address is 48 bits long and disseminates into six eight-

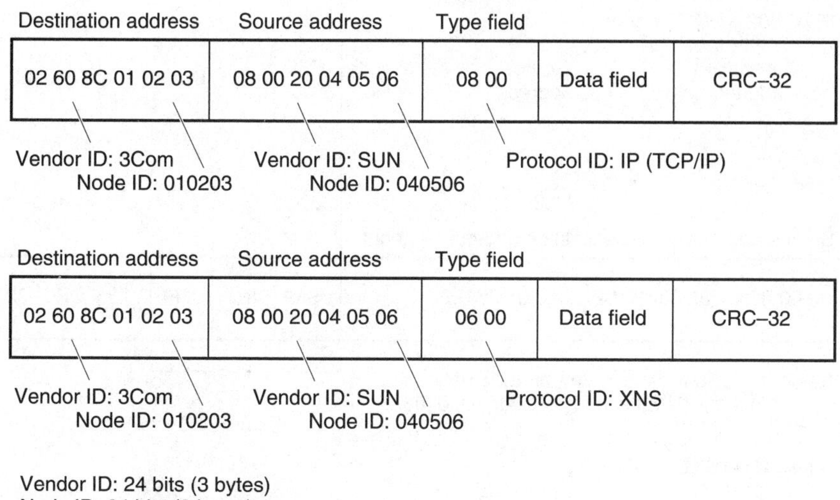

Figure 2.12 Generally defining the address fields.

bit fields. The first byte is on the leftmost side of the packet and is labeled byte 0. The last byte is on the rightmost side and is labeled byte 5.*

The first three bytes of the physical address, whether it is the source or the destination address, indicates the vendor. It was not intended to indicate the vendor—it just ended up this way. Originally, Xerox handed out these addresses. It is now the responsibility of the IEEE. The purpose of assigning the addresses by a central authority is simple. It ensures that there will not be a duplicate address by any network interface card.

Each vendor of a LAN interface card must register its use with the IEEE. IEEE will assign the vendor the first 3-bytes of the 6-byte total address. This is the first 3 bytes of the address. For example, 00-00-A2-00-00-00 is assigned to Wellfleet Communications. 02-60-8C-00-00-00 is assigned to 3Com Corporation. 08-00-20-00-00-00 is assigned to SUN Microsystems.

The last 3 bytes of the address can be assigned by the vendor. For example, with the first 3 bytes assigned to Wellfleet Communications (00-00-A2), Wellfleet is allowed to assign the last 3 bytes to their LAN cards for their routers. This means they are allowed to assign up to 2^24 individual addresses (16,777,215 in decimal) to their LAN cards, one per card.

* Although Token Ring and IEEE 802.3 frames transmit differently, the format of the address of the packet is the same.

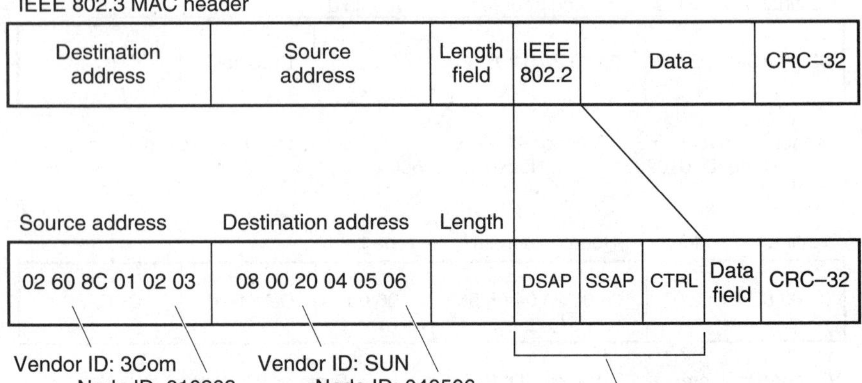

Figure 2.13 IEEE fields.

Each vendor is allowed to assign the last 3 bytes to whatever number they would like. Normally, these LAN cards are assembled in assembly-line fashion and each card produced is incremented by one in the last 3 bytes.

For example, in Fig. 2.12, the source address on both of the frames is 02-60-8C. This indicates the LAN interface card was manufactured by 3Com Corporation. The first three bytes were assigned to 3Com by the IEEE. Notice, the IEEE only assigned 3Com the first 3 bytes. The following 3 bytes are assigned by 3Com. The normal way to do this is to increment the node ID portion by one for each card they manufacture.

Notice in the bottom frame the destination address is different. The address is 08-00-20 which is the address assigned to Sun Microsystems. LAN controllers do not differentiate between vendors. The controllers read the whole 6-byte address as an address. The controllers do not care who manufactured the card.

The differences between an Ethernet and IEEE 802.3 packet should also be noted here. The largest difference is the type field. Ethernet packets use a type field, and IEEE 802.3 packets use a length field. How do these two fields correlate? They don't, except in their position in the packet. The type field is used to indicate the network protocol process that sent the packet. For example, in Fig. 2.12, a 0800 indicates that the packet originated from a TCP/IP process. A 0600 indicates the XNS process. If the field has an 8137, the packet was sent from a Novell NetWare station.

Refer to Fig. 2.13. IEEE 802.3 frames have the length field in place of the type field. This indicates the length of the data field, and the not the total length of the packet. How does the packet indicate what process sent the packet? IEEE 802.3 frames (with the exception of proprietary NetWare frames) should use IEEE 802.2 headers. This includes the Destination Service Access Point (DSAP), the Source Service Access Point (SSAP), and the control field. The DSAP indicates which destination process the packet is intended for. The SSAP indicates the source process that sent the packet. The control field is used for IEEE 802.2 link control. For example, if the DSAP and SSAP fields are both filled with an E0 and the control field is an 03, the packet is a nonproprietary Novell NetWare packet. It is stretching it, but you can think of these fields as the type field in an Ethernet packet. Refer to Chap. 3 for a detailed explanation of this field.

An IEEE 802.3 Ethernet controller can differentiate between the two types of packets by reading the twelfth byte of a packet. This byte will be either a length field or a type field. Ethernet type fields begin at 0600 (hex). The largest packet size of Ethernet is 1518 bytes; 1518 bytes is 05FE (hex). Therefore, if the number at byte 12 is equal to or greater than 0600 (hex), it is an Ethernet framed packet.

Bit-order transmission. The following text will use Figs. 2.14, 2.15, and 2.16. First refer to Fig. 2.14. This is an IEEE 802.3 frame. Most of the fields have been explained in the previous text. The purpose of this picture is to explain the way the bits in the bytes are transmitted. This is very important, for IEEE 802.3/Ethernet and Token Ring do it differently. This leads to many incompatibilities between the two architectures.

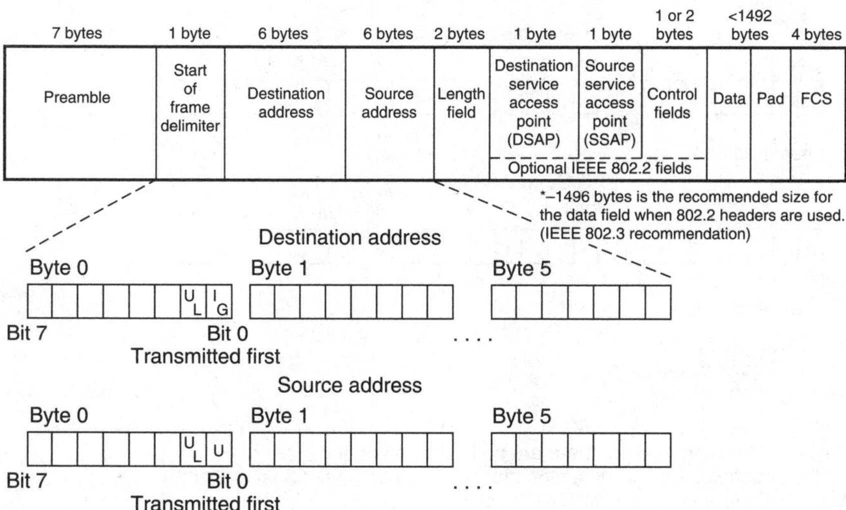

Figure 2.14 IEEE 802.3 CSMA/CD frame.

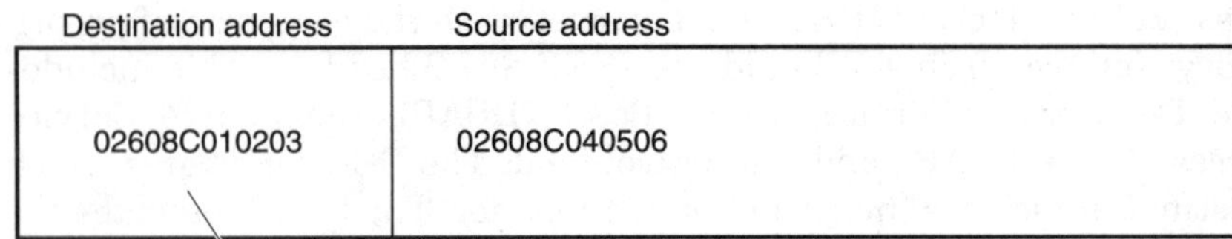

Figure 2.15 Ethernet/IEEE 802.3 bit order and transmission.

First, the IEEE 802.3 address fields are divided into 6 bytes. In this figure, the whole frame would be transmitted left to right, but the bits in each of the fields are transmitted right to left. Refer to the bottom of Fig. 2.14. This shows an exploded view of the address fields. Notice that bit 0 is the rightmost bit. This is called the least significant bit of the byte. It is transmitted first. The next bit transmitted is the bit to

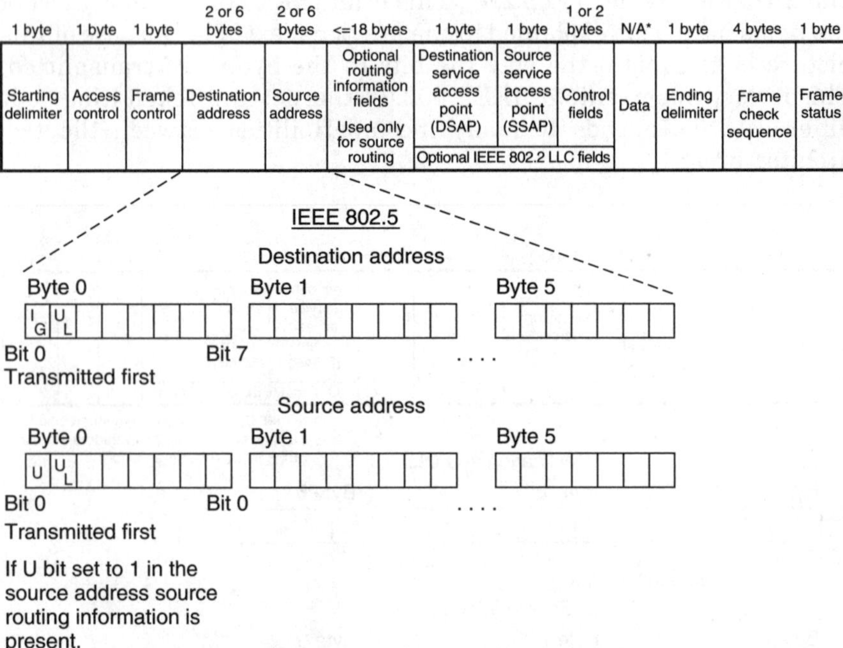

Figure 2.16 IEEE 802.5 frame format.

the left of bit 0. Once all the bits of the byte are transmitted, the next byte (byte 1) is transmitted. Once again, bit 0 is transmitted first.

For a better view, refer to Fig. 2.15. This figure shows a destination address of 02608c as the first 3 bytes. Four your convenience, it is converted to binary for you. Notice, though, when the bits are transmitted, each byte appears to be reversed. This is the way Ethernet/IEEE 802.3 frames are transmitted on a cable plant.

For IEEE 802.3 addressing, two other bits are important in the address. Refer to Fig. 2.14. For IEEE 802.3, bit 0 of byte 0 is on the right side of the first byte of the packet. If this bit is set, the packet is a multicast packet. IEEE 802.3 frames call this the Individual/Group address bit. It is the same as the multicast bit in the Ethernet V2.0 frame. This is the first bit transmitted on the LAN. Therefore, if the first bit transmitted on an Ethernet or IEEE 802.3 LAN is a 0, then it is an individual address. If the first bit is a 1, then it is a multicast address. For example, 02-60-8C-00-01-02, the first bit transmitted would be a 0. But for 03-60-8C-01-02-04, the first bit transmitted would be a 1. Therefore, this address is a multicast address. The second bit indicates whether it is a universally assigned address (the IEEE) or a locally assigned address (the local site). This bit is rarely used in Ethernet networks.

Token Ring is completely different. It is true, like Ethernet/IEEE 802.3, bit 0 is the first bit transmitted on a Token Ring LAN, but for Token Ring, *bit 0 is the leftmost bit of the byte*. Refer to Fig. 2.16. Like IEEE 802.3, this is the Individual/Group Address bit. It is the same as the multicast bit in the Ethernet frame. This is the first bit transmitted on the LAN. Therefore, if the leftmost bit (bit 0) of byte 0 is set to a 1, then the packet is a multicast packet. The next bit (bit 1) of byte 0 is the universal/local administration bit. If this bit is set, then the address has been locally assigned. This means that the address prom is not used to determine the MAC address of the card. It has been assigned by a network administrator of the LAN. This can have many advantages. Some LAAs have the phone number of the person that is using the address. Some LAAs are assigned by building, floor, and cube number. There are many way to assign these addresses. It will always have the 1 bit set. Therefore, LAAs always start with a 4 as the first digit.

The disadvantage of these addresses is that every address on the LAN must be unique. No two MAC addresses should be the same; therefore, the addresses are usually assigned by a central authority. This central authority is usually the LAN administrator's office. In other words, each company that uses LAAs is free to assign their own addresses, but it should be managed by one group of people. This can get to be an administrative nightmare. It also allows users to assign their own addresses. This can lead to a security breach. A lot of companies are applying filtering capabilities to their forwarding devices, known as bridges and routers, that can filter on a MAC address so that certain addresses are allowed on certain LANs and other addresses are "filtered" from entering some LANs. Token Ring controllers check for duplicate addresses upon start-up.

In summary, Token Ring and Ethernet/IEEE 802.3 both signify the left-hand byte as byte 0. They both state that bit 0 of byte 0 should be the first bit transmitted on the LAN. The problem is that Ethernet/IEEE 802.3 has the rightmost bit as bit 0 and Token Ring has the leftmost bit as bit 0. This is a bit reversal of the packet.

This leads to a complication. If Ethernet/IEEE 802.3 transmits and receives MAC addresses one way and Token Ring transmits and receives them in another way, how would network stations located on different LANs (one on Ethernet and one on Token Ring) communicate with each other? The answer is they cannot without the use of a device known as a router or a bridge (these devices are explained in the next section). Routers fully understand their specific protocol and what in their packet needs to be translated. Therefore, all routers and some vendors' bridges understand how to translate between the two LANs. We will come back to this problem at the end of the next section.

Bridges, Routers, and Basic Network Information

This section provides a brief introduction to transparent and source route bridges, multiprotocol routers, and network protocols.

In environments with a variety of computer resources (PCs, graphics workstations, mini, and mainframes), there are varying requirements for network bandwidth. For instance, clustered minicomputers, diskless workstations, or PCs sharing a file server place a great burden on a network because of numerous data transfers. When such traffic begins to seriously affect performance, the most efficient way to deal with the problem is to divide the network into separate networks. These separate networks are then brought together to form a internet using bridges or routers.

Bridges (Ethernet or IEEE 802.3)

Before the advent of bridges, everything that could be placed on one cable plant was placed there, regardless of the type of application. Refer to Fig. 2.17. Graphics workstations were on the same cable plants with equipment that used very little cable bandwidth (i.e., ter-

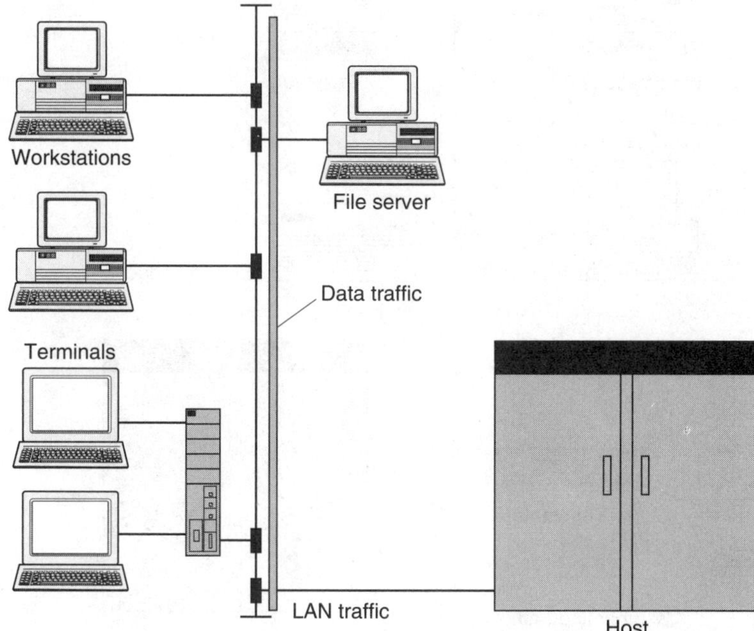

Figure 2.17 Typical Ethernet data traffic without bridging.

minal servers). The stations that do not generate much network traffic had to contend for use of the cable plant equally with the equipment that generated a lot of network traffic. Soon, people found that the network response was extremely slow. Some even went so far as to say that Ethernet had found its true limitations.

Before an uproar was started, a new networking concept arrived. Invent a device that would allow us to segment the cable plant based on network utilization, yet give us complete transparency. Refer to Fig. 2.18. The answer came in the form of a device called a *bridge*. The true name for the algorithm is *transparent bridging*.

Refer to Fig. 2.19. An Ethernet bridge* interconnects two or more Ethernet cable segments and watches all packets that traverse the cable. The bridge operates by inspecting all packets on the network for their addresses. An Ethernet bridge operates in a promiscuous mode. This means that it receives all packets, not just the packets with the destination address assigned to them.

---

* The true name for the algorithm is known as transparent bridging. Since it was originated for Ethernet networks first, and is commonly found on Ethernet networks, the text will call it Ethernet bridging. It should be noted that this same technology could be applied for Token Ring networks—but is usually not.

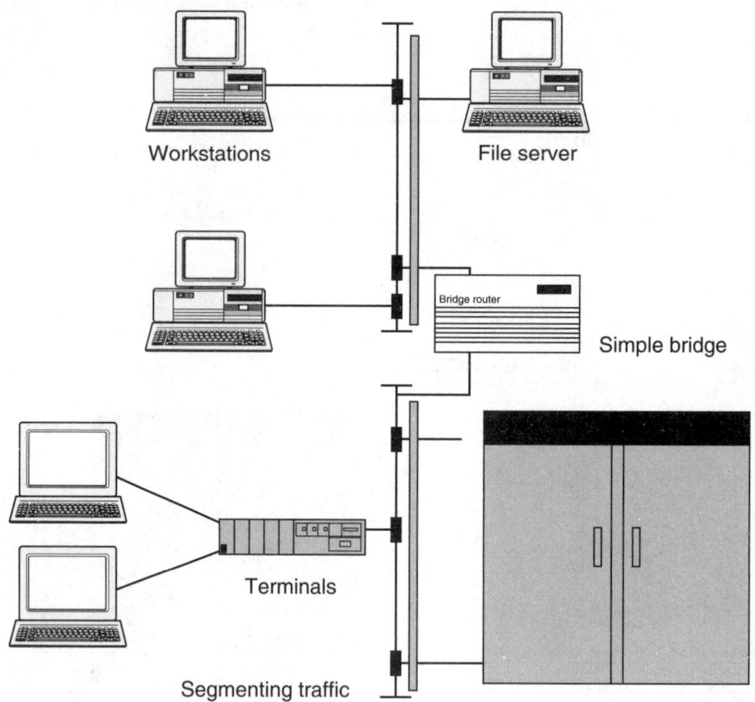

Figure 2.18 Bridged Ethernet environment.

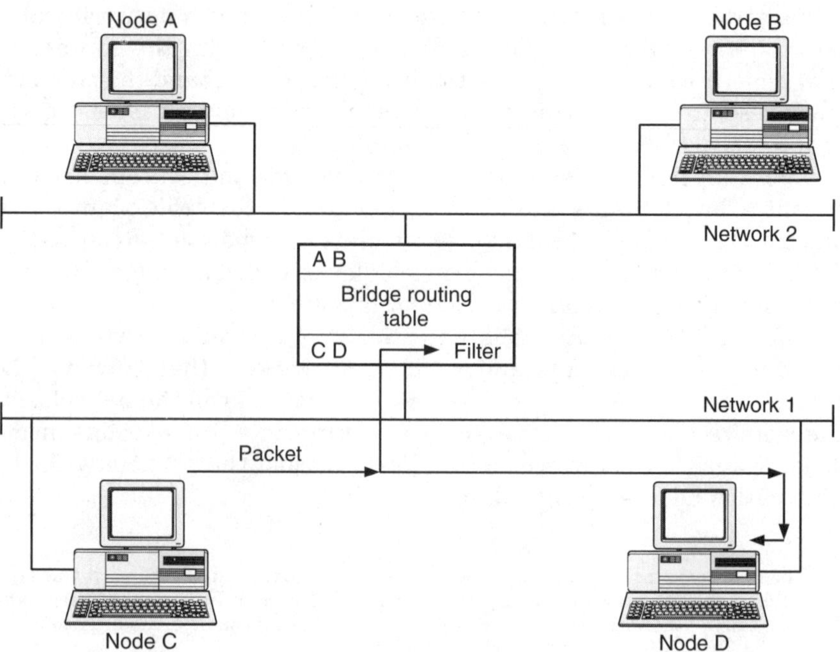

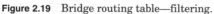

Figure 2.19 Bridge routing table—filtering.

In theory, a transparent bridge watches all cable segments that are attached to it (a bridge device may have more than two connections. Some vendors provide up to 52 connections per bridge). Two circumstances occur here for which the bridge will have to make a decision:

1. When the bridge receives a packet (remember that in broadcast mediums like Ethernet all stations on the same cable plant will receive any transmission on the cable plant), it is up to the controller to perform an address comparison and discard the packet if there is not a match. The point here is that, unlike routing technology, end-station transmitted packets are not directed towards the bridge. It will look at source address of the packet and enter this address into a database table of addresses (if the address is not already in the table). The bridge will keep a table of source addresses for each cable segment that it is attached to. This process is called *learning.* Any transmitted packet on the cable segment will suffice for the learning process. There are not special packets transmitted on the cable plant for the bridge to learn. Remember, this is called transparent bridging. An end station addresses the packet to the destination station with which it wishes to communicate. The end station does not know the bridge exists.
2. After receiving a packet, the bridge will look at the destination address of the packet. It will perform a lookup on all its database tables to find a match for that address. If a match is found in the local table (the table which is associated to the cable plant from which the bridge received the packet), the bridge will discard the packet. The packet will not be forwarded to any cable plant attached to this bridge. The destination was on the same cable plant as the source of the packet. This is known as *filtering.*

Refer to Fig. 2.19. If network station C transmits a packet to network station D, the bridge will receive the packet (not because it was specifically transmitted to it, but because it listens and receives all packets that are on a cable segment). It will perform a filter operation for the destination C in the same table as source A. Therefore, the bridge will not forward the packet to network 2. It will discard that packet. Again, since Ethernet is a broadcast network, Station D will receive that packet as if the bridge had not even been there. This reduces the amount of traffic on network 2, allowing for better utilization of that network.

If there is not a match in the local table, the bridge will look into each of the other tables that it has (under most circumstances, it will maintain one table for each cable segment attachment). Refer to Fig. 2.20. Node C transmits a packet to node A. If a match is found in one of those tables, the bridge will forward the packet onto that cable segment and

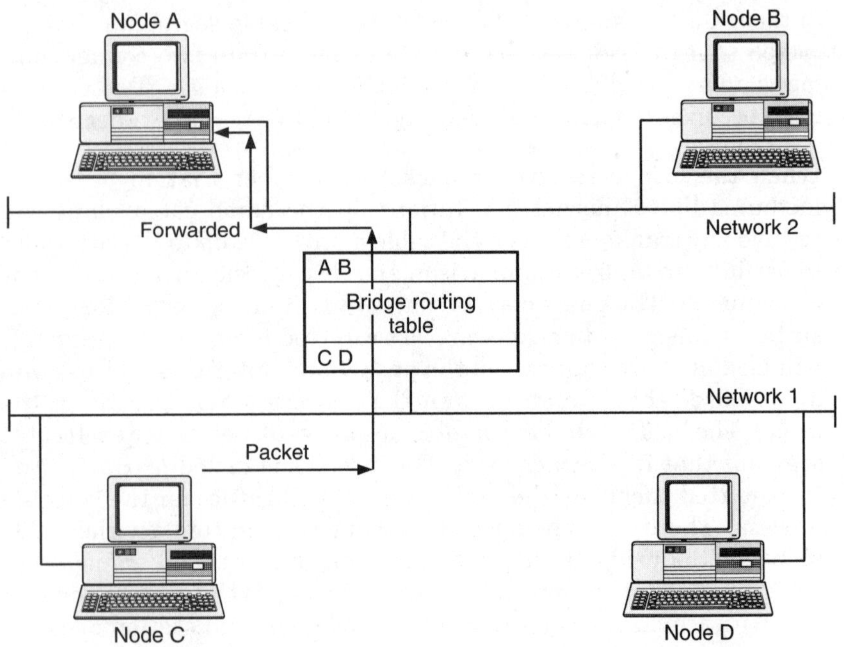

Figure 2.20 Bridge routing table—forwarding.

only that cable segment. In this case, the packet was forwarded to the LAN that has node A. This is known as *forwarding*.

Basically, a bridge performs three functions: learning, filtering, and forwarding.

Under certain circumstances, the destination address will not be found in any of the bridge's tables. If the bridge cannot find a match in any of the tables, it will forward the packet to all cable plants attached to it. There may be times when a bridge just has not yet learned the address and made an entry into one of its tables. When the bridge cannot find the address indicated by the destination address field, it will forward it to all active ports that the bridge has. This is known as *flooding*. Flooding it to all ports will not cause any errors on the network and the table will be quickly updated for when the destination station transmits a response to a packet, the bridge will then learn the address of that packet and place the address in the correct table, and it will not have to forward the packet to all cable plants after that. This is known as forwarding an unknown packet. It should not happen frequently. In most cases, unknown addresses are usually learned within one minute of bridge initialization. Bridges must forward to all active ports packets for which it does not know the destination address.

Some protocols must use multicast and broadcast addresses in order to properly operate with other stations on the network. With addresses such broadcast and multicast, the bridge will always forward these packets to every active cable segment that is attached to the bridge (flood the packet to all attached cable segments). The bridge can be configured to not forward these types of packets, but this is not usually the case. Bridges will flood multicast and broadcast packets.

Redundancy and the Spanning Tree Algorithm. In a bridged environment, it is possible to place two bridges in parallel. That is, two bridges that interconnect the same two or more of the cable segments. Refer to Fig. 2.21*a*. In this figure, there are two bridges that interconnect the same two Ethernet LANs. An active loop configuration is not allowed in Ethernet bridging. There is a protocol that allows the physical loop to exist, but not a logical loop. This protocol is the Spanning Tree Algorithm, or STA.

You might think that since they interconnect the same cable plants, each bridge will forward a copy of a packet destined for a remote cable plant. That is, if one station transmits a packet and neither bridge knew about the other, both bridges would forward the same packet to the other cable segment. This allows one packet to be transmitted

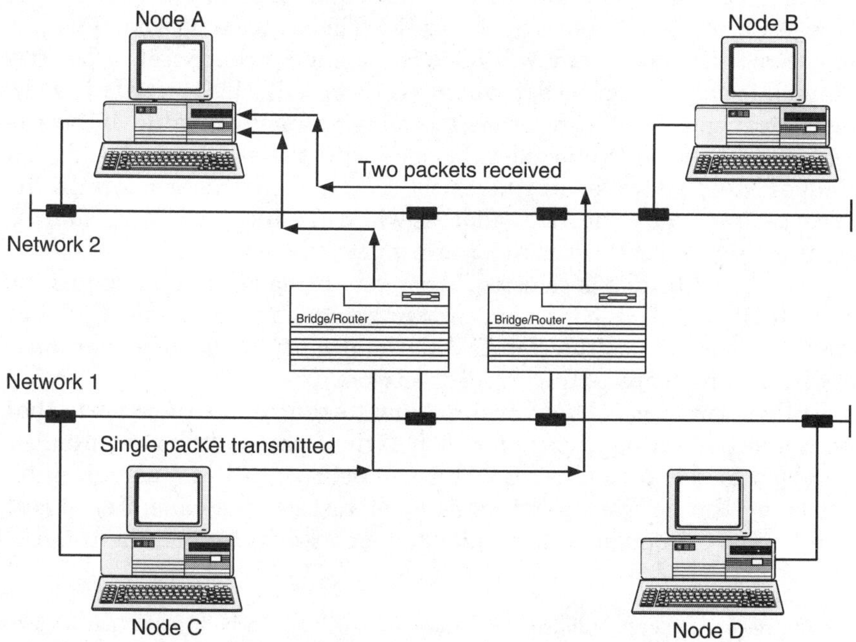

Figure 2.21 (*a*) Redundancy—loops.

and both bridges to forward the packet. This will allow two or more packets on the forwarded LAN. This can produce loops and fatal errors on the network. In fact, these environments will cause tremendous problems in bridged networks. For example, packets that are sent out in broadcast mode will be picked up both bridges. Each bridge will forward a copy of the packet to the next LAN. Each bridge will receive the other's broadcast on the forwarded LAN. Since the destination address is broadcast, each bridge will forward the packet back to the originating LAN. This loop will continue until one of the bridges stops forwarding.

Redundancy had to be allowed. Redundancy is the biggest use for parallel or looped bridges. For Ethernet, the Spanning Tree protocol enables this redundancy without the duplication of packets.

Spanning Tree is the protocol, approved by the IEEE 802.1d committee, which enables bridges to interconnect two or more of the same cable plants or to allow for a redundancy in the network. The protocol enables bridges to talk to one another using reserved multicast packets known as Bridge Protocol Data Units (BPDUs). These packets allow bridges to learn about one another and, if there is a loop (indicating parallel bridges), one bridge will become the ruler of the spanning tree LAN (known as the root bridge) and it will place all of its ports in the forwarding state. Other bridges will be placed in a blocking state.

The first stage to create a loop-redundancy network is that all the network bridges will select a root bridge. The bridge that wins the right to become the root bridge will have the highest priority set (a priority number is given to the bridge when it is installed). High priority is a low numerical value and a low priority is a high numerical value. If there is a conflict between two or more bridges with the same priority, then a bridges MAC address will rule as the tie breaker. The bridge with the lowest numerical value MAC address will win. Since each MAC address on an Ethernet LAN is unique, there will not be a tie again.

Once a root bridge is selected,* that root bridge then propagates the root BPDUs to find loops, and certain bridges will dynamically "shut down" one or more of their ports (known as a *port in the blocking state*) to disable any loops in the bridged network.

Bridges running STA determine how to shut down their ports that have a looped configuration, for each of their ports will have a number assigned to it known as a *cost.* This can be assigned as a default number or by the network administrator at installation time. These cost numbers are propagated throughout the network through the BPDUs.

---

* The network should stabilize very quickly but there will be bridges that assume they are the root bridge and will continue to transmit root BPDUs until another root is discovered.

The bridges that put their ports in the blocking state are the bridge ports that have the highest cost associated to the path to the root bridge. If there is a loop between two bridges, each bridge will determine who has the highest cost to the root bridge. The bridge that has the highest-cost port to the root bridge will put its port into the blocking state. The other bridge will keep its port in the forwarding state, allowing the forwarding of data frames.

Highest cost is inversely proportional to the line speed. For example, a T1 line which runs at 1.544 Mbps will have a higher cost than an Ethernet segment which runs at 10 Mbps. In other words, once the root bridge is selected, bridges that have the highest cost to get to the root bridge will shut down their ports. For those segments that all have the same cost, for example, a pure Ethernet environment (no serial lines), the bridges furthest away from the root bridge will put their ports into the blocking state. The whole purpose of this is to provide a loop-free topology.

This process of providing a loop-free topology usually takes about 30 to 35 seconds, depending on what the network administrator has set up on the bridge. When the bridges have invoked the STA, all forwarding of data will be stopped and bridge tables will be flushed (erased). Once a loop-free topology is established, the root bridge will transmit root

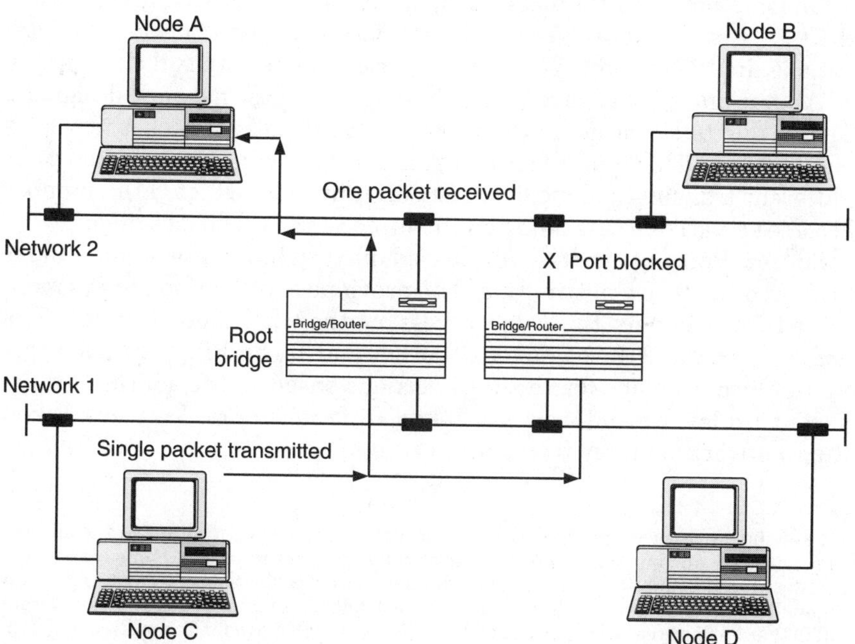

Figure 2.21 (*b*) Redundancy—blocked loops.

Hello BPDUs to the network (default every two seconds). Every bridge on the network waits for these Hello BPDUs, whether or not they are in blocking or forwarding mode. If it receives them, it assumes the root bridge is alive and the path to get there is good, for it received the Hello message. In the event that a bridge does not receive the Hello BPDU, maximum wait timeout is 20 seconds default, the bridge that discovered this will issue a topology change configuration BPDU, and the bridged network will reconfigure to establish another loop-free topology.

Refer to Fig. 2.21*b*. In this simple configuration, the bridge on the left was selected as the root bridge. Therefore, the bridge on the right will put one of its ports into the blocking mode.

Being in the blocking state does not mean the bridge is disabled. It is true the bridge will not forward any data packets or learn any addresses while in the blocking state, but the bridge will continue to listen for hello packets submitted by the root bridge. These hello packets are special packets submitted by the bridge to let all other bridges (active or blocking state) know that the root bridge is still alive. If a bridge with a port in the blocking state does not receive these hello packets for a certain amount of time, the LAN bridges will reconfigure and create a new tree topology.

Rule to remember: The Spanning Tree Algorithm allows only one path to any network in a bridged environment.

One last note on Ethernet (transparent) bridges. With all costs equal, the total amount of bridges in a linear (in a row) path between two stations is limited to eight. This is not a strict standard (i.e., defined in the STA), but one that is generally adhered to by most network designers. This is due to latencies that may start to occur after a packet traverses eight bridges. This is for the transparent bridges only. With unequal costs (different transmission medias: 56k serial lines FDDI, etc.) the number becomes a variable depending on the protocol that is being bridged.

Source Routing bridges (discussed next) allow only seven linear bridges or hops to a destination. The previous explanation always mentioned Ethernet as the cable access method for these bridges. The address format is the same for Ethernet and Token Ring.* Since transparent bridges make forwarding decisions based on the address, transparent bridging could work on Token Ring networks. Very few Token Ring networks employ transparent bridging.

---

* For the purposes of this book they are formatted the same. In actuality, the address length is the same but the bit order for transmission is not the same. Some bridge vendors have taken this into account and therefore provide for transparent bridging for Token Ring and Ethernet. There is a standard known as Source Route Transparent (SRT) that has not yet been released by the IEEE that will allow for Token Ring and Ethernet networks to transmit data across a heterogeneous bridge. This standard does not allow for Ethernet-to-Token Ring translation. There is another standard due to be released by the IEEE for this.

Bridges (Token Ring)

Token Ring environments enable a different type of bridging. The accepted method (at least by IBM and the IEEE 802.5 committee; it is not accepted by any other standards body) is an algorithm known as *source routing*. This method of bridging Token Ring LANs can exist only on Token Ring LANs. It will not work for Ethernet LANs. The algorithm for Source Routing is much more detailed that what will be described here. It will be only briefly described in the following paragraphs. For more information, please refer to the *IBM Token Ring Architecture Reference Manual* and the *Local Area Networking* books.*

Refer to Fig. 2.22*a*. Token Ring environments have a number assigned to each ring. This number is assigned when configuring the bridge ports. The ring on the left side of the picture has been assigned ring number 4. The ring on the right side has been assigned ring number 3. These numbers are not assigned in the network station. They are assigned when configuring the bridge for operation on the ring. The bridge on top is assigned number 5 and the bridge on the bottom is assigned number 6.

* The *IBM Token Ring Architecture Reference Manual* can be ordered from IBM, part no. SC30-3374-02. *Local Area Networking* can be ordered from McGraw-Hill.

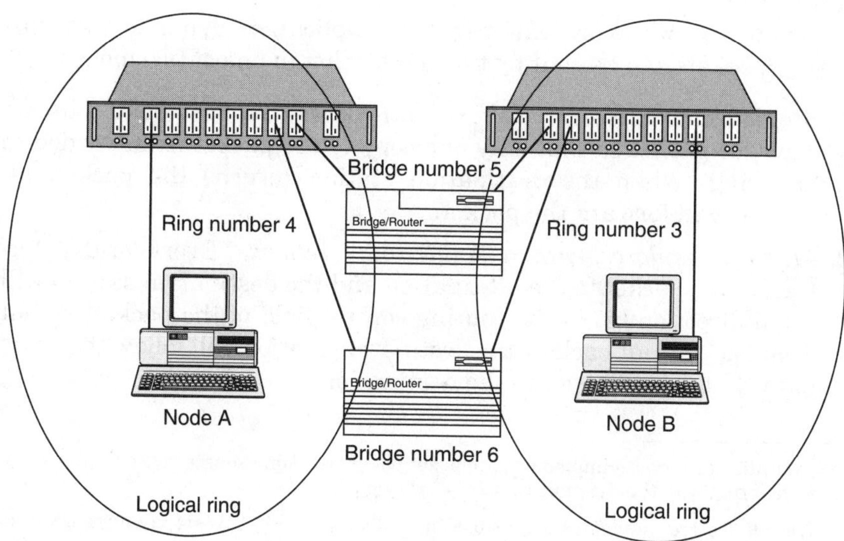

Figure 2.22 (*a*) Source routing.

The combination of the ring and bridge number creates a 2-byte field with the ring number being 12 bits in length (leftmost bits) and the bridge number is 4 (the rightmost bits). This allows for 4095 rings and virtually an unlimited number of bridges, as explained next. The ring numbers must be unique for each ring on the network. The bridge number does not have to be a unique number and if there are no parallel bridges (those bridges interconnecting the same two rings); all bridge numbers may be the same, allowing virtually a limitless number of bridges on a ring. The following text will show how a packet is forwarded through a Token Ring bridge.

If node A needed to communicate with another device, node B, it will transmit certain packets on the ring in order to find the other station. It will* first transmit a packet called the *all stations broadcast packet* in an attempt to find the destination. If the destination station is on the same ring, it should respond and the originator and the destination can set up a local session.†

If there is no response on the local ring, the originating station assumes that it may be on a remote ring. The originating station will then broadcast a *dynamic route discovery packet* in an attempt to find the destination on a remote ring. This packet will have routing indicators, i.e., the optional routing field, built into it that any bridge attached to ring will know what to do with. The originating station can submit an all-routes discovery packet (the actual name for this is the all-routes explorer, ARE, frame) or a single-route discovery packet. Refer to Fig. 2.22*b*. This figure will be explained throughout the following text.

Figure 2.22*b* shows the complete Token Ring packet format with the full RIF field.

Depending on the programmer of an application, dynamic route discovery packets can be sent by the end station in one of two modes:

1. *Single-route explorer with an all-routes return.* Send out an explorer packet so that only one copy of the packet is forwarded to any ring. When the destination station returns the packet, all bridges will forward the packet.
2. *All-route explorer with a single-route return.* Every bridge forwards this packet to the destination and the destination station will flip a direction bit in the routing control field of the packet so that each packet sent back by the destination station will follow the exact path that it took to get to the destination.

---

* Not all source route implementations support this. Some source route implementations go straight to the dynamic route discovery packet.

† Not all protocol implementations use this. Most now skip this step and transmit an all-routes broadcast, explained in the next paragraph.

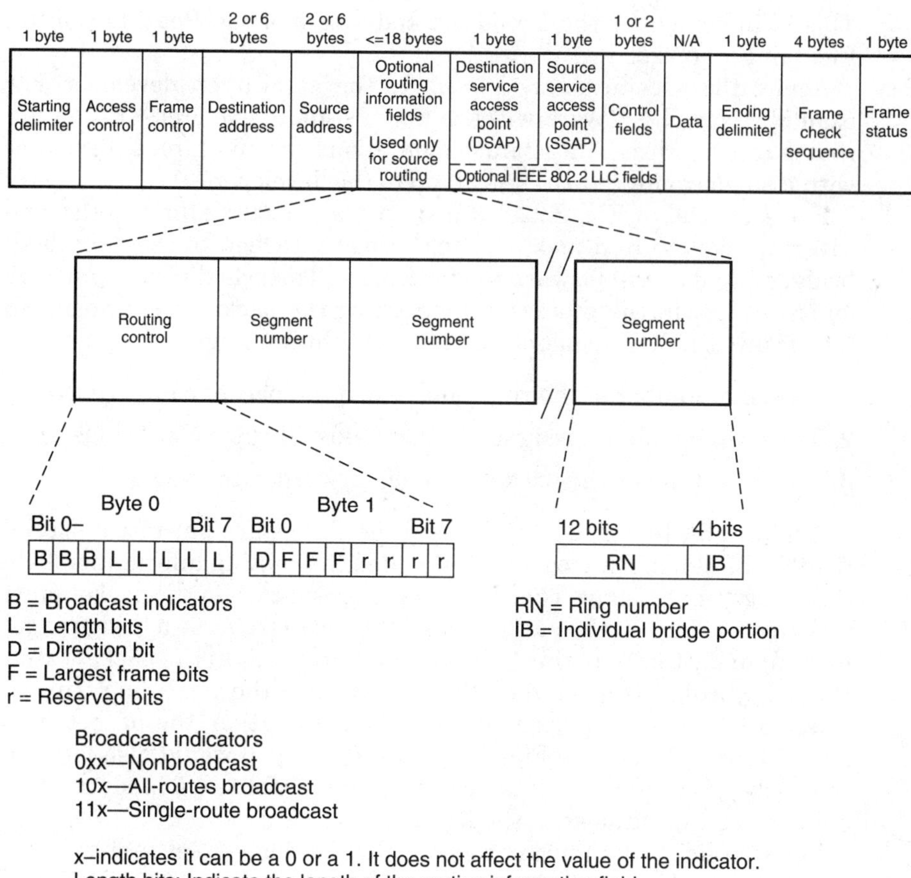

x–indicates it can be a 0 or a 1. It does not affect the value of the indicator.
Length bits: Indicate the length of the routing information field.

Largest frame bits: Indicated the largest frame that the bridge may handle.

000—up to 516 bytes
001—up to 1500 bytes is present in the information field
010—up to 2052 bytes
011—up to 4472 bytes
100—up to 8144 bytes
101—up to 11407 bytes
110—up to 17800 bytes
111—Used in an all-routes broadcast

Direction bit: Indicates to the bridge in which order to read the information in the routing information fields.
Ring number: Indicates the number for a particular ring.
IB: Indicates the number for the bridge.

Figure 2.22 (*b*) IEEE 802.5 frame format with defined RIF field.

This is indicated by the Broadcast Indicators of the Routing Control Field in Fig. 2.22*b*.

Again, the specific method is up to the application developer. For example, Novell NetWare will use a single-route explorer with an all-routes return. Most TCP/IP implementations use an all-routes explorer with a single-route return. It is all up to the developer.

For example, in Fig. 2.22*a*, if node A transmitted an all-routes discovery packet to find node B, each bridge attached to the ring (both bridges 5 and 6) will forward the packet to all attached rings connected on its bridge. In the process of forwarding the packet, the bridge will "stuff" into the RIF segment number field three things:

1. The ring number of the ring from which the packet came (ring 4)
2. The bridge number assigned to that bridge (bridge 5 or bridge 6)
3. The ring number the packet is being forwarded to (ring 3)

Again, refer to Fig. 2.22*b*. These three things are put into a special field in the Token Ring packet. It is called the routing information field (RIF) segment number. This field is only present when the packet must traverse a bridge. If the packet does not have to traverse a bridge to get to its final destination, this field will not be present in the packet. After this, the bridge will forward the packet onto the next ring, ring 3. Therefore, when the packet reached the destination, the packet from bridge 5 would look like Fig. 2.22*c*. Since bridge 6 would also forward the packet, it would be similar, except there would be a 6 in place of the 5 for the bridge number in the RIF field.

For simplicity, the routing control (RC) field is not set in Fig. 2.22*c*. The RC field contains information such as the length of the RIF field (the L bits), the largest frame size that a bridge (the F bits) can transmit. As the packet traverses each bridge, that bridge will set these bits as to the largest frame that it can transmit. The possible entries are given in Fig. 2.22*b*. If a bridge receives a packet that has the field set to 2052 and the receiving bridge can transmit only 1500 bytes, that bridge will reset the field to 1500. If the bridge can transmit larger packets, it will not enter anything into the field. It will leave it alone.

The direction bit indicates to a bridge which way to read the RIF field (right to left for a packet being transmitted from the destination to the source station, or left to right for the source station to the destination station). It is used on specifically routed frames, and responses

DA	SA	Data-link header	RC	0045	0030	Data	Packet trailers
				RIF field			

Figure 2.22 (*c*) IEEE 802.5 packet with filled-in RIF field.

to all-routes explorer frames. Instead of having a destination station rebuild the RIF field, it can set the direction bit and sent the packet back. In this way, bridges will read the information from last to first.

If the destination station received a frame that was sent to it as a single-route explorer, the responding station will not set the direction bit and send the packet back to the originator. It will build a new frame and send it as an all-routes response. See the preceding rules for what type of response packet is generated for single- and all-routes explorer packets.

The rrrr bits are reserved, but IBM is now allowing their use to indicate more largest-frame sizes.

Refer to Fig. 2.22*c*. The 0045 indicates the that packet traversed ring 4 through bridge 5 and then onto ring 3, which is where the destination station resides. The 0 following the ring 3 was put in by the bridge to fill out the field to a 16-bit boundary. If there were another bridge in the path to the destination, the next bridge would strip off that 0, put in its bridge number, and then add the next ring number followed by a 0 into the RIF field. Figure 2.22*c* shows the RIF field as if the packet traversed ring 4, bridge 5, ring 3.

Each bridge the packet traverses will insert that type of information into the packet. As the packet traverses the rings and bridges in the network, the path (ring received from, bridge number traversed, ring forwarded to) that it took will be inserted into the packet. Each bridge will insert its own information into the packet.

When the packet reaches the destination, the destination will respond with a response packet. Depending on whether the packet was originally sent as an all-routes explorer or a single-routes explorer, the destination will respond with the opposite of what it received. See the preceding rules on route explorers.

The packet will then follow that path back to the originator. If the packet was received as an all-routes explorer, the destination station flips the direction bit in the Routing Control (RC) field and immediately sends the packet back to the originator. Flipping this bit will tell the bridges to read the preformatted RIF field in the reverse direction (only if the packet was originally transmitted to the destination as an all-routes explorer). In this case, with the direction bit flipped, the bridges will not insert any information into the RIF field. They would simply read the RIF field and forward the packet if their ring/bridge numbers were in the RIF field. This response is not submitted as an all-routes packet. This response packet is returned as a specifically routed frame. It will not traverse any bridges except for the ones specified by the RIF field.

If the packet received was a single route Explorer, the destination will not flip the direction bit. Instead, it will build a new packet, MAC address it to the source station, and send it back as an all-routes explorer frame.

As shown in Fig. 2.22*a,* there is more than one route to the destination. Therefore, more than one ARE packet would make it to the destination. The destination will respond to each of the packets. Each packet will take the reverse path back to the originator.

Therefore, multiple packets will arrive back to the originator of the packet. Which path does the originator decide to take? The most followed rule is that the first response packet that makes it back to the originator wins. The station will use the route of the first response packet when the other packets arrive, the originating station may discard the follow on packets.

The previous text mentioned that a multiple-response packet may arrive back to the originator of a route discovery packet. This may happen as a result of two of more bridges interconnecting two or more of the same LANs. In transparent bridging for Ethernet, one or more of the bridge ports would be set to blocking, allowing only one path to be active at a time. In Source Routing for Token Ring* all bridge ports can be and usually are active. This will allow for multiple packets to arrive at the destination. Each packet will have different routing entries, for each ring number in a Token Ring LAN will always be unique. Only bridge numbers may be reused. This is because the RIF field is always read as the ring number in, the bridge number, and the ring number out.

One final note on source route bridges. The Spanning Tree protocol has been adopted to run with source route bridges. Therefore, STA will shut down rundandant loops only for SRE frames. This is only useful when the end station uses the single route explorer for route discovery. Bridges that have their ports enabled will forward this SRE packet. Bridges with the ports in the blocking mode will not forward the frame.

An end station that submits an ARE frame for route discovery will still have the frame forwarded by all ports on a bridge, whether it is in blocking mode or not. In this way, source route bridges are using the STA to use the cable plant more efficiently.

Differences. The differences should be seen here between the two types of bridges. Ethernet (transparent) bridges operate completely transparent to any of the stations on the network. Transparent bridges communicate only with other transparent bridges. Using transparent bridges, end stations are not aware of any bridges on the network. Ethernet network stations operate on the network as if the bridges were not there. Therefore, no modifications had to be made to the Ethernet algorithm or the packet format. With a few exceptions, you simply place the bridge on the network and let it start to work.

---

* Transparent bridging does not necessarily mean Ethernet bridging. The IEEE committee has adopted transparent bridging for all LAN standards. The Source Routing technique has been adopted only by the IEEE 802.5 committee (Token Ring only). Source Routing will not be found on any Ethernet networks.

Just the opposite, Token Ring bridges do not contain any intelligence, except to stuff the packet with ring and bridge numbers. Each one of the bridges must be assigned a ring number for each of its ports, and internally it must be assigned a bridge number. The end station on a Token Ring network has no idea what its ring number is. The bridge will handle this for it.

This algorithm forces the end stations to find each other, which produces a lot of overhead on the rings. (*Overhead* is defined as those necessary protocol packets which do not contain any user data.) While these packets are being transmitted, no other station may transmit. The packet format for Token Ring had to be modified to allow for the route information. End stations on a Token Ring network do know about the bridges on their network.

One clear advantage for the transparent bridges (Ethernet bridges) is that those bridges may operate on either Token Ring or Ethernet environments, although they are rarely found on Token Ring LANs. IBM supports Token Ring and Source Routing for their implementation and most vendors have followed this. Source Routing bridges will operate only on Token Ring environments.

The IEEE committee that sets standards for LANs has adopted the transparent bridge algorithm for all its LANs (802.3, 802.4, and 802.5). The IEEE 802.5 committee is the only committee that has adopted source routing for IEEE 802.5. It has not been adopted for any of the other LAN standards.

One big advantage of bridges (no matter what kind) is that they are protocol transparent. This means that any protocol may run on top of them: XNS, TCP/IP, DECnet, AppleTalk, etc., may all run through a bridge, whether it is transparent or Source Route. This represents a big advantage for bridges. At the time of their introduction, there was one router for every protocol on the network. Multiprotocol routers were in their infancy, and it would be years before they were easily available and reliable. Bridges offered this first off in 1985.

One last thing that may be noticed here. What if you want to transfer data between Token and Ethernet networks. The best solution is to route data between the two types of networks. This will yield the best performance and smallest problems. It has been said, "Route if you can, bridge if you must!"

When a protocol cannot be routed (NetBIOS or LAT protocols, for example), there is a standard as of this writing that is currently being adopted by the IEEE committee that will allow for seamless transmission between Ethernet and Token Ring. Currently, the specification is not out. Otherwise there are only proprietary implementations of bridges (the IBM 8209) that will allow bridge translation between Ethernet and Token Ring. Ethernet and Token Ring (translating) bridges must convert the MAC address between the two because of the bit order of transmission.

Routers

Theory. General router information will be covered here. As each protocol is discussed in each subsequent chapter, routers will be discussed in detail for each specific protocol.

Networks running the appropriate software are usually divided logically by a device known as a *router*. At one time (late 1984 to early 1985) routers were expensive, and were very slow for packet forwarding (300 to 1000 packets per second, or pps). Not only that, most commercial router configuration tables were manually configured, and this was a network management nightmare for medium and large networks. Bridges provided not only self-learning capabilities, they could make forwarding decisions within the cable speed of Ethernet (actually 10,000 pps in 1986 and 14,800 packets per second today).

Routers are devices that interconnect multiple networks, primarily running at the same high-level protocols (TCP/IP, XNS, IPX, etc.). They make forwarding decisions at the network layer of the OSI model. With more software intelligence than simple bridges, routers are well suited for complex environments or large internetworks. In particular, they support active, redundant paths (loops) and allow logical separation of network segments. (Each separate network in a routed environment is given a network number. This is analogous to the area code numbering system for the telephone system.)

Refer to Fig. 2.23. Unlike transparent bridging, routers work with network numbers (unlike bridges, which operate at the data-link layer and operate only on the MAC addresses in the packet) that are embedded into the data portion of the packet and determine the forwarding of each packet based on this network number. These network numbers are similar to geographic area code numbers. For local calls, one simply dials the seven-digit number. The switching offices of the telephone system will automatically route the call locally to its destination.

For long distance calls (i.e., a call to a number in another area code, say, from New York to Virginia), you must enter the area code before the number in order to complete the call. The telephone switching offices in New York will look at the area code and notice that it is assigned to Virginia. It will route the call to Virginia, where the local switching offices there will route the call to its final destination. This is similar to the routing functions in a WAN–LAN connection.

Packets that are bound for nonlocal networks (i.e., network stations that usually are geographically separated) are sent to a router by the software that resides in the network layer of the OSI mode. Depending

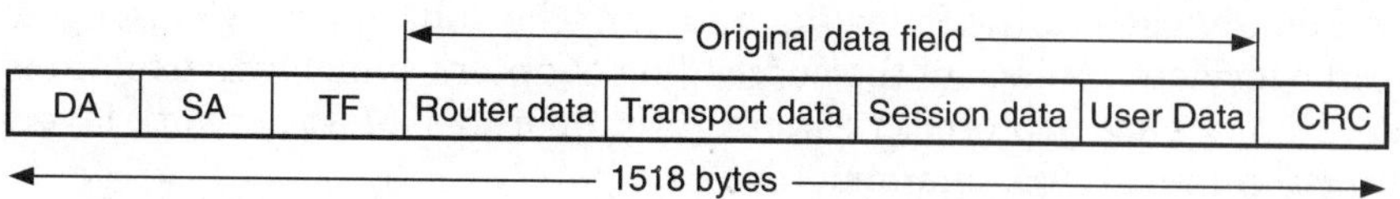

The Ethernet packet is still 1518 bytes possible in length. Routing information is filled into part of the data field. Transport-layer software (if there is any) is also placed in the data field.

Cut down the amount of space available for data but with 1500 bytes there is still plenty of room in the packet for user data. Router information can range anywhere from 20 to 60 bytes in length.

The receiving station will know where the router data starts and where it ends. It will not be mistaken for data.

Everything, whether it is user data or control information for the network stations, is stuffed into the packet and transmitted to the network.

Figure 2.23 Router information in packet.

on the type of network operating software (TCP/IP, XNS, IPX, etc.), there are many different ways of traversing the routers. The following example closely resembles the Internet Datagram Protocol (IDP) of the XNS (Xerox Network System) environment. Other routing protocols are similar and will be explained fully in each of the succeeding chapters of protocols. XNS was specifically designed to run on a network and it is the easiest to comprehend. It will be briefly explained here, and will be further explained in each of the following chapters. Each protocol implements routing a little differently.

Operation. Networks that allow the use of routers must employ what is known as a *network number.* This network number is not the same as a physical address that identifies a station on the network. The network number is the number assigned to identify a particular logical network. It usually is a single entity grouping multiple network workstations. Network stations are grouped together by a single network number. This constitutes a single LAN—a zip code, if you will. The combination of the network number and the physical address of the station on the network will uniquely identify any station on the internet. The *internet* is a term used when multiple single networks are grouped together to form a larger network though the use of routers.

If a network station has the network-layer software present,* thereby making it fully aware of a internetworked environment, it is

* Some network protocols do not employ a network layer. Representations of this are LAT from Digital and NetBIOS from IBM. These are session layer only protocols and must be bridged, for they do not employ the use of network numbers which routers require.

commonly used in the following manner. The subsequent text is a general overview for each of the succeeding chapters, which will explain in detail how each protocol's network layer operates. Most network layers function in a similar manner.

Refer to Fig. 2.24. When the network-layer software of the network operating system receives data from its upper-layer software that is bound for a station that is across a router, the normal process is to look at the network address (not the physical address) of the destination packet and compare it to its local network address. If the network number is different than its own, the network layer software will know that the packet is bound for a remote network. It will then attempt to find a router that can process this packet via the shortest route. Routers are the only device that may forward a packet to a remote

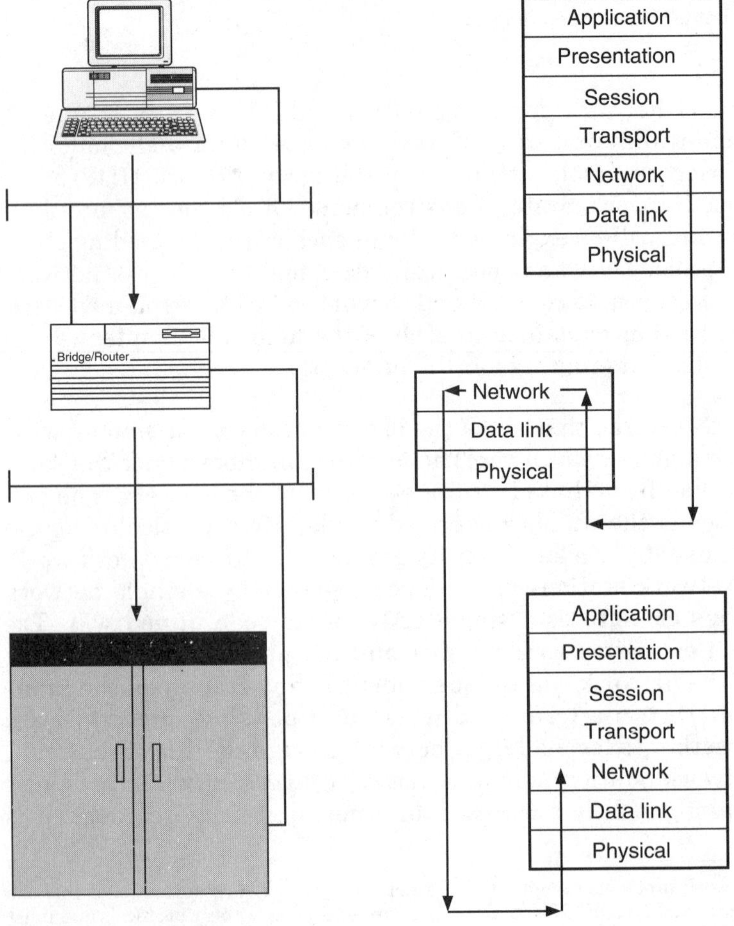

Figure 2.24 A routed environment.

device on an internet. Network numbers are assigned to a workstation in various ways. These ways will be identified in each of the following chapters.

The network-layer software that resides in an end station may hold a table of network numbers and their associated routers* that it knows about. These entries contain the router's physical address, whose network numbers the router is associated with, and the distance to the final destination. If the network number is not in the table, or the end station does not support holding a table, it will request the routers on the network to send it information about a particular destination.

The station will then use this returned information to address its packet to be handled by a router or a series of routers to enable the packet to reach its final destination. Once formatted, it will submit a packet to the network with the destination MAC address set, not to its final destination, but to a particular router. The final destination network number and host number will be embedded somewhere in the network-layer header of the packet. This is how each router in a path to the destination will know where to forward the packet: it reads the network header information in the packet to determine the final destination.

That router will receive and process the packet. The router reads the fields of the packet that contain the routing information, particularly the destination network number. If the destination network number is directly attached to the router, it will simply forward the packet, physically addressed to the final destination. If the destination network is not directly attached to that router, the router will have a list of other routers that it knows about. This is known as a routing table. The table should have the address of the router next in line to the final destination network. The router will then physically address the packet directly to that router. When the next router receives that packet, it will invoke the same algorithm as the previous router to get the packet to its final destination.

When the packet finally reaches the router with the destination network, that router will physically address the packet to that of the final destination. The physical source address of the packet will be that of the router, so that the destination will know how to address any response packets. Any return packets by the destination network station will be addressed directly to that router, and the response packet will be forwarded in the same manner to the originator of the packet.

---

* A source station may also know only one router on the network. This is known as a *default router.* The station will send all internet packets to this router, which will forward the packet to the destination. This can save RAM space and processing power.

It is important to remember that the originating stations, knowing the packet is destined for another network, will physically address the packet to the router and not to the final destination. This will enable the router to receive and process the packet. Remember that routers only process packets that are physically addressed to them. Embedded in the packet, in the network-layer header of a packet (refer to Fig. 2.23) will be the final destination network and destination network attachment. The router will use this network layer information to determine where to route the packet.

With bridging, an end station will physically address the MAC destination address to that of the final destination. In a bridged environment, all stations are assigned the same network number.

Conclusion

The information about routing is covered in much greater detail in each of the following chapters. The point of the previous text was to illustrate routing conventions. The next chapter will show the details of each protocol.

The following is a comparison between a router and a bridge.

Routers

1. Routers are self-configuring in that they know of all other routers and the best route to take on each interconnected segment. Routers exchange routing table information which show reachability of networks for the particular router.
2. Routers automatically allow for redundancy.
3. Routers offer some intelligence in that they will respond to any originating station when the destination is unreachable or if there is a better route to take.
4. Some routers allow for different-size packets on the network. If one segment of the network allows for only 1518 bytes (the maximum Ethernet packet size) and the other segment allows for 4472 (Token Ring maximum per 4 Mbps), most 16-Mbps networks will use the 4-Mpbs packet size of 4472. Routers will fragment the original packet and then reassemble it at the destination network.
5. Routers allow for multiple paths to exist to the same destination station. One network station could use one path to reach a destination and another network station might use an entirely different path but still reach the same destination.
6. Routers segment the network into logical subnets by assigning an ID number to an individual network. This allows for better network management, among other things.

7. Routers do not forward broadcast packets. This can eliminate what are known as *broadcast storms.*
8. Routers operate at the OSI network layer.

Bridges

1. Bridges are usually faster than routers. Bridges make simple filtering and forwarding decisions based on physical-layer addresses of the packet.
2. Bridges are less expensive than routers, although that cost is becoming negligible (usually within $500.00 of each other and some router vendors do not charge for bridge software if routing software is ordered).
3. Transparent bridges allow for loops but only one path can be active at any one time to a destination network.
4. Bridges are less complicated devices.
5. Transparent bridges are “invisible” or transparent to any other device on the network (except other bridges). Network stations do not need specialized software to operate with a bridge. This can reduce the network software executable size in a network workstation.
6. Bridges increase the available bandwidth of a LAN by physically segmenting network stations to their respective LANs.

One last device that has tremendous popularity is the multiprotocol bridge/router. This is a router and a bridge built into one unit. They were previously called *brouters* but now the term *multiprotocol router* is the most commonly used. They not only bridge but they can route many different types of network software—all out of the same box.

The operation of the multiprotocol router is straightforward, as shown in Fig. 2.25 and flowcharted in Fig. 2.26. With few exceptions, when the packet arrives at the router, the physical source address of the packet is checked and, if needed, it is added to the bridge table. Next, the router will check the destination address of the packet. If the destination address is that of the brouter, the multiprotocol router will attempt to route the packet (remember, in a routing environment, all packets to be routed will be addressed to a router and not to the final destination). If the address is not that of the multiprotocol router, the router will bridge the packet. Broadcast packets will be checked also. If need be they will be forwarded.

Another note on Source Route Bridging should be mentioned here. The capability of transferring data between two stations on two different LANs (i.e., Ethernet to Token Ring), is much more easily accomplished using a router that it is with bridging. A router will use the network IDs and pull the data out of the data field and reformat it for

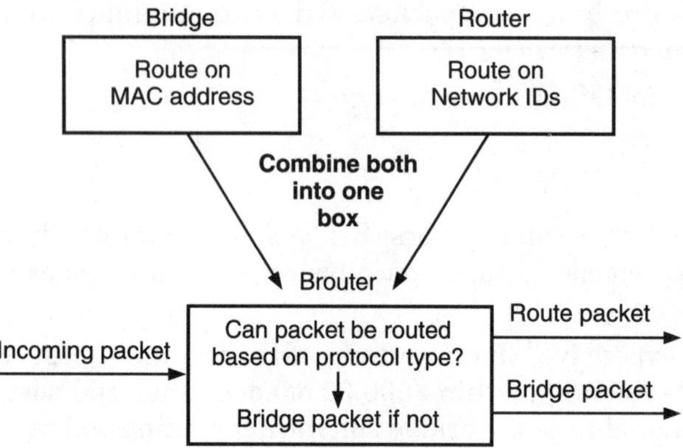

Figure 2.25 Multiprotocol bridge/routers.

the new network. It is the easiest and best way to transfer data between different LAN media types (Ethernet, Token Ring, and FDDI). Currently, there is not a standard by the IEEE committee allowing for the bridge translation of packets between Source Routing and Transparent Bridging. There is a standard by the IEEE committee, known as IEEE 802.5m, that allows for a bridge to receive a packet, read the first bit of the source address field. If it is set to a binary 1, then there is source routing information in the packet. If the bit is set to a 0, there is not source routing information in the packet and the packet should be transparently bridged. This is an SRT bridge capability, not a translating capability. It is best to use a router when mixing LAN types. Bridges do not easily accommodate this.

The algorithms used to transfer data between a Token Ring (with source routing) and an Ethernet network is still in its infancy. IBM supports this through their 8209 bridge. Most router vendors today do not support bridging between Token Ring and Ethernet. In these environments, routing is being used and the transfer between Ethernet and Token Ring using routing protocols is not a problem. This will become more apparent as each of the protocols are studied in the following chapters.

Again, it is best if the bridging and routing functions are allowed to reside in the same unit. This is called the multiprotocol bridge/router. This type of router will know when to bridge the packet and when to route an incoming packet. The two flowcharts in Figs. 2.25 and 2.26 show data flow in a multiprotocol environment and in a pure routing environment.

Now that bridges and routers have been explained, we will come back to the question of how do Ethernet/IEEE 802.3 networks converse with Token Ring networks.

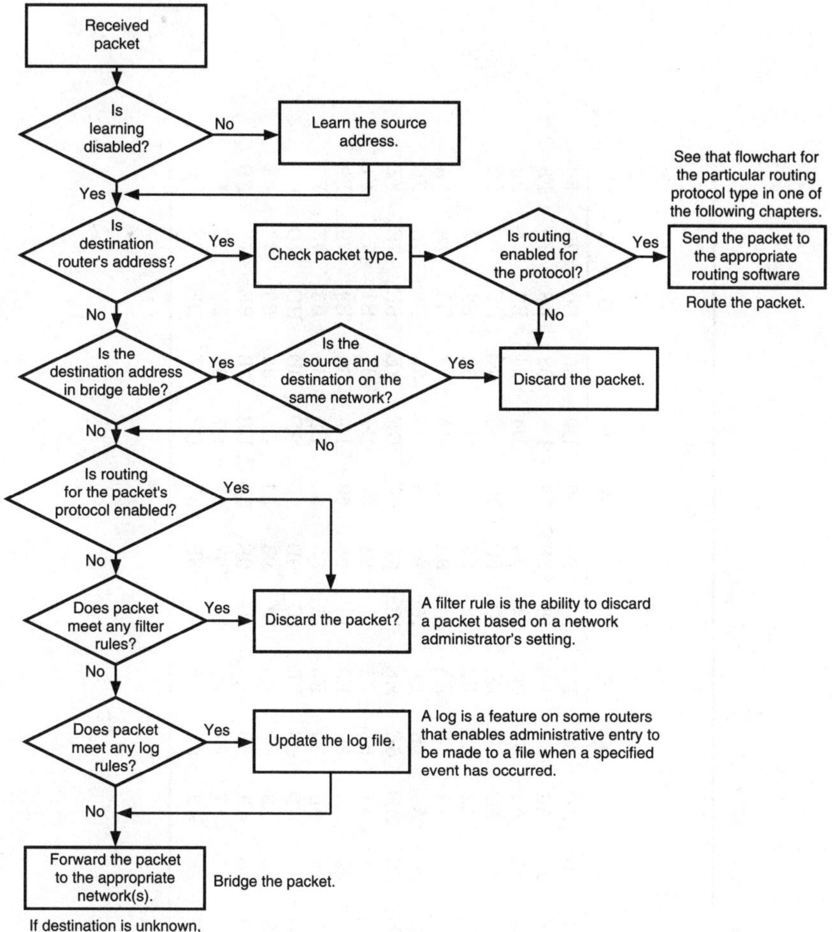

Figure 2.26 Multiprotocol router flowchart.

Due to the lack of a translation bridge standard from the IEEE committee, some bridges and all routers provide for the translation of Ethernet to and from Token Ring networks. The reason that routers easily provide this capability is that routers fully understand their protocols and the LANs (Ethernet, Token Ring, etc.) they are connected to. End stations send their packets directly to the router. This allows a router to build a new packet header when the packet is forwarded. Routers understand which part of their packet needs translation. Therefore, routers easily provide this address translation for packets that must converse between workstations that exist on different types of LANs.

TABLE 2.1 Bit Reversal Conversion Chart

Second four bits (across) / First four bits (below)		1	2	3	4	5	6	7	8	9	A	B	C	D	E	F
0	00	80	40	C0	20	A0	60	E0	10	90	50	D0	30	B0	70	F0
1	08	88	48	C8	28	A8	68	E8	18	98	58	D8	38	B8	78	F8
2	04	84	44	C4	24	A4	64	E4	14	94	58	D4	34	B4	74	F4
3	0C	8C	4C	CC	2C	AC	6C	EC	1C	9C	5C	DC	3C	BC	7C	FC
4	02	82	42	C2	22	A2	62	E2	12	92	52	D2	32	B2	72	F2
5	0A	8A	4A	CA	2A	AA	6A	EA	1A	9A	5A	DA	3A	BA	7A	FA
6	06	86	46	C6	26	A6	66	E6	16	96	56	D6	36	B6	76	F6
7	0E	8E	4E	CE	2E	AE	6E	EE	1E	9E	5E	DE	3E	BE	7E	FE
8	01	81	41	C1	21	A1	61	E1	11	91	51	D1	31	B1	71	F1
9	09	89	49	C9	29	A9	69	E9	19	99	59	D9	39	B9	79	F9
A	05	85	45	C5	25	A5	65	E5	15	95	55	D5	35	B5	75	F5
B	0D	8D	4D	CD	2D	AD	6D	ED	1D	9D	5D	DD	3D	BD	7D	FD
C	03	83	4C	C3	23	A3	63	E3	13	93	53	D3	33	B3	73	F3
D	0B	8B	4B	CB	2B	AB	6B	E8	1B	9B	5B	DB	3B	BB	7B	FB
E	07	87	47	C7	27	A7	67	E7	17	97	57	D7	37	B7	77	F7
F	0F	8F	4F	CF	2F	AF	6F	EF	1F	9F	5F	DF	3F	BF	7F	FF

Bridges operate at the MAC sublayer of the data-link layer and therefore they are transparent to network-layer protocols (remember that bridges forward based on the MAC address and therefore all protocols may be bridged). Bridges do not understand (besides the MAC address) which other parts of the packet must be translated. Examples of bridged-only protocols are SNA, LAT, and NetBIOS. The conversion of packets from Token Ring to/from Ethernet is more than a matter of how the MAC addresses are read. Remember, Ethernet and Token Ring transmit their MAC addresses differently. The importance of this is magnified for those protocols that carry the MAC address as part of the data of a frame. These protocols are discussed in detail in later chapters.

The first process that must happen when translating an Ethernet IEEE 802.3 frame to a Token Ring frame (or vice versa) is that the MAC address must be converted. Token Ring and Ethernet transmit differently at the MAC level. Therefore, an address of 02-60-80-01-02-03 on Ethernet will translate to 40-06-31-80-40-C0 on Token Ring. This is the first process: MAC address conversion. The address is simply bit reverse.

The second action is that the bridge must be informed of any protocol that may use the MAC address inside the packet somewhere. The most common protocol is IP-ARP. This packet is fully explained Chap. 6. Just let it be noted that the bridge must be made aware. Third, the bridge must be told that if a token packet needs to be translated to Ethernet, it must use either the Ethernet or IEEE 802.3 frame format. How the bridge accomplishes this is discussed under the SNAP section in Chap. 3.

Table 2.1 allows for easy translation of hex strings.

Example. The following MAC address needs to be converted: 02 C4 20 01 02 03. Let's try the first byte, 02. The left nibble (left-four bits or 0) are applied to the left-hand column. The right-four bits (the 2) are applied to the top row. Follow the two numbers across and down until they meet in the table. That number, 40, is the bit reversal of the column/row combination.

After applying the whole address to the conversion table: 40 23 04 80 40 C0.

From Table 2.1, it does not matter whether the address is Token Ring or Ethernet. Each type's MAC address may be applied to the table in the same manner specified to see what it would translate to on the other type of LAN.

Table 2.1 should be used to assist you in bit reversing. The disadvantages to this type of bridging is that addresses may be duplicated after the bit reversal process, when forwarded to the next LAN .

Chapter

3

IEEE 802.2

The purpose of this chapter is to explain the functions of the IEEE 802.2 protocol known as Logical Link Control (LLC). It is not intended as a tutorial to explain the complete workings of the protocol. It will explain the packet types and the functions that they provide. The reader will have an overall view of the protocol at the end of this chapter. For more reading information on the internal workings of this protocol, refer to references in the back of this book.

Logical Link Control, LLC, is the standard published by the IEEE 802.2 standards body. The IEEE 802 committee produces LAN specifications. The protocol of IEEE 802.2 LLC is actually a subset of another protocol. This protocol is High-Level Data-Link Control (HDLC), which is a specification presented by the international standards body known as the International Standards Organization (ISO). Specifically, LLC uses a subclass of the HDLC specification. It is formally classified as BA-2, 4. It uses the balanced asynchronous mode (ABM) and the functional extensions, options 2 and 4. The protocol of LLC allows network stations to operate as peers in that all stations have equal status on the LAN.

It is important to understand that IEEE 802 is a data-link protocol. It controls the link between two stations. It has nothing to do with the upper-layer protocols that may run on top of it. As shown in Fig. 3.1, the IEEE 802 committee divided the data-link layer into two entities: the MAC layer and the LLC layer. The MAC layer was explained in Chap. 2. This provided some benefits. First, it provides for a peer-to-peer connectivity between two network stations, which reduces the LAN's susceptibility to errors. Since it is a subset of the HDLC architecture, it provides a more compatible interface for wide area networks. It is independent of the access method (Ethernet, Token Ring, etc). The MAC portion of the data-link layer is protocol-specific. This

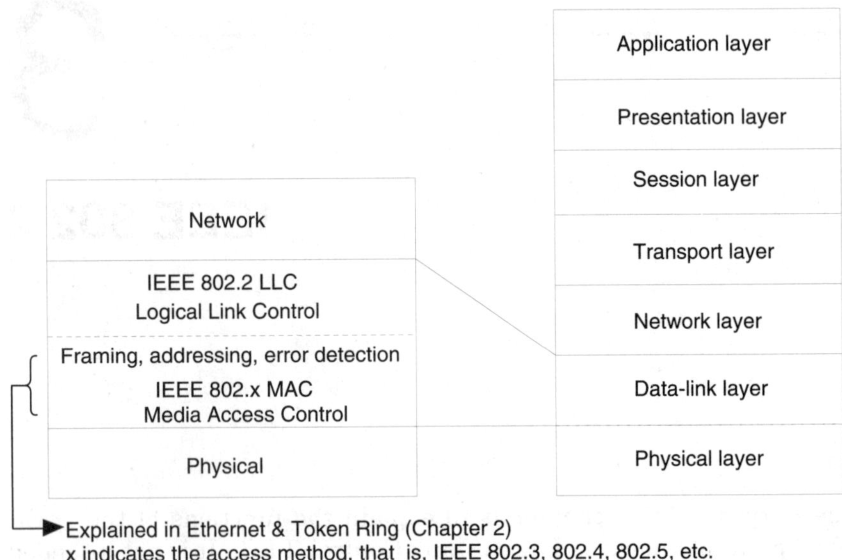

Figure 3.1 IEEE and the OSI model.

allows a IEEE 802 network more flexibility. LLC is placed between the MAC layer specification of the data-link layer and a network-layer implementation. LLC2 (connection-oriented) is used to link a Local Area Network to a Wide Area Network and between network stations and SNA hosts. Another example is the IBM Lan Server program. This is a network workgroup operating system is based on a session-layer protocol, NetBIOS, that operates functionally similar to Novell NetWare. IEEE 802.2 provides data-link services for the upper-layer protocols. This includes the data transfer and link establishment, control and disconnection between two stations.

When the IEEE started work on the LLC subset, they knew providing a connection-oriented service only (Type 2 or LLC2) would limit the capability of this protocol in the LAN arena. Most applications currently operating on a LAN do not need the data integrity functions provided for with the LLC2 protocol. Furthermore, time-sensitive applications could not tolerate the tremendous overhead involved with establishing and maintaining a connection-oriented session. Also, most LAN protocols already provided for this type of functionality in their software.

With this in mind, the IEEE 802 committee also provided a connectionless mode of the LLC protocol, as well as a connection-oriented specification.

Therefore, the IEEE 802.2 committee allowed for three types of implementation for LLC:

Type 1, known as LLC1, uses the UI (unsequenced information) frame which sets up communication between two network stations as unacknowledged connectionless service.

Type 2, commonly known as LLC2, uses the conventional I (Information Frame) and sets up acknowledged connection-oriented service between two network stations.

Type 3, using something called AC frames, sets up an acknowledged connectionless service between two network stations.

Type 3 will not be discussed in this chapter. Type 1 and Type 2 will be discussed in this chapter.

First, we will present an overview of connection-oriented versus connectionless. Connection-oriented service means that two stations that wish to communicate with one another must establish a connection at the data-link layer between the two before any data will pass between the two. When station A wants a connection to station B, station A will send control frames to station B to indicate that a connection is wanted. Station B will respond with a control frame that a session can be established, or it may respond to Station A that it may not have a connection. If a connection is allowed to be established, station A and station B will exchange a few more control packets that will set up sequence numbers and other control parameters. After this is accomplished, data may flow over the connection. The connection will be strictly maintained with sequence numbers, acknowledgments, retries, etc.

Connectionless service is just the opposite of connection-oriented service. A connection is not established (at the data-link level) before data is established. A connection will still be established, but it will be the responsibility of a particular network protocol (TCP/IP, NetWare, etc.) before data is transmitted. Connectionless service means that a frame will be transmitted on the network without regard to a connection at the data-link layer. It is the responsibility of the upper-layer software of a network operating system to perform these tasks.

In summary, this method of data transfer does not provide for error recovery, flow, or congestion control. There is not a connection established before the transmission of data. There is also no acknowledgment upon receipt of data. This type of functionality requires less overhead.

This protocol was allowed so that existing protocols, like TCP/IP, XNS, NetWare, etc., could migrate to the IEEE 802.2/802.3 protocol. The connectionless protocol of LLC specifies a static-frame format and allows network protocols to run on it. Network protocols that fully implement a transport layer will generally use Type 1 service.

TABLE 3.1 LLC Commands and Responses

Type of frame	Format	Command or response: Command	Response
Type 1		UI	
		XID	XID
		TEST	TEST
Type 2	I format	I	I
	S format	RR	RR
		RNR	RNR
		REJ	REJ
	U format	SABME	UA
		DISC	UA
			DM
			FRMR
Type 3		AC	AC

Table 3.1 shows the frame formats and the commands and responses used by the three types of LLC. This table will be used throughout the chapter. Each of the entries in this table will be explained in the next few pages.

LLC Type 2 Operation

Connection-oriented LLC2—Asynchronous Balance Mode (ABM)

This is the most complicated of the services, so it will be explained first. Connection-oriented services provide the functions necessary to provide reliable data transfer (similar to a transport-layer function). Connection-oriented services allow for error recovery, flow, and congestion control. They provide for specific acknowledgments that the connection is established or not. They provide for flow control, making sure that the data arrives in order as it was sent, and that the connection is not overloaded. This type of circuit has a tremendous amount of overhead compared to LLC1.

Connection-oriented link methods were originally used with data transfer through serial lines. Serial lines are used to connect networks together through the phone system (although it does not have to be so connected). Just a few years ago, serial lines tended to be noisy. Part of the High-level Data-Link Control (HDLC) protocol provides for the reliability of data. Although today data lines from the phone company are conditioned to handle data, there still are some lines that will remain noisy, and the connection-oriented services are used to handle this type of link. Connection-oriented services are used with LAN services today. Most common use for them is for protocols that do not invoke a transport or network layer. A good example of this type of protocol is NetBIOS. The

IBM LAN Server program, a client-server workgroup network operating system (similar in function to Novell NetWare), uses this type of connection. Most LAN protocols do not use this mode of LLC. Most LAN protocols have network, transport, and session layers built into the protocol and therefore use the connectionless mode of LLC.

Figure 3.2 shows the class of service compared to the LLC type. This figure shows that network stations supporting the Type 2 method can provide both Type 1 connectionless and Type 2 connection-oriented services. Type 1 can only provide Type 1 service.

Frame formats

An LLC frame is shown in Fig. 3.3. The following contains information on the frame types of IEEE 802.2. It may be confusing to read, but the end of the chapter will give examples of how they are used.

Destination Service Access Point (DSAP) identifies one or more service access points to which the LLC information field should be delivered.

Source Service Access Point (SSAP) identifies which service access point originated the message.

For LANs implementing LLC, SAPs identify a particular service that resides on a network station. It is used to send or receive a message. For those readers familiar with the Ethernet protocol, it is analogous to the Type field in the Ethernet frame. A SAP of FE indicates that the OSI protocol owns the packet. A SAP entry of F0 indicates

Classes of LLC	Type of Operation: 1	Type of Operation: 2
I	x	
II	x	x

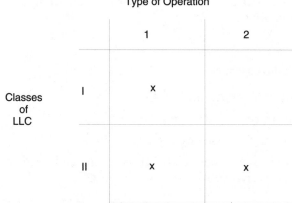

Figure 3.2 Classes versus Operation matrix.

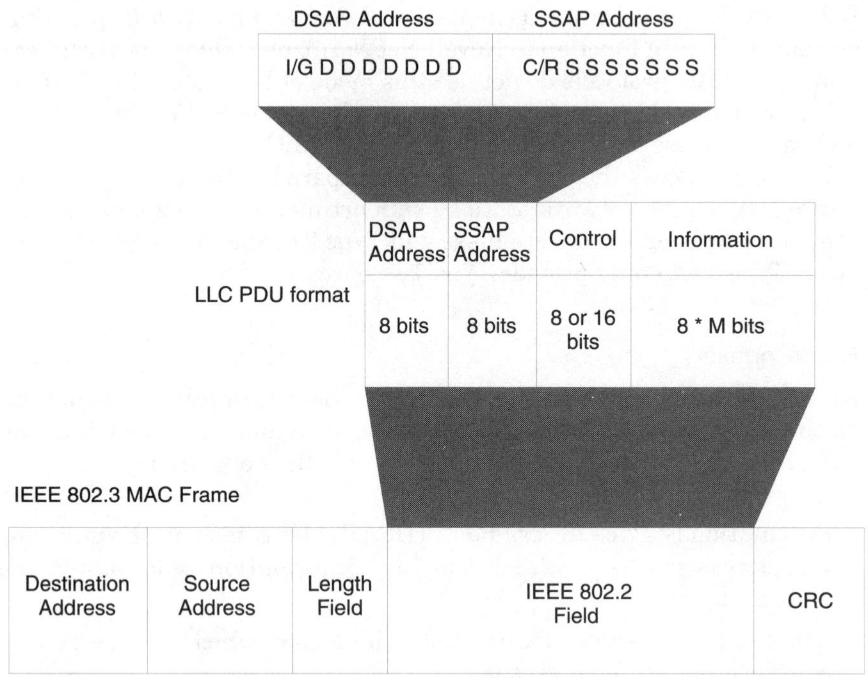

Frame shown is IEEE 802.3. The IEEE 802.5 frame also uses the IEEE 802.2 fields.

Figure 3.3 IEEE 802.2 fields. (*Courtesy IEEE.*)

NetBIOS. For a full listing of SAPs, refer to the end of this chapter. SAPs are used to tell the network layer which network process is to accept the packet and which network process submitted the packet. SAPs are registered by the IEEE. Companies must register their protocols with the IEEE to receive a SAP.

SAP addressing

There are four types of addresses:

1. Individual address, used by DSAP and SSAP
2. Null address, all zeros in the DSAP and/or SSAP
3. A group address, which is only used by the DSAP
4. Global DSAP, indicated by all ones in the DSAP field and used to designate a group of all active DSAPs on the network.

Each SAP address consumes exactly one octet. The DSAP address contains 7 bits of address (indicated by the D bits and 1 bit (I/G bit) that identifies the address as an individual SAP or a multicast SAP (intended for a group of SAPs). This is the leftmost bit of the DSAP field identified by the I/G bit in Fig. 3.3. This type of address shows that the packet is intended for a group of SAPs at the destination end of the link. If this bit is set to a 0, it is an individual address. If it is set to a 1, it is a group address.

The SSAP contains 7 bits of address (indicated by the S bits) and 1 bit to indicate whether the packet is a command or response type of packet. If this C/R bit is a 0, it is a command packet; if it is set to a 1, it is a response packet. This is explained further in a moment.

The control field is expanded as shown in Fig. 3.4. For supervisory and control frames this field may contain one or two octets which represent functions of the frame. For data frames, this field will contain sequence numbers when needed. This will be explained further in a moment.

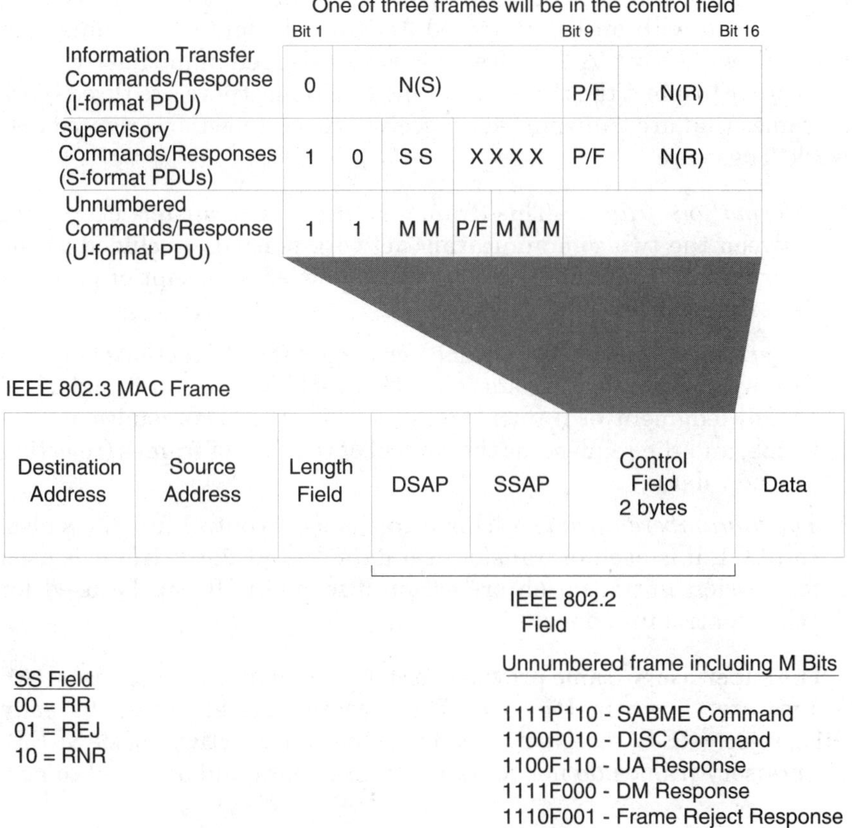

Figure 3.4 Control fields. (*Courtesy IEEE.*)

Poll and Final (P/F) bits. These bits are used between two communicating stations (termed a *primary* and *secondary*) to solicit a status response or to indicate a response to that request. It is a P bit when used by the primary station (the requester) and a F bit when used by the secondary station (the responder). In LLC, any station can transmit a frame with the P bit set or the F bit set. There is not a master-slave relationship with it.

A frame with the F bit set does not indicate the end of a transmission in Asynchronous Balance Mode (ABM), which is the mode used in LLC2. It is used as a housecleaning method between two stations to clear up any ambiguity between those two stations. It is used to indicate that the frame is an immediate response to a frame that had the P bit set.

For example, when a station wants to set up a connection with another station, it will submit a frame known as the Set Asynchronous Balance Mode Extended (SABME*). In this frame, the P bit will be set to a 1. The destination station, upon accepting a connection request, will respond with an Unnumbered Acknowledgment (UA) frame, and the F bit will be set. A P bit frame is acknowledged immediately.

In order to effect the three preceding functions, there are three types of frames that are transmitted or received in a connection-oriented network. These are:

1. *Information frame.* This frame is used to transfer user data between the two communicating network stations. Included in the information frame may also be an acknowledge receipt of previous data from the originating station.
2. *Supervisory frame.* This frame performs control functions between the two communicating stations. This includes control functions of acknowledgment of frame, the request for the retransmission of a frame, and the request for the control of the flow of frames (rejecting any new data).
3. *The unnumbered frame.* This frame is used control functions also. In LLC1, it is used to transfer user data. In LLC2, the frame is used for session initialization or session disconnect. It can be used for other control functions.

The supervisory frame provides for four commands or responses. (All frames are shown in Fig. 3.4.) These commands are receiver ready (RR), reject (REJ), receive not ready (RNR) and selective reject (SREJ). Supervisory frames do not contain any user data and are used to per-

* SABM and SABME are the same frame. SABME tells the destination station that the requesting station would like to use extended sequencing (modulo 128).

form numbered supervisory functions as mentioned before. Refer to Table 3.1 as you read the following text.

Receive ready (RR) is used by the source or destination station to indicate that it is ready to receive data. It is also used to acknowledge any previously received frames indicated by the N(R)* field. Some uses for this are for when the station had previously indicated that it could not receive any more data; by using the receive not ready (RNR), it will send the RR frame to indicate it can again accept new data. A network station may also use this frame to poll a destination station (an are-you-active type of poll). When running a protocol over IEEE 802.2 (SNA over Token Ring, for example), these packets will traverse the ring even when there is no data to send. It is a polling frame to ensure that the link is still good. It is usually sent (as a poll) every few seconds. This will consume bandwidth with nondata frames.

The receive not ready (RNR) is used by a receiving network station to indicate that it saw the data packet but was too busy to accept it. Therefore, a network station will send this frame to indicate to the source not to send any more information until further notice. The receiving network station will again indicate that it is ready to receive data by using the RR frame.

Reject (REJ) frame is used to indicate a request for a retransmission of frames (more than one), starting with the frame indicated by a sequence number in the field known as N(R). Any frames of N(R)-1 were accepted and are acknowledged. Sequencing is explained in a moment.

Finally, the unnumbered frame has commands and responses that are used for extension for the number of the data-link control functions. These commands are:

Set Asynchronous Balance Mode Extended† (SABME). This frame is used to establish a data-link connection to a destination network station. It will establish the link in asynchronous balanced mode and will be explained in a moment. No user data is transferred with this frame. The destination, in response to this packet, will send an Unnumbered Acknowledge (UA) frame back to the originator. All sequence counters are set to 0 upon receipt of a SABME and receipt of the UA.

Disconnect (DISC). This frame is used to disconnect a session between two communicating stations. No user data is sent with this frame. Upon receipt of the frame, the destination station should acknowledge it with a UA frame.

---

* N(R) is the state for sequencing. Sequencing will be explained shortly. For now, accept N(R) as a sequence number.

† SABME and SABM are the same frame. A requesting station that sends the SABME is requesting extended sequencing (modulo 128).

Unnumbered Acknowledge (UA). This frame is sent as an acknowledgment to the SABME and DISC commands.

Frame Reject Response (FRMR). This frame is different than the simple reject frame in that the sender of it is rejected. It is a noncorrectable frame.

Sequencing of data (LLC2)

Most LAN systems offer some type of sequencing for data delivery. Whether the sequencing is simplex, as in Novell's stop-and-wait method or complex, as used with LLC2 and TCP/IP, there will always be some type of sequencing to ensure proper data delivery.

The following text describes a generic method of sequencing—one is that is definitely used with LLC2 operation, but also one that has been around for many decades and whose modes and methods have been copied by many different LAN architectures. Most sequencing follows a method known as Automatic Return Request (ARQ). Examples of the method follow.

Sequencing of transmitted data ensures that when the data is received it will be presented to the receiver of the data in good condition and in the same order in which it was sent. Imagine sending data (a lawyer's legal text of a court trial, for example) between a PC and a host. During the transfer, the data got mixed up and was received at the host in the wrong order. Without sequencing of data, the host's application would receive the data as presented to it by the LAN software, and would then process the data (save it to a file, input it into a database, etc.). If the file was saved, the file would not be saved in the way it was sent. Needless to say, in any application, misordering LAN data can have catastrophic effects.

During the initiating of a connection, part of the handshaking that goes on is the establishment of a data window. For two communicating network stations, A and B, B will establish a window for A and A will establish a window for B. These windows are maintained by state variables. Another name for this is a *counter.* The transmitting station will maintain a send-state variable, V(S). This will contain the sequence number of the next frame to be transmitted. A receiving station will maintain a receive-state variable, V(R). This will contain the sequence number that is expected to be the next frame received. V(S) is incremented with each frame that is transmitted by a network station. This counter is also placed in a sequence field in a frame that is transmitted.

When a network station receives a frame, it will look for sequence number N(S) in the frame received. If this field matches its V(R), then it will increment its V(R) by one and place this number in a frame N(R) of some type of an acknowledgment packet that will be transmitted back to the originator of the frame.

TABLE 3.2 LLC2 Sequence Counter Definitions

V(R)	Receive-state variable. A counter maintained by a network station. This counter indicates the sequence number of the next in-sequence I PDU to be received on a connection. It is maintained in the network station and not the frame.
N(S)	Sequence number of the frame (called the send sequence number). Located in the transmitted frame, this field will only be set in information (I) packets (explained in a moment). Prior to sending an I frame, the value of N(S) is set to the value of V(S), the send-state variable. This is located in the frame and not in the network station.
V(S)	Send-state variable. This number indicates the next sequence number expected on the connection. It is incremented by one for each successive I-frame transmission. It is maintained in the network station and not the frame.
N(R)	Receive sequence number. This is an acknowledgment of a previous frame. It is located in the transmitted frame. All information and supervisory frames will contain this. Prior to sending that type of frame, it is set equal to the value of the receive-state variable V(R) for that connection. N(R) indicates to the receiving station that the station that originated this frame accepts all frames up to the N(R) minus 1.

If, during the matching of V(R) to the received sequence number, there was a mismatch, and usually after a wait timer expires, the station will send a negative acknowledgment packet to the originator. In this packet will be the sequence number of its value in V(R). In LLC2, this type of frame is a REJ or SREJ frame. In other words, the station expected one sequence number but received another. The number it expected will be transmitted back to the sender in hopes of receiving the correct packet and sequence number. Refer to Fig. 3.4 to see N(S) & N(R) in a frame.

When this packet is received by the originating station, it will look at the received sequence number N(R). It will also know that is has already sent this frame, but something went wrong in the process. If the station can, it will retransmit the old frame.

What is the ordering-for-sequencing numbering? Not all protocols operate the same. For LLC2, the sequence numbering starts at 0 and may go as high as 127 (known as modulo 128). For now, we'll stick with LLC2 sequence numbers, which is modulo 128. This means that sequence numbers may go as high as 127, but then must return (wrap around) to 0. This permits 127 frames to be outstanding (not acknowledged). It does not permit 128 frames to be outstanding, for the value of V(R) is the next expected sequence number.

It also guards against wrapping, for if a station has 127 outstanding frames (0–126), a sending station may not use 0 again until it has been acknowledged. This is a highly unlikely case. Most frames will be acknowledged within a few sequence numbers.

One important consideration of window sizes is the actual size of the window. While having a modulo of 128 is nice in that 127 frames may be transmitted with one acknowledgment, it is also a resource constraint. No transmitted frame may be erased in the sending network station's memory until it has been acknowledged. This means that a network station should have enough memory to store that amount of data until it is acknowledged.

The window can be shut down at any time, which will prevent any more frames from certain stations to be received. This allows for efficient use of resources and also allows a network station to tend to other stations on the network. In other words, it eliminates the possibility of one station hogging another station's time.

This window does slide. If a window size of 7 is opened to another station and six frames are outstanding to a network station, the window will be closed. If an acknowledgment is received for six frames, the window will be opened again for six frames. This is called the *sliding window.*

An advantage of a windowing system is known as *inclusive acknowledgments.* This means that if a network station has five outstanding (unacknowledged) frames (frames 0–4), and it receives an acknowledgment frame of 5, this can mean that the destination station has received frames 0–4, and the next frame the receiving station expects to see should have a sequence number of 5.

This has many advantages. For one, it keeps the receiving station from transmitting five acknowledgment frames. There will be less overhead on the network and the network stations (only one acknowledgment was transmitted instead of five).

This ability to detect and correct sequence errors is basically characterized by three types of retransmissions: Go Back to N, Selective Repeat, and Stop and Wait. With Selective Repeat, only the frame indicated needs to be retransmitted. The Go-Back-to-N method specifies not only a specific sequence number is to be retransmitted, but also any frames before that and up to the last acknowledged sequence number. Stop and Wait means send a packet and do not transmit another until that packet has been acknowledged. All three types have their merits.

The Selective Reject offers better bandwidth utilization in that only the out-of-sequence frame needs to be retransmitted. But the receiving network station must wait for that frame and, when it does arrive, it must reorder the data in the correct sequence before presenting it to the next layer. This consumes memory and CPU utilization.

Go-Back-to-N is a simpler method; however, it uses more network bandwidth and is generally slower than the Selective Reject.

LLC2 uses the Selective Reject methods. Other network protocols use a variance of the two.

The third is called the Stop-and-Wait method. This is said to have a window size of 1, for only one frame may be outstanding at a time. With this, a transmitting station will transmit a frame and will wait for an acknowledgment. It cannot transmit any more frames until it has received an acknowledgment for the previous frame. The sequence numbers used can be of two types. One can be a modulo number of some number and the other can be a 0–1 exchange. With the 0–1 exchange, a starting number is established between the two stations, say a 0. When the transmitting station transmits a packet, it will set the sequence number to a 0. When the receiver receives the packet, it will set its received sequence number to a 0 and then acknowledge the packet. When the response packet is received by the original station, it will notice the 0 sequence number and then set the next transmit sequence number to a 1. This sequence number will flip-flop throughout the length of the data transfers. The only two sequence numbers used are 0 and 1. Novell implements a variance of this protocol in the NetWare 3.11 and previous releases.

Sequence functions are confusing. There is an example of LLC2 sequencing at the end of the chapter.

Timer functions

Throughout this text, in the LLC2 mode of operation, timers are used throughout the operation of that mode. These timers include:

1. *Acknowledgment timer.* A data-link connection timer that is used to define the time interval for which a network station is expecting to see a response to one or more information frames or in response to one unnumbered frame.
2. *P-bit timer.* This is the amount of time that a network station will wait for a response frame in regards to a frame that was sent with the P-bit set.
3. *Reject timer.* The amount of time that a network station will wait for a response to a REJ frame sent.
4. *Busy-state timer.* The amount of time that a network station will wait for a remote network station to exit the busy state.

Three other parameters that are used in this text are:

N2 the maximum number of times that a PDU is sent following the expiration of the P-bit timer, the acknowledgment timer, or the reject timer

N1 the maximum number of octets allowed in an I PDU

k the maximum number of outstanding I PDUs (those which have not been acknowledged)

Connection-oriented services of the IEEE 802.2 protocol

There are two modes of operation for LLC2. These are operational mode and nonoperational mode.

Nonoperational mode will not be completely discussed in this text. It is used to indicate that a network station is logically (not physically) disconnected from the physical cable plant. No information is accepted when a network station has entered into this stage. Examples of possible causes for a network station to enter this mode are:

1. The power is turned on but the receiver is not active.
2. The data link has been reset.
3. The data-link connection is switched from a local condition to a connected on the data-link (on-line) condition.

In operational mode, there are three primary functions provided:

1. *Link establishment.* A source station will send a special frame to a destination indicating that a connection is wanted. This frame will be responded to with an acceptance or rejection to that attempt. Once a connection is established, the two network stations provide each other with a series of handshaking protocols to ensure that the other is ready to receive information.
2. *Information transfer.* Data from the user's applications is transferred from the originating station to the remote station and the data is checked for any possible transmission errors. The remote station will send acknowledgments to the transmitting station. During this phase the two network stations may send control information to each other indicating flow control, missing packets, etc.
3. *Link termination.* The connection between the two stations is disconnected and no more data is allowed to be transferred between the two stations until the session is reestablished. Usually, the link will remain intact as long as there is data to send between the two stations.

Details of LLC Type 2 operation

In operational mode, the data link enters into a mode known as the asynchronous balance mode (ABM). This type of operation means that a connection at the data-link layer has been established between two SAPs. Each end of the connection is able to send commands and responses at any time without receiving any type of permission from another station. There is not a master-slave relationship in this mode. The information exchanged between the two shall be command information (indicating sequence numbers, or that a station is busy and cannot accept any more data). It is also used for user data transfer.

ABM (LLC2) has four phases of operation:

1. Data-link connection phase
2. Information transfer phase

3. Data-link resetting phase
4. Data-link disconnecting phase

Data-link connection phase. Refer to Fig. 3.4. Any network station may enter into this state with the intention of establishing a session with another network station. It will use the unnumbered frame SABME. When the SABME frame is sent, an acknowledgment timer is set. If the frame is not responded to, it will be resent up to N2 times. If the frame is not responded to in that amount of time, the connection attempt is aborted. This type of frame has the P bit set.

The two responses that may be received back are the UA or the DM. DM stands for disconnect mode. This allows a network station to indicate a connection is not allowed. If a connection were already set up and a network station received this from the other end of the connection, the connection would be disconnected. The F bit will be set in the response packet. With the receipt of the DM frame, the acknowledgment timer is stopped and that network station will not enter into the information transfer stage. The connection attempt is aborted. It should report this condition to it upper-layer protocols.

Upon receiving a UA response frame back, the connection is then established and enters into the information transfer phase.

Information transfer phase. When a network station has sent a UA response packet or it has received a UA packet, that network station will immediately enter the information transfer phase. The connection will be established and the frames consist of sending and receiving I (information frames) and S (supervisory) frames. If a network station receives a SABME frame while in this phase, it will reset (not disconnect) the connection. It is used to return the connection to a known state. All outstanding frames are lost and sequence numbers are reset to 0. Retransmission of any outstanding frames will occur between the two network stations, and they will be acknowledged at this time.

When a network station has user information that needs to be sent (or resent as the case may be), it will do so with the I frame. In this sequence, numbers need to be put into the packet. Refer to Fig. 3.4, which shows the I-frame format.

Sequencing within LLC2 is accomplished with modulo 128. This means that the sequencing starts at 0 and reaches its upper limit at 127. From there, it starts back to 0. Zero is a higher number than 127.

Refer to Table 3.2 and Fig. 3.4. When a source sends an I frame to the destination, the N(S) field will be set (in the frame) to its current variable V(S), and the N(R) will be set to its V(R) for that particular connection. At the end of transmitting this frame, it will increment V(S) by one. In sending frames, a sending station may transmit more than one frame without receiving an acknowledgment for any of the frames. For each of the frames sent it will increment V(S) by one. This is an upper limit to the number of outstanding packets that may be unacknowledged. When this limit has been reached, the sending station will not send any more frames, but it still can resend an old frame.

The setting of the receiver of these frame counters is explained in a moment.

Also, if the transmitting station enters into the busy state, it can still transmit I frames. It just cannot receive any. If the source receives an indication that the destination is busy, then it will not send any more I frames until the receipt of a receive ready (RR) frame from the remote station.

One last case for the transmitting station is when it enters into the FRMR (frame reject) state. In this state, it will not transmit any more information for that particular link.

When the sending station transmits this frame, it will start an acknowledgment timer. This is in anticipation of receiving a response packet for its transmission. This is one of the many receive conditions which are discussed next.

Data-link disconnection phase. While in the information transfer phase, either network station may disconnect the session. This is accomplished by transmitting a DISC frame to the other network station.

When it sends this packet, it will start an acknowledgment timer and wait for a response. When it receives a UA or DM response packet, the timer is stopped and the station enters into the disconnected mode.

If this timer expires before receipt of a response packet, the originator will again send the DISC packet and restart the timer. When this has hit an upper limit of resends, that station will enter into disconnected phase, but will inform the upper-layer protocols that an error has occurred in attempting to disconnect from the remote station.

When a network station receives a DISC packet, it will respond to it with a UA packet and enter into the data-link disconnected phase. While in the disconnected phase, a network station is able to initiate sessions with other network stations and can respond to session requests. If it receives a DISC packet, it will respond with a DM packet; and if it receives any other Type 2 command with the P bit set to a 1, it will respond with the F bit set to a 1.

LLC2 frame reception

Frame reception for LLC2 has many more functions than the transmitting of a frame. When a network station is not in the busy condition and receives an I frame which contains the sequence number that is equal to its V(R) variable, it will accept the frame, increment the V(R) by one, and then:

1. If the receiving station has another I frame to transmit, it will transmit the frame as indicated previously, but set the N(R) variable in the transmitted packet to its V(R) and transmit the packet. LLC2 does not use separate packets to indicate an acknowledgment unless:
2. There are no more I frames to be sent. In this case, it will send a receive ready (RR) frame with N(R) set to its V(R).
3. It may also send a receive not ready (RNR) frame back, indicating that it is now busy, do not send any more data—but I acknowledges your packet, indicated by N(R).

If any frame is received as an invalid frame (wrong SAPs, etc.), the frame is completely discarded. Figure 3.5 shows the variable states of N(R), N(S), and V(R) and V(S) for a simple transmission between two network stations.

A live connection

Refer to Fig. 3.5. To establish a connection, station A will send a UI frame (a Set Asynchronous Balance Mode) frame with the P bit set. Station B allows the connection to send back a UA with the F bit set. The connection is now established.

Event	Operation
1	Station A requests a link to be established to station B by sending station B a SABME. Station B will respond with UA. Both the Poll and Final Bits are set to 1.
2	Station A sends an information frame and sequences the frame with N(R) = 0. The N(R) = 0 means station A is expecting to receive a frame with its field of N(S) = 0. The P bit is set to 0.
3–5	Station B sends information frames (I), number N(S) = 0 through N(S) = 2. Its N(R) field is set to 1, which acknowledges station A's frame sent in event 1 (it had an N(S) value of 0). Remember, the N(R) value states that the station acknowledges all previously transmitted frames. The N(R) value also identifies the next N(S) value that is expected from station A.
6	Station A sends an I frame sequenced with N(S) = 1, which is the value station B expects next. Station A also sets the N(R) field to the value of 3, which inclusively acknowledges station B's previously transmitted frames numbered N(S), 0, 1, 2.
7	Station B has no data to transmit. However, to prevent station A from "timing-out" and resending data, station B sends a receiver ready (RR) frame with the N(R) = 2 to acknowledge station A's frame with N(S) = 1 (sent in event 6).

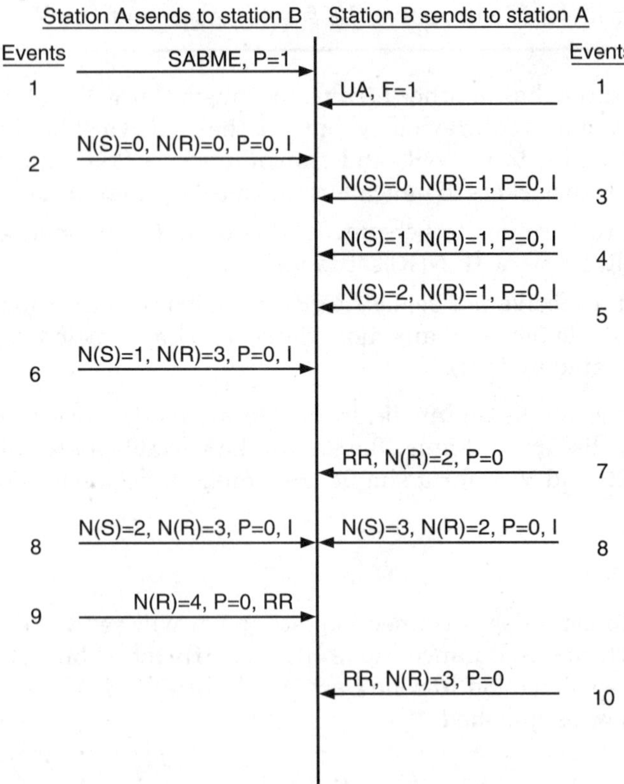

Figure 3.5 A sample user session.

8 The arrows depicting the frame flow from the stations that are aligned vertically with each other. This depiction means the two frames are transmitted from each station at about the same time and are exchanged almost simultaneously across the full-duplex link. The values of the N(R) and the N(S) fields reflect the sequencing and acknowledgment frames of the previous events.

9–10 Stations A and B send RR frames to acknowledge the frames transmitted in event 8. If neither side has data to send, each side will continue to send these frames to ensure the other side is active. The sequencing will remain the same throughout the RRs transmitted.

Refer to Fig. 3.6. This figure shows how LLC2 uses timers. It also depicts how the P/F bit can be utilized to manage the flow of traffic between two network stations.

Event	Operation
1	Station A sends a I frame and sequences it with N(S) = 3.
2	Station B does not respond within the bound of the timer. Station A times-out and sends a receiver ready (RR) command frame indicated by the P bit set to 1.
3	Station B responds with F = 1 and acknowledges stations A's frame by setting N(R) = 4.
4	Station A resets its timer and sends another I frame. It will keep the P bit set to 1 to force station B to immediately respond to this frame.
5	Station B responds with an RR frame with N(R) = 5 and the F bit set to 1.

Refer to Fig. 3.7.

Event	Operation
1	Station A sets up a connection with station B by sending an SABME, and station B accepts this request by sending back a UA.
2	Station A sends an I frame and sequences it with N(S) = 0. The N(R) = 0 means it expects station B to send an I frame with a send sequence number of 0.
3–6	Station B sends four frames numbered N(S) = 0, 1, 2, and 3. The N(R) value is set to 1 to acknowledge station A's previous frame. Notice the N(R) value does not change in any of these frames because station B is indicating that is still expecting a frame from station A with a send sequence number of 1. During these transmissions, we assume that the frame with N(S) = 1 is distorted.
7	Station A issues a (REJ) frame with N(R) = 1 and P = 1. This means that it is rejecting station B's frame that was sequenced with the N(S) = 1, as well as all succeeding frames.
8	Station B must first clear the P-bit condition by sending a non-I frame with the F bit set to 1.
9–12	Station B then retransmits frames 1–3. During this time (in event 9), station A sends an I frame with N(S) = 1. This frame has its N(R) = 2 to acknowledge the frame transmitted by station B in event 8.
13	Station A completes the recovery operations by acknowledging the remainder of station B's transmissions.

The preceding examples were taken from another HDLC exchange. LLC2 follows this flow very closely. It was presented mainly to show how a connection is set up and the exchange of sequence numbers. It also shows what happens during a frame loss.

The preceding text basically explained how most transport-level protocols work. They do not follow this exact interpretation of LLC2, but the functions are basically the same. LLC2 is primarily used when trans-

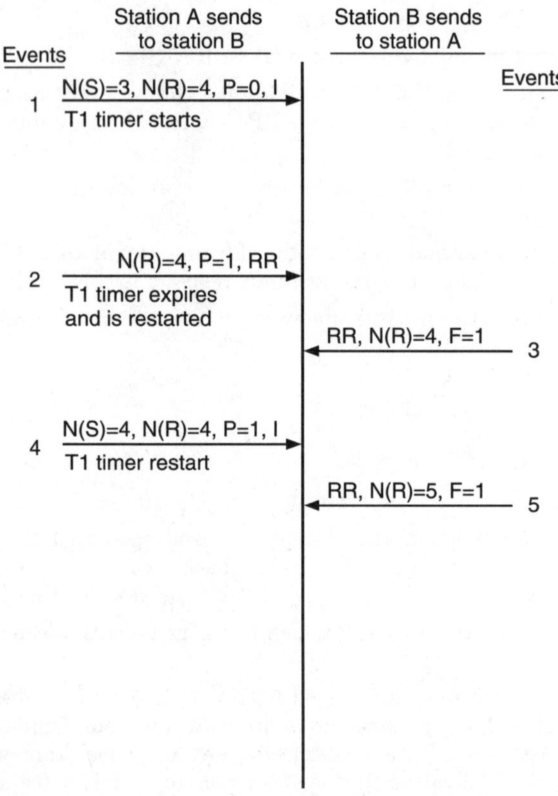

Figure 3.6 T1 timer. (*Courtesy of Uyless Black.*)

porting SNA traffic across Token Ring, when IBM LAN Server (IBM's alternative to Novell's NetWare) is being used, and with LANs that are implementing the use of serial lines with their network (bridges or routers that are using a telephone line to connect to a remote network). Usually, serial lines are conditioned to handle the digital traffic, but there may be instances where the serial line is not conditioned, and the LLC protocol ensures that data is reliably transferred across these lines.

LLC Type 1 Operation

With the exception of SNA and the IBM LAN Server Program, Type 1 is the most commonly used class of LLC. It is used by Novell, TCP/IP, OSI, and most other network protocols. There are no specific subsets for the operation of LLC Type 1. Type 1 operation consists of only one mode—information transfer—which will be subsequently described.

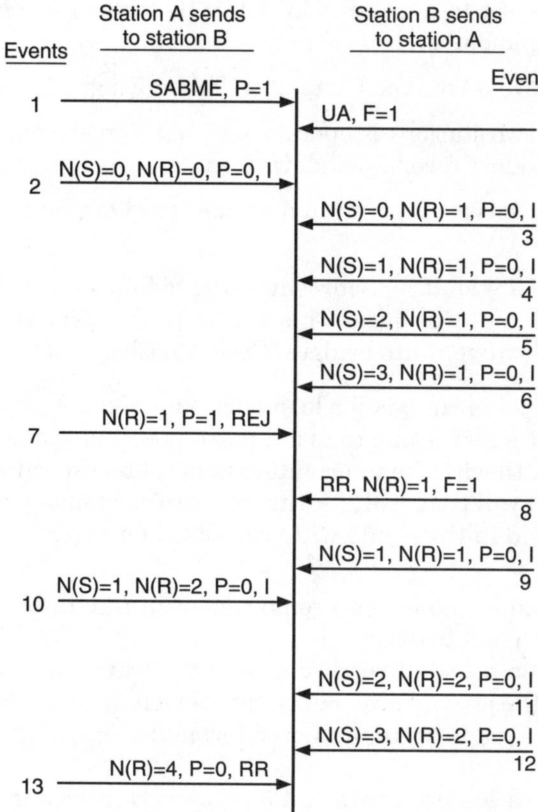

Figure 3.7 Selective reject. (*Courtesy of Uyless Black.*)

Information transfer

Type 1 operation does not require any prior connection establishment between the source and destination network stations before data is transferred between them. Once the SAP information field has been sent, information may be transferred between two network stations.

There are two other types of frames, besides information frames, that may be transmitted using LLC1 (XID and test frames can be used in LLC2 to perform the same operations) operation. They are the exchange identification (XID) and the TEST frames.

XID. The XID frame is used for the following functions:

1. An XID frame with a null SAP can be used to retrieve information from a remote network station. It is a form of the keep-alive packet that is used to test the presence of the remote station.

2. With the LSAP address set to a group SAP, the XID frame can be used to determine group membership.
3. To test for duplicate address (see the Chap. 2 on Token Ring).
4. If the link between the two stations is operating in LLC2 mode, this frame can be used to request receive-window sizes.
5. To request or identify a service class from a remote station (Type 1 or Type 2 LLC operation).
6. It can be used with IBM Token Ring Source Routing to find a remote station through source route bridges. This frame is the dynamic explorer frame used by source route bridges. (Refer to Chap. 2.)

The primary use of the test frame is for loop-back functions. A network station will transmit a test frame to test a path. It will be transmitted on a certain data path with the information field set to a specific entry. The network station will then wait for the frame to be responded to, and the information field in the frame will be checked for errors.

TEST. The TEST command frame is not a requirement in LLC1 operation, but the ability to respond to one is.

Although LLC1 operation does not require a response frame to any LLC1 command frame, these two previously mentioned frames do require a response, but are made in unnumbered format (no use of the P or F bits).

The most common application used with LLC1 is called SubNetwork Access Protocol (SNAP) and it is detailed subsequently.

SNAP

The most common implementation of LLC1 operation is through a special subsection of the IEEE 802.2 specification known as SubNetwork Access Protocol (SNAP). Most LAN vendors do implement this protocol, although the switch to true LLC1 operation is becoming more popular. The protocol of SNAP was introduced with LLC to allow network protocols an easy transition to the new frame formats that the IEEE 802.2 committee introduced. SNAP can be used with Novell, TCP/IP, OSI, and many other full OSI stack protocols. Any protocol may use this protocol and become a pseudo-IEEE-compliant protocol.

As stated previously, IEEE 802.2 defined two fields known as the Destination and Source Service Access Protocol (DSAP and SSAP, respectively). For the most part, the SAP fields are reserved for those protocols that implemented the IEEE 802.x protocols. There is one SAP that has been reserved for all non-IEEE standard protocols. To enable SNAP, the SAP value in both the DSAP and SSAP fields are set to AA (hex). The control field is set to 03 (hex). Therefore, many different protocols may be run using this one SAP. Therefore, to differentiate between the different protocols, any packet with the AA SAP address also has a 5-byte protocol discriminator following the control field. Refer to Fig. 3.8.

Since this is Type 1 operation, the DSAP and SSAP will be set to AA, and the control field (only 1 byte for Type 1 operation) will be set to 03 to indicate unnumbered information packets. Following this control field will be 5 bytes called *protocol discriminator.* This identifies the protocol family to which the packet belongs to.

Figure 3.8 shows an IEEE 802.2 with a SNAP header in an Ethernet packet. This packet contains four distinct parts:

1. The data-link encapsulation headers (destination and source address, and the CRC trailer)
2. The 3-byte 802.2 headers (set to AA, AA and 03)
3. The 5-byte protocol discriminator immediately following the 802.2 header
4. The data field of the packet

The important field to notice is the protocol discriminator. The first 3 bytes of this field indicate the vendor (080007 indicates Apple Computer, for example). The next 2 bytes indicate the type of packet it is (the EtherType field).

If the first 3 bytes of the protocol discriminator are set to 00-00-00, this indicates a generic Ethernet packet not assigned to any particular vendor, and the next 2 bytes will be the Type field of the Ethernet packet. The use of 3 bytes of 0s indicates the use of an Ethernet frame. This is useful when the frame traverses different media types. If that frame is transposed to allow passage on another media type, the field of 0s indicates that any time the frame is forwarded to the Ethernet media, it will be built as an Ethernet frame and not as an IEEE 802.3 frame. If this field contains an entry other than 0s, it indicates that the IEEE 802.3 frame (and not the Ethernet frame) should be used when forwarding to an Ethernet LAN. All 0s simply indicates an encapsulated Ethernet packet.

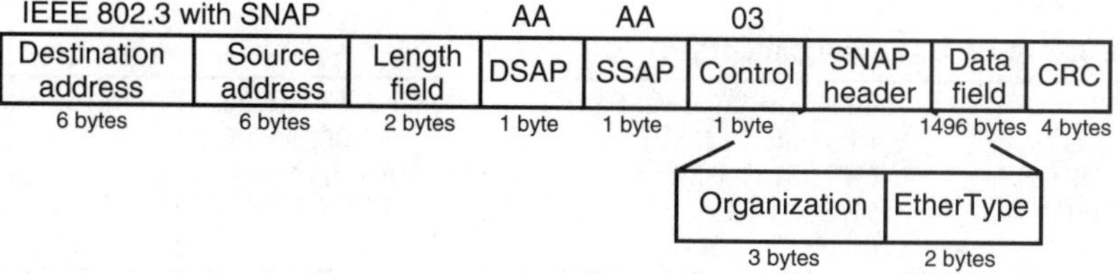

Figure 3.8 SNAP packet.

For example, a TCP/IP packet could have this field set to 5 bytes of 00-00-00-08-00. This signifies an organization ID (protocol discriminator) of 00-00-00 (which states that it is an Ethernet frame), and the Ethertype is a 08-00, which is the Ethertype for IP messages. Following this is the Ethernet data frame.

SNAP allowed for Ethernet vendors to quickly switch their drivers and network protocols over to the IEEE 802.x packet format without rewriting a majority of the code. Using this format allowed the vendors which had drivers written for the Ethernet system to port the network operating code quickly over to the Token Ring data-link frame format. A lot of vendors, in support of Token Ring, use the SNAP method to implement their existing code to run on top of Token Ring. It is quick, simple, and easy—and it also allowed for multivendor operation between different vendors.

Today, vendors are switching their code over to the LLC frame format. For example, Novell NetWare used to use SNAP. The format was AA-AA-03-00-00-00-81-37—AA for the DSAP/SSAP/Control fields, 3 bytes of 0's to indicate encapsulated Ethernet, and then the Ethernet Type field assigned to Novell: 8137. Novell has registered with the IEEE their NetWare operating system, and can now use the SAP address of E0 in their LLC frames. They use LLC1 for their transmission. This means that the DSAP and SSAP are set to E0 and the control field is set to 03 to indicate connectionless or LLC1 communication. Following these fields would be the IPX header starting with the checksum of FFFF.

The choice between connection-oriented networks and connectionless networks centers around the functionality that is needed. The connection-oriented system provides for the integrity of data, but with it comes the extreme burden of overhead. Connectionless systems consume less overhead but are prone to error.

Error rates on serial lines tend to be in the 1 in 10^3 range, while errors on a LAN tend to be in the 1 in 10^8 range. Therefore, it does not make a lot of sense to provide for connection-oriented services for a LAN. Error control is usually provided for by the application as well as the upper-layer software of a LAN (the transport layer).

Today, with LAN network protocols handling the connection-oriented services, connectionless methods are the most common.

TABLE 3.3 IEEE SAP Assignments

F0 OSI	42 Spanning Tree BPDU	F8, FC Remote Program Load
E0 Novell	FF Global LSAP	04, 05, 08, 0C SNA
F0 NetBIOS	F4 IBM Net Mgmt.	AA SNAP
06 TCP/IP	7F ISO 802.2	80 XNS
	00 NULL LSAP	

Ethernet Encapsulation Methods (Data-Link frame encapsulation)

Ethernet

Destination address	Source address	Type field	Data field	CRC
6 bytes	6 bytes	2 bytes	1500 bytes	4 bytes

IEEE 802.3

Destination address	Source address	Length field	Data field	CRC
6 bytes	6 bytes	2 bytes	1500 bytes	4 bytes

IEEE 802.3 with IEEE 802.2

Destination address	Source address	Length field	DSAP	SSAP	Control	Data field	CRC
6 bytes	6 bytes	2 bytes	1 byte	1 byte	1 byte/or LLC1	1496 bytes	4 bytes

IEEE 802.3 with SNAP

Destination address	Source address	Length field	DSAP	SSAP	Control	SNAP header	Data field	CRC
			AA	AA	03			
6 bytes	6 bytes	2 bytes	1 byte	1 byte	1 byte/ or LLC1		1496 bytes	4 bytes

Organization	EtherType
3 bytes	2 bytes

Novell-specific

Destination address	Source address	Length field	Data field	CRC
6 bytes	6 bytes	2 bytes	1500 bytes	4 bytes

30 bytes

FFFF	IPX header	Netware core protocol

IEEE 802.5 with IEEE 802.2 or IEEE 802.2 SNAP

Starting delimeter	Access control	Frame control	Destination address	Source address	Routing info field	DSAP	SSAP	Control	Data	End ring delimeter	Frame status	CRC
1 byte	1 byte	1 byte	6 bytes	6 bytes	up to 30 bytes	1 byte	1 byte	1 or 2 bytes	up to 17800 bytes	1 byte	1 byte	4 bytes

ORG	EtherType

SNAP

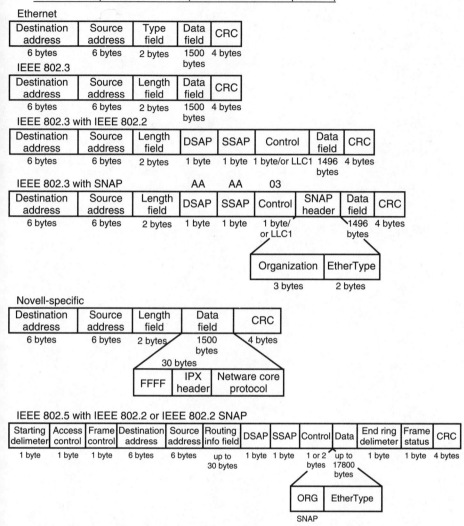

Figure 3.9 Ethernet, IEEE 802.3, and IEEE 802.5 Frame Formats.

To summarize all Ethernet/IEEE 802.3 and IEEE 802.5 with IEEE 802.2. data-link encapsulation types, refer to Fig. 3.9.

Figure 3.9 shows the IEEE 802.5 packet with SNAP. This packet can be used with or without SNAP. SNAP is shown with the IEEE 802.5 packet (and not as a separate packet) for space considerations only.

Chapter

4

Xerox Network System (XNS)

There are many variations of XNS, for XNS is basically an architecture and not a strictly adhered to standard. But it does provide a great insight into how a network protocol should operate. It is for this reason that I have chosen it as an introduction in generally learning the network protocols. It provides the architecture for the upper-layer protocols (OSI layers 3 through 7).

The protocols behind XNS can give implementors of network protocols a clear understanding of how to build a network protocol. The unfortunate thing about XNS is that the protocol allows for a tremendous amount of vendor-specific implementations. It was implemented by most vendors as an architecture to follow. There really was no strict standard for the vendors to follow. The architecture is very loosely written. XNS was derived to operate over a LAN—specifically, Ethernet.

XNS was the first protocol commercially implemented over Ethernet. It was implemented as an open document to show how a software protocol should run over a LAN. The protocol is fairly straightforward. This protocol was implemented by multiple vendors at the start of the network revolution in the early 1980s. All vendors implemented the protocol suite up to OSI layer 4 (the transport layer), the sequence packet protocol, or SPP. The OSI session-layer protocol known as courier, explained in a later section of this chapter, was not used by most LAN vendors. All vendors implemented their own session-layer schemes. Therefore, in the early 1980s, most network architectures were based on XNS, but all were developed as proprietary network systems. This meant that a protocol based on XNS from one LAN vendor would not work with another LAN vendor's XNS equipment.

This created a multitude of problems, primarily for the users of an XNS vendor's equipment. While the XNS protocol was a good protocol, it locked a company into one LAN vendor. For example, if you ordered network equipment from vendor A, and decided later to implement vendor B's equipment, the two vendors' equipment would not interoperate if both were using their own implementation of the XNS stack. Depending on your investment, this could represent a large investment to one vendor. If a company needed a certain type of networking equipment, and vendor A did not supply it but vendor B did, the company was faced with some very hard choices.

XNS is a good LAN protocol implementation. Unfortunately, no vendor implemented the exact same version. I have chosen XNS as the first protocol to study, for XNS does provide a good implementation from which to learn LAN protocols. It has all the pieces needed to construct a protocol suite for networking.

Other protocols such as TCP/IP proliferated as the type of standard for all protocols to run, for it allowed for multiple LAN and computer vendors to interoperate. Vendor A's equipment would interoperate with vendor B's, for they both implemented the TCP/IP protocol. The TCP/IP protocol was built as an open standard, and all vendors that implemented it had to follow one and only one standard. TCP/IP is covered in a later chapter.

Network Definition

Refer to Fig. 4.1. This figure shows a network (solid-line box) and an internetwork (dotted-line box). A network can be defined as a transmission medium that is used to carry internet packets through the network. A network is a collection of hardware and software that, when taken together, provide a means to share data and peripheral economically and efficiently. The dotted line surrounds all networks, and that is called the *internet.* The solid black line covers only one set of network components, and that is called a *network.* An internet is usually a composition of networks tied together by devices known as *routers.* Routers will be explained later.

There are many, many entities that comprise a network. For this introduction, a few important entities will be described further.

Hosts are classified into two groups: internetwork routers and network stations (nodes). Stations are classified as workstations or servers. This is true no matter what type of computing devices are attached to the network or internetwork.

A network is defined as a communication system that is used to carry internet packets that connect stations, and this, in turn, is connected to a router that will make up the internetwork (see Fig. 4.1). With a few exceptions, stations on the same network can communicate among

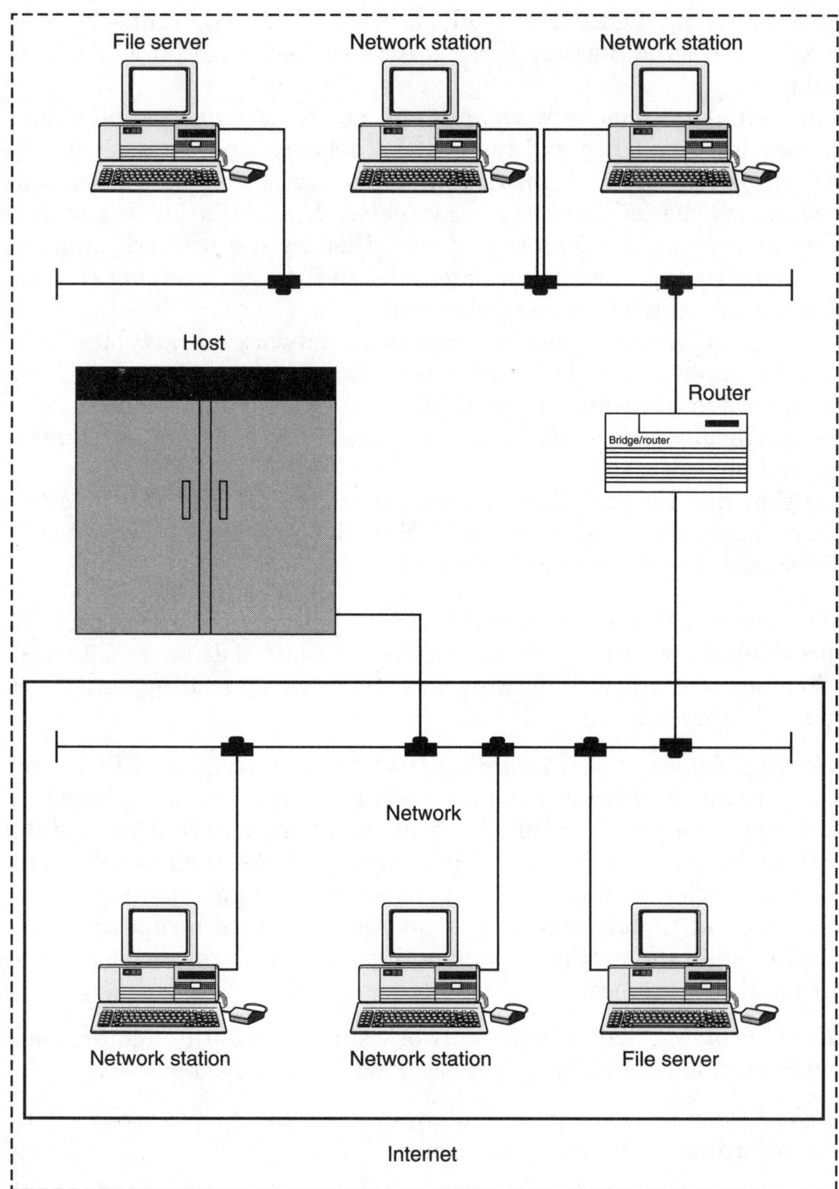

Figure 4.1 XNS Network/Internet.

themselves without the use of a router. Each and every network will be assigned a unique network number. This, in a crude way, is like the area code of the telephone system. Network numbers are assigned to every individual network, and even between routers that are connected together to form a circuit using leased lines (serial lines specially conditioned to handle digital data traffic or between directly connected networks). Data serial lines are like a static switched circuit. It will only be used for data.

Individual stations on a network will not be assigned an individual network number. They will take on the network number assigned by their network. This will mean that every station on that individual network will be assigned the same network number. In this way, a group of network stations can be identified by the network number. This greatly simplifies the routing tables in those devices that can forward data destined for other networks.

During the beginning of the commercial network marketplace, Ethernet was predominately found in most installations. Therefore, XNS became the most popular network protocol scheme implemented. XNS was specifically written as an architecture to use Ethernet as its data-link and physical layers.

As shown in Fig. 4.2, there are certain individual protocols involved that make up the architecture of XNS. This figure shows the protocols of XNS and how there were assigned to levels.

The Internet Datagram Protocol (IDP). This network-level protocol provides the routing functions needed to route data in an internet. This protocol provides network-level addressing, routing, datagram packet formatting, etc.

Routing Information Protocol (RIP). Similar to other RIP implementations, it provides dynamic updating of routing tables based on a distance vector algorithm. It should be noted here that the specification does not specify special routing algorithms such as split horizon or poisoned reverse. Most vendors are implementing them, though. Its update interval is 60 seconds. This terms are fully explained in the routing section of this chapter. Xerox developed the original RIP protocol.

Error Protocol. Allows one network station to notify another network station that an error has occurred in a received packet.

Echo Protocol. This protocol allows for testing of a network path or for recording round-trip delay times.

Sequence Packet Protocol (SPP). A transport-level protocol, this protocol allows for a reliable data exchange between two stations. An originator and receiver network station synchronize and establish a connection between themselves. During this process, a sequence number is established to mark the packets exchanged between the two. This sequencing is accomplished on a packet-level basis.

Packet Exchange Protocol (PEP). A request and response protocol used in transaction-oriented applications.

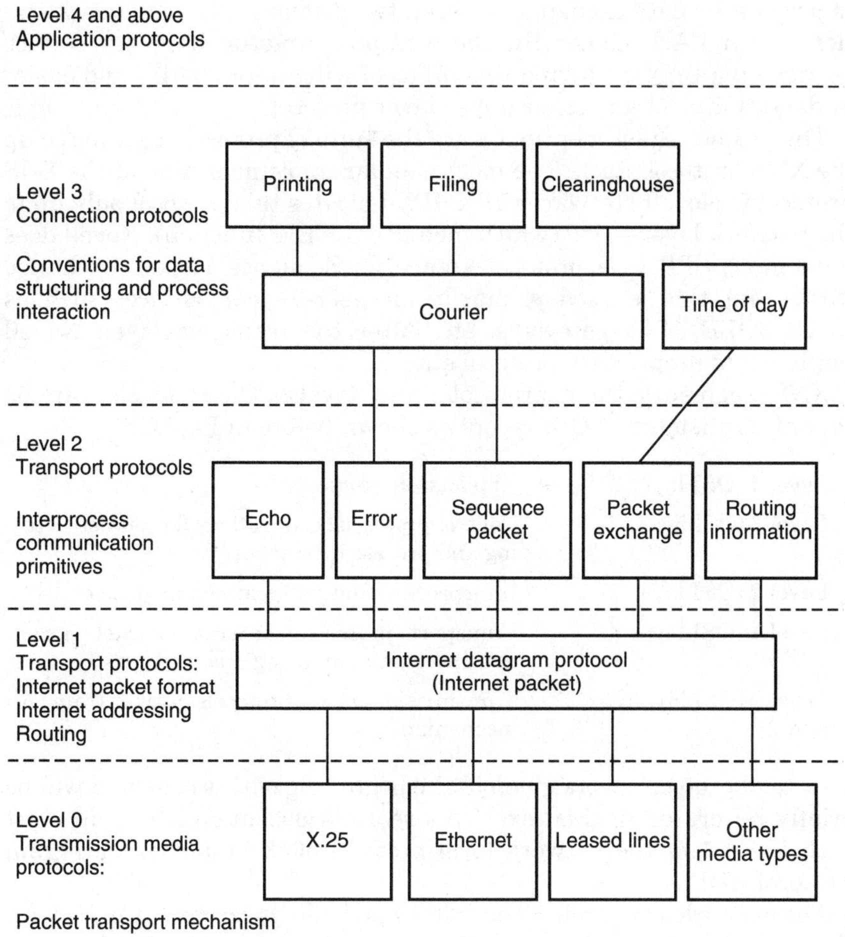

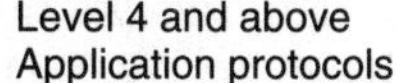

Figure 4.2 XNS model. (*Courtesy Xerox Corp.*)

Courier. A session-level protocol that provides remote procedural Call services (explained fully in a later section of this chapter).

Clearinghouse. Provides for the naming services to exist on XNS.

File Service. A file transfer service.

Printing Service. A remote printing service.

Time of Day. Provides date and time service.

With the exception of file service, printing service, and time of day, each of the aforementioned protocols will be discussed. The protocol of XNS provides an excellent example of how a software LAN protocol suite is built. Each of the services provided shows the functions needed to provide for data exchange between two communicating network stations on a LAN. Generally, there is one protocol for every service needed on a LAN. Studying this protocol will allow a better and easier understanding of any other upper layer protocol.

The protocols just mentioned are the suite of protocols that make up the XNS protocol stack. The most popular implementation of the XNS protocol is Novell NetWare's IPX. IPX imitates this protocol only up to the network layer—IDP (which includes the RIP function). Novell does implement SPP in a protocol known as Sequence Packet Exchange (SPX), but this is used primarily for peer-to-peer services such as RCONSOLE, SNA gateways, etc. After the transport layer, Novell implements proprietary protocol stack.

XNS segments their protocols into levels. These levels can be roughly translated to OSI layers as shown before in Fig. 4.2.

Level 4 (OSI layer 7)	Application protocols
Level 3 (OSI layers 5–7)	Control protocols: conventions for data structuring and process interaction
Level 2 (OSI layer 4)	Interprocess Communications Primitives
Level 1 (OSI layer 3)	Transport protocols: Internet packet format and Internet addressing and routing
Level 0 (OSI layers 1 and 2)	Transmission media protocols: packet transport mechanism

Level 0 protocols were given in the beginning of this book and will be briefly reiterated in this text. This real discussion on XNS will start with Level 1 or the network level protocol of the Internet Datagram Protocol (IDP).

The network level protocol operates much like the company of Federal Express. If you wish to send a letter to someone, you will write down the data in a letter. You will then insert this letter into an envelope and put the destination address and a return address on the envelope.

From here, you will put this envelope in the box, where Federal Express will pick it up. Federal Express will note the destination address of the letter and route the letter to its final destination. If Federal Express cannot find the recipient they will call the sender to inform the sender of this problem. The sender may then receive the letter back.

If the letter could be delivered, the recipient will read the letter and, if necessary, send a response. The recipient will know where to return the response by the return address you put on the letter. This letter will then be routed back by Federal Express to your address, where you will receive that letter.

I used Federal Express as an example, for Federal Express has checkpoints along the way to ensure that the letter will make it to its final destination. No letter should get lost without a message generated back as to what happened to this letter.

This may seem like a connection-oriented protocol. It is not. Most LAN network layer protocols are connectionless or datagram-oriented. But most offer checkpoint error detection for host or network address problems.

This is very similar to the service that a network layer provides. A network will add a few more features, like extensive error recovery and connection IDs, but the basic delivery service is the same. That is, basically, a network layer is a delivery service based on software or protocol addresses.

The IDP provides, like other network protocols, the network addressing, routing, and datagram packet formatting of data. It is this layer that provides not only for the routing of datagrams in the XNS internet, but also the network-level addressing.

XNS can run over any data link protocol, including Token Ring and Ethernet. We will start our discussion of the XNS system with the Internet Transport protocols. Since XNS was built to run specifically on top of Ethernet, it will be the medium of choice for the continuing discussion. XNS's general functions are shown in Fig. 4.3.

Terminology and definitions

Before the XNS levels are detailed, there are some terms that need to be defined. Every packet transmitted will have a source and destination address. This may be the MAC-layer source address or it may be a protocol address at the network layer. The MAC-layer address is the address directed at the physical interface to the network. The Ethernet card in a PC that connects to an Ethernet cabling system will be identified by this address, for example.

The data flow between the source and destination will always have the sender of the data and the recipient of that data clearly identified in the packet. They will be identified by their protocol address in the IDP header.

A *connection* is an association between two communicating stations (usually the sender and the receiver). After a connection is established, data should flow reliably between the two stations. A connection will usually have a *listener* and an *initiator*. The listener will wait for connection from remote sources, and the initiator will be the station that attempts to connect to other stations on the network.

A system that supplies services to others is called a *server*. Each service (file, print, terminal) in the server has a *supplier* and a *consumer*. Like the connection, the supplier "supplies" information upon requests from the consumer. An example of this is a user's workstation that has a connection to a file server.

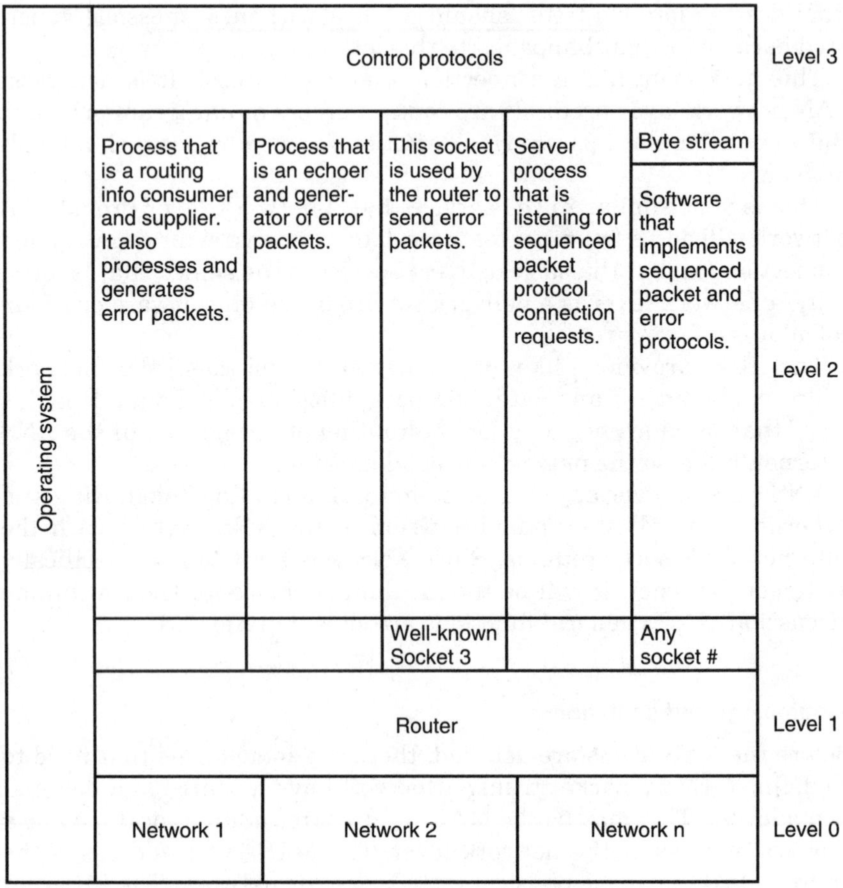

Operating system

Control protocols — Level 3

Process that is a routing info consumer and supplier. It also processes and generates error packets.

Process that is an echoer and generator of error packets.

This socket is used by the router to send error packets.

Server process that is listening for sequenced packet protocol connection requests.

Byte stream

Software that implements sequenced packet and error protocols.

Level 2

Well-known Socket 3

Any socket #

Router — Level 1

Network 1 | Network 2 | Network n — Level 0

Figure 4.3 Overall XNS model. (*Courtesy XEROX Corp.*)

A *network* is a transmission medium that is configured to carry internet packets. A *transmission medium* is any communications equipment that is configured to carry data. This includes the cable, the network interface card, and the software to send and receive packets (data).

A *host* can be a network station as long as it is supplied with a 48-bit address to identify it on the network. The host must supply communication protocols to enable other stations (hosts) on the network to communicate with it.

A *port* is an identified service in a host and is a source and/or destination of packets. It is an integer number that represents an application on a server on the internet. The service may be a file server application, a terminal service, or some type of communication service.

Data originates and is sent via ports. *Port numbers* are numbers that are assigned to services in a network station. These services are identified to the users with human, readable names. Network software uses port numbers. They identify which service is being requested and with which service a network station should respond to packets.

Socket numbers are the combination of host address, network address, and port number. The XNS documentation calls port numbers (just explained) a socket number. To be consistent with their documentation, this text will use the terminology of sockets to mean ports.

A network may be of three types: a broadcast network, a multicast network, or a point-to-point (nonbroadcast) network. A *broadcast network* is one in which all hosts on the network can receive the data. (It is possible to transmit to all hosts on the network with one packet.) Ethernet and Token Ring are examples.

A *multicast network* enables the communications software to transmit data to a subset of hosts on the network. Ethernet and Token Ring are examples, but the packets are addressed to a specific set of hosts on the network. An example would be the Spanning Tree Algorithm packets for Ethernet bridges.

A *point-to-point network* is a communication between two hosts only (an example could be two networks geographically separated, but connected to form an internet by telephone serial line communications).

Finally an *internetwork,* or *internet* as it is called, is the interconnection of networks that carry internet packets. Refer to Fig. 4.1.

Socket and routing definition. The Internet Transport protocols support data communication between *sockets* on a network. These sockets may be on the same host, or different hosts on the same network, or on different networks (the internet). Sockets will be explained in detail later. For now, a socket is an endpoint for communication in a network. It allows the network protocol in a workstation to understand the data's destination.

The function of switching or routing internet packets between sockets that reside on the same host, between sockets and networks (the same host is the source or the destination of the packet), and between networks is the function of *routing.* This routing function is found on every network station on a network or internet. Just because data is transferred between two sockets on the same host, or between two hosts on the same network, does not mean that the routing function is not enabled. The main purpose of the routing function is to deliver data between sockets no matter where the sockets reside.

Routing data between stations on the same LAN with the same network number is called *direct routing.* Sending data between stations on different networks is called *indirect routing.*

The router function maintains a table, known as a *forwarding table,* that will contain two important entries: a network number and cost to that network from the router. Each router will know of every network number on the XNS internet. Every network separated by a router will be assigned a unique network number. These numbers are propagated to all routers on the network. The routers will assign a cost, more commonly called a *hop,* to each network number. The *hop count* is the number of routers between a router and the associated network number on the internet. Routers update their tables dynamically using the routing information protocol. All of this is explained in more detail shortly.

Figure 4.1 shows the typical internet and the functions needed.

XNS at Level 0

The functions provided at this level are simply to transport data across the transmission medium (the broadcast, multicast or point-to-point network). At this level, the functions do not care what the data is; it is given to it by Level 1 protocols for the mere action of being transported over the medium.

Examples of broadcast transmission mediums:

Ethernet

Token Ring

FDDI

Nonbroadcast or point to point

Serial lines use the CCITT standard High-level Data Link Control (HDLC) protocol for data encapsulation. Data to be sent across the serial line will be wrapped in an HDLC frame so that the device at the other end of the serial line will understand what to do with the packet.

At this level, the packet is treated simply as data. Level 0 packets are only interpreted by Level 0 protocols. Refer to Fig. 4.4. Data handed to Level 0 by Level 1 is encapsulated (enveloped) by Level 0 headers and trailers to be transmitted over the medium. The exact encapsulation technique depends on the medium being transmitted onto. Ethernet will have one type of encapsulation; Token Ring, IEEE 802.3 another, etc. Refer to chapter 2 for an explanation of packet formats. The host that receives the data must be of the same type transmission medium for it to properly de-encapsulate the packet. A system

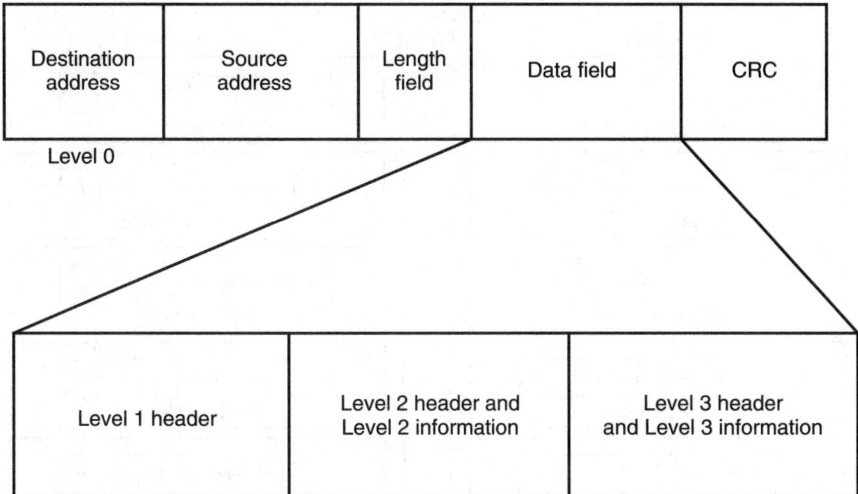

Figure 4.4 IEEE 802.3 frame with IDP headers.

that is not running the same Level 0 protocols should not appear on the same transmission medium as does the sender.

To explain further, packet encapsulation is the function of transforming Level 1 data (an internet packet) into whatever packet form is supported by the transmission medium, so that it simply appears as data. Generally, this involves the adding of headers (information at the beginning of the packet), trailers (information at the end of the packet), and error correction information, called a Cyclic Redundancy Check (CRC). The deencapsulation process will reverse this process at the destination host of the packet.

In order for the packet to be transmitted, the internet packet must be properly addressed according to the conventions of the transmission medium (for Ethernet and Token Ring, all Level 0 addresses are 48 bits in length).

For IEEE 802.3 transmission, the packet encapsulation is shown in Fig. 4.4. All upper-layer information is placed in the level 0 packet. All padding (to fill up the packet to the minimum number of bytes for transmission) is provided for at encapsulation stage. Since the internet packet has a length of its own, this extra padding will be removed by the destination station. Packet encapsulation from each layer is shown in Fig. 4.5. Figure 4.5 is introduced here to show each layer of the OSI model and the encapsulation that is used. Each layer will add its own information to the beginning of the encapsulated data. For example, as data is handed to it from the application layer, the presentation layer will add its own special information to it. Each layer

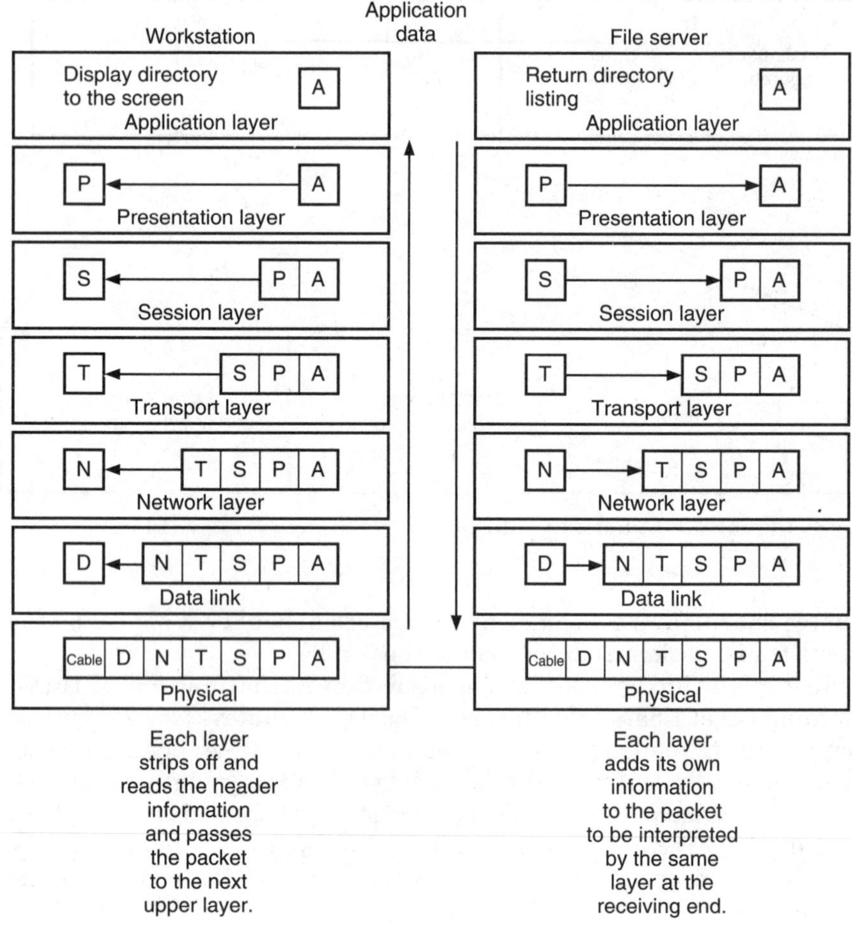

Figure 4.5 Layered encapsulation.

going down the OSI model will add its own special information. This special information is known as *header information.* When the packet is received, the network software at each OSI layer will read the header information and then process the packet accordingly.

Packet reception at level 0. When the internet packet is received, it must be de-encapsulated by the Level 0 protocols (address and CRC check), and then the rest of the packet is transferred to the Level 1 protocols. The process of de-encapsulation is simply the reverse of the encapsulation methods. Error checking is usually first done and if the packet is received in good condition (no errors), the packet will be de-encapsulated by level 0 and transferred to the Level 1 protocols for processing. Handing it the Level 1 protocols may be giving it to a socket, or it may re-encapsulate it and transmit it to another network (routing). If it is re-encapsulated, it must conform to the transmission-medium encapsulation methods of the new network. This is one reason why protocols that incorporate a routing layer can be delivered to different transmission mediums (received as a packet Ethernet and translated and then transmitted to a Token Ring network); bridging a packet cannot do this. Bridging essentially runs at level 0. XNS Level 1 encapsulation is shown in Fig. 4.6.

Level 0 protocols of Token Ring and Ethernet were explained in Chap. 2.

Internet Transport Protocols—Level 1

The design of the Internet Transport protocols is to treat all packets independently. Each packet is a datagram and is transmitted in what is known as connectionless or unreliable mode. It is a packet that is transmitted over the transmission medium, and an acknowledgment is not expected from the receiver of the packet at this level.

XNS defines only one protocol at Level 1. It is called the Internet Datagram Protocol (IDP). The purpose of this protocol is to address, route, and deliver standard internet packets. It provides the delivery system for data being transmitted and received on the internet. This process delivers a connectionless, best-effort delivery service. There is not a connection setup for the delivery of packets. The internet packet is transmitted and the protocol will continue with the next packet in the queue. If, for some reason, that packet never makes it to the final destination, another higher-layer protocol, usually a transport layer protocol, will time out and the packet will be retransmitted. But this is the function of the Sequence Packet Protocol (SPP), and this protocol will be discussed in a later section.

The format of the IDP header and its encapsulation in an IEEE 802.3 packet is shown in Fig. 4.6. It has a Source Network Address and a Destination Network Address. Its primary concern is dealing with the delivery of a datagram (formatted data) onto the network.

The network address totals three distinct fields. The 32-bit network number uniquely identifies a single network on the internet. The 48-bit host number, which allows for over 4 billion hosts, is a unique number for every network attachment on the internet. Whereas network numbers group network stations into a single entity, host numbers define a single host. The 16-bit port number uniquely identifies a socket within the operating system on the host.

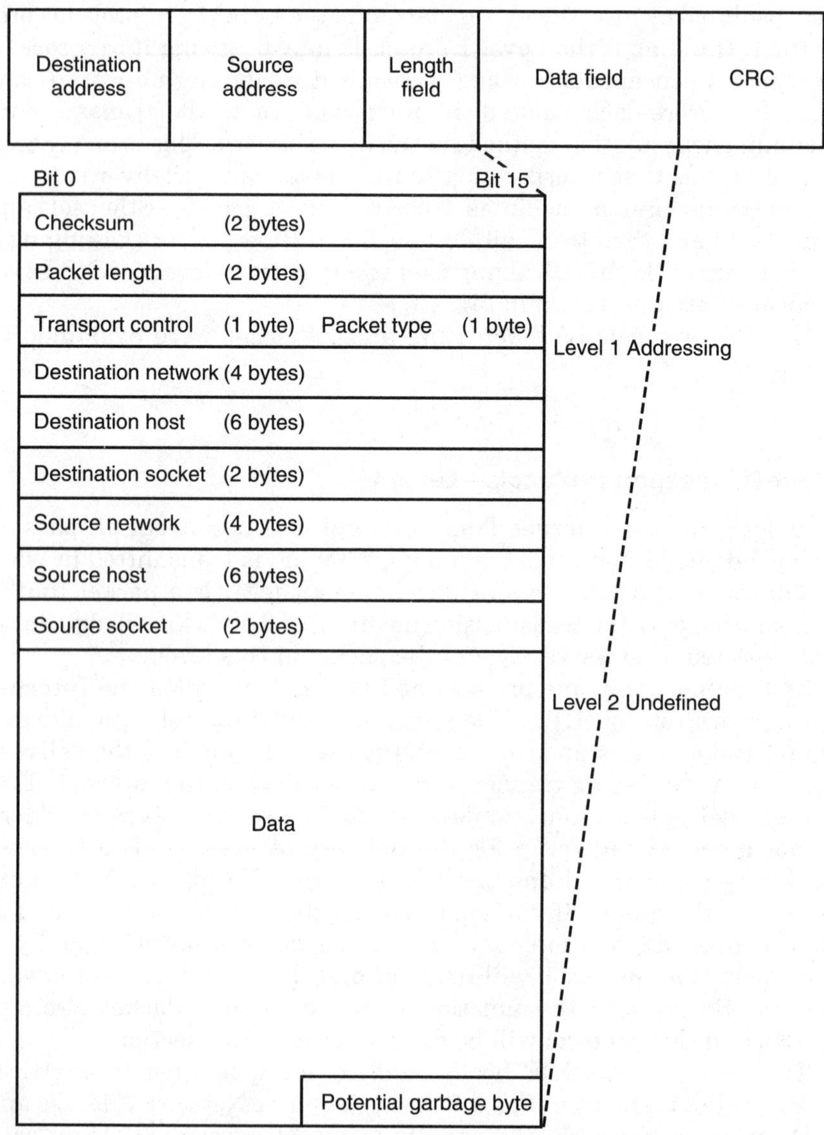

Figure 4.6 IEEE 802.3 frame with IDP headers. (*Courtesy XEROX Corp.*)

Host numbers

This field is exactly identical to the 48-bit physical MAC address of the network station. In the internet header, it identifies the originator of the packet, the source host number, and the final address (the destination host number) to which the packet is destined.

Applying it this way has many advantages compared to other network protocols (protocol address, TCP/IP, DECnet, AppleTalk, etc.). For example, when a host is moved from one network to another, it will not have to change its host address to the new network host address scheme (the network number may change, though). When the internet packet is encapsulated for transmission over the Ethernet, there will not be a separate process to provide a translation between the protocol address and the physical-layer address, as in TCP/IP or AppleTalk, thereby reducing the overhead needed for transmission. This also allows for the elimination of tables in the network station's conserving memory (at the time of XNS's popularity, memory was very expensive).

Network numbers

The host number identifies a particular host on the internet, and the network number can identify a group of hosts on the internet—specifically on one network. The network number is like the area code in the phone system. It serves an important role on the internet when hosts are separated by devices known as routers. With network numbers, routers need only to know a path to each network on the internet (a table of network numbers and the path to get there). This reduces the amount of information that a router must contain to perform its functions.

The routing function (direct and indirect) only uses the network number to route packets. It does not care about the host numbers until the packet reaches the final network. It is up the final router to determine how to address and deliver the packet to its final destination. Keeping track of network numbers instead of host numbers provides for more efficient routing. Network numbers are the only entries in the routing table. DECnet and OSI are the only protocols that take exception to this. DECnet routing is fully explained in Chap. 8, OSI in Chap. 10.

An internet packet addressed to a host will contain the network number on which the host resides. Routers will attempt to deliver the datagram to the host based on this network number.

All network numbers must be unique on the internet in order for routing to function properly. If two autonomous networks are merged, the network numbers must remain unique throughout the merged network.

Socket numbers*

A socket is an integer number assigned to a service on a host (destination or source). This will identify the process to which the originator or

* Socket numbers in this text actually refer to port numbers. In the true meaning, socket numbers are the combination of the port number, the host, and network numbers taken as a whole.

packet wishes to communicate (destination socket), and it will identify the process to which the recipient can return a response (source socket). Certain socket numbers are considered "well known." This means they are reserved for a specific use. They are also called *static sockets.* Table 4.1 shows the well-known sockets and their descriptions for XNS.

The other type of socket numbers are known as *ephemeral.* This means that they are dynamic and can be reused. These socket numbers do not need to be unique throughout the internet, for a socket number is combined to the host and network numbers to uniquely identify a network, host, and service needed on that host. In other words, the network address, host address, and socket address taken as one number will identify a service on the internet.

A socket number assigned to a file service (for example, 0451) may have multiple requests for connections to the server containing that socket number. Connection identifiers are used so that the host providing that file service will be able to differentiate between multiple incoming connections wanting access to the same destination socket number for the file service.

Simply stated, socket numbers identify a service running on a host (such as a file service, print service, or database service). The service is assigned a number by which a workstation may communicate to it. This number is the socket number.

Identifying the internet datagram fields

Checksum. This is an error-identifying number. It is a software checksum and is used in addition to the transmission media's checksum. This field is optional. A value of FFFF (hex) in this field indicates that checksumming is turned off at this layer. Novell's NetWare does not use the checksum field in their proprietary IPX implementation. This is the way some network software indicates a proprietary Novell encapsulated packet FF is a global LSAP.

Length. This field indicates the length of the internet packet measured in bytes. This includes the checksum field. It does not include the

TABLE 4.1 XNS Socket Types

Function	Well-known socket number (octal)
Routing information	1
Echo	2
Router error	3
Experimental	40–77
Dynamically assigned	4000–6000 (decimal)

transmission-medium encapsulation headers and trailers (Level 0). It equals the length of the data field plus 30 bytes. The 30 bytes is the length of the network-layer header. It will always be this length. The maximum length of the internet packet is 576 bytes and is summed by the following entries. All systems should be able to handle this maximum datagram size. XNS expects Level 0 protocols to provide fragmentation and reassembly (slicing up a packet to fit the transmission size of the transmission medium). The 576-byte packet was picked for the following:

30 bytes for network-header information

12 bytes for transport-layer information

22 bytes to be used for session-layer information (Level 3 information)

512 bytes which indicates a typical disk page (or a block of memory) for XNS systems

This does not mean that all XNS packets must be of this size. Two communicating stations may negotiate a different packet size, whether larger or smaller than the recommended packet size. An XNS recommendation is 576 bytes, and most XNS implementations (Novell NetWare) do not follow this recommendation.

Transport control. This is used only by routers and is used to manage the transport of internet packets on the internet. It is initialized to 0 by the initiator of a packet. As the routers change this field, the checksum (if enacted) will be recomputed. Each time a router forwards the packet to another network, it will add 1 to this field. This will indicate how many routers the packet has traversed. When this field reaches 16, the packet will be discarded by the router that set it to 16. This ensures that packets will not endlessly loop in an internet. Some implementations will send an error packet back to the originator of the packet by using the error protocol (explained later). With a maximum of 16 allowed in this field, only bits 4–7 are used. Bits 0–3 are not used and should be set to 0.

Maximum Packet Lifetime (MPL). This is used to estimate the maximum time any internet packet will remain in the internet governed by the Internet Transport Protocols. The recommended standard for this entry is 60 seconds. This was computed by estimating that the most time the router will delay forwarding a packet will be 1 second. A packet is allowed to traverse 15 routers before being discarded. This would allow for the number to reach 15. This number is multiplied by 4 for rare cases of extreme delay. This could be low-speed lines in a very large network.

It is recommended that network drivers that cannot transmit a packet within one-tenth of the MPL discard the packet.

Packet type. Refer to Fig. 4.7 and Table 4.2. This field is regulated by Xerox. Anyone following this protocol should call Xerox and register their packet type with them. This field indicates the format of the data field of the internet packet. It is a registry with Xerox for identifying the user of the packet. The types recommended are shown in Table 4.2. Experimental types are used when a vendor is developing a new protocol.

It primarily identifies the Level 2 function of the embedded data in the data field of the packet. Novell has a registry number of 17 (decimal) for their XNS implementation called Internet Packet Exchange (IPX).

The Level 1 protocol does not interpret this field; it merely reads it and then passes the packet information up to the appropriate socket identified by the packet type. It provides information on which "well-known process" the IDP should hand the packet to.

Source and destination network addresses. The source and destination network number identify two things: the originator of the packet (network and host addresses) and the intended recipient of the packet (network and host addresses). Providing this type of address, network, and host number is enough to identify any network address on the entire network. These fields were previously discussed.

Data. The data portion of the packet is nothing more than a sequence of bytes that is completely transparent to the Level 1 protocol. The length of the data is derived by subtracting 30 from length, and may have a value of 0 to 546 bytes. It could contain transport, session, and application data or it may contain commands. Level 1 does not care about this field.

Garbage byte. At the end of the data field, there may be an odd number of bytes in the packet. This type of packet cannot be transmitted. To get an even number of bytes, the Level 1 protocol may add a garbage byte which will be included in the checksum but not in the length field.

Any client may interface to the Internet Datagram Protocol by simply acquiring a socket from the network operating system and then beginning and continuing to send and receive data on that socket num-

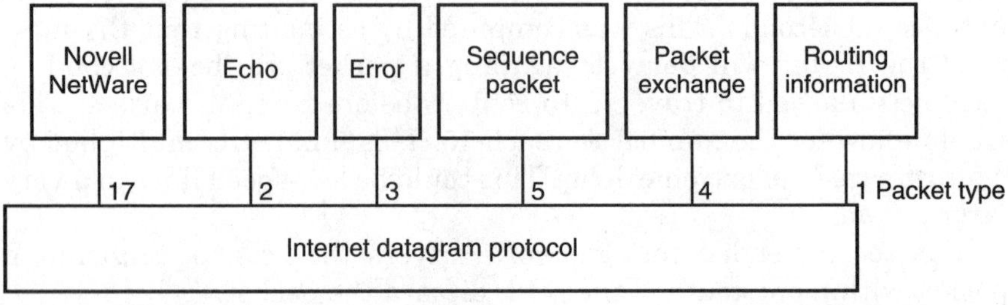

Figure 4.7 IDP demux efforts based on assigned packet types. (*Courtesy XEROX Corp.*)

TABLE 4.2 Packet Types

Protocol	Packet type (in octal)
Routing information	1
Echo	2
Error	3
Packet exchange	4
Sequence packet	5
Experimental	20–37

ber. At this time it should be noted that packets are sent on a best-effort delivery service. Packets may be lost even on the highest integrity type of network.

If the checksum is found to be in error, the packet may be thrown away and no error packet sent to the originator indicating there was a problem with the received packet. Packets may also be discarded due to buffer (RAM) constraints.

Part of the function of the Internet Datagram Protocol is the capability of a routing function. A router is a store and forward device that routes packets to different networks based on a network number and a routing table. The routing table must be updated dynamically (learn of other networks without user intervention). XNS accomplishes this using the Routing Information Protocol (discussed in a moment).

Packets may be sent directly to the destination (unique destination address) or it may be sent in multicast or broadcast mode (addressed so that many stations can receive the one packet). IDP packet flow will be shown later.

Level 2

The Level 2 protocols consists of the echo, error, sequence packet, packet exchange, and the routing information protocols. Each operates independently and is described following.

Routing information protocol

RIP is the most widely implemented routing update protocol in use today. Although it does have it drawbacks, it did provide a good beginning into dynamic routing protocols. A variation of this protocol is implemented on AppleTalk, TCP/IP, IPX, and XNS. A high-level overview of how distance vector protocols operate follows. Please refer to those specified protocols for more information on how they run the RIP protocol.

The routing of indirect routing of packets is accomplished using a special store-and-forward device known as a router. The router knows of other networks by means of a database table that lists the network numbers and the path associated with the network. The routing information protocol is the means by which this database is dynamically maintained. It is one of the protocols located at level 2.

All XNS routers perform two tasks: supply routing information to any station that requests information and update other routers about the networks that it knows about. A network workstation (nonrouter) must maintain a routing table or the capability to query a router. This table may be simple (with only one entry in the table) or it may be complex in that it maintains a routing table, just like a router, but does not update any other network station on the network.

The routing information requester uses the routing information to maintain a routing table cache.* This is a database table of network numbers and the associated cost required to reach that network that is usually maintained in RAM memory. The requester exists in all routers (workstations and internet routers), while a combination of the requester and the supplier exists in all internet routers. In other words, in an XNS environment, the requester (and its associated table) will exist in all network stations, whether or not they process the internet routing function or are simply a network station. The internet router maintains the ability of both the requester and supplier of routing information.

The main purpose of the internet router is to route packets to their destination. This is its primary job and usually exists as a separate entity on the network. It will also supply (upon request or at periodic intervals) routing information.

In order for routers to build a table of networks, routers must know the network numbers they are directly connected to. Routing requesters use the routing information protocol to discover the network to which they are attached.

For networks implementing RIP, an assumption is made that the internetwork is no larger than a few hundred networks. With this assumption, the network number space is called "flat." With RIP, there are no assigned area numbers separating the networks. It is a flat address space and all routers are considered equal with each routing table considered trusted (trusted in the sense that all routing information dispersed by any router is considered good and reliable information).

Implementing RIP. Some routing protocols allow routers to determine network paths based on concept known a *distance-vector.* Distance-vector means that the information sent from router to router is based on an entry in the table consisting of <vector, distance>. The routers exchange network reachability information with each other through

* A cache is simply an area of memory used to hold this table.

the broadcasting of this routing table information which contains a listing of distance-vector entries. Each entry in the table is a network number (the vector) and the amount of routers (distance) that are in between it and the final network. This distance is sometimes referred to as a *metric*. For example, if the source station wants to transmit a packet to a destination station that is four hops away, there are probably four routers separating the two networks.

Any time a datagram must traverse a router (thereby passing though a new network number), it is considered a hop (metric). The maximum diameter of 15 hops is allowed for any packet. If a data packet has traversed 15 routers and the sixteenth router receives that packet and it knows (there is a field in every XNS packet that indicates how many routers the packet has already traversed) it must traverse one or more routers beyond it to get to the destination network, the packet will be discarded at the sixteenth router. An error message may be sent back to the originator of the packet indicating the discarded packet. Again, XNS does not specify this, but some implementations of XNS allow this.

With distance-vector algorithms, each router will contain a table with starting entries of those networks that are directly attached to it.

A RIP request packet will have the destination network address set to a specific address if the router knows the identity of a routing information server process. If the destination network is unknown, the destination address will be set to broadcast. Refer to Fig. 4.8. This is a RIP packet. The operation field is either request or response, which will be explained later.

When a new host is initialized and possesses only the requester RIP process, it will broadcast a request packet onto its directly connected network and will build its table from all response packets received. The requester will be able to tell the directly connected network numbers by the RIP response packets that have the internetwork delay (the hop count is called *internetwork delay* in the XNS specification) set to 0. Any nonzero numbers in this field will indicate a nonlocal network. This is how a workstation finds out its network number without having it assigned by network administrator. The network administrator only has to assign a network number in the routers and the workstation will find out about it though the router RIP responses.

Network devices that possess the ability to supply RIP response packets will know their directly connected network number by the network administrator assigning them to the network device before the device is brought on-line. With this, their hop count will be set to 1* and they will broadcast this table immediately out to their directly connected networks. By doing this they will tell other routers

* It can be set to any number, but 1 is usually the default and the most commonly used.

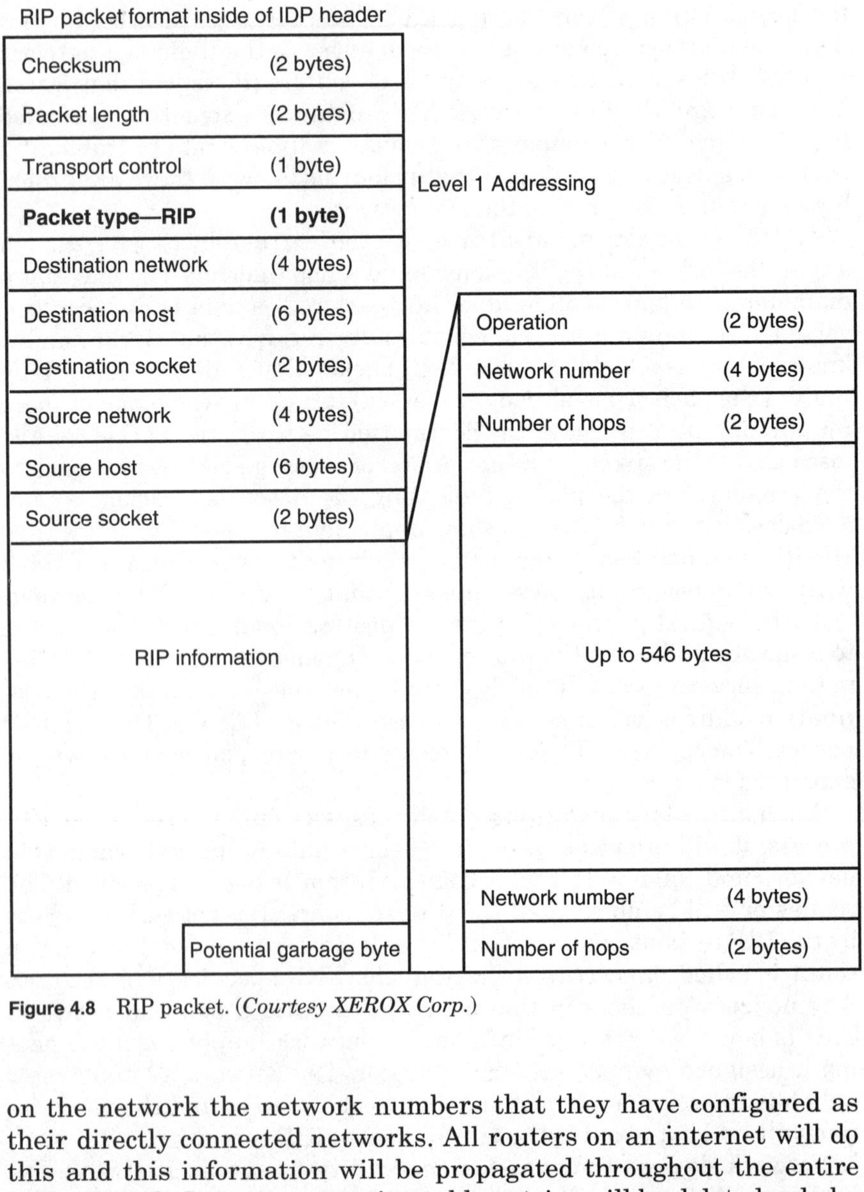

Figure 4.8 RIP packet. (*Courtesy XEROX Corp.*)

on the network the network numbers that they have configured as their directly connected networks. All routers on an internet will do this and this information will be propagated throughout the entire internetwork. In reverse, routing table entries will be deleted only by a time-out process expiring at three minutes. Any router that is gracefully taken down should report this by transmitting a RIP response packet to the network with all internetwork delay (hop count) entries set to 16, which means unreachable. This will indicate to other routers that that particular router no longer will be able forward packets to those networks.

The protocol of RIP was also built on the following assumptions: The network may contain Ethernet (broadcast networks), leased lines, and/or public or private networks (nonbroadcast networks) that use packet or circuit switching. Each of these networks has different bandwidth characteristics, but the metric (the length) for each delay is generally defined as hops or an internetwork router hop.

Internetwork routers use RIP to inform each other of the topology of the internetwork. With the predominate network being Ethernet, RIP utilizes the broadcast capabilities of the Internet Datagram Protocol and Ethernet to distribute this routing information. Public data networks may support broadcast addressing, or it may be too expensive, and therefore these types of networks must know the identity of the other routers with which they will be exchanging information (in other words, they must be statically configured with the other routers addresses in order to exchange information with them. There are limited dynamic exchanges between routers on public switch networks.

For RIP to work efficiently, it should not be implemented in large complex internetworks (although it is being used in some). There are many disadvantages for all internetwork routers to maintain complete database tables of all other networks in the internetwork and then to broadcast this information to all other routers on the internet. There will also be different bandwidth implementations (different speed leased serial lines and fast, reliable networks like Ethernet). This in conjunction with queuing delays (routers having delays in forwarding the packet) may cause extreme congestion on the internetwork and routing updates may be delayed to the farthest routers.

The fields of the RIP packet are defined as follows:

Operation. This field indicates the type of RIP packet. It can be one of two types:

1. A 1 in this field will indicate a request for routing information.
2. A 2 in this field will indicate a response to a request for information.

A request can be made by a router (upon startup of the router to get information immediately), but it is more commonly made by a workstation that needs to transmit a packet but does not know a router to send it to. A response is made only by a router that can respond with information about where to route the packet.

Contents. Each entry (there may be more than one) in the contents field will contain one or more tuples* that will consist of a 32-bit Object

* A tuple is an association that contains the network number and its cost (hop count) number.

Network (a network number) and a 16-bit Internet Delay in hops (how many routers away from the originator of a packet the final destination network is).

Depending on whether the packet is a request or response packet, the contents field can be filled in the following ways: If the RIP packet's operation field is a request, then specified in each tuple of the RIP packet is the object network number of the network in which the station that submitted the RIP request is requesting information about. The internetwork delay will be set to infinity (in RIP this means it will be set to 16). The other possibility for a RIP request packet is that, if the requester wants information about all the networks the router knows about, the contents field will be set to "all" (all FF's) with internetwork delay set to infinity.

If the operation is a response, this means that the router is responding to a request for information or it is a periodic update for other routers. The contents field will contain one or more tuples that contain the appropriate network number and the internetwork delay (the cost or hop count) that the router knows about. For example, if a request was received by the router for information on all networks that it knows about, the router would build a response packet in the format of Fig. 4.8 that would contain one or more tuples that consists of the network number and cost for each network number the router knows about.

When a routing information supplier transmits or broadcasts a packet that is a response, the following is characteristic of that packet: The internetwork delay (the cost, measured in hops) will be the delay that the packet will experience to be forwarded to that final network number as indicated by the object network number if the packet is forwarded by that router that generated the response. If the router forwards a packet to a directly attached network (the cable segment on the other side of a router), the internetwork delay would be 1. For each router the packet must traverse to reach the final destination, this number will increment by 1.

A delay of infinity (16) means the network cannot be reached or that the router does not know of the object network. For example, if the RIP request was sent out by a workstation for network X and a router responds to that request with the internetwork delay of 16, this will indicate that the router does not have that network number in its database table or that the network number was there and for some reason has been taken off the internetwork (the router that attached that network was taken down, for example). Finally, the delay to reach a router on a directly connected network will always be a 0.*

* In other words, to reach a router on a directly connected network, there is not a cost associated to it.

Routing table maintenance. RIP is used in every router and network station* on the network to maintain a cache (a portion of RAM memory) of network entries called the routing table. RIP is the algorithm that is used to maintain this routing table and serve several purposes. First it permits the quick initialization of a routing table when a network station starts. Secondly, it ensures that a routing table is up to date with any changes that could occur on the network. These changes could be new networks being added or a router becoming temporarily disabled.

As shown in Table 4.3, each entry in the table contains:

1. A network number (known as the object network).
2. A delay (measured in hops, the number of routers between it and the destination network).
3. a. The directly connected network. (There will be one entry for each attachment the device has. For example, if the device is attached to three Ethernet segments, there will be one entry in the table for each attachment.) or
   b. The host number of an internetwork router (only if the delay is not 0; in other words, it is not directly attached). This is used to forward a packet to another network by using another router.
4. A timer will be used to age out old entries—networks that have not been heard from for a specified amount of time.

During initialization, a network device will accomplish the following:

1. If the device is a requester only, called the RIP passive service (a user's workstation, for example), its table will contain an entry only for the network it is directly attached to. This will allow it to make a comparison between its network number and a destination station network number. If the two are different, the user's workstation will know that a router is needed to deliver the packet.

Routing tables can consume large amounts of memory. Therefore, in a nonrouting network station (a workstation) only one network number is held in the table. This network number is the number of the net-

* Not all network protocols place the ability for network workstations to maintain a router table in the workstation.

TABLE 4.3 An XNS Routing Table

Network number	Delay (hops)	Host number	Timer
1	1	02608c1234565	50
20	2	02608c123456	100
50	0	Local	34
20	0	Local	45
23	0	Local	40

work it is directly attached to. If it needs to communicate with a remote network station on the internet, it will ask a local router for the information. This will save RAM memory. Some network protocols do not allow a workstation to possess the RIP process. They give the network workstation the address of a local router and make it send all routable data packets to it. The router will figure out the shortest path and, if there is another router that can handle the request with a shorter path, it will inform the workstation of this and the workstation will then use the other router.

2. If the device is capable of being a requester and responder (a router, for example), the table will contain entries for both the directly connected networks and all other networks on the internetwork. Most routers, upon initialization, will enter the network numbers of their directly connected networks in the table, as the first entries in the table, and the cost will be set to a 0, indicating directly connected.

Routers perform two operations: responding to requests for routing information (event driven) and periodically transmitting their routing tables to their directly connected networks. This means, when a router transmits its table to the network, it will keep other routers to keep informed on the state of the internetwork.

Figure 4.9 shows the propagation of routing table information. This figure shows updating without using an algorithm known as split horizon. This is explained later. Also, this figure shows one direction of the update process.

After initializing router A adds its directly attached network numbers into its tables and marks these entries as local (directly attached). It will then transmit this table to network 2. It is transmitted as a RIP response. Each of the hop count entries will contain a 1 before being transmitted. They were initialized to a 0, for they are directly attached networks on router A.

Router B will receive this packet (it will be addressed to the RIP socket number and physically addressed to broadcast). The RIP cost assigned on that receive port of the router is a 1. Router B will therefore add a 1 to each entry of the received table. Router B will then compare the entries in the received table to its routing table. If there is not an entry of a network number, router B will add the network number. If the network number is already in the table, router B will compare the cost (hop count) of the received routing table with its own. If the hop count is lower, router B will change that entry in the table. If the received hop count is greater than its internal table, it will discard that entry of the received routing table. Once router B has updated its table, it will be transmitted out to network 3. Router C will receive this table and repeat the preceding process.

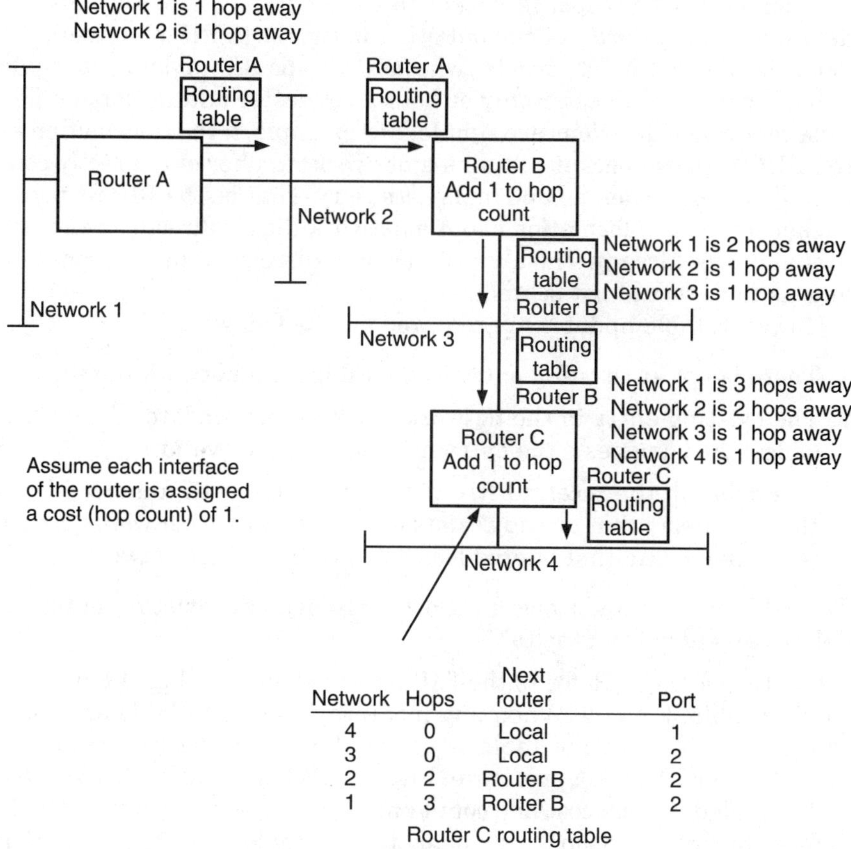

Network	Hops	Next router	Port
4	0	Local	1
3	0	Local	2
2	2	Router B	2
1	3	Router B	2

Router C routing table

Figure 4.9 A Routing Table Update (RIP) not implementing split horizon.

Reception of a RIP response. This type of packet is received in two ways. First, it may be received in return from a previous request that was transmitted requesting information about a network or a set of networks. Second, it could be received by "gleaning." This is the process by which a local router will be sending out its routing table periodically, and since this response packet is generated in broadcast mode, all stations will receive it. The needed information is gleaned from the packet. It was requested by another station, but since it is sent in broadcast mode any network station will take a receive and build a table based on the information found in the packet.

Decisions on updating the table. This was explained previously, but is given again here in greater detail. All routers perform this routine.

This is the real purpose of the RIP protocol. The ability to dynamically update a router's table periodically or when an event has occurred that forced a RIP response packet to be generated. When a network device receives information about other networks (a RIP response), the network device must decide whether it should update its table (whether it is a requester only or both a requester and responder, i.e., a router). Some decisions are simple. For example, if the information in the RIP response packet contains a network number of a directly connected network, then no update is necessary. That is, the RIP response packet contains information about a network that is directly connected to that device already. The algorithm would disregard that information and its table would not be updated.

However, table updates are required for the following:

1. There is not an existing entry in the table for a network number.
2. The existing entry in the network has not been updated for 90 seconds, which suggests the entry may no longer be valid.
3. The delay in the received RIP packet for a network number is less than the delay that already exists in the table. In other words, a new route was found that offered less delay to the target network.

The RIP process adds new networks, changes an existing entry, or deletes an entry from the table.

Updating the table. Refer to the RIP packet structure, Fig. 4.8 and the routing table, Fig. 4.9. When any modifications of the table are done, the host address in the table is set to the source host entry of the packet (see RIP packet structure, Fig. 4.8). When a packet is received, a 1* is added to each cost/hop count entry on the received routing table before any comparisons are made to the table. Located in a RIP response packet are network numbers from a router's table. These network numbers are networks to which the router can forward packets.

In other words, if they are from another router, it is assumed that, to reach those indicated networks, the packet will have to travel across that router. Anytime you traverse a router, the internetwork delay increments by 1. This is the reason the router automatically increments each entry by 1 before accomplishing any comparisons. Remember that XNS is being presented here as a generic example to explain network protocols. Therefore, this is a general rule. Not all protocols follow this. Some implementations add 1 to each entry before transmitting a RIP response packet, so when the RIP response packet is received, it does not add a 1 to each entry and then do a comparison. Either way works! The aforementioned is the way the XNS standard recommends.

---

* A 1 is used in this case. It assumes the cost assigned to the port that received the update table was assigned a 1. It could have been assigned a cost of 1–15. It were assigned a cost of 2, the update would have 2 added to it.

If the entry is not new, but a better route to an existing network was found, the old entry is completely replaced with the new entry; the information that was contained in the RIP packet is placed in the table. The delay in the table is set to the delay indicated in the RIP packet. If this delay exceeds 15, the object network is said to have become inaccessible. The internet delay is set to the internet delay indicated in the RIP packet plus the internet delay of the router. Usually this means setting the internet delay to the internet delay of the RIP packet plus 1.

For a change to be made, a 1 is added to the delay indicated in the RIP response packet and then compared to the delay in the table. If the delay in the RIP response packet is lower, the entry will be changed. If it is the same or it is higher, the entry in the RIP response packet is ignored.

Upon an update, the time-out entry for each update entry is set back to 90. Each entry in the table has its own expiration timer, initialized to 90 seconds.

Handling time-outs. The XNS standard states that for the network device that possesses only the RIP requester, timing out an entry is at twice the normal 90 seconds. Their table will be set with an internetwork delay of 16 (infinity) and may be discarded.

Routers may keep this infinity entry longer so that with each routing update, it is ensured that all routers on the internet know that this network path is no longer valid. During this time-out period, if the requester or a router receive new information about the object network, the table entry may be reinitialized and the network entry will become valid once again.

Timing for updating the network. Routers will transmit their complete routing tables once every 30 seconds to their directly connected networks. The packet is addressed to a MAC broadcast destination address. If the network is point to point (serial connections between routers), then the packet will be addressed specifically to those routers. If a router updates a routing table entry with a changed entry, it should immediately notify all other routers with a response packet. This is known as *event-driven updating*. In other words, if a router changes an entry in its table for internetwork delay, it will not wait for the 30 timer to expire before transmitting a RIP response packet. It will transmit this packet immediately, usually with only that entry in the packet.

Under XNS, a router should gracefully shut itself down by transmitting a RIP response packet with the internetwork delay set to infinity (16) for all network entries in its table. This allows the router to tell other routers that it will no longer be able to forward packets to those networks, even before it cannot do so.

Finally, when a responder replies to a requester and it does not know about the network being requested, it will respond to this request with the network entry in a response packet, but the internetwork delay will be set to infinity (16).

Complications of the RIP implementation. RIP exists primarily for those networks that are not large and complex and experience relatively few changes in topology (networks going up or down for whatever reason). Since most networks implementing XNS will be Ethernet, it could be said that the transmission speed is high and deemed reliable and the speed is constant. However, there are negative circumstances that will occur using this protocol.

When an internetwork router initializes, bringing a shorter route (or the only route) to a network than any other router knows about, all routing tables in all routers and nonrouters will have to be updated. This should occur within 30**n* seconds, where *n* is the number of hops (internetwork delay) from the newly initialized router to the furthest router distant from that router, and the 30 represents the normal broadcast interval of RIP routing updates (routers broadcasting their routing tables to their directly attached networks).

When an internetwork router is taken out of operation from the network, and if another route exists that the router used to forward packets, this new router for the replaced network number will be discovered within 90 seconds. This is the time that a routing table entry in any router becomes suspect as unreachable and this entry becomes eligible for replacement with another entry.

If a network goes away and there is not an alternative route to it, the entry in the routing tables in all routers for this network will be purged with 90 + 30*max(*n*, 15)* seconds (although it should occur much faster than this). RIP router updates occur every 30 seconds.

In a single router, an entry that has not been updated for 180 seconds is considered suspect and will be removed from the table if an update is not heard from in another 60 seconds. Therefore, an entry in a table will be deleted in 240 seconds (if the router does not hear from it).

It is possible during this time of a network being inaccessible and the purging of the routing table entries that a packet may get caught in a routing loop (described as a packet that will endlessly be forwarded by routers that are misinformed about a path to a network destination—for more information, see the RIP section in Chap. 6). XNS alleviates this problem, for any packet on the internetwork has a lifetime. Once the packet's lifetime is exceeded, the packet will be discarded.

---

* 30 times the maximum of *n* or 15 (whichever is larger).

In order to make RIP operate correctly, the following protocols were implemented:

1. Split horizon*
2. Poisoned reverse
3. Hold-down timers
4. Triggered updates

Routers will not broadcast their entire routing table out of all their active ports. There are certain entries in the table that will be omitted before the table is sent. This is the purpose of split horizon.

Referring to Fig. 4.10, with router A directly attached to network 1, it will advertise that route through all its ports as a distance of 1. Router B receives this and updates its table as network 1 with a distance of 2. Router C will receive this and update its table as network 1 with a distance of 3. Notice that all routers will broadcast all the information in their tables through all ports (even the ports from which they received the update).

Why would router B broadcast a RIP update of network 1 to router A, when router A already has a direct attachment to it? Wouldn't this confuse router A into thinking another route existed for network 1? Normally it would, but remember that the only changes that RIP will make to its tables is when then the distance is lower, it is a new entry, or if the next hop router path taken to a network changes its hop count. Since the received hop count is higher, router A will simple ignore that particular entry in the update table.

Using the aforementioned original algorithm, a serious problem occurs when router A loses it reachability to network 1. It will update its table entry for that network with a distance of 16 (16 indicates not reachable), but will wait to broadcast this information with the next scheduled RIP update. So far so good, but if router B broadcasts its routing table before router A (notice that not all routers will broadcast their tables at the same time), router A will then see that router B has a shorter path to network 1 than it does (a distance of 2 for router B versus a distance of 16 for router A). The new entry will be made. Now router A, on its next RIP update broadcast, will announce that it has a path to network 1 with a distance of 3 (2 from the table entry received from router B and 1 more to reach router B). There is now a loop between router A and B. A data packet destined for network 1 will be passed between routers A and B until the transport field is 16.

---

* This is usually the only correction made to XNS RIP. The other three corrections are explained here because this chapter is being used as an overview for all the following chapters.

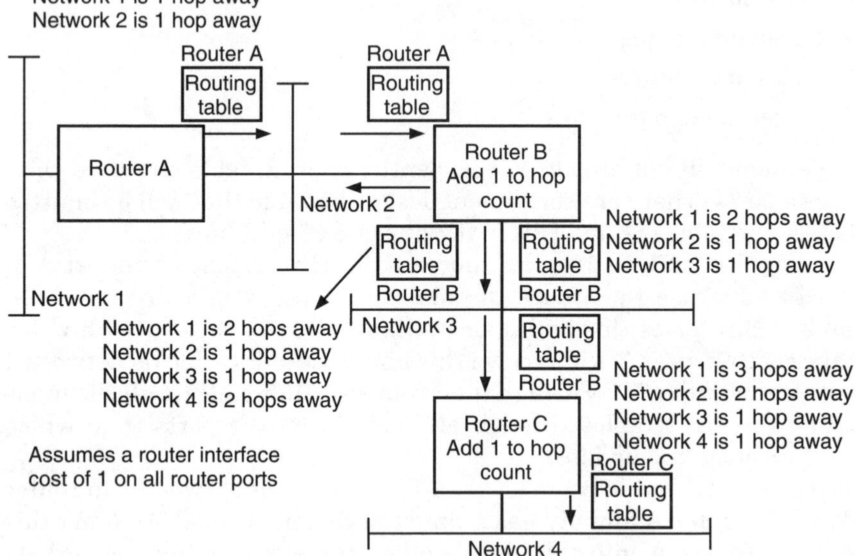

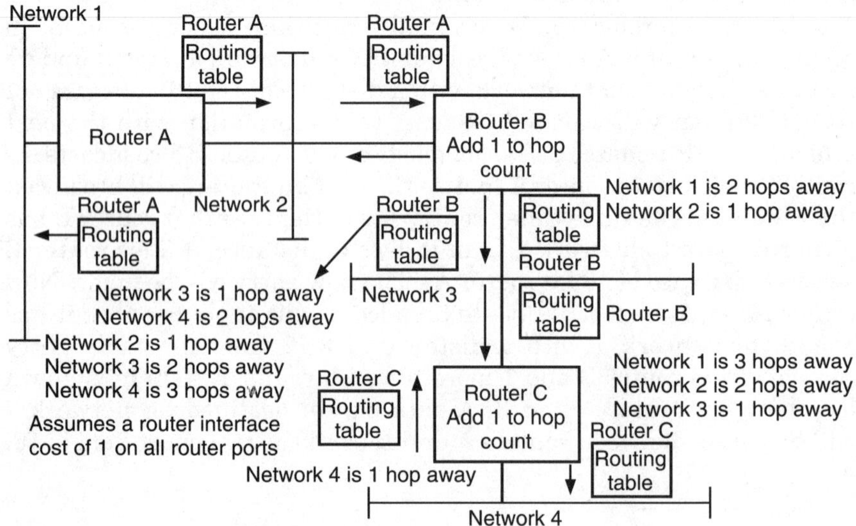

Figure 4.10 Routing Table Updates (RIP). (*a*) Not implementing split horizon; (*b*) implementing split horizon.

This is known as *loop*. Its cause is named *slow convergence*. The RIP protocol works extremely well in a stable environment (an environment where no routers or their networks ever change)—a *stable convergence*. Convergence is the ability of the network to learn about bad destinations and to correctly mark them as being unreachable in a timely manner.

Even future RIP updates will not quickly fix the convergence in this case. Each update (every 30 seconds default) will add 1 to the table entry, and it will take a few updates to outdate the entry. This is known as slow convergence and it causes errors in routing tables and routing loops to occur.

To overcome this and other problems, a few rules were added to the RIP algorithm. *Split horizon* states that any router will not broadcast a learned route through a port from which it was received. With this, router B would not broadcast the entry of network 1 back to router A. It learned of this route through router A. This would keep router B from broadcasting back to router A the reachability of network 1, thereby eliminating the possibility of a lower hop count being introduced when network 1 went away. Refer to the bottom of Fig. 4.10.

Without split horizon, every entry in a table is sent out every port of the router during a RIP routing update broadcast. As explained previously, this has no consequences except for the possibility of router A losing its connection to network 1, updating its hop count to 16 for that network and then waiting to transmit a RIP routing table update packet. In the meantime, router B broadcasts that it can reach network 1 with a hop count of 2. Router A receives this, notices that the hop count is lower than 16, and updates its table with the new entry. Now packets received by router B, destined for network 1, will be sent to router A. Router A will receive this packet and send the packet back to router B. This is a routing loop. The packet will time-out and be discarded, but it is impossible to determine how many packets could get caught is this loop. Eventually the loop will close, for future RIP updates will continue to increment the hop count, and eventually both sides will have a 16 in their hop count field for network 1. It is impossible to determine how long this could take.

The bottom of Fig. 4.10 shows how routers that implement split horizon would broadcast their tables. Notice they do not broadcast information about their directly connected networks from the same port as the directly connected network. In other words, router A does not include information about network 2 when broadcasting a routing table update from the port that is attached to network 2.

A router will not broadcast information out the same port that it learned it from. Router C, in broadcasting a routing update to network 3, will not include information it learned about through that port. In other words, information about networks 1, 2, and 3 are not included with the update.

The second is called a *hold-down timer.* This rule states that once a router receives information about a network that claims a known network is not reachable, it must ignore all future updates that include an entry (a path) to that network, typically for 60 seconds. Not all vendors support this in their routers. If one vendor does support it and another does not, routing loops may occur.

Another rule that helps eliminate the slow convergence problem is *poison reverse and triggered updates.* This rule states that once the router detects a network connection is disabled, the router should keep the present entry in its routing table and then broadcast network unreachable (metric of 16) in its updates. This rule becomes efficient when all routers in the internet participate using triggered updates. Triggered updates allow a router to broadcast its routing table immediately following receipt of this "network down" information. The XNS specification does call for this to be implemented.

The main advantages of the RIP protocol is that is a good protocol for networks that are stable, it provides adequate responsiveness, and is not complicated to implement. With most routing implementations, the user simply sets RIP to on and RIP will take care of the rest of the work. All updating will occur without user intervention. Remember, though, this is used with a flat network address space and each router is a trusted router. Each routers transmits its entire routing table, even when no change has occurred. Each router takes for granted that any router is a good and reliable router and their routing tables are without error. Propagation of the routing information is based on the previous routers table. If any errors occur on any router, then the error will be propagated throughout the network. RIP is a good router table update implementation for small networks with equal transmission-medium speeds (all Ethernet or all Token Ring) and where the network is stable (networks do not go up and down). Otherwise, hierarchical routing schemes prove to have many advantages over flat network address routing schemes. Refer to the DECnet routing in Chap. 8 or the IS-IS routing scheme in Chap. 10 for more information about hierarchical routing.

With the hierarchical internet, the internet is divided into areas, all of which are connected to a single "backbone" area.

By dividing an internet into areas, loops are avoided while still allowing for multiple paths and therefore redundancy. The area process also helps the routing table updates when a change occurs. With a hierarchical internet, a change will only affect the particular nodes that are in that area. The updates are not passed to those nodes that are not considered "trusted." That is, those routers that do not need to know about a change will not be updated and the network will still operate efficiently. With this network, overhead is drastically reduced.

To operate hierarchical networks, there are level 1 and level 2 routers. Level 1 routers update other level 1 routers within their own area. Level 2 routers update other level 2 routers for information between areas. There must be at least one level 2 router per area.

Refer to Fig. 4.11. In this figure there are three areas. In area 1, there are two level 1 routers that have connections to the Ethernet segments (EN). There is one level 2 router that has connections to other level 2 routers in areas 2 and 3.

For routing to occur, if the packet to be routed is in the same area, the level 1 routers will route the packet locally (it will not leave area 1). If a packet on area 1 is destined for area 2, it must be transmitted to the level 2 router for it to be delivered to the area 2 router. Once the packet has been delivered to area 2, it will be locally routed until it reaches its destination.

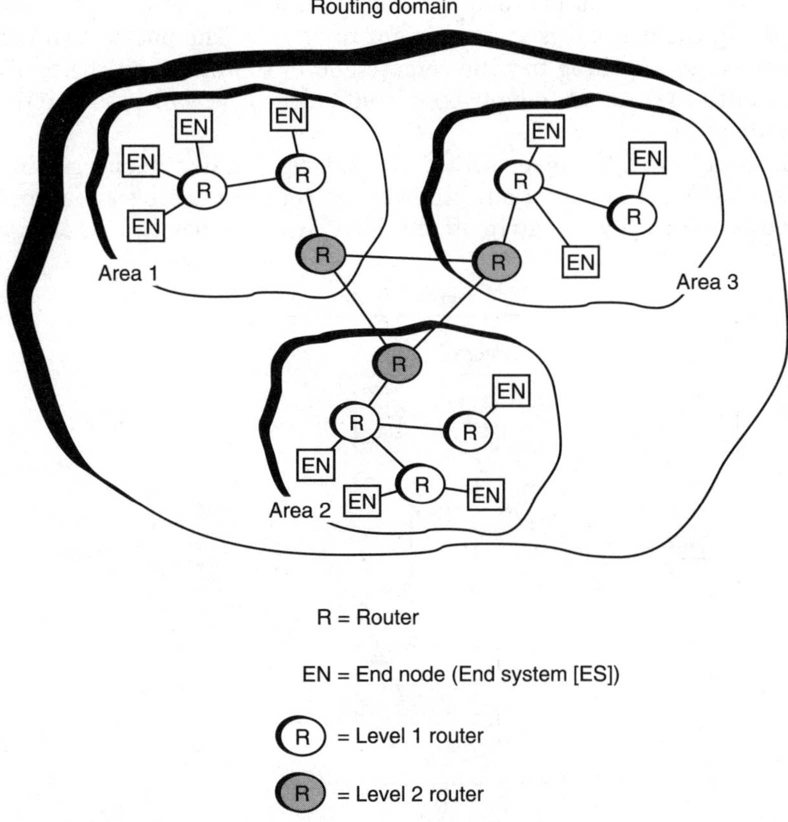

Figure 4.11 Level 1 and Level 2 routers. (*Courtesy Uyless Black.*)

Routing across a serial link. Refer to Fig. 4.12. When routing across a serial link (leased telephone line), the data-link and physical layers change, and so does the format of a packet. When we change from Ethernet to Token Ring, the packet headers changed for the data-link portion. This will hold true for transmitting data across a serial link.

When a packet is routed over a point-to-point link (two routers connected by a serial interface), the MAC headers of the packet when it was received by the router are not stripped off but serial data-link headers are put on. In other words, if a packet is received on the Ethernet and has to be routed to another router through a serial interface, the Ethernet headers (the address, the Ethertype field, and CRC) are not stripped off, but a serial line header is put on, and the packet is transmitted over the serial interface. When the packet is received at the remote end of the serial link, the Ethernet headers that pertain to that router that received the packet over the serial line will be placed in the packet and the packet then routed to its destination as if the packet were received by a LAN interface.

Since the serial link is a point-to-point connection (no intermediate stops along the way), it is most efficient to do this. The packet will not be received by anything but the remote end of the link, and the extra header data that needs to be transmitted on the link will consume little bandwidth.

This is allowed because, the MAC address header keeps getting changed by every router along the way en route to the packet's final destination. So, why not strip off the MAC headers before it is trans-

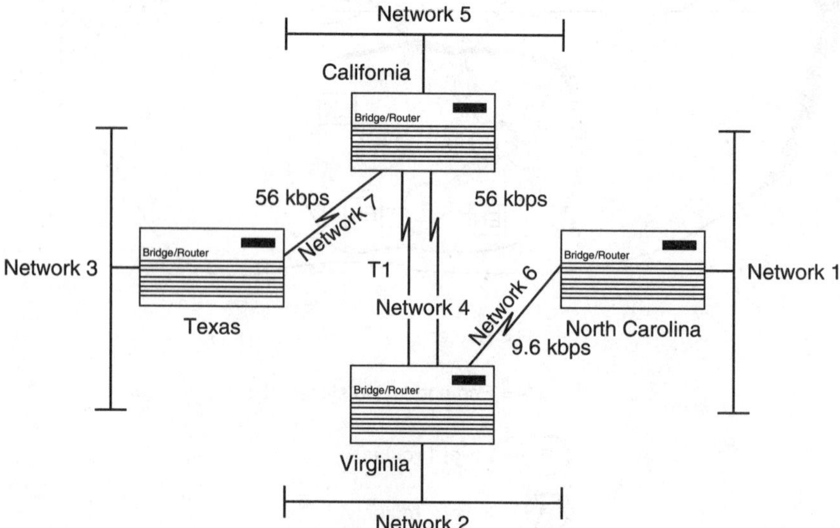

Figure 4.12 Wide Area Networking with serial lines.

mitted on the serial link? This really does allow for better utilization of the serial link. It will need new MAC addresses when it reaches the remote router, so it is left up to that router to do it.

Included in this case is when you are bridging a packet across a remote link. Since the bridging algorithm works with the MAC address, it must be left in tact before, during, and after crossing the link. This type of packet is encapsulated in a serial header and then transmitted on the serial link. The remote link will strip off the serial headers and bridge the packet just as if it was received on an Ethernet cable segment.

Notice also in Fig. 4.12 that serial lines are assigned network numbers. You cannot assign one network number for the all the serial lines. The one exception to this is shown for the routers between California and Virginia. These two lines are grouped together to form one logical connection between the two routers. This is a very common application for routers. Almost all router vendors support this. In this case, two lines are grouped together to form one connection between the two routers.

Data that is sent down these lines is usually load balanced, so that only one packet is transmitted down one of the links. (A single packet will not be transmitted down both links. This would cause duplication at the other end.)

Only in this case of grouping can two or more serial lines be assigned a single network number.

Packet flow. Figure 4.13 shows how a packet is formatted and sent to the router. The importance of this figure is to show how the MAC address changes and to show that the internetwork packets are addressed directly to the router. The final destination host and network address are embedded into the network header of the packet.

In this figure a network station A wants to transmit data to another station, server C. It is assumed here that the destination network station network and host address was found through a previous action on the workstation. This will be explained further in the Clearinghouse Name Service at the end of this chapter. For this example, though, the destination station address is already known.

Next, the workstation will compare the network address of the server C with its own network number. If it is the same network number, the network station would send the packet directly on the local LAN. If the network numbers are different, it must find a router to forward the packet for it. In this case, the network numbers are different and, therefore, workstation A must find a router to forward the packet to the destination.

Workstation A will send a RIP request packet out to network 1 and wait for a response. Inside the RIP request packet will be the network number needed. In this case, it will be network 2. Router B will receive

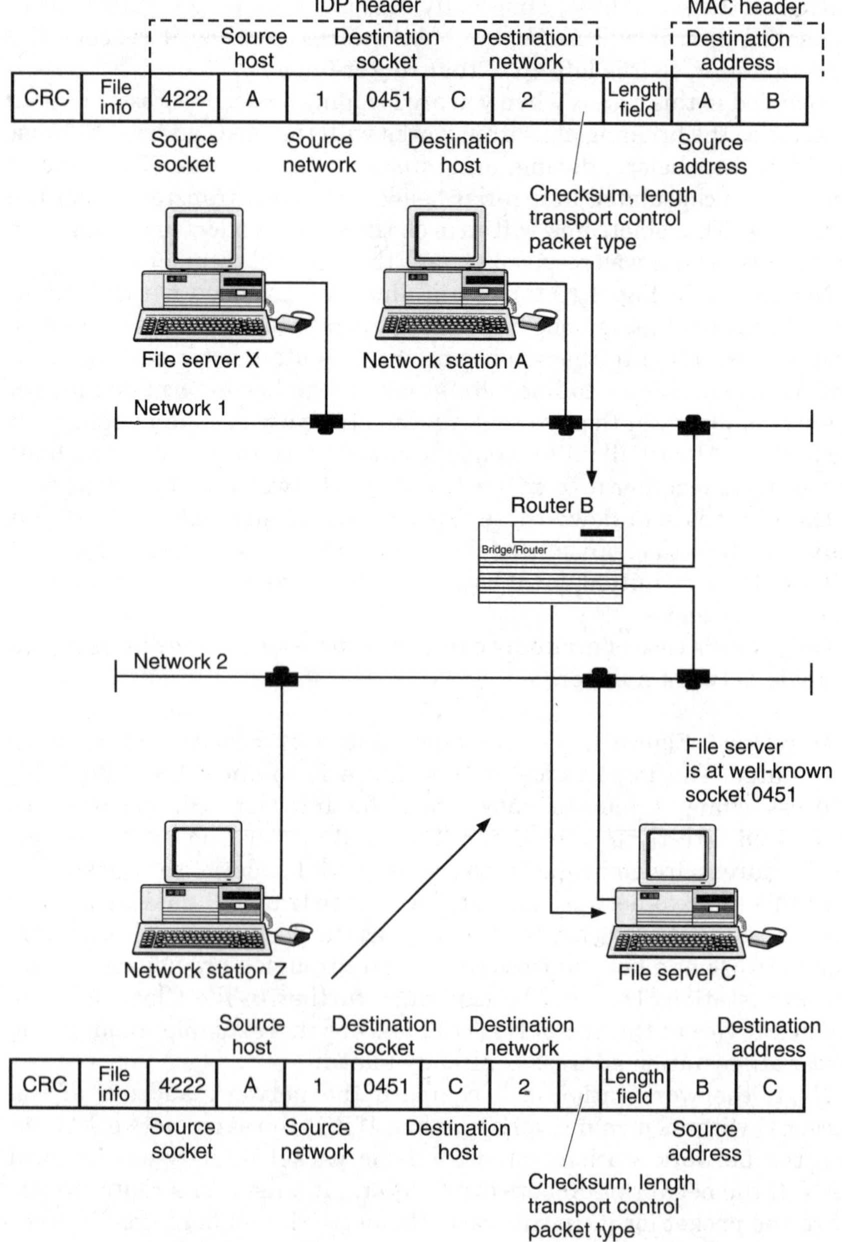

Figure 4.13 Abbreviated version of data transfer using IDP headers.

this packet and perform a routing table lookup. Router B will send a RIP response packet back to workstation A.

Workstation A will receive this router RIP response packet. Workstation A needs to format a packet to send to router B. It will fill out the network header with the source network number and host number set to its own. It will then ask the IDP layer for a dynamic socket (in the range of 4000 to 6000, decimal). The network station will then address the destination network and host with that of the final destination. The socket number in this case is set to 0451. This is a static socket (using this protocol) for a file server. Finally, the network station will assign the physical (MAC) address of the packet. The source will be its own and the destination will be set to the physical address of the router. It will then transmit the packet to the network.

Take a look at Fig. 4.13. It will show this previously mentioned packet format. At the top of the figure is the packet format built by workstation A. The MAC header contains two entries: the physical destination address of the router (B) and the source address of the workstation (A).

The IDP header will contain the following entries:

Destination network	2
Destination host	C
Destination socket	0451
Source network	1
Source host	A
Source socket	4222

The destination network and host in the IDP header is that of the final destination, not the router. The router uses this information to determine how to forward the packet.

The source network is used by the destination station (the file server). When the file server transmits a response to this packet, it will know the network to send a response to.

The router will receive this packet from workstation A and strip MAC headers, the length field (the physical addresses), and the data-link trailers (the CRC). What will remain is the IDP header. It will examine the destination network address and perform a routing table lookup.

From the routing table, the router will know that the destination network number is directly attached on the other side of the router since the packet will be directly delivered to the network and the packet does not have to be forwarded to another router. Router B will now format the packet and transmit it out the physical router port connected to network 2.

Router B will extract the destination host number out of the received IDP header and place this in the destination physical address (the

MAC address) field. It will place its own physical address in the data-link source address field. With a few exceptions, the rest of the packet will be left alone. It will be appended to the new data header that the router has just built. The router will then transmit the packet to the network. This is shown at the bottom of Fig. 4.13.

Notice the MAC header contains file server C's physical address as the destination address, and router's physical address as the source. The IDP header will remain the same, except for the CRC (checksum) and the hop-count fields. (These fields are not shown in this figure, but when the packet traverses the router, the transport control is incremented by 1 and the CRC is recalculated. The packet is then transmitted to network 2.)

File Server C will receive the packet, strip off the data-link headers, and then notice that this is a file server call of some type (the file info portion of the packet). It will process the packet according the call information and, if necessary, respond to the source.

The importance of the preceding paragraphs is that the destination MAC address of the packet will constantly change. Except for checksum and transport control, the IDP header will not change. A packet that is received by the router will determine the best route to the destination network and will address directly to the destination station (if the network is directly attached to the router) or it will physically address the packet to the next router in line to the destination station.

Finally, Fig. 4.14 shows the preceding paragraphs as a flowchart.

Level 2 error protocol

The error protocol is used by any service on the network (primarily in a network station) that noticed an error. If the error packet is generated by a well-known socket number, then the source socket in the error packet will be set to that number so the recipient of the packet will know what well-known service noticed the error. If the error was noticed by the IDP layer, it will be sent by the well-known router error socket. The packet is always sent to the source socket of the service that created the error. There is no acknowledgment of this type of packet, nor is one generated in response to a multicast or broadcast packet. The format of the error packet is shown in Fig. 4.15. The packet type of this packet is the error protocol as specified in Table 4.2.

The format of the packet is quite simple, and contains two 16-bit words that indicate the error number and the error parameter. The error number shows the kind of error, and the error parameter is a parameter for certain types of errors. These are shown in Table 4.4. This is followed by the first portion of the offending packet. Included in this is all of the IDP header and as much of the level 2 and higher levels as the implementor of the XNS protocol desires. Xerox recommends that at least 42 bytes be copied, since that will include the SPP header.

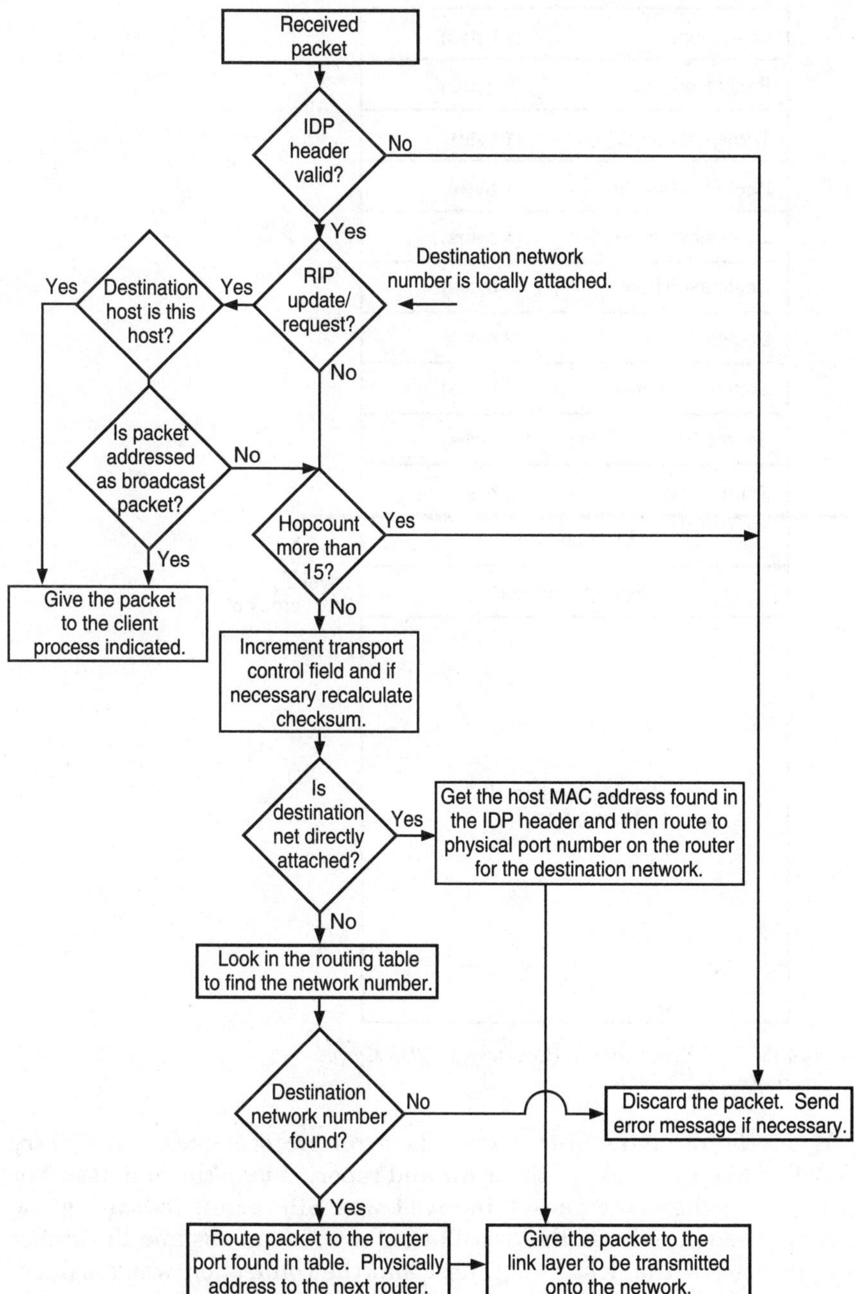

Figure 4.14 XNS routing flowchart.

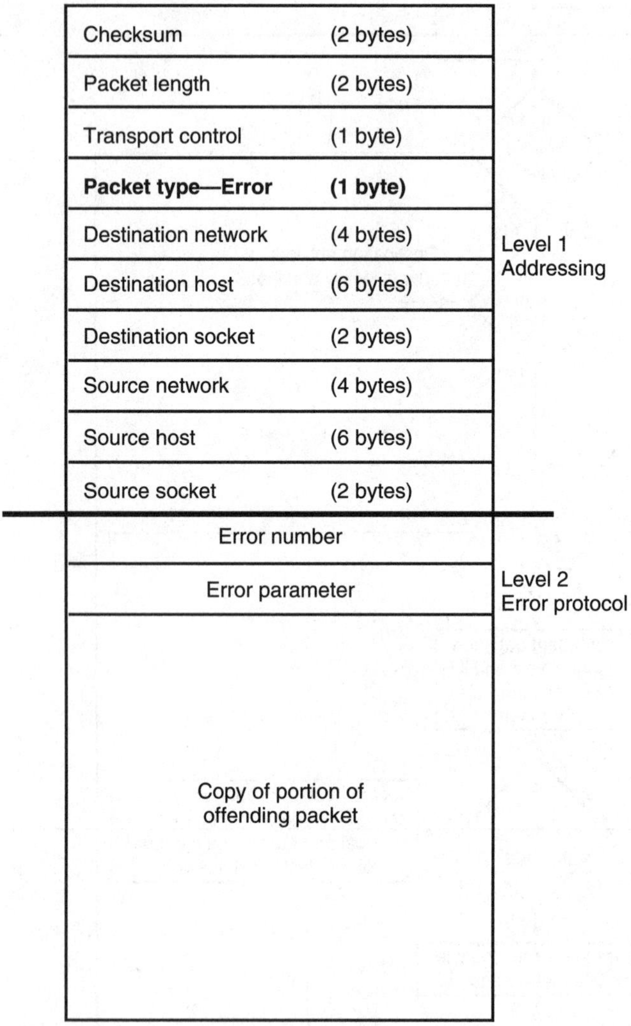

Checksum	(2 bytes)	
Packet length	(2 bytes)	
Transport control	(1 byte)	
Packet type—Error	**(1 byte)**	
Destination network	(4 bytes)	Level 1 Addressing
Destination host	(6 bytes)	
Destination socket	(2 bytes)	
Source network	(4 bytes)	
Source host	(6 bytes)	
Source socket	(2 bytes)	
Error number		
Error parameter		Level 2 Error protocol
Copy of portion of offending packet		

Figure 4.15 IDP Error packet. (*Courtesy XEROX Corp.*)

When the receiving process gets the error protocol packet, it will try to determine the cause of the error and report this to the end user. For example, if the error packet received was SPP error, indicating the socket does not exist at the destination host, it can assume the socket was deleted at the destination host and the connection was disabled. This would be turned into a descriptive response by the programmer so that the end user may understand what happened to the connection. It is up to the software programmer of the protocol to create a meaningful message. It may not be included at all.

TABLE 4.4 The Error Protocol Assignments

Error number (octal)	Description
0	An unspecified error is detected at destination.
1	The checksum is incorrect, or the packet has some other serious inconsistency detected at the destination.
2	The specified socket does not exist at the specified destination host.
3	The destination cannot accept the packet die to resource limitation.
1000	An unspecified error occurred before reaching the destination.
1001	The checksum is incorrect, or the packet has some other serious inconsistency before reaching destination.
1002	The destination host cannot be reached from here.
1003	The packet has pass through 15 internet routers without reaching its destination.
1004	The packet is too large to be forwarded through some intermediate network. The error parameter field contains the length of the largest packet that can be accommodated.

The error protocol may be used by any of the level 2 services.

Level 2 echo protocol

The echo protocol transmits an echo packet to a destination station to determine if a remote host is alive and operating, and to determine the path to that destination. This is a simple protocol in that an echo packet is sent out and the destination should send the packet back to the originator. The packet type will be set to the echo packet type as shown in Fig. 4.16.

The first word of the packet indicates the operation. It is set to a 1 for echo request and a 2 for echo reply. If checksumming was invoked on the request it will be checked and recomputed for the reply. If the packet received was an error, the error protocol will be invoked and the error protocol packet will be sent. The echoed data will be the same as the data that was in the echo request packet.

The echo protocol is often used to ensure the proper operation of the Internet Datagram Protocol since it uses this protocol to send the packet. The echo protocol packet can traverse routers.

Level 2 sequence packet protocol (SPP)

A transport layer implementation. When working with networks, you will often hear that the upper-layer protocols (the transport layer) will provide error correction for packets transmitted and also will guarantee packet transmission reliability. It is this layer that will do it. While the network layer delivers data on a best-effort service, if anything happens during this process, the transport layer will guarantee a retransmission for the reliable delivery of data. All packets sent over

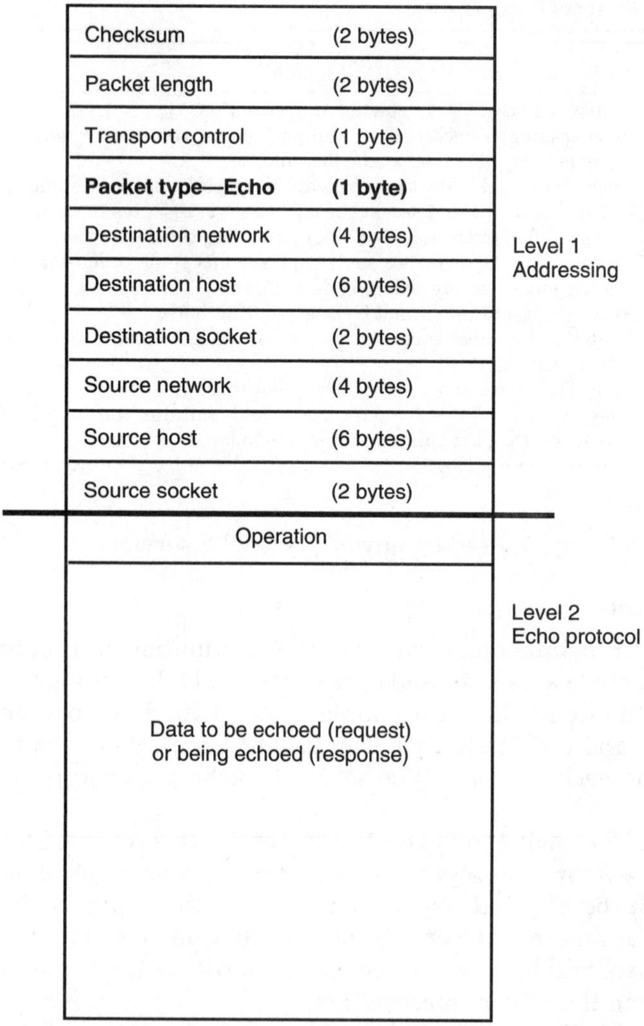

Field	Size	Level
Checksum	(2 bytes)	Level 1 Addressing
Packet length	(2 bytes)	
Transport control	(1 byte)	
Packet type—Echo	**(1 byte)**	
Destination network	(4 bytes)	
Destination host	(6 bytes)	
Destination socket	(2 bytes)	
Source network	(4 bytes)	
Source host	(6 bytes)	
Source socket	(2 bytes)	
Operation		Level 2 Echo protocol
Data to be echoed (request) or being echoed (response)		

Figure 4.16 IDP Echo packet. (*Courtesy XEROX Corp.*)

the network layer will be guarded by the transport layer to ensure proper delivery. It is the discussion that follows that explains this.

This layer establishes connections for the session layer. With this, SPP will establish a unique connection identifier for each connection the network station has. With each connection, the sequence packet protocol provides for reliable transmission of successive internet packets for the client process that requested it. For example, when a client process such as a file transfer program needs to send data to a destination, the SPP will provide the reliability for this transmission.

On a given connection, each packet will be given a sequence number (as part of SPP's header) and it will then given to the IDP layer for transmission onto the network. These sequence numbers are used for the following:

1. *Ordering of packets.* When packets are transmitted, all packets out may not be received in the same order they were sent. If the packet traverses routers, any packet may be dropped. It could have been lost while transmitting on the transmission medium (for example, Ethernet). In order to arrange the packets at the receiving end in the same order that they were sent, the packets must arrive in ascending sequence number order. Any packet received out of order will be requested again from the destination.
2. *Detect and discard duplicate packets.* If a packet was transmitted and there was a delay in getting to the destination, the originator may time-out waiting for an acknowledgment and resend the packet. In the meantime, the server acknowledges the original packet. The duplicate packet is then received. The transport layer software (SPP) will notice this sequence number has already been acknowledged and will discard the duplicate packet.
3. *The ability to acknowledge receipt of a packet.* Any sequenced packet that arrives in good condition at the destination station will be acknowledged.

XNS sequencing occurs on a packet basis. Every packet transmitted will have at most one sequence number. This is in contrast to protocols such as TCP/IP, where every byte of the data is assigned a sequence number. This is known as a *byte-oriented protocol.* SPP is a *packet-oriented* protocol.

A source network station may use sequence numbers up to and including the number specified by the recipient of the packets (the destination). There is a preestablished starting sequence number that will be known on both ends of the connection. The initiation of the connection will also initialize the sequence number to start with. The starting sequence number for XNS SPP protocols is 0.

A connection also establishes connection identifiers. These are 16-bit numbers, one specified by each end of the connection. An implementation of this is to assign a connection identifier by reading the clock register of the processor and assigning this as the connection identifier. This establishes a unique connection identifier at any connection attempt. Therefore, there is no need to maintain a cache table for connections already taken.

The maximum packet size for XNS packets, including SPP headers, is still maintained at 576 bytes, although many XNS implementations do not follow this. For example, Novell's implementation called Internet Packet Exchange (IPX) allows for packet sizes up to the maximum size of the transmission medium. This can be 1500 bytes for Ethernet and up to 4472 bytes for Token Ring. XNS still recommends 576 bytes for reasons explained in the earlier section on IDP. Upon connection time, two communicating network stations will negotiate for the maximum packet size.

SPP allows for different types of acknowledgments. This means that it can acknowledge a packet when it is received (some versions of Novell implement this). Other implementations allow for several packets to be received before an acknowledgment is sent. Upon connection time, the source station will tell the destination what type of acknowledgment it would like. (For more information on acknowledgment and sequencing algorithms, see Chap. 3.)

The packet format for SPP is shown in Fig. 4.17 and is explained as follows:

Connection control. The connection control field contains 8 bits, of which only 4 bits are used (0–3). It is used to identify the control actions of SPP. This field is shown in Fig. 4.17.

System packet bit. The system packet bit is used to send probes (to ensure that a connection is still alive, even when there is no data to send), or it may be used to return acknowledgments. The protocol of SPP needs to see data sequenced contiguously. System packets contain no data and are primarily used to maintain the connection. When there is no data to send to the destination, SPP will still ensure that the other side of the connection is active and can receive packets. To do this, it must send a system packet with the next unused sequence number; otherwise, the receiving end will send an error packet with a bad sequence number as the source of the problem. System packets are used to maintain the connection. The XNS standard does not specify how often these are to be sent. This is left up to the implementor of XNS.

Send-acknowledgment bit. This bit is set to ensure that the receiving end will immediately send an acknowledgment upon accepting the packet. If the receiving end has data to send back, the acknowledgment will be in that packet. Otherwise, it will send a system packet back as an acknowledgment. Acknowledgments may be sent at any time, even without this bit being set.

Attention bit. With this bit set, the source socket is telling the destination socket that this packet needs to be given immediate attention. The attention bit and the system packet bit cannot both be set at the same time. It is a way of immediately getting the destination's atten-

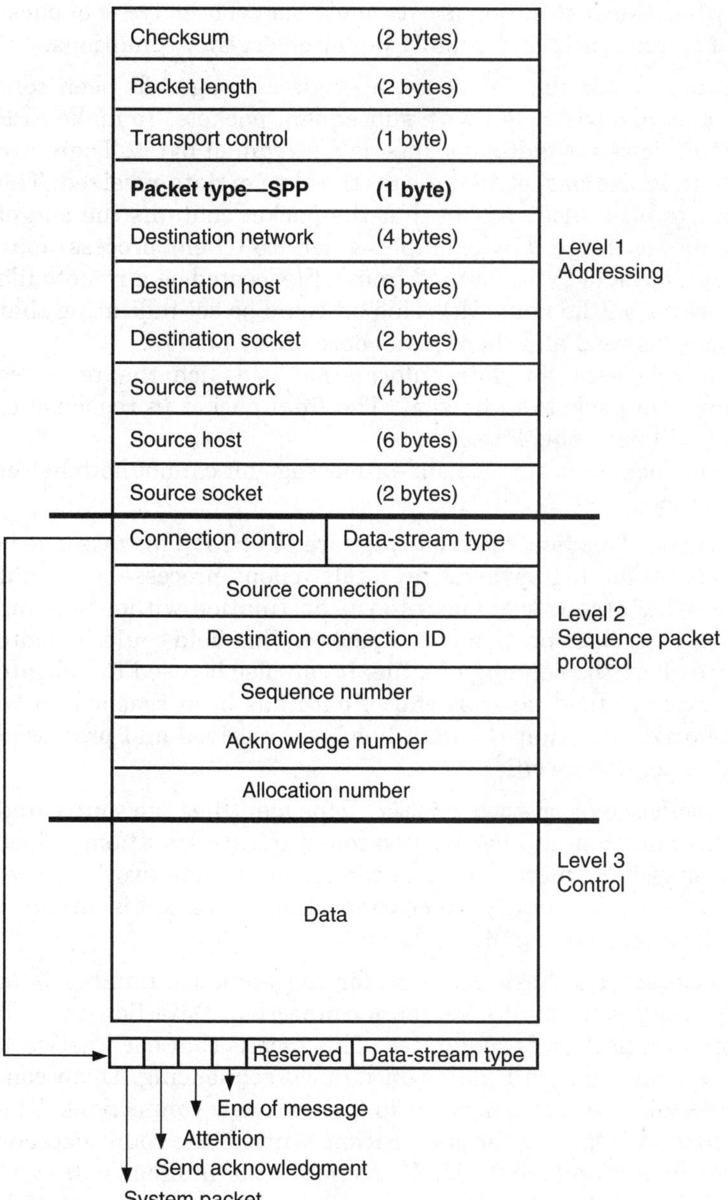

Checksum (2 bytes)
Packet length (2 bytes)
Transport control (1 byte)
Packet type—SPP (1 byte)
Destination network (4 bytes)
Destination host (6 bytes)
Destination socket (2 bytes)
Source network (4 bytes)
Source host (6 bytes)
Source socket (2 bytes)
Level 1
Addressing
Connection control
Data-stream type
Source connection ID
Destination connection ID
Sequence number
Acknowledge number
Allocation number
Level 2
Sequence packet
protocol
Data
Level 3
Control
Reserved
Data-stream type
End of message
Attention
Send acknowledgment
System packet

Figure 4.17 IDP/SPP packet. (*Courtesy XEROX Corp.*)

tion, even when the destination is extremely busy. These types of packets are sent infrequently and usually under emergency conditions.

End-of-message bit. If this bit is set, a single message has been sent and a new message will begin with subsequent packets. To make SPP efficient, SPP views incoming packets as a stream of bytes. There are not identifiers in the packet to indicate the type of data received. The end-of-message bit indicates only that the packet contains the end of that particular message. For example, a service (client process) may request that a block of bytes be read from a file located on a remote file server (wherever on the network). This bit could be set indicating that the full block was read and there is no more data to follow.

A request was sent for data information is which the response requires multiple packets to be sent. The final packet in response to this request will have this bit set.

The system packet bit and the end-of-message bit cannot both be set at the same time.

Datastream type. This field is actually ignored by SPP. This message is used exclusively for higher-level protocols (client processes) so that they may provide escape sequences to the destination without having to put this in their data portion of the packet. This field could indicate the means to abort the sending of a file. It can also be used to indicate data is in the data field, or that end of data has been reached, or to reply to the originator that the data has been received and processed correctly. It is vendor-specific.

Source and destination connection identifier. This identifies the source and destination connection number for two communicating stations. Since any station may have more than one connection to a network device, this serves as a way to identify which connection the packet is intended for. This will be discussed in detail later.

Sequence number. The basic function for the sequence number is to count the packets sent or received on a connection. Data flow in each direction on a connection is sequenced. This means that each network station on a connection will maintain its own sequencing. Upon connection, the sequence number is set to 0 for all new connections. The count will ascend from 0 (1 for each packet sent). If the count exceeds the number for a 16-bit field (65535 decimal), the number will start again from 0. This is how the destination knows how to order incoming packets (for a connection ID), to discard a duplicate packet, to acknowledge a packet, and to send control (maintaining the connection) information. If packets 4, 5, and 7 arrive, the destination knows that packet 6 is missing and will inform the source of this error. The source may then send packet number 6 or may send a stream of packets (4, 5, 6, and 7), depending on the control algorithm used for sequencing.

The three types of sequencing most commonly used are:

1. Go back to N
2. Selective
3. Stop and wait

Sequencing enables the workstation to synchronize the transmission of packets. For example, as shown in Fig. 4.18*a,* two stations have established a connection with each other. Workstation A and file server B have also established that sequence numbers will begin with 0. Next, workstation A will send five packets to file server B. File server B will respond with an acknowledgment packet. The acknowledgment number will be a 5. It is important to know the initial sequence number.* After this, workstation A sends five more packets to file server B and waits for an acknowledgment response.

If the file server, as shown in Fig. 4.18*b,* sent back an acknowledgment packet containing a 2, this means that certain packets were not received. The file server is telling the workstation that packets 0 and 1 were received okay, but packets 2, 3, and 4 were not. This indicates to the workstation to go back to the third packet and resend packets 2, 3, and 4 (the third, fourth, and fifth packets). After this, the file server sends the acknowledgment back to the workstation indicating all packets were received in good condition.

The selective reject is a way to indicate one packet was not received. In this case, the file server could have sent the packet a selective reject of 3, indicating to the workstation that packet 2 was not received.

Stop and wait is also called the *ping-pong sequence method.* When workstation A sends a packet to file server B, it stops and waits for file server B to send an acknowledgment packet for that one packet. Upon receipt of an acknowledgment from the server, the workstation may then transmit one more packet to the file server. As of this writing, this is the method used by Novell NetWare.

Sequencing is covered in complete detail in Chap. 3, "IEEE 802.2," under the section of data sequencing. XNS does not specify any particular method for sequencing of data.

The originator of a connection expects to receive an allocation number which will indicate that it may use sequence numbers up to and including a particular value.

---

* File server B will send back a 5 and not a 6. The reason for this is that the sequence numbers were established at 0. Therefore, workstation A sent packets 0, 1, 2, 3, 4 to file server B. This is a total of five packets and, therefore, file server B will send the acknowledgment back with a 5, indicating that packets 0 through 4 were received in good shape.

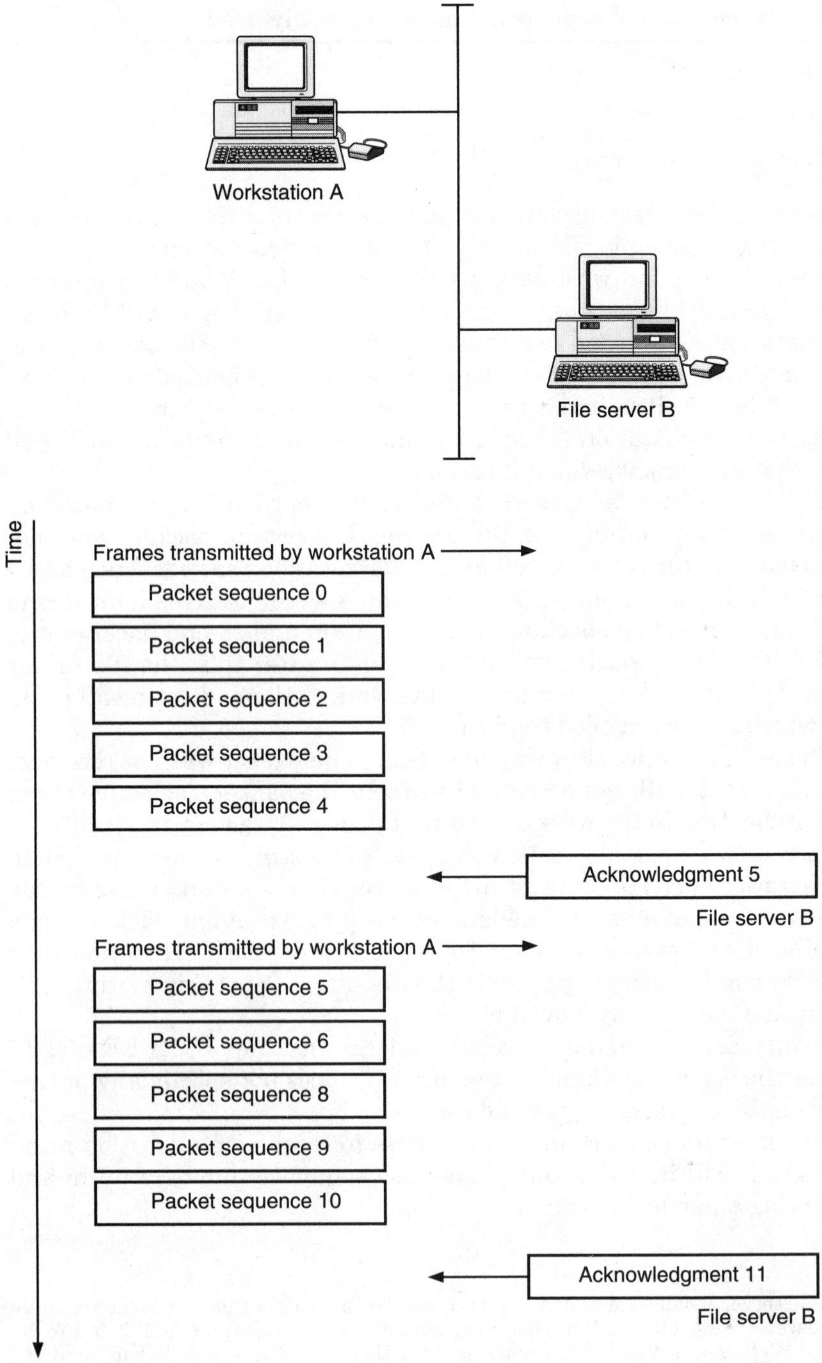

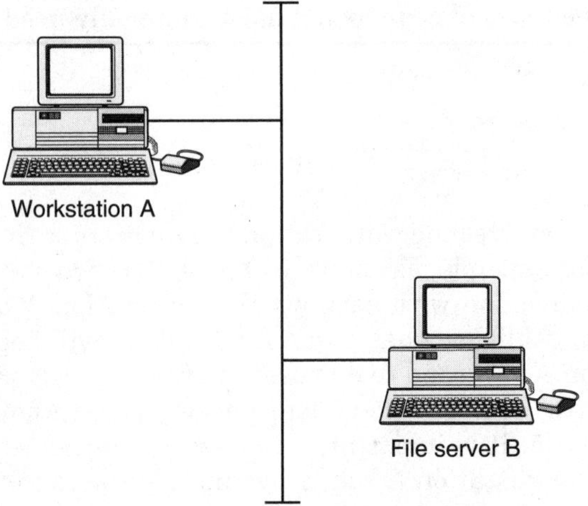

Workstation A
File server B
Time
Frames transmitted by workstation A
Packet sequence 0
Packet sequence 1
Packet sequence 2
Packet sequence 3
Packet sequence 4
Acknowledgment 5
File server B
Frames transmitted by workstation A
Packet sequence 5
Packet sequence 6
Packet sequence 8
Packet sequence 9
Packet sequence 10
Acknowledgment 11
File server B

Figure 4.18 (*a*) Sequencing.

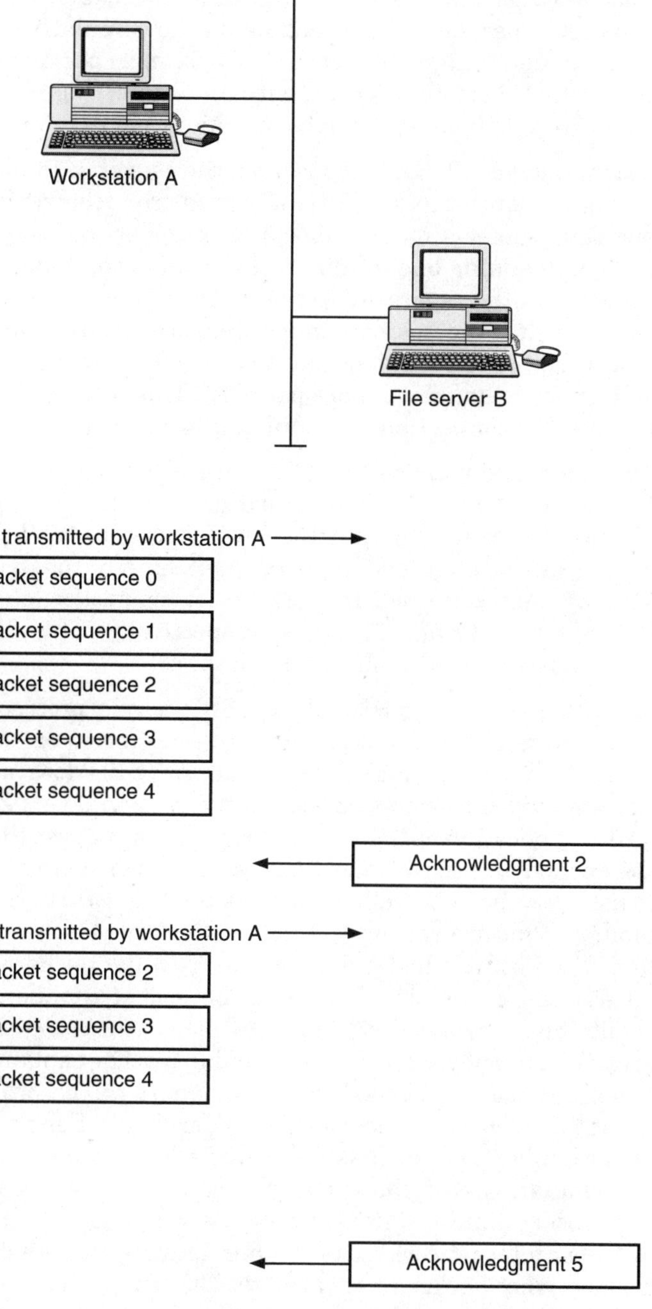

Figure 4.18 (*b*) Sequencing with error.

Acknowledge number. This field indicates the sequence number of the next expected packet. Acknowledgments are cumulative; by specifying the next sequence number expected, all previous packets are said to be acknowledged. This means that, with an acknowledge number of 7, all previous packets before 7 have been acknowledged.

Allocation number. This field specifies the sequence number up to and including which packets will be accepted from the remote end. This means that subtracting the allocation number and the acknowledge number, and adding one to this, will indicate the number of outstanding packets in the reverse direction. This is a good congestion control mechanism. It indicates how much data may be sent at one time. In other words, the destination may say, "received packets up to X, have enough space to handle *N* more packets). This is known as providing a window on the connection for sending information.

Data. This field will be filled with data only when the packet is not a system packet. This field is destined usually for the client process (a file server, for example), and the level 2 protocol will pass it to the client process without looking at it. The length of the data field is calculated by subtracting 42 from the internet packet length (IDP and SPP headers of 30 and 12 bytes, respectively). This field is recommended to have up to 534 bytes maximum.

Establishing and opening connections. SPP is the protocol that establishes, maintains, and disconnects sessions between sockets (client processes) on two communicating stations. SPP does not do this by itself. It provides this as a service to the session layer. The client process (the application or the session layer) must request that these sockets be opened and that connections be established. You can think that SPP listens only to the client process and does this according to the commands that are set by it. A connection between two network stations will be established only once the destination network and host numbers, the connection IDs, and the socket numbers are known. Without this, a connection cannot be established. Figure 4.19 shows the relationship of socket numbers and is further explained following.

A connection is established as follows. There will be two ends to a connection: the server and the consumer (the client). Server processes can be client applications such as file transfer, mail, name service, and terminal emulation. All these client processes must possess the well-known socket number. It will advertise this socket number on the network (or internetwork) so that other network stations on the network will know what socket to connect to. Otherwise, the network station must have this well-known socket number hard-coded into the software.

A server process will open up by establishing a relationship with the SPP protocols. In this, the server process will tell SPP to open up a

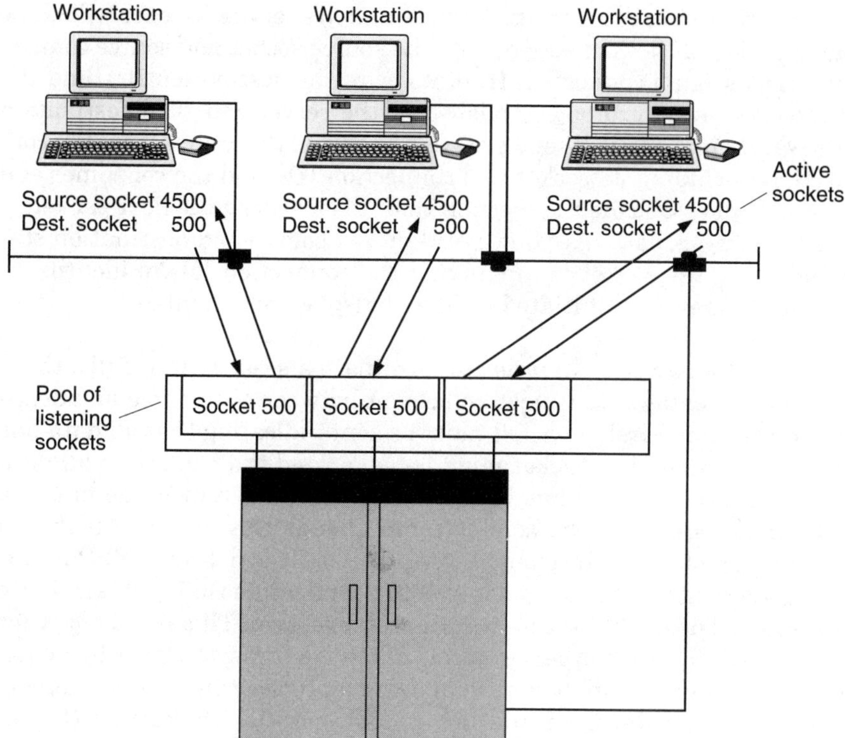

Figure 4.19 Socket Addressing.

socket (specified by the client process) and listen to the network for connection attempts for that socket. This is known as the *service listener process.* Refer to Fig. 4.19.

At the other end of the spectrum is the consumer, or the client, process. This process (the client end of a file transfer program, for example) will attempt to open a connection to the service listener process by asking SPP to open a connection to a specified service listener process. SPP in the workstation will build a packet using a dynamic, unassigned socket (not a static or well-known socket), will assign a connection ID to this connection attempt, and will build a connection type of packet and send it to the destination station. SPP has to create a source socket to use, so that the service listener station (the server) will know what entity in the requesting station to respond to when sending back a packet.*

---

* Different protocol implementations provide different ways of assigning socket numbers. Some allow the transport layer to provide it and some have the transport layer ask the network layer for this socket number.

Upon receipt of this packet, the destination's service listener will allow the creation of the connection, note the source socket and source connection ID, assign a connection ID of its own (the destination ID), and the connection is said to be established at the server end. The destination (the server process) will send a system packet to the originator of the connection (including its socket and connection ID), and the consumer end now has an established connection that it is awaiting the next packet.

At this time, data may flow between the source and destination stations using the socket numbers and the connection IDs to identify it. Sequence numbers (initiated at 0) will also be incremented.

Terminating sessions. In order to terminate a session gracefully, there are three messages that need to be sent between the source and destination station. First, a packet must be sent indicating that all data has been sent. Second, a packet must be generated that indicates all data has been received and has been processed. Third, a message must be sent indicating that the sender comprehends this action. All this is accomplished using the client-layer protocol. It is not up to SPP to terminate a session. It is a vendor-specific application that will terminate a session. The client process terminates a session. This is true only for XNS protocols. Most other protocols allow the transport layer to create, maintain, and terminate a session using a predescribed set of sequencing that is standardized and not vendor-specific. This action (terminating a session) is part of the reason why any vendor that implements XNS makes it proprietary for a lot of things. The way XNS operates is left up to the vendor and not set in the standard.

Some implementations of XNS use the following algorithm to end a session. The datastream type will be set to an "end" and the network station that wishes to end this connection will send this packet. It should be replied to by the remote end of the connection with a datastream-type "end reply." With this, the network station that sent the original "end" request will also reply with an "end reply." This will terminate a connection. During this, sequence numbers are still used; otherwise, the packet would be in error.

SPP implementations. The receiving end of a connection controls the flow of data to it. The originator of packets controls the flow of acknowledgments. In other words, the source station controls the acknowledgments and the destination station controls the data flow. With XNS SPP, Xerox gives guidelines only to implementors of this protocol to control the request for acknowledgments, the generation of acknowledgments, and the retransmission of packets. There is no standard based for it. Different sequence and acknowledgment protocols exist with the different implementations of XNS.

Once a connection is established, acknowledgments may be sent at any time (they do not have to be requested). Typically, the sender sets the send-acknowledgment bit in a packet with the sequence number corresponding to that permitted by the receiving end's allocation number (how many packets the receiving end can accept). The originator of a packet may send a probe packet, which is nothing more than a system packet with the send-acknowledgment bit set. This packet asks for an allocation number and/or an acknowledgment.

Acknowledgments and allocation numbers can be "piggybacked" to data packets. For example, if a packet is sent to a destination, and the destination has data to send back to this originator, it will also include in the packet and acknowledgment number an allocation number. This conserves not only processing cycles on the station, but also conserves bandwidth on the network. If there is no data with which to respond, these fields cannot be set, and the receiving end should respond with a system packet whenever one is requested.

The originating end of a connection will time when a packet was sent. Upon expiration of this time, if it has not received an acknowledgment, it will assume the packet was lost, and it has the capability to retransmit the packet. This timer is called the *round-trip delay* and is calculated by sending a send-acknowledgment packet and waiting for the response. This time is kept as the retransmit time. It is only a suggestion by Xerox.

SPP does use the error protocol when an error has occurred using SPP.

Level 2 packet exchange protocol

Refer to Fig. 4.20. The packet exchange protocol (PEP) (not to be confused with PUP—a no-longer-used XNS routing protocol) is used to transmit data between source and destination stations on a connectionless transport service. Unlike SPP, this transport-layer protocol does not establish a reliable session with the destination before data is sent over the link. The protocol is simple in architecture and is "single-packet-oriented." The protocol will submit a retransmit of a packet, but does not detect duplicate packets at the receiving end. It is primarily used for simplex types of transmissions.

This protocol can be used for network management, name service, time service, or any other protocol that can deal with the unreliable nature of the protocol. It is basically a transport mechanism for applications (services) that do not require the reliability of SPP. It is also used with protocols that have built into their application the functions provided for by SPP. There are many independent programs out there that are not public-user-oriented. This provides for a transport service for specialized programs as mentioned previously.

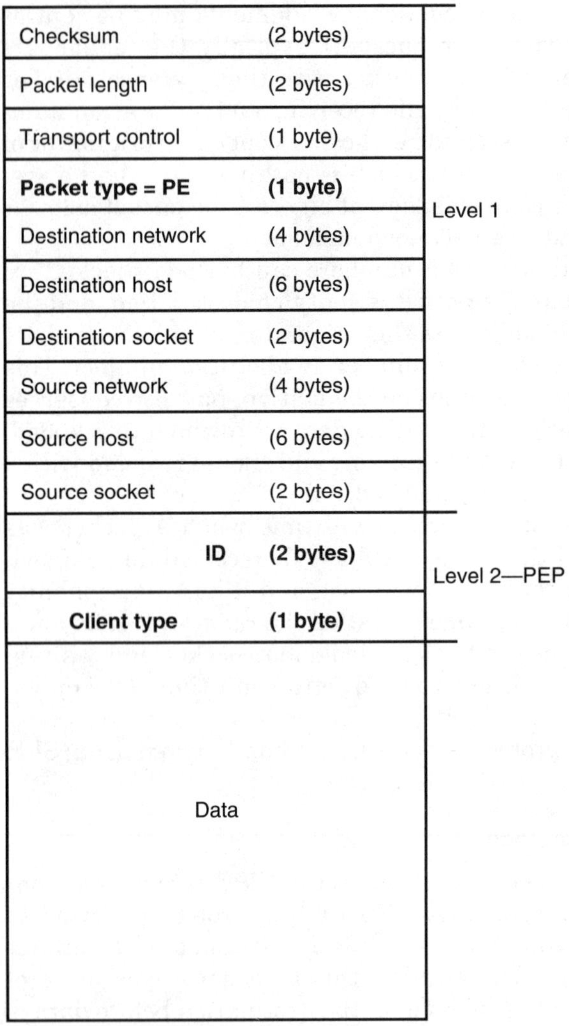

Checksum	(2 bytes)	Level 1
Packet length	(2 bytes)	
Transport control	(1 byte)	
Packet type = PE	**(1 byte)**	
Destination network	(4 bytes)	
Destination host	(6 bytes)	
Destination socket	(2 bytes)	
Source network	(4 bytes)	
Source host	(6 bytes)	
Source socket	(2 bytes)	
ID	**(2 bytes)**	Level 2—PEP
Client type	**(1 byte)**	
Data		

Figure 4.20 Packet exchange protocol packet. (*Courtesy XEROX Corp.*)

The structure of the PEP packet is shown in Fig. 4.20 and is defined following.

ID. This is a 32-bit field and the source will set it to a specific number. Upon receiving a reply, the source networks station will look at this field and, if it is the same as the packet previously sent, the packet exchange is said to be complete. That is, the source will send the destination a packet and will place a number in this field and then wait for a reply before any more information is sent. Upon receipt of this packet, the destination station will place the same ID back into this field and reply to the source network station. Of course, this destination will send a reply only if the source packet was received in good condition. Otherwise, it will discard the packet.

Client type. This field contains a registered field (registered with Xerox) that will identify the source and destination client (the service that submitted the request and the intended service for receiving the request). There will be a unique client type for every service offered under this protocol. Therefore, there will be one for time of day, name service, or a network management routine.

As shown in Fig. 4.20, the typical IDP packet header will be formed. This will include the source and destination network/host addresses and the socket address. This time, the socket will not identify a particular service being requested. The client type will specify this.

This protocol can be a faster protocol to use with services that do not require a connection-oriented routine to exchange data. There are many application programs that have been developed that take advantage of this protocol. Remember, though, that XNS implementations are usually specific to the vendor. This protocol will usually not work with implementations of another vendor's XNS protocol. Since XNS is a network architecture, it must include a connectionless transport protocol in order to be thorough in the transport-layer offerings. For examination of another protocol that uses a similar protocol to PEP, refer to Chap. 6, Sec. 2, "User Datagram Protocol (UDP)." For those readers familiar with Novell NetWare, PEP is used for SAP broadcasts.

Courier—the session-level interface. Courier is known as a remote procedural interface that not only establishes, maintains, and disconnects sessions between two communicating sessions, it also allows for (as the name implies) services to be invoked remotely. These services could be open a file, read a section of the file, close the file, etc. The following text is provided so that the reader may understand the beginnings of a remote procedural interface. It is not intended as a strict learning tool or to write code from. Courier is a different way of providing services on a network.

Other network protocols provide network services (file, print, and terminal) that use the session layer to establish and maintain a link with a remote network station, but use socket numbers to identify and invoke the remote service. This type (socket calls) has a client (the requester of a service) and server (the provider of a service) interface that allows the service to use the session layer to maintain the connection, while the application layer provides the service.

There are three sublayers to this session-layer protocol:

1. Sublayer one—the transport
2. Sublayer two—the data types
3. Sublayer three—the message types

With other protocols, once the physical-through-transport layers are defined, remote applications can be accessed by building a session to the remote network station and giving the remote station a port number with which you wish to communicate. For example, with TCP/IP, if you wish to communicate with the remote terminal application, you would build a packet (with the transport layer first establishing a connection to the remote network station) with the destination port number assigned to port 23. The remote station will spawn off a process with your network, host number, and source socket number to the TELNET application. It would then go back, waiting for more connection attempts at that socket number. The file transfer protocol is assigned a different port number and that application awaits connections only at that port number. Courier works similar to this but is different in many ways.

All calls to Courier are made to socket 5. If you wish to communicate with a remote station and wish to access a remote application, all requests go to port number 5. (Again, remember that Xerox calls their ports *sockets,* when in reality a socket is the combination of the network number, host number, and port number.) From this, in your packet, will be an application number. This number represents the application that you wish to communicate with.

These program numbers are all unique. No two program numbers may be assigned the same number. Those vendors who wish to use Courier at the session layer must register their applications with Xerox. Xerox will assign the company a block of application numbers for that vendor to use with their applications. This is similar to the process that Xerox used to do with Ethernet addresses and Ethernet type-field assignments.

Each program is also assigned a program name, but this has no significance to the Courier protocol. The application name will never be transferred in any packet exchanges and is said to have local significance only. Program names do not have to be unique. The program numbers distinguish the applications.

Furthermore, every application must also contain a version number, which is used to determine the version of the application being used. This is to ensure that both the source and destination stations will communicate using the same version of the application program.

A remote program will have one or more procedures with a full complement of error recovery and statements that should be used. When a program is used with the Courier protocol, it must declare itself with a program name (the identifier) and its version number. All procedures inside the program must be declared with an assigned number to each procedure. No two of these numbers can be used again in the program.

There are four messages defined at the message layer:

1. *Call.* For those that have written software programs, the program name is the name of the executable, and the procedures are nothing more than the functions that the program can call and execute. The following is an example which simply opens a file, reads a block of data, writes it to the screen, and then closes the file.

```
Program name readwrite 15 version 1
begin;
Credentials: Type = Record [user, password; string]
Mode: Type = {readpage(0), writepage(1), ReadAndOrWritePage(2)};
OpenFile: Procedure [credentials: Credentials, filename: string,
  mode:Mode]
returns [handle:unspecified, pagecount:cardinal]
reports [...NoSuchFile,...] = 0;
NoSuchFile:Error =2;
...
End
```

   The numbers in the function names are the procedure numbers that Courier requires a program to declare.

   With that declaration, the user's program will build a call message type to the procedure Openfile and use the user name Matt and the password Naugle and the file name of book.doc with the mode as readpage. This would be coded into a packet as follows:

```
call[
   transactionID:0
   ProgramNumber : 13, versionNumber : 1, procedureValue:0,
   procedure Arguments:[
      credential: [user, Matt", password: "Naugle"],
      filename : "book.doc",
      mode:readPage]];
```

   What this will do at the user's workstation is place a Courier call to the remote network station stating that it would like to invoke program number 13, procedure 0 (read), and the credential to get in is the user name and password. The file name would be transmitted as a string "book.doc". This would be formulated into a packet and be sent to the remote network station which would process this and return the information to the requester of it.

2. *Reject.* This message forms a reject message to the originator explaining why the request was rejected. This could be wrong ver-

sion number, the program does not exist, the procedure within the program does not exist, there was an invalid argument in the request. Otherwise, it will not indicate what the error was.

3. *Return.* The return message is a reply to a previous call. This usually contains some type of user data that the request indicated.
4. *Abort.* This message indicates an error occurred that was unspecified. This message will return the original arguments used in the request. These can be vendor-specific error codes.

With this information in hand the following shows a typical transaction using the Courier protocol:

```
FileAccess: program 13 version 1 =
begin
--(types and constants written here)
Credential: Type = Record[user, password: string]
Mode: Type = {readPage(0), writePage(1), readAndOr WritePage(2)};
PageContents: Type = Array of 256 of unspecified;

--procedures
OpenFile:Procedure [credentials: Credential, filename: string,
  mode: Mode]
returns [handle: unspecified, pageCount: cardinal] reports
  [NoSuchUser, IncorrectPassword, NoSuchFile,
AccessDenied, FileInUse, InvalidMode] = 0;
ReadPage: Procedure [handle: unspecified, pageNumber: cardinal]
  reports [NoSuchUser,
IncorrectPassword, NoSuchFile, AccessDenied, FileInUse, Invalid-
  Mode] = 1;

WritePage: Procedure [handle: unspecified, pageCount: cardinal,
pageContents: PageContent] reports (InvalidHandle, IncorrectMode,
  FileTooLarge] = 2;

CloseFile:procedure [handle: unspecified] reports [InvalidHan-
  dle] = 3;

--errors
NoSuchUser; error = 0;    --user unrecognized by server; user
  unregistered
IncorrectPassword;   error = 1;   --password specified not that
  of specified user
NoSuchFile;  error = 2   --filename unrecognized by server, file
  does not exist
AccessDenied; error = 3;    --user entitled to access file in
  specified mode
FileInUse   error [user:string] = 4   --file already open for
  specified user
InvalidMode   error = 5   --invalid mode, not read..., write...,
  or readAndOrWritePage
```

```
InvalidHandle  error = 6    --invalid handle, perhaps obsolete by
  Close File
IncorrectMode  error = 7    --requested operation inconsistent
  with open mode
NoSuchPageNumber   error =8    --requested page unreadable, not
  present in file
FileTooLarge   error = 9;    --requested page unwritable, file
  would be too large
end.
```

Clearinghouse Name Service—An Example Name Server. Any user may use the internet address to connect to any service on the network. But for a user to remember the addresses of all the network servers on the network is an impossible task. Users are more likely to remember names before they remember numbers. This is the purpose of the Clearinghouse Name Service. Without a name service, a user would have to remember the 6-byte MAC address, the 4-byte network number, and the 2-byte port (socket) number in order to get a connection to the remote station.

In order to easily understand how a network name service operates, a user should think of the "white pages," "yellow pages," and the operator in the telephone service. A network name service operates very similar to this.

When we want to call someone, we do not simply enter the name of the person into the telephone. We do enter the number of the person we are trying to reach. If we do not know the number of the person we are trying to find, we simply look in the telephone book to find the name of the person, and immediately following this is the telephone number. This is a simple example. What if we are trying to reach someone that is out of the area in which we are dialing? We must invoke the services of the telephone operator.

In this, we will ask the operator for the number of a person. This is accomplished by giving the operator the last name of the person that we are trying to reach. If the last name is Naugle, there is a good chance that the operator will be able to give you the number right away. If the name is Jones or Smith, the operator will usually ask for more information, like a first name or maybe a street address.

The other type of name lookup is the yellow pages. The yellow pages of the telephone system provide a more generic name-to-number lookup. Using the yellow pages, we will look up a number by category rather than by name. For example, if we need some electrical work done on the house, we can look up "electrical" in the yellow pages to get close to the number we are looking for. Once we get to that section of the yellow pages, we should be able to get some more specific information. We will be able to flip through a few pages to find the name of the specific electrical company that we want.

Therefore, there are three ways to find a number in the telephone system. These are by name, by number, or by subject. The telephone system has to have a number before it can make a connection between two users of the telephone. The users of the telephone do not like numbers and prefer using names. The problems that exist in the telephone system also exist in the network. Therefore, Xerox created the name system for XNS and called it the Clearinghouse Name Service (CNS).

CNS names are divided into name@domain@organization. This is a naming service based on organizations; within them are domains, and within the domains are the names. These three parts form a hierarchical naming structure so that two different names with the same value for the organization and domain parts are said to be in the same domain. As long as one part of the three is unique, the whole name is said to be unique. With this, there may be many domains within one organization and there may be more than one organization within the name structure.

There are two parts to this service: the client end (the part in the user's workstation) and the server end (a centralized server that contains a database of all the XNS internet address-to-name mappings).

Name server functions. As shown in Fig. 4.21, there are two entities to the name service. The client is a simple process that requests information from the name server. This request could be a connection attempt to a server. This connection request is accomplished by the user typing in the connection command and the name of the server to which the user wishes to connect. Another example could be a mail program for which the user wants to see all the users in a certain domain (to address the mail message). These requests are made to the

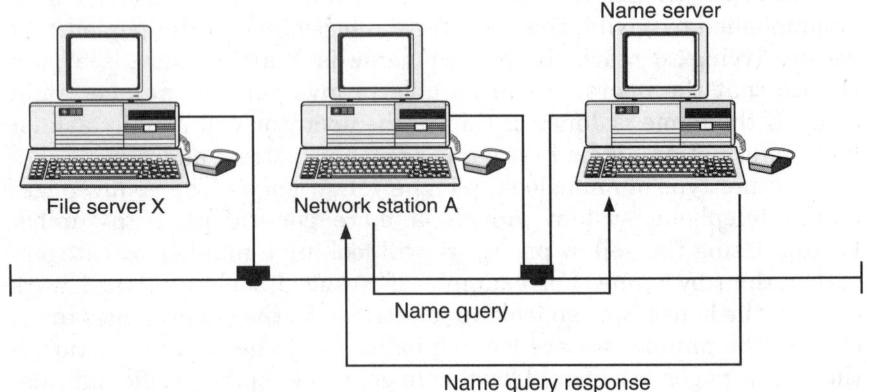

Figure 4.21 Example name service.

client side of the name service and the request is formed into a packet and sent out to the network. It is the responsibility of the server to receive this packet and try to find the internet address of the server or to respond with all the names in the domain requested. The client will first submit a packet to the name server to find the address of the file server. The name server should respond to this request and the client will be able to extract the internet address of the file server from this response. A name service may span routers. Not all protocols invoke this type of name service. Some name services are distributed. This means that the name service runs on multiple network stations and is synchronized. There is another type of name service in which each of the network stations will maintain a names directory for the name-to-internet address mappings. AppleTalk and NetBIOS are examples of this type of name service. The response that a name server provides will contain the full internet address (network number, host number, socket number) to the requested named service. For XNS, this is how workstations find network servers on the network. A user may request to be connected to Server1@Bldg5@Warehouse. This request would go out to the name server and the name server should reply with the full internet address (network number, host number, and port address) to the user's workstation. The user's network protocol would then be able to find the requested server by an address and not a name. The name is only used for human intervention. It is easier to remember a name than it will be to remember a list of numbers.

XNS uses a name server that is a centralized server that resides on the network somewhere. Although the XNS specification does not call for it, there can be more than one name server on a network. (This is known as *distribute* and requires the name servers to update each other, which is called *synchronization.*)

Upon receipt of a request, the name server will read the type of request it is. From this, the file server will respond to the user's request. Once the user has received its response, it may then proceed with whatever actions are necessary to complete its task. The name service is not invoked again until the next request.

Novell NetWare uses a name service but it is a variation of the distributed name service. NetWare services names are distributed throughout the network with the help of the routers. Routers maintain Service Advertisement Protocol (SAP)* tables, which contain the name of the server, the internet address, and the service provided, among a few other items.

---

*Not to be confused with the IEEE 802.2 SAP. These are two completely different entities.

Chapter

5

Novell NetWare

By far, the most frequently installed of workgroup client-server class of networks is Novell NetWare. The network operating system allows workstations and their associated file servers to exchange files, send and retrieve mail, provide an interface to SNA terminal emulation and database programs, among a host of other applications.

Novell NetWare's popularity grew very strong for its ability to provide not only file and print services, but also the ability to support multiple manufacturers' network interface cards and many different types of access methods (Ethernet, Token Ring, ARCnet, Proteon Pronet-10, FDDI). Novell's install base primarily includes DOS-based personal computers, but also offers connection services to Apple, Unix, IBM SNA, and OS/2 environments. Because of its low cost during the ramp-up of the LAN environment (early 1980s), the access method* of ARCnet was very popular with NetWare environments. NetWare supported the ability to "bridge"† packets to and from ARCnet, Ethernet, and Token Ring networks, and therefore gave users the ability to communicate to file servers and users no matter what access method they were working with. That is, since NetWare supported a native IPX router, it supports the translation between a variety of access methods.

As Ethernet and Token Ring became the access methods of choice, NetWare aided the migration to these networks from ARCnet. Furthermore, Novell supported almost any manufacturer of network interface cards (NICs). Novell grew a strong operating system from this environment and today is the number one manufacturer of workgroup computing operating systems (claiming 60 to 70 percent of the market).

---

* Access methods are the algorithms that allow data to be received or transmitted to the cable plant.

† Bridge is a term Novell used. The actual process was routing.

Finally, Novell's design goal was to be the most competitive as well as the highest performance LAN operating system.

This chapter will give you an understanding of how Novell NetWare operates on a LAN and WAN. The key topics for discussion are: (1) the user interface (workstations and servers), including the workstation shell, the NetWare File Service Core Program, the NetWare Core Protocol, and (2) the LAN operating system of Internet Packet Exchange (IPX). This chapter is not designed to teach you how to operate NetWare or how to apply the services provided with NetWare (although some of the services are used as examples). It is the objective of this chapter to provide you an insight on what goes on behind the scenes of this network operating system. When you start and log in to the NetWare network, exactly what happens and how does the file server and workstation communicate over the LAN or an internetwork?

For users in the Novell environment there are two primary or user-identifiable physical entities: a workstation and a server interconnected through a LAN. Refer to Fig. 5.1. The workstation is usually a personal computer (DOS, OS/2, Unix, or Apple operating systems) that makes requests for file and print services from an entity known as the *file server.* The file server runs a proprietary operating system known as NetWare Core Protocol (NCP) that services requests from the users' workstations and returns responses to these requests.

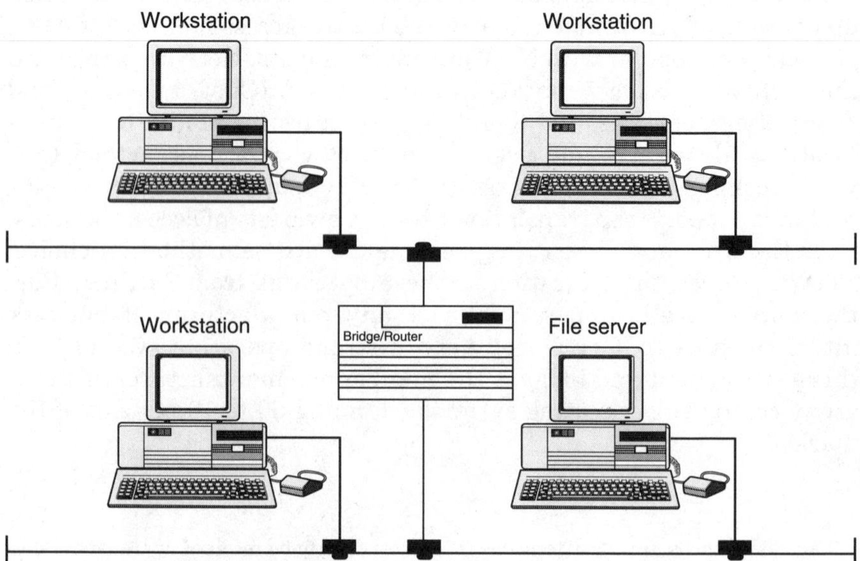

Figure 5.1 Basic Novell internet.

Introduction

For those who are new to NetWare, a brief description of the history of NetWare is necessary. When NetWare was first introduced, it was a small operating system primarily offering networked file and print services.

Version history

Advanced NetWare 86. 8086-based operating system required a keycard for copy protection. This was a hardware-based security adapter which was installed in the PC-based server. This version shipped with an adaptation of Xerox's networking-layer software known as Internet Packet Exchange (IPX).

Advanced NetWare 286 version 2.0a. Designed for the 80286 microprocessor. This version also required a keycard and the installation procedure was extremely complex (supported IPX only).

Advanced NetWare 286 version 2.11. With this release, Novell released their version of Xerox's transport-layer software known as Sequence Packet Exchange, which guaranteed reliable packet delivery. The complex installation procedure was simplified and the keycard procedure was now locally administered.

Advanced NetWare 286 version 2.12. With this release, Novell removed all keycard copy protection.

Advanced NetWare 286 version 2.15. This release supported the Apple Filing Protocol (AFP) for support of the Apple Macintosh workstation and LocalTalk cabling.

Advance NetWare 286 version 2.15c. Last release before 2.2. The most frequently installed NetWare to date.

Advanced NetWare version 2.2. As of this writing, the latest of the Novell 2.x releases. This version is basically the same as earlier releases but with a new installation program which combines all versions of 2.15 into one package. This includes SFT NetWare and all user versions.

Advanced NetWare 386 version 3.0. This was the first release supporting the 80386 microprocessor chip. The operating system was completely redesigned. It did allow coexistance with previous versions of software. First release supported only file and print services. Hard disks are now deemed reliable and COMPSURF (a proprietary disk-scanning utility that detected errors on a hard disk before the installation of the operating system) is now an option before the installation.

Advanced NetWare 386 version 3.1. With any new major release of software, major bugs were sure to be found. This release cleaned up most of the bugs in version 3.0. This version also supported more LAN adapters and provided better performance.

Advanced NetWare 3.11. As of this writing, the latest of the NetWare releases. This version added support for TCP/IP. It allowed NetWare packets to be encapsulated in an IP header for transmission on an IP network. The installation of the server was made very easy. Copy a few files to a DOS formatted hard disk, type the executable file name of "server," and basically feed diskettes for the rest of the installation. DOS can then be removed from the hard disk after the installation. This is done for speed purposes. The server may be brought down with the "DOWN" command and control is returned to DOS (if DOS was not removed from the hard disk).

Concepts

Novell NetWare is a LAN workgroup network operating system that permits workstations and their servers to communicate. The entities of NetWare that allow this are:

Access Protocols (Ethernet, Token Ring, ARCnet, ProNET-10, FDDI)

Internet Packet Exchange (IPX)

Routing Information Protocol (RIP)

Service Advertising Protocol (SAP)

NetWare Core Protocol (NCP)—run in the server and the workstation; in the workstation, known as the *shell*

Access protocols were covered previously and will not be further discussed in this chapter. Refer to Chap. 2.

Figure 5.2 shows the relationship between the OSI model and these NetWare processes. The ability to send NetWare commands and user data across the network relies on an XNS network layer Internet Datagram Protocol (IDP) derivative protocol known as IPX. IPX is a network-layer protocol implementation that allows data to be transferred across a local or a wide area network (through the use of routers in the WAN). IPX was derived using the IDP protocol of XNS.

The protocols that allow users access to their file servers is known as the NetWare Core Protocol (NCP) and the workstation shell program. Therefore, the remainder of this chapter will be divided into two parts: IPX and NCP (including the shell program). IPX will be discussed first.

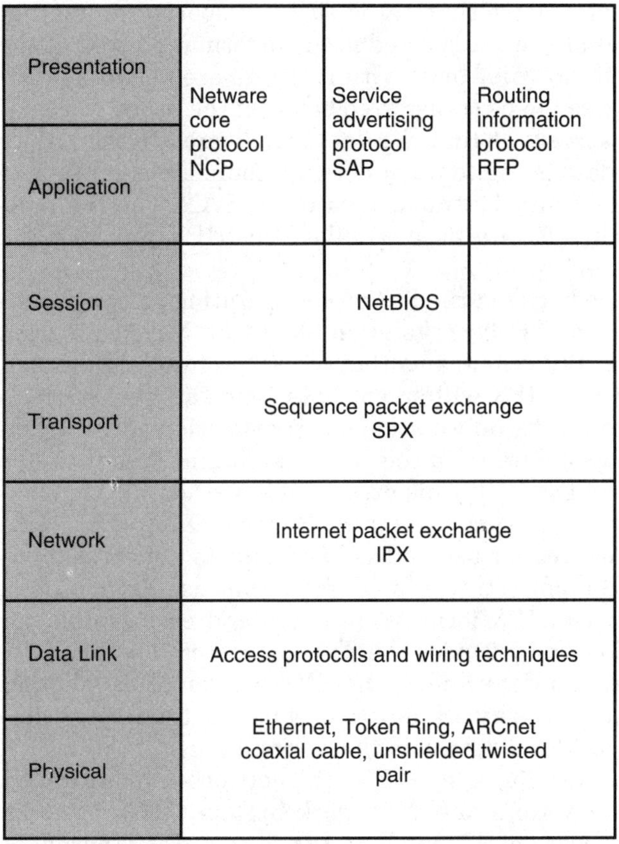

OSI layer			
Presentation Application	Netware core protocol NCP	Service advertising protocol SAP	Routing information protocol RFP
Session		NetBIOS	
Transport	Sequence packet exchange SPX		
Network	Internet packet exchange IPX		
Data Link	Access protocols and wiring techniques		
Physical	Ethernet, Token Ring, ARCnet coaxial cable, unshielded twisted pair		

Figure 5.2 The OSI model and Novell NetWare. (*Courtesy Novell, Inc.*)

Internet Packet Exchange (IPX)

Before networks and the architecture of distributed computing, files that resided on a personal computer remained on the personal computer and were transferred to another computer by copying the file to a diskette and physically transporting that diskette to the other computer. This delivery system was either by human intervention or by addressing the diskette and having a mail service deliver the disk. Initial network protocols did allow for files to be exchanged between computers but it was limited to that. They did not allow the files to be down-line loaded to the requesting station and to be seemlessly executed (like the files that were located on a local hard disk) once they were loaded to the requesting station.

With the advent of a network, data is still transported to another computer but the data to be transferred needs to formatted so that the network will understand what to do with it. There are network delivery commands that need to be transferred between the users' workstations and their file servers so that the data is delivered to the proper place. Whether the data is user data or network commands, it needs to be formatted so that it may be transferred to the LAN. The IPX software is the network software used to allow this. IPX provided the delivery service of data.

IPX is the interface between the file server operating software Network Control Program (NCP)/workstation shell (the Novell program that runs on the workstation) and the access protocols (Ethernet, Token Ring, or ARCnet). IPX will accept data from the workstation's shell or NCP and format the information for transmission onto the network. It will also accept data from the LAN and format it so it can be understood by the shell or NCP. This protocol follows Xerox's XNS network-layer protocol of Internet Datagram Protocol (XNS IDP). This protocol was implemented for use on local and remote networks. Novell followed the XNS architecture and adapted it for use in their environment. Simply stated, IPX formats (provides addressing) data for network transmission and provides the delivery system for this data. NCP is the program that determines, on a DOS workstation, whether the data is destined for a network device or whether the data is destined for a local device (local device on the workstation).

There are two purposes for using IPX as the network-level interface. First, since it follows Xerox's Xerox Network System (XNS) protocol, and this architecture was specifically built to run on top of Ethernet, it was designed to run on LANs. It was the only networking protocol designed to run on top of Ethernet. Other protocols such as TCP/IP, AppleTalk, etc., were adapted to run on top of Ethernet. Since the architecture was already written, and it was an open specification, Novell simply had to implement software to the architecture.

Second, not only will it carry data, it can easily route this data. This has many advantages. It allowed NetWare to support multiple network architectures easily. Novell calls this *bridging*. They called it bridging for it bridged together multiple networks. In reality, it was routing. This allowed ARCnet, Ethernet, Token Ring, and StarLAN networks to exchange data between the different LANs transparently. It is true that bridges did not enter the commercial marketplace until 1985, but this is well after Novell had established itself. With the release of NetWare 3.x, Novell has changed the term and now properly refers to this ability as *routing*.

Finally, by implementing only the network layer stack and a user interface (the shell), the amount of RAM consumed in a user's workstation was very small (sometimes as small as 20K of RAM). This was very important, for the first generation of PCs was limited to 640K of RAM to run application software. Applications could not be loaded into upper memory (later versions of the PC operating system allowed for this). As application software grew larger, the NetWare software remained the same and allowed larger applications to run.

Specifically, IPX is a full-implementation XNS IDP protocol with NetWare-adapted features. With this, the maximum packet size is 576 bytes* (although Novell does not strictly adhere to this when data is exchanged between two devices on a local LAN). The actual data size is 546 bytes, for the IPX packet header consumes 30 bytes. There are two entry points and two exit points for IPX. Data and commands are entered to and from either an application or from the LAN. Data is transmitted from IPX from the same two points. It all depends on the direction of the data flow.

Since data is packetized and is transmitted from the network-layer software, data is delivered on a best-effort basis (remember the transport layer is the protocol that provides reliable packet delivery). By implementing proprietary transport-layer software in NCP and simple transport software in the shell, NetWare did not have to implement full transport-layer software in the protocol stack of the client workstation. This saved valuable RAM at a time when DOS workstations had a limitation of memory in which to run applications. By implementing a small, reliable protocol stack such as this, the speed at which stations communicated with each other increased, especially when the medium was upgraded from ARCnet to Ethernet. Sequence Packet Exchange (SPX) was developed later and it is implemented into the shell. It is used primarily for peer-to-peer communications and utility programs such as RCONSOLE, SNA gateways, etc.

There are many functions provided by IPX, which can be grouped into two categories: packet formatting and data delivery. Packet formatting is discussed first.

IPX routing architecture

The data delivery system

Packet structure. Before developing a complete understanding of how data is transmitted and received on a network, some intermediate functions need to be addressed. The following text will address this.

---

* 576 bytes is the standard mandated by IDP. This allows enough room for network header information and allows for a typical memory block of data (512 bytes) to be transferred in a single packet.

Any data that is to be transmitted on a LAN needs to be formatted for transmission to the network. All data handed down to IPX from an upper-layer protocol is encapsulated into an entity known as *packet.* This process is similar to writing a letter. You write the letter and then put the letter into an envelope and address it to the receiver (the destination). On the envelope, you will put the destination address and your return address so the post office knows where to deliver the letter and the receiver knows where to send a response (if needed) to the letter. This is similar to the process IPX uses to format the data to deliver it to the network.

Let's take a look at the packet structure of IPX. Figure 5.3 shows a proprietary IPX packet,* and you will see that the IPX packet contains the following fields:

Checksum. This field contains the checksum (16 bits) for the IPX packet. The checksum can be thought of as a fancy parity check. Its objective is to ensure that the bits transmitted are the same bits that are received. In other words, no bits in the packet were transposed during the transmission. The sending station will perform the checksum algorithm on the packet and put the result of the checksum in this field. The receiving station will also perform a checksum on the IPX portion of the packet and generate a checksum. That checksum is checked with the checksum in the packet. If there is a match, the packet is said to be good. If the two do not match, that packet is said to contain an error and the packet will be discarded. Since this algorithm is performed at the data-link layer also (a CRC of 32 bits provides better accuracy than a 16-bit CRC), Novell has opted to disable this feature for IPX, considering it to be redundant and time-consuming—providing unnecessary overhead. With IPX, this field is set to FFFF to indicate that checksumming is turned off. (Some IPX routers use this field to check whether the packet is a Novell encapsulated IPX packet or of another type. This is explained in more detail later.)

Length. This field is used to indicate the total length of the IPX packet, including the IPX header checksum field. This means the length of the IPX header and data fields. The minimum length allowed is 30 bytes (the size of the IPX header fields) and its maximum number is 576 (indicating a maximum of 546 bytes total data field). For communications on a LAN, the number may be as high as the tranmission medium allows: 1500 bytes for Ethernet, 1496 for IEEE 802.3 (including IEEE 802.2 headers), and 4472 for 4-Mbps

---

* Other packet types are shown later.

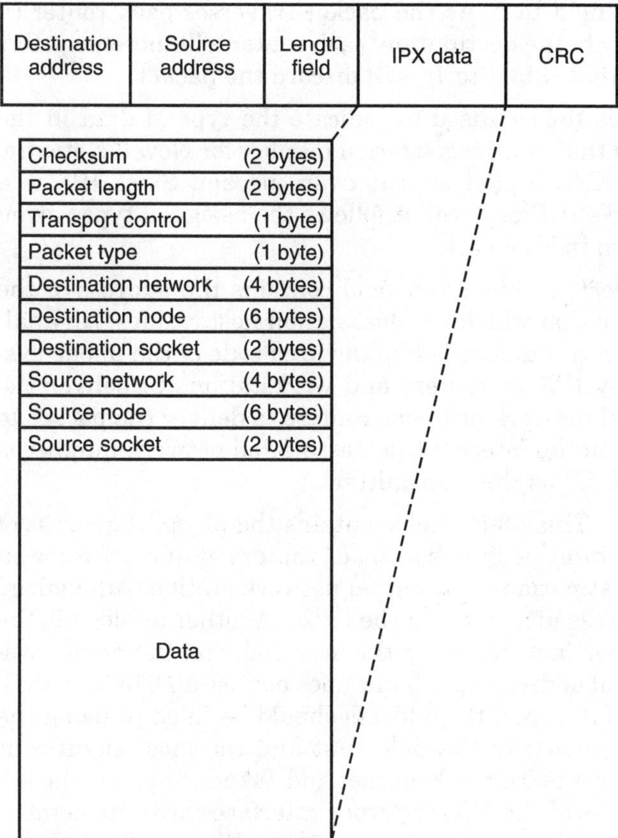

Figure 5.3 Novell proprietary (non-LLC) IPX packet format. (*Courtesy Novell, Inc.*)

Token Ring. Under Novell's packet burst mode, large packets may be transferred between two stations residing on different LANs. This is available under NetWare 4.0.

Transport control. This field is initially set to 0 by the sending station. This field counts the number of hops (the number of routers) the packet encountered along the way. Since the maximum number of routers a packet is allowed to traverse is 15 (a network 16 hops away is considered unreachable), the first 4 bits are not used. This is also used by routers that support Service Access Protocol (SAP) reporting and other file servers to indicate how far away a server (providing certain services) is from the recipient of the packet. The SAP process will be discussed later.

When a packet is transmitted onto the network, the sending station will set this field to 0. As the packet traverses each router (if needed) on its way to the destination, each router will increment this by 1. The router that sets it to 16 will discard the packet.

Packet type. This field is used to indicate the type of data in the data field. This is the Xerox registration number for Novell Netware. It identifies the XNS packet as a netware packet. Since IPX is a derivative of XNS's IDP protocol, it follows the assigned types given by Xerox as shown in Table 5.1.

Destination network. This 32-bit field contains the address of the destination network on which the destination host resides. An analogy is that a network number is like the area code of the phone system. It is used by IPX in routers and workstations to deliver the packet to the local network or to use routers to deliver the packet to another network on the internet (the destination network number is not on the same LAN as the transmitter).

Destination host. This 48-bit field contains the physical address of the final (not any intermediate hosts, i.e., routers, it may traverse on the way to the destination) destination network station. An analogy of this is the address displayed on the letter. Another analogy is the seven-digit number (not including the area code) on the phone system. If the physical addressing scheme does not use all 6 bytes (ARCnet and ProNET -10), then the address should be filled in using the least significant portion of the field first and the most significant portion should be set to 0s. For Ethernet and Token Ring, it is the 48-bit physical address of the NIC (network interface card). Remember that this address indicates the address of the ultimate (final) destination. It does not indicate any physical address of any intermediate stops along the way.

TABLE 5.1 Xerox-assigned Packet Types in Hex

Protocol	Packet type (hex)
Unknown	0
Routing information	1
Echo	2
Error	3
Packet exchange protocol (PEP) used for SAP (service advertisement protocol)	4
Sequence packet exchanged (SPX)	5
Experimental	10-1F
NetWare core protocol	11
NetBIOS	14

NOTE: Packets are set to a 11 (17 decimal).

*Destination socket**. This 16-bit field is an indicator of the process to be accessed on the destination station. Remember from our previous general discussion on XNS that a socket number is an integer number assigned to a specific process running on a network station (for example, the file service that runs on a file server). Each and every service that runs on a file server will be assigned a socket number. For example, the file service is assigned a socket number of 0451 (hex). Any workstation requesting this service must set this field to 0451 for it to be properly serviced by the file server. Novell Static sockets are shown in a moment. Since IPX follows the XNS standard, the socket numbers shown in Table 5.2 are reserved. Other socket numbers that are reserved and that may not be used without the permission of Xerox Corporation are in the range of 1-BB8. A number other than this may be used dynamically. This is covered in more detail under the source socket description.

Source network. This 32-bit field contains the network number of the source network. This indicates the network number from which the packet originated. A network number of 0 indicates the physical network where the source resides is unknown. Any packet of this type received by a router will have the network number set by the router. When IPX is initialized on a workstation, it may obtain the network number by watching packets on the LAN and derive its number from there. It may also find its network number from the router. Network numbers are not assigned to the workstation.

Source host. This 48-bit field contains the physical address of the source host (the network station that submitted the packet). This represents the host number from which the packet originated. Like the destination host field, if the physical address is less than 6 bytes long, the least significant portion of this field is set to the address and the most significant portion of the field is set to 0s (user for ARCnet and ProNET -10). Otherwise, it is set to the 48-bit address of the LAN interface card.

* The Xerox and Novell documentation misnames this as a socket. In actuality it is properly called a *port number.* The combination of the destination network, destination host, and port number is called a *socket.* For the purposes of this book, sockets (whether source or destination) and ports will also be interchangeable.

TABLE 5.2 Assigned Socket Numbers in Hex

Registered with Xerox	0001-0BB8
User definable	0BB9 and higher

Source socket. This 16-bit field contains the socket number of the process that submitted the packet. It is usually set to the number in the dynamic range (user definable range).

Source, destination host and source, and destination network are pretty much self-explanatory. Sockets are a little more elusive.

Multiple processes may be running on a workstation (OS/2, UNIX—usually not DOS), and definitely multiple processes will be running on a file server. Sockets are the addresses that indicate the endpoint for communication. A unique socket number indicates which process running on the network station should receive the data. Sockets represent an application process running on a network workstation. There are two types of sockets: static and dynamic. Static sockets are reserved sockets that are assigned by the network protocol or application implementor (in this case, Novell) and cannot be used by any other process on the network. Dynamic sockets are assigned randomly and can be used by any process on the network.

For example, to access the file services of a server, IPX would fill in the destination and source network, the destination host number of the file server, and source host number of its workstation. The destination socket number would be set to 0451 (hex). This is known as a well-known socket number, for it is static (it will never change). It has been defined by Novell. The source socket (assigned by IPX at the source workstation) will be a dynamic number and IPX will pick it randomly from the range of 4000 to 6000 hex. The source socket is used by the destination as a socket number to reply to. It indicates the socket number that made the request. In this way, when the packet arrives at the server, the server will know that the packet is destined for it (the host number) and will also know the transmitting station is requesting something from the server (socket 0451). Deeper into the packet will be a control code to indicate exactly what the transmitter of the packet wants (create a file, delete a file, directory listing, print a file, etc.).

Once the command is interpreted and processed, the server will return data to the transmitter of the packet. But it needs to know which endpoint of the workstation will receive this data (which process submitted the request). This is the purpose of the source socket number. The file server will format a packet, reverse the IPX header fields (source and destination headers), set the destination socket number to the number indicated in the received packet of source socket number, and transmit the packet. (See Table 5.3.)

Finally, the socket number (source or destination network number, source or destination host number, and source or destination port number) is the absolute address of any process on the network. With the combination of these fields, any process on any network on any

TABLE 5.3 Netware Assigned Port (Socket) Values

File server	
0451h	Netware core protocol
Router static sockets	
0452h	Service advertising protocol
0453h	Routing information protocol
Workstations sockets	
4000h–6000h	Dynamically assigned sockets used for workstation interaction with file servers and other network communications
0455h	NetBIOS
0456h	Diagnostic packet

network station can be found. IPX controls all socket numbering and processing.

That was one of the functions provided by IPX—the formatting of data into a packet so that it may be transferred across the network. How network numbers are found and how host numbers are found will be discussed later in this chapter.

The next (not in any order of precedence) function of the IPX protocol is the ability to route packets directly to a workstation on the same LAN or to a network station on a remote LAN. The following is a description of the Novell implementation that allows this. It is called *routing.*

Encapsulation at the data-link layer. Although this was covered in a previous chapter, Novell provides for support for a few more encapsulation methods. (Given its long history, it had to do this for supporting so many different vendors' network interface cards.)

The six methods of data-link encapsulation that Novell supports are:

1. Novell proprietary
2. IEEE 802.3 with IEEE 802.2
3. Ethernet
4. IEEE 802.3 with SNAP
5. Token Ring
6. ARCnet

Some of these packets are shown in Fig. 5.4. When installing a Novell network, the installer must choose between the encapsulation methods. Selection of one is needed. The software will not try to figure out the format. Once set, a transmitting station will format the packet and the receiver will read the packet according to the setting during the installation. Two communicating stations must use the same encapsulation type.

Some network installations perfer the Novell proprietary. This is basically the IEEE 802.3 MAC header encapsulation. Immediately following the length field, will be the beginning of the IPX header. This will be set to FFFF, indicating that checksumming is turned off. Some router vendors use this field to indicate that it is a Novell packet. IEEE 802.2 is not included in the packet.

The reason for all the packet formats is compatibility. During the ramp-up of Ethernet, different vendors supported different encapsulation techniques. The Ethernet packet header was the first encapsulation technique used with Ethernet networks. When IEEE 802.3 formally adopted CSMA/CD (Ethernet), they changed the packet format. Novell again changed the packet format to include this new type.

With the IEEE 802.3 packet format, Novell supports both the IEEE 802.2 and the SNAP protocols (These are fully discussed in Chap. 3, "IEEE 802.2"). Furthermore, Novell decided to support its own packet format.

The installer of a Novell network may choose any of the preceding. It all depends on the type of network interface cards that are installed in the network.

Of course, NetWare supports Token Ring encapsulation methods. The two methods supported are IEEE 802.5 with IEEE 802.2 and IEEE 802.5 with IEEE 802.2 SNAP. Figure 5.4 has some of the fields filled in. On the Ethernet frame, the Ethertype of 8137 identifies a Novell frame. On the IEEE 802.3 with IEEE 802.2, EO is the SAP address assigned by the IEEE to Novell. On the SNAP packet, the organization of 000000 identifies an encapsulated Ethernet packet and 8137 is the Ethertype for Novell. SNAP is fully explained in Chap. 3.

IPX routing functions

Novell routers. The routing function allows packets to be forwarded to different networks through the use of a device known as a router. An analogy would be when a phone number such as 749-4232 is dialed in Virginia, the local switching office knows by the first three digits (the local exchange number) that the number is local and should be routed to a destination on the local phone system. The call is switched between exchange offices (if necessary) in the local area to its final destination. But when a number such as 212-337-4096 is dialed, the local switching office knows the call is to be routed to a distant location. In this case, the call is to be routed to an exchange in the state of New York. This is a crude analogy, but shows how network IDs and routers work in networks.

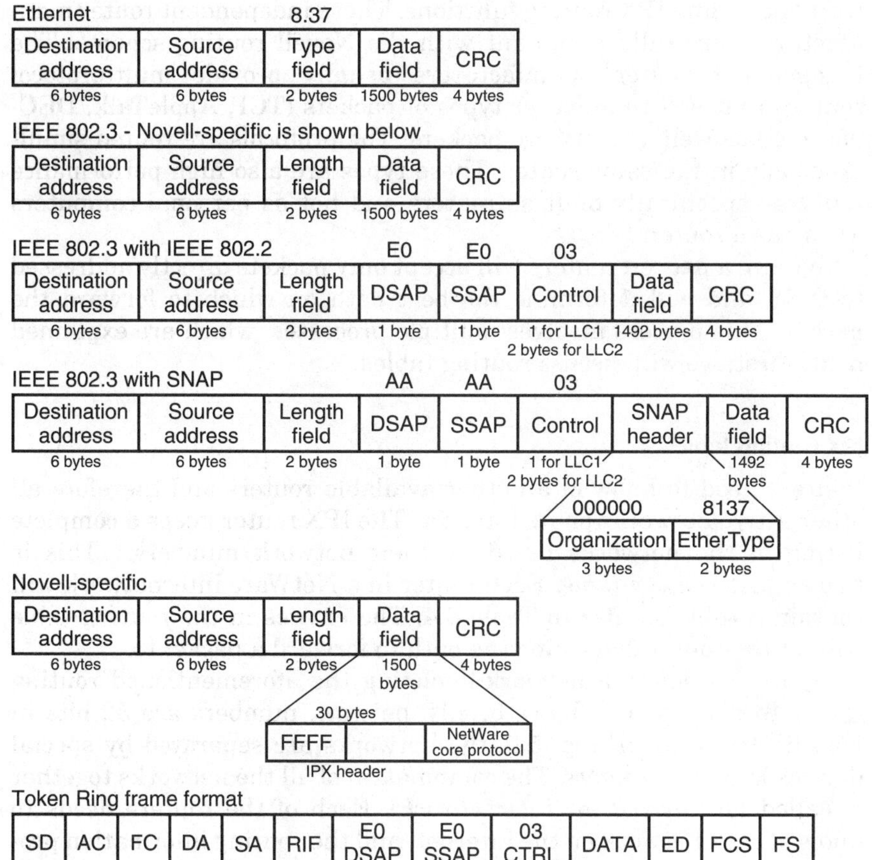

Figure 5.4 Encapsulation methods (data-link frame encapsulation).

There are two available types of routers on a Novell network. First, Novell implements a routing function in their operating system. Previous to Novell 3.x, Novell documention called their routers "bridges." But in reality they are routers. As of this writing, Novell has officially changed the names to *internal* and *external router.*

There are two types of NetWare supplied routers: internal and external. The internal router is one that is usually performing some other tasks, as well as the routing function. These tasks may be file and print services or a gateway service to SNA. The external router is a workstation (for example, a personal computer) consisting of multiple network interface cards, and its sole function is to route packets. There will be no other functions provided by this external router.

Second, independent router manufacturers (Wellfleet Communications, 3Com, cisco Systems, etc.) can also participate in a Novell network, providing IPX routing functions. These independent router manufacturers are fully compliant with the Novell routing scheme. The independent router manufacturers usually provide multiprotocol routers that will route other types of packets (TCP, AppleTalk, DECnet, etc.) as well as NetWare packets. The protocols are routed simultaneously in the same router. These types are also high-performance routers—specifically built as routers and not as personal computers acting as a router.

To route a packet, routers will accept only packets directly addressed to them and will determine the best path on which to forward the packet. This process involves multiple processes, which are explained next. First, we will discuss routing tables.

IPX routing tables

Routers need to know of all other available routers and therefore all other active networks on its internet. The IPX router keeps a complete listing of the networks listed by their network numbers.* This is known as a *routing table.* Each router in a NetWare internetwork will contain a table similar to Table 5.4. The entries in the routing table will let the router determine the path to forward a packet to.

Figure 5.5 shows a network depicting the aforementioned routing table. To discuss this figure briefly, network numbers are 32 bits in length. As shown in Fig. 5.5, the networks are separated by special devices known as *routers.* The combination of all the networks together is called an *internet* (or *internetwork*). Each of the routers needs to know of each network on the internet, and the routing information pro-

* Keeping a list of network numbers and the means to provide a path to get to that network is the basis of all routing algorithms, whether flat or hierarchial. For more information, see the routing introduction in Chap. 4.

TABLE 5.4 IPX Routing Table

Network number	Number of hops to network	Ticks to network	NIC	Intermediate address of forwarding router	Net status	Aging timer
00000020	1	2	A	Local		0
00000030	1	2	B	Local		0
00000040	1	2	C	Local	R	0
00000050	2	3	B	02608C010203		1
00000060	2	3	A	02608C040506		2
00000070	3	4	A	02608C010304		2

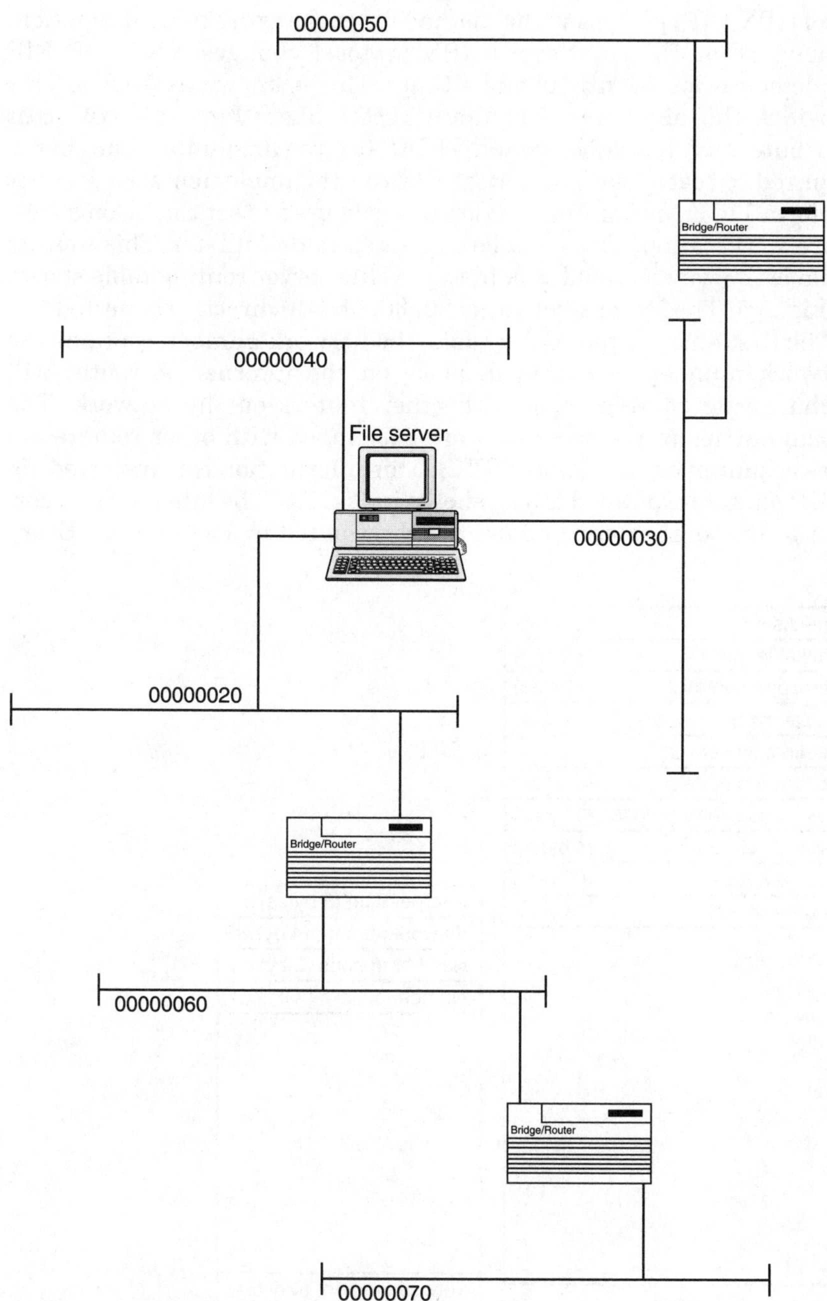

Figure 5.5 Network number assignments with routers.

tocol (IPX-RIP) process is the method for exchanging this information. Among other things, Novell's IPX protocol changes XNS IDP RIP implementation slightly to add a timer. This is known as TICKS. This provides the ability of a distance vector algorithm with true cost attributes, not just a hop count. TICKS are the amount of time that is required to reach that path. Most IPX routing implementations do not perform TICK counts. Today, it is primarily used to set timers on a NetWare workstation. Ticks will be explained in detail later. This routing table is the way it would look in the PC file server routing table shown in Fig. 5.5. The PC has networks 20, 30, and 40 directly connected.

The first entry of the router table, the network number, contains the network numbers that are in place on the internet. A router will exchange its routing table with other routers on the network. The actual entries in the table that are exchanged with other routers are network number, hops, and TICKS. This information is transferred via a RIP packet (explained later), shown in Fig. 5.6. The other entries pertain to the local router and are not distributed by each router. Every

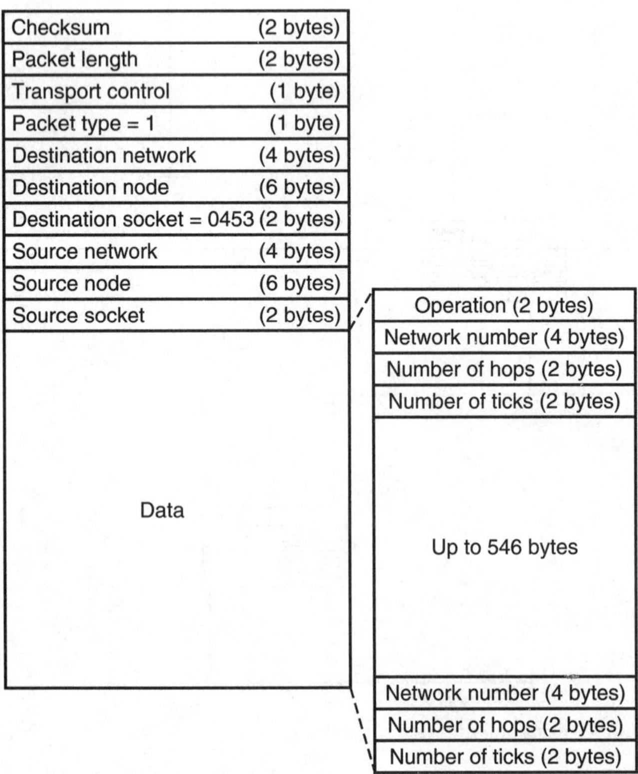

Figure 5.6 IPX RIP packet format. (*Courtesy Novell, Inc.*)

router will build its own entries. A router will receive these updates (routing tables) from other routers on the internet through a process known as RIP, which will be explained in a moment. From this received information, a router will build its own table and thus a picture of the intenet.

The second entry shows the number of routers that must be traversed to reach this network. Anytime that a packet must traverse a router to reach a destination, the process of traversing the routers is known as a *hop*. Therefore, if a packet must cross over four routers to reach the final network, it is said the network is 4 hops away. The term hops is also called a *metric*. Four hops is the same as a 4-metric count.

The next entry is the tick counts. This number indicates an estimated time necessary to deliver a packet to a destination on that network. This time is based on the segment type. A tick is about $\frac{1}{18}$ second. This number is derived from an IBM-type personal computer clock being ticked at 18 times a second. In actuality there are 18.21 ticks in a personal computer clock for every second elapsed. At a minimum, this field will be set to a 1; 18 would indicate 1 second.

For locally attached segments with more than 1 Mbps transmission speed (Ethernet and Token Ring), the NIC driver will assume a tick of 1. For serial network segments (X.25, synchronous line of T1 and 64 Kbps, and asynchronous), the driver will periodically poll to determine the time delay. For a T1 circuit, the tick counter is usually 6 to 7 ticks per segment, Any changes in this time will be informed to the router and propagated to other routers on the network. These numbers in the tables are cummulative. This means that as each router broadcasts its routing table, this number will not be reset. It is the sum of all the paths' TICK counts to reach a destination network.

The network interface card (NIC) entry field records the NIC number from which the network can be reached. It indicates the controller card from which the router received this reachability information. A Novell file server can hold four network interface cards or NICs. It is the same as a physical port number in a stand alone-router (not a personal computer, file server, acting as a router). The Intermediate Address entry contains the physical node address of the router that can forward packets to each segment. If the network is directly attached, the entry will be empty. If the network to be reached requires the use of another router, this entry contains the physical address of the next router to send the packet to. This physical address is extracted from RIP updates (a router broadcasting its table) sent by those routers. An entry in the NIC field would be valid only if the router were located in a PC. Otherwise, this field would indicate the router physical port number.

The Net Status entry indicates whether the network is considered reliable.

The Age entry is used to indicate how long it has been since a routing update has been made. This field is used to age-out (delete) entries for networks that have not been heard from in a certain amount of time. These timers follow the XNS specifications. This number can be in seconds or in minutes, depending on the manufacturer of the router.

In short, a routing table contains a listing of network numbers and an associated path (whether direct or indirect) in order to deliver the packet to its final destination network.

One last note is that, with the exception of the next hop router address, the entries in the routing table do not contain any physical addresses of the network stations that reside on the internet (this is true of most routing algorithms). The only physical address in the table is that of another router to which a packet, destined for a remote network, may be addressed. Routers do not know which other end stations are on the networks they connect to. The final destination (physical address of the final destination) is embedded in the IPX header (the destination host). Once the router determines that the final destination network number is directly attached to the router, it will extract the destination host number from the IPX header and address the packet and deliver it to the directly attached network segment. This will be discussed in detail later.

IPX routing information protocol (RIP)

To exchange their tables with other routers on the internet, IPX uses an algorithm known as *routing information protocol* or RIP. The RIP algorithm is the most widely used routing algorithm in use today. Variations of this protocol exist on TCP/IP, AppleTalk, IPX, XNS, and a host of other proprietary XNS vendor implementations. IPX RIP is not compatible with other protocol versions of RIP. This is why a multiprotocol router will force the network administrator to configure RIP for each protocol that is implemented on the router. The origins of RIP date back to the XNS protocol. A full discussion of it may be found in Chap. 4.

The functions of the RIP protocol are:

1. Allow workstation to attain the fastest route to a network by broadcasting a route request packet which will be answered by the routing software on the Novell file server or by a router supporting IPX RIP.
2. Allow routers to exchange information or update their internal routing tables.

3. Allow routers to respond to RIP requests from workstations.
4. Allow routers to become aware when a route path has changed.

There are multiple ways for a workstation (not a server) to determine its network number. IPX on a workstation will extract information from the network by watching the RIP responses on the network to dynamically determine a workstation network number. It also may retrieve from the router during a RIP request or during a SAP (discussed in moment) request. The point to take here is that a workstation is not predefined (during installation) with a network number. Server and router network numbers, however, are implemented during the installation of that server or router. If the network number is obtained during a SAP request during workstation startup, the network number will not be known. The workstation will send out the SAP request with the IPX header network number entry set to all 0s. The destination node field will be set up to all FFs.

IPX will format an IPX RIP packet, and this is shown in Fig. 5.6. This is the IPX RIP packet. Notice the destination socket field is set to 0453(h) to indicate the destination process. The packet type is set to a 1. The static socket for RIP is 0453. It should be noted that RIP data (the routing table) is enveloped by an IPX header (the IPX packet will be encapsulated by the data-link header), and the packet is then transmitted onto the network. All network requests will use IPX, as shown in later figures. The RIP request is placed in the data area of an IPX packet. This is what is meant, as not all packets contain user data. Some network packets will contain information known as *control information,* also known as *overhead.* It is necessary data for the network, but it is still overhead. This is one of those packets.

Refer to Fig. 5.6. A RIP request will have an operation field of 1 and a RIP response will have an operation field of 2. Following the information field will be one or more (depending on the number of known routes) sets (network number, distance, and TICK count) of information. The sets of information will contain a network number followed by the number of hops to that network and the associated delay cost (ticks) to that network. Due to the 576-byte limitation of an IPX packet, a single RIP packet can contain 68 sets of known route information. If more routes (a larger table) are known, multiple packets will be sent by a router.

XNS's IDP protocol does not define a TICKS field in an XNS IDP RIP packet. NetWare incorporated this so that a shell could determine the delay time in receiving a response from a file server (The Receive Timeout). If there are multiple paths to the same destination of equal hop count, the routers will use the route with the shortest tick time. These fields (ticks) are only valid for an IPX RIP response packet.

Router operation

An individual router, like any other network attachment, attaches directly to a LAN. A router will have at least two attachments.* The router separates two cable segments. The cable segments that it attaches to are known as the *directly connected cable segments.* That term will be used throughout the course of this book.

When an IPX router first initializes, it will place the network numbers of the directly connected routes into the routing table. These network numbers are manually entered during the configuration of the router during installation. Once integrated, the router will then send a broadcast packet to the network (on each of its directly connected cable segments) containing these routes (the network numbers of the directly attached cable segments) that the router will now make available. Other routers on those cable segments will read this information and update their tables. The RIP cost that is entered into the table at initialization is usually set to a 1. This is configurable in some routers.

The router will then transmit another RIP packet *requesting* information from other routers on its directly attached network segments (a RIP request). This request will be responded to by any other active routers on the directly connected segments. The term directly connected segments is used here because request and response packets are sent in broadcast mode. This means that all stations on the local network will receive and process this packet. These broadcast packets are not forwarded to other networks by the routers. Routers update their tables and, in turn, will broadcast their updated tables to their directly connected cable segments. Figure 5.7 shows router A sending† out its routing table to network 2. Router B will pick up this packet and add 1 to each hop count entry in the received table. The router will then compare the received table to its own table.

If a network number was found in the received table that is not in its table, it will add this entry into its table. If a network number matches a network number in its table, it will check the hop count. If the received table's hop count is lower than the one in its table, it will change the entry in its table with the entry from the received table. If the hop count of the received table was larger, the entry will be discarded.

Once its table is checked, it will broadcast its table (if the 60-second RIP update timer expired) to network 3. Router C will perform a similar comparison. (In actuality, it will broadcast table entries out both of its ports, but because of the algorithm of split horizon, only network

---

* Exceptions to this are DECnet and AppleTalk.

† In Fig. 5.7, an algorithm known as *split horizon* is not implemented. This feature is the router's ability to not broadcast a network number table entry out the same port it received it from. Therefore, if split horizon were implemented, router A should not broadcast information about network 2 out that port. This is explained in more detail later.

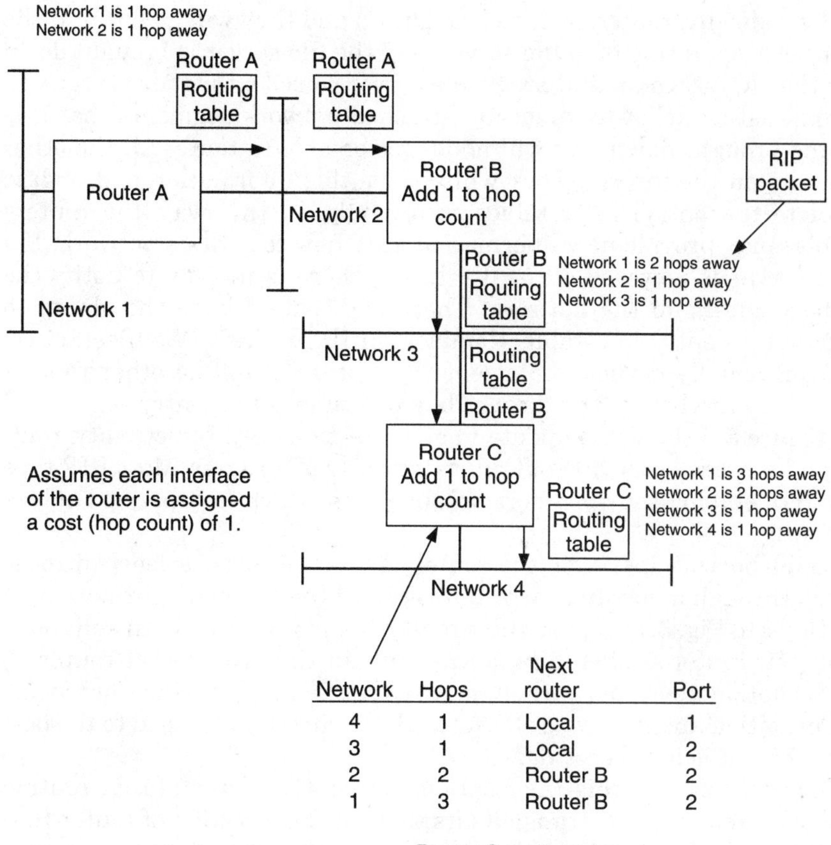

Network	Hops	Next router	Port
4	1	Local	1
3	1	Local	2
2	2	Router B	2
1	3	Router B	2

Router C routing table

Figure 5.7 A routing table update (RIP) not implementing split horizon.

numbers of its table that it did not learn from a port will be broadcasted out that port. Until split horizon is discussed, this example will do.)

Once these events have taken place, the IPX router will place itself in the operation of receiving information (processing RIP requests, routing packets, and maintaining its routing table). In addition to these updating tasks, all routers will broadcast their routing tables every 60 seconds. This is different than other implementations of RIP. For example, TCP/IP RIP broadcasts every 30 seconds and AppleTalk broadcasts every 10 seconds. These other routing tables are received by other routers so that they know about other networks on the internetwork. In this way, all routers will remain synchronized. Every router may transmit its table at different times. Each router must broadcast this every 60 seconds. In other words, the routers do not broadcast their tables at the same time.

Periodically, routers will be brought up and they will go down. If the router is operating on a file server, and the file server is brought down by the DOWN command at the file server console, that file server will broadcast a packet to its locally attached network segments that it is being brought down and will no longer be able to route. All the other routers on the internetwork will receive this information and update (delete the entry) their tables accordingly. In this way, the routers tables may provide new information as to how to get to a network. If a file server is powered off or it crashes, there is no way to notify the other routers on the network. Therefore, routers have the ability to age-out an entry in a table. Commercial IPX routers (Wellfleet, cisco, 3Com) usually do not implement the feature of telling other routers that they are being shut down. They will time out an entry.

Figure 5.7 shows an update in one direction only. In actuality, routing tables are broadcast out all active ports of a router. Most RIP-type routers employ the split horizon algorithm which is explained subsequently.

Split horizon instructs the router not to broadcast a learned route back through a port from which it received the learned information.

Refer to Fig. 5.7, in particular router B and router C. With split horizon set, router B should broadcast out (in the direction of router C) information about network 1 and network 2 only. It will not broadcast information about network 3. Network 3 is directly attached to the port on which it is broadcasting.

Upon receipt of this information, router C will update its routing table. When router C transmits its table in the direction of router B, it will include information only on network 4. It learned about networks 1 and 2 from router B (actually it received information about those networks from that particular port) and, therefore, it will not broadcast the same information about those networks out that port. Router C will still broadcast information about networks 1, 2, and 3 out the router port connected to network 4, but it will not broadcast information about network 4 out that port. Split horizon prevents this.

This and other RIP concepts are explained in more detail in Chap. 4.

Aging of the table entries. Every time routing information is received about a certain route, this entry is set to 0. If this entry is incremented to four minutes, the router will assume that the path to that network is down and will broadcast this information to other routers on its local segments. This information will be propagated on to other routers on the network to update their routing tables.

Determining a local or remote path. When a router is fully operational, it will make network numbers known on the internet, and other network stations may then use that router to forward a packet to those remote networks. Any time a network station wishes to send information to a destination station, it must have the network address as well as the physical (data-link or MAC) address of the destination station. If the two stations are communicating on the same network (they have the same network number), the transmitting station can send the packet directly to the destination without invoking the use of a router.

However, if the destination station lies on a different network than the transmitting station,* the tranmitting station must find a router to submit the packet to for final delivery. In order to find a router, the network workstation must transmit a RIP request packet. Inside this packet is the destination address (network number) of the final destination. This request will be answered by routers only on the immediate (same network as the requesting station) network. Routers that are not directly connected to the same network will not see this request because it is transmitted in data-link broadcast (all FFs in the data link address fields) destination address. Local routers can respond to this type of packet but will not forward this or any direct broadcast packet. Any router that has a path to that destination will respond, and the network workstation will choose the router to forward the packet to. Usually, this will be based on the lowest tick or hop count.

In the response packet from a router is the router's physical address (in the data-link header). The requesting network station will use this address to physically address its packet to the router. In the case of multiple responses to a route request (there are multiple routers on the requesting station's network), the workstation will choose which router to submit its packet to.

When the originating station receives the router response, it will extract the router's MAC address out of the response packet and prepare its data for transmission in the following way (Fig. 5.8*a*† shows the dialogue between network station A communicating to file server C through the intermediate router B):

1. Place the final destination's, not the router's, full internetwork address (a socket address consisting of network address, host address, port address) in the IPX destination header information fields (refer to Fig. 5.8*a*).

---

* It will determine this by comparing its own network address to that of the destination station. If they do not match, a router must be found to route the packet to the destination for that station.

† For simplicity, full addresses are not used. This figure shows an example, using alphabetic letters to identify nodes on the network.

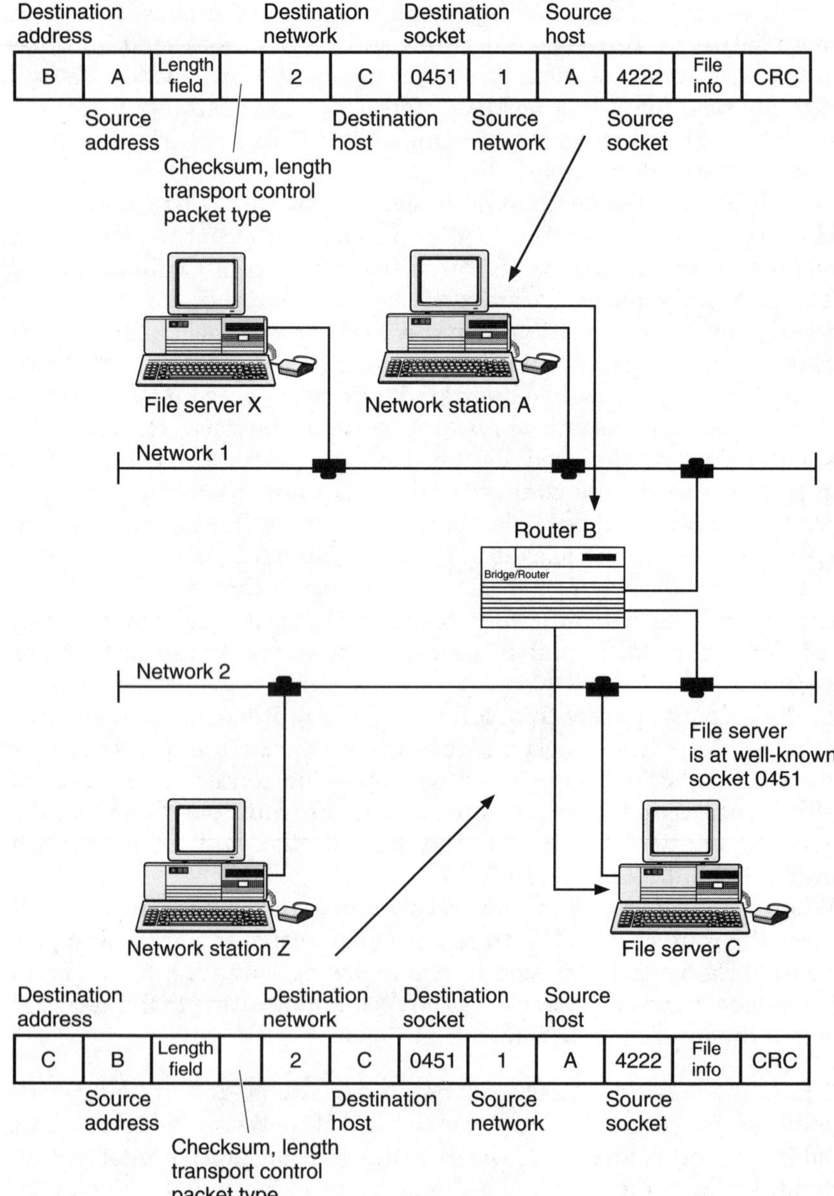

Figure 5.8 (*a*) Abbreviated version of data transfer using IPX headers.

2. Place its own full internetwork address in the source header information fields of the IPX header (network number, host number, and a dynamically assigned socket number).
3. The router's physical address that was extracted from RIP response packet is then placed in the data-link destination header field (refer to Fig. 5.8*a*) and its own physical address in the source address data-link header field.

Once all the fields have been filled out, the network station will transmit the packet. When the router receives this packet, two possibilities exist for the router:

1. If the network number of the end-station destination (indicated by the network address in the IPX header) is directly connected to the router, the router will extract the data-link destination address (the host address) from the IPX destination host address field, and place it into the data-link destination address header. Next, it will place its own physical host address in the data-link source address field and send the packet to the directly attached network. Throughout the course of a packet being forwarded, the IPX header will be read to make route determinations. It will never be written into. It will never be changed, with the exception of transport control and the checksum field (if used).
2. If the destination network is not directly connected to the router, the router must send the packet to next router in the path to that network. To do this, the router will place the data-link MAC address of the next router in the path in the data-link destination address field and will place its own address in the data-link source address field and submit the packet to the network that has the next router attached. It knows the next router's data-link MAC address, for it is one of the fields in the routing table. Refer to Table 5.4. The router will not touch the original data in the IPX header field (except for the transport control field which will be incremented by 1). When the packet reaches the next router, it will start this decision process over again starting from the preceding number 1.

   If the transport control field is set to a 16, indicating that 15 routers have been traversed, the router will discard the packet. Upper-layer protocols on the originating station will time-out and the packet will be retransmitted.

This is how routers know where to deliver a packet and this is the purpose of the destination host field in the IPX header. Again, when a packet reaches the destination router (the router that is directly connected to the destination network as indicated by the destination network number field in the IPX header), it will determine it is connected to the final network and will then extract the end-station host number (destination host) and put that number in the destination address of the data-link header and transmit the packet to the end network workstation.

The sending station of a packet will find out about the final destination host number through a protocol known as *service access protocol.* This is discussed in a moment.

Routing supplementals. With NetWare versions 2.15c and after, if more than one route (multiple routers to the same destination network) exists to a network, only the routing information that is equal (same number of hops and ticks) will be kept in the routing table; for a path will be selected only if it has the fastest route. Prior versions used to keep tables of all available routes, regardless of hops and ticks in the routing table.

The table shown in Table 5.4 is exclusive to Novell and its routing scheme. It uses a process similar to other routing schemes (TCP/IP, XNS, and AppleTalk) in that it uses the functions of a table and RIP to distribute that table. You will hear that if you know XNS you know IPX. This is somewhat true but the differences are:

- Router table (TICK entry)
- Format of the IPX RIP packet
- Not broadcasting complete tables across slower-speed serial lines (telephone lines)*
- Broadcasting information that a server is going down (routing functions will cease and may be a path to a network)
- The workstation can obtain its network address by watching the network cable and "gleaning" the address from other packets on the network. Upon start-up, if IPX has not determined the network number for the network station (not the server), and NETx.com has started (loading the shell program is discussed later), IPX will determine the network address from a RIP or SAP response packet that it uses during loading of the shell and the login program.

This completes the NetWare data delivery system known as IPX. Remember, any process that has to transmit or receive over the Novell NetWare environment must use IPX to deliver and receive the data.

Finally, Fig. 5.8*b* summarizes the router's functions in a flowchart.

---

* Not available on all IPX routers.

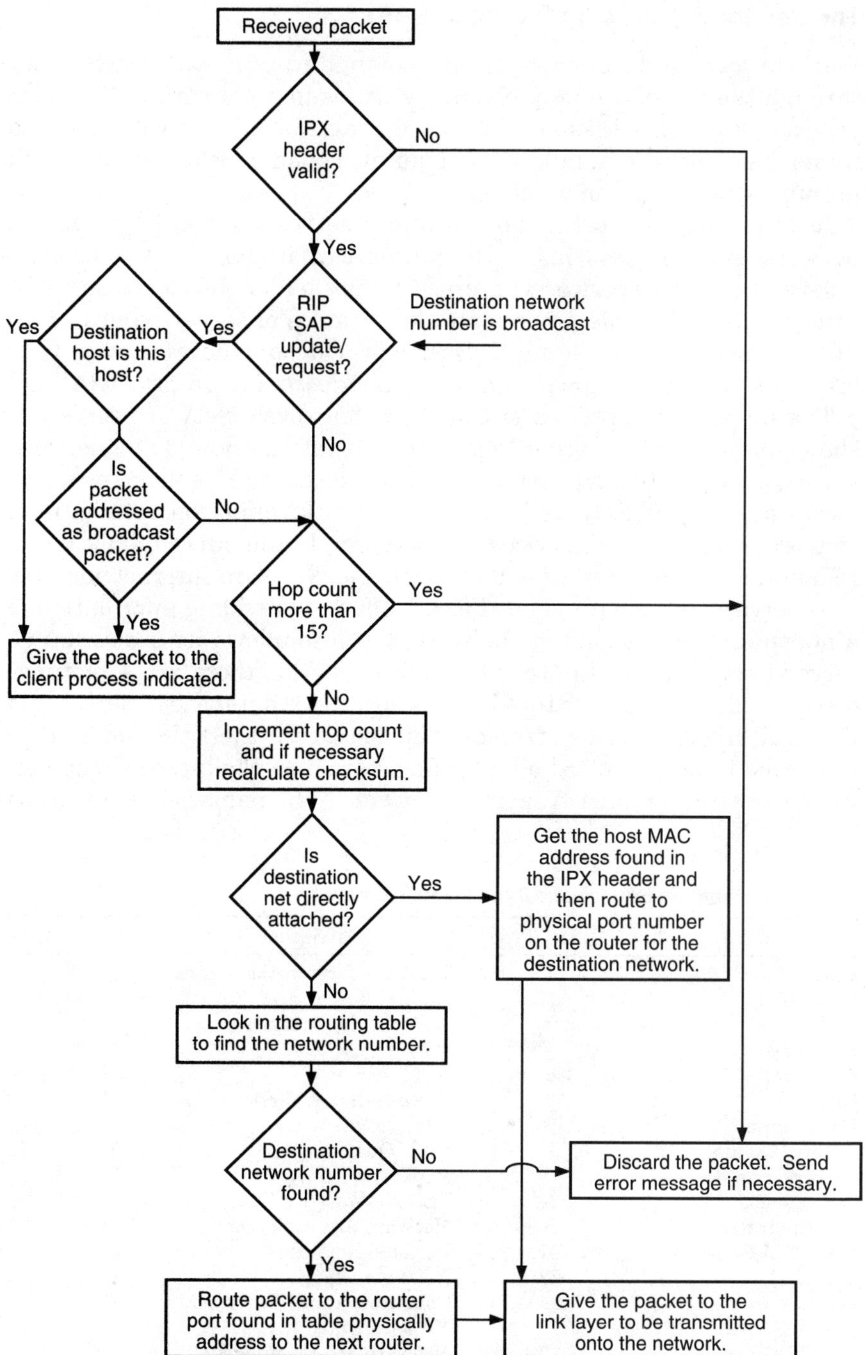

Figure 5.8 (*b*) Summary of router functions.

The Service Advertising Protocol (SAP)

Workstations and servers initiate communication with each other through the use of a name. Naming entities in a network is an easier way for users to access services on the network. Requiring users to remember network numbers, host numbers, and socket number will prohibit efficient use of a network.

In order for the workstation to find a server's name, log in to the network, or to use printing or E-mail services, it must be able to locate a server and the services running on that server. Routers are intricately involved in this process and keep tables of server names, their full internet address, the services they provide, and how far away they are. This process is known as the *service advertising protocol* (SAP).

There are many services provided by the Novell NetWare server, as shown in Table 5.5. In order to provide this information to any network station on any network (an internet), Novell NetWare implements a protocol known as SAP. A NetWare internetwork cannot operate without this protocol. It allows services of a server to be announced to local and remote networks, no matter how large the NetWare internet may be. This service not only provides the capability of providing information to a network station about the network, but also allows for a distributed server name service. In other types of networks, there are sometimes distributed name servers that keep a centralized database of names and their full internetwork addresses. This is true for the XNS and TCP/IP protocols. In order to find a particular station on the internet, the network workstation must transmit a packet to the name server to which

TABLE 5.5 NetWare Service and Type Identification

Description	Object Type	Description	Object Type
User	1	Time Synchronization Server	2D
User Group	2	Archive Server SAP	2E
Print Queue	3	Advertising Print Server	47
File Server	4	BTrieve VAP 5.0	4B
Job Server	5	SQL VAP	4C
Gateway	6	Xtree Network Version	4D
Print Server	7	BTrieve VAP 4.1	50
Archive Queue	8	Print Queue User	53
Archive Server	9	WANcopy Utility	72
Job Queue	A	TES-NetWare for VMS	7A
Administration	B	NetWare Access Server	98
NAS SNA Gateway	21	Portable NetWare	9E
NACS	23	NetWare 386.x	107
Remote Bridge Server	24	Communications Executive	130
Bridge Server	26	NNS Domain	133
TCP/IP Gateway	27	NetWare 386 Print Queue	137
Gateway	29	Wildcard	FFFFFFFF

the name server will respond with the full internet address of that remote network workstation. Once the originator of that packet receives a response from the name server, it can then attempt a connection.

While a centralized name service is good, it does have its deficiencies. The name server's full internet address must be manually entered in every network station on the network; otherwise, the network station will not know where the name server is. (This entry is entered into a static table and does not have to be entered in every time a name service is needed.) If the centralized name service is down, users must manually find and enter the full internet address of the remote network station. While all these problems are easily overcome, NetWare provides dynamic name service capabilities, plus much more, through their SAP protocol. This protocol is used for server names only.

NetWare name services operate just a little differently than standard name services such as that in the example of the Clearinghouse Name Service of the XNS protocol. There is not a central name server on the network. The NetWare operating system provides a function that allows any server on the internet to broadcast to the network some of the server services that it can provide by name and type. These services are shown in Table 5.5. This information is propagated throughout a NetWare internet by the routers on the internet (including any bridges or routers) through the use of the following types of packets: broadcast SAP information packets and SAP query packets (also known as Service Identity Packet).

A Service Identity Packet is broadcast from each active server to inform the routers or other servers on the internet of the services that particular server offers. A Service Query Packet is used the find any other active server on the network. SAP is a protocol that uses IPX encapsulation to transmit and receive these packets. Routers and other file servers, not user workstations, maintain tables that contain the address of the server and the service that it provides to the network.

The SAP makes the process of adding and removing servers and their services on the internetwork dynamic. When file servers are initialized, they broadcast their available services (again, the services are shown in Table 5.5) using the SAP. When the file servers are brought down, they will broadcast that their services will no longer be available using the SAP process. Routers, in turn, will then delete this information from their tables.

The SAP process allows workstations on the network to find a service and to connect to that service. This is accomplished completely transparently by the user. All the user wants to know is where a server is in order to connect to it. Using SAP, this is easily accomplished.

The propogation of this information is very similar to the way routing tables are updated using the RIP protocol. Using the SAP, network workstations can determine which services are available on the network. Inside a SAP broadcast packet is up to seven entries. Each entry will contain a server name, the service number, and the full internetwork address of the server that contains a service. Obtaining the full internet address of the server is important for a workstation and server to communicate with this address. They do not communicate using names.

SAP tables are maintained in the routers. SAP is not part of the routing services, but routers will update their SAP tables in each of the routers, just like the RIP protocol. Each router on the IPX internet would contain a table of SAP entries. Tables are maintained in each of the routers known as Server Information Table—all services known on the entire internetwork as maintained in each router. Any service that a client wishes to connect to will be provided by the client's local router. Refer to Fig. 5.9.

Figure 5.9 shows servers and workstations on an internet. The file server broadcasts information about the services that it is providing to the network. This information is received by the router and maintained in the SAP table of the router. Workstations at the top of the figure, when they need to communicate with a file server, will broadcast SAP Query packets to the network. The router will perform a SAP table lookup for the workstation and, if a service name is found, it will return the full internet address of the server so that the workstation may connect to it. At the bottom of the figure, the workstation will ignore any SAP updates that the file server broadcasts. It will perform only SAP Queries just like the workstations at the top of the figure. File servers have the routing function built in so they can act as both requestors and responders for RIP or SAP. The file server and router will update each other.

Like all other NetWare services, the SAP process uses IPX to broadcast its services. Figure 5.10 shows this packet format. The first entry in this packet identifies the operation being requested. It can perform five different operations as follows:

1. A network workstation request for the name and address of the nearest server of a certain type
2. A general request, by a router, for the names and addresses of either all the servers or all the servers of a certain type on the internetwork
3. Respond to Get Nearest Server request (from a workstation initializing onto the network, discussed later in this chapter) or a general request
4. Periodic updates by servers or routers
5. An information change broadcast

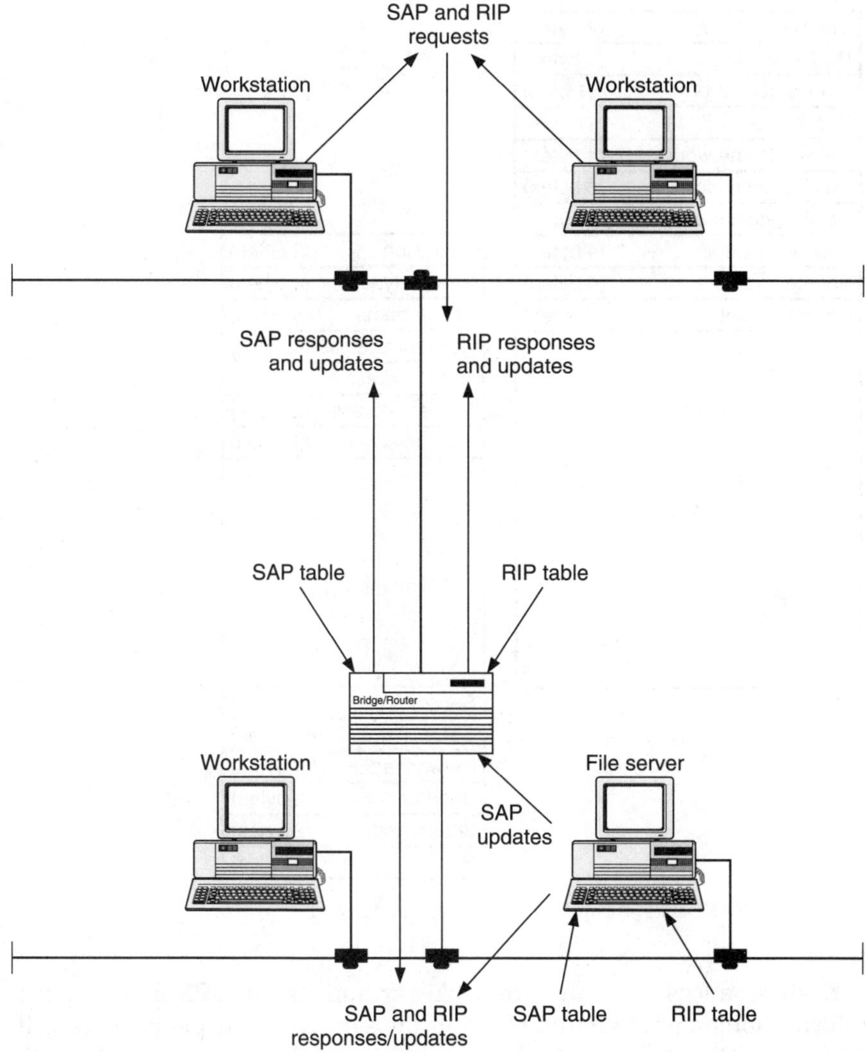

Figure 5.9 SAP and RIP processes on the network.

Any server that is implementing this protocol will contain a small database (a SAP table) to store accumulated broadcasted server names, service types, and their associated network addresses. This table is shown in Table 5.6. These tables are kept in the servers and the routers that are present on the network. With these tables, a NetWare workstation may then broadcast a packet to the network to query information from the servers and/or routers. The purpose of keeping these tables in the routers allows file servers to be located on a different LAN than the workstation. Routers will respond to workstation queries.

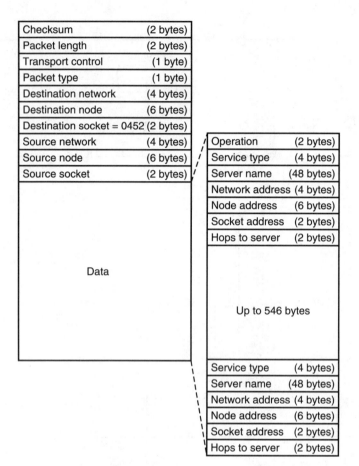

Checksum	(2 bytes)
Packet length	(2 bytes)
Transport control	(1 byte)
Packet type	(1 byte)
Destination network	(4 bytes)
Destination node	(6 bytes)
Destination socket = 0452	(2 bytes)
Source network	(4 bytes)
Source node	(6 bytes)
Source socket	(2 bytes)
Data	

Operation	(2 bytes)
Service type	(4 bytes)
Server name	(48 bytes)
Network address	(4 bytes)
Node address	(6 bytes)
Socket address	(2 bytes)
Hops to server	(2 bytes)
Up to 546 bytes	
Service type	(4 bytes)
Server name	(48 bytes)
Network address	(4 bytes)
Node address	(6 bytes)
Socket address	(2 bytes)
Hops to server	(2 bytes)

Figure 5.10 SAP packet format. (*Courtesy Novell, Inc.*)

Each broadcast SAP update packet tranmitted by IPX may contain information on a maximum of seven file servers. Multiple packets will be transmitted if the SAP table is larger than this.

SAP operation

When the file server is first started, its SAP operation will place the appropriate entries (the services that users may connect to) in its SAP table in the format shown in Table 5.6. The SAP process will then broadcast its table out all its directly connected ports (network interface cards, serial lines, etc.). These SAP broadcasts are transmitted with the physical address set to all FFs. This is a local network broadcast in that the routers will not forward this onto other networks. Once a file server/router has updated its table (including adding one to the

TABLE 5.6 A Sample SAP Table

Server name	Server's full internet address (MAC address, network number, socket number)	Server type (as listed in Table 5.5)	Hops to server (number in the transport control field)	Time since changed (in seconds)	NIC number (if in a PC server; otherwise, port number on the router)
Server 1	02608c01020: 00000002 0451	4	1	20	3
Print server	02608c025678 00000003 0451	7	2	50	4

hop count for that router), that router will broadcast its updated SAP table to its directly connected networks. In this way, all information will eventually be distributed (propagated) to all file servers and routers on the Novell internet. This will update all other servers and routers on those directly connected networks that a new server has become available, and all other servers will know which services are available on that server.

After this initial broadcast the server will then request SAP tables from other servers on its directly connected network. Other file servers and routers will respond to this request, and the information returned will allow the new server to find other servers on the network and build a SAP table for its use.

Once fully operational, the server will broadcast its SAP table to its directly connected network every 60 seconds. This is known as a *periodic broadcast.* The initiation procedure for those devices that are not file servers (i.e., routers only) is the same, but it will not accomplish the first initiation broadcast. This is because routers only route packets and do not provide server services. Routers will initialize their SAP table and transmit an initial request for SAP information from other routers or file servers on the network and then start a timer which will broadcast its SAP table every 60 seconds.

When a router or file server is gracefully brought down (i.e., it has not crashed or it has not been abruptly powered off), it will notify the network of this by broadcasting to the network that it will no longer broadcast its SAP table of servers. This is transmitted on the directly connected networks of that file server or router. This information will eventually be propagated to the rest of the network by the remaining file servers or routers on the internet.

SAP requests to find a server, using the server's name, are usually made by a workstation to find a server or some type of service. The SAP process in the router will answer this request. With this response, the workstation will extract the full internet address of the server out of the response packet and attempt a connection using that information. This internet address returned by the router may be a server on the local network or a server on a remote network. If the server is across a router or many routers, the network workstation will issue a Get Local Target packet (RIP request) to the local network and that's how it will find a router to use. It will address the packet accordingly and transmit the packet to the router.

Now that the networks providing services have been defined, the final part of this chapter explains how NetWare uses these entities to provide file and print services on a network. All the functions previously discussed must be operational for NetWare to operate. The file/print service architecture (workstation-to-server communication) operates over these functions. The discussion on the NetWare interface will be accomplished in two parts: the workstation and the file server. This will be discussed in a moment.

Data integrity. Novell NetWare does not use a separate transport layer (for example, SPP*). Transport-layer services provide reliable packet delivery. It uses connection IDs, sequence numbers, and acknowledgment packets to number or acknowledge the incoming packets or outgoing packets. In this way, the transport-layer software can determine if a packet has been lost during transmission. The file server knew what the last sequence number was and, if the next packet (Novell only, in this case) is not one above that previous sequence number, a packet was lost somewhere.

Sequence numbers are intialized to a 1 following the connection sequence packet exchange between a workstation and its connected file server, and will be incremented by 1 as each packet is received. Novell (and XNS for that matter) use packet-level sequencing as opposed to byte-level sequencing. Byte-level sequencing, like the one used in TCP/IP, is accomplished by assigning a sequence number for each data *byte* in the packet. Packet-level sequencing is incremented by 1 for each *packet,* not bytes, submitted. Packet-level sequencing provides for and is accurate for high-performance LANs (Ethernet and Token Ring), for they use a highly reliable access method scheme. TCP/IP is a byte-level sequencing scheme since its initial use was over noisy copper synchronous lines. TCP/IP was not architected for LANs.

---

* Novell does support an XNS SPP look-alike known as Sequence Packet Exchange (SPX). This is used for peer-to-peer services and not for shell-to-server connections and communications.

Therefore, its sequencing had to be more regimental in order to guarantee the reliability of the data.

NetWare has embedded the transport-layer function into its network operating system of NCP. Novell uses a stop-and-wait mechanism (or a window size of 1) packet sequencing. This means that each packet transmitted by the workstation must have an acknowledgment by the file server before the next transmission from the workstation is allowed to occur. This type of sequencing is used with the current release of NetWare—every packet sent must have an acknowledgment. There is a new version of the shell and NCP currently in beta test (as of this writing), known as *packet burst mode.* This product allows for multiple packets to be transmitted without an acknowledgment for each packet. This means that the server will acknowledge a sequence of packets, not just one at a time. This speeds up some NetWare networks 400 to 500 percent. As of this writing, this software has not yet been released by Novell. The following text will refer to the older method of sequencing. The new methods are fully discussed at the end of this chapter. This is available under Novell 4.0.

Right after a connection has been established, the connected *file server* will tell the *shell* what unique (not duplicated) connection number has been assigned to it. This connection number allows the file server to differentiate between users that are attached to this file server.

The shell (on the workstation) starts the packet transfer by setting the initial data packet with a sequence number of 1. The server will acknowledge this packet and return the same sequence number. The server will place this sequence number into an entry as its connection table (shown later). The workstation will wait for a response from the file server with that same transmitted sequence number. Once it receives that response packet from the file server, the next packet (for that connection to that file server) will increment by 1.

If the shell does not receive a response packet, it will submit the request again until it receives a response from its server or it reaches a certain upper limit.

When the server receives the next packet from a particular connection, it will extract the sequence number from the received packet and compare it with the sequence number entry as its connection table. If the sequence number equals the sequence number in its connection table, the server will respond to the request again (duplicate the response). If the sequence number is one more than the entry in the connection table, this represents a new request and the file server will respond to the new packet. This will be continued in more detail under the "File Server" heading.

This concludes the discussion on the LAN operating interface for NetWare.

An Introduction to Workgroup Client-Server Computing

Throughout the following text, refer to Fig. 5.11. This figure shows a network that has file and print services available from a server. The user's workstation accesses the server for these services over the network.

The 1980s brought on the importance of file servers and the ability of users to communicate to file servers through a LAN. The applications that originally ran on a user's PC were now located on the file server, located somewhere on the network. This file server would service user requests (file and print) from their PCs. The majority of requests made to a server are file and print.

Physical and virtual drives

A connection to a file server is accomplished through the concept known as *virtual drives*. Drives that are physically located on a user's

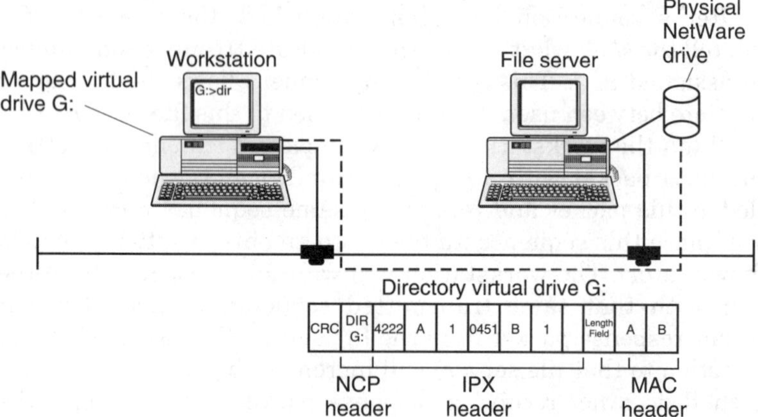

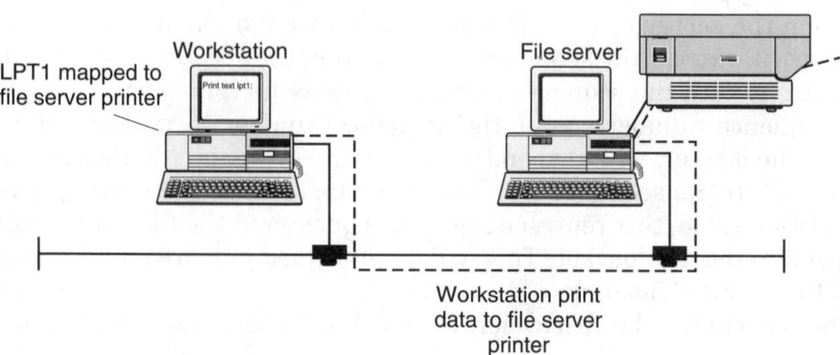

Figure 5.11 A network with virtual file and print services.

PC are known as physical drives. DOS is the operating system that allows access to these physical drives (usually denoted by the letters A:, B:, C:, D:, and E:). These are the physical drives that are located on the local workstation. The network operating system (NCP) grants access to the file server's file system through the use of these virtual drives. In other words, the user will send a command to the file server, requesting not only a connection to the file server, but access to the file server's file and directory system. If a workstation has a local drive assignment of C:, it should not be used for a virtual drive (a drive assigned to the file server connection).

On the user's workstation, the virtual drive identifier goes right along with DOS. The virtual drive to the workstation may have a drive identifier of F: or G:. The drive identifier is requested when the user asks for a connection to a server. With Novell, the command is the MAP command. The MAP command, used from the DOS workstation command prompt, will allow the user to use the file server as an extension of its own file service.

For example, if an application resided on the file server and the user logged in successfully, the user (at the command prompt on the workstation) might use the MAP command to link to a directory on the file server using the following command:

```
MAP G:= NOVA/sys:public
```

Using this command would give the user access to the directory public on the file server named NOVA. If access rights to this directory were granted for the user, the user would switch to that virtual drive and begin to use that directory of files as if the files were located on the user's physical drives. The shell on the workstation will know whether any commands typed on the user's workstation were meant for the server or whether the command should be passed to DOS on the user's local workstation. Figure 5.12 shows how the shell intercepts all DOS commands to see if the commands are meant for the network. If the commands are not, the shell will pass the command back to DOS for local processing. Otherwise, the shell will format a network command and give this information to IPX to be passed over the network. The shell is part of the NCP program.

Running an application from the virtual drive. When an application is requested from a virtual drive, the application will not run on the file server. Instead, it is as if the user had the application stored locally. The file server will download the file to the requesting workstation, and then the application is run locally on that workstation. The file server will remain idle (except for housekeeping chores) until the next request is received. When the user is done with the application, the

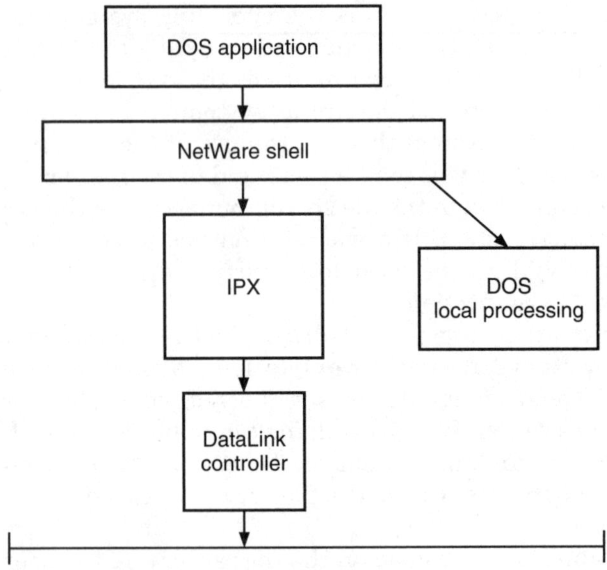

Figure 5.12 Shell command interception.

user will exit the application. The application file is exited as a normal DOS application exit. The connection to the file server is still active. Only the application was exited. The file server does nothing here.

The application is not uploaded to the file server. If the user wanted to store data files from the application on the file server, the data files would be uploaded from the user's PC to the file server and then the application would exit.

Printing using a server

File servers also contain the ability to accept print requests from users on the network. This is accomplished using queues. Using the MAP command, the user would redirect the local printer port (LPT1:, for example) to a named printer queue on the file server. The shell program intercepts all calls made to the local LPTx: port from the applications requests. The shell maps this request to a network call and gives the request to IPX to deliver to the file server. The file server would decode the request and send the information to a print queue on the file server. A print queue is nothing more than an area that contains print requests. Usually, the entries in the file server's print queue are stored as files on the file server's local disk. When an entry in a print queue is ready to be printed, the print service on the server would read the information from its disk and print it to its printer. By redirecting (or mapping, in NetWare terms) the workstation's local printer port to a file server queue, any information that was printed to the local printer would then be redirected to the file server and it would print the information out on the file server printer. The shell would intercept all printer activity to see if the information needs to be redirected, or mapped, to a server service.*

There are many advantages to client-server computing:

1. *Software updates.* Updating an application program need be done only on the file server and not on all the workstations.
2. *Lower printer costs.* Only one laser printer needs to be purchased, instead of one for each user.
3. *Central respository for files.* Only one copy of an application program needs to be loaded (depending on the number of users).
4. *Relaxed PC requirements.* Only the file server has to be the most powerful computer (depending on the user's application).
5. *Electronic messaging (electronic mail).* Files and messages could be moved between users through the file server. This eliminates the "sneakernet" and reduces the amount of paper associated with corporate interoffice mail.

This concept will be covered in greater detail in the following text. Users were granted a connection by the file server and then the users could access the files on the file servers (given the correct permission requirements).

The NetWare interface

The final entity on a Novell network is the NetWare interface. This is more commonly known as the user interface. Actually, there are many interfaces that a workstation or server may use to transmit information to a network. These interfaces include: a datagram interface, a virtual connection interface, a session interface, and a workstation shell interface. The subject of the following text is to explain the workstation shell interface and the file server interface. It should be noted that any application may use any of these interfaces to transmit data on the network. In other words, an application running on a network workstation need not use the NetWare shell to talk on the network. Any application may call the IPX interface directly, therefore bypassing the shell, or may choose to call a session interface such as NetBIOS (E-mail programs, SNA programs).

---

* The information given here pertains to Novell NetWare, but the text is generic to any file/print client-server system similar to Novell NetWare.

DOS. All DOS function calls in a NetWare environment are passed to DOS from the shell. The shell intercepts all calls from the workstation and determines whether the information is for the network or if it should pass the information to DOS. DOS does not know that the call was passed to it from the shell program and will process the call as if the call were made directly from the application program.

This method of intercepting the DOS calls before DOS gets a chance to read them started from the initial release of NetWare. In those days, most system calls (disk calls, screens calls, serial port, and parallel port calls) were made directly to the hardware, sometimes through a prom known as ROMBIOS. Therefore, the shell interface intercepted these calls and then made the decision: Is it a network call or is it a local DOS function call? With these earlier releases of DOS, DOS had no idea that a network was installed and could not pass network calls to NetWare. So NetWare passed the calls to DOS.

Today, DOS is network-aware, and Microsoft provides for a simple way to make system calls. Most system calls are made through a software interrupt known as INT21. All DOS system calls are made using this interrupt. The shell still intercepts these calls just as it intercepted the previous hardware calls.

IPX. This software interface handles the transmission and reception of network data to and from the shell program. It envelopes the data handed to it from the shell and transmits it to the network. Upon reception of a packet from the network, it will strip off the IPX envelope and pass the data to the NCP shell program or the server NCP program.

Network interface. This interface may be in the form of a network interface card (Ethernet, Token Ring, or ARCnet). Data passed to it from IPX is enveloped with the particular network interface header information (network addressing and CRC error checking) and transmitted on the physical cable plant. This network interface will also receive packets from the cable plant, strip off its headers, and pass the rest of the information to IPX for processing.

Application. An application that is run on the workstation operates as a normal DOS application. Normally, the application is not network-aware (i.e., it does not know that it is operating on a network). An application would simply be started on the workstation as if it were to run locally. All calls that are made from the application are intercepted by the NetWare shell to see if the call is made to a network resource. Special application programs such as a mail package or a 3270 SNA terminal emulator may also run on this workstation. These types of applications are usually written to a special interface called NetBIOS.

All NetBIOS calls are translated into IPX calls for transmission on the network. NetBIOS over IPX has a packet type 20 (decimal).

A PC application on the workstation will make system (DOS) calls through an Interrupt sequence known as INT21. These are DOS system calls to ask the workstation to provide some type of processing function (read a file, get a directory listing, delete a file). All INT21 calls are intercepted by the shell program to see if these calls are meant for a network device. If they are, the DOS INT21 function call will be mapped to an NCP call and passed to IPX for transmission on the network. If the call is for a local device, the shell will pass the call to DOS and wait for the next INT21 function call.

IPX data contains the data submitted by the application program and maybe control information from NCP.

The workstation

NetWare clients operate on many different types of operating systems (OS/2, Unix, DOS, and even SNA). The following text conforms to the DOS interface. A summary of the other operating environments is given at the end of the chapter.

There are two files that are executed in a DOS workstation that allow a NetWare system to communicate: NETx.com and IPX.com. These are not device drivers, but are executable programs started from the command line interface (usually started from a start-up file like autoexec.bat on DOS PCs). For a workstation on a Novell network, the NetWare interface is contained in an executable program commonly named NETx.com (x signifies the major version of the current active DOS being used on the workstation). There is a version of the shell called NETx.com (where x is literally part of the file name) that will automatically determine the operating system version and start up the correct shell for that version of DOS. This is available under NetWire on Compuserve.

Any data that is destined for a local device on the workstation (the disk drive or printer) is transferred to DOS by the shell for local processing. The shell maps the DOS request to a network-type request and will pass this mapped information to IPX for delivery to the network.

In order for data to pass between the workstation and the file server, there must be some mechanism in the workstation to capture the data and format it for use on the network. This mechanism is known as the NetWare *shell*. Refer to Fig. 5.12. NETx.com is the shell program and it is a terminate-and-stay resident (TSR) program in the workstation that intercepts all input (from the user at the workstation) as if it were the actual DOS command interpreter. In other words, the shell intercepts all information on the workstation to see if the data is for the network or if the data should be passed to DOS for local processing. Also, the NetWare shell is the interface between an application (WordPerfect, Lotus 1-2-3, etc.), running on a workstation and its associated file server. For the purposes of this chapter, input to the shell comes from two places: (1) an application or (2) directly from the user.

As stated before, it is the NetWare MAP command that redirects local device identifiers (D:, E:, LPT1:, etc.) to the server, whether this device is a virtual disk driver or a printer queue. The MAP command also establishes a table of mappings. In this table will be a listing of all the MAP redirect requests that were issued successfully. This table will contain a listing of the drive identifier and the mapped name of the server that it belongs to. For the printer, the table will contain the local physical printer port identifier (LPT1:, etc.) and the name of the server and printer queue to which the mapped printer port was redirected. In this way, the shell interface will know whether the imputed DOS function call should go to the network or be handed to DOS for processing. If the call does not map to a virtual drive or printer queue in the table, it is handed to DOS.

For example, if you mapped the E: drive to the file server NOVA and typed into the command prompt "DIR E:", the shell would intercept this and determine that you wanted a directory listing of the E: drive. The shell does a lookup on its table and determines that the E: is a mapped virtual drive to the file server NOVA. The shell would format a packet with the NCP command for the DIR and submit this to IPX for delivery. Once the file server receives this packet, it will process the packet (do a directory command on the mapped portion of its hard disk) and return the results to the workstation that requested the DIR (using IPX for delivery). The shell would then print the directory listing to the workstation's screen.

This action is taken whether an application submits a DOS function call or whether the user types in the function call directly to the command prompt.

These operations of the shell include establishing, maintaining, and disconnecting a connection from a file server, as well as file-related operations such as creating, reading, or deleting a file. The shell will provide any file operations that you may perform on your workstation without a network.

Connection establishment

Before any communications take place between a workstation and its associated file server, a connection must be established between the two. Table 5.7 shows how this is accomplished. The numbers under the CALL heading are shown in the sequence of events. The shell uses a combination of the processes of NCP, RIP, and SAP to establish a con-

TABLE 5.7 Initial Connection Sequence of the NetWare Shell

Call	Source	Destination	Protocol
1. Get Nearest Server	Client	Broadcast	SAP
2. Give Nearest Server	Router	Client	SAP
3. Get Local Target	Client	Broadcast	RIP
4. Give Local Target	Router	Client	RIP
5. Create Connection	Client	File Server	NCP
6. Request Processed and Connection Number Assigned	File Server	Client	NCP
7. Propose Packet Size	Client	File Server	NCP
8. Return Maximum Packet Size	File Server	Client	NCP

nection to a file server. There are two methods that the shell can use to connect to a file server: (1) the shell program and (2) the preferred server shell.

The shell program. When IPX.com and NETx.com (IPX is loaded first) are loaded, the workstation will automatically attach to the first server that responds to it. This provides for fast login service to the network. During this process, the workstation will be able to identify its network number, if it does not already have it.

The response is an automatic connection to virtual drive seen as F: on the user's PC screen.* This gives the user access to two other utilities LOGIN.exe and ATTACH.exe. These applications allow the user to log in to a file server and attach to another server (not the login server). Login.exe provides user authentication. Without this, the user has just logged into the network but has yet to log into any server. The user may then use the ATTACH commands to reach a desired network server. Table 5.8 shows this sequence of events.

To accomplish this, the shell must find the file server's address and the nearest route to that server. To find the server's address, the shell invokes the services of SAP. This is called the Get Nearest Server Request. All routers on the local network (the network that the workstation is attached to) should respond with the SAP information. The contents of this information are: the nearest server's name, its full internetwork address, and the number of hops required to reach the server (how many routers are between the shell and its requested server).

Once this information has been received by the shell, it will try to find the best route to a server. The shell will invoke the routing services of IPX for this request. This process is known as the Get Local

* The drive ID will be one more than the lastdrive statement in config.sys. If none is stated, F: will be used.

TABLE 5.8 LOGIN.exe Sequence

1. Query Bindery for Preferred Shell	Client	File Server X	NCP
2. Address of Preferred Server	File Server X	Client	NCP
3. Get Local Target	Client	Broadcast	RIP
4. Give Local Target	File Server X Router	Client	RIP
5. Create Connection	Client	File Server Y	NCP
6. Request Processed and Connection Number Assigned	File Server Y	Client	NCP
7. Propose Packet Size	Client	File Server Y	NCP
8. Return Maximum Packet Size	File Server Y	Client	NCP
9. Destroy Service Connection	Client	File Server X	NCP

Target request. When the response packet is received, IPX will compare the network number returned (this network number was obtained through the Get Nearest Server request) in this request with its own network number. If the two numbers match, IPX will inform the shell that the server is located on this local network and to send requests directly to the server on the local network.

But if the network numbers do not match, IPX will submit a broadcast routing information request to the network through RIP request packet. The routers located on the local network will respond with the known routes to this server. IPX will find the shortest route, discard all others, and will return the address of that router to the shell. The shell then uses the address and submits a Create Connection Request packet to the router (for a connection to the server, not to the router). These requests are illustrated in Table 5.8.

The IPX header will contain the actual addresses of the file server that it wishes to communicate with. The packet will then be transmitted on the network and accepted by the router. The router will look at the final destination address (destination network number) and route the packet to that network.

Preferred server shell. There is a new shell known as the *preferred server shell,* which contains new features that enable the user to tell the shell which server it wishes to connect to. This may be either at the command line or located in a file called SHELL.CFG. As shown in Table 5.9, the first eight steps are still the same. The ninth step causes a lookup in the nearest server's database table to acquire the preferred server's address. Steps 11 and 12 might not be used if the preferred server is on the same local network (not separated by a router). The shell skips this and submits a connection request directly to the server.

One other difference between the old shell and the new shell is the process of Give Nearest Server responses. Previous shells accept the first response they receive and discard all other responses. The prob-

TABLE 5.9 Preferred Server Shell Connection Sequence

Call	Source	Destination	Protocol
1. Get Nearest Server	Client	Broadcast	SAP
2. Give Nearest Server	Router	Client	SAP
3. Get Local Target	Client	Broadcast	RIP
4. Give Local Target	Router	Client	RIP
5. Create Connection	Client	File Server X	NCP
6. Request Processed and Connection Number Assigned	File Server X	Client	NCP
7. Propose Packet Size	Client	File Server X	NCP
8. Return Maximum Packet Size	File Server X	Client	NCP
9. Query Bindery for Preferred Shell	Client	File Server X	NCP
10. Address of Preferred Server	File Server X	Client	NCP
11. Get Local Target	Client	Broadcast	RIP
12. Give Local Target	File Server X Router	Client	RIP
13. Create Connection	Client	File Server Y	NCP
14. Request Processed and Connection Number Assigned	File Server Y	Client	NCP
15. Propose Packet Size	Client	File Server Y	NCP
16. Return Maximum Packet Size	File Server Y	Client	NCP
17. Destroy Service Connection	Client	File Server X	NCP

lem that arose with this is a server will respond even if it has no free connections available for the shell. Shells will then not be able to establish a connection to that server.

The preferred server shell will accept the first response, but it will save up to the next four responses it receives. This is used in case a connection cannot be made to the first response. If the first server response cannot be connected to, the shell will use the next response and try to establish a connection to that server.

Logging in to a server. Anytime after the initial connection is made, users may then log in to a file server. The utility LOGIN transmits the user's name and password to the file server for validation. LOGIN can also create a new connection to a file server, if prompted to on the command line. Table 5.8 shows this. Please note that steps 3 and 4 are not needed if the file server is located on the same local network.

During this connection process, the shell and the file server will exchange a few packets. (This is commonly called *handshaking.*) The workstation will request of a file server that a connection number be assigned to the shell and the two need to negotiate a maximum packet size that each will accept.

A workstation may attach to eight different servers at one time, no matter where the servers are located on the NetWare internet. This means that a workstation does not have a one-on-one relationship with just one server. A shell will maintain a local table that has entries in it for all the connections that it has on the network. Looking at shell connection Table 5.10, each entry in this table contains the name and full internetwork address of the server it is connected to. If the shell and its connected server are separated by a router, the address of that router will be placed in the Router's Node Address Field. Next, the shell's connection number to that server is stored, along with the current sequence number. Finally, there are two time-outs stored: Receive Time-out and Max Time-out.

The Receive Time-out is dynamically set and is the amount of time that a shell will wait for a response from a server. If this timer expires, the shell will retransmit a packet to the server. Once set, the timer will change due to changing network conditions. Changing conditions may be a router going down, the file server becoming congested (experienced by the number of retransmissions count), or the file server response speeds up.

Max Time-out value is preset at operating system initialization and represents the maximum value for timing out a connection.

Once the preceding connection sequence and a login has been established, the shell will place all needed entries into a table. Using this table, the shell will know which packet is which and where a packet should be sent.

Again, please note that the full internet address consists of the MAC address, the network number, and the socket on which the service is available. The combination of these numbers is call the *full internet address* or the *socket address.*

File server concepts

The server. When a workstation requests a service of a file server, it builds a packet and submits the packet to the network for delivery to

TABLE 5.10 Shell's Connection Table

Server's name	Full internet address	Intermediate router's node address	Packet sequence number	Connection number	Receive time-out	Maximum time-out

the server. Once the server receives the packet, it needs to know what operation to perform for the workstation. It could be a connection request, a data request, or maybe a print request. In any case, the server needs to know the operation.

In the packet received by the server will be an NCP function code that the server will use to determine which operation is to be performed by the requesting packet.

Novell file servers provide many services as detailed below:

Accounting Services. This service keeps track of transactions that occur on the server and it provides a detailed output of service usage.

AppleTalk Filing Protocol (AFP). This service provides the capability to allow both DOS and Apple files to reside on the server. These files can be accessed by both DOS and Apple personal computers.

Bindery Services. A bindery is simply a database and is used in the server as a lookup table to provide information on resources to clients.

Communication Services. This service has many features, including providing an interface for application programs to extension services of asynchronous communication services (ACS).

Connection services. The connection between a client workstation and its file server.

Directory and File Services. Allows users to manage files on the file server.

Message Service. Allows broadcasting of messages (up to 55 bytes in length) to other servers, clients, or both.

Print Services. Allows a client to access the server for use of the printer services through the use of queues. Network workstations do not attach directly to a server's printer. They attach to a queue name which, in turn, is used by the print service to access the server physical printer.

Value Added Processes (VAPs). For NetWare 2.1x, these are applications that are not Novell-native. These are external programs that run in a Novell server such as a database program or an electronic mail (E-mail) system. In other words, these are applications that run external to the server's NCP, but act like a direct server service.

NetWare Loadable Modules (NLM). For NetWare 3.x, these are applications similar to VAPs. The applications access the NetWare operating system and act as a NetWare service. These applications are developed from third-party application developers. These are, in a sense, VAPs for NetWare 3.x.

A file server may accept many connections from remote workstations and applications, and the process of managing these connections is assisted by the use of a server connection table. As shown in Table 5.11, the file server maintains a table of connections and associated specifics to each connection.

Address entries. Used for supplying the MAC header addresses to response packets. It is also used for security. When the server is presented with a service request, the request contains the connection number of the requestor. The server will match the packet's full IPX internetwork address (see Table 5.12) with this connection and associated address in the table. If there is not a match, the server will discard the request.

Sequence number. Used for packet-level error checking. The data-link layer will provide bit-level data integrity and, if there was any error in the packet during reception, the data link will discard the packet. The problem here is that the data link will not inform the upper-layer software (the shell or IPX) that an error occured. A method is needed to ensure that all packets sent are received correctly, in the same order they were sent. This is the purpose of the sequence number and is part of Novell's implementation of transport-layer software. Each single packet sent must be responded to by the file server. This is commonly called a packet window with a length of one (known as the *stop and wait*). There is a new protocol design called *packet burst mode,* which allows multiple packets to be sent by the shell, which will require only one acknowledgment. The workstation initiates this number and uses it to ensure that it has received a response to a particular request.

In NetWare, the sequence number is the responsibility of the shell. Each service request that a shell submits to the server will contain a sequence number (an integer number). NCP for the server will respond to this request to the workstation with the same sequence number. This request packet (received by the server) must contain the number that is one more than the previous packet; otherwise, the file server will think that it is a duplicated packet. If the sequence number is 2 or higher, the server will inform the workstation of the last known sequence number.

Error detection and correction. When a client is communicating with a file server, there will be conditions when a file server may not respond to a client's requests. These conditions are depicted in Figs. 5.13 and 5.14.

The main conclusion here is the file server fails to respond to a transmitted request. Three variations of this follow.

TABLE 5.11 File Server Connection Table

Connection number	Node address	Network address	Socket number	Sequence number	Watchdog count	Watchdog timer	NIC number	Intermediate routers address

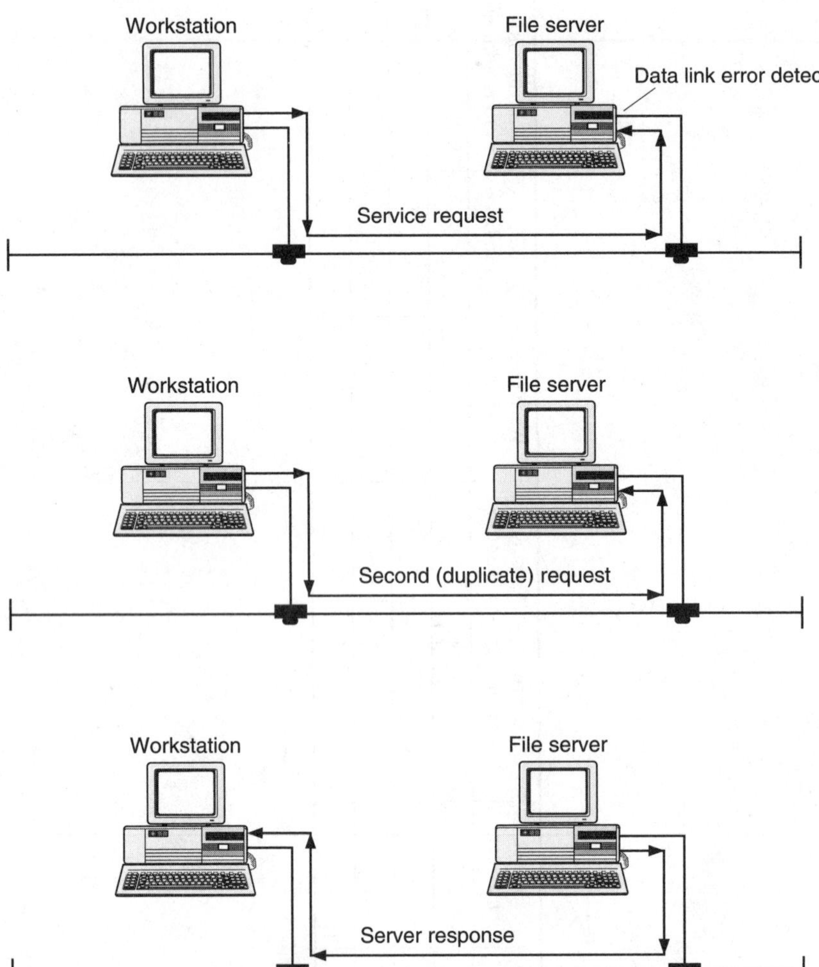

Figure 5.13 Packet timeouts and duplicate requests.

The File server does not respond to a request. This could be a case of the packet getting lost either going to the server or coming from the server. In either case, the shell does not receive a response. (See Fig. 5.13.)

Second, the file server missed the packet (it was busy doing something else) or it has not yet finished processing the request. The common cause here is a database lookup on a large file. In any case, the shell will time-out and retransmit the request. (See Fig. 5.14.)

Figure 5.13 shows a request being made of a file server where the data link (Ethernet card) finds an error in the packet. The packet is discarded and the data link does not inform the upper-layer software of

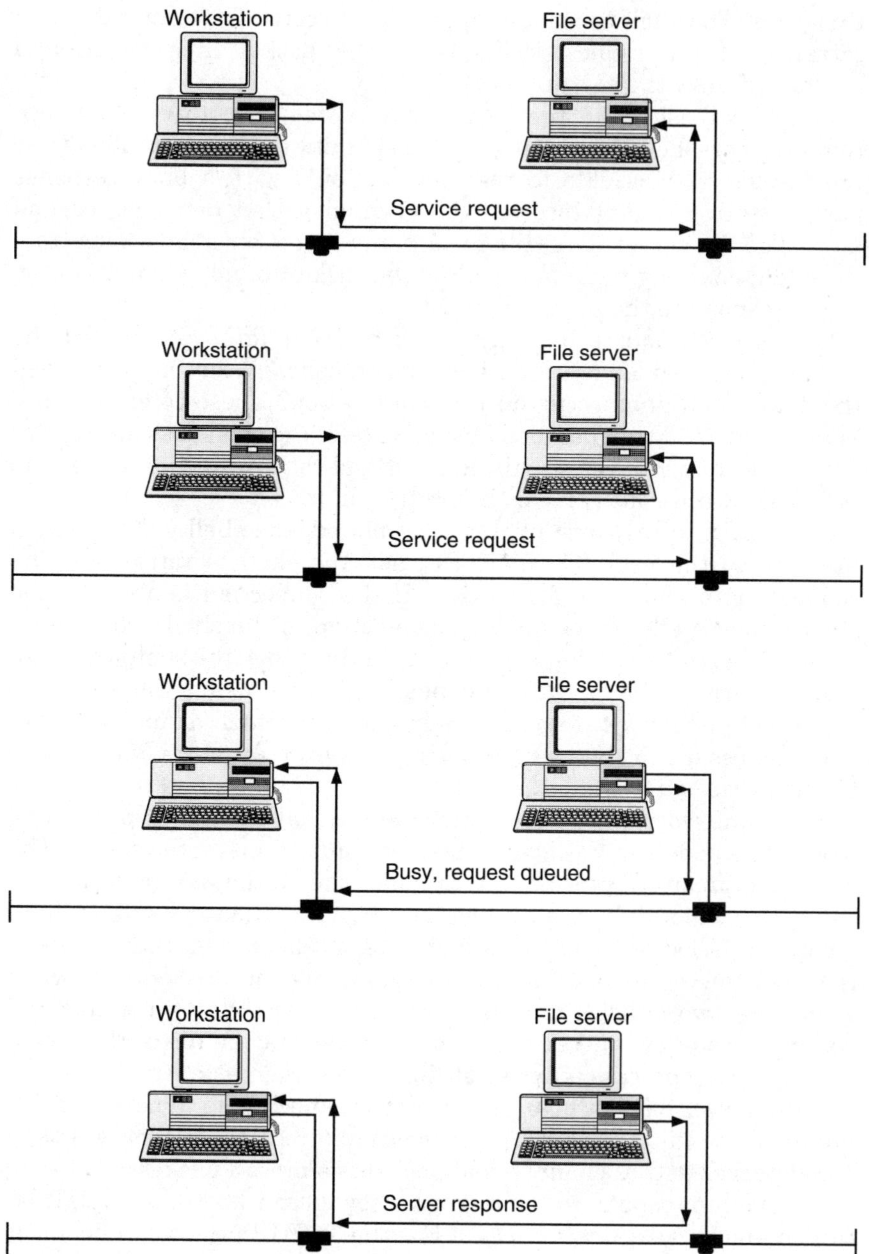

Figure 5.14 Queued packets on a busy file server.

this error. The shell times-out, adjusts its Receive Time-out value and retransmits the request. This time, the packet is accepted and responded to by the server.

Figure 5.14 shows a file server that is too busy to respond to a request. The shell times-out and retransmits the request. This time the file server was able to respond, but only with a busy response packet stating that it received the original packet and will respond later. The file server does this to stop any more retransmissions from the shell, enabling itself to complete the task at hand; when it is free, it will respond to the service request.

One other serious error may occur: *complete failures.* What if the server is powered off, or the server's disk crashes? What happens when the same conditions occur on the workstation? These conditions are known and are easily handled by NetWare. If the shell does not receive a response to a request, it will time-out and retransmit the request up to the MAX time-out value or IPX retry count.

If there is no response in this time period, the shell will display a message to the user. The user can ask the shell to retransmit the request or to abort the connection. If the connection is aborted, the shell removes all entries for that connection in the shell's connection table. If there are no other connections in this table, the shell will automatically try to connect to the nearest server using the sequence explained previously. If no servers respond, the shell displays the following message to the user: *You are not connected to any file servers. Current drive no longer valid.*

Since unused connections require additional RAM and processing power, it is beneficial to clear all unused connections on the server. The watchdog timer is a process that provides this. If the workstation fails, the server will still have a connection for that station in its table. If, in a certain period of time, the server does not hear from that workstation, the server invokes a process known as the *watchdog process.* There are two entities in this process: the watchdog timer and the watchdog counter. There is one timer for each of the file server's connections. This process is active all time the server is active.

If the server has not heard from client connection for a period of five minutes (the initial watchdog timer has expired), the server will send a poll packet to that client. A poll packet is simply a packet asking the client shell to respond to the request. (For those who know AppleTalk, this is known as a *tickle packet.*) For the TCP/IP protocol, a client or server can send a packet with a known bad sequence number to see if the other side responds. The other side of the connection, if alive, should respond with the next sequence number expected.

If the client responds to that packet, the watchdog timer is reset for that connection. If the poll is not responded to, the watchdog process will reset the timer to 0 and increment the watchdog counter from 0 to 1. It will then submit a poll every minute. If the client shell does not respond, it increments the counter by 1 until it has reached the count of 10 (indicating it has not heard from the client shell for 15 minutes—the original 5 minutes plus the poll count). At this point, that connection is cleared from the server's connection table. If the client responds, all watchdog timers and counters are reset and the process starts from step 1. Current versions of Novell 3.1x support adjustable watchdog timers.

Server system calls

The protocol that a workstation and a server use to communicate with one another is called the NetWare Core Protocol or NCP. This primarily runs at the session through the application layers of the OSI model. It is a language that the workstation and the server use to communicate.

This communication enables the workstation and the server to understand what each side of the connection needs. NCP is a proprietary protocol and the specification is not released by Novell.

The two main messages that NCP provides are request and reply messages. A request is usually made by the workstation and the reply comes from the server. NCP builds its own header into the packet and this is shown in Fig. 5.15*a* and *b*.

There are literally hundreds of requests that a workstation may ask of the server, but the basic requests are usually file reads and writes and printer queue requests. The request-field functions are shown in Table 5.12.

When a workstation requests a connection to a server, it will use the Create Service Connection Request, which is type 1111. When the workstation no longer needs this connection to the server, it will issue a Destroy Service Connection Request (5555).

Refer to Fig. 5.15*a*. As stated before, once a connection has been established between the server and the workstation (known as the *client*), there are literally hundreds of request that the workstation may ask of the server. Instead of providing a separate request function for each request, Novell provides a general request function (2222) for the workstation and then further down in the header is the specific request function called the *function code*. The function code could be a 76 to indicate to the file server to open a file. The file to open would be found further into the packet. The function code could be a 66 to indicate to the file server to close a file. The workstation shell program (NCP) creates an NCP header based on the information that it intercepted at the workstation. For example, if the user is in a WordPerfect file, and the user requests WordPerfect to open a file that was located

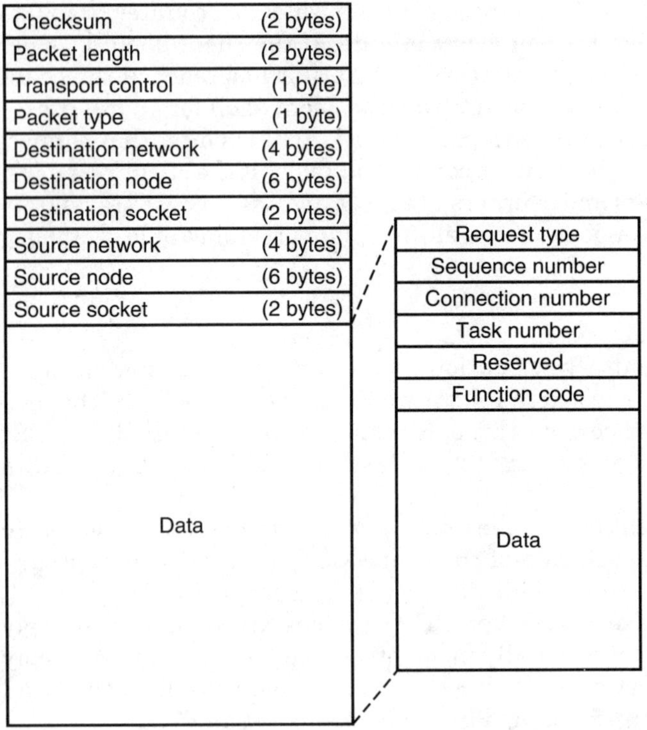

Figure 5.15 (*a*) Client NCP request packet format. (*Courtesy Novell.*)

on a server, NCP (the shell) would intercept this call and build an NCP header with function 2222 and function code of 76. The name of the file would be further down in the packet. The workstation would then request IPX to send this packet to the server.

The connection number contains the service connection number that was assigned by the server and given to the workstation during the connection login attempt between the workstation and the file server.

The task number indicates to the server which client task is making a request. The server uses the task number to deallocate resources when a task is completed.

The NCP reply packet is shown in Fig. 5.15*b*. The reply type can be:

1. 3333—Service reply
2. 7777—Burst mode connection
3. 9999—Request being processed

The only difference between the header and the request header is the addition of the completion code and the connection status fields.

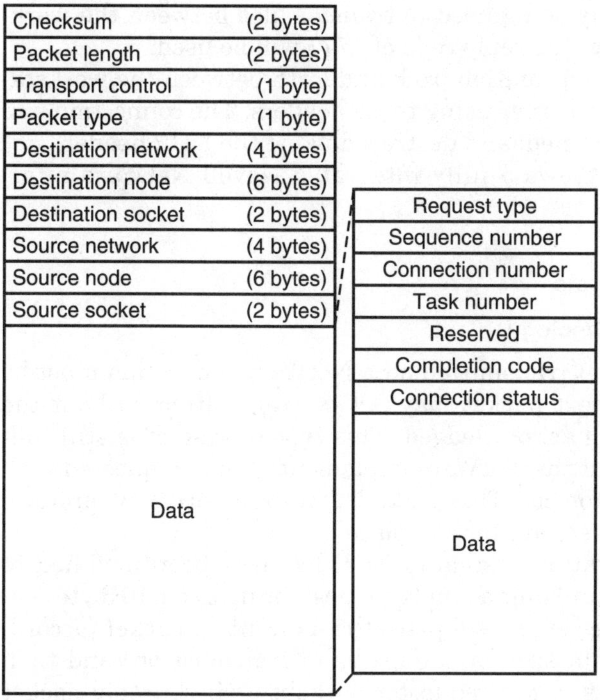

Field	Size
Checksum	(2 bytes)
Packet length	(2 bytes)
Transport control	(1 byte)
Packet type	(1 byte)
Destination network	(4 bytes)
Destination node	(6 bytes)
Destination socket	(2 bytes)
Source network	(4 bytes)
Source node	(6 bytes)
Source socket	(2 bytes)
Data	

Data
Request type
Sequence number
Connection number
Task number
Reserved
Completion code
Connection status
Data

Figure 5.15 (*b*) Server NCP reply packet format. (*Courtesy Novell.*)

This allows the server to inform the workstation as to whether the previous request was successfully completed. This is indicated by the field-of-completion code. A completion code of 0 indicates a successful completion. Any other value indicates it did not complete.

The connection status flag is used by the workstation to indicate the status of its connection to the file server. Every incoming packet received by the workstation will have this field. This packet is used by the server when the command DOWN is given to the file server. The DOWN command is used to gracefully bring the file server down. A workstation that receives this packet will know that the file server is no longer up.

TABLE 5.12 NCP Types

System calls	
1111	Create service connection
2222	Request (to the file server)
3333	Reply (from the file server)
5555	Destroy service connection
7777	Request burst mode
9999	Request being processed response (ACK with wait)

When burst mode is being used to transfer files between the workstation and the server, the reply code of 7777 will be used.

NCP will transfer information back and forth between the workstation and its associated server using these headers. The connection will be established, maintained, and destroyed using the NCP header.

Finally, Fig. 5.16 shows a fully integrated Novell NetWare internetwork.

NetWare Supplementals

Packet burst mode technology

Currently, each packet transmitted on a NetWare connection must be acknowledged. The next packet may not be transmitted without the previous packet being acknowledged. This type of system is still full-duplex connection, but the NetWare implementation is requested with a response type of protocol. This make NetWare a very slow protocol when large file transfers are to take place.

The NetWare operating system of NCP has now been modified to allow a requestor to transmit a single request for up to a 64-Kbyte segment of data. The file server will place the data into a packet (according the maximum data size for the media of transmission) and then reply with all packets to the requestor without a single reply packet being issued until the final packet has been transmitted. In some instances, this has improved response time by 300 to 400 percent.

This process is known as *providing a data window.* The window is how many packets may be transmitted without an acknowledgment. Packet burst mode takes this a couple of steps further. NCP provides a sliding window with a theoretical maximum of 125 (512-byte packets) before a reply packet needs to be generated.

The second process enacted by this protocol is the between-packet delay timer. This allows a window of packets to be transmitted, but there is a "settable" delay between the packets. This allows for the receiving to free up buffer space to hold more information, and also prevents a station from "hogging" the network while it transmits packets back-to-back.

Determination of these two values (the window size and the packet delay timer) is autonomous to each client on the network. Each workstation's shell configures these parameters based on the clock speed of the workstation, the amount of free RAM associated with the receiver's communication buffers, and the latency time between two communication workstations. Certain conditions—such as received bad packets and missed packets—are monitored while two network workstations are communicating. As these conditions improve, the parameters may change. This means that the values are dynamic in that they can change automatically depending on the conditions on the network.

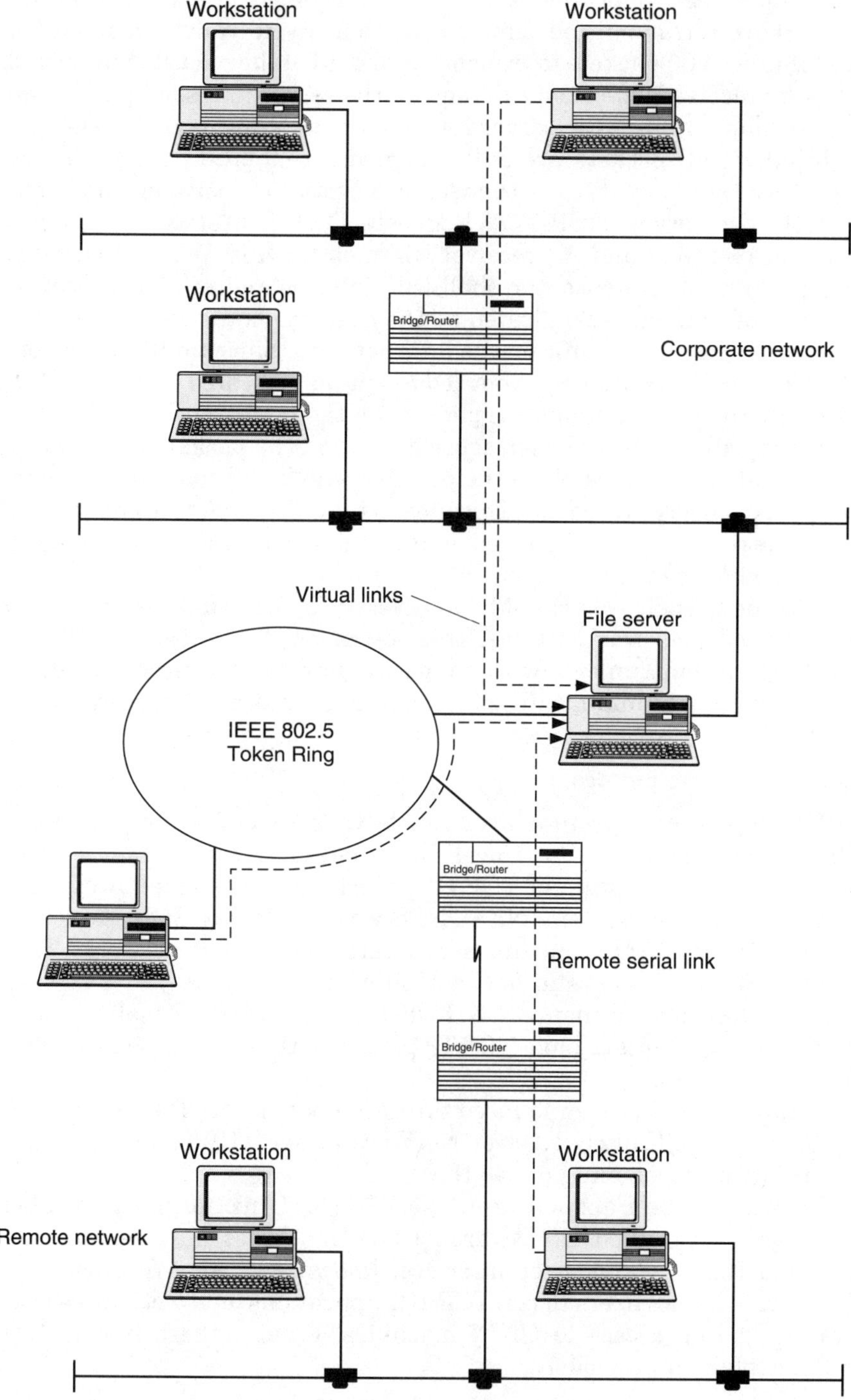

Figure 5.16 Fully integrated Novell NetWare internetwork.

One last feature of this new shell is that only the packets that are missed are retransmitted. This means that if you transfer a small file and it takes 200 packets to transmit it and all of the packets but 40 and 85 were received, the shell can request the server to resend packets 40 and 85 and not have the server retransmit the whole transmission.

In effect, all packets are still assigned a sequence number. These sequence numbers start at connection negotiation between the client and the file server (NCP 7777 Request). Each packet sent is given a sequence number and the receiver will monitor this. When a packet is received out of sequence, the shell will flag this and ask for a retransmission of that packet indicated by the missing sequence number.

There is also less traffic on the internetwork. Since multiple packets may be sent without any acknowledgment (as indicated by the window size), there are that many less packets on the network.

Speed will also be affected, especially when the packets have to traverse multiple routers. With the previous shell, each packet transmitted had to be acknowledged. This means that if the connection is across multiple routers, the acknowledgment must traverse the same routers. This can be a slow process.

This new shell is available for NetWare 3.11 and NetWare 4.0 servers and their workstations. This new mode of operation still allows the shell to communicate with nonpacket burst mode servers while at the same time communicating to the packet burst mode servers.

Multiple NetWare protocols

IPX is not the only protocol over which NetWare currently runs. With the advent NetWare 3.1x, Novell has allowed access to their system using the protocol suite of TCP/IP. At first, access was allowed with the Network File System (NFS). NFS was written by SUN Microsystems to allow UNIX machines to share disks on a network. This allows NetWare workstations not only to have access to NetWare servers, but also to mount UNIX disk drives. Next, Novell allowed IPX to be encapsulated in a TCP/IP packet so that it may be routed on TCP/IP network.

Finally, Novell has announced direct support for TCP/IP. Currently in beta, this will allow NCP or NetWare to use TCP/IP directly as a transport protocol, and not use IPX.

NetWare is one Unix platform—NetWare for Unix (formerly portable NetWare, now called UNIXware). UNIX machines may be accessed through their TCP/IP user interface, known as LAN Workplace for DOS. This allows users to run TCP/IP applications on a NetWare workstation, giving access to UNIX machines. Finally, there is NetWare NFS, explained previously.

LAN Workplace for DOS 4.0 uses a data-link library interface known as Open Data Link Interface. This interface is a library of routines that allows multiple protocols to reside on a workstation. In essence, these protocols are terminate-and-stay resident protocols that can be brought up and down at the user's discretion. This means that IPX can load as the transport for NetWare commands and data. At the same time, TCP/IP can be loaded so that connections may be made to both a NetWare file server and a TCP/IP host. ODI can multiplex both protocols on the same data link.

Chapter

6

Transmission Control Protocol/Internet Protocol (TCP/IP)

Transmission Control Protocol/Internet Protocol (TCP/IP) is one of today's most widely used networking protocols. A TCP/IP network is generally a heterogeneous network, meaning there are many different types of network computing devices attached.

Before TCP/IP, network protocols were proprietary and known to only a few individuals. Users and network administrators were held to proprietary network environments and proprietary network applications, which deterred network development and enhancement in all corporate environments. TCP/IP allows public access to network protocols and allows seamless integration between all computing environments that wish to operate in a network environment. Commercial success of this protocol happened unexpectedly. TCP/IP was never envisioned as a commercial network system and was not envisioned to gain the widespread use it has today. Had the open protocol of TCP/IP not flourished, the network environment would possibly be in the same situation as the operating system world was in the 1970s. Everyone had their own proprietary operating system, and users were stuck with one operating system. TCP/IP not only gave the network world the groundwork for future protocols (OSI), it allowed open access so that users may choose this network operating system without having to choose a single vendor along with it. We should be thankful for this. There are many more advantages to this protocol that will be pointed out throughout the text.

TCP/IP allowed for open communications to exist and also allowed for the proliferation of LAN to LAN to LAN to WAN connectivity between multiple operating environments. The only people hurt by this open protocol are the network companies that do not support it. All other companies have flourished based on it.

From this, one would tend to think that this operating system was developed by a large-scale R&D center like that of IBM or DEC. It wasn't. It was developed by a team of research-type people, but these individuals were college professors, graduate students, and undergraduate students from major universities. This should not be hard to believe. These individuals are the type who enjoy not only R&D work, but who also believe that, when problems occur, the fun starts.

Many years from now we will look back on the TCP/IP protocol as the protocol that provided the building blocks of future data communications.

The following text will show the inner workings of the TCP/IP protocol. The text will not enable the reader to write code or perform protocol analyzer traces on protocol packets, but will merely provide an alternative to the current theory books.

Introduction

The suite of protocols that encompass TCP/IP were originally designed to allow different types of computer systems to interact. It was developed by a project underwritten by an agency of the Department of Defense known as the Advanced Research Projects Agency (DARPA).

There are many reasons why TCP/IP became popular, two of which are paramount. First, DARPA provided a grant to allow the protocol suite to become part of Berkeley's UNIX system. When TCP/IP was introduced to the commercial marketplace, UNIX was always mentioned in every story about it. Berkeley UNIX and TCP/IP became the standard operating system and protocol of choice for a lot of major universities, where it was used with workstations in engineering and research environments. In 1983, all U.S. government proposals that included networks mandated the TCP/IP protocol in all the government proposals.

Second was the capability of the protocol to allow dissimilar systems to communicate through the network. At the time of the TCP/IP influx, other protocols were in use and very popular with the LAN vendors. Variations of Xerox's XNS and Digital's proprietary DECnet/LAT were the most popular. One drawback for users of these protocols is that the protocols were *vendor dependent.* Running XNS on one system did not guarantee compatibility of communication to any other system except for the same vendor. This was good for the vendor, but it tended to lock users into one vendor.

TCP/IP eliminated this. TCP's beginnings were rough (interoperability issues), but the protocol stabilized and the interoperability between different computer and operating systems became a reality. For example, a DEC system running the VMS operating system combined with

TCP/IP running as the network operating system can communicate with a Sun Microsystems UNIX workstation running TCP/IP. The two systems could communicate by taking advantage of the protocol and the specific applications written for the protocol, primarily by being able to log on to one another and by being able to transfer files between the two across a network.

When interconnecting computers and their operating systems with TCP/IP, it does not matter what the hardware architecture or the operating system of the computer is. The protocol will allow any computer implementing it to communicate with another. What follows are the methods used to accomplish this.

Fundamentals

TCP/IP originated when DARPA was tasked to bring about a solution to a difficult problem: allowing different computers to communicate with one another as if they were the same computer. This was a difficult task considering that all computer architectures in those days (the early 1970s) were highly guarded secrets. Computer manufacturers would not disclose either their hardware or software architectures to anyone. This is known as a *closed* or *proprietary* system.

The architecture behind TCP/IP takes an alternative approach. TCP/IP developed into an architecture that would allow the computers to communicate without grossly modifying the operating system or the hardware architecture of the machine. TCP/IP runs as an application on those systems.

The original result was known as the Network Control Program (NCP). The protocol was developed to run on multiple hosts in geographically dispersed areas through a packet switching internet known as the Advanced Research Project Agency network—ARPAnet.* This protocol was primarily used to support application-oriented functions and process-to-process communications between two hosts. Specific applications, such as file transfer, were written to this network operating system.

The first few years of this design proved to be an effective test, but had some serious design flaws. A research project was developed to overcome these problems. The outcome of this project was a recommendation to replace the original program known as NCP program with another called Transmission Control Program (TCP). The protocol responsible for routing the packets through an internet was termed the Internet Protocol. Today, the common term for this standard is TCP/IP.

---

* ARPAnet was the term used to describe the public TCP/IP network that links universities and scientific centers. Due to the large growth of this network (which now includes many different private, government, and public agencies), it is now known as the Internet.

With TCP/IP replacing NCP, the NCP application-specific programs were converted to run over the new protocol. The protocol became mandated in 1983, when ARPA demanded that all computers attached to the ARPAnet use the TCP/IP protocol.

In order to perpetuate the task of allowing dissimilar government computers to communicate, DARPA gave research grants to UCLA, University of California at San Bernadino, the Stanford Research Institute (SRI), and the University of Utah. A company called BBN provided the Honeywell 316 Interface Message Processors (IMPs) which provided the internet communications links. In 1971, the ARPAnet Networking Group dissolved and DARPA took over all the research work. Between the years of 1975–1979, DARPA had begun the work on the Internet technology which resulted in the TCP/IP protocols as we know them today.

Around 1980, the Internet was started when DARPA began to move their machines and research networks over to the TCP/IP protocols.

Around 1983, the Office of the Secretary of Defense mandated that all government computers be switched over to the new TCP/IP protocols. Also during this year, the ARPAnet was split into two networks:

1. The Defense Data Network (DDN)—also known as the MILNET (military network)
2. The DARPA Internet—a new name for the old ARPAnet network.

In 1985, the National Science Foundation expanded the use of the Internet by using it as the vehicle to network as many scientists as possible. This program was started as network access to their six super computer sites. The NSFNET was formally established in 1986.

There are two prominent items in the architecture of this protocol that need to be understood: the architecture itself and the elements that control the architecture.

First, the protocol is well defined. The TCP/IP protocol is known as an open protocol. The architecture is defined in public documents for anyone who would like to build a TCP/IP operating system. What governs the protocol? Refer to Fig. 6.1*a*. The TCP/IP protocol suite is governed by an organization known as the Internet Activities Board (IAB). This group was originally set up by DARPA to allow information to be exchanged between the major individuals involved in the ARPAnet. Each member of the IAB heads a group known as the Internet Engineering Task Force (IETF) that is responsible for investigating a problem or a set of issues. Each IETF has a chairperson known as the Internet Architect whose responsibilities include future directions, coordination of the activities, and technical directions.

Finally, there are documents written known as Request for Comments (RFCs) that define the processing functions of this protocol.

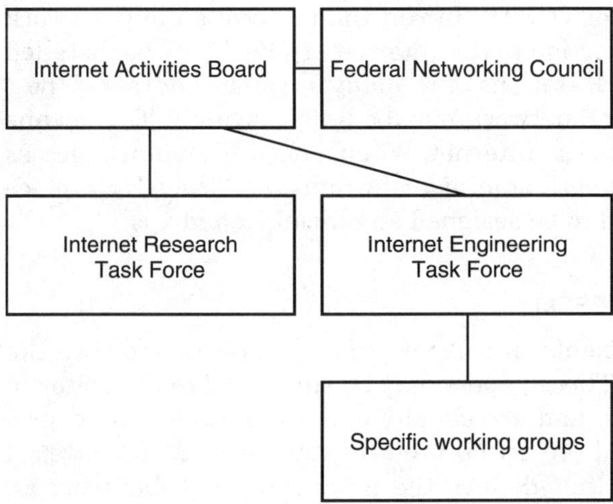

Figure 6.1 (*a*) Internet structure.

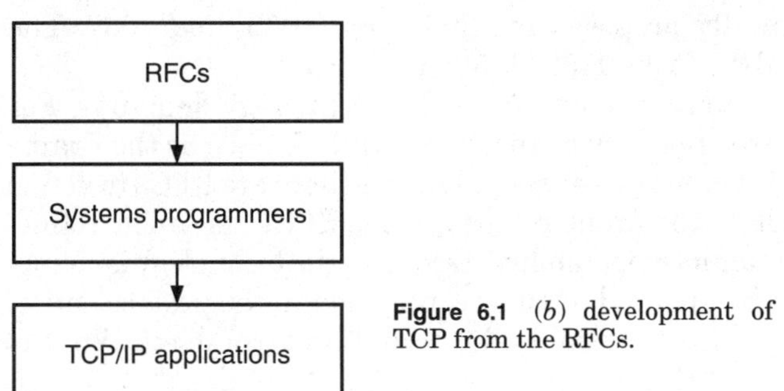

Figure 6.1 (*b*) development of TCP from the RFCs.

These documents are placed in the public domain for all who are interested to read. The address and phone number to purchase the RFCs is:

Network Information Center
14200 Park Meadow Drive
Suite 200
Chantilly, VA 22021
(703) 802-4535

The ARPAnet changed names and is now known as the Internet. What is significant here is when talking about the Internet (the ARPAnet), it will always be spelled with a capital I. When talking generally about a collection of networks that form an internet it will be spelled with a lowercase i.

One last distinction of TCP/IP. To run the protocol on any network does not require a connection to the Internet. TCP/IP may be installed on as few as two network stations or as many as can be addressed (possibly millions). A TCP/IP network may be built privately. This means that there is no access to the Internet. When a network requires access to the Internet, the network administrator must call the NIC to place a request for access and to be assigned an official IP address.

Request For Comments (RFCs)

The Request for Comments are papers (documents) that define the TCP/IP protocol suite. These papers may be submitted to the editor in chief of NIC by anyone, and are usually about reports for work, proposals for protocols, and the actual protocol standards. As a matter of fact, there is an RFC that defines the procedure for submitting an RFC. The following text will be mentioning the RFCs periodically, for any modification to the TCP/IP protocol is defined in these RFCs.

Each RFC is assigned a number in ascending sequence (Newer RFCs have higher numbers and they are never reassigned). Newer RFCs may make older RFCs obsolete. For example, the SNMP network management was originally proposed in RFC 1065, 1066, and 1067. The latest adopted SNMP RFC is 1155, 1156, and 1157.

The RFCs are continuing to evolve as the technology demands. For example, the wide area network connection facility known as the Frame Relay specification is becoming very popular, and there are RFCs to define how to interface TCP to the frame relay protocol. RFCs also allow refinements to enhance better interoperability. As long as the technology is changing, the RFCs must be updated to allow connection to the protocol suite.

The second part of this protocol is the actual protocol itself. What is TCP/IP?

Let's start with understanding the functions and protocols by studying their placement in the OSI model. In looking at Fig. 6.2, we can see that there are distinct protocols that run at each layer of the OSI model, starting from the network layer to the application layer. The heart of the TCP/IP network protocol is at layers 3 and 4. The applications for this protocol (file transfer, mail, and terminal emulation) run at the application layer.

As you can see, this protocol runs independently of the data-link and physical layer. At these layers the TCP/IP protocol can run on Ethernet, Token Ring, FDDI, serial lines, X.25, etc. It has been adapted to run over these protocols. TCP/IP was first used to interconnect computer systems through synchronous lines and not high-speed local area networks. Today, it is used on any type of media. This includes serial lines (asynchronous and synchronous) and high-speed networks such as FDDI, Ethernet, and Token Ring.

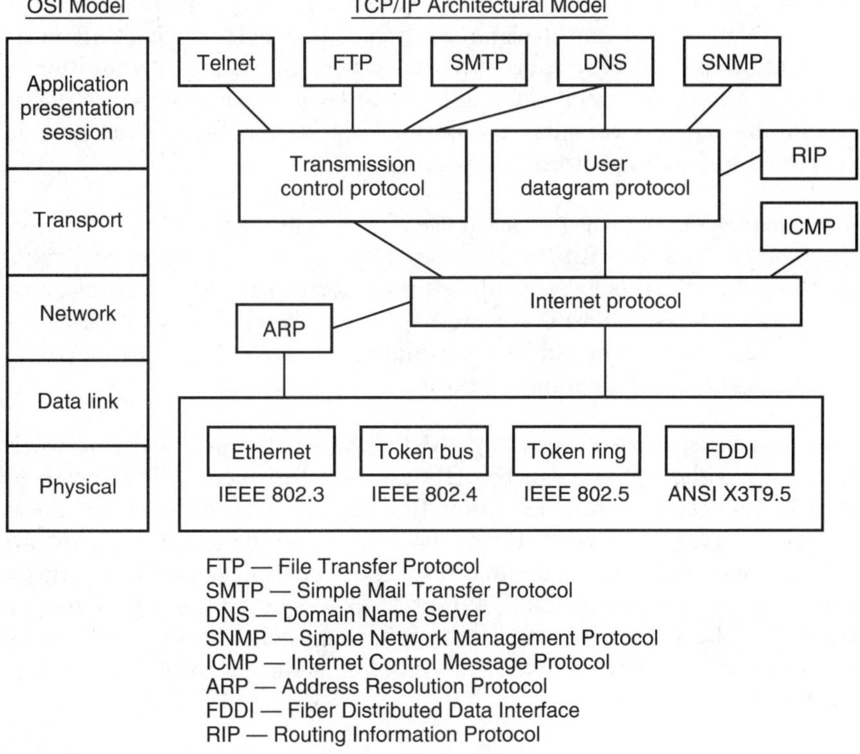

Figure 6.2 OSI model and TCP/IP architectural model.

The protocol suite

TCP/IP is actually a family of protocols working together to provide a path that allows internet data communication.

In this chapter, the TCP/IP protocol suite will be discussed in three phases:

1. The Internet Protocol (IP)
2. The Transport Control Protocol (TCP)
3. The suite of applications that were specifically developed on top of TCP: TELNET, File Transfer Protocol (FTP), Domain Name Service (DNS), and Simple Mail Transfer Program (SMTP), to name a few

A brief summary of these three section is given below:

Overview

Section 1: the network layer

Internet Protocol (IP). This protocol is designed to interconnect packet-switched communication networks to form an internet. It transmits blocks of data called datagrams received from its upper-layer software to and from source and destination hosts. It provides a best effort or connectionless delivery service between the source and destination—connectionless in that it does not establish a session with the destination before it transmits its data. This is the layer that is also responsible for the protocol addressing.

Internet Control Message Protocol (ICMP). Not really part of the IP layer, this works directly with the IP layer. Reports certain error conditions on the network. Basically, it allows internet routers to transmit error or test messages. These error messages may be that a network destination cannot be reached or they may generate/reply to an echo request packet (PING, explained later).

Address Resolution Protocol (ARP). ARP is not really part of the network layer, it resides in-between the IP and data-link layers. It is protocol that translates between the 32-bit IP address and a 48-bit Local Area Network address. Since TCP was not originated to run over a LAN, an address scheme was implemented to allow each host and network on the internet to identify itself. When TCP/IP was adapted to run over the LAN, the IP address had to be mapped to the 48-bit data-link or physical address that LANs use, and this is the protocol that accomplishes it.

Section 2: transport layer protocols

Transmission control protocol. Since IP provides for a connectionless delivery service of TCP data, TCP provides application programs access to the network, using a reliable connection-oriented transport-layer service. This protocol is responsible for establishing sessions between user processes on the internet, and also ensures reliable communications between two or more processes. The functions that it provides are:

1. to listen for incoming session establishment requests
2. to request a session to another network station
3. to send and receive data reliably
4. gracefully to close a session

User datagram protocol. UDP provides application programs access to the network using an unreliable connectionless transport-layer service. It allows the transfer of data between source and destination stations without having to establish a session before data is transferred. This protocol also does not use the end-to-end error checking that TCP uses. With UDP, transport-layer functionality is there, but the overhead is low. It is primarily used for those applications that do not require the robustness of the TCP protocol. For example, mail, broadcast messages, naming service, and network management.

Section 3: applications

TELNET. For new users to the TCP/IP protocol, this is not Telenet, a packet-switching technology using the CCITT standard X.25. It is pronounced TELNET. This is an application-level protocol that allows terminal emulation to pass through a network to a remote network station. TELNET runs on top of the TCP protocol and allows a network workstation to appear to a remote device (i.e., a host) as a terminal as if the terminal were a local device.

File Transfer Protocols (FTP, Trivial FTP). FTP is similar to TELNET in terms of control, but this protocol allows for data files to be transferred on the internet. FTP resides on top of TCP. TFTP is a simplex file transfer protocol (based on an unreliable transport layer called UDP). It is primarily used for boot loading of configuration files across an internet.

Simple Mail Transfer Protocol (SMTP). This is an electronic mail system that is robust enough to run on the entire Internet system. This protocol allows for the exchange of electronic mail between two or more systems on an internet.

Domain Name Service (DNS). This is a centralized name service that allows users to establish connections to network stations using humanly readable names instead of cryptic network addresses. It provides a name-to-network address translation service.

The aforementioned protocols are the topics for this chapter. Since the TCP/IP protocol suite basically begins at layer 3, the Internet Protocol, it will be the protocol that we will study first.

Section 1: The Network Layer

Internet protocol (IP)

The main goal of IP is to provide interconnection of subnetworks to form an internet in order to pass data.

The IP protocol provides four main functions:

1. Basic unit for data transfer
2. Addressing
3. Routing
4. Fragmentation of datagrams

Basic unit for data transfer—connectionless, best-effort delivery service. The IP layers provide the entry into the delivery system used to transport data across the internet.

Usually, when anyone hears of the name IP, they automatically think of the devices commonly known as *routers* which connect multiple subnetworks together. It is true the IP performs these tasks, but the IP protocol performs many other tasks, as mentioned previously. The IP protocol runs in all the participating network stations that are attached to subnetworks so that they may submit their packets to routers or directly to other devices on the same network. It resides between the data-link layer and the transport layer.

Declarations. The primary goal of IP is to provide the basic algorithm for transfer of data to and from a network. It provides a connectionless delivery service for the upper-layer protocols. This means that IP does not set up a session (a virtual link) between the transmitting station and the receiving station prior to submitting the data to the receiving station. It encapsulates the data and delivers it on a *best-effort basis.* IP does not inform the sender or receiver of the status of the packet. It merely attempts to deliver the packet and will not make up for the faults encountered in this attempt. This means that if the data link fails or incurs a recoverable error, the IP layer will not inform anyone. It tried to deliver a message and failed. It is up to the upper-layer protocols (TCP) to perform error recovery. In other words, TCP will time-out for that transmission and will resend the data.

IP submits a properly formatted data packet to the destination station and does not expect a status response. Because IP is a connectionless protocol, IP may receive and deliver the data (data sent to the transport layer in the receiving station) in the wrong order from which it was sent, or it may duplicate the data. It is up to the higher-layer protocols (layer 4 and above) to provide error recovery procedures. IP is part of the network delivery system. It accepts data and formats it for transmission to the data-link layer. (Remember, the data-link layer provides the access methods to transmit and receive data from the cable plant.) IP also retrieves data from the data link and presents it to the requesting upper layer.

IP will add its control information, specific to the IP layer only, to the data received by the upper layer (transport layer). Once this is accomplished, it will inform the data link (layer 2) that it has a message to send to the network. The unit of information that IP transfers is known as a *datagram.* This datagram may be transferred over high-speed networks (Ethernet, Token Ring, FDDI). When it is transmitted over these networks, it will be called a *packet.* For simplicity, considering the primary focus of the book is network protocols over high-speed networks, datagrams and packets will be synonymous. It is important to remember that IP presents datagrams to its lower layer (the data-link layer).

The IP protocol does not care what kind of data is in the packet. All it knows is that it must apply some control information, called an IP header, to the data received from the upper-layer protocol (presumably TCP or UDP) and try to deliver it to some station on the network or internet.

The IP protocol is not completely without merit. It does provide mechanisms on how hosts and routers should process transmitted or received packets, or when an error should be generated and when an IP packet may be discarded. To understand the IP functionality, a brief look at the control information it adds (the IP header) to the packet will be shown. Refer to Fig. 6.3. This figure shows the IP header encapsulated in an Ethernet frame. This is shown to indicate the position of the header in the packet.

The other part of Fig. 6.3 is the IP header. This shows the standard packet header for an IP datagram. The following text will study the functions of the IP datagram delivery through a look into the header information in the IP datagram.

The fields are defined as follows:

VERS. Defines the current version of IP implemented by the network station. Version 4 is the latest version.

HLEN. The length of the IP header (all fields but the IP data field). Not all the fields in the IP header need to be used. The field is measured in the amount of 32-bit words. The shortest IP header will be 20 bytes. Therefore, this field would contain a 5 (20 bytes = 160 bits; 160 bits/32 bits = 5). This field is necessary, for the header can be variable in length depending on the field called options.

Service Type. Which is further divided:

Precedence	D	T	R	Unused

Precedence. This field may have an entry of 0 (normal precedence) and up to 7 (network control), which allows the transmitting station's application to indicate to the IP layer the priority of sending the datagram. This is combined with the D (delay), T (throughput), and R (reliability) bits. These bits indicate to a router which route to take. This field is known as a Type of Service (TOS) identifier.

D bit—request low delay when set to a 1

T bit—request high throughput

R bit—request high reliability

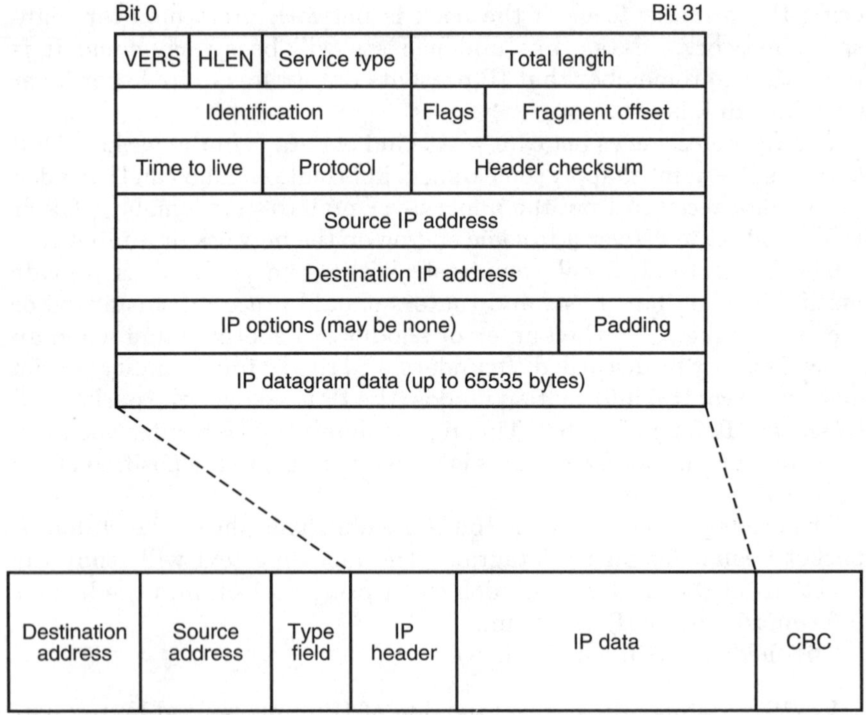

Figure 6.3 IP header encapsulated in an Ethernet frame.

For example, if there is more than one route to a destination, the router could read this field to pick a route. This becomes important in the OSPF* routing protocol, which is the first IP routing protocol to take advantage of this. If the transaction to take place is a file transfer, you may want to set the bits to 0 0 1 to indicate that you do not need low delay or high throughput, but you would like high reliability. TOS fields are set by applications (i.e., TELNET or FTP) and not routers. Routers only read this field. Routers do not set this field. Based on the information read, routers will select the optimal path for the datagram. It is up to the TCP/IP application running on a host to set these bits before transmitting the packet on the network. It does require a router to maintain multiple routing tables—one for each type of service.

---

* Open Shortest Path First (OSPF) is a routing protocol that allows devices known as routers to determine the topology of the TCP/IP internet. With this, routers will be able to forward packets correctly to their destination. OSPF will not be covered in this chapter. Another routing protocol known as Routing Information Protocol (RIP) will be covered later.

Total length. This is the length of the datagram measured in bytes (this field allots for 16 bits, meaning the data area of the IP datagram may be 65535 bytes in length).

Fragmentation. There may be times when a packet transmitted from one network may to be too large to transmit on another network. Consider transmitting a frame from a Token Ring network (which typically supports 4472 bytes as the maximum transmission size) to an Ethernet LAN (which supports only 1518 bytes as the maximum transmission size). A TCP/IP router must be able to "fragment" the larger packet into smaller packets. TCP will set up packet sizes for a connection, but what if the two communicating stations are separated by multiple types of media, each supporting different transmission sizes? Fragmenting a packet into smaller packets suitable for LAN transmission or heterogeneous LAN routing is another task accomplished by the IP layer. The following fields are used to accomplish this.

Identification, flags, fragment offset. These indicate how to fragment a forwarded datagram that is too large for the attached network. TCP/IP can run on top of almost any data link. When trying to send data to different networks, the maximum size of the data that may be sent at one time may vary on those networks. Ethernet holds its packet size to a total of 1518 bytes (including all headers). Token Ring allows for around a 17800-byte* data size (16 Mbps, 4472 bytes for 4 Mbps) and FDDI allows for a 4472-byte data size.† Any of the networks may have the largest frame passing on it. IP allows for the exchange of data between all these networks via its ability to fragment packets.

Each IP header from each of the fragmented datagrams is almost identical. The identification field indicates which datagram fragments belong together. It identifies a group to which datagrams belong so datagrams do not get mismatched. The receiving IP layer uses this field and the source IP address to identify which fragments belong together.

The flags field is used to indicate the following:

1. Whether more fragments are to arrive or whether no more data is to be sent for that datagram (no more fragments)
2. Whether or not to fragment a datagram (a don't-fragment bit)

Fragmenting is by far the most important feature to notice if the networks to be traversed employ different frame sizes. Readers who

---

* The maximum number of bytes is typically 4472 for ring-type circuits (FDDI and 16/4 Token Ring).

† Taken from *IBM Token Ring Architecture Reference Manual,* 1989.

understand bridges know that bridges do not have this capability. If a bridge receives a packet that is too large for the forwarded network, as mandated by the IEEE 802.1d, it will drop the packet and notify no one that it has done so. Higher-level protocols will time-out the packet and will respond accordingly. Once a session is established, most protocols have the capability to negotiate the maximum packet size that each of the stations may handle and, therefore, it will not effect bridge operation.

The total length and the fragment offset fields IP can reconstruct a datagram and deliver it to the upper-layer software. The total length field indicates the total length of the original packet, and the offset field indicates to the node that is reassembling the packet the offset from the beginning of the packet. It is at this point that the data will be placed in the data segment to reconstruct the packet.

Time to live (TTL). There are error conditions that may occur that would cause a packet to endlessly loop between routers on the internet. The initial entry is set by the originator of the packet. Time to live is a field that is used by routers to ensure that a packet does not endlessly loop around the network. This field (currently defined as the number of seconds) is set at the transmitting station and then, as the datagram passes through each router, it will be decremented. With the speed of today's routers, the usual decrement is 1. One algorithm is that the receiving router will notice the time when a packet arrived, and then, when it is forwarded, the router will decrement the field by the number of seconds the datagram sat in a queue waiting for forwarding. Not all algorithms work this way. A minimum decrement will always be 1. The router that decrements this field to 0 will discard the packet and inform the originator of the datagram that it cannot be forwarded.

The time-to-live field may also be set to a certain time (i.e., initialized to a low number like 64) to ensure that a packet stays on the network for only a set time. Some routers allow the network administrator to set a manual entry to decrement. This field may contain any number from 0 to 255.

Protocol field. This field is used to indicate which higher-level protocol sent the frame and which receiving protocol should get the frame (i.e., TCP or UDP). There are many protocols that may reside on top of IP. IP is not specific as to the protocol that runs on top of it. Currently, the most common transport implementations are TCP and UDP (explained in Section 2). In order for IP to know how to correctly deliver the packet to the correct entity above it is the purpose of this field. It will be explained in more detail in Section 2. If the protocol field is set to TCP, the packet will be handed to the TCP process for further frame processing. The same is true if the frame is set to UDP.

Checksum. This is a Cyclic Redundancy Check of 16 bits. This is beyond the scope of this book, but the idea behind it is to ensure the integrity of the header. A CRC number is generated from the data in the IP data field and placed into this field by the transmitting station. When the receiving station reads the data, it will compute a CRC number. If the two CRC numbers do not match, there is an error in the header and the packet will be discarded. Stretching it, you may think of this as a fancy parity check. As the datagram is received by each router, each router will recompute the checksum. This is because the TTL field is changed by each router the datagram traverses.

The IP options field. This is also beyond the scope of this book. Basically, it contains information on source routing (nothing to do with Token Ring), tracing a route, time stamping the packet as it traverses routers, and military security entries. For more information on these entries, please refer to the TCP/IP references at the end of this book. These fields may or may not be in the header (which allows for the variable length header).

The fields of IP source and destination address. These are particularly important, for users will be most aware of this when starting their workstation or trying to access other stations without the use of a domain name server or an up-to-date host file. These fields indicate the final destination IP address that the packet should be delivered to and the IP address of the station that originally transmitted the packet.

All hosts on an IP internet will be identified by these addresses. IP addressing is extremely important and a full discussion follows.

IP addresses, subnetting, and the Address Resolution Protocol (ARP)

The ideas and concepts that evolved the protocol of TCP/IP were devised before any data-link protocols of Ethernet and Token Ring were developed. Hosts were not attached to a local high-speed network (like Ethernet or Token Ring). Initial work on the TCP/IP protocol started in the 1970s (about the same time the Ethernet protocol was being developed), and hosts communicated with each other through low-speed point-to-point serial lines (telephone lines). Ethernet and Token Ring controllers have addresses known as MAC addresses, which identify the controller on the LAN. (For more information refer to Chap. 2, "Ethernet and Token Ring.") Therefore, an addressing scheme to identify TCP/IP hosts and where they were located was implemented. The addressing scheme used to identify these hosts is called the 32-bit IP address. This is also known as a protocol address.

Addressing's purpose was to allow IP to communicate between hosts on a network or on an internet. IP addresses identify both a particular node and a network number where the particular node resides on an internet. IP addresses are 32 bits long, separated into four fields of 1 byte each. This address can be expressed in decimal, octal, hexadecimal, and binary. The most common IP address form is written in decimal as is known as the *dotted decimal notation* system. This format will be shown in a moment.

There are two ways that an IP address is assigned. It all depends on your connection. If you have a connection to the Internet, the network portion of the address is assigned through a central authority known as the Network Information Center (NIC). Their address and phone number are located on p. 245. If your network will not have a connection to the Internet, the IP addresses for your internet can be locally assigned by the network administrator of your network.*

Individual host IDs are not assigned by the NIC and will always be assigned by the local network administrator of the network whether the network attachment has access to the Internet or not. When the NIC assigns your network address, it will be the network number only—the host portion of the address is locally assigned.

Whereas XNS uses the 48-bit MAC address as its host address, IP was developed before high-speed local LANs and, therefore, it has its own numbering scheme.

IP addressing was later adapted to the physical-layer addressing of Ethernet and Token Ring and will be discussed in a moment.

IP address format. Each host on a TCP/IP network is uniquely identified at the IP layer with an address that takes the form of <netid, hostid>. The address is not really separated and is read as a whole. The whole address is always used to identify a host. There is not a separation between the fields. In fact, when an IP address is written, it is hard to tell the distinction between the two fields without knowing how to separate them.

The following shows the generalized format of an IP address:

```
<Network Number, Host Number>
```

IP classes. 128.4.70.9 is an example of an IP address. When looking at this address, it is hard to tell which is the network number and which is the host number. In order to understand how this is accom-

* IP addresses may be local to your network. That is, commercial businesses may assign their own addresses on their network. But, in order to connect to the Internet, the address connecting to the Internet must be assigned by the NIC.

plished, let's look first at the how IP addresses are divided. The structure of an IP address takes the following form:

Byte	Byte	Byte	Byte	
1	2	3	4	
xxx	xxx	xxx	xxx	Decimal
<Network	Number,	Host	Number>	

As shown in the this table, there are four bytes that are used to represent an IP address. The network number can shift from the first byte to the second byte to the third byte. The same can happen to the host portion of the address. xxx represents a decimal number from 0 to 255 (the reason for three x's), in decimal.

IP addresses are divided into five classes: A, B, C, D, and E. Classes A, B, and C are used to represent host and network addresses. Class D is a special type of address used for multicasting (for example, OSPF routing updates use this type of address). Class E is reserved.

For those trying to figure out this addressing scheme, it is best if you also know the binary numbering system and are able to convert between decimal and binary. Finally, IP addresses are sometimes expressed in hexadecimal and it is helpful to know. The most common form is decimal. This book shows most addresses in binary and decimal.

Classes A, B, and C are the most commonly used. Referring to Fig. 6.4*a* and *b,* we can see how the classes are actually defined. How does a host or internet device determine which address is of which class? Since the length of the network ID is variable (dependent on the class), a simple method was devised to allow the software to determine the class of address and, therefore, the length of the network number.

IP class identification. The IP software will determine the class of the network ID by using a simple method of reading the first bit(s) in the first field (the first byte) of every packet. IP addresses contain four (4) bytes. Refer to Fig. 6.4*a*. The IP address is broken down into its binary equivalent. If the first bit is a 0 of byte 0, it is automatically a class A address. If the first bit is a 1, then the protocol mandates reading the next bit. If the next bit is a 0, then it is a class B address. If the next bit is a 1 and the third bit is a 0, it is a class C address. If the third bit is a 1, the address is a class D address and is reserved for multicast addresses.

Class A. Class A addresses use only the first of the four bytes for the network number. It is identified by the first bit in the first byte of the address. If this first bit is a 0, then it identifies a class A address. The last three bytes are used for the host portion of the address. Class

A addressing allows for 126 networks (using only the first byte) with up to 16 million hosts on each of the 126 network numbers (the last three bytes, 24 bits in binary) and are used for networks with a large number of hosts attached to each logical network. Why only 126 networks when there are eight bits? First, 127.x (01111111 binary) is reserved for a loop-back function. It cannot be assigned to identify a network number.

Second, since the first bit is reserved and will always be set to a 0, it leaves seven bits to assign to a network number (01111111). Seven 1s in binary is 127 in decimal. The last three fields we do not care about, for

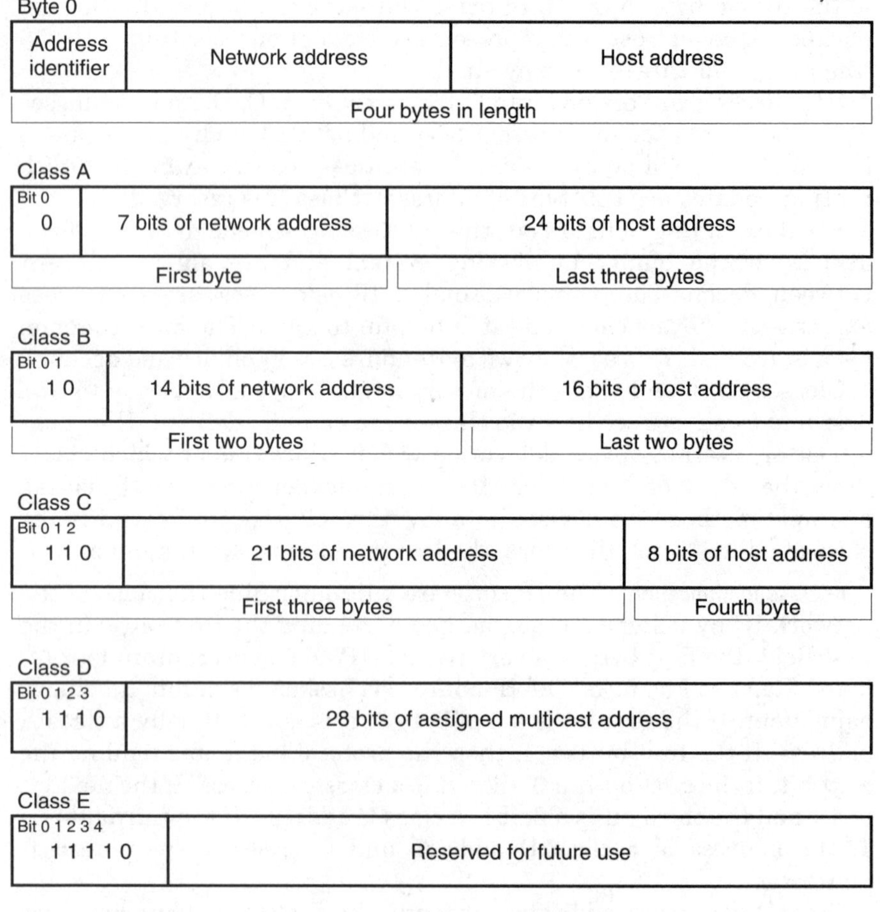

Figure 6.4 (*a*) 32-bit Internet addressing scheme.

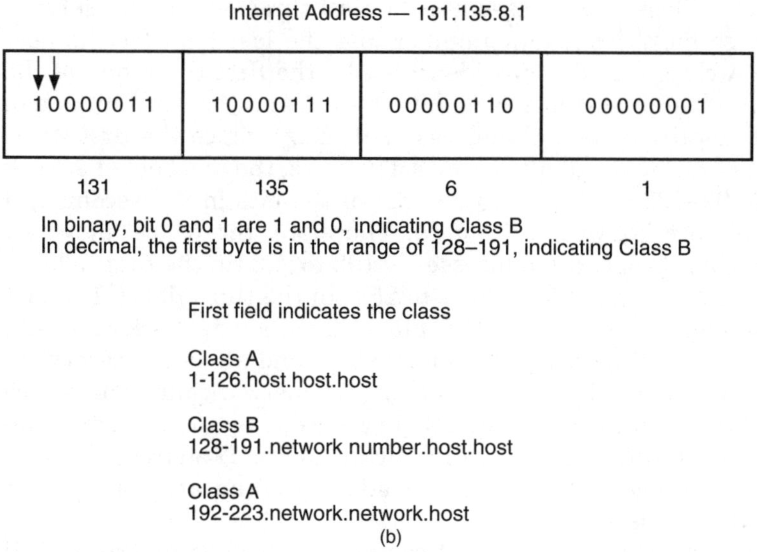

Figure 6.4 (*b*) Dotted decimal notation.

they are assigned to hosts. Class A network addresses will always be in the range of 1 to 126 (127 is reserved), with each of the last three bytes in the range of 1 to 254. The last three bytes are assigned locally.

Class A addresses take the 4-byte form <network number.host.-host.host>, bytes 0, 1, 2, and 3.

Class B. Class B addresses use the first two bytes of the four bytes for the network number and the last two fields for the host number. It is identified by the first two bits of the first byte. If the first bit is a 1, then the algorithm checks the second bit. If the second bit is a 0, this will identify a class B address.

This allows for 16,384 network numbers (10111111.11111111.-host.host), with each network capable of supporting 65,354 hosts (net.net.11111111.11111110). Since it reserves the first two bits to identify the class type (in binary, a 10xxxxxx in the first field), there are limited address numbers that may be used in the first field. This translates to 128 to 191 (in decimal) as the allowable network numbers in the first field. Since the first field identifies the class, the second field is free to use all eight bits, and can range from 1 to 255. The total range for network numbers for class B addresses is 128 to 191 (in the first field), 1 to 255 (in the second field) and xxx.xxx (x represents the host ID) in the third and fourth fields. This is the most popular class of addresses.

Class B addresses take the form <network number.network number.host.host>, bytes 0, 1, 2, and 3.

Class C. Class C addresses use the first three out of four fields of the address for the network number and the last field for the host number. A class C address is identified by the first three bits of the first field. If the first and second bits are a 1 and the third bit is a 0, this will identify a class C address (110xxxxx). Since the first three bits in the first field will always be a 110xxxxx, the allowable network range is 192–223 in the first field. All of the bits in the second and third fields are allowed to be used. Therefore, the whole allowable range for class C network addresses is 192 to 223 (in the first field), 1 to 255 (in the second field), and 1 to 254 (in the third field). The last field will range from 1 to 255. This allows 2 million network numbers, each capable of supporting 254 hosts (all 0s and all 1s are reserved). Class C addresses allow only 254 hosts per network number. Notice that the largest number in the first field may go up to 223. Any number over 223 in the first field will indicate a class D address. Class D addresses are reserved as multicast addresses and are not used an individual addresses.

Class C addresses are the most commonly assigned by the NIC. If you can prove a need for a class B address, they will assign one to you. Usually, they assign a class C.

Class C takes the form of <network number.network number.network number.host>, bytes 0, 1, 2, and 3.

For anyone new to this protocol, the easiest way to remember IP addresses and their associated class is this: the *first byte* will always identify the *class address.* A is the *first letter* in the alphabet and therefore a class A network address is only the *first byte* leaving the last three fields for host addressing. B is the *second letter* in the alphabet and therefore the network portion of the address is the first *two bytes* of the address leaving the last two fields for host address. C is the *third letter* in the alphabet and the network portion takes up the first *three bytes* of the address and leaves one field for host addresses. As for remembering which number is associated to which class, the only field that is important is the first field. Memorize the starting network number for each class.

Let's review. Refer to Fig. 6.4*a* and *b*. All IP addresses are actually the grouping of four bytes that represents both a network number and host number. This number is usually represented in decimal. With the first bit reserved (set to 0xxxxxxx) in a class A address, the network numbers can range from 1 to 126. Number 127 is reserved as a local loop-back IP address and must not be assigned to a network number and broadcast on the network. With the first two bits reserved in a class B (10xxxxxx) or three bits in a class C (110xxxxx) address, the network numbers for class B range from 128.1.0.0 to 191.255.0.0 and for class C, they range from 192.1.1.0 to 223.255.255.0.

Examples

192.1.1.1	node assigned with a host ID of 1, located on a class C network of network 192.1.1.0
200.6.5.4	node assigned with a host ID of 4, located on a class C network of 200.6.5.0
150.150.5.6	node assigned with a host ID of 5.6, located on a class B network of 150.150.0.0
9.6.7.8	node assigned with a host ID of 6.7.8, located on a class A network of 9.0.0.0
128.1.0.1	node assigned with a host ID of 0.1, located on a class B network of 128.1.0.0

Notice that to represent a network number only, only the network number is written. The host field will be set to 0. This type of network number display will become apparent when looking at routing tables.

For those not familiar with binary, you need to memorize the starting and stopping points of the first byte of an IP address:

Class A	1 to 126 in the first field
Class B	128 to 191 in the first field
Class C	192 to 223 in the first field

Restrictions

1. Addresses cannot have the first four highest bits (in the first field) set to 1111. This is reserved for class E networks only (a reserved network classification).
2. The class A address of 127.x is for a special function known as the *loop-back function.* This is provided so that processes which need to communicate through TCP that reside on the same host will not send packets out to the network. x is usually set to 0, although it can be set to 1. Routers that receive a datagram addressed this way will discard the packet.
3. The bits that define the network and host portion of the address cannot be set to all 1s to indicate an individual address.* This is a special address to represent a broadcast packet to all hosts on that particular network. Broadcast addresses indicate that every host on the network (not necessarily the internet) should receive and interpret the datagram. If each byte of the IP address is all 1s (all 255 in decimal), this is known as a *limited broadcast* (the packet will be received by all network stations on the local network). Routers will not forward a limited broadcast datagram. This takes the form of

* The exception to this rule is the subnet mask. This concept is explained later.

255.255.255.255. Routers, explained later, use this type of address. They use this to update other routers with network number and hop-count updates. Routers are explained later.

4. Another form of broadcast is when the network portion of the address is set to a specified network address but the host portion of the address is set to all 1s. This is known as *directed broadcast.* Routers will forward this type of datagram. An example of this is 128.1.255.255. This signifies a broadcast address to all stations on network number 128.1.0.0.

   Other types of broadcast formats will be shown in the subnet section of this chapter.

5. Any address with all 0s in the network portion of the address is meant to represent "this" network. For example, 0.0.0.120 is meant as host number 120 on "this" network (the network from which it originated).

6. There is an old form of broadcasting known as the *all-0s broadcast.* This will take the form of 0.0.0.0. This form is discouraged from being used. 0.0.0.0 is used to indicate a default router (explained later).

Class D or multicast addresses are used to send an IP datagram to a group of hosts on a network. This will prove to be very beneficial when routers need to update their neighbor routers (in some routing algorithms). It is a more efficient way of broadcasting to use a multicast address rather than a broadcast address, for the upper-layer software will not always be interrupted every time a broadcast packet arrives. With a multicast address, each individual IP station must be willing to accept the multicast IP address before the transport-layer software will be interrupted. With a broadcast address, all stations will interrupt their upper-layer software no matter what type the packet is.

Remember that the Network Information Center (NIC) assigns all IP addresses for those stations with an attachment to the Internet. No one is allowed to attach to the Internet with their own assigned address (the network number portion of the address). The NIC is the only source for an IP address. You can assign your own IP network numbers if you will *never* have access to the Internet.*

Addresses cannot be out of the 255 (decimal) range for any for the four bytes. Therefore, an address of 128.6.200.655 is not a valid address. Likewise, an address of 420.6.7.900 is not a valid address. Each of the fields must be less than 255 for network and host assignments and the host fields should be 255, or all fields set to 255, if it is a broadcast address.

* There is an exception to this rule, as noted in a previous footnote.

Subnetting. Now that IP address assignment has been shown, let's confuse the issue some more by looking at subnet masks. In short, this is an easy way of assigning some of the bits normally used by the host portion of the address and reassigning these bits to the network portion of the address. This is accomplished for the reasons that follow.

When a site is assigned (by the NIC), a network number or a LAN administrator devises an address scheme; the individual site may be assigned only one network number. This can create many problems. Why use only one network number when the desire is to segment the network into many more manageable network numbers? The NIC is running short of IP network number assignments and assigns them sparingly.

There is a desire among most companies using TCP/IP to break their network into many logical networks. Why use a single class B network address and have 65534 hosts assigned to it? Most sites will not have this many network attachments. Why not use part of the host portion of the IP address and reassign it to a network address? This is possible using a method known as *subnet masking.*

Figure 6.5 shows the three classes of networks, each with an address. This time, each of the addresses has been assigned a subnet mask. In this example of the classes A and B addresses, only the first field following the network ID portion of the address is used to indicate a subnet. The class C address uses the first three bits of the host portion of the address for the subnet. In reality, with any of the addresses, any of the host bits (except for 2 bits, there must be at least one host on a network) may be used for subnetting. For example, a class B address may use all of the third octect and two bits of the fourth octet for subnetting. This would give 1022 possible subnetwork numbers (1023 would indicate a broadcast address), with each network holding 62 hosts (63 would indicate a broadcast).

When doing this, host numbers are being taken away and given back to identify a subnet of a network address. Figure 6.5 depicts this. The subnet is a real network. In looking at the address, it appears that there is one class B address. With subnetting a class B address, we can take any amount of the bits in the third or 6 bits of the fourth byte (1 through 8 bits; they should be contiguous, starting from the left) of the IP address and make it part of the network number (a subnet under the network number). The format of the IP address would now be: <network number | subnetwork number | host number>. For example, if the address assigned to a particular host is 128.1.1.1, the network portion would be 128.1 and the host portion would be 1.1. With subnetting (assuming all eight bits of the third field were consumed for a subnet address), the address would be defined as network number 128.1 and subnet 1, with a host ID of 1.

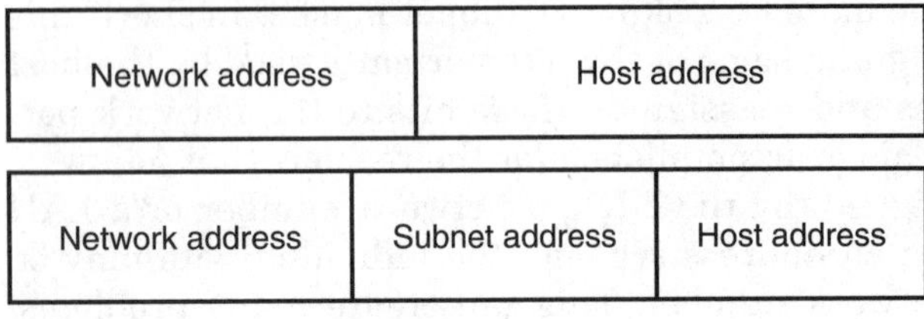

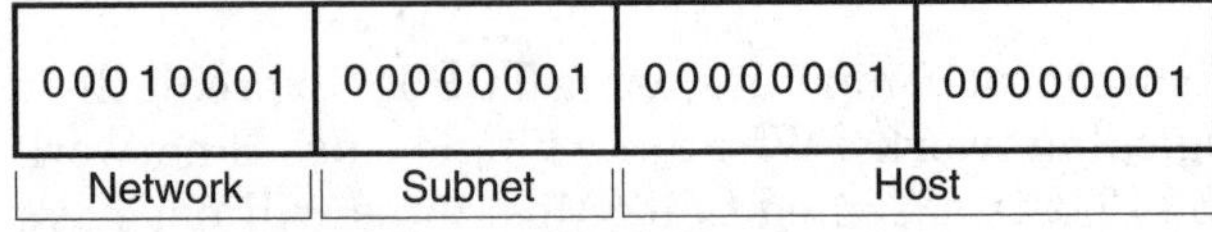

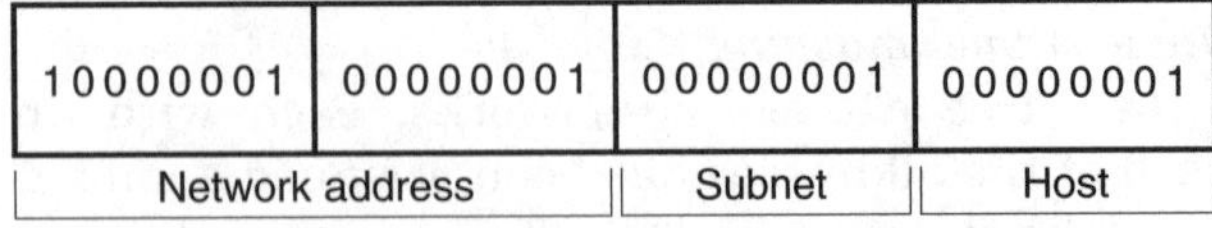

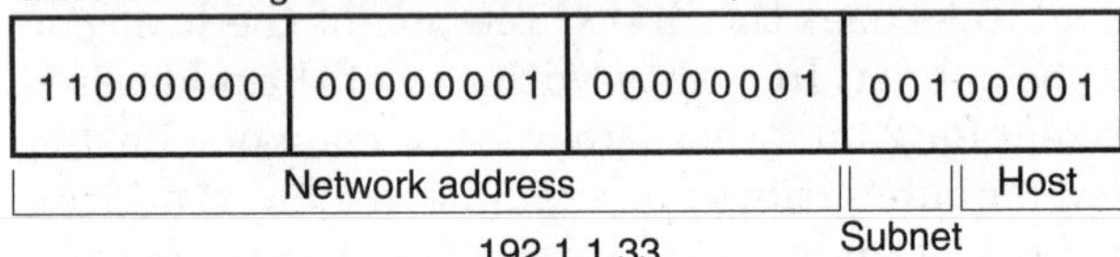

Figure 6.5 IP network addressing.

To illustrate further: If the class B network address of 130.1.0.0 is assigned to a site, it may be subnetted into the following: 130.1.xxx.0. x here indicates the decimal-formatted field that may be consumed for subnetting. The field may be subnetted using any of the bits in the field (translating binary into decimal, you may have one subnet using the most significant bit of the third field or use all the bits in the third field, which would give you 254 subnets with 254 hosts per subnet).

Refer to Fig. 6.6*a*. Suppose the first five bits (starting from the left; they should start from the left and remain contiguous going to the right) are reserved in the third field for assigning subnet numbers. Convert those first five bits of that octet to binary. All five of those bits are now assigned to the subnet number and may not be used for host IDs. To assign a unique subnet number, one rule must be adhered to. This is that a subnet must not have all 0s or all 1s (they are used for

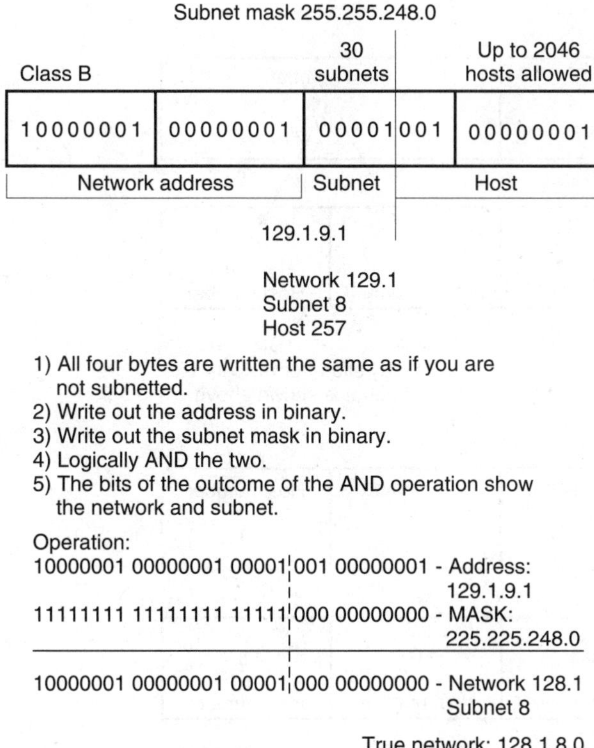

Figure 6.6 (*a*) Subnetting a class B with 5-bit subnet mask.

broadcasting). Applying this rule, we could have subnet numbers of any combination of the first five bits.

To identify the subnets is a little tricky. Please read this paragraph carefully. As shown in Fig. 6.6*a*, the vertical line separating the host and subnet portions of the address is the dividing line. The first bit in the subnet portion of the address is set to a 1. The subnet would not be a 1. In calculating the value of the subnet, the whole third field is taken into consideration. Therefore, since that bit is set, it is actually a binary 8 (the fourth bit). Therefore, the first subnet number will be an 8. Each subsequent subnet will be a multiple of 8. Some of these subnet numbers are 192, 128, 96, 64, 56, 32, 24, 16, 8, and so on. The address is still read as if subnetting has not been turned on. The address is 129.1.9.1. But, as shown, this is network 129.1, subnet 8, and host 257. This is a little tricky, but subnetting is found on almost all TCP/IP networks installed. Each field will still never read beyond 255, but by using subnetting, you can have a host number higher than 255.

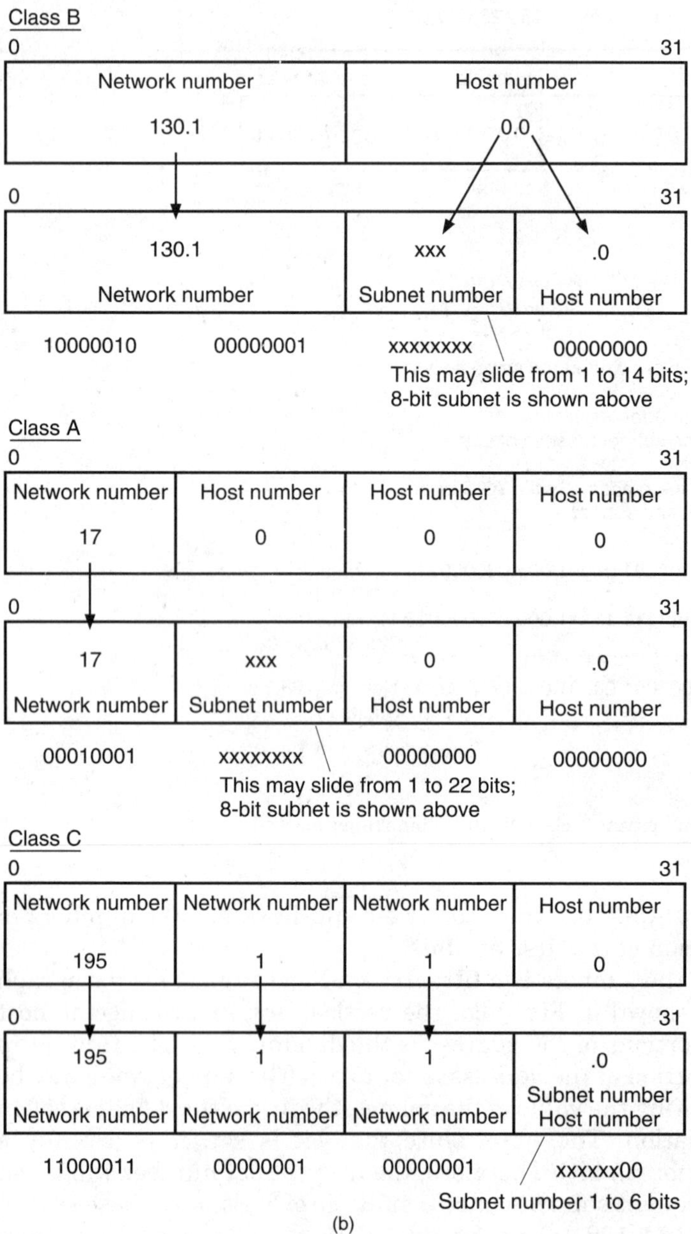

Figure 6.6 (*b*) Subnetting a network number.

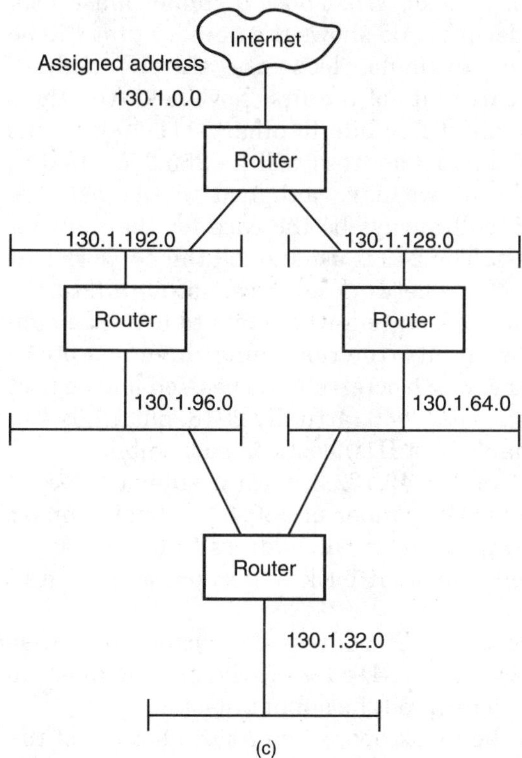

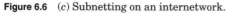

Figure 6.6 (*c*) Subnetting on an internetwork.

This takes in all possible combinations with the exclusion of all 0s and all 1s. In the previous example with each of those subnetwork numbers, we could possibly have 2046 hosts per subnetwork number. This is a little more realistic than not subnetting. With subnetting, we did not have to use many unique class B addresses. We used one class B network number and have 30 subnets available to us from the one class B network. Without subnetting, we would have one network number and up to 65535 hosts assigned to it. Now, we used one network number and made 30 subnetworks from it. All zeros or all ones are not allowed in any of the subnet or host fields.

How did we get 30 possibilities? Using five bits for the subnet mask gives us 32 possible combinations (0 to 31). Since all 1s or all 0s cannot be used (subtract 2), that gives us 30 possibilities. The subnet mask could have used all eight bits, which would give us 254 subnet numbers (all 0s and all 1s not used).

How does a router or workstation know when a subnet is being used. It employs the use of a *subnet mask*. What does a subnet mask look like? It is always written in decimal and shows the number that will be use to mask the bits. For example, let's use the IP address 130.40.132.3. Using the first five bits of the first host field (the third octet) yields 248 (convert the first five bits to binary 11111000). This means the subnet mask for that IP address will be 255.255.248.0 in decimal. This is the mask that we have assigned to the network address of 130.40.132.3. 255 will always be the case for the network number portion of the address. The 248 is used to tell the network station to use the first five bits of the network address, not for a host ID, but for a subnet. It tells a network station which bits to use for a subnet mask. The remaining eleven bits (the remaining three bits of the third octet and eight bits of the fourth octet) should be used for the host ID. This allows for 30 subnets with 2046 (actually 2048, but all 0s and all 1s are not allowed assignable host IDs) hosts on each subnet.

Therefore, the IP address of 130.40.132.3, with a subnet mask of 255.255.248.0, yields the network number of 130.40, subnet number 128, and host ID of 1027. (*Hint:* convert the address to binary, apply the mask in binary, and then convert it back to decimal as shown in Fig. 6.6*a*.

An operation is performed on an IP address. It is called a bitwise AND operation. The IP address is AND'ed with the subnet mask to allow the network station to determine the subnet mask.

Again, Figure 6.6*a* shows the mask operation. At the bottom of the figure is the IP address in binary. This address is logically AND'ed with the mask. The bits that drop out of this operation will indicate to any TCP/IP station the network address. It masks out the host address and leaves the network address.

One last rule: when a network is subnetted, the whole network (all stations assigned to that network number) must be subnetted exactly the same. This is for networks using the IP RIP routing update protocol. When the network number changes (not the subnetwork number), the subnet mask may change. You cannot assign one network number with different subnet masks. The exception to this rule is the routing algorithm of OSPF, which is beyond the scope of this book.

For example, if using the RIP routing protocol (explained later), the subnet mask must remain the same throughout a single class B assignment. For example, if the network assignment is 130.1.0.0 and the subnet mask assigned is 255.255.255.0, this subnet mask must remain the same throughout the 130.1.0.0 network. If the network address changes—for example, to 131.1.0.0—the subnet mask may also change. If the network is using the OSPF routing protocol, the subnet mask may change within one network address.

As stated before, the subnet mask for a class B address could extend into the fourth octet. For example, the subnet mask for a given IP address could be 255.255.255.192. This would indicate a 10-bit subnet mask and this would allow for 1022 subnets with 62 hosts on each of the subnets.

Figure 6.6*c* shows a subnetted network topology connected to the Internet. It is assigned a class B address and uses an 8-bit subnet mask. The Internet knows of the IP address 130.1.0.0. It does not know the subnets involved. This allows the Internet address (routing) tables to remain smaller.

Do you need more hosts than networks? Or more networks than hosts? Unless the network employs the routing protocol of OSPF when choosing a subnet mask, a compromise is usually the case in deciding the mask. If the site is assigned only one network number, there can be only one subnet mask assigned to the whole network. Without a routing protocol that supports multiple subnet masks within a single network number, expansion and network design must be thought about. The only other alternative is to assign multiple network numbers to a single site and, unless the network is private, these addresses are hard to come by.

If the network station moves to a new network, does the IP address for that station change? Like the telephone system, IP addresses must change when the network station is moved to a new network that employs a different network number. If the network station is moved on the same logical network, the IP address may remain the same. For example, if a network station moved to a different part of the network, but the network portion of the address (including subnetting) did not change, the whole IP address may stay the same. If the network station was moved to a network that has a different network address, the IP address of the network station must change.

New with TCP/IP is the ability to assign more than one network number to the same network. This means that one network may employ more than one network number on the same physical cable plant. A router will take the steps necessary to allow network stations to converse on the network. Implementations are different; therefore, the amount of network numbers that may be assigned to the same cable plant varies.

In doing this, multiple class C network numbers may be assigned to the same cable plant. Class C addresses allow only for 254 host IDs per network number. This is a rather low number, and some sites will have more than 254 network stations attached to a cable plant. This means that multiple stations on the same cable plant may have different network addresses. A router must be used to translate between two stations that are located on the same cable plant with different network addresses.

An unfortunate circumstance involving IP addressing becomes very visible when an IP network address must be assigned to a serial link (two routers using a leased phone line to connect). The serial link between two routers has its own network number assigned to it even though the only attachments will be the two routers that are linked together. A serial link will consume a network number and associated host IDs. Therefore, a unique network number will be assigned and, instead of being able to use all available hosts IDs, it will be possible to use only two hosts IDs (there will be only two addressable points on that network). Figure 6.7 depicts this situation.

The rest of the host IDs will be lost for that network number and will now be assigned and used for that serial link and will not be able to be assigned to any other links. If you have a large site that will encompass many serial links and you do not have the ability to assign a large number of network numbers, use subnet addressing and the routing protocol of OSPF. OSPF supports variable length subnet masks, which will collapse that serial link into two hosts within a network number and, therefore, no host numbers are wasted on serial links. Variable length subnet masks are beyond the scope of this book, but they allow a single network number to use multiple masks (unlike RIP). This allows more bits to be assigned back to the network, allowing a more efficient use of the address.

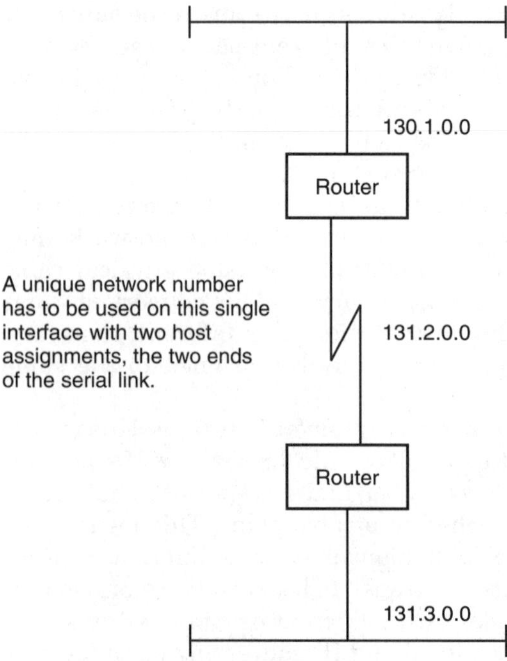

Figure 6.7 Serial line IP address assignment.

Note:

Class A addresses can use the second, third, or fourth (not the whole fourth router field) field for subnets.

Class B addresses can use the third or fourth (not the whole fourth field) field for subnets.

Class C is tricky. The only field left is the single host field. Subnetting this is allowed, but you must use up to 6 of the bits in the fourth field. You need to have a couple of hosts somewhere!

Address resolution protocol (ARP). The IP address does not physically identify those stations on a high-speed local area network (Ethernet, Token Ring, etc.). IP addresses are meant to identify IP hosts and networks at the network layer of the OSI model. It is an IP address and not a physical or MAC address. (For more information on physical-layer addressing, please refer to Chap. 2). The designers of Local Area Networks (LANs) allotted 48 bits to identify a network attachment. This is known as their *physical address* or *MAC address.** Physical addresses identify stations at their data-link level. IP is an addressing scheme used at the network level. On a local area network (Ethernet, Token Ring, etc.), two communicating stations can set up a session only if they know each other's physical address.

An RFC resolved this problem. The resolution was simple and it did not affect the already established IP addressing scheme. It is known as *Address Resolution Protocol* or *ARP.* This is an IP-address-to-physical-station-address resolution (actual name is *binding*) and is explained as follows: If you are trying to connect to a host on the same network number as the one you are currently residing on, the TCP/IP protocol will use ARP to find the physical address of the destination station. (Finding a remote station—one with a different network number address than yours—is explained in a moment.)

Refer to Fig. 6.8. In order to attach to another station on a TCP/IP network, the source station must know the designation station's IP address. Station 129.1.1.1 wants a connection with 129.1.1.4 (no subnet addressing is used here). Therefore, the network address of this class B address is 129.1.0.0 and the personal computer's host address is 1.1; hence the address 129.1.1.1.

With ARP, it is assumed that the IP address of the destination station is already known either through a name service (a central service or file on a network station that maps IP addresses to host names, explained in more detail later) or by using the IP address itself. To reduce overhead on the network, most TCP network stations

* Physical- and MAC-layer addresses are synonymous throughout this book.

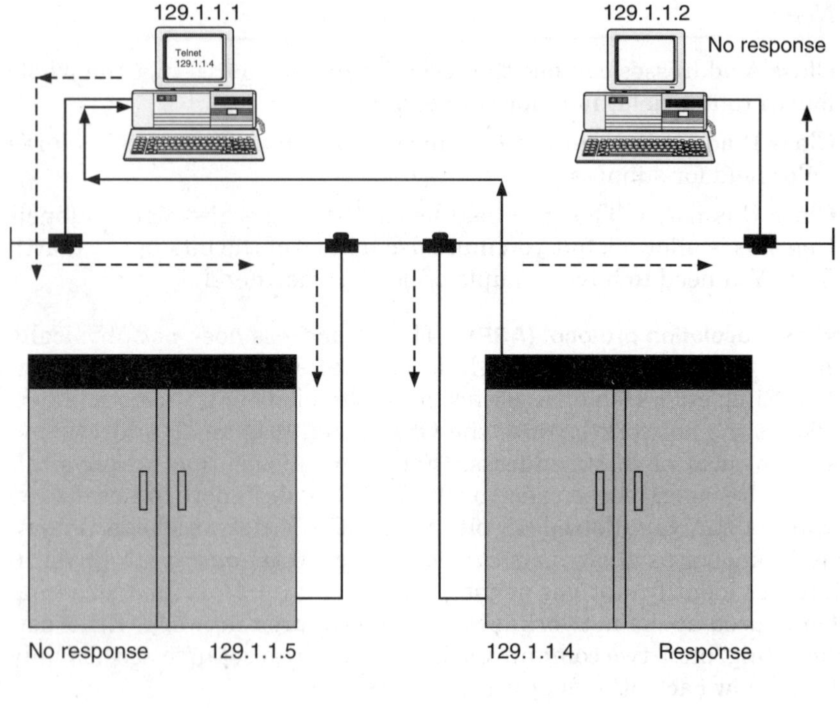

Figure 6.8 ARP request and response.

will maintain a LAN physical-address-to-IP-address table on their host machine. The ARP table is nothing more than a section of RAM memory that will contain data-link physical (or MAC addresses) to IP address mappings that it has learned from the network. Although vendor independent, the first entry in the table should contain the physical address and the IP address of the station on which ARP is currently residing. The second entry in this table may contain the broadcast mapping for the physical address.

Once the IP address is known for the destination station, IP on the source station will first look into its ARP table to find the physical address for that destination IP address. If a mapping was found, no ARP request packet will be transmitted onto the network. IP can bind (place the physical addresses on the data-link headers of the packet) the IP address with the physical address and send the IP datagram to the data link for transmission to the network. (See Table 6.1.)

TABLE 6.1 ARP Table for Station 129.1.1.1

Physical address	IP address
02-60-8C-01-02-03	129.1.1.1
FF-FF-FF-FF-FF-FF	148.9.255.255
FF-FF-FF-FF-FF-FF	255.255.255.255
00-00-A2-05-09-89	129.1.1.4
08-00-20-67-92-89	129.1.1.2
08-00-02-90-90-90	129.1.1.5

If the address is not located in the ARP table, the ARP protocol will build an ARP request packet and send it physically addressed in broadcast mode (destination address FF-FF-FF-FF-FF-FF). This packet is shown in Fig. 6.9*a*. Since the packet is sent out in broadcast mode, all stations on the physical network will receive the packet, but only the host with that IP address will reply. In Fig. 6.8, host 129.1.1.4 will reply to the request packet with an ARP response packet. It will be physically addressed to station 129.1.1.1.

When the host whose IP address is in the request packet responds, it will respond with an ARP reply packet not addressed to destination broadcast but with the source address set to its address (physically and inside the ARP reply packet), and the destination address is the origi-

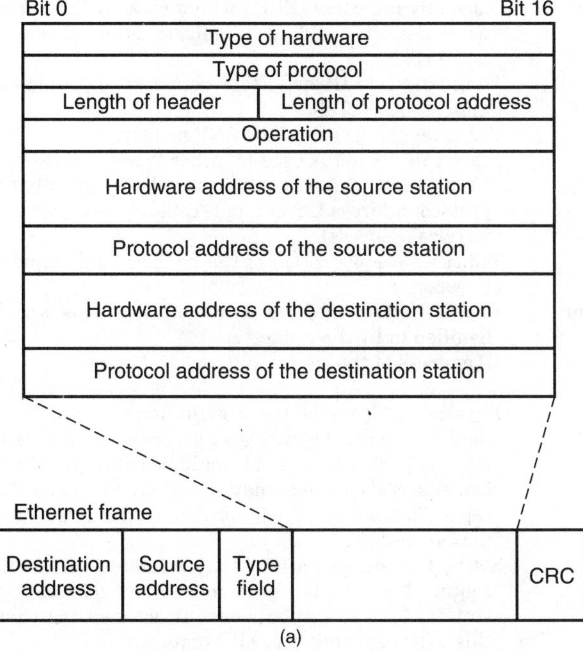

Figure 6.9 (*a*) ARP packet format.

nator. Once the originator of the request receives the response, it will extract the physical address from the source address in the packet and update its ARP table. Now that it has the mapping, it will try to submit its IP datagram to the destination station using the proper addresses (IP and physical address).

This process is completed as an involuntary act to the user. The user will typically be using one of TCP's applications (TELNET for terminal service, SMTP for mail service, or FTP for file transfer service) attempting a connection. This ARP request and reply will happen automatically in the connection. Most TCP vendors supply a utility program that allows a user see the entries in the ARP table.

To improve the efficiency of the protocol, any station on the physical network that received the ARP packet (request packet) can update the ARP cache. In looking at the packet format, the sender's physical and IP addresses will be in the packet. Therefore, all stations can update their ARP tables at the same time.

Figure 6.9*a* shows the ARP packet format. It is encapsulated in an Ethernet packet as shown. (See also Table 6.2. This ARP process works for stations communicating with each other on the same LAN (the

TABLE 6.2 Definition of the ARP Packet

Type of hardware	Normally indicates IEEE 802 network for local area networks. It could also indicate other types of networks.
Type of protocol	Would indicate IP for TCP/IP networks. It could also indicate AppleTalk.
Length of header	Indicates the length of the ARP header.
Length of protocol address	Since this header is used for other types of networks (AppleTalk), this field indicates the length of the protocol address (IP or AppleTalk address, not the physical address).
Operation	Indicates the operation of the header: ARP request or response.
Address of the source station	Physical address of the source station. This would be filled in by the requester.
Protocol address of the source station	IP address of the source station.
Hardware address of the destination station	Physical address of the destination station. This field is usually, but not always, set to 0s if it is a request packet. This field would be set to the physical address of the destination station if it is an ARP reply. This field is filled in by the responding destination station.
Protocol address of the destination station	Set by the source station (ARP requester). This will contain the IP address of the wanted destination station. Only a station whose IP address matches this will respond to the ARP request.

same network number). If they are not on the same LAN, the ARP process still works, but an address of a router will be found. This is fully explained later. Summarizing the ARP process is shown in Fig. 6.9*b*.

Rules for ARP

1. ARP is not a part of the IP protocol and therefore does not contain IP headers.
2. ARP requests and responses are transmitted with a destination physical broadcast address (all Fs) and therefore never leave their logical network.*
3. Since ARP is not part of the IP protocol, new Ethertypes were assigned to identify this type of packet. 0806 is an ARP request and 0806 is an ARP reply. Some ARP implementations can be assigned the 0800 Ethertype, for IP will be able identify the packet as an ARP request or ARP reply packet. Not all implementors of IP use these types. Some still use the Ethertype of 0800 for ARP.

---

* All stations broadcasts (all FFs in the MAC destination header) will not be forwarded by a router.

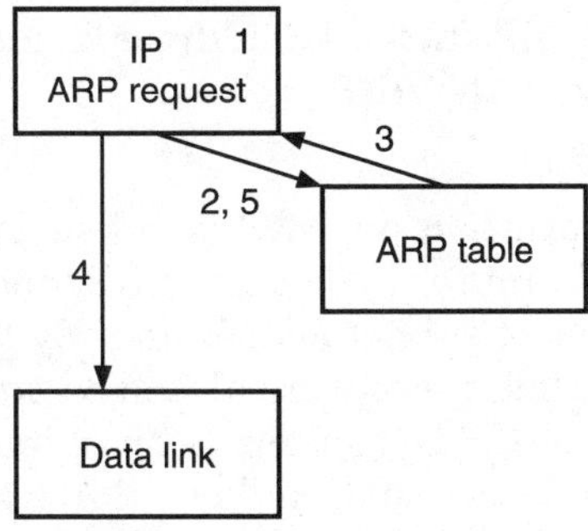

1. IP requests a MAC address to IP address translation.
2. Searches ARP cache table for possible entry.
3. ARP cache will either return the MAC address (if it is in the table) or not.
4. If the address is not in the table, generates an ARP request packet to the network (localized packet). If the address mapping is in the table, reply to IP with the MAC address.
5. Upon an ARP reply, ARP updates its table and reports the address back to IP.

(b)

Figure 6.9 (*b*) the ARP process.

TABLE 6.3 Ethertype Field Entries for ARP

ARP request	0806h
ARP reply	0806h

4. ARP contains an aging entry to delete entries that have not been used for a period of time. This reduces the ARP look-up time and saves memory.
5. If a machine submits an ARP request for itself, it must reply to the request.

Reverse address resolution protocol (RARP). This protocol is used when a network station knows its MAC address but does not know its IP address. When would this happen? This is a common application for diskless workstations (Sun Microsystems, for example).

The requesting client machine will send out a RARP request to a server located on the physical network somewhere that has the RARP server service running on it. This RARP server will respond to the request with that particular station's IP address.

The packet format for a RARP packet is the same for as for ARP. The only difference it that the field that will be filled in will be the senders physical address. The IP address fields will be empty. A RARP server will receive this packet, fill in the IP address fields and reply to the sender. It is the opposite of the ARP process.

Proxy ARP. One last variation on ARP is called Proxy ARP.* Proxy ARP is the capability of a router to be able to respond to an end station (host) that does not support subnet addressing. By the time IP subnet addressing became adopted, there were already a tremendous amount of hosts established with TCP/IP as their networking protocol. Subnetting was implemented later, so if a host did not support subnet addressing, it could incorrectly mistake an IP network number (the subnet portion of the IP address) for a host number. The router tricks the transmitting station into believing that the source station is on the local LAN.

As shown in Fig. 6.10, the host on network A may not attach to other devices on network B since it has no concept of subnetting. When the IP layer does a comparison of its address to the destination IP address, it will think the packet is locally addressed and, therefore, will not transmit it to a router for delivery. Instead it will invoke the algorithm

* This is also known as promiscuous ARP or ARP hack.

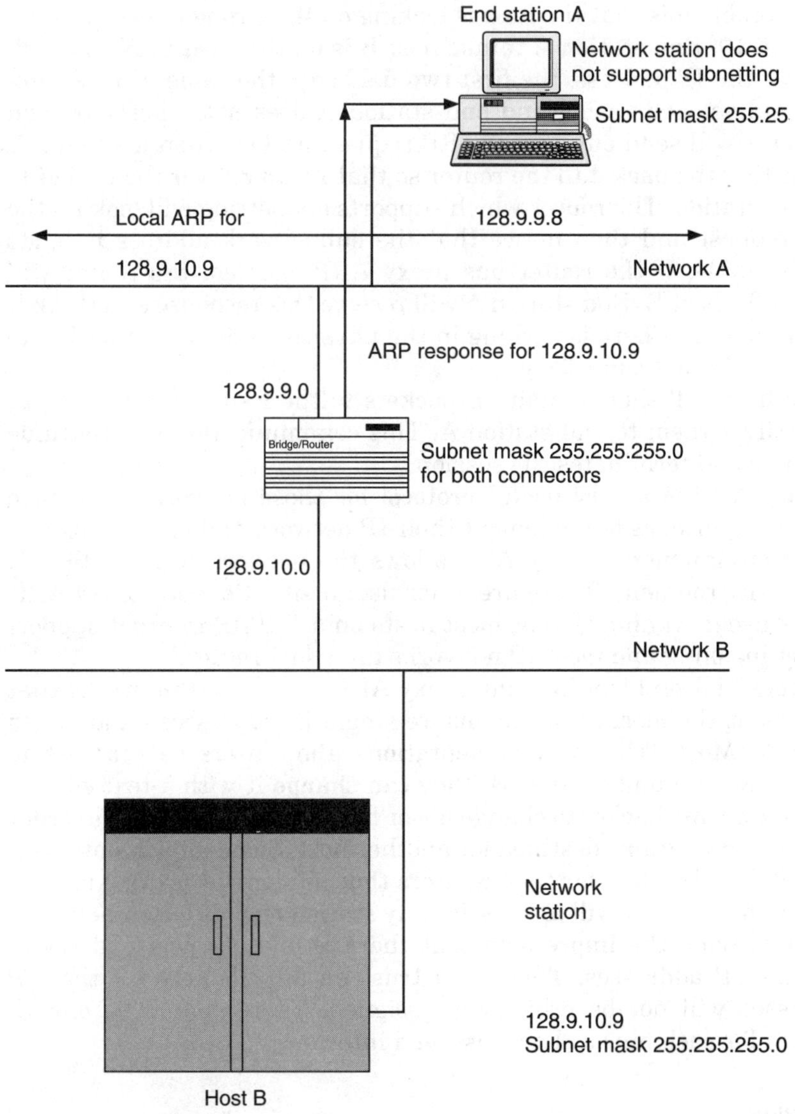

Figure 6.10 Proxy ARP.

to deliver it locally. Unless the local router is running proxy ARP, the packet will not be answered and the host will think the destination station is not available. Furthermore, different subnet masks are not allowed within the same network number (unless you are running a routing protocol that supports the broadcasting of subnet masks in its routing updates, like OSPF).

The problem is that the host is looking on the wrong network. Refer to Fig. 6.10. End station A thinks host B is on the local LAN. By deciphering the IP address, the first two fields are the same. Host B supports subnet addressing and end station A does not. Therefore, end station A will send out a local ARP request packet when it should be submitting the packet to the router so that it can deliver the packet to the end station. The router which supports subnetting will look up the ARP request and then notice that the subnetwork address is in its routing table. If the router has proxy ARP enabled, the router will answer for host B. End station A will receive this response and think it is from host B. There is nothing in the physical address of a packet to indicate where it came from.

The host will then submit all packets to the router and the router will deliver them to end station A. This communication will continue until one end terminates the session.

Proxy ARP is a very useful protocol for those networks that have been using bridges to implement their IP network and are moving to a router environment. Proxy ARP allows the network to migrate to a routed environment. There are other useful situations for proxy ARP, but its use is waning. Today, most hosts on a TCP/IP internet support subnet masking and most IP networks are using routers.

A potential problem in using proxy ARP is for those networks that implement the mechanism to ensure single IP addresses on are each network. Most TCP/IP implementations allow users easy access to their network number (that is, they can change it with a text editor). This allows any hacker to change his or her number to another in order to receive datagrams destined for another host. Some implementations of TCP/IP will detect for this. Routers that implement proxy ARP will get caught, for they will answer for any station on a different network, thereby giving the impression that there is one physical address to multiple IP addresses. There is a trust on any IP network that IP addresses will not be arbitrarily assigned. There should be one IP address for each physical address on a internet.

IP routing

Routing fundamentals: interior gateway protocols. To make any network more manageable, it will be split into many networks. The interconnection of these networks is accomplished by routers. Routers enable data to be forwarded to other networks in a very efficient manner. It will always be easier to manage many smaller networks than it will be to manage one large network. In order for routers to forward data to other networks, they use special protocols to enable them to internally draw a map of the entire internet for the purposes of routing. To accomplish this, there are two types of protocols used. Interior Gateway Protocols (IGPs) and Exterior Gateway Protocols (EGPs). The exterior gateway protocol that is used with IP (known as EGP) will not be covered in this book. For the purposes of this book, only one type of routing protocol will be shown. It is an Interior Gateway Protocol known as the Routing Information Protocol (RIP).

In the previous section, the text referred to network numbers, routers, and packets that must get to a network different from their own. This section will fully explain those items.

Referring to Fig. 6.11, end station B and host A are located on different networks. In order to communicate with one another, they must employ the use of a router. A TCP/IP internet consists of multiple physical networks with network devices attached. All these local networks can be interconnected by special devices known as routers to form an

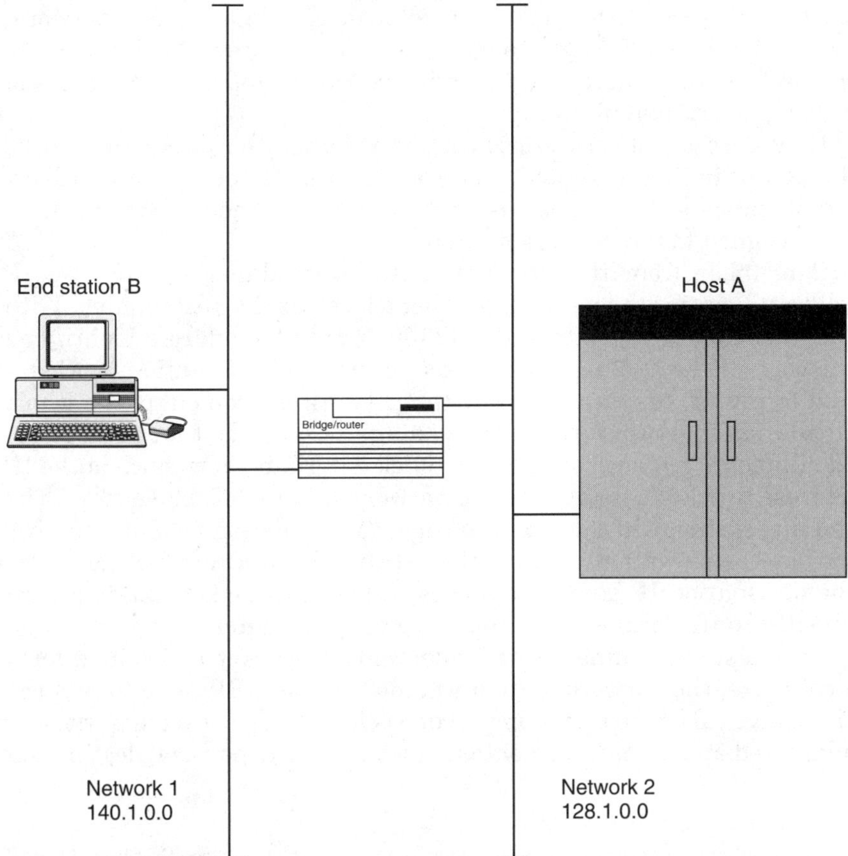

Figure 6.11 A routed environment (no subnets).

internet. These routers are used to connect two or more networks and allow internet traffic to pass through them.

Routing data. Throughout this section, different network numbers will be used. The examples will not employ the use of subnets. Subnets effectively act like network numbers. Subnetworks are also separated by a router. For example, in Fig. 6.11, the network numbers could be 140.1.1.1 on the network with end station B and 140.1.2.1 on the network containing host A. Using a subnet mask of 255.255.255.0 would yield two different networks: 140.1.1.0 and 140.1.2.0. For simplicity in explaining routers, I have chosen to use completely different network numbers.

For a packet to be transmitted and received on a local network or an internet, it must be routed to the remote network station by using the IP network layer. Packets may be routed on a local LAN (two stations on the same physical network, i.e., not separated by a router). This is known as *direct routing.* If the packet is destined for another network, it must be routed through a device known as a router. This is known as *indirect routing.* Therefore, data may be transferred using two types of routing: direct and indirect.

How does a network station know whether the packet has to be directly or indirectly routed? For the network station, it is a relatively simple process. The whole basis for routing is in the IP network number assigned to the network station.

Remember from the previous section on addressing that an IP address contains the network number as well as the host number. With the first 1, 2, 3, or 4 bits of the 32-bit IP network address identifying the class of the address, this allows for any network station (workstation or router) to quickly extract the network portion out of the whole IP address.* In other words, by reading up to the first four bits of the IP address, a network station can quick determine how much of the IP address to read to determine the network number of the address. The sending station will compare the packet's destination network number to that of its own network number. If the network number portion of the destination IP address matches it own, the packet can be routed directly on the local LAN, without the use of a router.

Once this determination is made, and the packet is destined for a local route, the network station would check its ARP table to find the IP to physical address mapping. If one is found, the packet is physically addressed and transmitted onto the network. The physical destination

* For a subnetted network, two actions are required: one to read the first bits of the IP address to identify the class and another to check the subnet mask to identify if a subnet is being used.

address (located in the data-link header) will be that of the receiving station. If the station's address is not in the ARP cache, the ARP request process is invoked.

If the host resides on a network with a different network number (not on the local LAN), then the transmitting station will have to use the services of a router. The transmitting station will address the physical destination address of the packet to that of the router (using ARP, if necessary, to find the physical address of the router) and submit the packet to the router.* The router will, in turn, deliver the packet to either its locally attached networks (finding the destination's physical address and submitting the datagram directly to that network station) or to another router for delivery of the data. Notice here, the destination physical address is that of the router and not the final destination station. This type of routing is indirect routing. The destination IP address is embedded in the IP header.

Sending a packet to its final destination may be accomplished by using both direct and indirect routing. For example, when a packet is to be delivered across an internet, the originating station will address it to the router for delivery to its final network. This is *indirect routing.* No matter whether the final destination network ID is directly connected to that router or whether the packet must traverse a few routers to reach its final destination, the last router in the path must use *direct routing* to deliver the packet to its destination host.

It should be noted here that none of the IP routing protocols will alter the original IP datagram, with two exceptions: the TTL (Time-to-Live) field and the Cyclic Redundancy Check fields. If an IP datagram is received by a router and it has not arrived at its final destination, the router will decrement the TTL field. If TTL > 0, it will forward the packet based on routing table information. Otherwise, the IP datagram's header contents will remain the same (with the exception of an error-detection field known as the Cyclic Redundancy Check (CRC). Since the TTL field changed, the CRC must be recalculated throughout all the networks and routers that the datagram traverses. Otherwise, the only alterations that are made are to the data-link headers and trailers. The IP addresses in the IP header will remain the same, as the datagram traverses any routers in the path to its destination.

Routers deliver on a connectionless basis and therefore do not guarantee delivery of any packet. They operate at the network layer which provides best effort or connectionless data transfer. Routers do not establish sessions with other routers on the internet.

---

*ARPs are used only on the local network to either find the MAC address of a local station or to find the MAC address of a router for a nonlocal destination.

These routers forward packets based on the network address of the packet (in the IP header) and *not* on the physical address (the 48-bit address for Ethernet and Token Ring) of the final destination (the receiver) of the packet. When the router receives the packet, it will look at the final network address (embedded in the IP header of the packet) and determine how to route the packet. Routers only route packets that are directly addressed to them. They do not operate in promiscuous mode (watching all LAN traffic).*

For a full explanation of the router forwarding process, refer to the flowchart in Fig. 6.12.

Before complete confusion takes over here, there are some entities that need to be explained about the IP layer that allow the internet to operate. In other words, when a router receives a packet, how does it know where and how to send these packets? In order for a packet to be delivered through a router, the router must know which path to deliver the packet to in order for the packet to reach its final destination. This is accomplished through IP routing algorithms, which involves two steps: maintaining a table of known routes (network numbers) and learning new routes (network numbers) when they become available.

Routing data based on routing tables. Some routing protocols allow routers to determine network paths based on concept known a vector-distance. Distance-vector means that the information sent from router to router is based on an entry in a table consisting of <vector, distance>. Vector means the network number and distance means what it costs to get there. The routers exchange this network reachability information with each other by broadcasting their routing table information consisting of these distance-vector entries.

Each entry in the table is a network number (the vector) and the amount of routers (distance) that are in-between it (the router) and the final network (indicated by the network number). This distance is sometimes referred to as a *metric.* For example, if the source station wants to transmit a packet to a destination station that is four hops away, there are probably four routers separating the two networks.

Any time a datagram must traverse a router (thereby passing through a new network number) it is considered a hop (metric). For RIP, the maximum diameter of the internet is 15 routers (hops). A distance of 16 is an indication that the network is not reachable. In other words, if the network is more than 15 routers away, it is considered unreachable.

As shown in Table 6.4, each router will contain a table with starting entries of those networks that are directly attached to it. For a router

---

* Multiprotocol routers operate in promiscuous mode, but this concept is beyond the scope of this book.

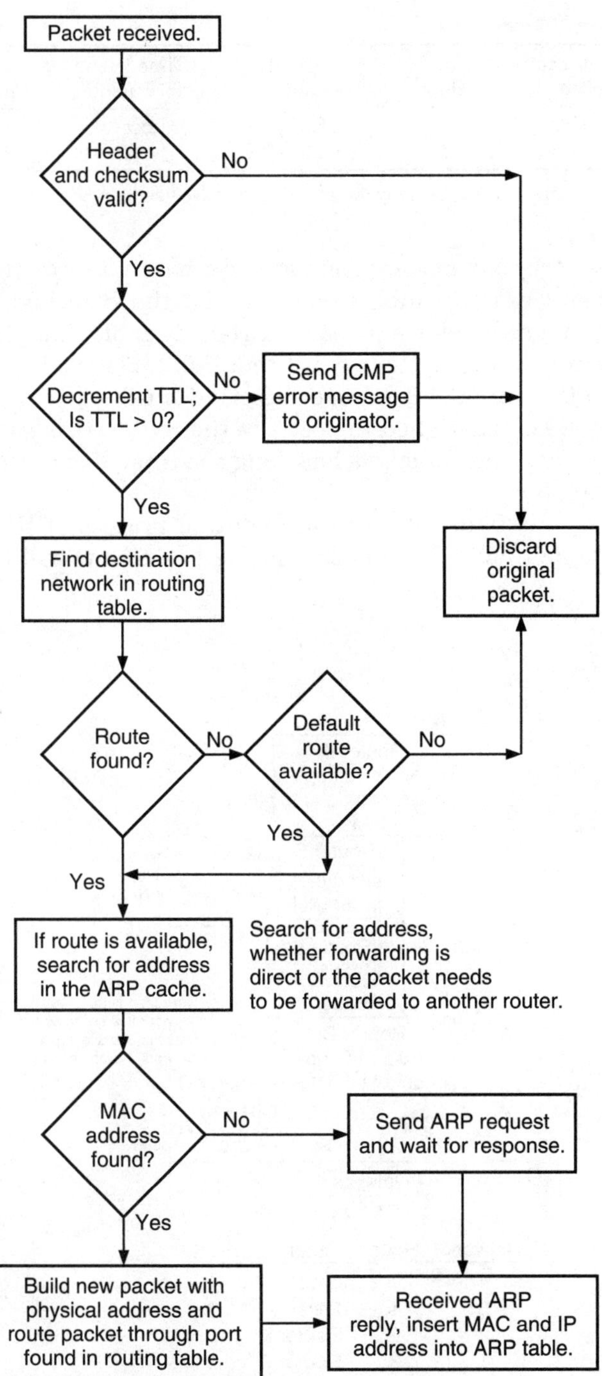

Figure 6.12 IP routing flowchart.

TABLE 6.4 Routing Table Entries*

Network number	Next router to deliver to	Hops	Learned from	Time left before delete	Port
134.4.0.0	Direct route	1	RIP	xxx	1
133.3.0.0	Direct route	1	RIP	xxx	2

* Actual verbiage of the entries in the table may differ from vendor to vendor.

that has only two network connections (there are no other routers on the internet), the initial entries in the table would look like the following:

There are actually more header entries in a routing table, but the significant portions are shown in Table 6.4. From this table, we know that networks 134.4.0.0 and 134.3.0.0 are directly connected to this router. Network 134.4.0.0 is assigned to port 1 of the router. It is running the RIP protocol, and xxx indicates how long the route has before it is deleted from the table.

Refer to Fig. 6.13. This figure shows the updating process of RIP. Parts of a router's table (network number and the hop count) will be

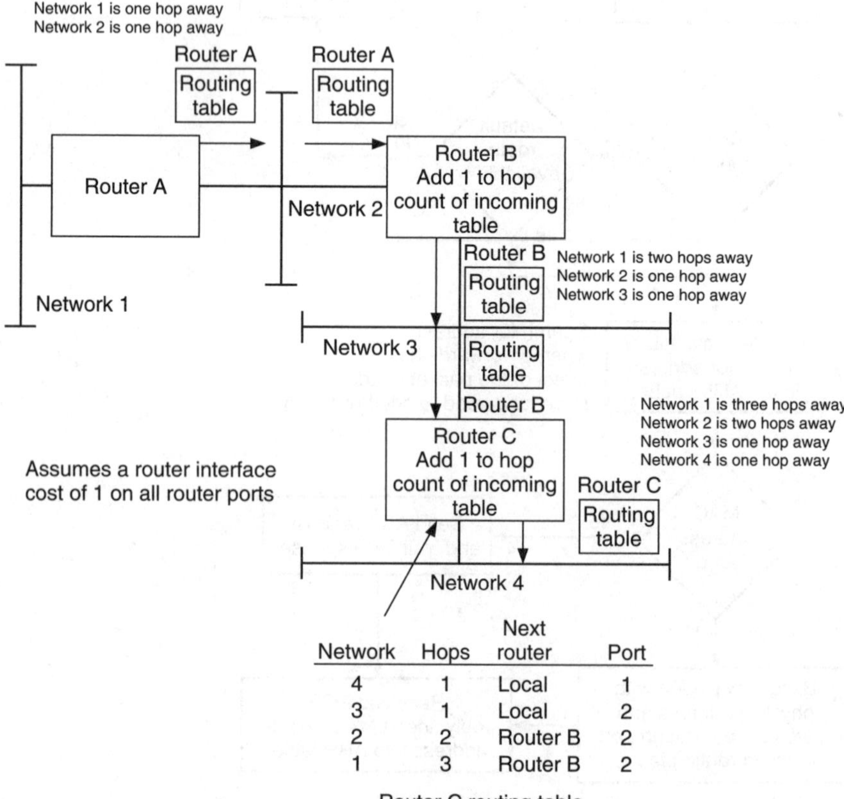

Figure 6.13 Routing table updates (RIP); split horizon is not implemented here.

broadcast to the local networks to which the router has directly attached. There are a few exceptions, which will be explained in a moment. Any router that is located on the same network will receive the packet, read the routing table data, update its table if needed, and then discard the packet. Routers will not forward any update packets they receive. All participating routers will accomplish this. As each table is received, the routers are building a picture of the network. As each broadcast is transmitted, more and more information is being propagated throughout the network. Eventually, all routers will know of all networks in the internet.

The tables are encapsulated in a packet which is physically and logically addressed to broadcast mode. All local routers will receive and interpret the table against their own tables, but they will not forward the received table through their network ports. (Remember that routers will not forward packets addressed to broadcast.) Instead, once a router has updated its table, it will then broadcast its newly updated table out its directly attached ports. All routers on that network will receive the datagram and update their tables. This is how routing table information is propagated throughout a network.

There are three possibilities that can cause a router to update its existing table based on just-received information:

1. If the received table contains an entry to a network with a lower hop count, it will *replace its entry* with the new entry containing the lower hop count.

2. If a network exists in the just-received table that does not exist in its own table, it will *add the new entry.*

3. If the router forwards packets to a particular network through a specified router (indicated by the next hop router address) and that router's hop count to a network destination changes, it will *change its entry.* In other words, if router A normally routes data for a network X through router B, and router B's hop count entry to that network changes, router A *changes its entry.*

Figure 6.13 shows what happens when router A submits it routing table out of its port connected to network 2. (For simplicity, the figure will show the updating through one port only. In reality, routing tables are submitted out all ports of a router, with a few restrictions on which entries of the table get transmitted.)

Router A transmits its table containing two networks: 1 and 2. Each of these networks is one hop away (they are directly connected). Router B will receive this packet and it will add one to each hop count entry in the received table. (This is accomplished assuming the RIP cost assigned to that port of router B is 1. It could be set to something else.)

Router B would examine its table and notice that it does not have an entry for network 1. It will add this entry to its table as: Network 1, available through port 1, two hops away. It will then check the next entry. Network 2 will not be added, for router B already has network 2 in its table with a cost of 1. Since the incoming table reports network 2 has a cost of 2, router B will ignore this entry. (There are rules that will prevent router A from sending out information about network 2 and these rules will be discussed later.)

Once its table is updated, router B will transmit its table out every 30 seconds its ports (again, for simplicity only one port is being shown). Router C will receive this table from router B and will perform the same steps as router B. Eventually, all information about all networks on the internet will be propagated to all routers.

IP routing tables. Referring to Tables 6.5 and 6.6, the significant entries in a routing table for the network shown in Figure 6.14 consist of three elements:

1. Network number
2. Hops to that network number
3. The next router in the path to that network

Routing tables vary, depending on the update mechanism used. The following table is a sample of a routing table used by the routing information protocol (RIP) for the IP protocol.

TABLE 6.5 Router A's Routing Table

Network number	Next router to deliver to	Hops	Learned from	Time left before delete	Port*
132.2.0.0	Direct route	1	RIP	xxx	1
133.3.0.0	Direct route	1	RIP	xxx	2
130.1.0.0	Direct route	1	RIP	xxx	3
134.4.0.0	133.3.0.4	2	RIP	xxx	2

* This indicates the physical port on the router from which the router learned the route and where it will forward a packet to if one is received with the network number.

TABLE 6.6 Router B's Routing Table

Network number	Next router to deliver to	Hops	Learned from	Time left before delete	Port
134.4.0.0	Direct route	1	RIP	xxx	1
133.3.0.0	Direct route	1	RIP	xxx	2
132.2.0.0	133.3.0.3	2	RIP	xxx	2
130.1.0.0	133.3.0.3	2	RIP	xxx	2

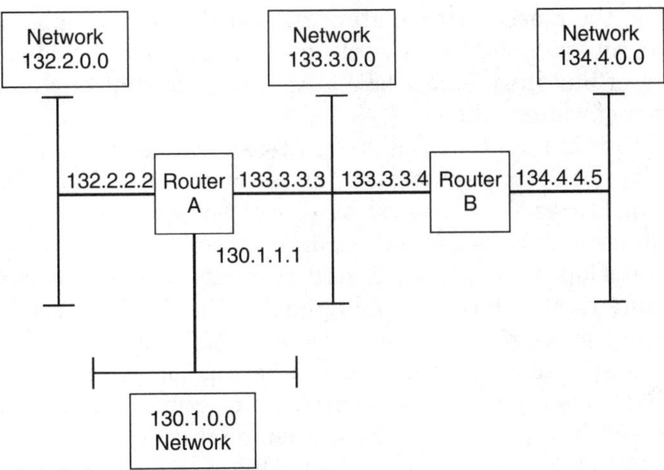

Figure 6.14 IP addressing for routers.

Tables 6.5 and 6.6 are defined as follows:

Network number. A known network ID.

Next router to deliver to. The next router that the packet should be delivered to if the destination network is not directly connected. A directly connected network is one that is physically connected to the router, since most routers today have more than two connected networks.

Hops. This is the metric count of how many routers the packet must traverse before reaching the final destination. A one indicates a local route.

Learned from. Since many routing algorithms may exist in a router (i.e., RIP, OSPF, and EGP may exist in the same router), there is usually an entry in the table to explain how the route was acquired.

Time left to delete. The amount of time left before the route will be deleted from the table.

Port. The physical port on the router from which the router received information about this network.

The routing information protocol (RIP)

How the table is created. Dynamic updating is the process by which routers update each other with reachability information. Before the advent of dynamic updates of routing tables, most commercial vendors supported manual updates for their router table. This meant entering network numbers, their associated distances, and the port numbers manually into the router table. As networks grew larger, this became a cumbersome way of building tables. RIP is the protocol that enables automatic updates of router tables.

The RIP algorithm is based on the distance-vector algorithms just described. RIP placed the fundamentals of distance-vector in a simple routing algorithm. It was first devised by Xerox Corporation as the routing algorithm used by Internet Datagram Protocol of XNS.

An RFC was developed for the XNS RIP standard to be incorporated into IP, and it was formally adopted by the IAB in 1988. Although it was not primarily intended as *the* routing algorithm for TCP, it gained widespread acceptance when it became embedded into the Berkeley UNIX operating system through a service known as routed* (pronounced "route d"—d is for the daemon process that runs the protocol in UNIX). The protocol was actually in widespread use much before 1988, for the protocol was distributed in Berkeley 4BSD UNIX and gained widespread acceptance through the vast number of installations of this operating system.

With RIP information, any router knows the length of the shortest path (not necessarily the best) from each of its neighbor routers (routers located on the same network) to any other destination. Keep in mind that RIP understands only the shortest route to a destination. This route may not be the fastest. RIP understands only hop counts. For example, there may be two paths to a destination—one that traverses two T1† lines (three hops) and another that has 2 hops but is a 9600 baud serial line. RIP would pick the 9600 baud line, for it is shorter (two hops). There are variations of RIP that allow the network administrator to assign an arbitrary RIP hop count or cost to a route to disallow for this RIP problem. This solves one problem but creates another. This incremented RIP number adds to the upper limit of a 16-hop diameter in RIP.

As shown in Fig. 6.15*a*, the RIP packet is quite simple. This figure shows the RIP header and data encapsulated in an Ethernet packet.

There are two types of RIP packets that traverse a network (indicated by the command field). One type of RIP packet is to request information and the other is to give information, a response packet. Most RIP packets that traverse a local network will be the periodic RIP table updates. Remember that RIP packets will not leave their local network. All participants in the RIP protocol (for example, routers) will receive the packet, update their tables if necessary, and then discard the packet. They will compute the reachability of net-

---

* Remember that TCP/IP was also embedded into the Berkeley 4BSD operating system by a research grant provided by DARPA.

† T1 is 1.544 Mbps. It is a serial data line provided by the telephone characters.

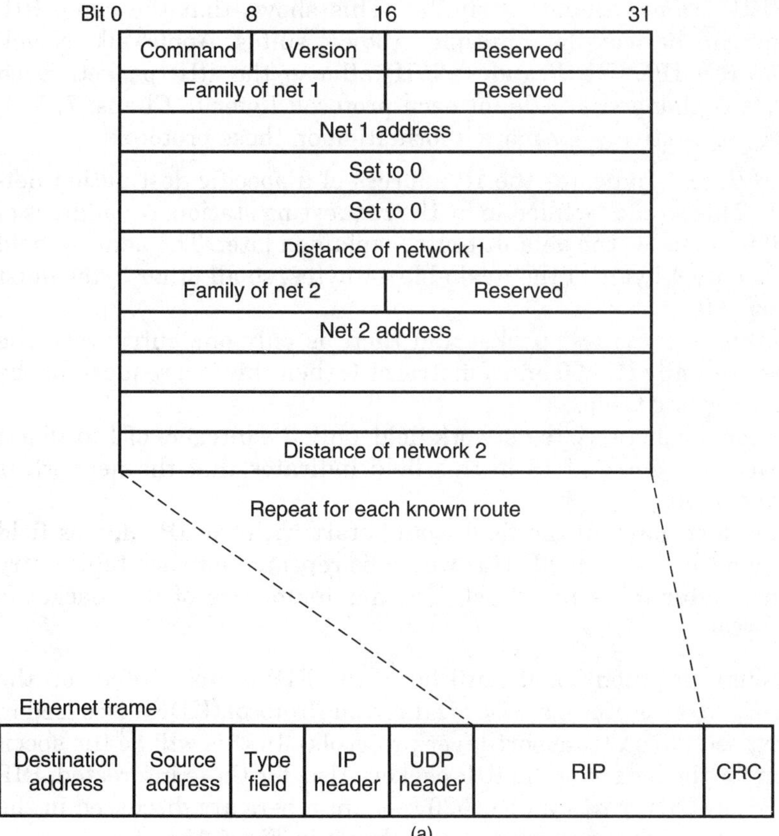

Figure 6.15 (*a*) RIP packet format.

works based on adding a cost (usually 1) to the just-received tables or count entry, and then broadcast their tables out their ports (usually being mindful of a protocol named split horizon, which is explained a little later).

The fields in the RIP packets are:

Command	*Description*
1	Request for partial or full routing table information
2	Response packet containing a routing table
3–4	Turn on (3) or off (4) trace mode (obsolete)
5	Sun Microsystems Internal use

Version. Used to indicate the version of RIP. Currently set to 1.

Family of net x. Used to show the diversity of the RIP protocol. This is used to indicate the protocol that owns the packet. It will be set to 2 for IP. Since XNS could possibly be run on the same network as IP, the RIP frames would be similar. This shows that the same RIP frame can be used for multiple protocol suites. AppleTalk, Novell NetWare's IPX, XNS, and TCP/IP all use the RIP packet. Each packet is changed a little for each protocol. Refer to Chaps. 7, 5, 4, and 6, respectively, for more information on those protocols.

IP address. Indicates the IP address of a specific destination network. This would be filled in by the requesting station. An address of 0.0.0.0 indicates the default route, explained later. The address field needs only 4 bytes of the available 14 bytes, so all other bytes must be set to 0.

If this is a request packet and there is only one entry, with the address family ID of 0 and a metric of 1, then this is a request for the entire routing table.

As for the distance to network field, only the integers of 1 to 16 are allowed. An entry of 16 in this field indicates that the network is unreachable.

The next entry in the field would start with the IP address field through the metric field. This would be repeated for each table entry of the router to be broadcast. The maximum size of this packet is 512 bytes.

Although not mentioned until later, the RIP protocol relies on the transport-layer protocol of User Datagram Protocol (UDP, discussed in the next section on transport-layer protocols). In this will be the specification for the length of the RIP packet. Also, for those interested, RIP operates on UDP port number 520 (port numbers are discussed in the UDP section). This encapsulation in shown in Fig. 6.15*b*.

Finally, both routers and individual hosts can implement the RIP protocol since RIP has two entities: *active* and *passive*. As active, RIP both listens to RIP broadcasts from other network stations (and builds

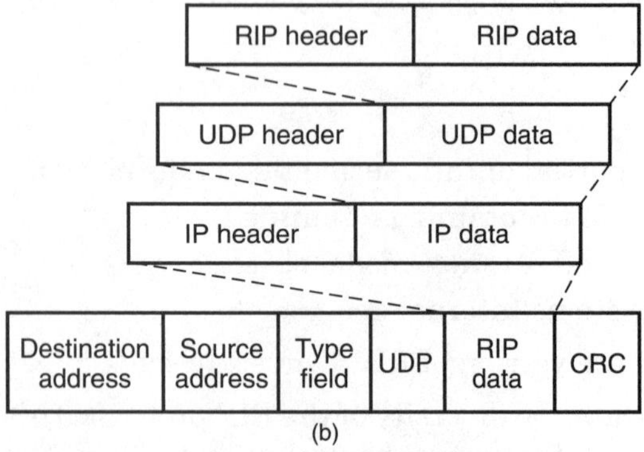

Figure 6.15 (*b*) RIP packet encapsulation.

it own internal tables) and transmits its own broadcasts to respond to requests from other stations.

In passive mode, RIP listens only for RIP updates. (It may build its own tables or it may not. If it does build a table, it will not broadcast these tables.) It will build a table so that it will not have to request information from other routers on the network when it needs to. Passive end is used for nonrouting network stations. This is also useful when using simplex devices such as a DOS personal computer with TCP/IP or maybe a terminal server. These devices have no reason to broadcast updates, but have every reason to listen for the updates. Today, most DOS PC computers will use a concept of a default gateway, explained later.

Using the RIP passive protocol allows the host to maintain a table of the shortest routes to a network and designates which router to send the packets to. This does consume a considerable amount of RAM for both the table and the algorithm. Without it, TCP/IP requires the use of a default gateway entry which specifies that when a packet is destined for remote network, the host must submit the packet to a specified gateway for it to process, even if this gateway does not have the shortest path to that network. Passive implementations add no more overhead to the network, for they listen only to routing table updates that are on the network. Without passive RIP, these devices had to maintain their own tables or implement a default route.

Default routes. On a TCP/IP network, there is a concept known as the *default route.* This is not part of any other network protocol (i.e., XNS, AppleTalk, IPX, etc.). The default route can be maintained in two places: the router and the end station.

For an end station that does not support the passive function of the RIP protocol, thereby allowing it to find a route dynamically, the default router (commonly called a default gateway) is assigned to it. The IP layer in the end station would determine that the destination network is not local (no direct routing) and that the services of a router must be used. Instead of implementing the RIP protocol, the end station may submit the packet to the default router as assigned by the default route number. The router will take care of ensuring the packet will reach its final destination. If that router did not have the best route, it would send a message to the end station to inform it of a better route. This will be explained later.

A router may also be assigned a default route. It is indicated by a 0.0.0.0 in its routing table. This is implemented for when a router receives a packet and does not have the network number in its table. The router will forward the packet to another router for which it has as an assigned default route. This means that when a router has received a packet to route, and its table does not contain the network number indicated in the received packet, it will forward the packet to another router in hopes that the default router will have the network number in its table and will be able to properly forward the packet. That router will receive the packet and, if the network number is in table, it will forward the packet. If the network number is not in its table, it, too, may have a default router—and it will forward the packet to that router.

The problem with default routes in workstations is that a workstation's default router may go down and the workstation will not know if there is another router on the network. The network number may change or there may be a better path for the workstation to take. The default gateway does allow for the elimination of routing tables in the network station and routers, and allows the routing tables to become small by allowing groups of networks to become available through the default route.

Disadvantages of the RIP protocol. As noted before, the acceptance of RIP in the Internet community was based on its implementation into the popular Berkeley 4BSD UNIX operating system through a process known as routed. Unfortunately, it was implemented before the rapid growth of the TCP/IP. It has many disadvantages that were not considered limiting at the time it became accepted. Before RIP was implemented, most router tables had to be constructed manually (a very tedious and dangerous job). RIP allowed these table to be updated dynamically, which was a real advantage at that time. The disadvantages follow.

Routing table updates received are only as accurate as the router that submitted them. If any router made a computational error in updating its routing table, this error will be received by all other routers.

What may also be apparent is the fact that the routing tables could get very large. If the network consisted of 300 different networks (not uncommon in larger corporations), each routing table of every router would have 300 entries. Since RIP works with UDP (connectionless transport-layer service), the maximum datagram size of a RIP packet is 512 bytes. This allows for a maximum of 24 <network number, distance> tuples in each packet (refer to RIP packet description Fig. 6.15*a*). Therefore, it would take 13 packets from each router to broadcast its routing table to all other routers on all the local networks in the internet. This would be broadcast every 30 seconds by each of the 300 routers. This is an unnecessary consumption of bandwidth, especially over slow-speed serial lines.

This leads to the second disadvantage. RIP broadcasts (data-link physical address of all FFs) to the network, normally every 30 seconds, even across slower-speed serial links. This will make the data link pass the packet up to the upper-layer protocols on all stations on the network, even if the stations do not support RIP.

The third disadvantage is RIP routes datagrams based on the shortest distance to the destination network. The protocol does not take into effect the throughput associated with any path taken. In the RIP protocol, if the path to a destination network contains three hops and another path contains two hops to the same destination, the router will always select the path with two hops, even if the path with two hops is 56 Kbps serial lines running and the one with three hops is running at Ethernet speeds of 10 Mbps. To overcome this, some RIP implementations provide a mechanism to manually assign an artificial hop count to a path.

But this creates another problem. The limit for the number of hops that a network may be distanced from any network station is 15, for a hop count of 16 is considered unreachable. If you add additional hops to a path, you have decreased the total number of routers allowed in a path.

RIP does not handle growth very well. This problem is twofold. The first limitation is that a destination network may be no more than 15 hops away in diameter (a distance of 16 in any routing table indicates the network is unreachable). This does not allow for large networks to be based on RIP. Careful planning is needed to implement large-scale networks based on the RIP protocol.

The other scale problem is the propagation of routing information. Four terms need to be understood here, for they are used quite frequently: *split horizon, hold-down timer, poison reverse,* and *triggered updates.*

Refer to Fig. 6.16*a*. With router A directly attached to network 1, it will advertise that route through *all* its ports as a distance of 1 (whatever the RIP-assigned cost of that port that attaches to that network is). Router B receives this, updates its table as network 1 with a distance of 2. Router B then broadcasts its table (at the 30-second update timer) and router C will receive this and update its table as network 1 with a distance of 3. Notice that all routers will broadcast all the information in their tables through all ports (even the ports from which they received the update).

Why would router B broadcast a reachability of network 1 when router A already has a direct attachment to it? Wouldn't this confuse router A if network 1 is located? Normally it would, but remember that the only changes that a router will make to its tables is when the hop count distance is lower, is a new entry, or if the next hop router path taken to a network changes its hop count. Since that hop count is higher, router A will simply ignore that particular entry in the update table.

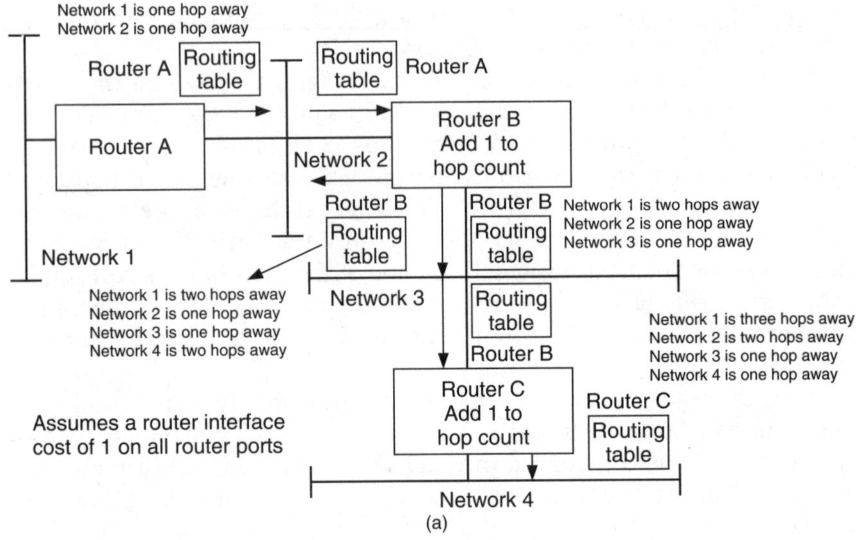

Figure 6.16 Routing table updates. (*a*) Not implementing split horizon.

Using the foregoing original algorithm, a serious problem occurs when router A loses it reachability to network 1. It will update its table entry for that network with a distance of 16 (16 indicates not reachable) but will wait to broadcast this information with the next scheduled RIP update. So far so good, but if router B broadcasts its routing table before router A (notice that not all routers will broadcast their tables at the same time), router A will then see that router B has a shorter path to network 1 than it does (a distance of 2 for router B versus a distance of 16 for router A). Router A will change its entry for network 1. Now, router A, on its next RIP update broadcast, will announce that it has a path to network 1 with a distance of 3 (2 from the table entry received from router B plus 1 to reach router B). There is now a loop between routers A and B. A packet destined for network 1 will be passed between routers A and B until the TTL counter is 0. When router B receives a packet destined for network 1, it will forward the packet to router A; router A will forward it back to router B; and this will continue until the TTL field reaches 0. This is known as *loop*. The RIP protocol works extremely well in a stable environment (an environment where routers and their networks rarely change). The process of clearing out dead routes and providing alternate paths is known as *convergence*.

Even future RIP updates will not quickly fix the convergence in this case. Each update (every 30-second default) will add 1 to the table entry, and it will take a few updates to outdate the entry in these routers. This is known as *slow convergence,* and it causes errors in routing tables and routing loops to occur.

To overcome this and other problems, a few rules were added to the IP RIP algorithm:

1. *Split horizon.* Implemented by every protocol that uses a variation of RIP (AppleTalk, IPX, XNS, and IP), this states that a router will not broadcast a learned route back through a port from which it was received. Therefore, router B would not broadcast the entry of network 1 back to router A. This would keep router B from broadcasting back to router A the reachability of network 1, thereby eliminating the possibility of a lower hop count being introduced when network 1 became disabled. Figure 6.16*b* shows how the routers would send their tables if split horizon were used. Notice which routes are not included in their updates. Compare Fig. 6.16*b* with Fig. 6.16*a*.
2. *Hold-down timer.* This rule states that once a router receives information about a network that claims a known network is not reachable, it must ignore all future updates that include an entry (a path) to that network, typically for 60 seconds. Not all vendors support this in their routers. If one vendor does support it and another does not, routing loops may occur.
3. *Poison reverse* and *triggered updates.* These are the last two rules which help to eliminate the slow convergence problem. They state that once the router detects a network connection is disabled, the

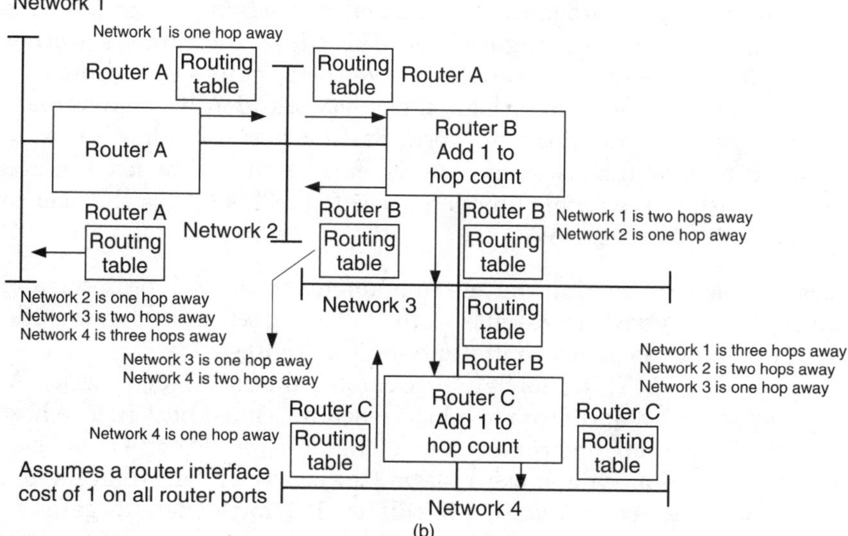

Figure 6.16 Routing table updates. (*b*) Implementing split horizon.

router should keep the present entry in its routing table and then broadcast network unreachable (metric of 16) in its updates. These rules become efficient when all routers in the internet participate using triggered updates. Triggered updates allow a router to broadcast its routing table immediately following receipt of this "network down" information. The two most common are split horizon or poison reverse.

Static routes

Static versus dynamic routing. The last topic of discussion is the capability of routing protocols to accept information for their tables from two sources: the network or a user.

Although the RIP protocol allows for automatic updates for routing tables, manual entries are still allowed and are known as *static entries.* These entries must be entered manually. They can be configured to be included or not included in a dynamic update. Static routes refer to the process of manually updating the tables. For any given port on the router, the network administrator may update that port table with a static route.

Static tables have many disadvantages. First, as discussed before, static tables are not meant for large networks that incur many changes such as growth. As the topology changes, all the tables must be manually reconfigured. Second, in the case of router failure, the tables have no way of updating themselves. Dynamic tables overcome the disadvantages of static entries.

The primary advantage that a static entry may have is for security, for static tables can be configured *not* to broadcast their routes to other routers. In this way, users can customize their routers to become participants on the network without their network identity being broadcast to other routers on the network. Static rates also allow a user to update a routing table with a network entry that will be used in end stations with the dynamic function turned off. This allows the user to maintain the routing table.

Packet routing. Now that routing fundamentals, the RIP protocol, and routing tables have been discussed, the following will show how a datagram is routed via direct routes and indirect routes.

Refer to Fig. 6.17. In this figure we can see that a PC (end station A) is trying to pass a datagram to a host machine, called host B. The host machine is one hop (one router) away. The IP layer of the PC (end station A) knows that it must use a router (the source and destination network addresses are different), and will use RIP or the default gateway to determine the IP address of the router to use. Upon determining the router's physical address, it will physically (MAC layer) address the

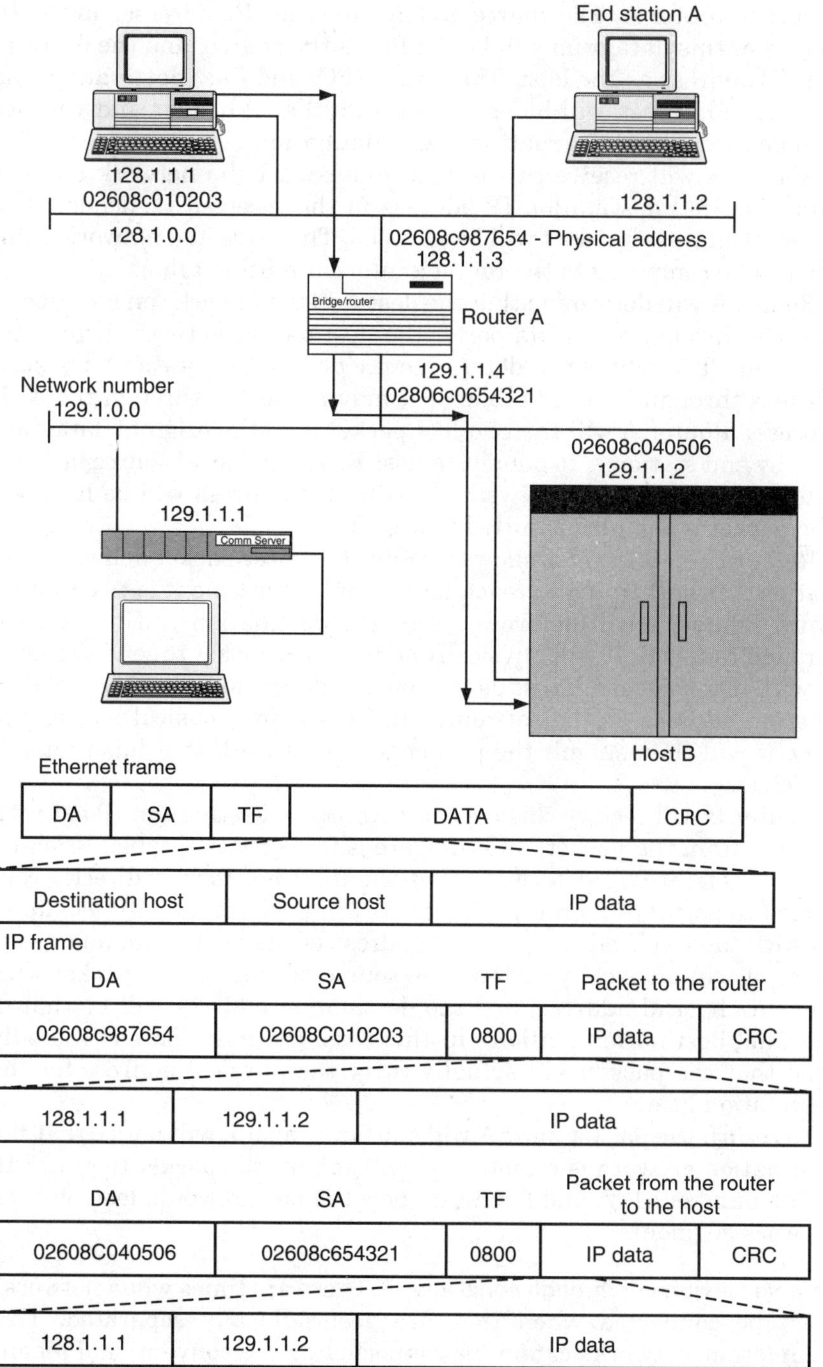

Figure 6.17 Packet flow in a routed environment.

packet to router A. The source and destination IP addresses in the IP header of this datagram will be the PC as the source, and the destination IP address as the host. The source (PC) and final destination (the host) IP addresses will be embedded into the IP header and will not change throughout the routing of this datagram.

Router A will receive this packet and extract the network number from the final destination IP address in the received IP header. The physical address headers will be stripped. The extracted network number will be compared to the router's internal routing table.

Router A will determine that the destination network can be reached directly through one of its ports (the destination network is directly attached). The router will determine the destination station's physical address through its ARP table (or it may request it through the ARP process). Router A will then build a packet with the original datagram sent by end station A to submit to host B. The physical source address will be the router's, the physical destination address will be host B's. The packet is then transmitted to host B.

Refer to Fig. 6.18. This shows a router-to-router packet delivery. End station A is still trying to reach host B, only this time it is two routers away. Router A will determine that the destination can be reached through router B. It will physically address the packet to send to router B, with its physical address as the source address and the physical destination address as that of router B. This is for physical addressing only. It will then submit the packet to the network that has router B attached.

Router B will receive this packet, extract the destination IP network address from the packet, and compare it to its routing table. From its router table, it will determine that the final network is directly connected to port 2 of its router. Router B will perform an ARP lookup in its ARP table to find the physical address of the host. If an address is there, it will physically address the source address of the packet with its own physical address, and the destination address will be that of the final destination station—in this case, the host. This is the only time that the packet will actually carry the physical address for the destination host.

To return the packet, host A will start over again, will notice that the destination network is remote, and will submit the packet to router B.

The numbers 1, 2, and 3 indicate how the packet would look on each network segment.

Remote networking through serial lines. There are times when networks must be connected when they are geographically separated. This means that networks cannot be connected by the conventional means of a LAN interconnect. This could be when a network in New York and

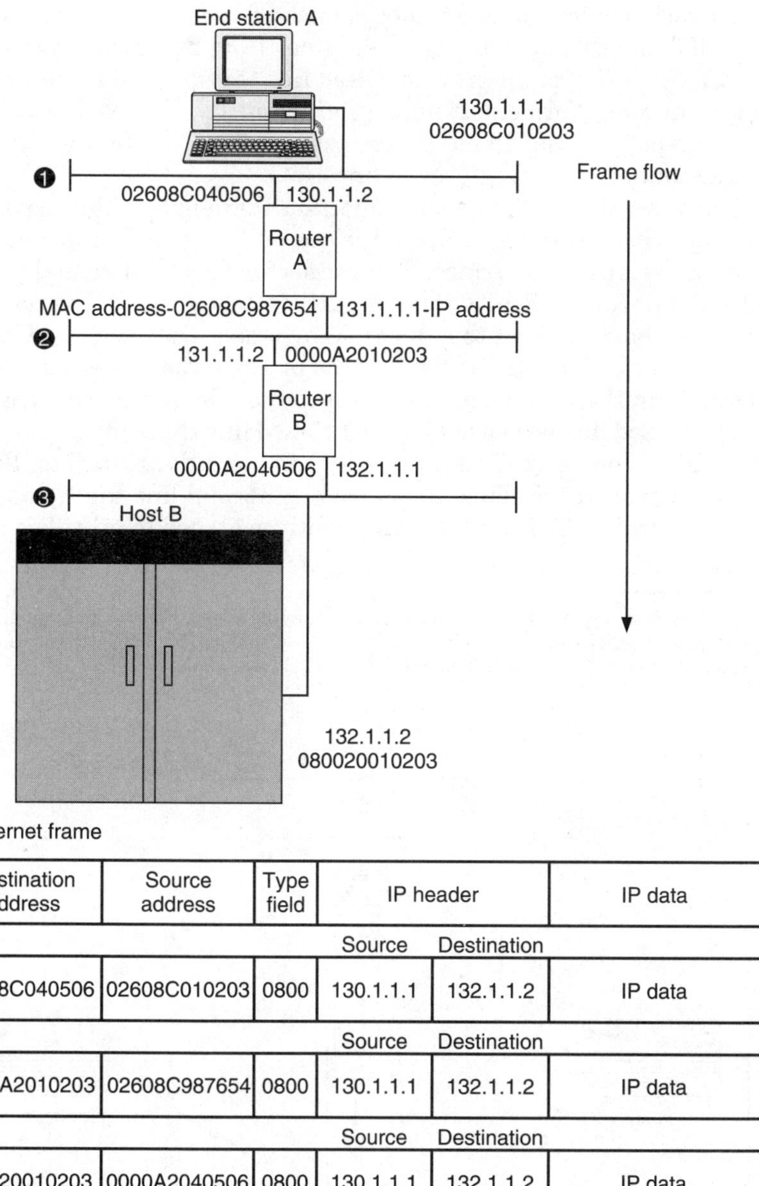
End station A
130.1.1.1
02608C010203
Frame flow
❶
02608C040506
130.1.1.2
Router A
MAC address-02608C987654
131.1.1.1-IP address
❷
131.1.1.2
0000A2010203
Router B
0000A2040506
132.1.1.1
❸
Host B
132.1.1.2
080020010203
Ethernet frame
Destination address
Source address
Type field
IP header
IP data
Source
Destination
❶ 02608C040506 02608C010203 0800 130.1.1.1 132.1.1.2 IP data
❷ 0000A2010203 02608C987654 0800 130.1.1.1 132.1.1.2 IP data
❸ 080020010203 0000A2040506 0800 130.1.1.1 132.1.1.2 IP data

Figure 6.18 MAC address assignments.

a network in Virginia need to be connected together. The only feasible way of doing this is by using leased lines from the telephone company. AT&T, MCI, Sprint all provide leased line service for data networks. It comes in many forms, but again, for simplicity, this book will explain point-to-point serial lines. Refer to Fig. 6.19. This figure shows networks connected through serial lines.

Likewise, the router has a connection that enables this type of connection. Instead of the LAN interface on the router, the router will have a serial line interface. The connector for this is usually a V.35, EIA-232 (formerly RS-232-D) or an RS-449 connector.* The connection will then be connected to a device known as a Data Service Unit/Customer Service Unit (DSU/CSU). This is a box that receives the serial signal from the router and repeats it to the telephone switching office.

The leased line is a specially conditioned line that will be provided by the phone company. This line has been conditioned to handle high-speed digital traffic. This line is not the normal line that is used with voice switching. This line is permanently switched to provide a connec-

* The type of connector used will depend on the line speed. For the most part, only two types of connections are used: EIA-232 for lines speeds at 19.2 Kbps (thousand bits per second or less) and V.35 for line speeds above 19.2 Kbps (56K, T1, etc.).

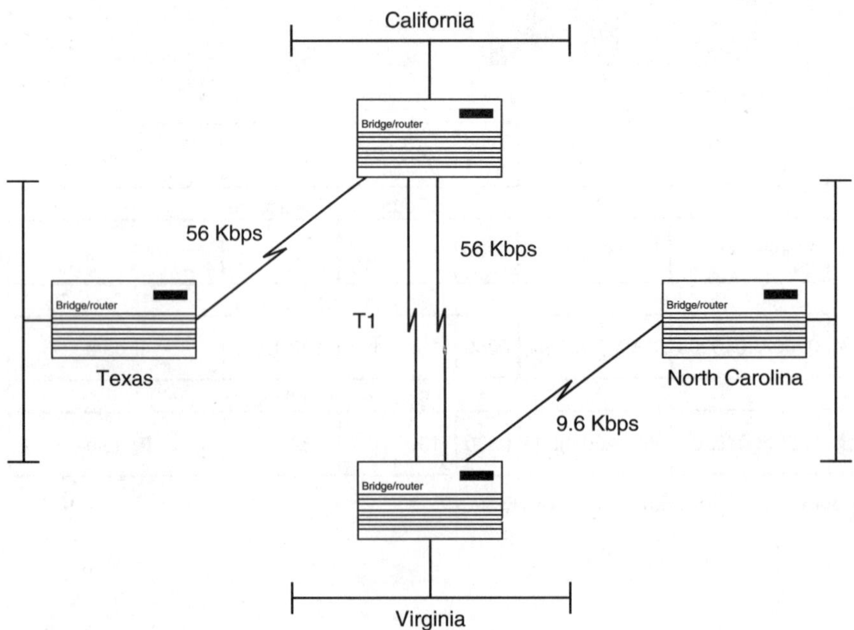

Figure 6.19 Wide area networking with serial lines.

tion between two points. Therefore, it is sometimes called a point-to-point link. It is analogous to dialing a number, receiving a connection, and never hanging up.

The router at the remote end will also be attached to a DSU/CSU. It will be able to receive the signals generated at the remote end. The typical speeds at which these lines run vary. The most common are: 56 Kbps and T1.* These lines are called leased lines because the customer does not own the line. It is leased from the phone company and the rates vary depending on the length of the line. Rates are usually cheaper for short runs (the other point of the network is a few miles away) and more for longer runs. Rates also vary depending on the speed of the line.

The serial line provides a simple interconnect between two routers that cannot be connected directly by a LAN. The real problem in using them in an IP internet is that they consume a full network number or a subnet number. There have been methods to overcome this (variable length subnet masking available only with the routing algorithm known as Open Shortest Path First—OSPF, not discussed in this book); otherwise, they generally act as a full network even when there are only two points connected.

Internet control message protocol (ICMP)

Refer to Fig. 6.17. What would happen if router A could not find the end station (the end station was not in the router's ARP cache and it did not respond to the router's ARP request)? This is one of the reasons for the ICMP service. The router would send an ICMP message back to the originator of the datagram, end station A, that the destination node cannot be found. This message will be transmitted to the user as an error message on the user's screen.

Before the dynamic routing algorithm RIP was formally accepted in 1989, static routes were fairly common in routers. Therefore, if a router has a packet for which no route can be found, it should discard the packet. If a default route was assigned, the router would not discard the packet, but forward it onto the router assigned in the default route. If the default router could find the route, the default router would discard the packet and notify the originating station of this action through a control protocol known as ICMP.

Since IP is a connectionless, unreliable delivery service, allowing routers and hosts on an internet to operate independently, there are certain instances when errors will occur on the internet. Some of these errors could be: a packet is not routed to the destination network, the router is too congested to handle any more packets, or a host may not

---

* Kpbs is thousand bits per second and T1 runs at 1.544 million bits per second (Mbps).

be found on the internet. There is no provision in IP to generate error messages or control messages. ICMP is the protocol that handles these instances for IP.

Figure 6.20 shows the packet format for ICMP.

ICMP controls many entities on an internet. As Table 6.7 shows, there are 13 control messages that ICMP uses.

ICMP datagrams are routable since they use IP to deliver their messages. Since they use the IP protocol and not TCP protocol (the transport layer), these messages themselves have the capability of being lost or generating an error. IP is a connectionless protocol and does not have mechanisms to detect whether datagrams were delivered to their proper destination. Therefore, there is not a mechanism in ICMP to detect lost ICMP messages. As a result, no ICMP messages will ever be generated for an erred ICMP message. Furthermore, ICMP messages are not generated and received by a user on the network. The message is intended for the IP software in another network station. A message may be generated to your screen, but this is up to the programmer. ICMP software only talks to other ICMP software.

Figure 6.20 shows how an ICMP message is encapsulated in an IP packet.

One of the most common uses for ICMP is the PING program. PING (packet internet groper) is an ICMP message that tries to locate other stations on the internet to see if they are active or to see if a path is up. It can also be used to test intermediate networks along the way to the destination.

To see if host number 129.1.2.3 is alive, all the user has to do is type: "ping 128.1.2.3" at his or her workstation (provided the TCP/IP proto-

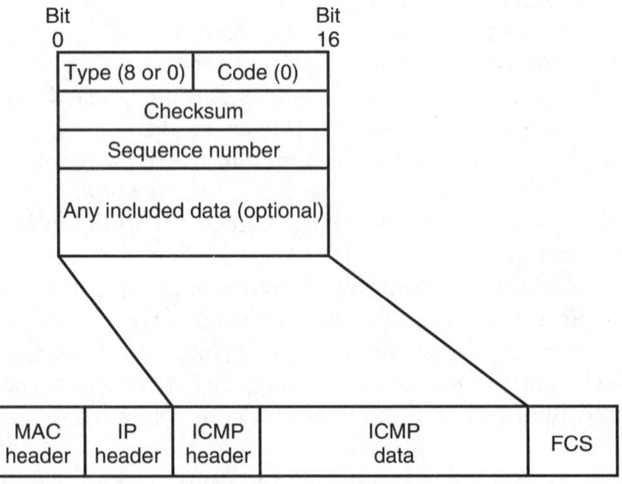

Figure 6.20 ICMP packet format echo request or reply.

TABLE 6.7 ICMP Message Types

Type field	Message description
0	Echo reply—PING
3	Destination unreachable
4	Source quench—a form of flow control
5	Redirect—there is a better route to take
8	Echo request—PING
11	Time exceeded for a datagram—TTL is zero
12	Parameter problem on a datagram
13	Timestamp request
14	Timestamp reply
15	Information request
16	Information reply
17	Address mask request
18	Address mask reply

col is active on the user's workstation). If the host is active, the host will respond with an ICMP echo reply and the message the user will usually see on the screen is "129.1.2.3 is alive." This is a simple way to check for hosts on the network. There are some times where TELNET will not connect with the destination host; using the ping command, you can at least check to see if the host is active or if the path to the destination is up. Another usage of the PING command is to check for network delays along a path. The response to a ping request can report the response delay. This delay is usually measured in milliseconds.

A lot of network management software uses this command to determine the status of a given station. Network management software will build maps to show the topology and placement of network stations on the map. Using colors (green for active, yellow for possible errors, and red for not responding) a network manager can trace problems on the network. A lot of the work is done through the use of the utility ping.

Another use is to find the address mask of the local network. ICMP running in a router can respond to a host's request to find the subnet address mask for its network. A host, upon start-up, can request of a router the subnet mask assigned to the network.

Source quench is the end station's ability to indicate to the *originator* of a message that the host cannot accept the rate at which the sender is submitting the packets. A source quench packet is continually generated to the originator until the rate of data flow slows down. The intended recipient of a source quench is will continue to slow down its data rate until it receives no more source quench packets. The station that was requested to slow down will then start to increase the data rate again. This is similar to a flow control, except that it is more like throttle control. The data is not stopped, merely slowed down and then increased again. It is generated by any network station on the internet to indicate that the node cannot handle the rate of the incoming data.

There are many other uses of the ICMP protocol. When a router receives a datagram, it may determine a better router that can provide a shorter route to the destination network. This is an ICMP redirect, and this message informs the sender of a better route.

If the TTL field is determined to 0, a router will inform the originator of this through an ICMP message.

A user's workstation can request a time stamp from a router asking it to repeat the time when it received a packet. This is used for measuring delay to a destination.

Section 2: Transport Layer Protocols

User datagram protocol (UDP)

A transport layer allows communication to exist between network stations. Data is handed down to this layer from an upper-level application. The transport layer then envelopes the data with its headers and gives it to the IP layer for transmission onto the network. In TCP/IP there are two transport-layer protocols: UDP and TCP.

The functionality of UDP should sound familiar. It is a connectionless, unreliable transport service. It does not provide an acknowledgment to the sender upon the receipt of data. It does not provide order to the incoming packets, and may lose packets or duplicate them without issuing an error message to the sender. This should sound like the IP protocol. The only offering that UDP has is the assignment and management of port numbers to uniquely identify the individual applications that run on a network station. UDP tends to run faster than TCP, for its has low overhead involved in the function that it performs. It is used for applications that do not need a reliable transport. Some examples are network management, name server, etc.

Any application program that incorporates the use of UDP as its transport-level service must provide an acknowledgment and sequence system to ensure that packets arrive, and that they arrive in the same order as they were sent. That is, the application program using UDP must provide this type of service.

As shown in Fig. 6.21, an applications data is encapsulated in a UDP header. The transport layer has its own header, independent of all other layers, that it prefaces to the data handed to it from its upper-layer protocol. The UDP header and its data are then encapsulated in an IP header. The IP protocol would then send the datagram to the data-link layer which would then encapsulate the datagram with its headers (and/or trailers) and send the data to the physical layer for actual transmission.

Upon receipt of the packet, the data link would interpret the address as its own, strip off its header (and/or trailers), and submit the packet

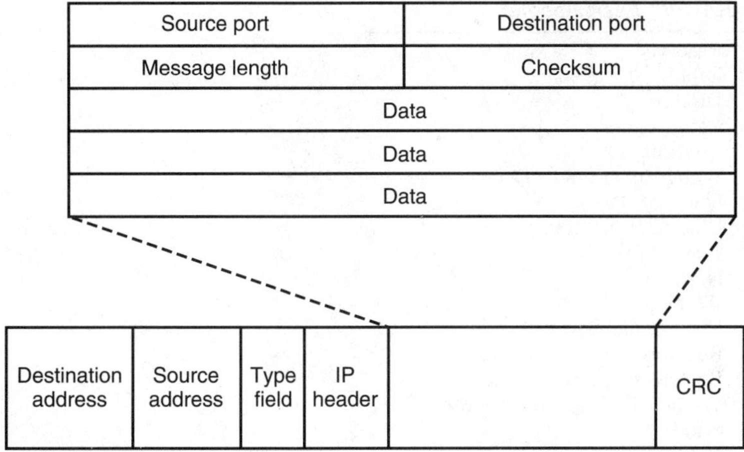

Figure 6.21 UDP header.

to the IP layer. IP would accept the packet based on the correct IP address in the IP header, strip off its header, and submit the packet to the UDP-layer software. The UDP layer accepts the packet and now has to demultiplex the packet based on the port number in the UDP header.

Port numbers. Since many network applications may be running on the same machine, a protocol needed to be developed to allow access to these applications, even though they reside on the same machine. If they reside on the same machine, each application can be accessed by a sending node addressing its packet to that machine. A problem arises here in how you differentiate between all the applications on one machine that contains one IP address.

It would not be advantageous to assign each process an IP address, nor would it be advantageous to change the IP addressing scheme to include a marker to identify a unique application in the machine. Instead, the User Datagram Protocol provides a concept known as *ports.**

Ports, along with an IP address, allow any application in any machine on an internet to be uniquely identified.

Refer to Table 6.8. This table shows the reserved port numbers' UDP. When a station wishes to communicate to a remote application, it must

* Ports are sometimes incorrectly referred to as sockets. For the purposes of this text, ports and sockets will be interchangeable. In actuality, sockets are a station's full internet address plus the associated port number.

TABLE 6.8 UDP Port Assignments*

0	Reserved
7	Echo
9	Discard
11	Active users
13	Daytime
15	Who is up or NETSTAT
17	Quote of the day
19	Character generator
37	Time
42	Name server
43	Who is
53	Domain name server
67	Bootstrap protocol server
68	Bootstrap protocol client
69	Trivial File Transfer Program (TFTP)
111	Sun RPC
123	Network time protocol
161	SNMP net monitor
162	SNMP traps
512	UNIX comsat
513	UNIX rwho process
514	System log
525	Timed

* If you are looking for a port number here and cannot find it, the application may be using TCP as its transport and, therefore, you should look up the port number in the TCP section.

identify that application in the packet. For example, if a station wished to use a simple file transfer protocol known as *trivial file transfer program* (TFTP) on the station 130.1.1.1, it would address the packet to station 130.1.1.1 and insert destination port number 69 in the UDP header. The source port number identifies the application on the local station that requested the file transfer, and all response packets generated by the destination station would be addressed to that port number on the source station. So, when the IP layer demultiplexes the packet and hands it to UDP, UDP will pass the data to the locally assigned port number for it to process the data. Port numbers are explained in detail later.

In looking at Fig. 6.21, the packet header for UDP is small, but functional. The source port indicates the process ID from the sender. This is used for replies from the remote station. If it is not used (broadcast RIP update tables), it should be set to 0. The destination port number indicates the process on the remote station. The message length indicates the size of the UDP header and its data in bytes. The minimum packet size for UDP is 8 bytes (the size of the header). The checksum is used to check for the validity of the UDP header and data. It does not have to be implemented and would be set to 0 if not implemented.

In thinking of the OSI model (refer to Fig. 6.2), an application would talk directly to UDP for it to transport the data. UDP would then use the services of IP to actually send the data to the network.

UDP accepts data from the application layer, formats it (UDP header) with its information, and presents it to the IP layer for network delivery. UDP will also accept data from the IP layer and, depending on the port value, present it to the appropriate application. As shown in Fig. 6.22, UDP is responsible for directing the rest of the packet (after stripping off its headers) to the correct process according to the port number assigned in the UDP header. This process is called *demultiplexing*. There are many different types of port numbers to indicate any application program running on the network station. UDP reads the destination port field of the UDP header (demultiplex) and gives the data to the application. When the application program (identified by the port number) initializes, the station's operating system works in conjunction with it and provides a buffer area for which information may be stored. UDP will place the data in this area for retrieval by the application program. UDP does provide one error mechanism for ports which are not valid. It can generate an ICMP port unreachable message to be sent to the originator of the packet.

Since the TCP/IP protocol suite include applications that are specifically written to it (TFTP, Domain Name Service, etc.), there are statically assigned port numbers that identify these applications. Certain

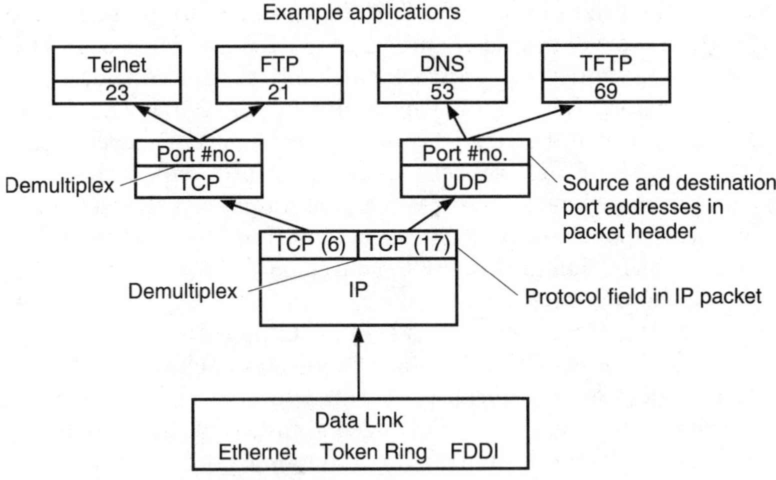

Telnet—A remote terminal program
FTP—File Transfer Program
DNS—Domain Name Server
TFTP—Trivial File Transfer Program

Figure 6.22 IP port assignments.

port numbers are reserved and cannot be used by any unknown application program. They are reserved by the applications that are defined in the RFCs. The reserved port numbers are specified in RFC 1060.

Dynamic and static assigned port numbers. In the TCP/IP protocol, UDP port numbers are both static and dynamic. Table 6.8 lists some of the port numbers that are static. No matter which implementation of TCP/IP (i.e., which vendor's TCP) is in use, those applications listed beside the port number will always be the same. There are known as *globally assigned numbers* or *well-known port numbers.* These are assigned by a central authority. In this case, the RFC 1060 spells out which processes are assigned to which port numbers. If station A wanted to access the TFTP process on station B, it would call it in the UDP header with a destination port number of 69 (decimal). The difference between the two types is: static port numbers are reserved and dynamic port numbers may be used by any network station.

TCP/IP also implements dynamic port numbers. These are available for dynamic use. Since the port number field in the UDP header is 16 bits long, 65535 ports (minus the static port assignments) are available for individual use. One use for a dynamic port is for a source station that is requesting the services of TFTP on a remote station. The source station would dynamically assign itself an available port number (usually above size) to use so that the remote station would know what port to access when it transfers the file. In other words, if a user initiated a trivial file transfer (TFTP), the TFTP request packet sent to the TFTP server would include in its UDP header a dynamic port number of the requesting network station that wanted the TFTP, called the *source port.* Let's say it was assigned port 2000. The destination port number would be 69. In this way, the server will accept the packet, give it to the TFTP process in the host and, when the host responds, it will know how to address the port number in the response packet. In the response packet, the server would fill out the UDP header with a destination port of 2000, source port of 69, and send the packet back to the requesting station.

Another use is when network vendors implement proprietary schemes on their devices—for example, a proprietary scheme for a network station to boot or a proprietary scheme to allow network management statistics to be gathered. All these applications are valid and may run on any TCP environment using a dynamic port assignment.

The disadvantage to dynamic ports occurs when a broadcast IP datagram is transmitted to the network using a dynamic port. This port could be used by another vendor on the network, and another network station may invoke a process to accommodate that request. This is rare, but has been known to happen.

Dynamic port numbers are assigned at the local workstation. They can be duplicated from workstation to workstation. This is because an application on any network station is uniquely identified by the network number, host number, and port number. When taken as a whole number, it is called the socket, and cannot be duplicated on an IP network except by negligence.

Transport control protocol (TCP)

TCP/IP hosts originally were connected via telephone lines (commonly known as serial lines). This communication facility was not the same in the early 1970s as it is today. These line were extremely noisy and were not conditioned to handle data. Therefore, the TCP protocol has strict error detection algorithms built in to ensure the integrity of the data. The following paragraphs explain the TCP protocol and show the strictness with which it is structured to ensure the integrity of the data.

TCP is also a transport-layer protocol. Unlike the UDP protocol, the purpose of the transport-layer software TCP is to allow data to be reliably exchanged with another station on the network. It, too, provides the demultiplexes of port numbers to identify an application in the host, but also provides reliable transport of data.

The analogy is as mentioned before: suppose you are standing next to someone and you are telling a story to this person. If that person stands there and does not acknowledge you and your conversation, you would not be able to tell if the person was understanding what you were saying. If the person acknowledges you with something like a nod of the head or a verbal "yes," then you would know that what you were saying was understood and you could continue with your conversation.

The protocol of TCP uses sequence numbers and acknowledgments to converse with another station on the network. Sequence numbers are used to determine the ordering of the data in the packets and to find missing packets. Since packets on an internet may not arrive in the same sequence as they were sent (for example, a single packet in a series of packets being transmitted was discarded by a router), sequencing the data in the packets ensures that the packets are read in the same order that they were sent. Also, a receiving station may receive two of the same packets. The sequence number with acknowledgments is used to allow a reliable type of communication. This process is called full duplex, for each side of a connection will maintain its own sequence number for the other side.

TCP is a byte-oriented sequencing protocol. This means that every byte in each packet is assigned a sequence number. This does not mean that TCP transmits a packet containing only 1 byte. TCP will transmit data (many bytes) and assign the packet one sequence number. Assigning one sequence number per byte in the packet may sound repetitious, but remember that TCP/IP was first implemented over noisy serial lines and not reliable high-speed LANs. Packet sequencing, such as that used with IPX and XNS, applies a sequence number to each packet transmitted and not to each data byte in the packet. Refer to Fig. 6.23. In this figure three packets are transmitted. Each packet is assigned one sequence number. Notice how the sequence number jumps by the same amount of bytes that are in each packet. The receiver of these packets will count the amount of bytes received and increment its sequence number of received packets. The first packet received has a sequence number of 40 and contains 4 bytes. The receiver expects the next sequence number to be 44. It is, and that packets also contains 7 bytes of data. The receiver expects the next packet to be sequence number of 51. It is. This is how the byte sequencing of TCP works.

Not all networks use a separate transport-layer software to converse on a network. The best example of this is Novell with their LAN workgroup operating system of NetWare. As you read in Chap. 5, they rely on the network-layer software to transport their data and the NetWare Control Protocol to provide the sequence numbering of the packets. There is nothing wrong with this, and it generally speeds up the communication process between two stations on the network. The overhead of a full transport layer is gone, but without the full transport-layer software there is no way to guarantee the data will be transmitted in a reliable fashion.

Shown in Fig. 6.24 is the TCP header for the TCP. It will be referenced throughout the discussion on TCP. Do not try to fully understand the header now. Most of the fields in the header will be discussed in the text following.

Source port. The port number of the originating station.

Destination port. The port number for the receiving station.

Sequence number. A number assigned to a TCP packet to indicate the beginning byte number of a packet unless the SYN bit is set. If this bit is set, the sequence number is the initial sequence number (ISN) and the first data byte is ISN + 1.

Acknowledgment number. Number sent by the destination station to the source station, indicating an acknowledgment of a previously received packet or packets. This number indicates the next sequence number the destination station expects to receive. Once a connection is established, this field is always set.

Data offset. Indicates how long the TCP header is (i.e., the number of 32-bit words in the TCP header). It indicates where the data begins and the TCP header stops.

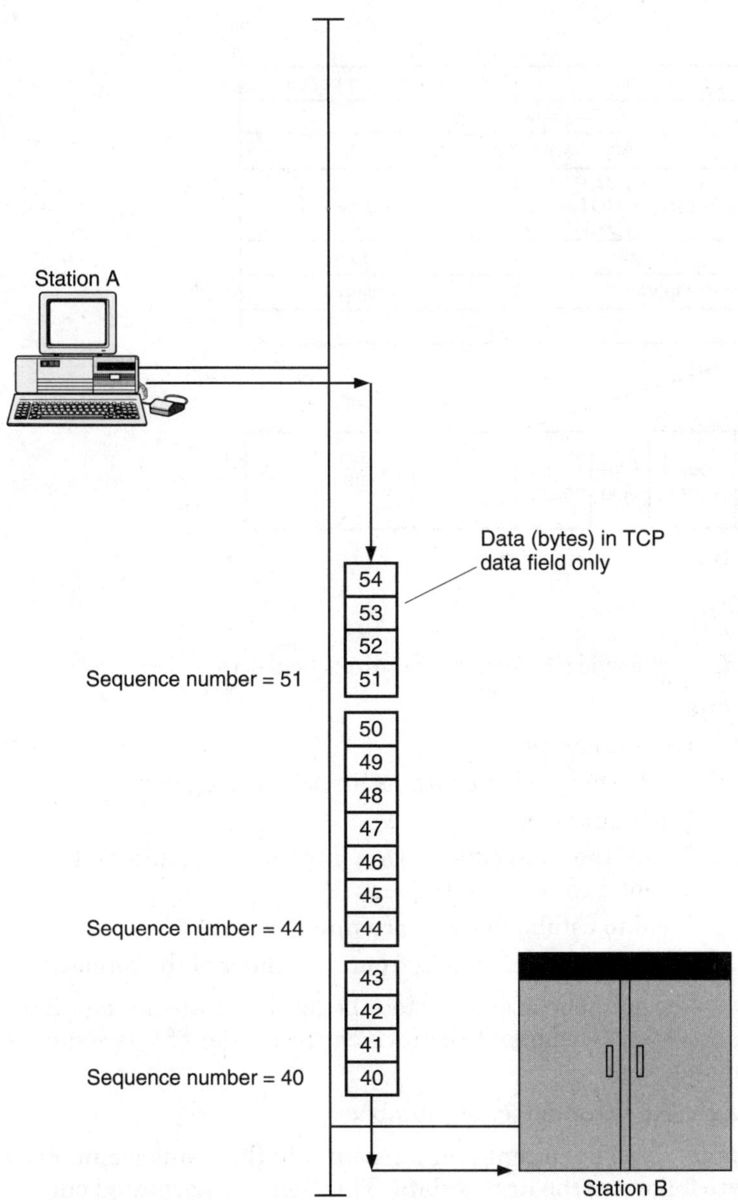

Figure 6.23 TCP byte sequencing.

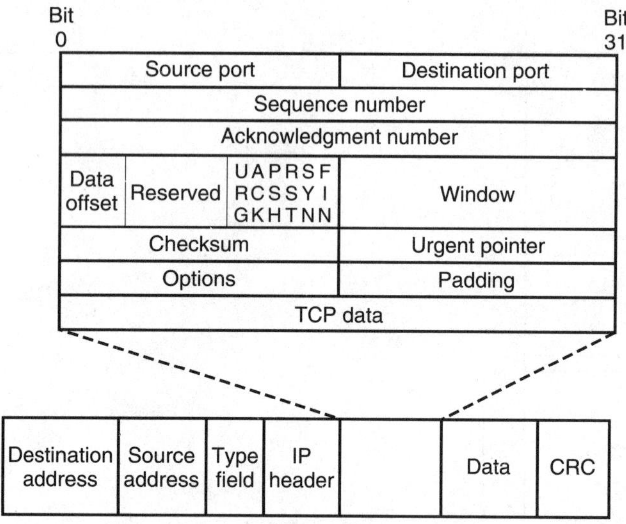

Figure 6.24 TCP header information.

Reserved. Reserved for future use. Must be set to 0.

Control bits

URG	Urgent pointer.
ACK	If set, this packet contains an acknowledgment.
PSH	Push function.
RST	Reset the connection. One function for this is to not accept a connection request.
SYN	Used to establish sequence number.
FIN	No more data is coming from the sender of the connection.

Window. The number of data octets beginning with the one indicated in the acknowledgment field which the sender of this segment is willing to accept.

Checksum. An error detection number.

Urgent pointer. The urgent pointer points to the sequence number of the byte following the urgent data. This field is interpreted only in segments with the URG bit set.

Options. Variable in length, it allows for TCP options to be presented. These are:

End of option list

No operation

Maximum segment size

The main services provided by TCP are:

1. Establishing, maintaining, and terminating connections between two processes
2. Reliable packet delivery—through an acknowledgment process
3. Sequencing of packets—reliable transfer of data
4. Mechanism for controlling errors
5. The ability to allow multiple connections with different processes inside a particular source or destination host through the use of ports
6. Data exchange using full-duplex operations

General TCP data flow. A network application such as TELNET (for remote terminal emulation discussed further under Sec. 3) or a file transfer program such as FTP actually transmits data by placing a call to the TCP software and then passes data to it. TCP encapsulates this data into "segments" and, in turn, places a call to the IP software for it to transmit the data to the destination. The receiving host's TCP software deencapsulates the data from the packet and notifies the appropriate process that it has data to be retrieved.

As we learned previously, the IP layer is a connectionless delivery service and therefore is deemed unreliable. TCP must be a robust and complex protocol to ensure that data is delivered with no errors and also is received in the same order that it was transmitted. TCP allows for this.

TCP functions. Each function will be explained separately and then it will all tied together at the end of this section.

Connection establishment. Unlike the UDP protocol, a TCP connection between two stations on a network must be established before any data is allowed to pass between the two. Applications such as TELNET and FTP communicate using TCP through a series of function calls. These calls include OPEN and CLOSE a connection, SEND and RECEIVE to that connection, and to receive STATUS for a connection.

When a connection to a remote station is needed, an application will request TCP to place an OPEN CALL. There are two types of OPEN CALLS: *passive* and *active*. A passive OPEN is a call to allow connections to be accepted from a remote station. This usually occurs when an application starts on a network station (such as TELNET, FTP, or SMTP), and it will indicate to TCP that it is willing to accept connections from other stations on the network. TCP will note the application through its port assignment and will allow connections to come in. This end of the TCP actions is known as the *responder* TCP. It will open up connection slots to accept any incoming connection request. This may be thought of as the server end of TCP. These passive open calls do not await for any particular station to attach to it.

An active OPEN is made when a connection attempt to remote network station is needed. Looking at Fig. 6.25, station A wishes to connect to station B. Station A issues an active open call to station B. In order for the connection to be made, station B must already have issued a passive open request to allow incoming connections to be established. In the connection attempt packet is the port number that station A wishes to use on station B. Station B's operating system will spawn a separate process on its system to maintain that connection. This process will act as if it is running locally on that station. TCP will then await another incoming connection request. This process is similar to the way a multitasking operating system handles multiple applications.

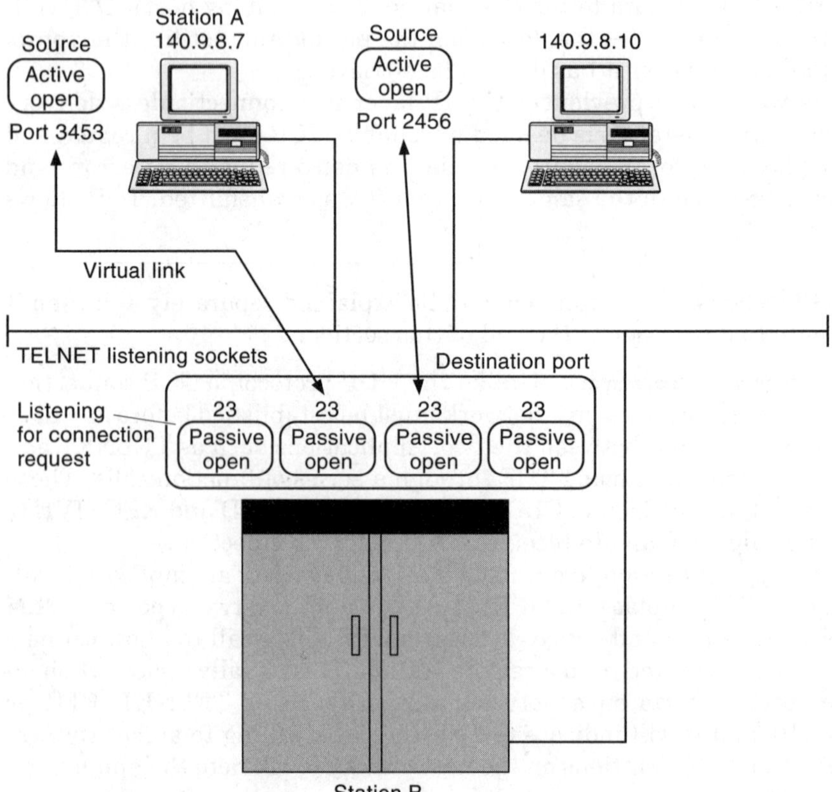

Figure 6.25 Passive and active connection.

A connection will only be an active connection after the sender and receiver exchange a few control packets to establish the connection. This is known as the *three-way handshake.* It is shown in the top portion of Fig. 6.26. Its purpose to synchronize each end of the connection with sequence numbers and acknowledgment numbers.

Refer to the bottom picture on Fig. 6.26. Station A will place an active open call to TCP to request connection to a remote network station's application. Station A will build a TCP header with the SYN (the sync bit shown in Fig. 6.24) bit set and then assign an initial sequence number (say, 100) and place it in the sequence number field. Other fields will be set in the TCP header (not pertinent to us at this time) and the packet will be given to IP for transmission to station B.

Station B will receive this packet and notice it is a connection attempt. If station B can accept a new connection it will acknowledge station A by building a new packet. Station B will set the SYN and the ACK bits in the TCP header shown in Fig. 6.24, place its own initial sequence number (200) in the sequence field of the packet, and the acknowledgment field will be set to 101 (the station A sequence number plus 1, indicating the next expected sequence number).

Station A will receive this response packet and notice it is an acknowledgment to its connection request. Station A will build a new packet, set the ACK bit, fill in the sequence number to 101, fill in the acknowledgment number to 200 + 1, and send the packet to station B. Once this has been established, the connection is active and data and commands from the application (such as TELNET) may pass over the connection. As data and commands pass over the connection, each side of the connection will maintain its own sequence number tables for data being sent and received across the connection. They will always be in ascending order.

Once the connection is established, TCP will allow data to flow between the source and destination station through something known as a *segment.* A TCP segment will contain the TCP header (shown in Fig. 6.24) and its data. The data handed to TCP for transmission is known as a *stream*—more specifically, an *unstructured stream.* A stream is a flow of bytes of data and an unstructured stream is unknown type of data flow of bytes. This means that TCP has no way of marking the data to indicate the ending of a record or the type of data that is in the stream. When TCP receives a data stream from the application, it will divide the data into segments for transmission to the remote network station.

A TCP segment may be as long as 65535 bytes, but is usually much less than that. Ethernet can only handle 1500 bytes of data in the data field of the Ethernet packet (Ethernet V2.0, 1496 bytes for IEEE 802.3 using IEEE 802.2). On the other hand, FDDI can handle a maximum

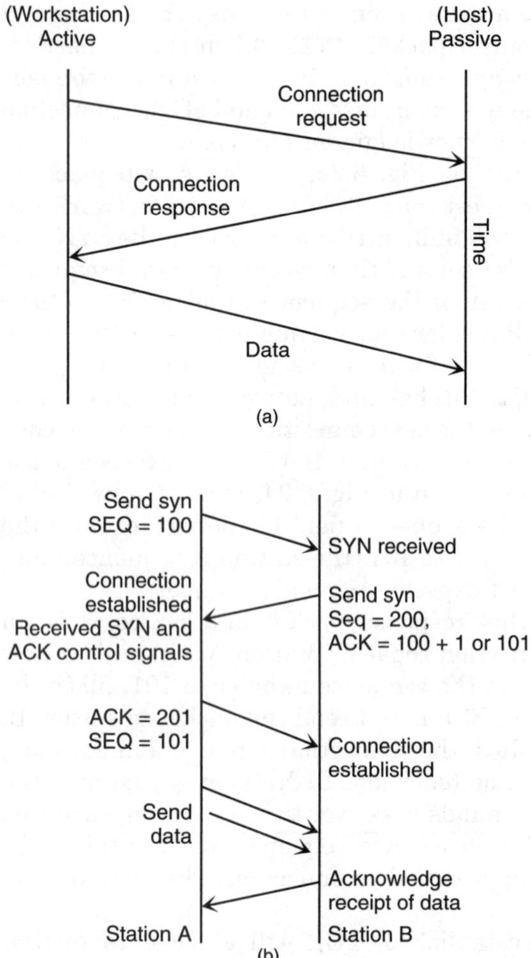

Figure 6.26 Block diagram of the three-way handshake.

of 4472 bytes of data in a packet and Token Ring packet size varies depending on the speed. For 4 Mbps, the maximum size is 4472 bytes. For 16 Mbps, the maximum size of the packet is 17800* bytes, but is usually set to 4472 bytes. To negotiate a segment size, TCP will use one of the options fields located in the TCP header to indicate the largest segment size it can receive, and submit this packet to the remote network station.

TCP does not care what the data is. Once the connection is established, TCP's main job is to maintain the connection (or multiple con-

* Although it may be this large, it is usually set to 4472 or below.

nections if there are). This is accomplished through the sequence numbers, acknowledgments and retransmissions, flow control, and window management.

Since the connection between stations A and B is now established (by way of a successful three-way handshake), TCP must now manage the connection. The first of the management techniques to be discussed is sequence numbers.

Sequence numbers and acknowledgments. TCP calculates a sequence number for each byte of data in the segment taken as a sum. For each *byte* of data that is to be transmitted, the sequence number *increments by one.* Let's say a connection was made between stations A and B. Refer to Fig. 6.23. Station A sends a packet to station B with a sequence number of 40 and knows the packet contained 4 bytes. It will increment its sequence number to 44. Upon acknowledgment from station B (containing the ACK number of 44), station A will then transmit the second packet to station B and know that 7 bytes are being transmitted. Station A's sequence number increments to 51, and it will wait for an acknowledgment from station B.

Each packet will contain as many bytes as will fit into the transmission window (windows are discussed in a moment). The sequence number is set to the number of the first byte in the packet being sent. The TCP segment (the data) is then given to IP for delivery to the network.

Each packet transmitted must be acknowledged. Multiple packets may be sent with one acknowledgment to all received good packets. This is called an inclusive ACK. TCP accomplishes this bidirectionally across the same connection. Each packet transmitted will have the ACK bit set. With the ACK bit set, TCP will read the acknowledgment field to find the next byte number that the other end of the connection expects. In other words, the number in the ACK field equals the sequence number of the original packet transmitted plus the number of the bytes successfully received in that packet plus 1. The ACK number is stuffed into a data packet to make TCP more efficient. There is usually not a separate packet on the network used just for ACK packets. All data bytes up to but not including the ACK number are considered good and accepted by the receiver.

Since TCP is a byte-oriented transport protocol, sequencing and acknowledgments are accomplished for each byte of TCP data. To ensure the integrity of the data, TCP had to become a robust protocol that took every byte and ensured that it would make it across to the destination. Local Area Network protocols such as Novell NetWare and Xerox XNS were developed to work on high-reliability mediums (shielded copper cable in controlled environments). Their sequence numbers are based not on bytes in the packet but on the number of packets. These protocols are discussed in detail earlier in the book.

As shown in Fig. 6.26, the connection was established using an initial sequence number from the sender and an initial sequence number supplied by the receiver (the destination). Each side will maintain its own sequence number, which may be in the range of 0 to 2,147,483,647. Each side of a TCP connection knows the upper and lower limits of the sequence numbers, and once the limit has been hit, it will roll over to 0. The initialization sequence numbers are selected at random. Each side must ACK each packet's sequence number.

ACK NO = Sequence number + good bytes read in the segment + 1

This is a clean, fast, efficient way of determining which bytes were successfully received and which ones were not. The sender of data must retain a copy of transmitted data until it receives an acknowledgment for those bytes from the remote network station of a connection.

Acknowledgment packets are not necessarily separate packets with only the acknowledgment number in the packet. This would be inefficient. For example, if station A opened a connection to station B and station A and station B were sending data to each other, the ACK packet can be combined with the response data packet. In other words, one packet transmitted contains three things: the data from station B to station A, the acknowledgment from station B of the data previously sent from station A, and the sequence number for the data B is sending to A.

If the sender does not receive an acknowledgment within a specified time, it will resend the data starting from the first unacknowledged byte. TCP will time-out after a number of unsuccessful number of retransmissions. The retransmission of a packet is accomplished using the Go-back-to-N routine. Any number of outstanding packets may be not acknowledged. When the destination station does acknowledge the receipt of a series of packet, the source will look at the ACK number. All sequence numbers up to but not including the ACK number are considered received in good condition. This means that if a source station can start the sequence number with 3 and then send two packets containing 100 bytes each. When it receives an ACK from the destination of 203, it will know that both packets sent previously are considered received in good condition.

The number of outstanding packets allowed is the next topic of discussion.

Control through window management. Two functions are required of TCP in order for the protocol to manage the data over a connection. They are called *flow control* and *transmission control.* Do not confuse these functions with the ICMP source quench mechanism. Source quench is for a host to inform the source of transmissions that the host is full and the host would like the sender to slow its rate of transmission.

For those readers who do not understand flow control, it is a mechanism used to control the flow of data. For example, if data is being received at a destination station faster than that station can accept it, it needs to tell the source station to slow down or to stop completely until it can clear out some space (replenish buffers) to receive the data.

There are many methods employed for flow control. The method that is used by TCP is a window and is explained subsequently.

How many packets may be outstanding at any one time? Data management using a "window" is accomplished as shown by the following. Data for TCP to transmit to the remote network station will be accepted by TCP from an application. This data will be placed in memory where it will wait to be sent across a connection to a remote station (for IP to send the packet). TCP places a "window" over this data in which to structure the data: data sent and acknowledged, data sent but not acknowledged, and data waiting to be sent. This is called a *sliding window,* for the window will slide up the data segment as each data packet is sent and that segment acknowledged.

Refer to Fig. 6.27. Sequence numbers 100 to 104 have been transmitted to the destination station and the destination station has acknowledged receipt of these packet. Packets containing sequence numbers 105 to 108 have been transmitted by the source station, but it has not received acknowledgment of these packets. Packets containing sequence numbers 109 to 114 are still in the source station and are waiting to be sent. Packets containing 115 to 118 are not yet in the window.

The important thing to notice is the black box covering the sequence numbers. This is the window. It will constantly move in ascending sequence order upon receipt of acknowledgments from the destination station.

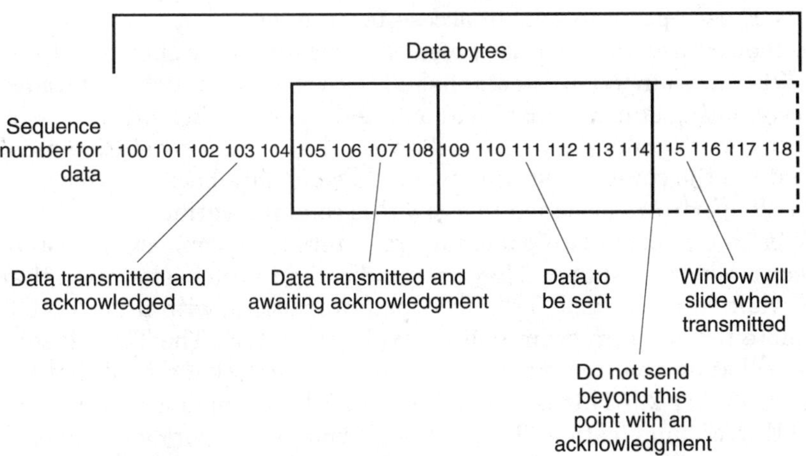

Figure 6.27 TCP segment.

When the receiving station (the destination station) is running low on buffer space (an area of memory to store incoming data), the receiver of this data has a capability to inform the sender to slow its transmission rate. This is accomplished through the window field in the TCP header packet. The destination station will inform the source station as to the amount of data it can accept. This is indicated by the window field of the TCP header. This field will contain the number of bytes (by indicating the range of sequence numbers) that the destination station is willing to accept. Figure 6.24 shows the TCP header, specifically the window field in the TCP header.

When the remote network station cannot accept any more data, it may set this window field to a 0. It will continue to submit these zero packets until it can again accept data (that is, the sender can send data to a host, and this host should respond with the ACK set to the previous ACK sent and a window set to 0). When buffer space is freed up, it can again submit a packet with the window size set to a nonzero number to indicate it can again accept data.

The one instance it may accept data, even with the window set to 0, is when it receives a packet with the urgent bit set, indicating the packet cannot wait. Any packet with the urgent bit set means that the packet must be received immediately. This is indicated by the URG bit in Fig. 6.24.

This connection management technique allows TCP to maintain control of the data transfer over a connection by informing TCP on the sending side how much data the receiver is willing to accept. This enables a sender and receiver of data on a connection to maintain consistent data flow over the connection.

Differentiating connections through PORTS. Like the UDP transport protocol, TCP uses ports to enable access to an application program. The well-known (also known as reserved or static) ports are shown in Table 6.9. When a connection is established between two network stations, the originating station must be able to tell the receiving station which application it would like to use. Likewise, the originating station must indicate to the receiving station where to send data back. As shown in Fig. 6.25, ports are assigned to allow this communication.

Refer to Fig. 6.28. Two personal computers have connections established to a host computer. They each indicated to the host station that they wanted to establish TELNET communications with it (TELNET, a remote terminal program will be explained later). The TCP/IP software will know this, for the incoming connection packet stated that the port is number 23. This is a well-known port assignment reserved for the TELNET application. The personal computer's port assignments (source port indicated in the TCP header, see Fig. 6.28) were chosen at random by the TCP software running in the personal computer. Any

TABLE 6.9 TCP Port Assignments*

0	Reserved
1	TCP multiplexor
5	RJE
7	Echo
9	Discard
11	Active users
13	Daytime
15	Network status program
17	Quote of the day
19	Character generator
20	FTP—data connection
21	FTP—command connection
23	TELNET
25	Simple mail transport protocol
37	Time
42	Name server
43	Who is
53	Domain name server
77	Any private RJE service
79	Finger—find a active user
93	Device control protocol
95	SUPDUP protocol
101	Network info. center host name server
102	OSI-transport service access point
103	X.400 mail service
104	X.400 mail sending
111	Sun Microsystems remote procedural call
113	Authentication service
117	UNIX to UNIX copy (UUCP) path service
119	Usenet news transfer protocol
129	Password generator protocol
139	NetBIOS session service
160–223	Reserved

* Some port numbers are assigned with the same numbers as UDP. This means that the application may use TCP or UDP as its transport service.

random port assignment can be issued by the personal computer's TCP software as long as it is above 512. With the field for ports in the TCP header being 16 bits wide, up to 65535 ports (minus the first 512 reserved ports) may be dynamically assigned.

One final note on TCP. The merits of this protocol are far reaching. A lot of the structures used to build TCP were incorporated into the OSI protocol of OSI known as TP4.

As stated before, the combination of the internet address and its port number is known as a *socket*. Port numbers indicate only the end connection point (application program identifier) of the connection. When a port number is used with the internet address of a network station, it becomes the socket number.

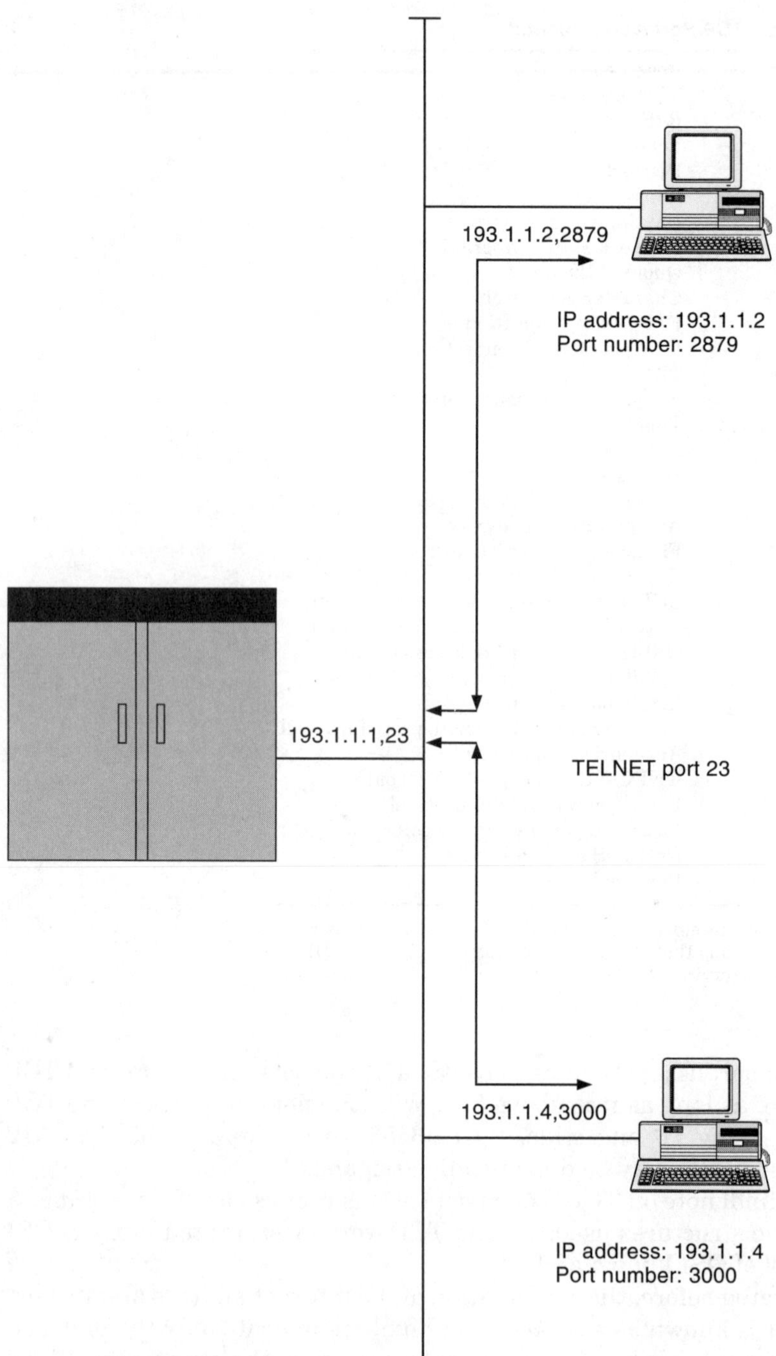

Figure 6.28 Telneting to the same host.

The second thing to notice about Fig. 6.28 is that the host TELNET server has accepted two TELNET connections. Both personal computers gained access to the host computer using port 23. What makes each connection unique in this case is the dynamic port assignment on the personal computer. Each TELNET connection initialed on the personal computer is using a different port number.

Each *active* call on a TCP/IP internet will assign its own port numbers above 512. The host has two TELNET connections connected to the port 23 on the host computer. The host computer will spawn each connection as a process to the operating system. Each connection will be uniquely identified by the socket address. The host computer will then return to waiting for any incoming connections, depending on how many *passive* open calls it has allowed. (See Table 6.10.)

Connection state. This describes the current status of the connection. This could be in the listen mode, in the process of termination, closed, etc.

Local address. Contains the local IP address for the TCP connection. If this connection is in the listen state, it should be filled in with 0.0.0.0.

Local port. Contains the local port number for the connection

Remote address. contains the remote IP address for the connection.

Remote port. contains the remote port number for the connection.

Termination of a connection. Finally, TCP must be able to gracefully terminate a connection. This is accomplished using the FIN bit in the TCP header. Since TCP offers a full-duplex connection, each side of the connection must close the connection. Refer to Fig. 6.29 for two communicating devices, end station A and host station B. The application running on end station A indicates to host B that it wishes to close a connection by sending a packet to host station B with the FIN bit set. Host station B will acknowledge that packet and will now no longer accept data from end station A. Host station B will accept data from its application to send to end station A, though. End station A will continue to

TABLE 6.10 TCP Connections

	Connection state	Local address	Local port	Remote address	Remote port
Connection 1					
Connection 2					
Connection 3					
Connection x					

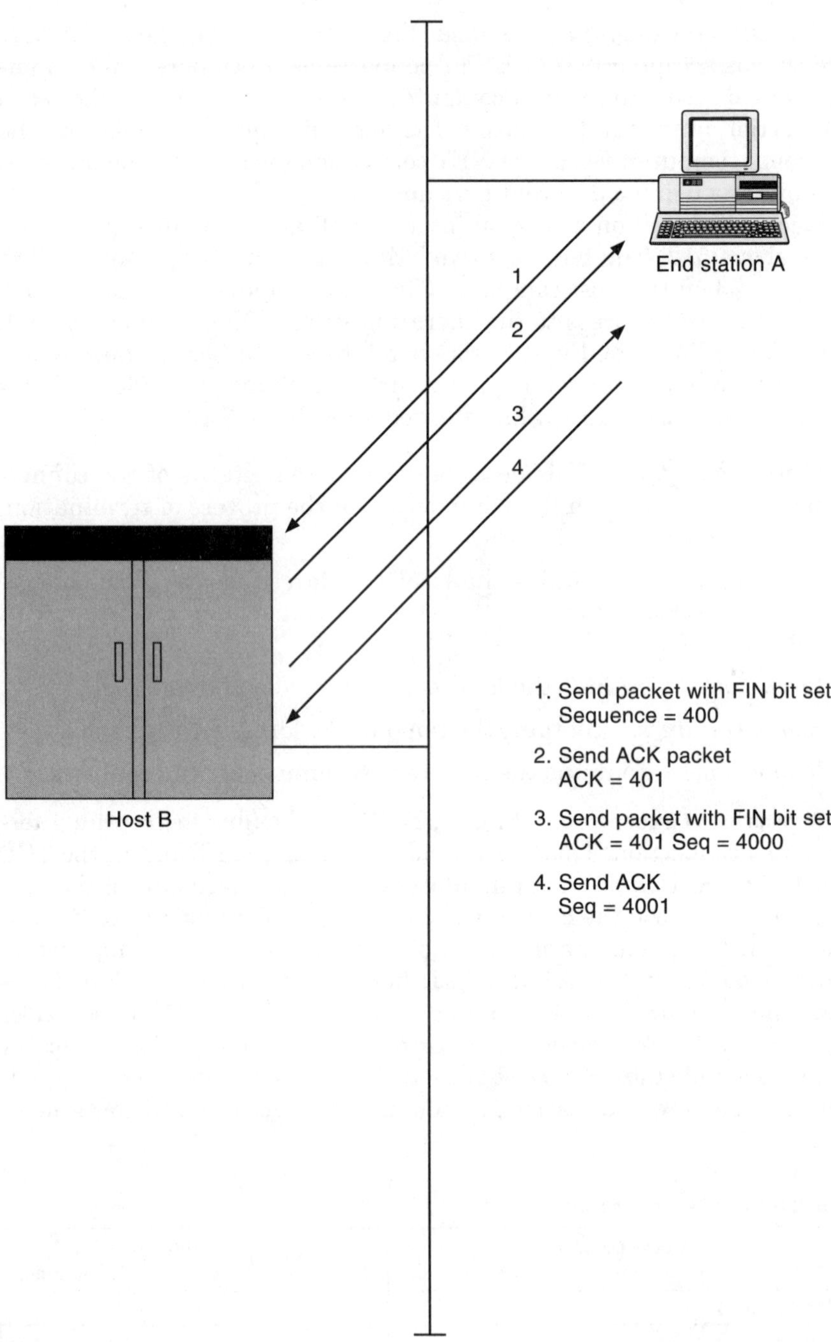

Figure 6.29 Terminating a session.

accept data from host station B. This way, station A can, at a minimum, accept a FIN packet from host station B to completely close the connection. To finalize the closing of this connection, host station B will send a packet to end station A with the FIN bit set. End station A will ACK this packet and the connection is closed. If no ACK is received, FINs will be retransmitted and will eventually time-out if there is no response.

Retransmission timer. One last function to discuss is TCP's capability to know when to send a retransmission of a packet. Retransmissions occur when a segment of data has not be acknowledged within an *allotted time.* This allotted time is dynamic (not held to one number) and is accomplished as follows: When TCP submits a packet to be sent, TCP records the time of the transmission and the sequence number of the packet. When TCP receives an acknowledgment to that sequence number, it will again record the time. TCP actually records the difference in time between the packet sent and the acknowledgment that was received. TCP uses this time to build an average time for a packet to be sent and an acknowledgment to be received.

This calculation of time used for TCP is a transport-layer protocol that was devised to run on multiple network-layer protocols. TCP knows that the packet to be transmitted may run through long delays on multiple types of networks. Therefore, it is impossible to accurately (in advance of sending the packet) gauge the amount of time it will take to receive an acknowledgment. TCP uses this timer to determine when to send a retransmission. The time is dynamic and has the capability to constantly change.

Section 3: Selected TCP/IP Applications

This section will give you an introduction to TELNET, FTP, SMTP, and DNS.

There can be many applications written for the TCP/IP environment, and many exist today. There are word processing systems, CAD/CAM systems, mail systems, and so on. The four most common applications that run on the TCP/IP network system are:

1. TELNET
2. File Transfer Protocol (FTP)
3. Simple Mail Transfer Protocol (SMTP)
4. Domain Name Service (DNS)

These applications are fully documented in the RFCs and almost always will be delivered with any TCP/IP protocol suite in the market today. These applications are usually included with every vendor's implementation of TCP/IP. These means that you can switch to almost any type of computer using TCP applications software and the commands and functions of these programs will be the same.

The applications were specifically written for TCP/IP and basically provide almost all the applications that users need to access on any network. Database programs, word processing programs, and so forth, are all viable programs, but are not pertinent to the operation of a TCP/IP network. Using the foregoing application, a user can find any other needed application on the internet. The ones listed previously are the bare minimum needed to create a networked user environment in which all users can actively communicate and share data with each other across the network.

One nice thing about these available network applications is that they run on TCP/IP no matter which operating system is being used. The commands, their connection techniques, the commands that control the application, and the interface to the user almost always will be the same. So, if you normally work with UNIX and then switch for a day to DOS, the same FTP commands that operated on the UNIX machine will be there in the DOS machine. It is hard to say that with most applications that run on any system today. The discussion starts with the TELNET protocol.

The protocols are covered briefly. Please refer to the TCP/IP books at the back of this book for more information about these protocols.

Telnet

This is pronounced TELNET and not Telenet. Telenet is a wide-area packet-switching technology based on the CCITT X.25 recommendation. TELNET is a TCP/IP application that provides remote terminal services.

TELNET allows a user from his or her network workstation to log in to a remote network station across the network and act as if the terminal were directly connected. The network may be local or it may be geographically distant (i.e., Virginia to Texas). TELNET is a relatively simple protocol compared to the complex terminal emulators that are represented in the personal computer arena today. In effect, it is a completely different application, for those emulators usually provide asynchronous terminal emulation connection, whereas TELNET provides network terminal emulation. The main reason for its popularity is that it is an open specification (in the public domain) and is widely available throughout all the TCP/IP company product offerings. There is even a version which provides 3270 emulation across TELNET connections. It is called TN3270. It does require a TN3270 server program at the host end.

As shown in Fig. 6.30, the TELNET protocol is encapsulated in a TCP header. The user starts the TELNET protocol at his or her work-

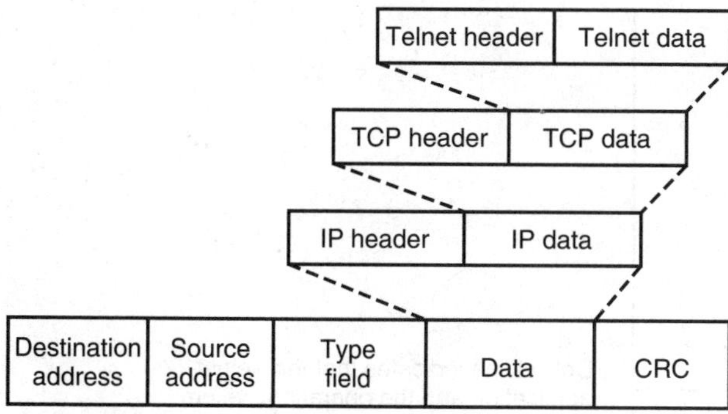

Figure 6.30 Telnet encapsulation.

station, usually by typing *TELNET <domain name or IP address>*. The TELNET application may be started with or without an argument.* The argument allows a simpler procedure to be invoked so that the TELNET process would automatically try to connect to the host signified by the argument statement. The TELNET application would start and attempt to establish a connection to the remote device (by accessing the services of the domain name server or directly with the IP address; DNS will be discussed later). If an argument was not supplied, TELNET would wait for the user to OPEN a connection using the DNS or an IP address.

Refer to Fig. 6.31. This figure shows the TELNET process and its association with a computer and operating system. The TELNET protocol was written so that it would work on a variety of operating systems. Therefore, before a connection is made to the remote device, the TELNET protocol has some work to do in order to synchronize the connection with the remote device. For example, the DOS operating system for personal computers requires that a CR-LF (carriage return-line feed) be used to terminate a line of text. Other systems such as UNIX require a line of text to be terminated with an LF. Another example is the echoing of characters. Upon connection attempt, the TELNET protocol will negotiate with the remote device as to who will do the echoing of typed characters to the initiator of a connection.

During the connection attempt between a source and destination station, the two stations will communicate options. These options indicate how each end of the connection will respond on the TELNET connection. These options include:

---

* An argument is a parameter that is typed in after the application name is typed in on a workstation. For example, if you wanted to invoke the TELNET application and wanted a TELNET connection to destination host 129.1.1.1, then 129.1.1.1 is the argument to the TELNET application program.

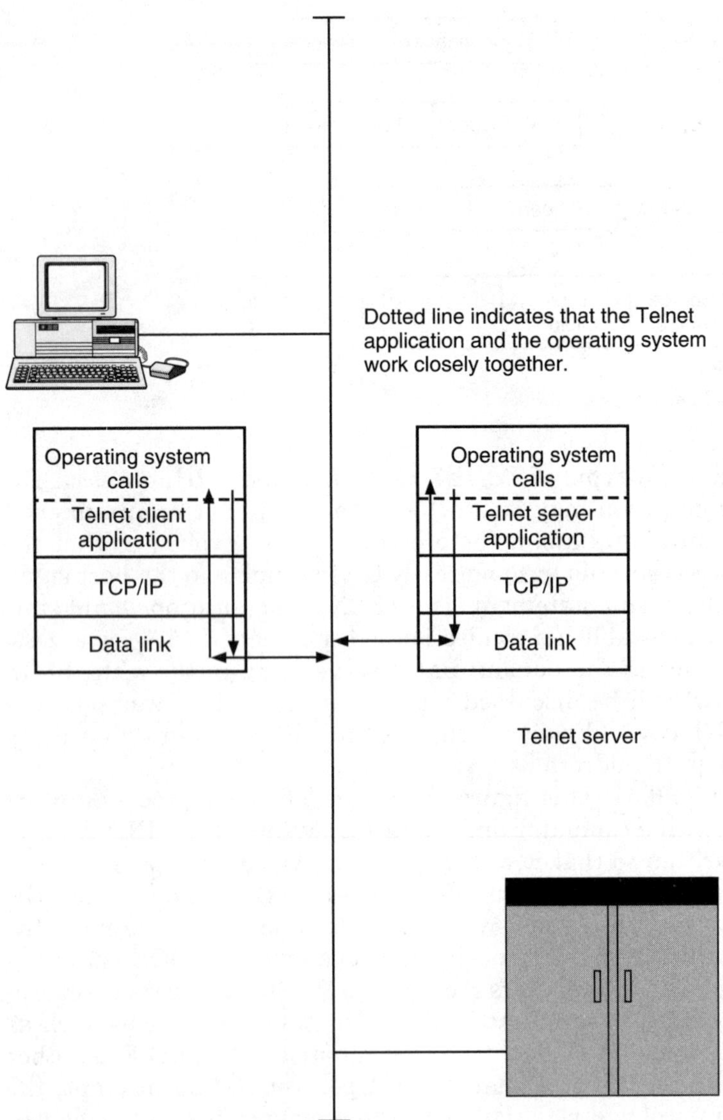

Figure 6.31 The Telnet process.

1. The ability to change from 7-bit text to 8-bit binary
2. Allowing one side or the other to echo characters
3. Specifying a terminal type
4. Requesting the status of a TELNET option from the remote connection
5. Setting a timing mark to synchronize two ends of a connection
6. The ability to terminate a record with an EOR code
7. Setting line mode so that strings of characters may be sent instead a character-at-a-time transmit
8. Stopping the go-ahead signal after data

The options are negotiated between the two network stations in the following manner:

Request	**Response**
Will <option>	Do or Don't <option>

For example, will echo from station A is requesting that station A will provide the echoing of characters. The response will either be DO echo, meaning the remote end agrees, or Don't echo, meaning the remote end will not allow station A to echo.

Agreement between the two TELNET ends communicated for a DO <option> will be responded to with a Will <option> or Won't <option>.

An example of this option negotiation: If the TELNET application was running on a DOS personal computer and it was set up for local echo, upon the connection setup, the TELNET option from the PC would be WILL ECHO and the response should be DO ECHO. If the PC had been set up without the local echo option and you wish the remote end to provide echo, the PC should negotiate echo with DO ECHO and the response would be WILL ECHO.

Using the WILL, WON'T and DO, DON'T provides symmetry. Either side of the connection can provide the command or the response. One side provides services in exactly the same manner as the other side.

The TELNET connection simply allows a terminal service over the TCP/IP network. Remember from Chap. 1 that computers and terminals were connected by a cable and the terminals were directly attached to the host computer. The TELNET service provides a terminal service for the network. It can emulate many different types of terminals, depending on the manufacturer of the TELNET program. There are TELNET programs that emulate DEC VTxxx series of terminals, IBM3270 terminals, etc.

The advantage to the TELNET program is that, with access to this program, a user may log on to any host on the TCP/IP internet (providing security options are allowed). Sessions are set up over the TCP/IP network.

Figure 6.32 shows a typical TELNET connection on a TCP/IP network.

File transfer protocol (FTP)

TELNET provides users with the ability to act as a local terminal even though users are not directly attached to the host. One other TCP/IP application that provides network services for users on a network is a file transfer protocol. With TCP/IP, there are three types of file access protocols in use: FTP, Trivial File Transfer Protocol TFTP, and Network File System (NFS). This FTP protocol provides for files to be transferred reliably across the network.

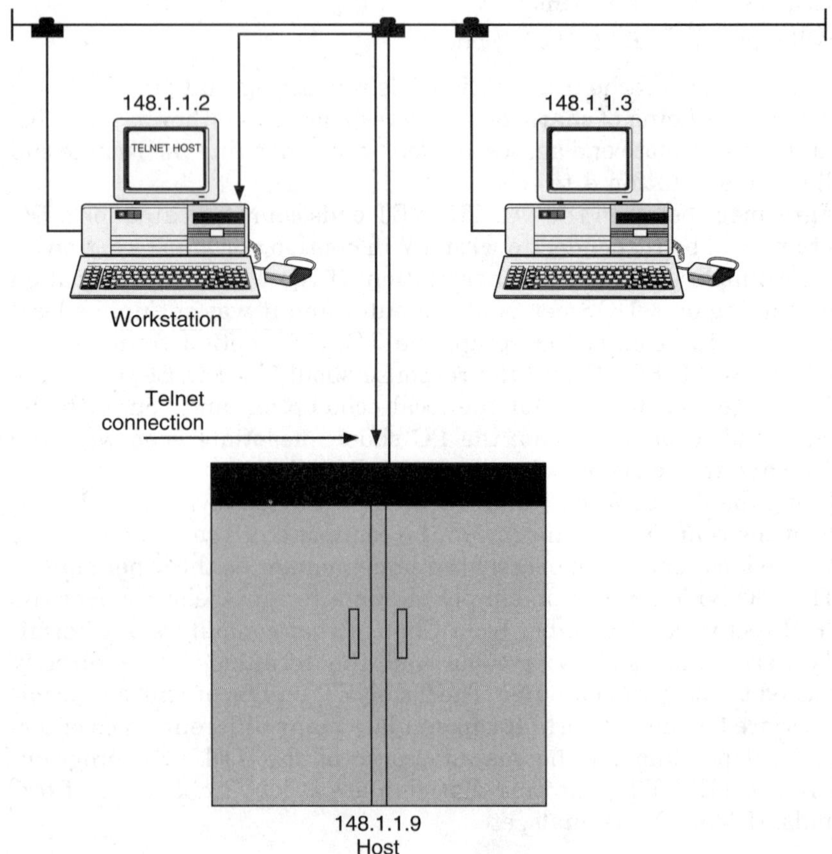

Figure 6.32 Remote terminal emulation over the network.

FTP is very robust. In Sec. 2, there was an in-depth discussion on port and sockets: how they are established and used. The FTP protocol actually uses two port assignments (and therefore two connections): 20 and 21. Remember that most connections between two network stations are made via one source port and one destination port. A network station wanting a connection to a remote network station must connection to two ports on the destination station in order for FTP to work.

Port 20 is used for the initial setup of the connection and is used as the control connection. No data passes over this circuit except for control information. Port 21 is used for user data (the file to be transferred) to pass over the connection.

Once the connection is established, the server process awaits a command from the client. To transfer a file from the server to the client, the user would type in: get <a name of a file>, which will be transmitted over to the remote network station. With this, a second connection is established between the server and client FTP process. It is known as the *data connection.* Now we have two connections, but only during the file transfer process. Once the file is transferred, the data connection port is closed.

All data connections are made with port number 20. This is the well-known (or static) FTP data port. From a user's standpoint, to establish a connection between itself and a remote station, the command is similar to TELNET; FTP <domain name or IP address>. A user could also type in FTP and wait for the FTP prompt. At the prompt, the user would use the open command to establish the connection. Table 6.11 lists the available commands in FTP.

There are a lot of commands listed but, in reality, only a few are used. They are:

TABLE 6.11 FTP Commands

!	cr	macdef	proxy	send
$	delete	mdelete	sendport	status
account	debug	mdir	put	struct
append	dir	mget	pwd	sunique
ascii	disconnect	mkdir	quit	tenex
bell	form	mls	quote	trace
binary	get	mode	recv	type
bye	glob	mput	remotehelp	user
case	hash	nmap	rename	verbose
cd	help	ntrans	reset	?
cdup	lcd	open	rmdir	
close	ls	prompt	runique	

open	open a connection to a remote resource
close	close a connection to remote resource
bye	end this FTP session
binary	indicate that the file transfer will be a file of binary type (i.e., executable file, lotus file, etc)
get	get a file from the remote resource; get <filename>; mget <multiple files, wildcards included>
put	put a file to the remote resource; put <filename>; mput <multiple files, wildcards included>
cd	change directory on the remote device; to change the directory on the local end use: lcd
dir	get a directory listing on the remote device; to get a directory listing on the local end use: ldir
hash	Display hash marks on the screen to indicate a file in being transferred

Data transfer. Refer to Fig. 6.33. If a user wanted to establish an FTP connection between 148.1.1.2 and an FTP server process on 148.1.1.19, the following sequence of events would take place on a DOS PC (for other operating systems, the prompt would change, but the commands are all the same in every FTP implementation):

```
C> FTP
```

The user would establish the connection via one of three possible ways:

1. FTP (entered with no arguments)
   FTP> OPEN <IP address or domain name>
2. FTP <IP address>
3. FTP <domain name>

The FTP client process would return information to the screen, showing a connection had been made, and then ask for a user name and password. Once the authentication has been approved, the FTP prompt would return. From this, the user would enter one of the listed commands.

Since FTP is about file transfer, we shall get a file:

```
FTP> get <remote_file_name> <local_file_name>
```

This means *get* the file specified (remote_file_name) and copy it to the local file system under the name of <local_file_name>. If <local_file_name> is not specified, the remote file would be copied to the local file system with the same name.

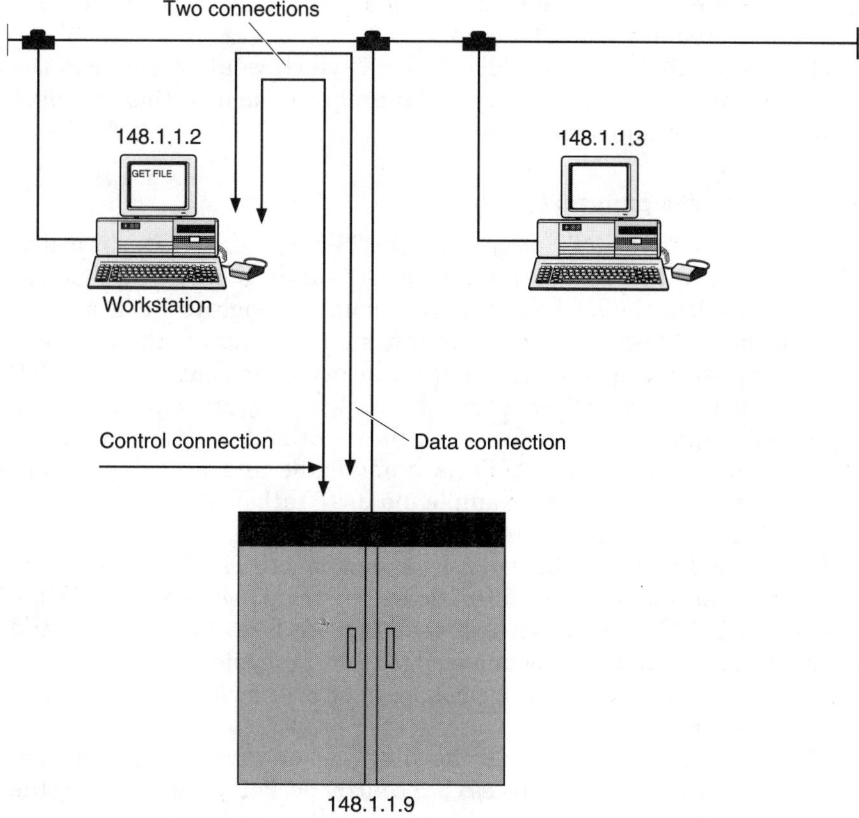

Figure 6.33 FTP process.

The FTP process would then determine that a data connection was being set up and whether or not the transfer was complete. At this point, the user could get more files or put more files, and just quit the program by typing:

```
FTP> close
FTP> quit

C:>
```

If multiple files were needed, the user could use the command MGET or MPUT, which stands for multiple GET and multiple PUT.

Table 6.11 listed the available commands under the FTP prompt. If the file we wanted was a binary file (a spreadsheet and an application are examples of binary files), the user would have to type in the keyword "binary" at the FTP prompt. This would indicate to the FTP program that file to be transferred is a binary file. Any of the commands may be entered at the FTP prompt.

The user could also enter "disconnect," which would disconnect the current connection but leave the FTP program open so that the user could enter another connection.

Trivial file transfer program (TFTP)

An alternative to the FTP program is the TFTP program. This is a simplex file transfer program and is primarily used to bootstrap diskless network workstations (the program is small enough to fit in a ROM chip on the diskless workstation to initiate a boot across the network) or even network components (network bridges and routers). The FTP program is an extremely robust and complex program, and situations exist that require file transfer capabilities without complexity. Hence, FTP is also a larger file. TFTP is a small file and provides a more restrictive file transfer (for example, no user authentication); it is also a smaller executable software program.

There are differences between FTP and TFTP. TFTP does not provide a reliable service; therefore, it uses the transport services of UDP instead of TCP. It also restricts its datagram size to 512 bytes, and every datagram must be acknowledged (no multiple packet windowing). There are no windows for packets to be acknowledged. It could be said that it has a window of 1.

The protocol is very simple. The first packet transmitted from the client process to the server process is a control packet, which specifies the file name and whether it is to be read or written (get or put command). Subsequent packets are data packets and file transfer is accomplished with 512 bytes transferred at one time. The initial data packet is specially marked with a number of 1. Each subsequent data is incremented by 1. This is the sequence numbering system for TFTP. The receiving station will acknowledge this packet immediately upon receipt, using this mark number. Any packet of less than 512 bytes in length signifies the end of the transfer. Error messages may be transmitted in place of the data in the data field, but any error message will terminate the transmission. Also notice that only one connection is made to the remote resource. FTP has one for data and one for control information. The commands of get and put are used the same as the FTP program.

The sequencing of the data is accomplished through TFTP, not the transport-layer service of UDP. UDP provides only unreliable, connectionless service. TFTP is keeping track of the sequencing of the blocks of data and the acknowledgments that should be received. For those readers familiar with NetWare, this is the same type of transaction accomplished between the NetWare Control Protocol (NCP) and its underlying delivery system, called IPX. This is fully discussed in Chap. 5.

Domain name service (DNS)

The IP protocol mandates the use of IP addresses. Any user may use this address to connect to any service on the network. But for a user to remember the addresses of all the network servers on the network is an impossible task. Users are more likely to remember names than they are to remember numbers. The architects of the TCP/IP protocol also noticed this and started work on the naming service for TCP/IP.

The first entry to an IP naming scheme was a public domain text file known as HOST.TXT. The Network Information Center (NIC) at Stanford Research Institute maintained this file, which listed the names of networks, gateways (routers), and hosts on the Internet and their corresponding addresses.

This type of name service was a simple text file that anyone could download (using FTP) to their hosts. If a user wanted to use an application like TELNET to connect to a remote station, he or she could do so with a name instead of an IP address. The application would look for the host name in the host-text file. This was simple enough for the early days of the Internet. With the expansion of the Internet, this file was becoming extremely hard to maintain. Therefore, in 1983, the Internet administrators decided to create the Domain Name Service (DNS).

DNS is hierarchical in structure, as shown in Fig. 6.34. This type of structure is exactly the same as an organization chart for any company. When you look at this type of chart, you will notice there is one person at the head of the chart with the subordinates branching out from this "root."

The advantage of this structure is that at the bottom of the chart, users can assign their own names. These users will use the upper-level names when they must access nodes outside of their region.

The domain name takes the form of local-part@domain name. The local part is usually a name of a host, a name of a user, etc. It is assigned by the local network administrator and not the NIC. For example, when applying for a network number, the NIC will also assign a company a Domain Name. As shown in Fig. 6.34, the Domain

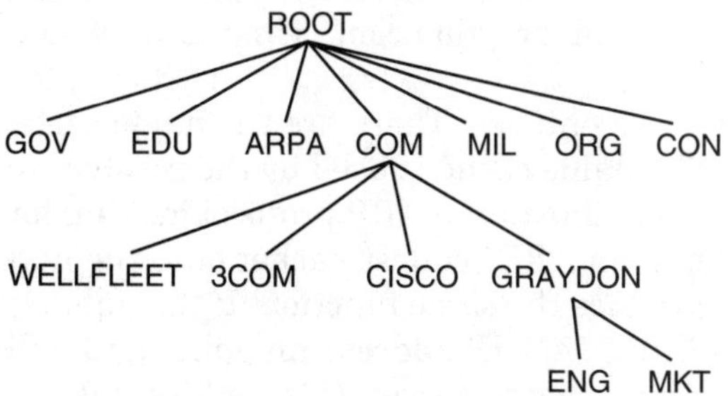

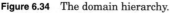

Figure 6.34 The domain hierarchy.

Name for the company Graydon would be: Graydon.com. Once this is assigned, the Graydon company could implement their own domain name scheme. For example, a user in the engineering department could be assigned the domain name mnaugle@ENG.Graydon.com. This would be a user known as mnaugle located in engineering at the company called Graydon. This is a commercial company as assigned by the NIC.

The other abbreviations are as follows:

GOV	A government body
EDU	Educational body
ARPA	ARPA-Internet host identification
COM	A commercial entity
MIL	Military
ORG	Any other organization not previously listed
CON	Any country using the ISO standard 3166 for names of countries

DNS is defined in RFC 1035.

Going down the chart, we can pick out a domain name such as research. Wellfleet.com. This would signify the research department at Wellfleet, which is defined as a commercial entity of the Internet.

Mapping IP addresses to domain names is the object of RFC 1035. There are two entities that will provide this mapping. These are the *name resolver* and the *name server.* Refer to Fig. 6.35. A user at workstation 148.1.1.2 types in the TELNET HOST command. This workstation must have the domain name resolver installed on it. This program would send out the translation request to a domain name server to resolve the host-name-to-IP address. If the host name is found, the domain name server would return the IP address to the workstation. The workstation then attempts a connection to the host using the IP address and not the name. The preceding example used only part of a name: host. This is known as a *relative name.* It is part of a larger name known as the *absolute name.* The absolute name for the preceding example could be host.eng.graydon.com. This name would be in the domain name server.

Figure 6.36 shows a couple more entities. There are the name cache and the foreign name server. The name cache is used by the resolver to find the address locally. This is similar to the ARP protocol looking for a physical address before placing an ARP request packet onto the network. The name resolver will produce the same function. If the name is found in the local cache, it will use that IP address mapping and will not transmit a query to the network name server. If the address is not in this table, it will try to find a name server to produce the mapping.

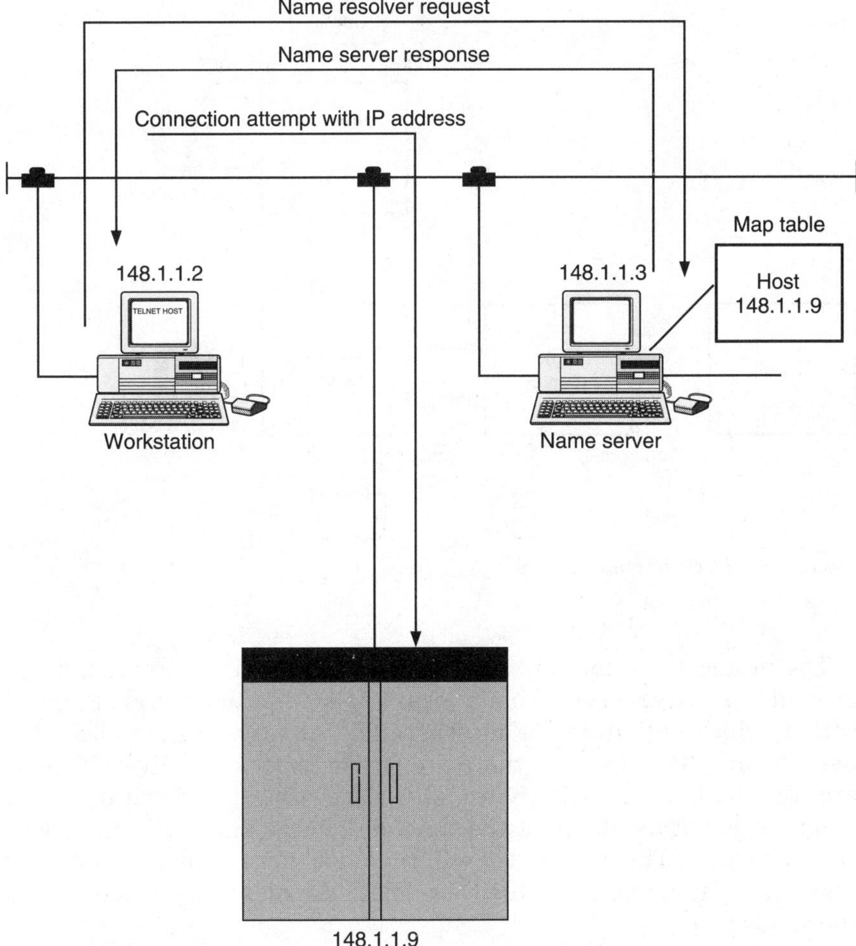

Figure 6.35 Functions of the domain name server.

The other entity is the foreign name server. Once a name server has received a request for a name-to-IP address mapping, it must look this up in its table. If the name server cannot find the mapping of the request, it may pass it off to another server. This server should be able to find the mapping or it will inform the user that it could not find the address.

Domain name servers are used simply to map IP names to IP addresses. The main name service entries may be downloaded from the Internet.

Simple mail transfer protocol (SMTP)

This is a protocol that allows users to transmit messages (mail) between other users. It is one of the most widely used applications of the TCP/IP protocol.

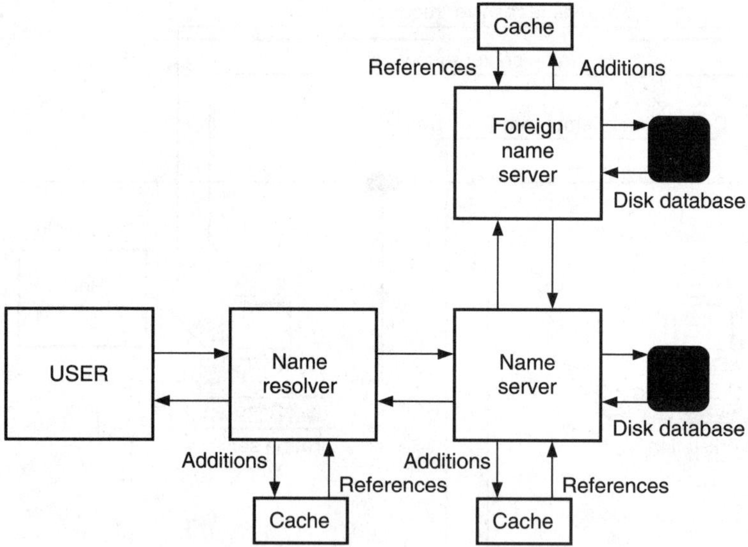

Figure 6.36 Block diagram of DNS.

The protocol is relatively simple. A message will be created, properly addressed, and sent from a local application to the SMTP application, which will store the message. The server will then check (at periodic intervals) to see if there are any messages to deliver. If there are, the mail server will try to deliver the message. If the intended recipient is not available at the time of delivery, the mail server will try again later. The mail server will try a few times to deliver the message and, if it cannot, it will either delete the message or return it to the sender.

The protocol of SMTP is found in two RFCs. RFC 822 defines the structure for the message, and RFC 821 specifies the protocol that is used to exchange the mail between two network stations.

Address field format. The address has the general format of local-part@domain-name. By this, you should recognize the Domain name format. For example, an address at the SMTP header could be naugle@vax1.wellfleet.com. This would indicate that message is addressed to a user named Naugle at the commercial entity known as Wellfleet, specifically on computer name VAX1.

From here the user would enter a data message and send this message off to the network to be handled by the mail server. Figure 6.37 shows the SMTP model.

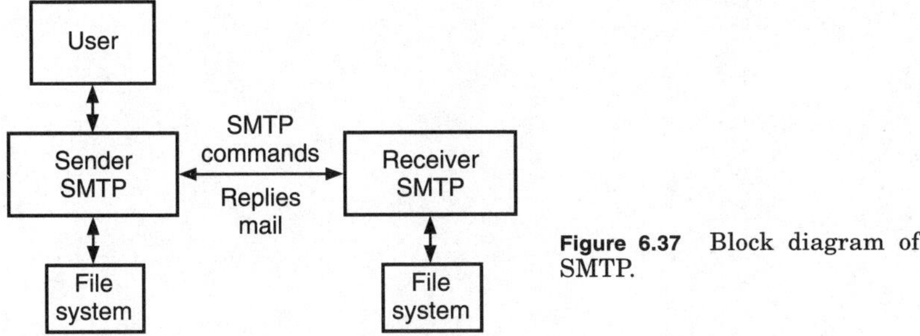

Figure 6.37 Block diagram of SMTP.

There are two entities to this system. The Sender SMTP and the Receiver SMTP.

The sender SMTP will establish communications with a receiver SMTP. The sender will send the command "mail" and the receiver should return an acknowledgment. The last step would be to transmit the data, a line at a time, and end it with a special control sequence. The server should terminate the process with a QUIT command.

Chapter

7

AppleTalk

This chapter will explain the underlying AppleTalk architecture—the architecture that enables Apple computers and printers to be shared. It is assumed that the reader has some experience with an Apple Macintosh computer.

In 1983, Apple was about to introduce its new personal computer line known as the Macintosh computer. At this same time, networks were becoming popular in the business community. Apple engineers decided to incorporate a networking scheme into the Macintosh. The major drawback of networks at that time was the complexity and expensive cost associated with the implementation of a network. The AppleTalk networking scheme was designed to be innovative but to adhere to standards wherever possible. Apple's main goal was to implement a network in every Macintosh inexpensively and seamlessly. Their first implementation was to link a LaserWriter (Apple's laser printer) to the Macintosh. File sharing between Macintoshes came later.

The key goals of the AppleTalk networking system are:

- Simplicity
- Plug and play
- Peer to peer
- Open architecture
- Seamless

When designing this system, the standard Macintosh user interface was not to be disturbed. Users should be able to implement an Apple network and not know that they are running on one. A user should be able to look at the screen and notice the familiar icons and window interfaces as if the Macintosh were operating locally. All exterior actions on a Macintosh were implemented in the chooser,* and this is where the network extensions were also provided. The network menus should be as friendly to use as the operating system itself. The engineers overwhelmingly accomplished this.

Even the wiring scheme used to fit into these goals. Users should need only to plug in the network cable for the Apple operating system to be able to detect the network and work accordingly. The beginnings of AppleTalk gave us two entities to work with: (1) LocalTalk, which is the access method (physical and data-link layers); and (2) AppleTalk (more commonly known as AppleShare), which is the network operating system (OSI network through application layers).

The following text is written to explain the underlying technology of the AppleTalk network operating system—the network system that cannot be seen. It is an uncomplicated system and was an inexpensive solution at a time when other networking solutions were expensive. Macintosh computers have two large components that have given Apple computers a clear advantage in the personal computer marketplace: built-in networking and an easy-to-use object-oriented operating system. The object-oriented operating system provides users with computing capabilities based on objects. When working with the Apple personal computer, components of the operating system or application programs are accessed with icons that appear on the screen. Users use the mouse to access the icons which provide an entrance into the operating system or to an application program.

The focus of this chapter is the network portion of AppleTalk. The AppleTalk network operating system consists of two entities: network protocols and hardware. Appletalk protocols are arranged in layers, with each layer providing a service to another layer or to an application. We will show how data flows on an AppleTalk network.

Figure 7.1*a* shows the layout of the AppleTalk protocols. Figure 7.1*b* shows the subset of the protocols to be fully described in the following chapters.

The network protocol is the software version of AppleTalk and the wiring scheme is the hardware component of AppleTalk. The hardware portion consists of the physical wiring, the connectors, and their physical interfaces. It also includes the network access methods used with AppleTalk. Currently, AppleTalk can run over LocalTalk (Apple cabling and access method scheme), and the two other most popular

---

* The chooser is the program which allows peripheral access to the Apple operating system. This includes changing networks, printers, and other utility programs designed to change the default settings on the Apple Macintosh.

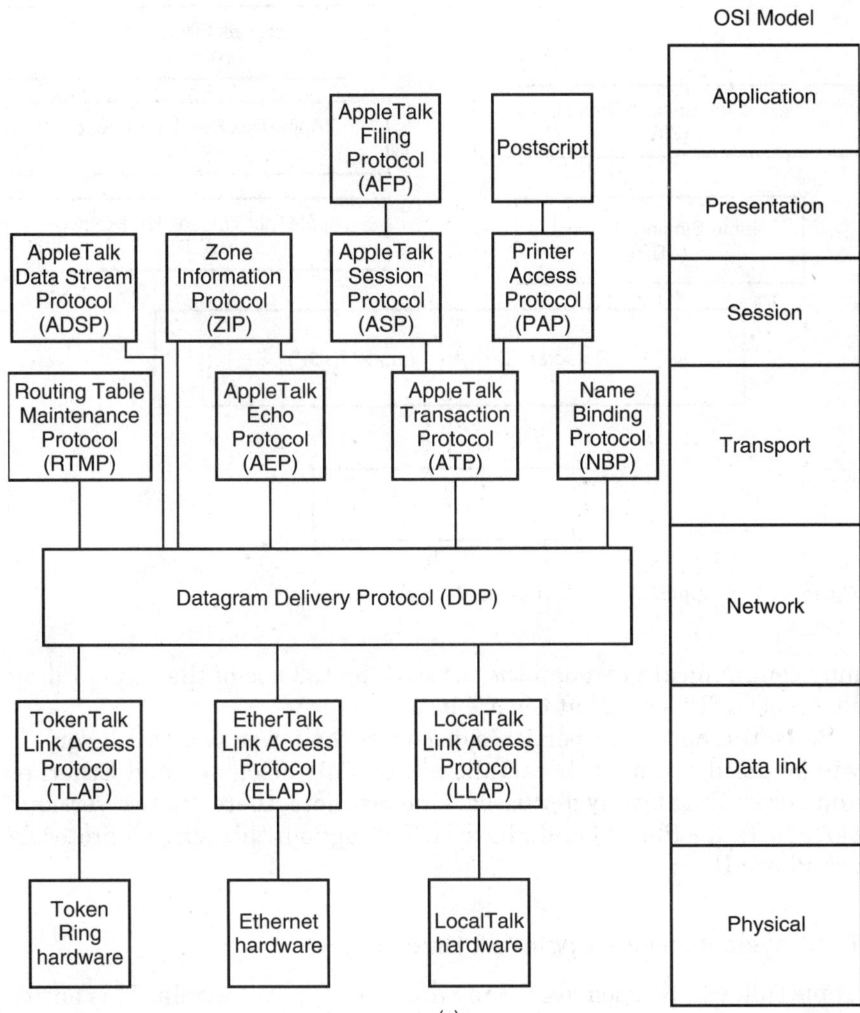

Figure 7.1 (*a*) AppleTalk and the OSI model. (*Courtesy Apple Computer.*)

access methods: Ethernet and Token Ring. (These protocols were discussed in Chap. 2. They will be briefly discussed again in this chapter.)

The software portion of the AppleTalk stack consists of the OSI network layer through the application layers. The network layer has the ability to direct messages locally or through network-extending devices such as routers. The stack also contains transaction-oriented transport- and session-layer routines, which enable messages to be sent reliably through the network. Printing is also incorporated into the AppleTalk session layer. Finally, network workstations and servers

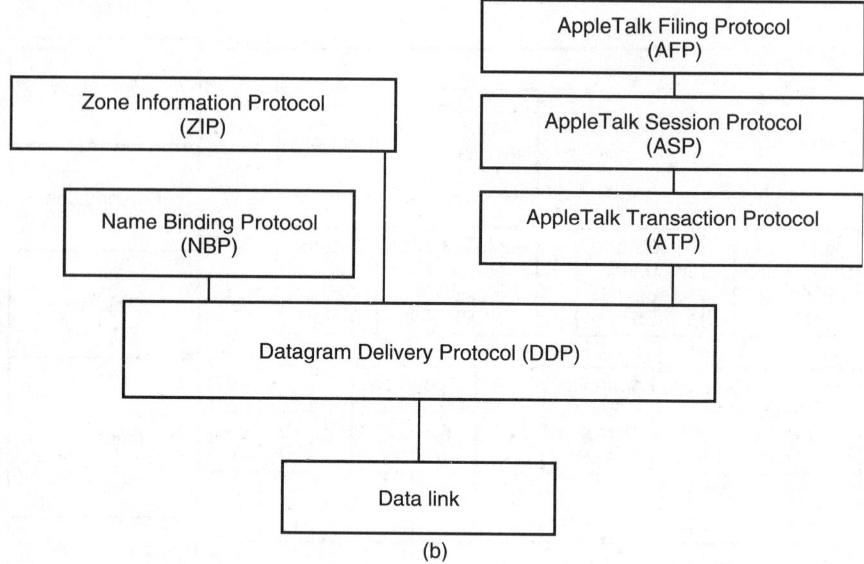

Figure 7.1 (*b*) AppleTalk stack. (*Courtesy Apple Computer.*)

may communicate through the network by the use of the Apple Filing Protocol (AFP) located at the application layer.

Since the hardware portion consists of the lower two OSI layers, it will be discussed next. LocalTalk will be fully discussed and Ethernet and Token Ring briefly discussed. One last note: there are two versions of AppleTalk—Phase I and Phase II. Throughout this text, all protocols are Phase II.

The Physical Layer—AppleTalk Hardware

AppleTalk can be used over many different types of media. This entity is comprised of the network controller and cabling systems used to allow users to communicate with each other. The current media capable of handling the AppleTalk system include: LocalTalk (for Apple proprietary networking), EtherTalk (for use on Ethernet systems), TokenTalk (for use on Token Ring networks), and LANSTAR AppleTalk from Northern Telecom.

First, we'll discuss the hardware requirements of the access methods.

LocalTalk

Apple's low-cost network implementation of LocalTalk consists of the wiring (cable segments) and access methods to transmit data on the wiring. AppleTalk with LocalTalk is embedded into every Macintosh computer. The access method of LocalTalk is used only with Apple Macintosh computers and the related network devices like printers and modems. It is not used with any other network protocol.

Just as Ethernet defines the access methods that govern the transmission and reception of data on a special type of cable plant, LocalTalk accomplishes the same functions and is an inexpensive way to connect workstations and their associated peripherals into a network. As shown in Fig. 7.2*a*, a LocalTalk network consists of the devices which connect AppleTalk network stations on a bus topology.

The devices used are:

1. LocalTalk connector module shown as the two device connectors
2. A 2-meter LocalTalk cable with locking connector shown as the bus cable
3. A LocalTalk cable extender
4. The DIN connector shells

The device connector module is a small device with a cable attached to it that connects a network node to the LocalTalk cable. There are two types of connectors associated with it. An eight-pin round type connector (DIN connector, shown as the upper-left device in Fig. 7.2*a*) is used to connect to the Apple IIe, Apple IIGS, Macintosh Plus, Macintosh SE and Macintosh II computers, the LaserWriter II NT and LaserWriter II NTX printers, and the ImageWriter II printer with the LocalTalk option installed. The nine-pin rectangular connector, shown

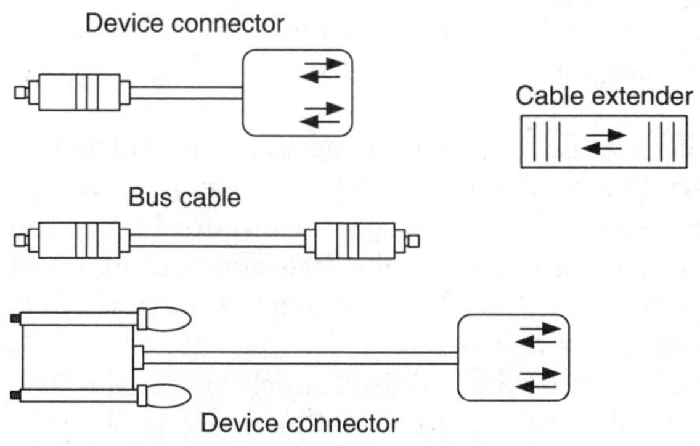

See basically two devices in LocalTalk networks

1. Device connector (2 types)
2. Twisted pair cable with DIN or RJ-connectors

Others include: cable extenders

(a)

Figure 7.2 (*a*) LocalTalk devices.

as the lower device connector in Fig. 7.2*a* is used on the Macintosh 128K, 512K, and Macintosh 512K enhanced computers and the LaserWriter and LaserWriter Plus printers.

LocalTalk cable is available in 10- and 25-meter lengths. Apple also sells a kit for custom-made lengths. Included in the kit are the connectors. Therefore, to run a longer cable between two network devices, a cable extender adapter is used to connect these cables to make longer runs of cable. In order for a network station to transmit and receive on the cable, a special device known as a *transceiver* is used. The Apple engineers have built this device into every Macintosh computer, so all the user has to do is connect the cable directly into the computer. It connects into the printer port in the back of the Macintosh. Printers participate in the AppleTalk scheme as autonomous devices and need not be directly connected to the Macintosh. The AppleTalk specifications state that the longest single cable length is 300 meters. Other companies that have compatible wiring for AppleTalk have made modifications to this scheme and allow cable segments of up to 1000 meters. Cables are made available in different lengths, and the total length of the cable plant may run as high as 1000 meters. The text in this chapter follows Apple Computer's recommendations.

This style of cabling is similar to the thin Ethernet cable scheme. Refer to Fig. 7.2*b*. In order to build the LocalTalk cable plant, it must be connected together. Devices are connected to the LocalTalk network by connecting the DIN connector to the printer port of the Apple Computer (the MAC 128, 256, 512, 512 enhanced, LaserWriter, and LaserWriter Plus use the 9-pin rectangular connector). The connector block at the other end of this connector has two RJ-11 plugs.* The bus cable is connected into this and network stations are more or less concatenated to each other.

Similarly to Ethernet coaxial cable, the two end stations on the bus cable will have one connection to the bus and the other plug will be self-terminating. Phonenet systems must have a terminator jack in the other plug. Figure 7.2*b* depicts this. Only the two end stations will have the terminator in their block. All other stations will have the bus cable plugged into both connector blocks.

The speed on LocalTalk is 230.4 Kbps. This is much lower than the speed of Ethernet (10 megabits per second) or Token Ring (4 or 16 Mbps). The components used in the LocalTalk system were inexpensive and the cabling system was built on inexpensive wire. This set limitations on the LocalTalk system that forced a low speed.

---

* Traditionally, LocalTalk uses DIN connectors. The more popular Phonenet by Farallon system uses the RJ-11 connectors.

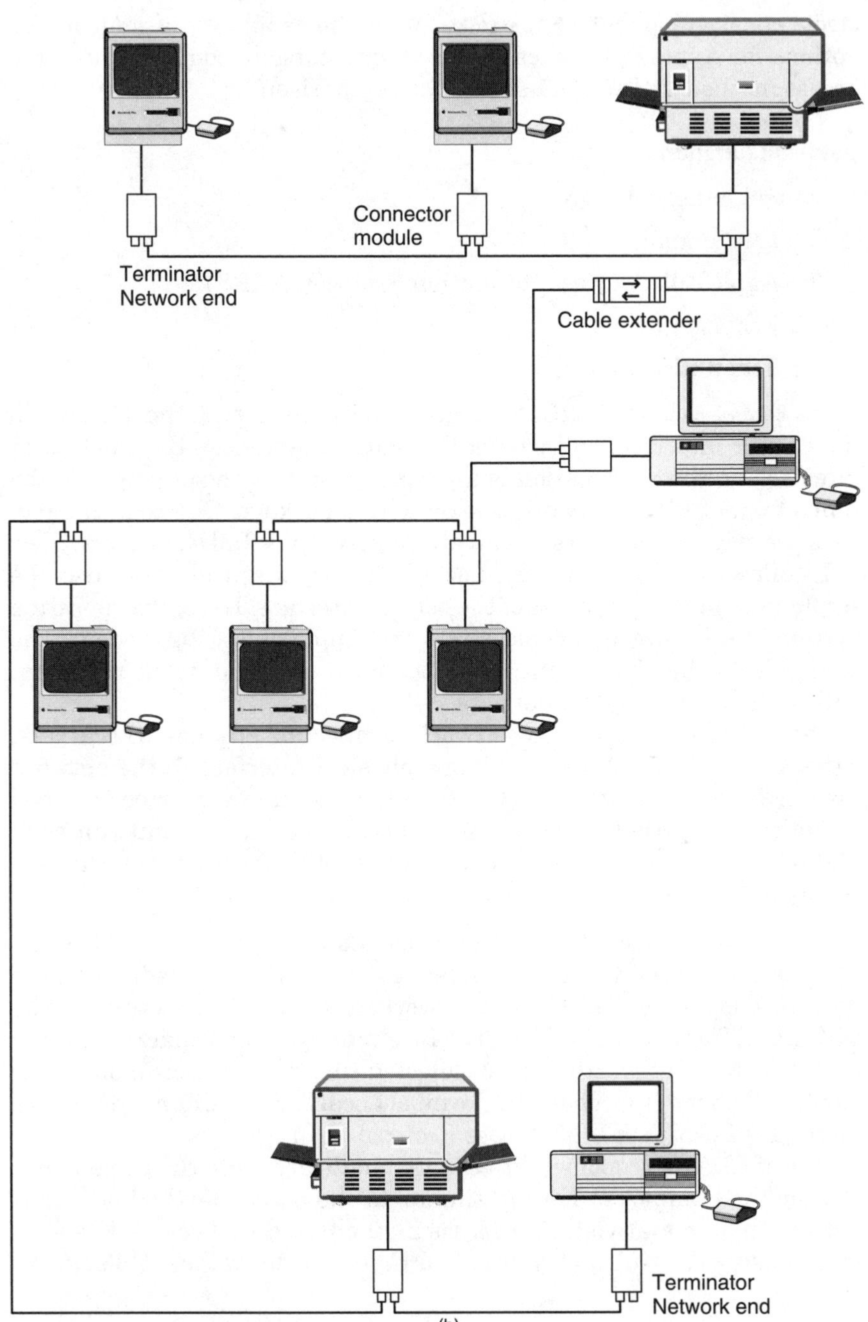

Figure 7.2 (*b*) A LocalTalk network.

Media considerations for AppleTalk. With the capability of multimedia options for AppleTalk comes the need for a table to compare the three access methods.* Table 7.1 shows the comparison.

Data-link functions

Control panel software

The LAP manager

The AppleTalk Address Resolution Protocol (AARP)

The Ethernet driver

The Token Ring driver

The control panel. AppleTalk makes extensive use of the Macintosh (Mac) user interface, and part of the window system in the Apple user interface on the workstation is an icon called the control panel. In the control panel is the network control device package. The control panel uses the system folder to store all alternative AppleTalk connection files.

To allow connection to the LocalTalk bus, the user must use the Apple icon on the menu bar of the screen interface. Here, the operating system allows multiple choices into the Apple operating system. The user selects the chooser menu. In the chooser menu, icons represent each possible action on a network.

The user can select a network connection to use (LocalTalk, EtherTalk, or TokenTalk). Only one physical interface to the network may be in use at a time. That is, the network station may be attached to both an Ethernet network and a LocalTalk network but can send and receive data only on one or the other (not both). A user may attach to any network device on the *active* network.

Link access protocol (LAP) manager for LocalTalk. This entity (LAP manager) is used to send and receive data over the selected media. It is the data-link layer for LocalTalk. For workstations that are connected to both LocalTalk and EtherTalk, the LAP manager sends packets to that network connection the user selected in the control panel. For AppleTalk networks operating over a LocalTalk medium, the access method is LocalTalk Link Access Protocol or LLAP.

One of LLAP's responsibilities is to handle access to the cable plant. The method employed here is similar to the access method of Ethernet—with a small twist. The access method used by LocalTalk is Carrier Sense with Multiple Access and *Collision Avoidance* (CSMA/CA).

---

* Since most Token Ring cables terminate in a central MAU or concentrator MAU, the length of the lobe cable (cable that connects the network station to the MAU) is usually 100 meters in length.

TABLE 7.1 LocalTalk and Ethernet Media Considerations

	LocalTalk	Thick Ethernet	Thin Ethernet	LANSTAR AppleTalk
Medium	Twisted pair	Coaxial	Coaxial	Twisted pair
Link access protocol	LLAP	IEEE 802.3	IEEE 802.3	LLAP
Transmission rate	230.4 Kbps	10 Mbps	10 Mbps	2.56 Mbps
Maximum length	1000 feet	Segment: 1640 ft Network: 8202 ft	Segment: 656 ft Network: 3281 ft	2000 ft to star
Minimum distance between nodes	No minimum	8.2 ft	1.5 ft	No minimum
Maximum number of nodes	32 Physical network: 1023	Segment: 100 Physical network: 1024	Segment: 30	1344
Maximum number of active AppleTalk nodes per physical cable segment	32	Unlimited	Unlimited	1344

NOTES:

1. Cable segment is a piece of cable not separated by a repeater device.

2. Network segment is the total number of devices on all cable segments not separated by a network-extending device such as a bridge or a router.

Ethernet uses *Collision Detection* (CSMA/CD). Collision avoidance is explained in a moment.

LLAP packet types

lapENQ	Inquiry packet used by the station to assign itself an address
lapACK	A packet sent back in response to a lapENQ
lapRTS	Sent to a destination station to indicate that a station has data for it
lapCTS	Sent in response to a lapRTS to indicate to a source station that the destination station can accept data

Figure 7.3 shows a LocalTalk/AppleTalk packet structure. It will be used throughout the LAP section.

LLAP-directed transmissions (station-to-station communication). The following text assumes that the source stations know the identity of the destination stations. How this happens is discussed later.

Since there is only one cable plant and all stations need access to it, all active network stations compete for sole use of the cable plant for a limited amount of time. To gain access to the cable plant, one at a time, is the algorithm used in LLAP. LLAP uses Carrier Sense Multiple Access with Collision Avoidance (CSMA/CA) as defined following.

Refer to Fig. 7.4. First, it performs *carrier sense* (*CS*). This is the process of checking the cable plant to ensure that no one is currently using the cable to transmit (it senses electrical activity on the cable). If the cable is busy, the transmitter is requested to defer (the process of holding the data until the cable plant is clear). Once the line activity is quiet—and it has to have been idle for at least one *interDialog gap* (IDG), which is 400 microseconds—it will wait an additional amount of random time. This random time is the result of the number of times the node had to previously defer and the number of times it assumes a collision has occurred (explained in a moment).

If the cable remains quiet throughout this whole time period (if the line became busy at any time during this interval, the whole process will be started over), the network station will send a Request-to-Send (RTS) packet to the destination station. The destination station must reply with a Clear-to-Send (CTS) packet to the originator within the *InterFrame Gap* (IFG) of 200 microseconds. When the originator receives this packet (CTS packet), it knows the destination is active and willing to accept packets. The source is now able to send data to the destination station. It must send data within the IFG time period. If the destination needs to respond to the packet (an ACK or a data response), it must repeat the foregoing procedure starting with an RTS packet. Once one station has transmitted any packet, the cable is free to anyone to try and gain control over it. This is one of the reasons that the network operates at a slow rate (LocalTalk operates at 230.4 thou-

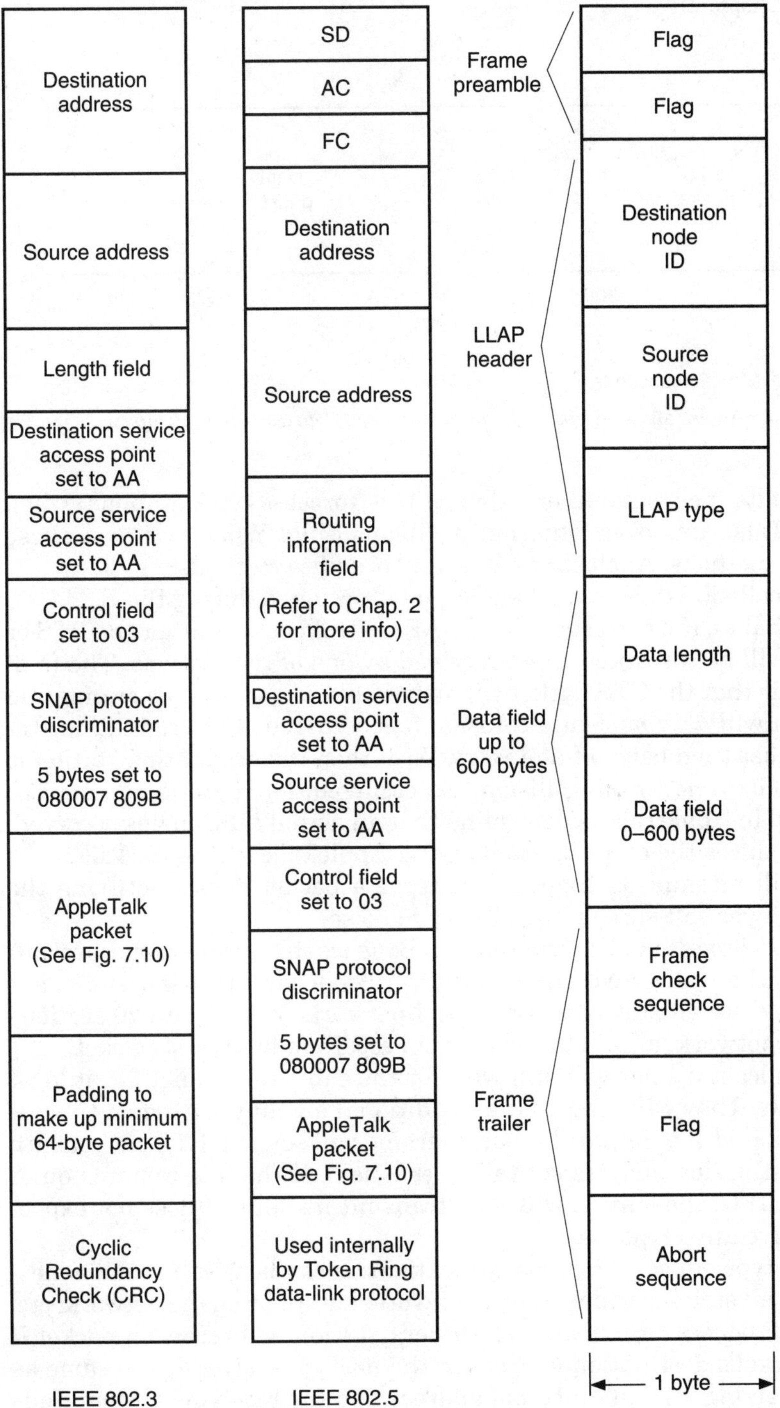
Destination address
Source address
Length field
Destination service access point set to AA
Source service access point set to AA
Control field set to 03
SNAP protocol discriminator
5 bytes set to 080007 809B
AppleTalk packet (See Fig. 7.10)
Padding to make up minimum 64-byte packet
Cyclic Redundancy Check (CRC)
IEEE 802.3
SD
AC
FC
Destination address
Source address
Routing information field
(Refer to Chap. 2 for more info)
Destination service access point set to AA
Source service access point set to AA
Control field set to 03
SNAP protocol discriminator
5 bytes set to 080007 809B
AppleTalk packet (See Fig. 7.10)
Used internally by Token Ring data-link protocol
IEEE 802.5
Frame preamble
LLAP header
Data field up to 600 bytes
Frame trailer
Flag
Flag
Destination node ID
Source node ID
LLAP type
Data length
Data field 0–600 bytes
Frame check sequence
Flag
Abort sequence
1 byte

Figure 7.3 LocalTalk. (*Courtesy Apple Computer.*)

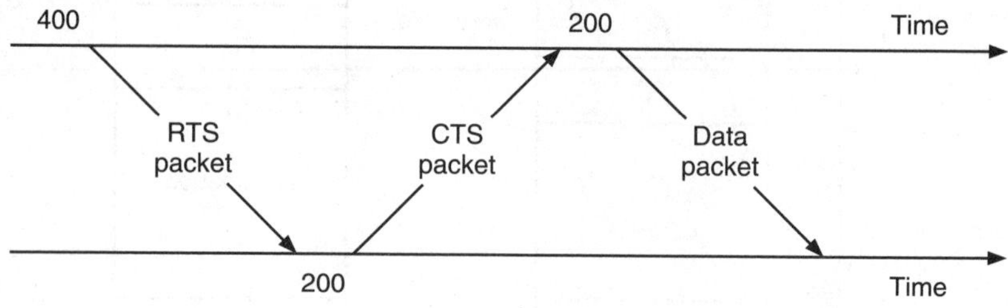

All time is in microseconds.

Figure 7.4 AppleTalk with LocalTalk data transfer. (*Courtesy Apple Computer.*)

sand bits per second or Kbps). This process in not done when AppleTalk runs over Ethernet or Token Ring. When run over these access methods, AppleTalk follows their access methods.

If a collision did occur (it should have occurred during the RTS-CTS handshake), the corresponding LLAP control packet (either the RTS or CTS) will be corrupted when received by one of the stations. The final result is that the CTS packet will never be received and the originating station will *assume* that a collision has occurred. The originating station must then back off and retry. With this, the originating station is said to *assume* that a collision has occurred, for there is no circuitry defined in AppleTalk to determine that an actual collison has occurred. This reduces the cost of implementing AppleTalk with LocalTalk.

It will attempt 32 times to transmit a packet before notifying the upper-layer software of its inability to do so.

LLAP broadcast transmissions. Broadcast transmissions are different than directed transmissions. Broadcast transmissions are intended for all stations on the local network. If there are 20 stations on the network, all 20 stations should receive a broadcast packet.

Broadcast frames will still wait for the cable to be quiet for at least one IDG. They will then wait an additional amount of random time. If the link is still quiet, the broadcast frame will send an RTS packet with the destination address set to 255 (FF hex). If the line remains quiet for one IFG, the station will then transmit its data. It does not expect to receive any responses.

This type of packet has many functions. It can be used to send a message to all stations at one time, to find other stations on the network, etc.

LLAP packet receptions. A network station will receive a packet if the packet's destination address in the packet received is the same as the receiving station's internal address and the receiving station finds no errors in the packet's Frame Check Sequence (FCS).

A frame check sequence is an algorithm to verify the data that was sent is the same data that was received. For simplicity, you may think of this algorithm as a complex parity checker. This data check guarantees the transmission of the packet to be 99.99 percent free of errors. The transmitting station computes the FCS upon building the packet. When the receiving station receives the packet, it will compute its own FCS. It will then compare its FCS with the one received. If there is a discrepancy between the two, the receiving station will discard the packet.

The LLAP of the receiving station will also drop a packet for other reasons, such as one that is too large or too small or one of the wrong type. It will handle this without interrupting the upper-layer software.

The next protocol in the data-link layer of AppleTalk is the AppleTalk Address Resolution Protocol (AARP). This will be discussed by studying EtherTalk and TokenTalk.

AppleTalk addressing. To communicate with another station requires more than sending RTS and CTS packets on the network. A packet must be addressed so another station may receive this packet and decide if it is meant for that station.

AppleTalk was designed to run on top of LocalTalk. Unlike Ethernet and Token Ring, LocalTalk does not have an address "burned" into a prom of the LocalTalk hardware. With Ethernet and Token Ring, the physical address (also known as the MAC address) of the controller card is usually assigned by the manufacturer of the controller card.* During initialization, network software that runs on these controller cards will read the address of the controller card and assign this as the address on the network. AppleTalk has an addressing scheme, but the address of a network station is decided by the network station's AppleTalk software during the initialization of the network software. This type of address is also known as a *protocol address* (originally, AppleTalk with LocalTalk, there were no physical addresses, only AppleTalk addresses).

As with any other protocol that operates over a network, any attachment on the network must be identified so any other device may communicate with it. As studied before, each device on a network is assigned a unique node address and a group network address. Since LocalTalk was devised as the hardware complement to AppleTalk, the following text describes the AppleTalk addressing scheme. The address scheme will be used again when mapped to an Ethernet or Token Ring MAC-layer address.

The AppleTalk addressing scheme was not changed when AppleTalk was migrated to Ethernet and Token Ring. The AppleTalk address is combined with the Ethernet or Token Ring physical address. This requires the use of a new protocol known as AppleTalk Address Reso-

---

* Token Ring allows for Locally Assigned Addresses (LAAs). See Chap. 2 for more information.

lution Protocol, AARP. This protocol allows for a translation of the AppleTalk software address to Ethernet and Token Ring physical addresses. AARP is discussed at the end of this section.

There are many addresses on every network. There will be one for each attachment (workstations, routers, servers) to the network. On an AppleTalk network, each network station possesses a unique identity in the format of a numeric address. The assignment of this address to the network attachment is a *dynamic* process in AppleTalk. This creates two advantages over hard-coded* addressing schemes (like the ones used in Token Ring and Ethernet). First, there is less hardware required, for the address is not fixed (burned into a prom). Secondly, there is no central administration of IDs from vendor to vendor (Ethernet and Token Ring vendor ID are required from the IEEE standards committee). However, dynamic node assignment can create large problems when combined with network-extending devices such as a bridge.

The AppleTalk address will actually be two numbers: a 16-bit network address and an 8-bit node ID. A network address is similar to an area code in the phone system. The node ID is similar to the seven-digit phone number. The node ID ranges from 0 to 255 and the network number ranges from 0 to 65535. Each network attachment on the network will be identified by these two numbers together. For example, a single network station can be found on any AppleTalk internet if the network number and node ID are known. Knowing the network number will track it down to a group of network stations, and knowing the node ID will single out a network station within that group. Again, AppleTalk addressing takes the form of <network number, nodeID>, with the network number being 16 bits in length and the node ID being 8 bits in length. This is the process and format for the AppleTalk address. This address will be mapped to a MAC address through a process known as AARP, which will be discussed later.

For AppleTalk Phase II, there are two addressable types of networks: nonextended and extended. AppleTalk Phase I did not have the concept of extended networks. Nonextended networks are individual networks that contain one network number and one zone name.† LocalTalk and AppleTalk Phase I/Ethernet are examples of nonextended networks. Likewise, extended networks are those individual networks which can contain more than one network number and multiple zone names.

* The address on Ethernet and Token Ring is 48 bits in length and the first 3 bytes are assigned by a central authority named the IEEE. The last 3 bytes remain unique from the vendor. All of these addresses are burned into a ROM and are read the by the network software at network software initialization time. See Chap. 2.

† A zone is the logical grouping of network stations into a one common name, no matter where the stations are located on the internet. This is discussed in detail later in this chapter.

Extended networks were devised to allow for more than 254 node IDs on a single physical network (i.e., for Ethernet and Token Ring).

There are some restrictions placed on the AppleTalk addresses. The network number of 0 indicates that the network number is unknown, and is meant to specify a local network to which the network station is attached. In other words, packets containing a network address of 0 are meant for a network station on the local network segment. Network numbers in the range of FF00h through FFFEh are reserved. They are used by network stations at start-up time to find their real network number from a router and at times when no router is available.

Node ID of 0 also has a special meaning. A packet with this address is destined for any router on the network as specified by the network part of the address. Packets utilizing this address will be routed throughout an internet and will be received by a router whose network address, not node ID, is included in the network ID field. A protocol such as the name binding protocol (NBP, discussed later) is one example of this type of addressing. It allows processes within routers to talk to each other without having to use up a node ID. Node ID 255 is a reserved as a broadcast address. A packet containing this address is meant for all stations on the network. For AppleTalk Phase II, node ID of 254 is reserved and may not be used.

With LocalTalk only, the available 254 node IDs are divided into two sections: those reserved for servers and those reserved for workstations. Table 7.2 shows this. This eliminates the chance that a station was too busy to answer an inquiry packet. It also allows for the separation of workstations from acquiring a server ID, which could be disastrous on an AppleTalk network. Because of the high speed and reliability of Ethernet and Token Ring, the EtherTalk and Token Talk protocols do not implement this separation of node IDs.

An AppleTalk node may acquire any address within those restrictions just stated. Remember, this is a dynamic process, meaning the number is randomly chosen by the AppleTalk protocol running on a network station. All stations on the network will participate in the selection of a node ID for a network station.

TABLE 7.2 Node ID Definitions

Node ID range	Assignment
0	Not allowed or unknown node
1–127	User node IDs
128–254	Server node IDs
255	Reserved for broadcast
Network number 0 and node ID	Networkwide or zone-specific
255	Broadcast

Nonextended node ID address selection. On a nonextended* network, server and workstation node IDs range from 1 to 254 (0 and 255 are reserved). This type of network is assigned exactly one network ID and exactly one zone name (zone names will be discussed later). An example of this type of network is LocalTalk or Phase I AppleTalk with Ethernet framing. When the network station starts up, it will assign itself a node ID. The station will then send out a special packet, known as an inquiry control packet containing this address, to see if any other station has already reserved this number for its use. If no response is received, the node will then use this number. If a response is received to this inquiry packet, the requesting node will randomly choose another number and submit another inquiry control packet and wait for a response. It will continue this until it can acquire a unique ID.

The node will then send out a request to the router to find out the 16-bit network number that has been assigned to the particular network. If a response is not received, the node will assume that no router is currently available and will use network ID of 0. If a router later becomes available, the node will switch to the new network number when it can. (It might not switch immediately, for previous connections may have been established.) If a response is received, the response packet will contain the network number assigned to that network and the node will then use that.

Extended network node ID selection. AppleTalk Phase II introduced a new network numbering scheme and a concept called an *extended network*. An extended network is a network cable segment that consists of multiple network numbers and, theoretically, may have up to 16 million network attachments on it. It can afford this expansion, for each network station is assigned a combination of a 16-bit network ID and an 8-bit node ID. Network IDs are like area codes in the phone system. They usually, but not always, identify groups of nodes with common network IDs assigned to them. Extended networks can also be assigned multiple zone names. (Zoning is discussed in a moment.)

With extended networks, there is one less node ID allowed. Node ID FE (decimal 254) is reserved; therefore, there are only 253 node IDs allowed per network ID. Implementation of AppleTalk network IDs is different from other network ID implementations in that multiple network IDs are allowed on the same cable segment. In order to allow AppleTalk to run on Ethernet and Token Ring networks, this had to be taken into account, for the maximum number of network attachments on a extended cable segment of Ethernet is 1024. Token Ring is still 260.

---

* An nonextended network is a physical cable plant that contains one network number and one or no zone name.

For those network stations operating on an extended network, the network ID acquisition is a little different. First, the network station will assign a provisional node address to itself. This is assigned by the data link and its only purpose is to talk to a router. The start-up network ID is taken from the range of FF00h to FFEEh.* This range is reserved for use with start-up stations and may not be permanently assigned to any network.

A unique twist to this acquisition process is that, if the network station was previously started on the network, it will have reserved its previous node ID and network ID on its disk. This is known as *hinting*. When the network station starts up, it will try this address first. If this address is no longer valid, it will start from the beginning.

Otherwise, the network station will send out a special packet to the router. The router will respond with a list of the valid network IDs for that network segment. The node will then select a network number from that range. If no router is available, the reserved start-up network number is used and will be corrected later when the router becomes available.

One noteworthy point here for those familiar with the manual filtering capabilities of bridges or routers: since node IDs and network IDs are dynamic, it is impossible to guess which network station is assigned to a network number. The manual filtering of bridges or routers for AppleTalk is generally reserved to zone names.

AppleTalk phase I and phase II. When AppleTalk Phase I was implemented, no more than 254 network stations could attach and be active on a single network cable segment. One network number and one zone name existed for each cable segment (not separated by a router). This protocol also supported the Ethernet framing format.

With AppleTalk Phase II, the network addressing was extended so that many network numbers could exist on a single cable plant. This network number is 16 bits wide, allowing for the possibility of over 16 million network stations per network segment (in reality, an unrealistic number but it will allow for it). Support for the Ethernet framing format was also changed to the IEEE 802.3 with SNAP headers frame format (this format was shown in Chap. 3). AppleTalk Phase II allows 253 network station addresses per network number (one less than Phase I). But now, you may have multiple network IDs on the same cable plant. AppleTalk Phase II also supports Token Ring networks using 802.2 SNAP frames. Most Apple network implementations today have switched over to AppleTalk Phase II.

* This range is reserved for start-up purposes only.

The AppleTalk address resolution protocol (AARP). The aforementioned AppleTalk addressing scheme is the one that Apple Computer developed to work with LocalTalk. Since AppleTalk's inception, Ethernet and Token Ring have taken over as the network implementation of choice (especially since the price has dropped considerably for the controller cards). LocalTalk is still used in smaller network environments and is by no means a dead access method.

In order to have AppleTalk run on an Ethernet or Token Ring network, the AppleTalk address previously described must be mapped internally to conform to the 48-bit MAC address (also known as the hardware, or physical, address) used in Ethernet and Token Ring. AARP is the protocol that accomplishes this.

There are three types of packets that AARP will use:

1. *Request packet.* Used to find other node's AppleTalk address/MAC address. In order to send information to another station (on a local network), the station must know its MAC address and its AppleTalk address. This packet is sent out to find the address.
2. *Response packet.* Used to respond to a node's request for an address mapping.
3. *Probe packet.* Used to acquire an AppleTalk protocol address and to make sure that no one else on the local network is using this address. This packet is sent out up to 10 times, once every 200 ms (1/5 second), 10 times in 2 seconds.

To identify all software and hardware protocol stacks operating within a network station, they are addressed with integer numbers. As previously discussed, when Appletalk and LocalTalk were first devised an 8-bit wide integer was selected for this purpose. Ethernet uses 48-bit addresses for network attachment identification (6-byte source and 6-byte destination MAC-layer address). To interpret the differences between this, a software entity was devised to translate between the two. For those readers familiar with TCP, AARP is similar to IP's ARP protocol. AARP resides between the Link Access Protocol and the LAP Manager. AARP performs the following functions:

Functions provided by AARP

1. Selection of a unique address for a client
2. Mapping the protocol address to the specific physical hardware address
3. Determining which packets are destined for a specific protocol

This process is only used when implementing AppleTalk on top of Ethernet or Token Ring. AARP is not implemented for LLAP (LocalTalk).

We have not replaced the AppleTalk software address. We have merely devised a scheme to work with it. This is similar to the process that TCP/IP uses to map the 32-bit TCP/IP addresses to the Ethernet or Token Ring MAC hardware address. If you know that protocol, called the Address Resolution Protocol (ARP), you will know how AARP functions.

AARP address mappings. Each node that uses AARP maintains a table of address mappings. In the example of Ethernet, it maintains a table of the AppleTalk protocol address and its associated IEEE 802.3 physical address. This table contains the mappings for every network station on the network—not for every station on the internet, just the local cable segment. This table is the Address Mapping Table (AMT). (See Table 7.3.)

Instead of requesting the mapping each time a station needs to talk to another station on the network, the AMT is a table that will have a listing of all known network stations on its local network. The entries in the table are an AppleTalk address and the MAC hardware address for the AppleTalk address. When a network station needs to talk to another station on the network, it will first look up the mapping in the AMT. Only if it is not there, will it send out a request packet.

Once an entry in the AMT is accomplished, AARP maintains this table. AARP will age out (delete after a certain time) old addresses and update with new ones.

AARP receives all AARP request packets, since they are sent out with a broadcast MAC destination address. AARP will discard the packet if it does not need to respond to the packet; but it will check something first—the sender's hardware (48-bit address) and AppleTalk node address (8-bit address) embedded into the AARP request packet. It will extract this information, use it in its initialization table and then discard the packet. Table 7.3 shows an example of an AMT for a given network station. This shows four entries. When a network station that contains this table would like to talk to another station, it must find the hardware address of the remote station. It will first consult this table.

In order to communicate with another station over Ethernet or Token Ring, a network station must know the destination's AppleTalk and MAC address. If the requesting station wanted to talk to station 16.3, it would look in this table and find the MAC address for 16.3.

TABLE 7.3 An AMT Table

16.3	02608c010101
16.4	02608c014567
16.90	02608c958671
17.20	02608c987654

Therefore, it will build a packet and, in the data-link header for addressing, it would put 02806c010101.

If the entry for 16.3 were not in this table, AARP would build a request packet and transmit the packet to the network. Upon receiving a response, it would add the contents of the response packet to the AMT and then build a packet for 16.3.

AARP node ID assignment. When a network station initializes, AARP assigns a unique protocol address for each protocol stack running on this station. Either AARP can perform this or the client protocol stack can assign it and then inform AARP.

For AARP to assign the address, it must accomplish three things:

1. Assign a tentative random address that is not already in the Address Mapping Table (AMT).
2. Broadcast a probe packet to determine if any other network station is using the newly assigned address.
3. If the address is not already in use, AARP permanently uses this number for the workstation.

If AARP receives a response to its probe packet, it will then try another number and start the whole algorithm over again until it finds an unused number.

When a network operating system submits data to the data-link layer to be transmitted on the network, the protocol will supply the destination address. In AppleTalk, this will be supplied as a protocol address. This address will then be mapped to the corresponding MAC address for that particular destination station. This mapping is what AARP accomplishes.

Examining received packets. When AARP receives packets, it will operate only on AARP packets. All other packets are for the LAP. In other words, AARP does not provide any functionality other than AARP request, response, and probe packets.

Once AARP has provided the mapping of addresses, the data-link protocol may then accomplish its work. The access protocol of Ethernet remains unchanged to operate on an AppleTalk network. AARP does not interfere with the operation of Ethernet or Token Ring.

LAP manager for EtherTalk and TokenTalk

Ethernet was developed in Xerox's Palo Alto Research Center (PARC).* First known as the Experimental Ethernet, it was first utilized in

* A detailed explanation of Ethernet is covered in Chap. 2.

1976. In 1980, a cooperative effort by Digital, Intel, and Xerox led to a public document known as the "Blue Book" specification. Its formal title was Ethernet Version 1.0. In 1982, these three companies again converged and came out with Ethernet Version 2.0. This is the standard by which Ethernet operates today.

At that time, though, the components that made up an Ethernet network were extremely expensive and were out of most companies' cost reach. Since Ethernet is an open architecture (one that is publicly available) and not proprietary, many companies have jumped on the bandwagon and have developed Ethernet products of their own. Since Ethernet is an open specification, all Ethernet products are compatible with each other. You may buy Ethernet products from one company and more Ethernet products from another company and the two will work with each other (at least at the data-link layer). Changes in cabling strategies and mass production of the chip sets have also led to price reductions in Ethernet and, currently, Ethernet is the most popular—second in cost only to ARCnet networking scheme. For more information on Ethernet and related documents, refer to references in the back of this book or to Chap. 2.

The origins of Token Ring date back to 1969. It was made popular when IBM selected it as its networking scheme. It was adopted by the IEEE 802.5 committee in 1985, and offered some advantages over the Ethernet scheme. Some of these advantages included a star-wired topology and embedded network management. The cost of Token Ring was extremely high at first. The price reductions throughout the last few years and its advantages over Ethernet have let this networking scheme become very popular.

AppleTalk was derived as an alternative to this high cost of networking. AppleTalk, with LocalTalk, operates at all layers of the OSI model. It is a true peer-to-peer network and is built into every Macintosh computer. It is a simplex "plug and play" type of networking that easily allows users to access the services of a network.

But Ethernet and Token Ring are still the most popular of networking schemes with many advantages over the LocalTalk access method, and, therefore, AppleTalk has been adapted to allow for this. To allow these networks compatibility with AppleTalk, the primary layer that is replaced is the LocalTalk data-link layer and the way LAP manager works with it.

When an AppleTalk network station wishes to communicate with another AppleTalk network station, it must provide its data link with an AppleTalk protocol address which consists of a 16-bit network number and an 8-bit node ID.

When Ethernet and Token Ring are used as the medium, a major change is invoked here. The address technique used with these access methods is 48 bits long. The AppleTalk protocol address must be translated into this format before a packet may be transmitted on an Ethernet or Token Ring network.

Extensions were made to AppleTalk's LAP in the form of EtherTalk Link Access Protocol (ELAP) and TokenTalk Link Access Protocol (TLAP) to accommodate Ethernet and Token Ring access methods. This LAP manager also uses a new function known as AppleTalk Address Resolution Protocol (AARP) to translate the 48-bit addresses to the AppleTalk addresses. ELAP and TLAP function according to their access methods of Ethernet (CSMA/CD) and Token Ring, respectively.

Theory. Simply enough, EtherTalk and TokenTalk are the Ethernet* and Token Ring access methods that have AppleTalk running on top of them. We stripped out the LocalTalk access method and replaced it with either Ethernet or Token Ring.

If you have an Ethernet network, EtherTalk will allow AppleTalk to run on that network. The same is true for TokenTalk. The major changes were made in the LAP manager. All layers above (network layer and above) are still AppleTalk. Refer to Fig. 7.5. One noticeable change should be in Fig. 7.5 (which shows the attachment for an Ethernet system): the printers are now usually connected to an AppleTalk file server and not directly to the LocalTalk network. Ethernet and Token Ring interfaces, for direct attachment of Apple printers, are not in widespread use.

Token Ring packets are shown in Fig. 7.3. Compare them to the AppleTalk with the LocalTalk packet headers shown in Fig. 7.3. As far as AppleTalk is concerned, it is running on top of LocalTalk. Only the LAP manager is changed.

To allow AppleTalk Phase II to operate over Ethernet and Token Ring, the easiest method was through the use of the Institute of Electrical and Electronics Engineers (IEEE) protocol specification called IEEE 802.2 Type 1. This protocol is discussed in detail in Chap. 3. SNAP is discussed fully at the end of that chapter. Please refer to Chap. 3 for a complete discussion of the protocol. It will be briefly discussed in the following text.

IEEE 802.2 (pronounced 802 dot 2) data-link specification consists of two types. Type 1 is a connectionless protocol (meaning that an established link between a source and destination network station does not have to exist before data transmission occurs) and type 2 is connection-oriented (meaning the opposite of type 1). EtherTalk and TokenTalk use IEEE 802.2 type 1 packet formats for transmission over the network.

---

* Although stated as Ethernet, AppleTalk Phase II uses the IEEE 802.3 framing format. Ethernet is stated to refer only to the access method.

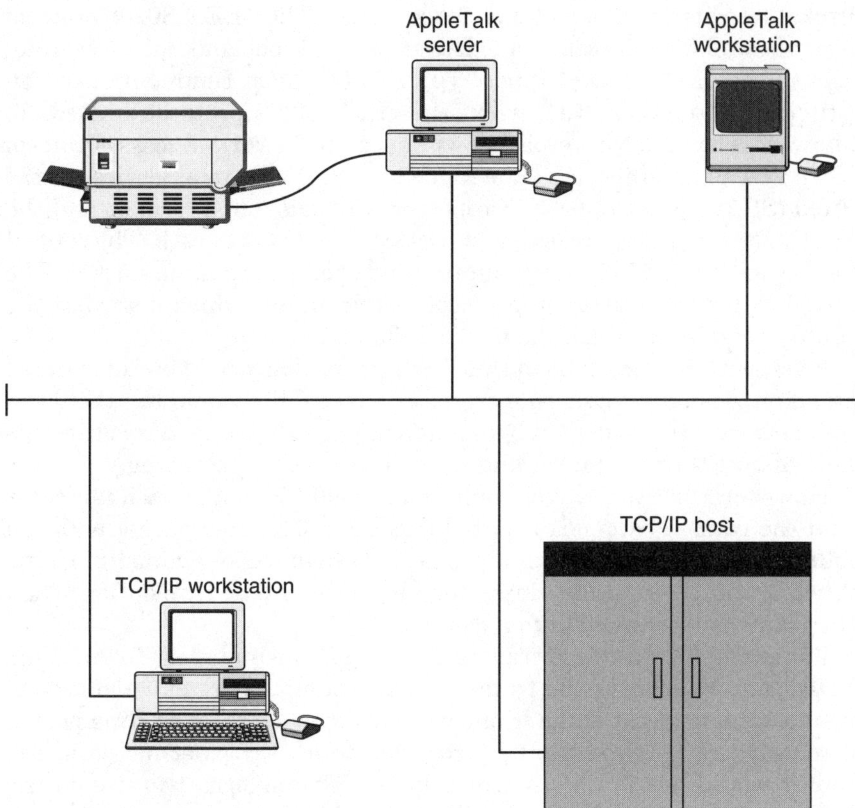

Figure 7.5 AppleTalk on Ethernet.

A subpart of that protocol is defined here and is called SubNetwork Access Protocol or SNAP. Refer to Fig. 7.3. For those familiar with the Ethernet specification, the IEEE 802.2 specification replaced the concept of the type field with the concept of a Service Access Point or SAP. SAPs allow for the distinction of a single protocol within a packet. It was determined when IEEE 802.2 was being written that many protocols may exist on a network station or on a network. When a packet is transmitted, it should be known which process of the protocol stack submitted the packet and to which process of the protocol stack the packet is destined. For example, you may have AppleTalk, Xerox Network Systems (XNS), and Transport Control Protocol/Internet Protocol (TCP/IP) all running on the same network station. All three may send and receive packets from the same network connection (in this case, Ethernet). To determine which protocol stack any received packet is for, a SAP number is used. SNAP allowed those non-IEEE protocols to run on the IEEE 802.x data link. It allowed an easy port of existing LAN protocols.

Packet formats for Ethernet and Token Ring. The IEEE 802.2 protocol also allowed for migration of existing packet types and network protocols to the IEEE packet type. Type 1 is the most commonly used on Ethernet and Token Ring when the IEEE 802.2 protocol is used. To allow for this, a protocol known as SubNetwork Access Protocol (SNAP) was invented. As shown in Fig. 7.3, the Source Service Access Field (SSAP) is set to AAh (h represents hexadecimal format) and the Destination Service Access Field (DSAP) is also set to AAh. The control field is set to 03h to indicate an unnumbered information packet. The next 5 bytes represent the protocol discriminator which describes the protocol family to which the packet belongs.

First, with 3 bytes of 0s in this field, the packet would be determined as an encapsulated Ethernet framed packet. This would tell the data-link software that the next byte following the SNAP header is the type field of an Ethernet packet and to read the packet accordingly.

However, the first 3 bytes could read 08-00-07 (hex), which indicates that the frame is an encapsulated IEEE 802.3 framed packet with the following 2 bytes indicating a protocol ID field. As explained in Chap. 2, what the protocol discriminator allows is proper translation when the frame is forwarded onto a network.

For example, if a frame traversed multiple media types (Token Ring, FDDI, and Ethernet), the frame format would change for each type of media traversed. So, if the frame were received on a Token Ring port of a router, and it needed to be forwarded to an Ethernet network, the router would need to know which type of frame/format to use on the Ethernet—Ethernet V2.0 or IEEE 802.3. This is the purpose of the protocol discriminator. If the first 3 bytes were 00-00-00, then it would use Ethernet V2.0 frame format. If this field is set to a number other than 0, it will use the 802.3 frame format.

The one exception to this is when you are bridging (not routing) an AARP frame. Bridges employ a translation table to indicate special occurrences, and will format this correctly. This is according to the IEEE 802.1h specification.

The SNAP address of 00-00-00-80-F3 is used to identify AARP packets. Following this is the AppleTalk data field which will contain the AppleTalk OSI network-layer protocol of Datagram Delivery Protocol (DDP) information. The last 2 bytes are the protocol ID, and it is set to 809B (hop) to indicate the packet is an AppleTalk packet.

TLAP packet formats are like ELAP packet formats, with the exception of the internal fields for the Token Ring controller and the source routing fields for packet routing with bridges. All IEEE 802.2 SNAP fields are the same.

Referring to Fig. 7.3, the first couple of bytes pertain only to the data-link layer of Token Ring. These bytes include the Access Control field and the Frame Control field. These fields indicate to the Token Ring data-link controller how to handle the packet and which type of packet it is.

The next byte is similar to Ethernet packet address. It is the 48-bit physical address of the network station for which the packet is intended. The source address is the 48-bit physical address of the network station that transmitted the packet to the ring. The next fields are the routing information fields according to the source routing protocol defined by IBM and IEEE 802.5 committee. This, too, was discussed in the beginning of the book.

Following the routing fields are the IEEE 802.2 SNAP headers of DSAP, SSAP, and control. The DSAP and SSAP fields contain AAh, and the control field will contain 03h. Following this is the protocol discriminator, which is set to 080007809B to indicate AppleTalk is the protocol for this packet.

The ELAP packet format is shown in Fig. 7.3. The first 6 bytes are the physical destination address of an Ethernet network station. The next 6 bytes are the physical address of the Ethernet station that transmitted the packet. The next field is the length field, which indicates to the data link the amount of data residing in the data field, excluding the pad characters.

What follows the length field is how AppleTalk easily resides on an Ethernet network. At byte 14 (starting from byte 0 at the top) is the IEEE-assigned SNAP DSAP header of AAh, and the next byte is the SNAP SSAP of AAh. AA is assigned by the IEEE to indicate that the packet is for the SNAP format, and all data-link drivers should read the packet as such. Following the DSAP and SSAP bytes is the field to indicate the control. This byte indicates to the data link that it is a type 1 (connectionless) IEEE 802.2 packet (03h).

Following this is the SNAP protocol discriminator. 08-00-07-80-9B indicates AppleTalk and the data link should read the packet according to AppleTalk protocol specifications. If that particular node is not running the AppleTalk protocols, the network station software will simply discard the packet. If it is running the AppleTalk protocols, it will accept and decipher the packet according the AppleTalk protocol specification.

Operation. When the AppleTalk protocol is started, ELAP or TLAP will ask AARP to assign a dynamic protocol address to it. All we did here was replace the link layer. AppleTalk above layer 2 remained the same. No changes were made to it. The data-link layer changed to accommodate the new access technique of Ethernet or Token Ring. Figure 7.6 shows how three LAP managers may be installed but only one may be used at a time. The upper-layer protocols may switch to any of

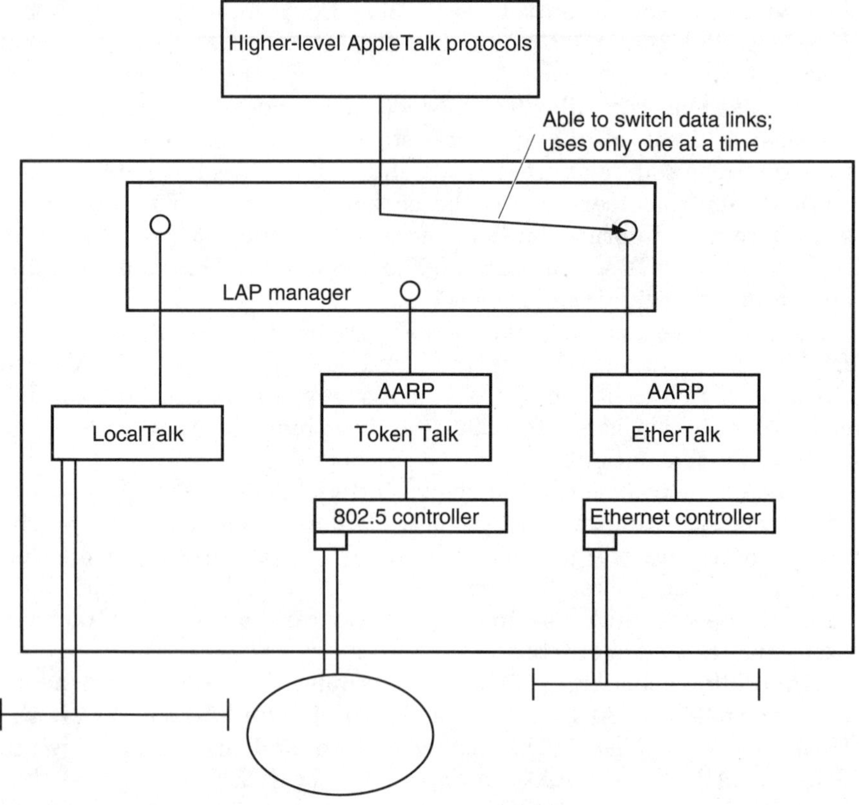

Figure 7.6 LAP manager.

the three protocols. There was one small change to the LAP manager and that came in the form of AppleTalk Address Resolution protocol (AARP).

Those were the data link and physical layers for AppleTalk. The software portion of AppleTalk begins here with the network-layer entity of Datagram Delivery Protocol (DDP). The previous protocols can be intermixed and used throughout any networking scheme. The following discussion concerns AppleTalk.

The AppleTalk Network Layer: End-to-End Data Flow

Datagram Delivery Protocol (DDP)

The DDP layer resides at the OSI-network layer and allows data to flow between two or more communicating stations on the network. There are actually multiple entities that make up this layer:

- The Datagram Delivery Protocol (DDP)
- The Routing Table Maintenance Program (RTMP)
- The AppleTalk Echo Protocol (AEP)

There are many functions provided by the DDP, which include data delivery, routing, and socket assignment. The first to be discussed is the concept of sockets.*

The data-link layer is nothing more than a car that carries passengers. It accepts the passengers and will take those passengers to the destination they indicate. Whereas the data link delivers data (given to it by the network layer) based on a node-to-node relationship, DDP establishes a concept called *sockets.* When data is transmitted or received by a station, the packet must have someplace in the network code to attach to. This is the purpose of the socket. Since many processes may be running on a network workstation, the DDP must be able to identify which process the packet should be delivered to.

With DDP, communication between two stations is now on a socket-to-socket basis for data delivery and reception. All the communication is accomplished on a connectionless service, meaning the data is delivered to a process known as a socket and, once delivered, the receiving station does not acknowledge the originating station.

Sockets. To communicate with another device, a network workstation will need an addressable endpoint to connect to. In other words, the initiator of the communication transfer must indicate the final destination—a software endpoint—for this data. The socket number tells the network station software to deliver the incoming packet to a specific process or application in the network station. This is the only purpose of the socket.

Socket numbers are addressable endpoints in any network station that actually represent an application program or another process running in that network station. There will be one unique socket number for each process that is running in a single network station. Since many processes may be running in a network station at any one time, each process must be uniquely identified with a socket number. If you know the socket number, you will know the process or application that owns it. Socket numbers are also used to identify the process that submitted the packet. If a file server receives a data packet and must

* Do not confuse sockets with ports. The combination of the network address, node ID, and the port number is the socket number. Apple calls this the internet socket address. Ports refer to a service. A port number is part of the socket. Apple uses the term socket; therefore, it will be used here.

respond to it, it needs to know the socket number in the source station that will receive this data.

All communications between a source and a destination station on the network will "attach" to each other through a socket. A socket is abstract to the user. It is not a physical device and is used by the networking software as an end connection point for data delivery. There are source and destination sockets. The source socket is from the originator of the connection and the destination socket indicates the final connection point (the end addressable point on the destination station). A source station will initiate communication with a source socket identified in the DDP header of a packet so that the destination station will know where to attach when a response is generated.

AppleTalk implements sockets a little differently than other network protocols. In other protocols, sockets are assigned as static (well-known sockets) and dynamic sockets. AppleTalk well-known sockets are those sockets which are directly addressed to DDP only. There are no well-known sockets for applications that run on the internet. The well-known sockets are listed in Table 7.4. When a packet that has a known socket is received by a network station, DDP will act upon the packet. These types of sockets are used by the DDP process and no other process. This is the difference between AppleTalk and other types of protocols for using sockets.

Other protocols (TCP/IP, NetWare, for example) will assign static sockets for every known process in the network station. A committee will assign these socket numbers, and once a process is assigned this socket, no other service may duplicate it. This well-known socket is universal. All applications that are written will be addressed to these socket numbers. AppleTalk allows its processes (file service, mail service, print service, etc.) to ask DDP for a socket number, and it could be different every time the service is started on the network. Like the node ID assignment, socket numbers are also assigned dynamically.

For example, the router table update process that runs in AppleTalk is statically assigned socket number 1. Any process that wishes to com-

TABLE 7.4 Socket Values

DDP socket value (hex)	Description
00h	Invalid
FFh	Invalid
01h	RTMP socket
02h	Names information socket (NIS)
04h	Echoer socket
06h	Zone information socket
80h–FEh	Dynamically assigned

municate to the router process must identify the packet with a destination socket number 1. A listing of the router sockets and their associated applications is shown in Fig. 7.7. The only well-known sockets used by DDP are shown in Table 7.4.

Dynamic sockets are assigned at process initiation. For example, when a process on a workstation initiates, it will request a socket number. It is the DDP layer that assigns the dynamic socket numbers. To connect to a process that is not directed for DDP, for example, an application wishing to use the Apple Transaction Protocol (ATP—the transport layer protocol for AppleTalk, discussed later) would use a locally dynamically assigned socket to connect to the destination station's DDP process. DDP would accept this packet and look into the type field in the DDP header. For ATP, this field would contain a value of 3. DDP type fields are shown in Table 7.5. DDP will strip the DDP packet headers off of the packet and pass the rest of the packet to the ATP process. ATP would then act upon the packet according to the information in the ATP headers.

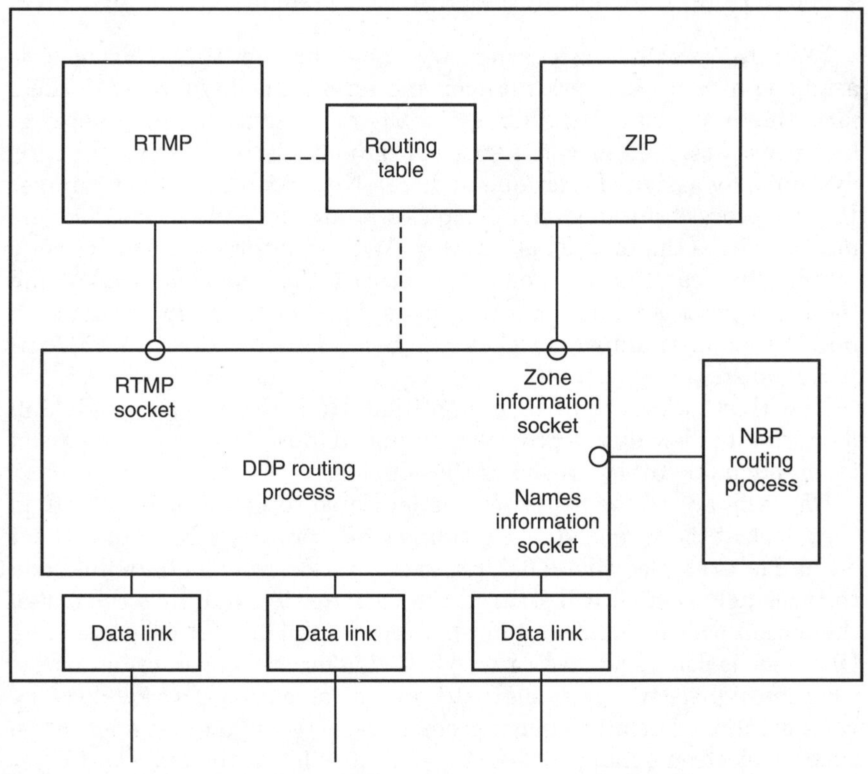

Figure 7.7 DDP. (*Courtesy Apple Computer.*)

TABLE 7.5 DDP Type Fields

DDP type field value	Description
00h	Invalid
01	RTMP response or data packet
02	NBP packet
03	ATP packet
04	AEP packet
05	RTMP request packet
06	ZIP packet
07	ADSP packet

Valid socket numbers are numbered 01 to FEh and are grouped as follows:

- 01h to 7Fh—Statically assigned sockets
- 3h and 05h—Reserved for Apple Computer's use only
- 40h to 7Fh—Experimental use only (not used in released products)
- 80h to FEh—Dynamically assigned for node-to-node communications

From the previous discussion, we know that an AppleTalk node is assigned a 16-bit network number and an 8-bit node number. Sockets form the final part of the addressing scheme used by Apple. A network number is assigned to each network segment. Each network station is dynamically assigned a unique node ID. Now, with the socket number ID, any process running on an AppleTalk internet can be identified, no matter where the process is running. With this three-part addressing scheme, you can find the node, the network that the node lies on, and the exact process running on that node. It takes the form of <network number><node number><socket number>. This is called the *internet socket address.*

Now that sockets have been identified, DDP also has a type field in its packet to identify the process running on top of DDP that the packet is intended for. Table 7.5 shows these fields.

DDP will accept the packet on the indicated socket number. It will, in turn, look at the type field to determine which process to hand the packet off to. For example, when DDP receives a packet from its data link, and the type field is 06, it will strip off the DDP headers and turn the rest of the packet over to the Zone Information Protocol for further processing. DDP's job is done, and it returns to listening for packets or for interrupts from the higher-level protocols (listed in the Table 7.5) for packet delivery.

As mentioned before, when a process starts (it could be an application such as electronic mail, file server, etc.), it will ask the transport-layer protocol of Apple Transaction Protocol (ATP, discussed later) to assign it a socket number (a dynamic socket number). ATP will pass this call to

DDP, which will find an unused dynamic socket number and pass it back to ATP. ATP will then pass this socket number back to the calling process.

The calling process will then pass the socket number to the Name Binding Protocol (NBP, discussed later), which will bind this socket number to a name. DDP logs this to a table to ensure that it will not be used again (socket numbers are not allowed to be duplicated in the same network station). All processes on an AppleTalk network are available to users through names and not socket numbers. NBP provides this service to the users, but uses socket numbers to find users and services on the AppleTalk internet. NBP and the use of sockets is discussed later.

The second function of the DDP is routing. This is the ability to forward packets that are destined to remote networks. DDP provides a dynamic routing protocol which is similar to the Routing Information Protocol (RIP) that is found on XNS, TCP/IP, and Novell NetWare networks.

Routers, routing tables, and maintenance

Another function of DDP is to allow networks to form an internetwork through the use of routers. As stated before, an internet consists of a number of local LANs connected together into an internet through special devices known as routers (also incorrectly called gateways). These devices physically and logically link one, two, or more individual networks together. In doing this, a network is transformed into an internet. One of DDP processes is the process through which network stations may submit their packets to the router in order to route to a destination on a different network (LAN). In order for DDP to accomplish this, it uses static sockets (socket 1) to deliver special messages known as routing table updates.

Router description. A router is a special device that enables a packet destined for networks other than the local network they were transmitted on. Routers are usually separate boxes on the network that contain at least two or more physical ports, each connected to a cable plant (See Fig. 7.8). The router shown in Fig. 7.8 contains two physical ports: two DB-15 Ethernet DIX* connectors. They would be the physical connection point of the routers.

By Apple's definition,† AppleTalk routers are available in three forms: local, half, and backbone. Local routers are attached to local net-

---

* Routed LocalTalk connections to Ethernet are provided by special devices such as FastPath from Shiva Corporation.

† Most AppleTalk routers do not conform to this. Most routers are treated as local routers. Even half-routers that use serial lines to connect to geographically separate networks together are considered local routers. This is done for simplicity. It will not affect interoperability and performance.

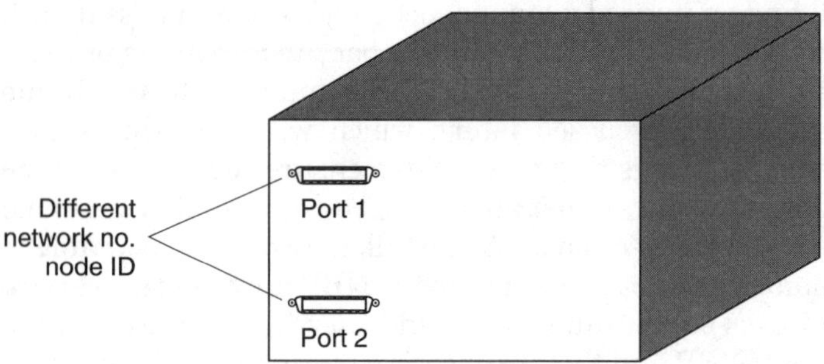

Figure 7.8 AppleTalk router.

works, i.e., networks that are located geographically close together (on the same floor or between multiple floors in a building). Local routers interconnect local LANs. This is usually multiple network segments with *all* segments having station attachment.

Local routers are connected directly to the network. There is not an intermediate device between the two networks and the routers. For example, an Ethernet-to-Ethernet router is a local router. See Fig. 7.9*a*. Each segment separated by a router will be assigned a network number or a range of network numbers. This is shown by the middle network having the range of 200 to 300. This means that network numbers 200 through 300 are reserved for this network segment. Notice that the different network numbers are the two routers connected to this network. Their network numbers are different but they are assigned to the same cable segment. When assigning a range to a network, the network numbers should be contiguous.

Half-routers are used to connect geographically distant networks together. This type of connection is usually done through the telephone system on what are known as leased lines. These are special lines that the phone company has "conditioned" to accept digital data. They are not standard voice lines, for standard voice lines are too noisy to carry most high-speed data. Typical data rates are 56 Kbps and T1 (1.544 Mbps); although now most telephone companies are using fiber, T3 (45 Mbps) is becoming more available. Half-routers are important to note for their hop count. Since the router is separated by a serial line, each router on each end of the line is considered a half-router. The two taken together are considered one router. Therefore, no network number is assigned to the serial link, and a network separated by a serial line to another network is considered one hop away. Please note that not all router vendors support this method. Some router vendors will assign a network number to the serial line and the two networks separated by a signal line are considered two hops away. This will be discussed in a moment.

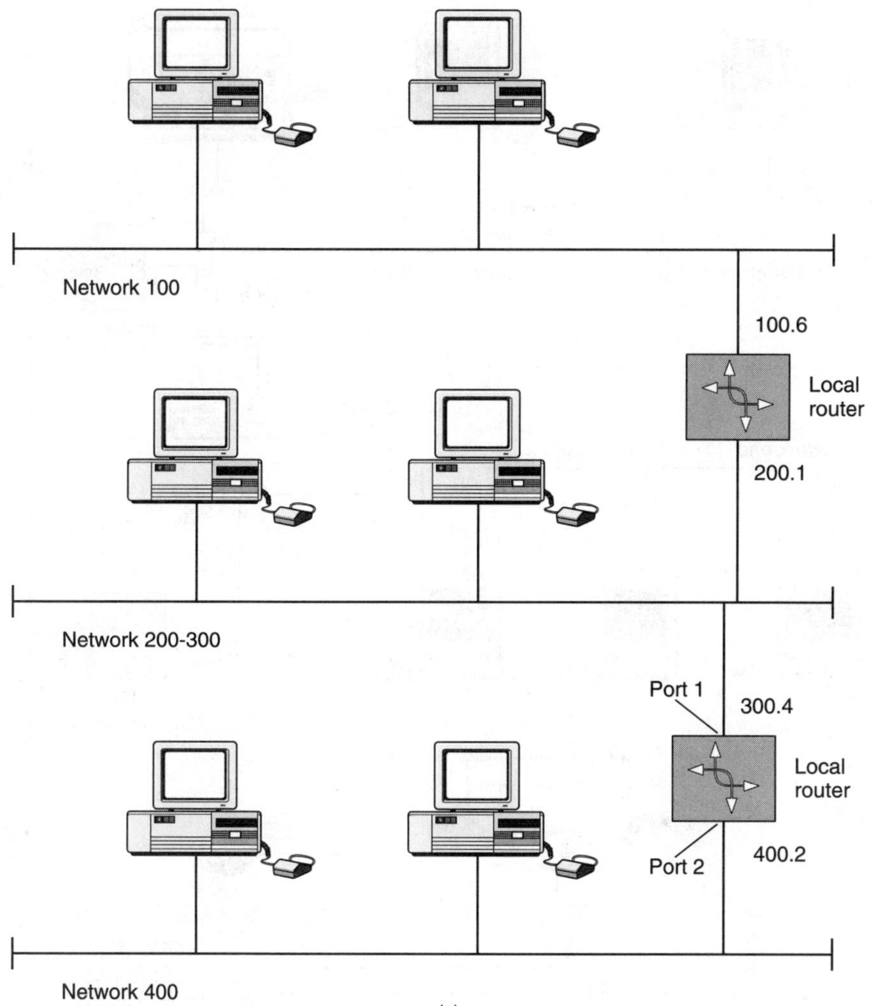

Figure 7.9 (*a*) AppleTalk internet.

Backbone routers are those routers which connect AppleTalk network segments to a backbone network segment. Backbone network segments are networks connected to a backbone cable segment that is not AppleTalk. This type of network is shown in Fig. 7.9*b*. Apple defines backbone router as one which connects to a network having a higher throughput than the one to which it interconnects. Examples of these are FDDI backbones, 16 Mbps Token Ring, etc.

Any time that a packet must traverse a router to get to another network, the term used to display this action is known as a *hop*. Through-

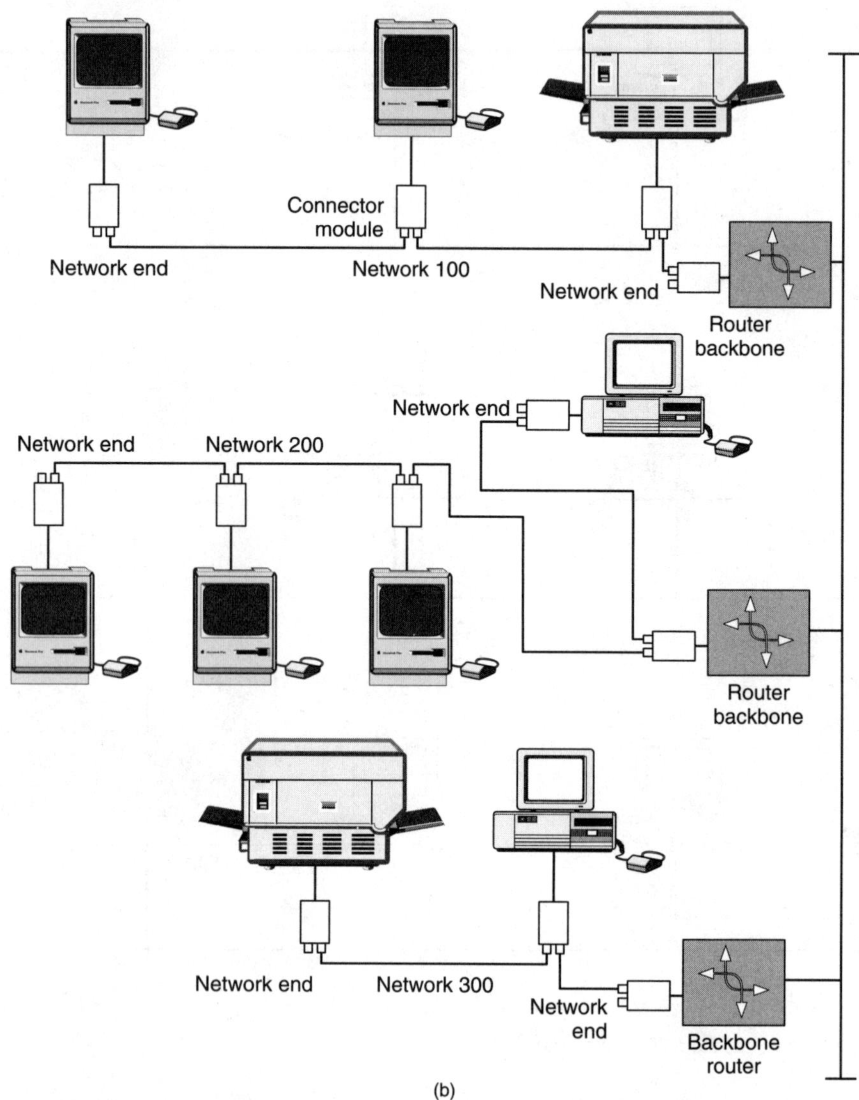

Figure 7.9 (*b*) LocalTalk to backbone connection.

out an AppleTalk internetwork, a packet may traverse no more than 15 routers (i.e., a distance of 16 hops is considered not reachable).

Operation. Routing of AppleTalk packet reduces the maximum size of a DDP packet to 586 bytes, even though the frame capacity of Ethernet and Token Ring is much higher.

In an AppleTalk internet, there are two types of devices for data. These are routing and nonrouting nodes. For the purposes of this chapter a routing node will be a device that accomplishes only that. Its main purpose is to route data for the internet. This function is usually located in a separate box known as a router. See Fig. 7.9*a*.

The other type of node is called a nonrouting node. The usual case for this is a user's workstation or even a file/print server. Routers are devices that are usually autonomous from the other devices on the network, and their main function is to receive packets from other nodes on the network and forward them to their appropriate network. Routers on AppleTalk internets accomplish more than this (zones) but that will be covered later.

When a network station has data to transmit, it will determine whether the packet is to be transmitted locally (to another network station on the same LAN) or to a network station that is remote (separated by router). The network station accomplishes this by comparing the destination network number* to its known network numbers. Remember that with AppleTalk, there can be more than one network number assigned to a single network. Therefore, the destination network number cannot match any of the network numbers assigned to that network.

If there is a match, the packet may be locally transmitted. If there is not a match, the network station must employ a router to get the packet to its final destination. In that case, the network station would find a router and address the packet to the router. The router will then forward the packet to its final destination. A router will discard a packet for an unknown destination network.

Simply stated, a router accepts packets directed to it, looks up the network address in a table, and forwards the packet to either a locally attached network or another router that will further route the packet to its destination.

The functional block diagram of the internal functions of a router are shown in Fig. 7.7. Each router will contain the following:

1. A data-link handler (ELAP, TLAP, or LLAP)
2. A DDP routing process

---

* The address of the destination on the remote network is found through a scheme that involves the naming concept involved in AppleTalk. This will be discussed in a moment.

3. A routing table
4. A process to update the routing table (RTMP)
5. A physical hardware connector (known as a *router port*)

The router ports may be connected to any of the previously mentioned router types, but no two active router ports may be attached to the same network cable (this is done with other routers to allow for dynamic redundancy). You may connect two router ports to the same network as long as one of the router ports is disabled. When the active router port fails, the disabled router port can then be made active. This allows for manual redundancy.

Each router port contains a port descriptor which contains the following four fields:

1. *A connection status flag.* An indicator to distinguish between an AppleTalk port and another type port (a serial link, a backbone network, etc.).
2. *The port number.* A number assigned to a physical port of a router. Used to identify a port to forward packets.
3. *The port node ID.* A router node ID for that port.
4. *The port network number.* The particular network number of the LAN connected to it.

When a port is connected to a serial link (indicating a half router), the port node address and port network number are not used.* When a port is connected to a backbone network, the port network number range is not used and the port node address is the address of the router on the backbone network.

It should be noted here, again, that not all router vendors support this method. Some router vendors treat AppleTalk routing like any other RIP routing protocol. In other words, there are no such things as separation of backbone, half router, and local router. A router is a router and network numbers will be assigned to each and every port of the router no matter what the connection is. In other words, AppleTalk packets are routed just like any other RIP routing environment.

This is necessary to point out because routing of AppleTalk packets may be different from that of vendor to vendor. The concept of the backbone, half, and local routers is specific to the AppleTalk specifications. It is the methods by which AppleTalk is recommended to be implemented.

---

* This is not true for routers that do not support the half-router function.

The router table. To find other networks and their routers, AppleTalk routers use an algorithm similar to that of TCP/IP, XNS, and NetWare's IPX. It is known as a *distance-vector algorithm.* The router maintains a table of network numbers (the vector) and the distance to the network number (distance, hop, or metric number).

In order for the router to know where to forward the packet, it must maintain a table that consists of network numbers and the routes to take to get there. Each entry in an AppleTalk router table contains three things: the port number for the destination network, the node ID of the next router, and the distance in hops to that destination network. Refer to Table 7.6 and to the bottom router in Fig. 7.9*a*. The table consists of the following entries:

Network range. This is the vector. This is a known network number that exists on the internet.

Distance. This is the number of routers that must be traversed in order to reach the network number. By Apple's standards, this entry will have a 0 for locally attached networks.

Port. The physical port on the router which corresponds to the network number. If the hop count is 0, then this is the network number range assigned to that port. If the hop count is greater than 0, it is the port from which the network number was learned. Likewise, it indicates the port that the router will forward a packet to if the network number is so indicated in the packet.

Status. Indicates the status of the path to that network.

Next router. If the network number is not locally attached to the router, this field indicates the next router in the path to the final destination network. If the network number is directly attached to the router, there will not be an entry in this field. The router will forward the packet directly to that cable plant.

In order for the router to maintain its table, a process must be invoked to allow the routers to exchange data (their routing tables) for periodic updates. This allows the router to find shorter paths to a destination and to know when a new router is turned on or when a router has been disabled. Possibly, a new path must be taken to get to a par-

TABLE 7.6 AppleTalk Router Table

Network range	Distance	Port	Status	Next router
400	0	1	Good	N/A
200–300	0	2	Good	N/A
100	1	2	Good	200.1

ticular network. The process that enables this maintenance is called the Router Table Maintenance Program (RTMP).

A routing table like the one previously described is maintained in each of the routers that are on the AppleTalk internet. The table simply tells the router the network number and how to get there. But where did the router get this information?

All router tables are constructed from information that comes from other routers on the network. In other words, each router will tell another router about its routing table. The protocol that maintains this is the Routing Table Maintenance Program (RTMP).

Routing table maintenance program (RTMP). The Routing Table Maintenance Program provides the logic to enable datagrams to be transmitted throughout an AppleTalk network through router ports. This protocol allows routes to be dynamically discovered throughout the AppleTalk internet. Devices which are not routers (workstation, for example), use part of this protocol known as the RTMP stub to find out their network numbers and the addresses of routers on their local network.

Some DDP packets are shown in Fig. 7.10*b* and *c*. Figure 7.10*a* shows the general DDP packet. The type field would be filled in appropriately for each packet type of RTMP, NBP, ATP, AEP, ADSP, and ZIP. Figure 7.10*b* and *c* shows the RTMP and NBP packet type. RTMP packets are further described in Fig. 7.11. The hop field indicates how many routers a packet has traversed.

Routing tables in the routers are exchanged between routers through the RTMP socket. By addressing the packet with this socket number, DDP, upon receipt of the packet, will know exactly what the packet is and will interpret it without passing it on to another process. In other words, the DDP socket number of 1 indicates a routing update or request packet.

Each RTMP (DDP socket number 1—source sockets may be any number but the packet must be addressed to destination socket 1) packet includes a field called the routing tuple in the form <network number, distance> for nonextended networks. Extended networks contain the header form <network number range start, distance, network number range stop, unused byte set to 82h>; then come routing tuples. In the routing tuple is the network number, which consumes 2 bytes, and the distance, which consumes 1 byte. The routing tuple contains a network number and the distance traveled in hops from the router to that network. When the router receives this packet, it will compare it to the entries already established in the table. New entries are added to the table and distances may be adjusted, depending on the information in the packet.

There are two ways a router may receive its network number. One way is to configure the router as a seed router. The network administrator must manually assign the network numbers to each port on the

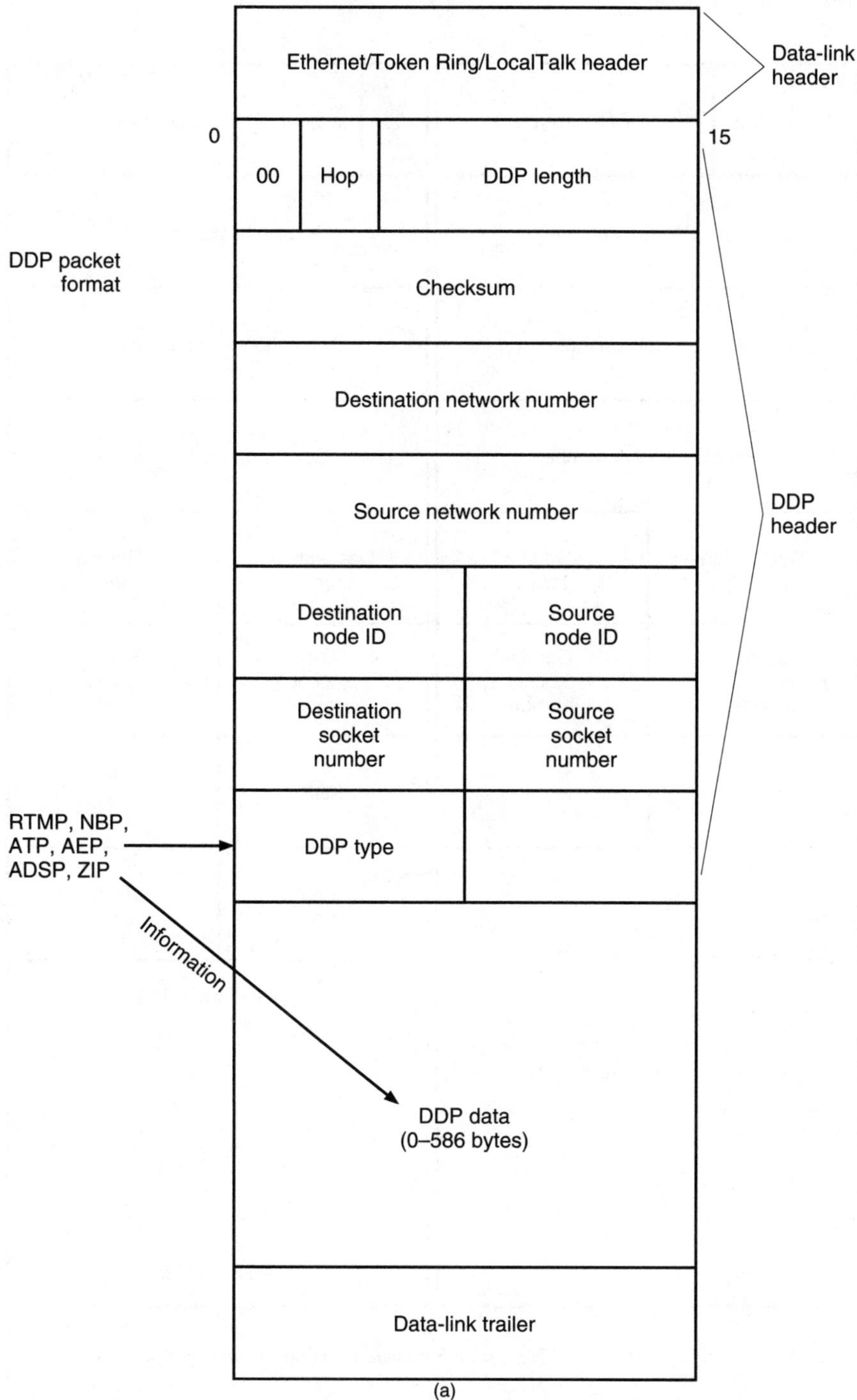

Figure 7.10 AppleTalk packet format. (*a*) General DDP packet header format. (*Courtesy Apple Computer.*)

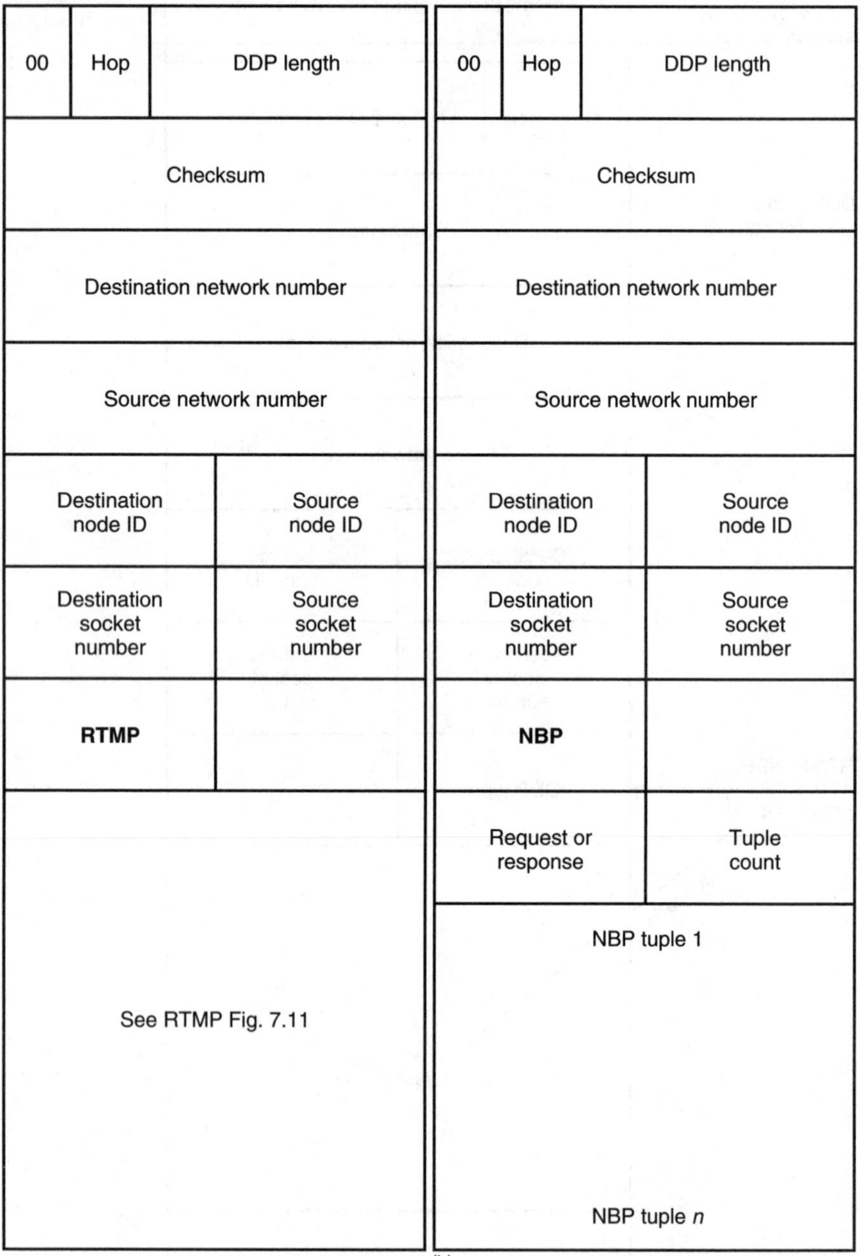

00	Hop	DDP length
Checksum		
Destination network number		
Source network number		
Destination node ID	Source node ID	
Destination socket number	Source socket number	
RTMP		
See RTMP Fig. 7.11		

00	Hop	DDP length
Checksum		
Destination network number		
Source network number		
Destination node ID	Source node ID	
Destination socket number	Source socket number	
NBP		
Request or response	Tuple count	
NBP tuple 1		
NBP tuple *n*		

(b)

Figure 7.10 DDP packets. (*b*) RTMP and NBP packet format. (*Courtesy Apple Computer.*)

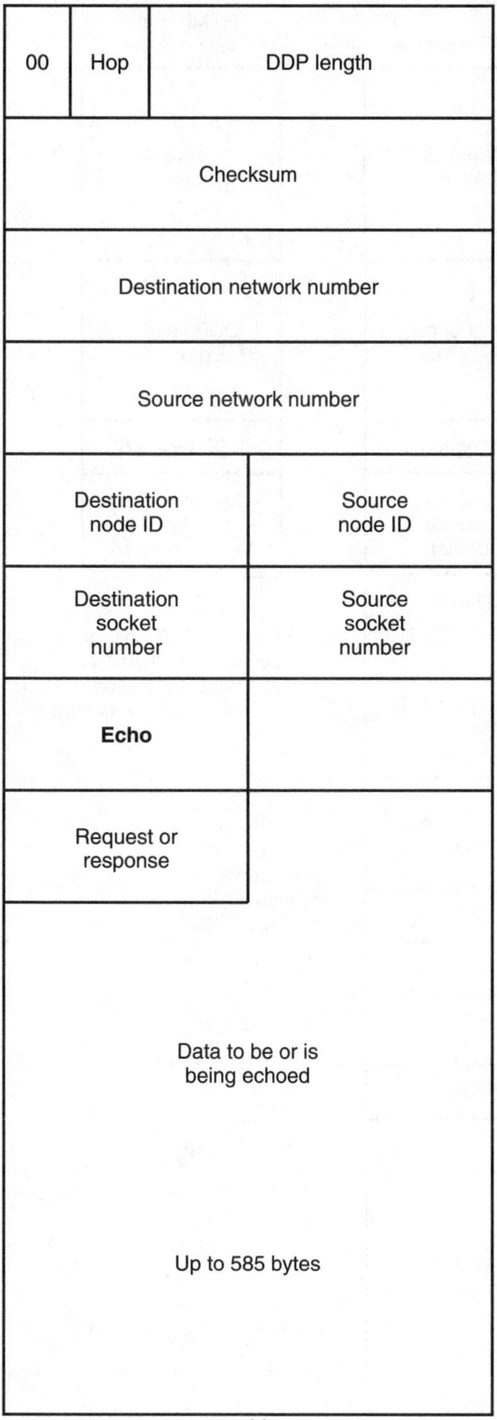

00 | Hop | DDP length

Checksum

Destination network number

Source network number

Destination node ID | Source node ID

Destination socket number | Source socket number

Echo

Request or response

Data to be or is being echoed

Up to 585 bytes

(c)

Figure 7.10 DDP packets. (*c*) Echo packet format. (*Courtesy Apple Computer.*)

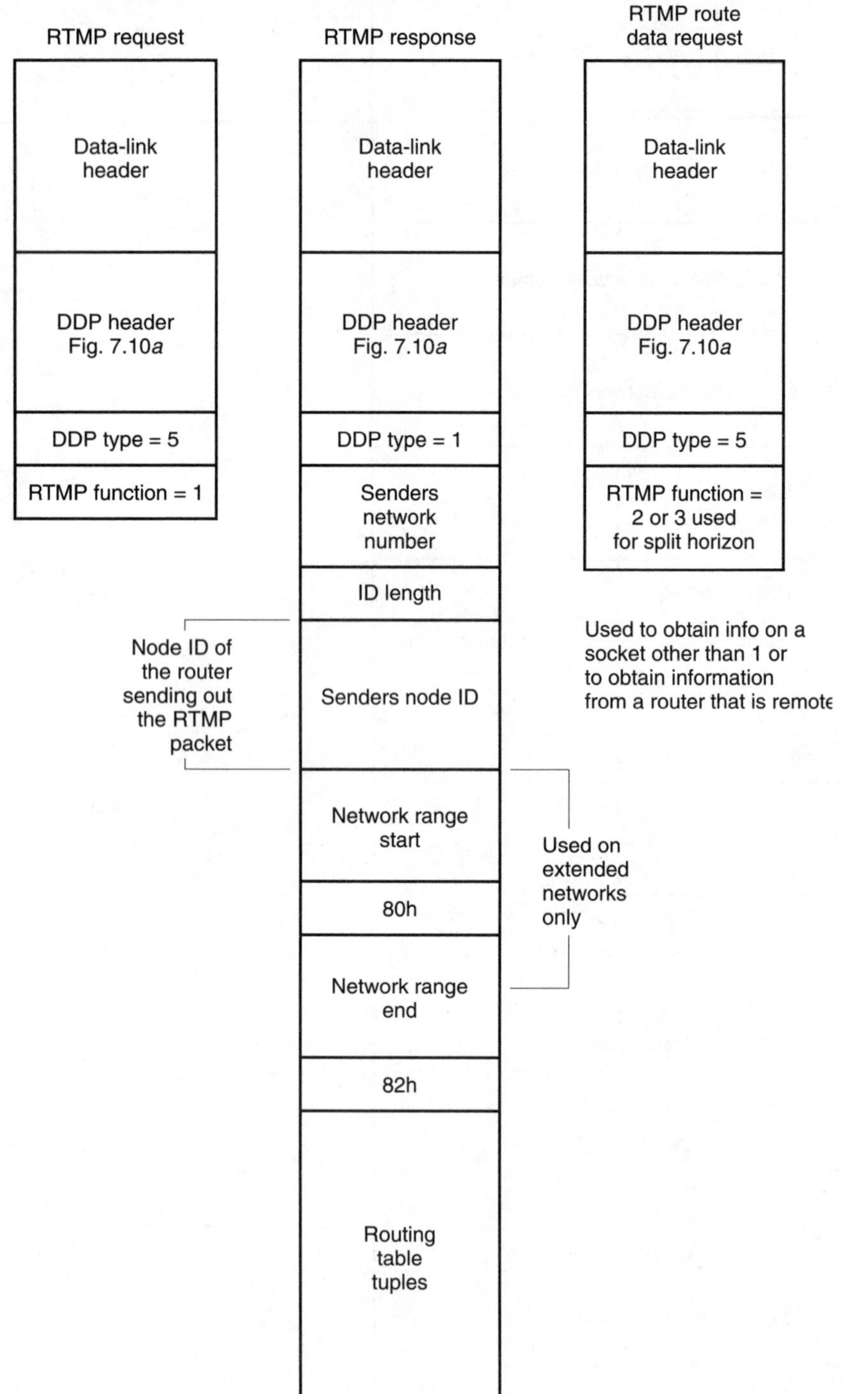

Figure 7.11 RTMP packets. (*Courtesy Apple Computer.*)

router. Each port must be configured as a seed router or a nonseed router port.

When a seed router starts up, it will enter the network numbers assigned to its local ports into the table. Other routers on the network will obtain their network numbers from the seed router.

For a network that is served by multiple routers (each router has the same network numbers assigned to it), the seed router will distribute the network numbers to the rest of the routers on that network. There is at least one seed router per network. There can be multiple seed routers per internet. Again, the purpose of the seed router is to inform the other routers of their network numbers.

Nonseed routers will learn their network numbers and zone names through the seed router. In an extreme case, all routers may be configured as seed routers. Configuring all routers as seed routers allows the network administrator to statically assign the network numbers on each of the router ports. The seed router will contain a list of network numbers on a per-router-port basis. The seed router can also contain a zone name listing on a per-port basis.

Once a router has found its local port network numbers and entered them in its table, it will submit its router table to its locally attached network segments, being conscious of split horizon. This will inform other routers on those segments of the networks that router knows about. Those routers will update their tables and then submit their tables to their locally attached cable segments. With this process, each router on the internet will eventually know about all network numbers and their associated routers. When a router updates its routing table with a new or changed entry (network number), the hop count is incremented by one more than the hop count number indicated in the table that it received. After this, the router will transmit its table to the directly attached cable segments. This does not occur for entries in the table that are not new or are not changed from the previous update.

Nonrouting nodes (i.e., user end stations) are not expected to maintain routing tables like a router. A nonrouting node may acquire its network number and a router address (a router to which to submit packets for forwarding data to another network) in one of two ways:

1. It may listen to the routing update messages sent out by routers on its local network. In these packets will be the local network number and the address of the router that sent the update.
2. It may also ask any router to respond by submitting a request for this information. With this, the requesting node should get a response packet back that looks like a routing update packet but it contains no routing update entries. Instead, embedded in this packet will be the network number and address of the router that

sent the response packet. Also, this packet is a directed response packet. It is not sent in broadcast mode.

For nodes that are on extended networks, the end node will transmit a special packet known as the ZIP* GetNetInfo request. This is a request to the router's Zone Information Protocol (ZIP). A router will respond to the packet with the network number range assigned to that zone. Normally, nodes on extended network do not submit a routing request for network number information, but the AppleTalk specification does not disallow it. This request is studied in more detail later in the chapter.

The router that first responds to the request to an end node on either the extended or nonextended router is called the end nodes A-router. This is the router to which the nonrouting node (a user's workstation, for example) will send its packets that must be routed. The entry in a nonrouting node for A-router may change if a different router responds to another routing request.

Aging table entries. In actuality, the end station's (nonrouting node) A-router will change each time a routing update is transmitted by a router.

AppleTalk is also one of the few routing protocols that use a hop count of 0. Any network number associated with a hop count of 0 is considered to be the local network number.

Each entry in a router table must be updated periodically to ensure that the path to a destination is still available. Otherwise, a route would stay in the table and may not be valid. To age out old entries, a timer is started upon receipt of each routing tuple. After a certain amount of time (called the *validity timer,* set to approximately 20 seconds) has expired without notification of a particular route through RTMP (no routing tables received contained that network number), the router will change the status of the select entries from "good" to "suspect." After more time has expired, a suspect entry is changed from "suspect" to "bad" and then finally it is deleted from the routing table. If, at any time, the router receives an update pertaining to that entry in the routing table, it will place the entry status back to "good" and start the timer process over again.

Aging of the A-router in a nonrouting node is set to 50 seconds.

RTMP packets are shown in Fig. 7.11. There are three types. A request packet, a response packet, and a router data request. The request packet is used to obtain information from a router about a network or networks. In response to a request, a router will send the

---

* Zone Information Protocol (ZIP) is the protocol that enables network stations to be grouped together into a common zone name. Users needing connection to any network station will first choose a zone and then a network station. This is explained in full detail later.

response packet. This will contain information about a network number, such as how many hops away the requested network is.

The route data request is used by a router to obtain information about another router, such as whether one router supports a protocol known as split horizon. Split horizon is the ability for a router to not announce information about a network on the same port from which it learned about the network. This means if a router learned about network 1 through port A, do not announce this information back out port A. One last thing to notice is the response packet—specifically, the network range field. Any station on the network that reads this packet will know from this field what the network range for its network is.

RTMP routing update packets are transmitted by the router every 10 seconds. This means that a router will transmit its table to its locally backed cable segments every 10 seconds. This is the most frequent of any of the protocols that use RIP as their updating protocol. Novell's implementation of RIP is 60 seconds, and TCP/IP and XNS is 30 seconds.

Finally, AppleTalk routers do employ the split horizon protocol. Routers find out about this from other routers by an indication in the RTMP Route Data Request Packet, which is a special type of routing information inquiry packet that does not require network number updates.

Finally, Fig. 7.12 shows a flowchart for router information flow.

AppleTalk Echo Protocol (AEP)

The AppleTalk Echo Protocol (AEP) resides as a transport-layer protocol, and allows any station to send a packet to another station which will return the same packet (echo it). This allows stations to find other active stations (even if you just wanted to test if the station was active or not) on the network but more important is that it allows a network station to determine packet round-trip delay times.

This protocol is used when a network workstation has found the destination station it wishes to talk to and submits an echo packet to "test" the path. It will submit an echo packet (DDP socket number 4) to the destination and will wait for a reply. When the reply does come, it notes the time and submits the packet to establish a connection to that station. This can be used to establish timers for packet time-outs. The packet format for AEP is shown in Fig. 7.10*c*.

That was the delivery system for AppleTalk. It included the data-link and network layers. All data is submitted to these layers for transmission on the network. The network and data-link protocols do not care what the data is. The only job that these protocols are tasked to do is to provide a transportation service for the upper-layer protocols.

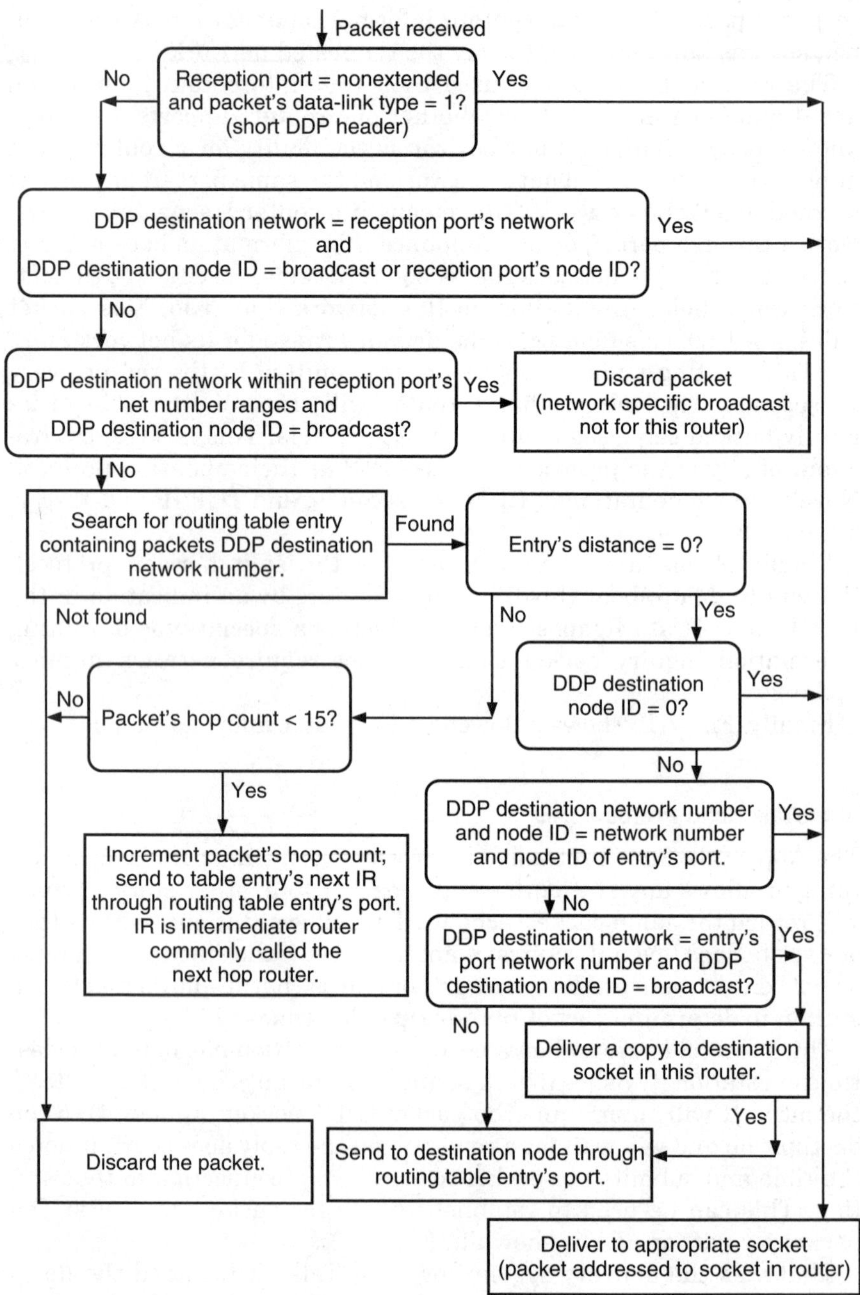

Figure 7.12 AppleTalk routing. (*Courtesy Apple Computer.*)

The following protocols (transport and session layer protocols) allow for a session to be set up and maintained and ensure that the data is transmitted and received in a reliable fashion.

Names on AppleTalk

Throughout this section, refer to Fig. 7.10*a*. As discussed in the previous text, the delivery system depends on certain numbers in order to deliver data. There is one physical address for every network station on the internet. There are network-layer addresses so that the network layer is able to route the data over the internet if needed. Socket numbers are needed so that once data arrives at the final destination, it is forwarded by DDP to the appropriate software process. In other words, there are many addresses used throughout the AppleTalk internet.

To eliminate the need for users to remember all the network addresses, node addresses, sockets, and so forth of the network and data-link layers, a naming scheme has been devised. Also, since network addresses may change frequently (dynamic node IDs, etc.), all services (file, print, mail, etc.) on a network are assigned user-definable (string) names. These string names may not change frequently, so AppleTalk uses a name process to identify network stations on an internet. This accommodates two things: (1) it is easier for a user on the internet to remember names and not numeric addresses and (2) it enables network stations to acquire different network addresses while retaining a static name. All of this is accomplished transparent to the users.

Names on an AppleTalk network are usually assigned by the network administrator. Anyone needing access to these services usually cannot change the names that are being used.

Names are used to request a service to be processed. This includes attaching to a file server or maybe sending a print job to a network-attached printer. All of these processes on the network are assigned numbers so that the network stations may communicate with each other. Network stations do not communicate with each other using the string names we type into the network station. String names are only for users on the AppleTalk network. When network stations communicate with one another, they still use the full internet address of the network station and not the user-defined name of the network station.

Defining the names on AppleTalk. Within a network, AppleTalk has a concept known as *network visible entities* (NVE). The actual physical devices can be seen by the user. These devices are file and print servers, routers, etc. The actual services within these physical devices cannot be seen by the user. These services are represented on the network as sockets, and each socket is assigned a numeric address. In this way, a network station may logically attach to the service and not to the actual device. For those who use electronic mail, the user is not visible to the network but the electronic mailbox service is.

A Network Visible Entity (NVE) is any process on an AppleTalk internet that is accessible through a socket in DDP. In other words, the application processes to which users attach from their network stations are the NVEs.

An entity can assign an *entity name* to itself. This name consists of three fields, and each field may contain a maximum of 32 characters. Any of the fields may be "user-defined," meaning there is not a defined method for assigning the names. For example, the object could be a printer name whose the type is laser, which is located in some zone name on the internet. The form taken for this name is:

```
object:type@zone
```

An example of this name structure is Server1:Postoffice@Vienna. The naming of this entity name is case-insensitive. The object mentioned here is server1. This would indicate the name of a server (although this is user-defined). The type is post office, which could possibly indicate a mail server. This server is located in an internet zone name of Vienna. This NVE form will become more apparent as the text proceeds.

Now that we have identified the names and what constitutes a name, these names must still be mapped to an internet address so that network stations on the network may attach and pass data.

The protocols that handle names on the AppleTalk network are:

The Name Binding Protocol (NBP)

The Zone Information Protocol (ZIP)

These protocols are described here briefly and in more detail later.

The process to translate (or map) between numbers and names (not zone names) is the process invoked by NBP. NBP maintains a table that translates between character names and their corresponding full internet addresses. The name-binding process is the process by which a network station will acquire the internet socket address of a destination network station by use of its string name. It converts the string name to the numeric address used by internally network stations. This process is accomplished completely transparent to the user. All of these name-to-address mappings are maintained in tables.

The Zone Information Protocol maps network numbers and zone names. A zone is a logical grouping network stations no matter where these network stations are located on the internetwork. Furthermore, zones do not reflect on network addresses. Network stations grouped into a zone many have many different network addresses. The grouping of zones is called the AppleTalk internet. Each network number requires at least one zone name.* Network station placement in a zone is fairly liberal. Network stations may participate in one zone or many zones. Zones may cross networks (across a router or routers). In other words, these zones may be spread through many different network numbers. You claim a zone name and add NVEs to this zone. Zone names originate in routers. The network administrator will assign the zone name and broadcast this to the network. This is what brings logic to this chaos. Routers maintain a listing of zone names and their associated network numbers through a table known as the Zone Information Table (ZIT). A simplex AppleTalk zone is shown in Fig. 7.13.

Before any NVE can be accessed, the address of that entity must be obtained through a process known as *name binding.* This is the process of mapping a network name to its internet socket address (the network number, the node ID, and the socket, or port, number). A network visible entity (file, print, database, E-mail, etc.) will start and ask ATP for a socket number. ATP will return a socket number (given to it by DDP) and the NVE process will then determine its network and node addresses (by methods previously discussed). All of these numbers combined (network ID, node ID, and socket number) form the internet socket address. The process will then call NBP to bind the internet socket address to a name.

Each network station must maintain a *names table,* which contains an NVE name-to-internet address map for all entities in that particular network station (remember that entities are those processes visible to the network, such as a print or file service or maybe a mail service). NBP does require the use of special nodes called name servers. NBP is distributed on all network stations on the AppleTalk internet. The process that maintains this table is available through the Names Information Socket. This socket (static DDP socket number 2) is also responsible for accepting and servicing requests to look up names from within the network station and from the network.

Then a separate table is used, called the *names directory,* which contains a distributed database listing of all the names tables on the internet. As described before, the names table contains only those internet socket address-to-name mappings of the NVEs on the local network station. The names directory contains a listing for NVEs on the internet.

Names table. Name table for services running on a single network station.

Names directory. Name table for all services on the AppleTalk internet. A compilation of all names tables on the internet.

* All text in this chapter refers to AppleTalk Phase II.

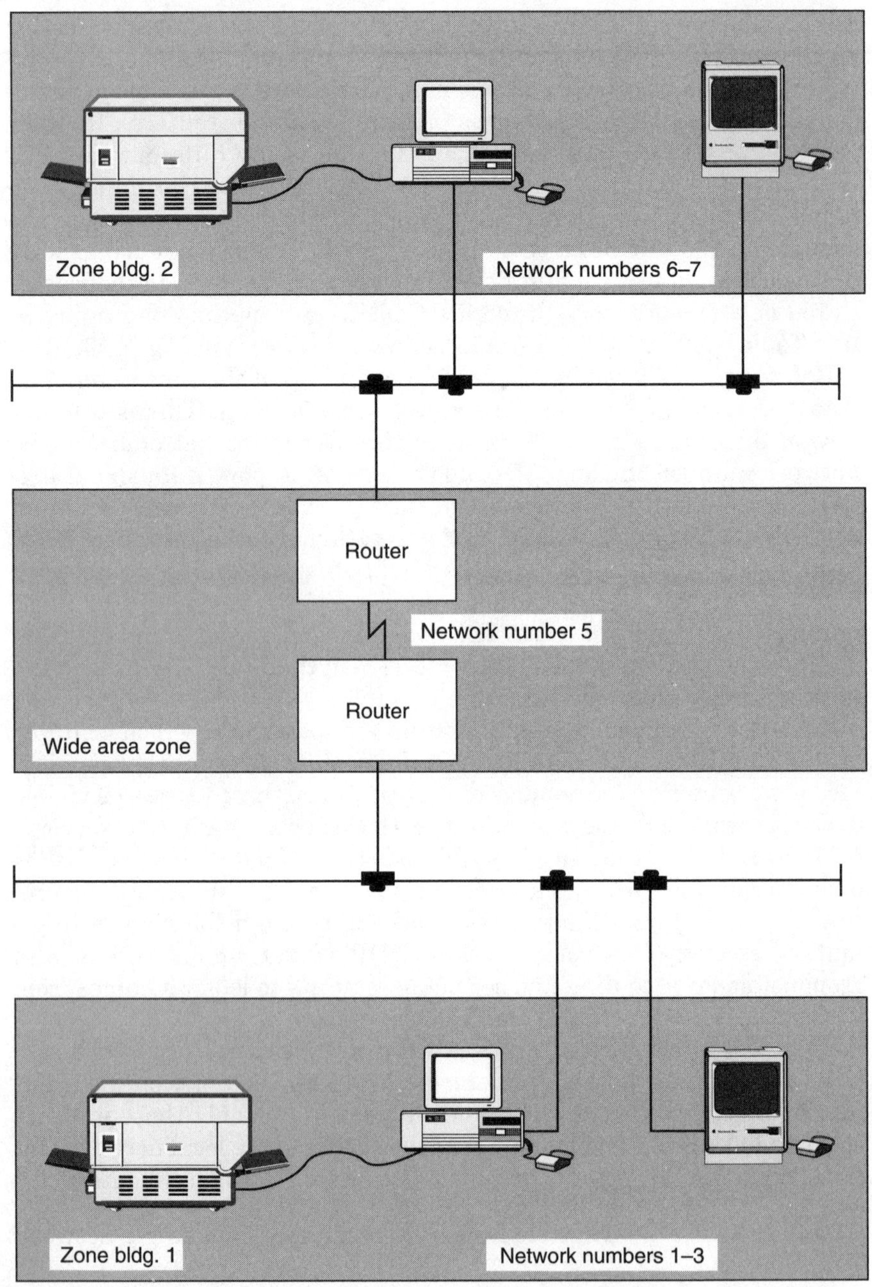

Figure 7.13 Zone names.

Simply put, NBP handles the names table and name lookup requests from client processes or requests from the network. Every network station on the AppleTalk internet has this process whether it is providing services for the network or uses the services of the internet.

NBP is a distributed name service. This means that each network station acts as a name server. Use of a centralized name service, a single station on which all names reside, is not usually found on AppleTalk networks. According to the AppleTalk specification, centralized name service is allowed to exist on an AppleTalk network, though.

The NBP process provides four types of services:

1. *Name registration.* Register its name and socket number on its local node name table.
2. *Name deletion.* Delete a name and its corresponding socket.
3. *Name lookup.* Respond to a name registration.
4. *Name confirmation.* Affirm a name registration.

Briefly, when any process starts on a network station it will register its name and associated socket number in the names table. When this process removes itself from the network station, it will also ask NBP to remove its name and socket number from the names table. NBP will then place the NVE in the name directory. Name lookup occurs when a request for a name-to-internet address binding is required, and name confirmation occurs to check the validity of the current binding. Routers participate in this process through the use of zone mappings.

Name registration. Any NVE working on the internet can place its name and corresponding internet socket address into its names table. This allows the entity to become visible on the network. First, the NBP process will check to see if the name is already in use. If it is, the attempt is aborted and the process will be notified. Otherwise, it is placed into the table. The NBP process then places this name-to-address mapping in the names directory. It should be noted that any entry in the names table is dynamic. It is reconstructed every time the network station is started. Using this process, every network user is registered on the internet.

When the entity wants to delete itself from the names directory, it will do so by telling NBP to delete the entry.

On a single network, mapping a name involves three steps:

1. The requesting network station's NBP process broadcasts an NBP lookup packet addressed to the Name Information Socket number to the network. A lookup packet contains the name to be looked up.

2. Every active network station that has an NBP process will receive this packet and will perform a name lookup on its table not directory for a match to that name.
3. If a match is found, a reply packet is generated and transmitted to the requesting socket. Included in this packet is the name's address.

If there is no response to this packet, the requesting network station assumes that the named entity does not exist on the local network and the name is added. This is a name confirmation.

On an internet, two extra steps are added to find an NVE on an internet (those networks connected by a router.) An NBP-directed broadcast request containing the NVE to be found is first sent out to all available routers on the station's local network. A router will pick up this request and will send out a broadcast lookup request for all networks in the requested zone. This process is done for zones and may stretch across multiple networks. The process then continues with the second step.

Zones. A zone is a group of networks that form an AppleTalk internet. The Zone Information Protocol (ZIP) is the protocol that maintains an internetwide map (a table) of zone-to-network names. NBP uses ZIP internet name mappings to determine which networks belong to a given name. It is easier to address network stations based on their zone. An AppleTalk internet is a collection of network stations grouped together by zones.

An extended network can have up to 255 zones in its zone list. An AppleTalk internet can theoretically have millions of zone names. A nonextended network can have at most one zone name.

The ZIP process uses routers to maintain the mapping of the internet network numbers to the zone names. ZIP also contains maintenance commands so network stations can request the current mappings of the zone-to-internet network numbers.

A router's participation is mandatory in an AppleTalk internet zone protocol. Just as a routing table is maintained in a router, a Zone Information Table (ZIT) resides in each router on the AppleTalk internet. There is one ZIT for each physical router port on the router. Each table provides a list of the mappings between the zone name and internet addresses for every zone on the AppleTalk network. It looks like a routing table, but lookups are on the zone name instead of network numbers. This is similar to Novell NetWare's Service Advertisement Protocol.

This table may consist of one zone name mapped to one network number or it may contain one zone name with multiple network numbers or it may contain multiple zone names with multiple network numbers assigned to those zones. With the last, it should be noted that zones may overlap each other. An example of three logical zones is shown in Fig. 7.13. An example of a zone overlap would be that the printer in zone building 2 could exist in zone building 1, except that it is still attached to the segment of network numbers 6 to 7. Not all routers support zone names on serial backbones as shown in Fig. 7.13. Some routers do provide for support of half routers which allow point-to-point links (such as the serial line) between the two routers, but there is no zone name on the point-to-point link.

To establish the zone table, the zone process in a router will update other routers through the ZIP socket. The requesting router will form a ZIP request packet, input into this packet a list of network numbers, and transmit it to the node's A-router. This router will reply with the zone names that it knows about (with the associated network numbers included). Since this process is accomplished over DDP (best-effort delivery service), the request contains a timer and, upon expiration of that timer, ZIP will retransmit a request.

To maintain a ZIT, ZIP monitors the router's routing table (not the ZIT) for changes in the entries in the table. If a new entry (meaning a new network number) has been found on the internet, ZIP will send out request packets to other routers in an attempt to find a zone name associated for the new network number. Therefore, ZIP maintains its zone name table by monitoring the routing table.

When a network number is deleted from the routing table (eventually, the network number will be deleted from all routing tables on all routers on the internet*), ZIP (ZIPs on all routers) will also delete its zone name entry for that network number.

Any network station on the internet may request the mappings from ZIP by transmitting a ZIP request packet to the network. If the router does not know the zone name, it will not reply.

For a user's workstation, there are special ZIP packets that enable it to operate properly with the ZIP. These are:

GetZoneList	Requests a list for all zones on the internet
GetMyZone	Gets the zone name for the local network (nonextended networks only)
GetLocalZones	Obtains a listing of all the zones on the requesters network

* Remember that routing table entries are maintained by routers broadcasting their routing tables to each other. If a network number has not been heard from, the router will expire a timer for that entry and the router will delete the entry from its routing table. ZIP will notice this and delete its name entry on the ZIT. This name deletion is not broadcast, for all routing tables on the internet will delete the network entry and the ZIP on each router will then delete the zone name. ZIP is reliant on the information in the routing tables.

Just as a network station may keep its last known node ID stored (the hinting process), a network station, upon start-up, may have a previous zone name that it was using (the last time the station was active on the network). If so, the network station, upon start-up, will broadcast a packet called the GetNetInfo* to the network. In this request packet will be the last zone name it worked with or, if the zone name is unknown, the packet will not contain a zone name. Routers on this network will respond to this request with information on the network number range and a response to the zone name requested. If the zone name requested is okay, the network station will use this zone name. If not, the router will respond with the zone name used on that network.

To see the ZIP in action is as simple as signing onto the network and requesting connection to a service on the network. The Apple Mac chooser will bring up a listing of zone names for logon or to access a service. This is an example of the ZIP protocol finding out all the zone names for the user.

Transport-Layer Services

Reliable delivery of data. The preceding documentation consisted of information for stations to identify themselves, gain access to a network, find zones, names, routers, and how to connect to an NVE via internet sockets. All of this allows communication to exist with data being delivered on a best-effort, connectionless method. With the connectionless delivery system, there is no guarantee that the data was delivered or, if it was delivered, that the packets in a data segment transferred arrived to the destination in the same order in which they were sent.

Consider transferring a file that is 250 Kbytes long. This is larger than any network protocol could transfer in one packet. Therefore, many packets are used to transfer the data. If we used only a connectionless protocol, the data might arrive in the wrong order, or one packet out of the thousand packets that were transferred might never make it. A protocol to allow information to flow reliably is called the AppleTalk Transaction Protocol (ATP). It is the next protocol to be examined.

Without transport-layer services, we would have to rely on the application itself to provide this purpose. To require every application to build this into their software is like reinventing the wheel. The network software should provide this for every network application, and ATP is the protocol that does.

---

* The GetNetInfo request is also used to find the network number for a network station.

AppleTalk provides two methods for data delivery: transaction-based and data stream (the AppleTalk Data Stream Protocol, ADSP). Transaction-based protocols are based on the request-response method commonly found on client workstation-to-server communication. Data stream protocols provide a full-duplex reliable flow of data between network stations. The protocol to be studied here is the transaction-based transport layer. It offers something different than other protocols shown in this book. Therefore, the ADSP protocol will not be discussed here.

The protocols that make up this OSI transport layer consist of the following:

1. AppleTalk Transaction Protocol (ATP)
2. Printer Access Protocol (PAP)
3. AppleTalk Session Protocol (ASP)
4. AppleTalk Data Stream Protocol (ADSP)—not discussed in this chapter

These protocols guarantee the delivery of data to its final destination. Two stations use the AppleTalk Transaction Protocol to submit a request to which some type of response is expected. The response is usually a status report or a result from the destination to the source of the request.

AppleTalk Transaction Protocol (ATP)

ATP is the protocol on AppleTalk that provides reliable delivery service for two communicating stations.

There are three types of packets that are sent:

1. Transaction Request (TReq)—a transaction request initiated by the requester
2. Transaction Response (TResp)—the response to a transaction request
3. Transaction Release (TRel)—releases the request from the responding ATP transaction list

There is a Transaction Identifier (Tid) that assigns a connection number to each transaction. Each request and response between a source and destination is as simple as the three preceding commands taken as a whole.

Refer to Fig. 7.14. First, the requesting station submits a TReq. The destination station will respond with TResp. The requesting station will then acknowledge the transaction response by sending it TRel.

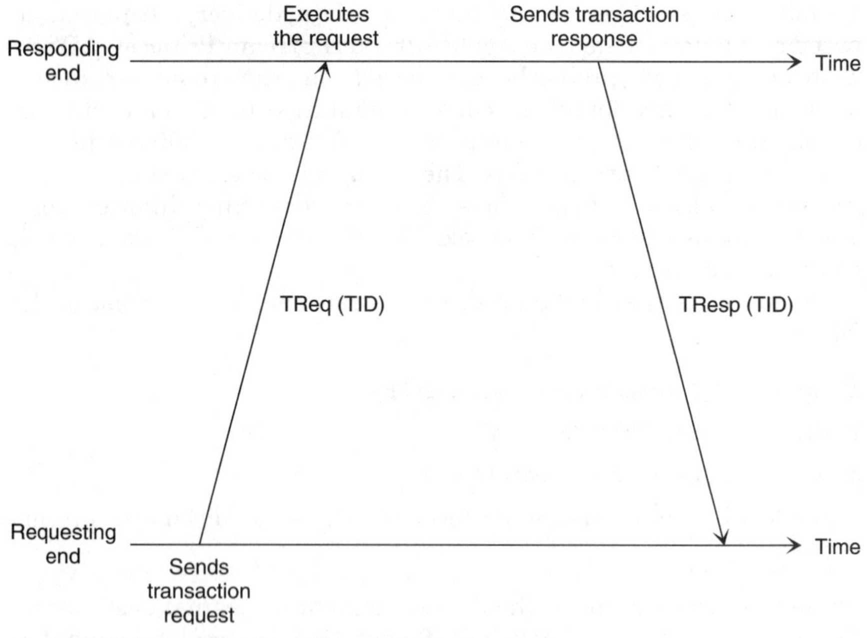

Figure 7.14 ATP transaction. (*Courtesy Apple Computer.*)

This handshaking will continue until the session is released by the session layer.

ATP provides adequate services for most sessions. Since most network protocols restrict the size of their packets on the medium, multiple packets may be needed for a TResp. TReq packets are limited to a single packet. Multiple requests are sent as multiple TReqs. A TResp is allowed to be sequential packets. When the requester receives all the TResp packets in response to a TReq, the request is said to be complete and the message is delivered as one complete message to the client of ATP. ATP will assemble the message as one complete message and then deliver it to a client of ATP.

Every ATP packet has a sequence number in its header. This field is 8 bits wide. This does not mean that it has 255 sequence numbers (counting in binary). Each bit is a sequence number. Therefore, if bit 0 is turned on, this is sequence number 0; if bit 1 is turned on, this is sequence number 1, etc.

In a TReq packet, it will indicate to the receiver the number of buffers available on the requester. When the receiver receives this packet, it will know how many response packets the requester is expecting.

When this field is set by a TResp packet, it is used as a sequence number (0 to 7). As stated before, each bit is not taken as a binary number; each bit represents an integer number (in the range of 0 to 7). This will indicate the number of the packet in the sequence of the response packets. Therefore, the sequencer on the requester can place the incoming packets in the appropriate buffer. As each good packet is received, the requester makes a log of this. For each packet not received in a sequence, the requester can make a request for a retransmit of this packet in the sequence. This is a selective reject type of retransmission (refer to Chap. 3 for more information on sequencing).

For example, if a TReq is transmitted and the sequence bitmap is set to (00111111), it is indicating to the destination that it has reserved six buffers for a response. In other words, the requester expects six packets of TResp in this response. As the TResp packets are sent back, the TResp packets will have a bit-map set to indicate the number of the packet that is being responded to. If the requester receives all packets except number 2 (00000010), it will send another TReq for the same information with its sequence bitmap set to (00000010). The destination should respond with that and only that TResp packet.

In the ATP data field (not the ATP header) would be an indication of what type of service is being requested, such as a read of a disk file on a file server. This type of information would be the session header and the application header, which will be discussed in a moment.

Printer Access Protocol (PAP)

The Printer Access Protocol uses the connection-oriented transport (meaning a connection is established between the client and server before data is passed between the two). This is the protocol used to deliver data that a client workstation would send to a printing device on the network. This is the protocol that allows an application to write to the printer across the network.

PAP uses the services of NBP and ATP to find the appropriate addresses of the receiving end and to write data to the destination.

PAP provides five basic functions described in the following four steps:

1. Opening and closing a connection to the destination
2. Transferring of data to the destination
3. The ability to check on the status of a print job
4. Filtering duplicate packets

PAP calls NBP to get the address of the server's listening socket for printer services (the SLS). Data can be passed only after this socket is known. After the connection is established, data is exchanged. There is a two-minute timer to determine if either end of the connection is closed. If the timer expires, the connection is closed. Either end of the connection may close the connection.

A workstation may determine the status of any print job. This may be executed with or without a connection being established. As for filtering duplicate packets, sequence numbers are assigned to each packet. A response from either end must include the original sequence number. Sequencing is fully explained in the ASP section which follows.

Figure 7.15 shows the block diagram of the PAP. Notice how the printer has the AppleTalk protocol stack in the printer software. This architecture is shown for a printer connected to the LocalTalk network. For EtherTalk or TokenTalk networks, the printer software is a spooler that resides in the Mac network server. The printer is directly attached to the Mac's printer port. The Mac uses AppleTalk to communicate between the Mac and the printer.

AppleTalk Session Protocol (ASP)

The AppleTalk Session Protocol does not care about the delivery of data. It does not care about the sequencing of data to ensure reliable delivery of the data. ASP's sole purpose is very straightforward. ASP, like most session-layer protocols, opens, maintains, and closes sessions and sequences requests (not data) from upper-client software. It uses the lower-layer protocol ATP to sequence these requests.

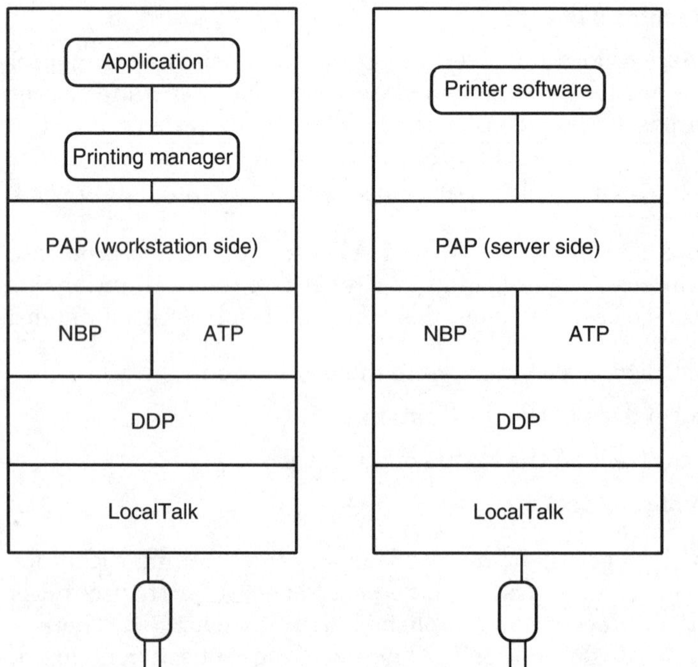

Figure 7.15 Printer connections. (*Courtesy Apple Computer.*)

ASP does provide a method for passing commands between a network station and its connected service. ASP provides delivery of these commands without duplication and makes sure the commands are received in the same order in which they were originally submitted. This orderly retrieval of commands is then responded to as the results become available. Like the other layers of the OSI model, the session-layer ASP communicates only with another ASP layer on another network station.

ASP is based on a client-server model. Upon initiation, a service (NVE) on a server will ask ATP to assign to it a socket number. ATP should respond to this request with a socket number received by DDP, and this number is the one used by the service on the server to let the network know about the service. The service will then notify NBP of the name and its socket number. This will be placed in the names table of that network station offering this service. This will allow any network station to find the service on the network. ASP will then provide a passive open connection on itself so that other stations on the internet may connect to it. This is known as the *server listening socket* (SLS).

Before we continue, there are three types of named sockets that the text will be referring to:

1. Session Listening Socket (SLS)—a service being offered listens on this socket.
2. Workstation Session Socket (WSS)—identifies a socket in the requesting workstation when a connection attempt is being made to a service.
3. Server Session Socket (SSS)—identifies to the workstation, once a connection is made, the socket number to which to refer all future transactions.

Figure 7.16 depicts this interaction of sockets. The client side of ASP, upon seeking a connection to a remote resource, must find the full internet address of the remote service (the NVE). ASP is said to place an active open connection request. In this, ASP will find the full internet address of the remote service and give itself a socket number, the workstation session socket (WSS), and will then request a connection of the remote resource. The server should have open sockets residing on DDP and will accept the connection request on one of these sockets. The virtual circuit (the connection or session) is then maintained between these two sockets (the WSS and the server socket, now known as the SSS).

ASP builds upon ATP to provide a secondary level of transport service that is commonly required by client-workstation environments.

Since the most common application found on AppleTalk networks is the sharing of file and print services, the remainder of the text will

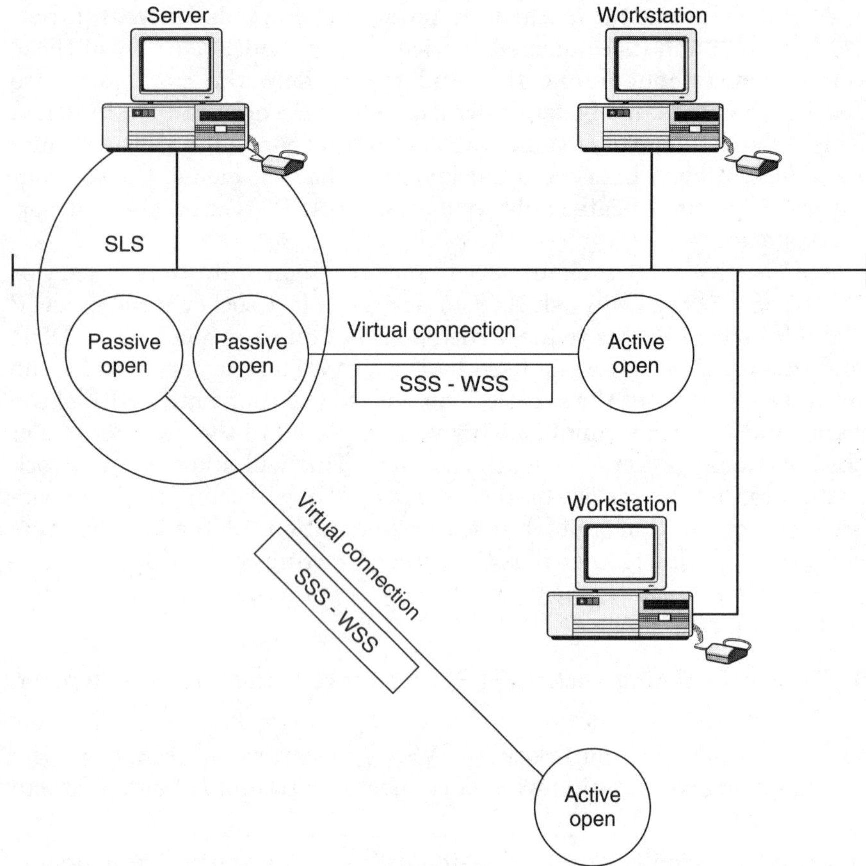

Figure 7.16 Connection attempts and sessions using sockets.

deal with how a workstation and its file server communicate over the internet.

Establishing a session. Two handshaking protocol steps must be performed before any session is established between a workstation and its file server.

1. The workstation and server must ask ASP to find out the maximum allowable command and reply sizes.
2. The workstation must find out the address of the server session listening socket (SLS) number by issuing a call to NBP.

The session listening socket, previously described, is an addressable unit to which the workstation will send all requests. This socket is opened by ASP, and the file server will make this socket well known on the network by broadcasting this socket to known entities through the use of NBP. This is the socket number for which the file server, for example, is listening for connection requests.

Refer to Fig. 7.17.

1. The workstation will ask ASP to open a session with a particular service on a file server.
2. ASP will transmit a session request packet to the file server. This packet will contain the workstation's socket number to which the file server may respond. This WSS is an addressable unit in which the file server knows which process in the workstation to respond to in the workstation.
3. If the server accepts the session request, it will respond with the following:

   Acceptance indicator. An entity within the packet to indicate to the workstation that the request is accepted.

   Session identifier. An integer number that the server assigns to identify any particular session on the file server. Each unique workstation request is assigned an identifier.

   Address of the server session socket (SSS). Upon accepting a connection from a remote workstation, the server will respond to this requester with a new socket number that will uniquely identify that session on the server.

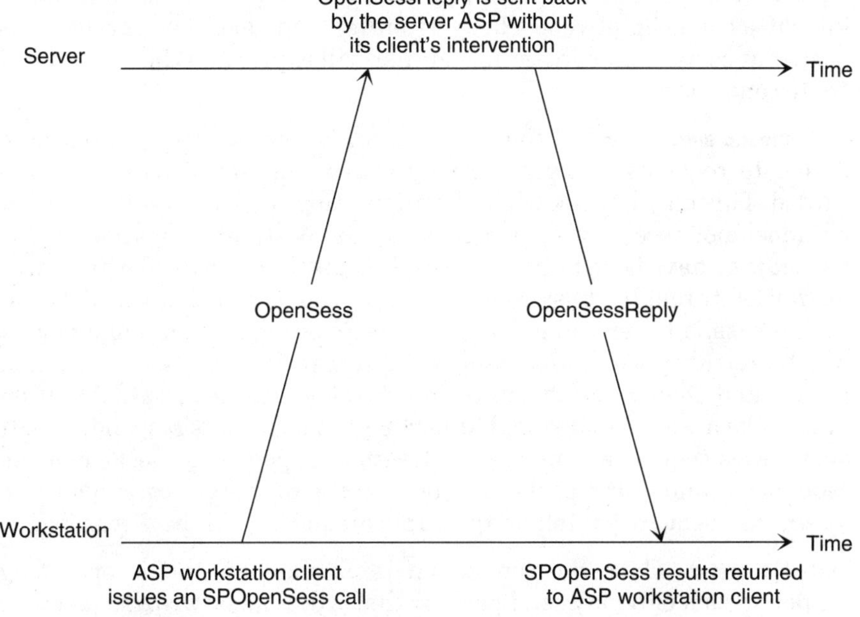

Figure 7.17 Session requests. (*Courtesy Apple Computer.*)

The session is now considered established and all communication will continue between the two, using the WSS, the connection ID, and the SSS.

Session maintenance. Once the session is established, ASP must maintain the session. There are maintenance commands specific to the management of any AppleTalk session. Three are to be discussed here:

1. Tickling
2. Command sequencing
3. Discarding duplicate requests

Once a session is established, it will remain active until one end of the connection decides to quit the session. One other possible occurrence for session termination is when the path has become unreliable or one end has become unreachable. There will be times when the session will not be passing data or commands from one end of the connection to the other. You may establish a connection, start up an application and then not enter any data for a while. When this occurs, each end of the circuit does not know if any circumstance may have occurred which would make the session inoperable.

In order to find out if the other side is operating normally, AppleTalk employs a protocol known as *tickling*. With this, each network station involved in a connection will periodically send a packet to the other to ensure the other end is functioning properly. (In other protocols, this is known as a keep-alive packet.) If either end does not receive this packet at certain time intervals, a timer will expire and the session will be disconnected.

Command sequencing. If the same packet is received twice, discarding duplicate requests is the process by which the second request is discarded. This may happen when the originating station submits a packet and does not receive a response for it. The destination station of this packet may have been busy, or the packet may have delayed while being forwarded through a busy router and the response packet was delayed. In any case, a timer will expire in the origination station and a packet will be retransmitted. Meanwhile, the server responds to the original packet and then receives the retransmission. The destination station must have a way of knowing that particular packet was responded to. It does—with sequence numbers. Each incoming packet is checked for the sequence number. If a packet received on the file server corresponds to a response sequence number, the duplicate packet will be discarded.

Data transfer. Once the connection is established and is operating properly, each end may send packets that will read or write requests to the respective sockets. These reads and writes are actually data transfers between the two network stations.

ASP handles all requests from the workstation and the server. ASP is an initiator of requests and a responder to any requests on the network. Any of these commands will translate into ATP requests and responses. There are three formats for ASP:

1. Commands
2. Writes
3. Attention requests

As shown in Fig. 7.18*a*, ASP commands ask the file server to perform a function and to respond to these requests. Any command will translate into an ATP request of the session server socket (SSS). The reply will translate into an ATP response.

A write is performed in Fig. 7.18*b*. ASP on the server issues a single write command with its appropriate transaction ID. The workstation responds, stating that it is okay to continue writing on Tid 12, which the server will do. At a certain point in time, the workstation replies to the writes ending with a TResp for Tid 12. After all the write replies are sent to the server, the workstation acknowledges the end by a TResp on Tid 11 for the server's Tid.

If the workstation's command to its file server was to read part of a file, the response would be in multiple packets returned to the file server (if the file was larger than the largest packet size allowed on the network).

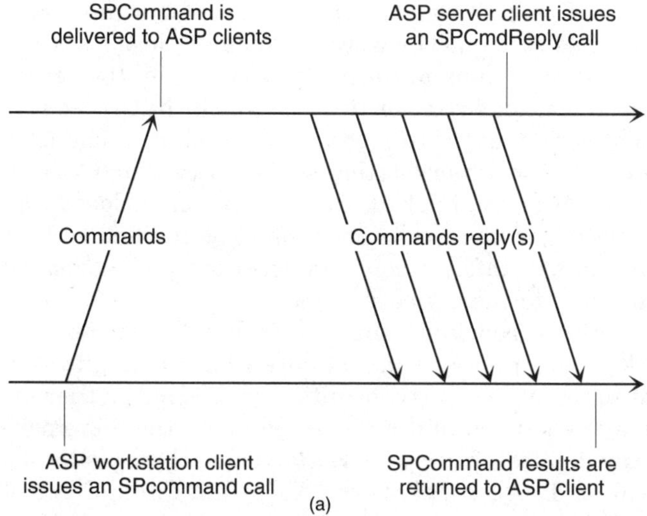

Figure 7.18 (*a*) Data transfer. (*Courtesy Apple Computer.*)

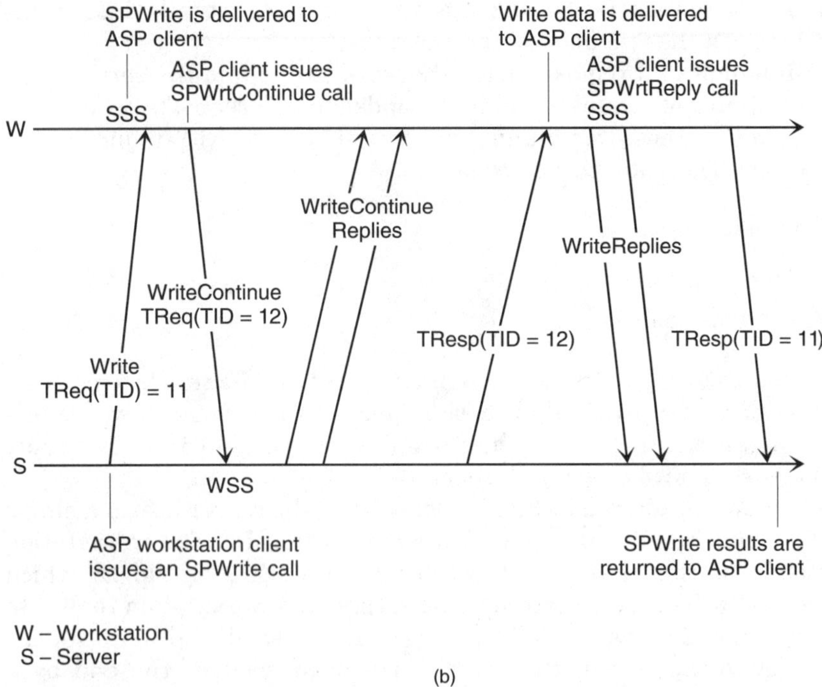

Figure 7.18 (*b*) ASP write. (*Courtesy Apple Computer.*)

Attention requests are those requests that need immediate attention. No data will follow this packet.

Session end. Refer to Fig. 7.19 *a* and *b*. The workstation or the server may close an established session. The workstation may close a session by sending a close session command to the same socket on the server (known as the server session socket or SSS) in which the server was first established. The server may close a session by sending a command to the workstation socket (the workstation session socket or WSS) in which the session was first established. After a session is closed, the ASP on both the server and the workstation must be notified so that each may delete the proper information from their session tables. All entries for those sessions in the tables are deleted.

The previous sections conclude the protocols needed for the AppleTalk network. These protocols accept data from the application layer and format it so that it may be transmitted or received on the network. A session may be started and maintained using the aforementioned protocols. Any application may be written using those protocols. The largest application for AppleTalk is the AppleTalk Filing Protocol (AFP). This protocol allows network stations to share file and print services with each other.

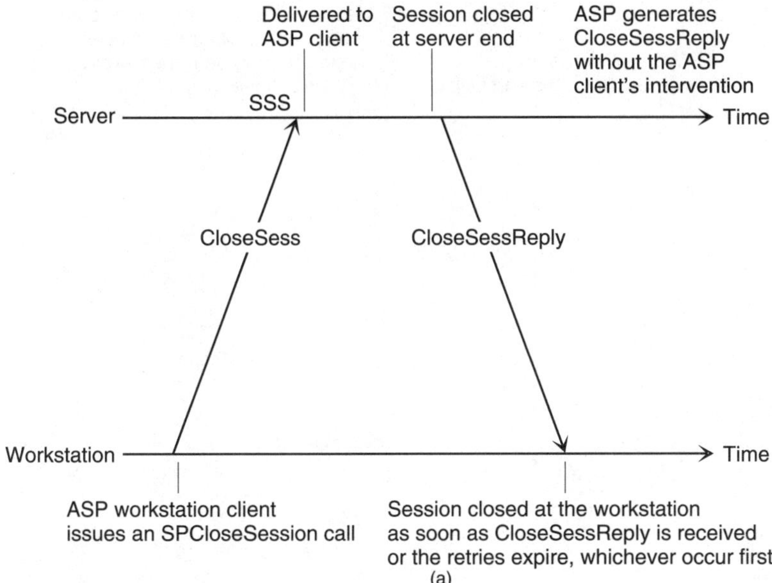

Figure 7.19 (*a*) Workstation session close.

AppleShare and the AppleTalk Filing Protocol (AFP)

In order for a workstation to access files and other services of another workstation, the requesting station must invoke a high-level service known as Apple Filing Protocol. This is Apple's method of controlling server, volume, directory, file, and desktop calls between a client and workstation on an AppleTalk network. For those familiar with other protocols, Microsoft's Server Message Block (SMB), Novell NetWare Control Protocol (NCP), and Sun's Network File System (NFS) are all similar in function to Apple's AppleShare and AFP. Apple decided not to follow these implementations, for they were in various stages of completion and SMB was written for DOS and NFS was written for UNIX. Neither could implement all of Apple's file structure easily. So Apple created a new remote file system using a protocol call AFP. The name given to use this is AppleShare. Simply stated, AFP is a service that uses the AppleTalk protocols to allow network stations to share data over the internet.

There are entities within the AppleTalk network that must be known before fully understanding the AppleTalk file/print network. These entities are:

File servers. A file server is a device on the network that acts as a repository for files. These files can include applications as well as user data. File servers are usually the most powerful network sta-

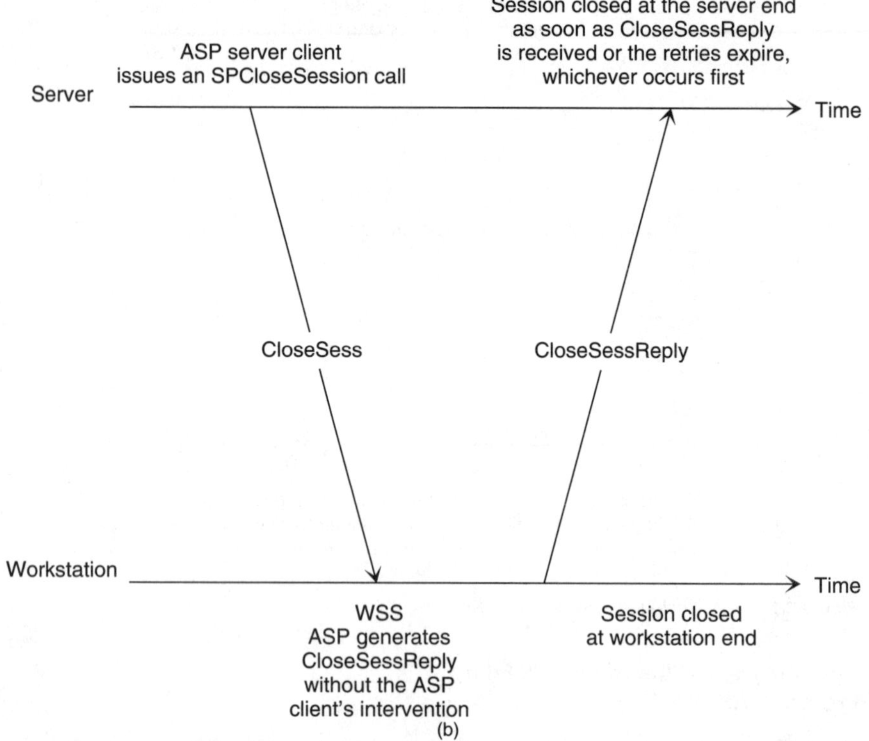

Figure 7.19 (*b*) Server close.

tion and contain a large-capacity hard disk. Multiple file servers are usually found on any network, and can be segregated to file server, data server, and printer server.

Volumes. A volume is the top level of the Apple directory structure. Volumes may be separated as an entire disk drive or may be many partitions of a disk drive.

Directories and files. These entities are stored in each volume. In any Apple machine, they are arranged in a branching-tree structure. Directories are not accessed as a file. Directories are an addressable holding area for files. They may branch into other directories, for they carry a parent child relationship.

File forks. A file consists of two forks: a resource and a data fork. A resource fork contains system resources such as the icons and windows. A data fork contains the data in the file in unstructured sequence.

The protocol known as AppleShare allows an Apple computer to share its files with other users on the network. Every network station on the

AppleTalk network may be set up to share files with any other station on the network. Or they may be dedicated file servers on internet and all station may have access to these servers (provided the network administrator allowed for this). Each AppleShare folder has an owner and that owner will determine the access rights for that folder. The access rights are private, group, or all users and are self-explanatory. The ownership can be transferred to another owner.

Communication between a user's workstation and an AppleShare file server is accomplished using AFP.

AFP runs as a client of ASP. It is an upper-layer protocol to ASP. It will use ASP to allow a connection (known as a session) between a client and a file server. This session is a virtual connection which will allow protocol control information and user data to flow between the two network stations.

Prior to session establishment, a requesting station must know the address of the server it wishes to communicate with. Specifically, it must obtain its session listening socket or SLS. Servers will ask ATP for this (this was explained previously). After this is accomplished, the server will use NBP to register the file server's name and type on the socket just received.

For a workstation to find a server, the workstation will place a lookup call to NBP. NBP should return the address of all the NVEs within the zone specified by the workstation. To find the names of all the file servers on a particular zone, the workstation would use: =:AFPServer@<zone name>. NBP should respond to this lookup string with a listing containing all the active file servers specified in the zone name specified. Included in this listing will be the internet socket address (the SLS). The workstation will then choose a server. To get a particular server, the user could enter <server name>:AFPServer@<zone name>. This would return the SLS of the server which the user would then connect to it. This is all accomplished in the Chooser. It all sounds complicated, and it is—behind the user's screen. This is where the simplicity becomes involved. All the user has to do to connect to a file server is select Chooser under the Apple icon on the menu bar. Under Chooser, the user will then select the AppleShare icon. Chooser will then ask the user to select a zone.

Once the user selects a zone, the Chooser will ask the user to choose a file server. This is all accomplished using the mouse with windows and icons displayed on the user's screen.

The user would then log in to the server. Once the authentication is accomplished, the workstation would establish a session to the server and communication would begin.

On the server side, once the server has opened the file server's socket and registered the file server's name, the server is ready to accept workstation requests, and workstations will call NBP to obtain the server's address and name. Once accomplished, the workstation will call ASP to open a session to that server.

All the resources are secured in three ways. Upon login, AFP provides user authentication (basically a password), volume password protection, and directory access controls based on the user authentication information.

Since its inception, AFP has continually undergone changes, mostly enhancements. Therefore, different versions of AFP will exist on an AppleTalk network. To determine which version the workstation will use with a server, the server (during the connection process) will tell

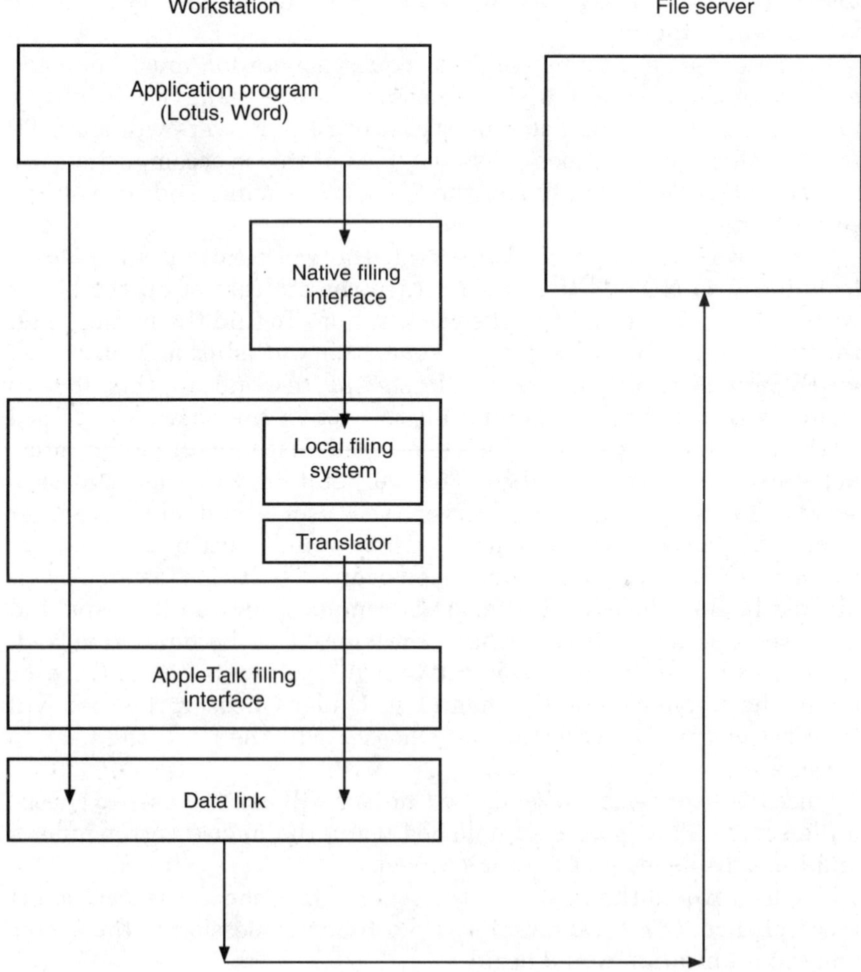

Figure 7.20 AppleTalk Filing Protocol (AFP). (*Courtesy Apple Computer.*)

the workstation which versions it supports. The workstation will then choose among the versions.

If the logon process is completed without error, the workstation will tell the server what it wants by issuing AFP calls to the server. Some of these calls are listed at the end of this chapter. When the workstation is done using the file services of a file server, the user should disconnect from that file server, allowing other connections to be established and to free up memory and processing of other transactions continuing on that file server. Once connected to file server, the user can then select file volumes on the file server to attach to. These attached file volumes will show up as a network connection folder on the user's screen.

Previous figures showed a workstation and file server connection. Once the workstation and file server have a session built, it is up to the workstation to determine which system calls are local and which are destined for a remote resource. The selected volumes will show up on the user's screen as a file folder with a local talk connection to it. This is an icon. It is accessed just as the local hard disk is accessed. The user will double-click on the networked file folder icon.

Apple's native file system commands are converted to AFP calls by being sent to the translator. These AFP calls are then sent to the file server. As shown in Fig. 7.20, a workstation program may send AFP calls directly, without having to use the translator. These are application programs that directly use a network. Applications such as these are network mail programs, etc.

AFP functions. AFP operates on a series of calls. Calls are the commands that a workstation will submit to a file server. AFP calls are comprised of the calls listed in Table 7.7. These calls are completely transparent to the user. It is given here to show the reader the list of commands that are performed by AppleShare.

TABLE 7.7 AFP Calls

Call	Function
	Server Calls
FPGetSrvrInfo	Obtains descriptive information about the server
FPGetSrvrParms	Retrieves file server parameters
FPLogin	Establishes a session with a server, specifies the AFP version and user authentication to use
FPLoginCont	Continues the logon and user authentication process begun by FPLogin
FPLogout	Terminates a session with a server
FPMapID	Maps a user ID or group ID to a user name or group name
FPChangePassword	Allows users to change their passwords
	Volume Calls
FPOpenVol	Makes a volume available to a workstation
FPCloseVol	Informs a server that a workstation will no longer use a volume
FPGetVolParms	Retrieves parameters for a volume
FPSetVolParms	Sets the backup date for a volume
FPFlush	Writes to disk any modified data from a volume
	Directory Calls
FPSetDirParms	Sets parameters for a directory
FPOpenDir	Opens a directory
FPCloseDir	Closes a directory
FPEnumerate	Lists the contents of a directory
FPCreateDir	Creates a new directory
	File Calls
FPSetFileParms	Sets parameters for a file
FPCreateFile	Creates a new file
FPCopyFile	Copies a file from one location to another on the same file server
	Combined Directory-file Calls
FPGetFileDirParms	Retrieves parameters for a file or directory
FPSetFileDirParms	Sets parameters for a file or directory
FPRename	Renames a file or directory
FPDelete	Deletes a file or directory
FPMoveAndRename	Moves a file or directory to another location on the same volume and optionally renames it
	Fork Calls
FPGetForkParms	Retrieves parameters for a fork
FPSetForkParms	Sets parameters for a fork
FPOpenFork	Opens an existing file's data or resource fork
FPRead	Reads the contents of a fork
FPWrite	Writes to a fork
FPFlushFork	Writes to disk any of the fork's data that is in the server's buffer
FPByteRangeLock	Prevents other users from reading or writing data in part of a fork
FPCloseFork	Closes an open fork
	Desktop Database Calls
FPAddIcon	Adds an icon bitmap to the Desktop database
FPGetIcon	Retrieves the bitmap for a given icon
FPGetIconInfo	Retrieves an icon's description
FPAddAPPL	Adds mapping information for an application
FPRemoveAPPL	Removes mapping information for an application
FPGetAPPL	Returns the appropriate application to use for a particular document
FPAddComment	Stores a comment with a file or directory
FPRemoveComment	Stores a comment with a file or directory
FPGetComment	Retrieves a comment for a file or directory
FPOpen DT	Opens the Desktop database on a specific volume
FPCloseDT	Informs a server that a workstation no longer needs the volume's Desktop database

Chapter

8

Digital Network Architecture (DNA)

The original of protocol of computer-to-computer communications, DECnet,* was developed before any of today's LAN protocols were developed. Currently, DECnet is about to enter its fifth phase, known as DECnet Phase V. This will be the DECnet that will incorporate Open Systems Interconnect (OSI) into the architecture.

History

DECnet Phase I was introduced in 1975 and ran on Digital's PDP-11 computers under the RSX operating system. It allowed for program-to-program communication, such as file transfer, and remote file management between two or more computers. It supported asynchronous, synchronous, and parallel communication devices. It was simplex compared to today's topologies and protocols, but it did allow for most of the same capabilities of today's internets. It was quite simplex but very powerful for those times.

With this release and the next two releases, the DEC PDP-11 computer was the network. All computers communicated to each other through the PDP-11. Ethernet was not available until the release of DECnet Phase IV. The data link for this network was a control message protocol, known as Digital Data Command Message Protocol, which ran on serial links between the PDP-11's.

* DNA is the architectural model for DECnet. These terms will be used interchangeably.

DECnet Phase II was introduced in 1978 and provided several enhanced features over DECnet Phase I. Included in this release was support over more operating systems: TOPS-20 and DMS. Also enhanced were the remote file management and file transfer capabilities. DECnet Phase II could support a maximum of 32 nodes on a single network. Most important with this release was the modularity of the code. The code that provided DECnet was rewritten. With this and all subsequent DECnet releases, Digital kept the end user interface the same. Only the underlying code changed.

DECnet Phase III was introduced in 1980. Included in this release was adaptive routing (the ability to find a link failure and route around it) and the support of 256 nodes. Remote terminal, known as Remote Virtual Terminal capability, was first introduced in this release. This allowed end users to remotely log in to remote processors as if the user were directly attached to that processor. The addition of downline loading operations, which allowed for a program to be loaded and run in another (remote computer), was included. Finally, this phase was the first phase that supported IBM's SNA architecture.

DECnet Phase IV. The release that is by far the most popular and most found on Digital's products is called DECnet Phase IV. This was introduced in 1982. With this release came the support for Ethernet and the expansion of the number of nodes supported.

Since Digital was one of the originating companies to develop Ethernet into a standard (Xerox invented it and Digital, Intel, and Xerox developed it as a standard), they incorporated this into DECnet Phase IV. The second most noticeable improvement was the idea of area routing. This routing technique is similar today to OSI's IS-IS routing. It remains the strongest link in the DECnet architecture.

The number of nodes (DEC terminology for network stations, workstations, routers, etc.) supported was increased to 64,449. This number is split into the concept of areas and nodes. It is a 16-bit number with the first 6 bits assigned to the area and the remaining 10 bits allotted to the node number. Nodes are separated into distinct logical areas. The specification allows for 63 areas to be defined with 1023 nodes in each of 63 separate areas. This was shortsighted on Digital's part. This may seem like a lot of addresses, but it disallows building large Digital internets that interoperate. With DECnet, even personal computers need to be assigned a full node address.

Digital's routing is different than all other protocol type routing in that the routers keep track of all the end nodes (user workstations) in an area. This greatly increases the size of a router's routing table. Separating nodes into areas not only reduces the traffic of updating routers, but also decreases the size of routing tables per area. DECnet addressing and routing will be discussed in a moment.

The network terminal concept introduced in Phase III was reinvented as network virtual terminal in Phase IV. Also introduced with this release was X.25 packet switch network support.

Excluded in future versions of this release was support for TCP/IP and Token Ring. Both network (TCP/IP and Token Ring) protocols became very popular throughout the 1980s, but Digital did not allow these protocols to run on DECnet Phase IV nodes. Around 1990, DEC finally delivered its version of TCP/IP for the VMS operating system after years of allowing a company known as Wollongong to provide this functionality.

Previous to the direct support of TCP/IP on VMS, DEC did provide TCP/IP functions for Ethernet through its Ultrix operating system. This operating system was actually the Berkeley UNIX operating system adapted to run on VAX computers.

As shown in Fig. 8.1, DECnet closely follows the seven-layer OSI model. The following text will talk about the protocol of Ethernet. DEC's support for Token is not yet public. It is to be released in 1993. The first two layers of Ethernet, physical and data link, were described in Chap. 2. Digital also includes support at the physical layer for:

1. X.21
2. EIA-232-D
3. CCITT V.24/V.28
4. All wiring concepts for Ethernet

DECnet capabilities	DNA layers	
Network virtual terminal Remote file transfer and remote record access Remote resource sharing Downline loading/upline dumping Remote command file/batch submission	User Network application	Network management
Program-to-program communication (Task-to-task communication)	Session control Transport	
Adaptive routing	Routing	
	Data link Physical link	

Figure 8.1 DECnet capabilities and DNA layers. (*Courtesy Uyless Black.*)

At the data-link layer, DNA not only supports Ethernet (IEEE 802.2/IEEE 802.3), but also a proprietary protocol known as Digital Data Communication Message Protocol (DDCMP). DDCMP is beyond the scope of this book. It is now a seldom used protocol since the introduction of Ethernet Phase IV support. Most companies have switched to Ethernet local and wide area networks for their Digital minicomputers. Figures 8.2 and 8.3 review the physical and data-link DNA layers. Figure 8.4 shows the network routing layer.

Where Digital differs from other protocol implementations starts at the network layer. Here is where DECnet also becomes proprietary. This means that it is not an open protocol. Not just anyone can build this software protocol suite, for Digital holds the patents and copyrights to the architecture.

The Routing Layer

DECnet Phase IV routing

Definitions. Before studying the routing methods, some specific terms will be used throughout the text. Some definitions include terms that have not been defined yet. The following list of terms is to be used as a reference for the text that follows.

Adjacency. According to the DECnet specification, it is a [circuit, nodeID] pair. For example, an Ethernet with n attached nodes (network stations) is considered as $n - 1$ adjacencies (it does not include itself) for that router on that Ethernet. Basically, it is a node and its associated data-link connection. This could also be a synchronous connection to a router provided by a phone line.

Broadcast Endnode Adjacency (BEA). An endnode connected to the same Ethernet as this node.

Broadcast Router Adjacency (BRA). A router connected to the same Ethernet as this node.

Circuit. An Ethernet network (not internet) or a point-to-point link.

Connectivity algorithm. The algorithm in the decision process whose function is to maintain path lengths (or hops). The routing function.

Cost. An integer number assigned to a router interface. This represents the cost of the port for routing. (See *Path cost.*)

Designated router. The router on the Ethernet chosen to perform additional duties beyond that of a normal router. This includes informing end nodes on the circuit of the existence and identity of the Ethernet routers. Also used for the intra-area routing for end nodes (discussed later).

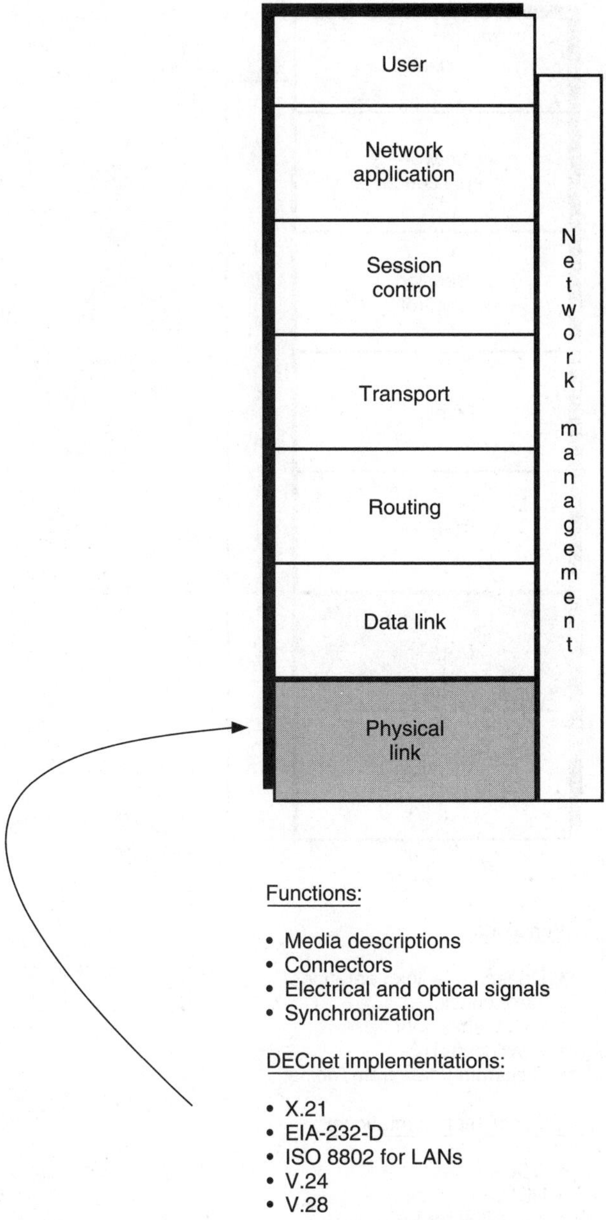

Figure 8.2 The physical layer. (*Courtesy Uyless Black.*)

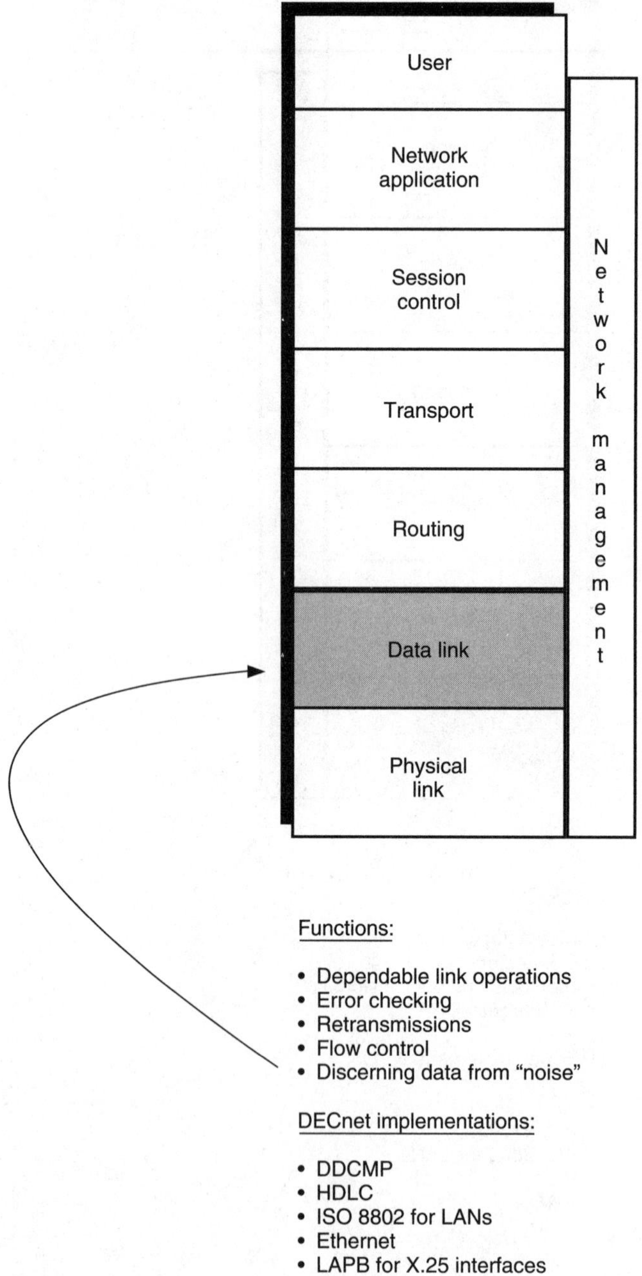

Figure 8.3 The data-link layer. (*Courtesy Uyless Black.*)

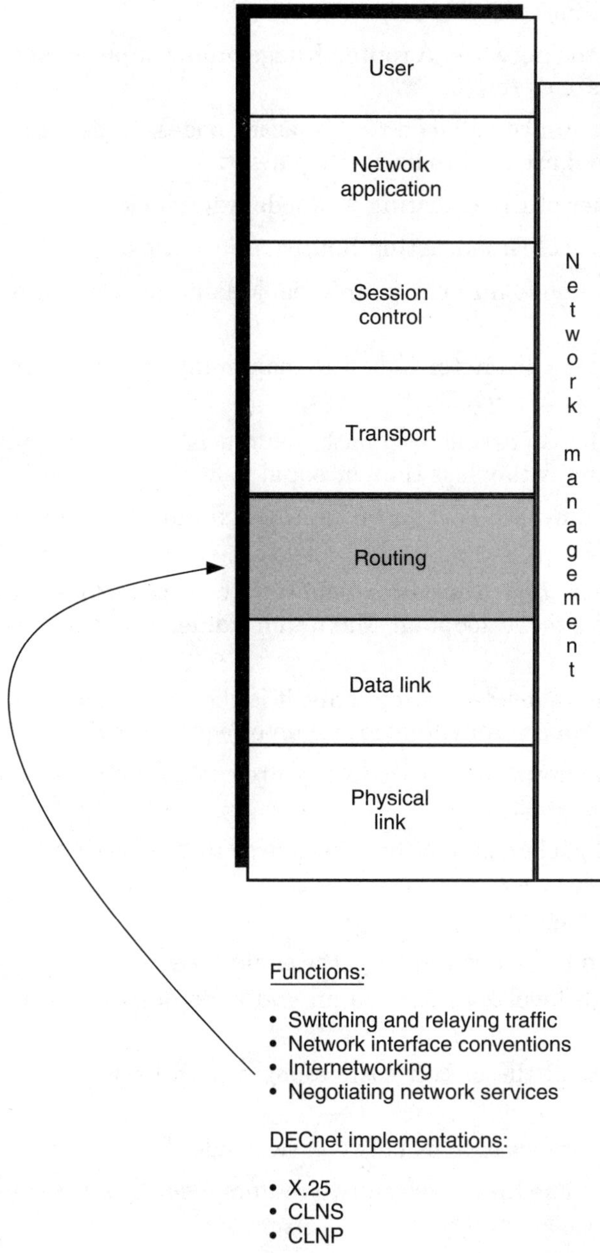

Figure 8.4 The network layer. (*Courtesy Uyless Black.*)

Endnode. A node that cannot route.

Node. A device on the network. A router, bridge, minicomputer, and personal computer are examples.

Hop. The logical distance between two adjacent nodes. Nodes that are directly connected are said to be one hop away.

NBEA. The Number of Broadcasting Endnode Adjacencies.

NBRA. The Number of Broadcasting Router Adjacencies.

NN. The maximum node number in an area. Maximum value: less than 1024.

NA. A level 2 router parameter only, the maximum area number. Maximum value: less than 64.

Maxh. Maximum hops possible in a path to a reachable node in an area value. Maximum value: less than or equal to 30.

Maxc. The maximum path cost in an area. Maximum value: less than or equal to 1022.

Maxv. Indicates how high the visits field may become before the packet is considered to be looping. Maximum value: less than or equal to 63.

AMaxh. Pertaining to level 2 routers only, it is the maximum path length to any area. Maximum value: less than or equal to 30.

AMaxc. Actual maximum path cost to any area. Maximum value: less than or equal to 1022.

Path. The route a packet takes from the source to the destination node. There are three types of paths:

1. End node to end node (direct routing)
2. End node through level 1 router(s) in the same area
3. End node through level 2 routers to an end node destination in another area

Path cost. The sum of the circuit costs along a path between two nodes.

Path length. The number of hops between two nodes.

Point-to-point link. The link between two routers, usually a remote serial line connecting two routers.

Traffic assignment algorithm. The Algorithm in the decision process that calculates the path costs in the routing database.

Functions of DECnet routing. DECnet provides a first glimpse into hierarchical routing. Unlike other dynamic routing methods, routing tables are not distributed to all nodes on the entire internet. Routing tables are held to the local area routers with end nodes (those that do not provide routing functions) reporting their status to their local routers.

The routing method of DECnet divides the DECnet internet into areas. There are 63 areas total allowed in a DECnet network. Each area may have up to 1023 addressable nodes in one area. Routers that provide routing functions between other routers in a local (one) area are known as level 1 routers. Routers that provide routing between two areas are known as level 2 routers.

Upon start-up, end nodes report their status to the router with a MAC destination multicast address "all routers." This is called the end node hello packet. All level 1 routers will pick up these packets and build a level 1 database table of all known end nodes for the circuit (Ethernet, for example) they are attached to. These end node multicasts will not be multicast across the router. This means that a router that receives an end-node hello will consume the packet. The router does not forward this packet.

Instead, level 1 routers will transmit their database tables (of all known end nodes) to other level 1 routers. In this way, all level 1 routers will be updated with all known end nodes in a particular area. Level 1 routers also maintain the address of the nearest level 2 router. To reduce the memory required to keep track of all end stations, DECnet routing is split into distinct areas. Level 1 routers track only the state of the end nodes in their area.

Level 2 routers maintain a database of all known level 2 routers in the entire DECnet internet. Level 2 routers must perform level 1 functions as well as level 2 functions. Therefore, they adhere to all level 1 routing functions, including receiving all local level 1 updates for their area. They do provide the additional ability to route between areas.

Finally Fig. 8.5 shows the services and components used in DECnet routing. Again, this figure is to be used as a reference for the text that follows.

Addressing. The addressing scheme used by DECnet Phase IV is based on area and node numbers. The total address is 16 bits long with the area number being the first 6 bits and the node number being final 10 bits. To carry this addressing scheme from Phase III over to Phase IV, which supports Ethernet (Ethernet physical addresses are 48 bits long), an algorithm was derived to produce the conversion. This is as follows. Whereas other protocols use a translator function to map a protocol address to a MAC address, DECnet literally maps its protocol address directly to the MAC address. A DECnet address is used in the DECnet packet header, but the trans-

DECnet Routing Layer Functions

Service	Component
Packet paths	Determines path for packets if more than one path exists.
Topology changes	Alternate paths are used if a node or circuit fails; routing modules are changed to reflect changes.
Packet forwarding	Forwards packet to end communication layer at destination node or the next node if packet is not destined for the local node.
Node visits	Limits number of nodes that a packet can visit.
Buffer management	Manages buffers at nodes.
Packet return	Returns packets to end communication layer if packets are addressed to unreachable nodes (if requested by end communication layer).
Data-link monitoring	Monitors errors detected by the data-link layer.
Statistics	Gathers event data for network management layer.
Node verification	If requested by the network management layer, exchanges passwords with adjacent node.

Figure 8.5 Services and components in DECnet routing. (*Courtesy Uyless Black.*)

lation of it to a MAC address overrides the burnt-in MAC address of the LAN controller. A table is not maintained to map a DECnet address to a MAC address.

Conversion.

Example DECnet address 6.9 (area 6, node number 9).

Put into binary with 6 bits for the area number and 10 bits for the node ID:
`000110.0000001001`

Split into two 8-bit bytes gives:
`00011000 00001001`

Swap the two bytes:

00001001 00011000

Convert to hex:

0918

Add the HIORD (Digital's constant high-order bytes, AA 00 04 00, explained next) gives AA 00 04 00 09 18 as the 48-bit physical address for a nodes residing in area 6 and a node ID of 9.

Allowing for 6 bits of area address and 10 bits for node ID gives a total of 65535 possible addresses in a DECnet environment.

Figure 8.6 shows another example.

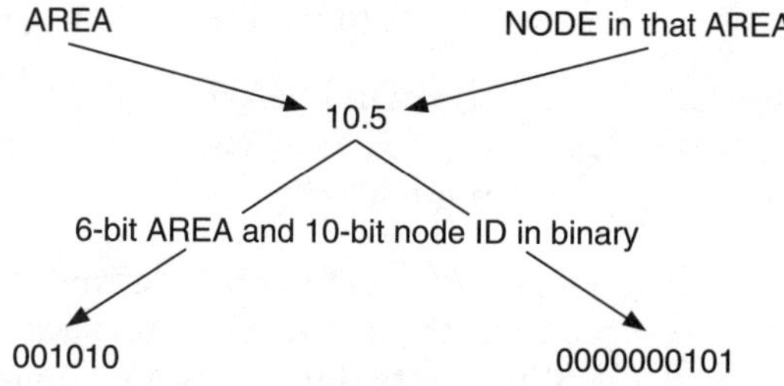

Combine into two 8-bit bytes

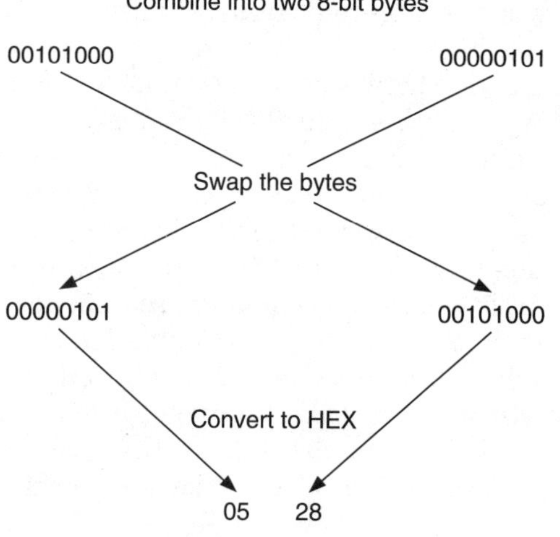

Add the HIORD (4 Hi-order bytes assigned by DEC which are AA 00 04 00)

Gives the following 48-bit physical address
AA 00 04 00 05 28

Figure 8.6 MAC address conversion for a DECnet address.

Address constants. The following addresses are reserved by Digital for the following usage*:

HIORD (Hi-order bytes)	The 4 bytes placed on the beginning of a 48-bit converted DECnet address. This is used after the address conversion is accomplished to complete the 48-bit DECnet address. These bytes are AA 00 04 00 xx xx.
All Routers	This is the multicast address for packets that send out information that pertains to all the routers—AB-00-00-03-00-00.
All Endnodes	This is a multicast address used by packets that contain information for all end nodes in an Ethernet segment (a circuit)—AB-00-00-04-00-00.

The protocol (Ethernet Type field) should be set to 60-03, which indicates an DECnet packet. DECnet uses the Ethernet frame format. DEC supports SNAP† for Token Ring packets.

Areas. With this, a DECnet network is split into definable areas (63 total). To accomplish area routing, there will be two types of routers: level 1 and level 2. Level 1 routers route data within a single area and keep track of the state of all nodes that are in its area. Level 1 routers do not care about nodes that are outside their area. When communication takes place between two different areas, the level 1 routers will send the data to a level 2 router.

Level 2 routers route traffic between two areas. Level 2 routers keep track of the least-cost path (not necessarily the fastest) to each area in the internetwork as well as the state of any of the nodes in the area.

Refer to Fig. 8.7. This figure shows three areas: 10, 8, and 4. Level 1 routers are those routers which forward data within their own area. They will not forward data outside of their area. This is the function of the level 2 router. If a data packet is destined for another area, the level 1 router will forward the packet to its "nearest level 2 router." A level 2 router automatically assumes the function of a level 1 router in that area.

In turn, this router will ensure the packet makes it to the final area. Then a level 1 router will forward the data to the final destination node. Level 2 routers perform both level 1 and level 2 routing functions in the same router.

Finally, the Fig. 8.7 shows level 2 routers being connected through serial lines. This is not always the case. Level 2 routers may connect two segments of Ethernet cable. Each Ethernet segment would be defined as a different area. Unless there are multiple routers defined

---

* xx means the result of the computation stated previously.

† Refer to Chap. 3 for more information on SNAP.

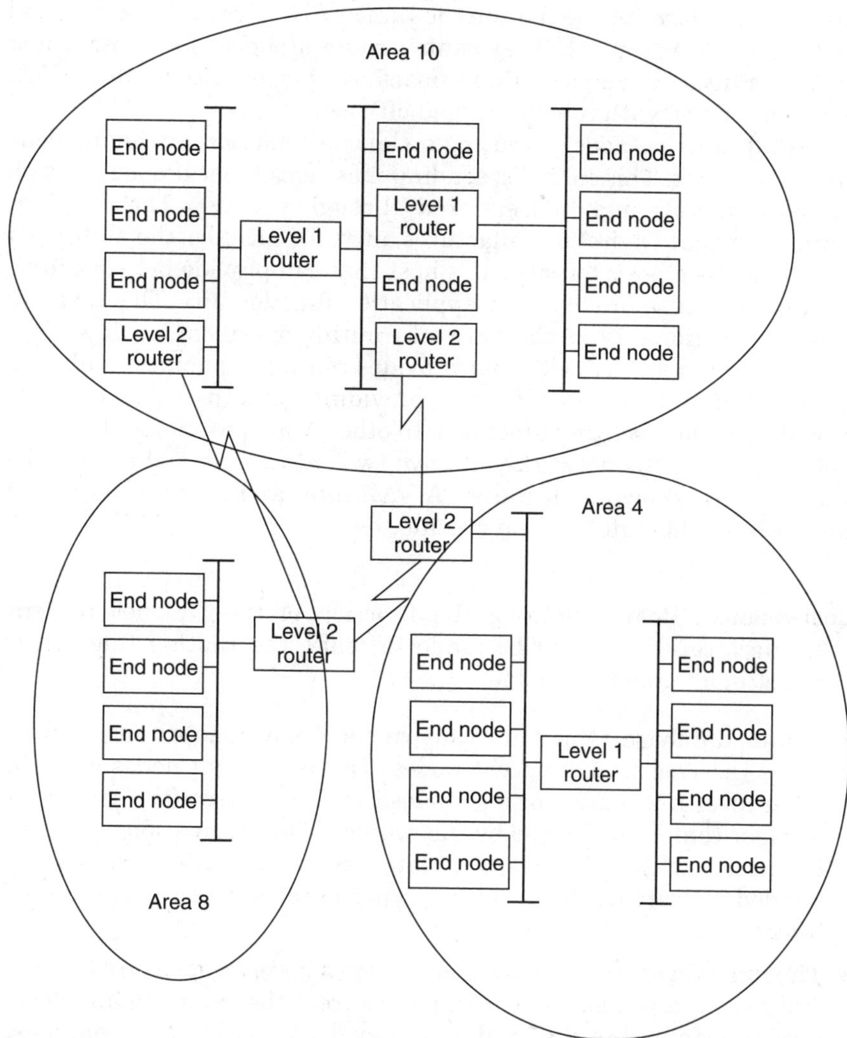

Figure 8.7 DECnet areas. Level 2 routers can be Ethernet-to-Ethernet as well as Ethernet-to-serial connections, as shown here.

with a different area number connected to the same cable segment, there is only one area per cable segment. Unlike TCP/IP or AppleTalk, DECnet supports only one area per cable segment. This will be shown at the end of the routing section.

The routing database. There are two types of nodes in DECnet areas:

1. End nodes are stations that do not have a routing capability. What this means is that they cannot receive and forward messages that are intended for other nodes. An end node can send data (packets)

to another adjacent node (i.e., on the same LAN, whether that is an end node or another router). They cannot route a packet for another end node or router. Examples of end nodes are personal computers, VAX minicomputers (with routing turned off), etc.

2. Full function node (a routing node) can send packets to any node on the network. This includes sending messages to local nodes as well as nodes that are in a different area (through a router). The computer equipment that Digital manufactures and sells includes the ability not only to act as a host, but also as a host that can provide network functionality and also provide user application functionality. This text will include functionality of the network routing specification. It will be written in terms of a device that provides routing capabilities only and not the dual functionality of a host providing application functionality plus the network routing functions. In other words, to explain the function of routing, the network will have two entities: an end node and a single device known as a router. A VAX mini and an external router can both provide full function routing.

Declarations. Before defining the function of the DECnet routers, some declarations should be made to make the routing function of DECnet more understandable.

- Router database tables are constructed from update routing messages received from adjacent nodes. These adjacent nodes could be other level 1, 2 routers or end nodes in the local area (the same area number that is configured by the router). The information contained in these tables will be shown later. Since a DECnet internet is divided into areas, there are two types of tables: level 1 and level 2 tables.
- The function of level 1 routers is to store a distance measured by cost and hop information. This distance is from the router to any destination node within the local area. Level 1 routers receive database updates from adjacent level 1 routing nodes. This means that once a level 1 router builds a table containing a listing of end nodes that the router knows about, it will send this information to other level 1 routers (known as *adjacencies*) on its network. Therefore, the level 1 routing database table is updated periodically by the update routing message received from adjacent level 1 routing nodes. Included in this message is the router's listing of known active end nodes in the unique area.
- To update other level 1 routers, a routing node sends update routing messages to its adjacent routing nodes with cost/hop information. All level 1 routers will transmit this information to all other level 1

routers. This will allow all level 1 table information to be eventually propagated to all routing nodes. Level 1 routers will not propagate their information to other areas. This information is propagated to routers in their own area.

- Level 1 routers can function on Ethernet (broadcast circuits) or point to point (router to router through a serial line).
- Level 2 routers perform level 1 routing functions as well as level 2 routing. They store cost and hop values from the local area to any other destination area. This is the main function of the level 2 routers—to route information to other areas on the DECnet internet. Level 2 routers receive database updates periodically from adjacent level 2 routing nodes.
- Level 2 routers can function on Ethernet (broadcast circuits) and point-to-point circuits (router to router across a serial line).
- DECnet routers are adaptive-to-topology changes. If the path to a destination fails, the DECnet routing algorithm will dynamically choose an alternative path (if available). If, at any time, a physical line in the network goes down, all paths affected by that circuit will be recalculated by each routing node. Any time these algorithms reexecute, the contents of the databases are revealed to all other adjacent nodes on each respective network.
- Adaptive-to-different circuit types include such things as X.25, DDCMP, serial links, and Ethernet.
- Event-driven updates mean that other routers are updated immediately to any changes in the network that would affect routing of a packet.
- Periodic updates are timed intervals at which routing updates, test, and hello messages will be sent. These timers are settable.
- An unknown address or network unreachable packet will be returned (if requested).
- The number of nodes a packet has visited is tracked to keep it from endlessly looping in the network.
- Node verification–password protection is performed.
- Information is gathered for network management purposes.

Forwarding of packets. As stated before, DECnet uses not only adaptive routing, but also area routing. This means that DECnet is hierarchical in its routing. In other words, there is more than one layer in the routing (see Fig. 8.7). The routing techniques used by DECnet are not the same as those used in most networks today. When a source station is trying to send data to a destination station, the path its takes to transmit this data is called the *path length* and is measured by the number of hops. A path between the source and destination station may never exceed the maximum number of hops for the network.

An example of hierarchical, or area, routing is the phone number system for calling the internal United States, Mexico, or Canada. There is a 10-digit system that is used to identify any phone in the United States, Mexico, or Canada. The first number is an area code, which identifies which area (according to the phone system) you live in. For example, 703 is the northern part of Virginia. The second three numbers are called the exchange number. This further identifies which subpart of the area you live in. The last four digits actually indicate the phone itself. Therefore, it you wanted to call in the local area, you would not have to use all 10 digits. By using just the last seven digits, the phone company switches (analogous to data routers) would identify the exchange number and switch (route) the call. If another area is needed, the first three digits are used and the phone company's switch recognize this and will switch the call to another switch in that area. The long distance call would then be routed to the exchange number and, finally, to the individual phone. The preceding example will not work in every case, but for those readers trying to grasp an understanding of area routing, it will suffice.

Although DECnet uses hops, DECnet is not based on a distance-vector algorithm. (For more information on distance-vector, see Chap. 4.) DECnet routes are based on a different "cost" factor. In other words, what is the cost to reach another destination on the network? The path with the lowest cost will be chosen as the path a packet will take. This allows realistic multiple paths to a destination to exist*. The network manager may also assign a cost to each circuit (connection to the data link) on each station. The cost is an arbitrary number that will be used to determine the best path for a data transfer. The total cost is the cumulative number that is between a source and destination station.

With this, a router not an end node will pick a path for data to travel based on the least cost involved. This path may contain the most number of hops, but it will have the least cost. Refer to Fig. 8.8. The path to node D can take many different routes. Before data is sent, node A must decide which is the lowest cost to node D. As shown in Fig. 8.8, A to B to C to D offers the lowest cost, so it is chosen as the path. Notice that this path has more hops than option 1. Hops are used in DECnet to determine the diameter of the network and to determine when a packet is looping,

* Other routing algorithms (i.e., RIP) allow for multiple paths to exist to a destination. But their "cost" is associated to only a hop count. With DECnet, the cost is a user-definable number to truly indicate the cost, not just a hop count.

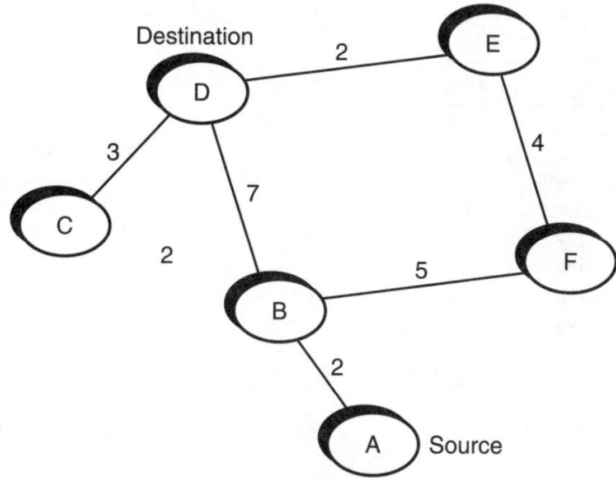

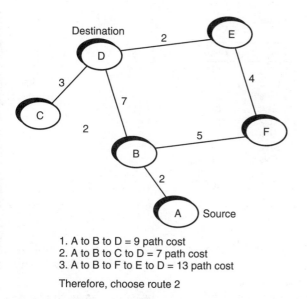

1. A to B to D = 9 path cost
2. A to B to C to D = 7 path cost
3. A to B to F to E to D = 13 path cost

Therefore, choose route 2

Figure 8.8 DECnet least-cost routing. (*Courtesy Uyless Black.*)

among other things. Assigning a real cost is a much more efficient way of routing. Imagine we based this on hops. Option 1 would have been taken. But if the path from B to D is a 9600-baud sync line and the paths B to C and C to D are T1 serial lines, the hop algorithm will select the 9600-baud line, for it has the lowest hop count. Assigning costs allows the network administrator to effect the best path. One exception to cost-based routing is when a node can be reached in two different ways and each path has the same cost. The router will arbitrarily select the route.

Router tables will not keep two known paths to the same destination. The most cost-effective route is the only one kept in the routing table. The one exception to this is when there are two paths to the same destination and the costs are equal.

Cost numbers for circuits are arbitrarily assigned by a network administrator. There is not a strict standard in choosing them. The DECnet architecture does have an algorithm for assigning them, though. The general thought behind it is, the slower the circuit (the link) the higher the cost. For example, a 9600-baud line will have a much higher cost than a T1 line. Table 8.1 shows the cost number most usually assigned.

Depending on the type of level of a router node, each routing node in a DECnet network maintains at least one database. On a level 1 router, the database contains entries on path length and path cost to every node (workstation, host, etc.) in its area. It also maintains an entry for the whereabouts of a level 2 router in its area.

TABLE 8.1 Possible Cost Parameters Based on Line Speed

Speed	Cost	Speed	Cost
100 Mb/s	1	64 Kb/s	14
16 Mb/s	2	56 Kb/s	15
10 Mb/s	3	38.4 Kb/s	16
4 Mb/s	5	32 Mb/s	17
1.54 Mb/s	7	19.2 Kb/s	18
1.25 Mb/s	8	9.6 Kb/s	19
833 Kb/s	9	7.2 Kb/s	20
625 Kb/s	10	4.8 Kb/s	21
420 Kb/s	11	2.4 Kb/s	22
230.4 Kb/s	12	1.2 Kb/s	25
125 Kb/s	13		

Level 2 routers add a second database, known as an area routing table, which determines the least-cost path to other area routers in the network (not only the local area).

Node reachability explains that a node can be accessed if the computed cost and the hops it takes to get there are not exceeded by the number that is configured for that router.

A lot of parameters may be configured for a DECnet router. This is to allow for efficient utilization of memory in the router. If the DECnet network is small and has only a few nodes in a few areas, there is no need to configure the parameters with large entries. The memory will never be used. Most DECnet routers will allocate memory space based on the configuration parameters. It is important to know the DECnet topology before configuring a DECnet router. The memory space will not be allocated dynamically based on what the router finds on the network.

Remember, in a DECnet environment, routers are not necessarily separate boxes that perform routing functions only. Routers may be contained in a Micro VAX, a VAX, or any other node on the network.

Routing the data. There are two types of messages that a router node may receive: data and control messages (network overhead, nothing to do with data).

Data messages contain user data that is transferred between two communicating stations, specifically at the End-to-End Communication Layer (OSI transport layer). The process of routing will add a route header to the packet that will enable the routers to forward the packet to its final destination based on the information that is in the route header portion of the packet. Control messages are exchanged of the routers that initialize, maintain, and monitor the status between the routers or end nodes.

Figure 8.9*a* shows the end station hellos from nodes 5.3, 5.2, and 5.1, respectively. These are multicast packets that will be received by the 5.4 router. The 5.4 router is simply a level 1 router, for it has no other area to talk to. It will transmit level 1 routing updates from its Ethernet port.

Figure 8.9*b* shows two types of update packets that the routing function uses. One is for Ethernet and the other is for non-Ethernet (i.e., serial lines). The routers in Fig. 8.9*b* are level 2 routers. As shown in Fig. 8.9*b* the packet types used on broadcast networks (i.e., Ethernet), are:

1. Ethernet end node Hello message—Picked up by level 1 and level 2 router
2. Ethernet router Hello message—Sent to all routers on the Ethernet by the router
3. Level 1 routing message—Sent by the level 1 router and contains the end node database
4. Level 2 routing message—Sent by the level 2 router and contains level 2 routing table information

The packets that are transmitted between the routers on the serial lines, nonbroadcast networks, use the following routing messages only:

1. Initialization message
2. Verification message
3. Hello and Test message
4. Level 1 routing message
5. Level 2 routing message

The definitions of the six types of routing control messages that DECnet Phase IV uses:

1. The routing message contains information that is used for updating the routing database of an adjacent node. Inside this message are the path cost and path length values for specific destinations.

2. The Ethernet router Hello message is used to initialize and monitor routers on an Ethernet circuit. This is a multicast packet and contains a list of all routers on the Ethernet circuit that the sending node has recently received via the Ethernet router Hello messages. This packet is multicast periodically to all other stations (routers and end nodes alike) on the same Ethernet circuit. This is done so that all routers are updated with the most current status of any other routers on the circuit. By transmitting this message, the designated router

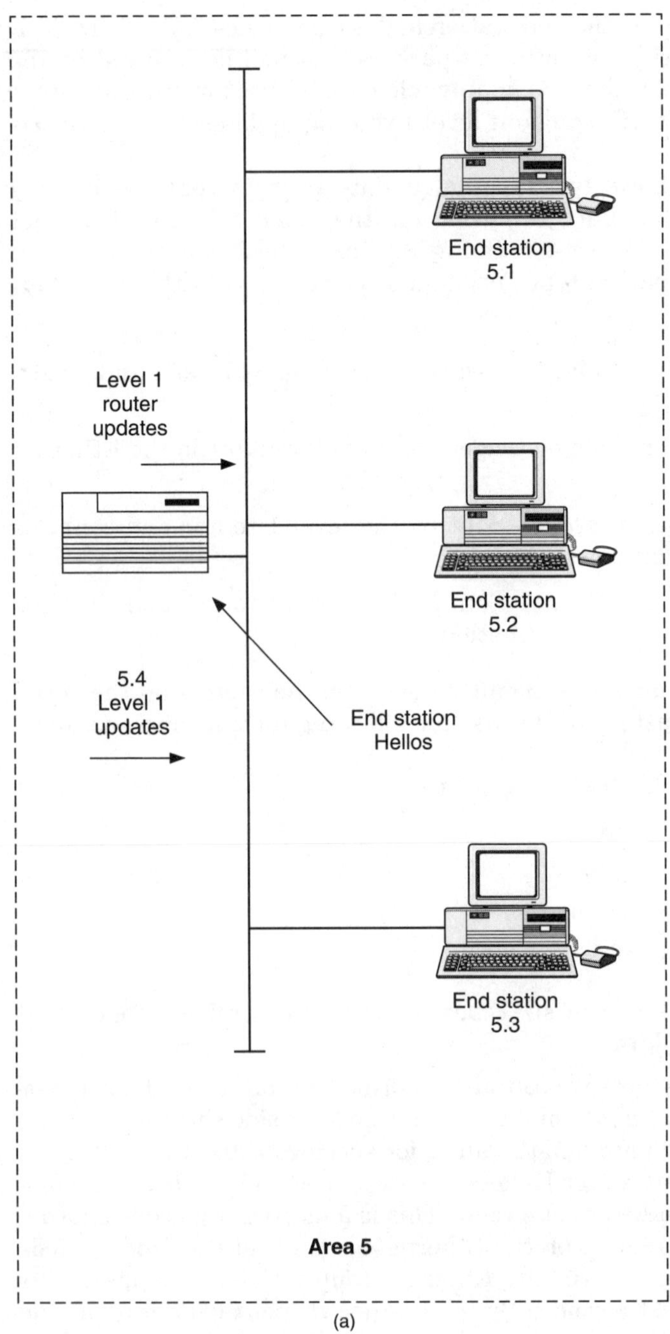

Figure 8.9 Level 1 routing updates.

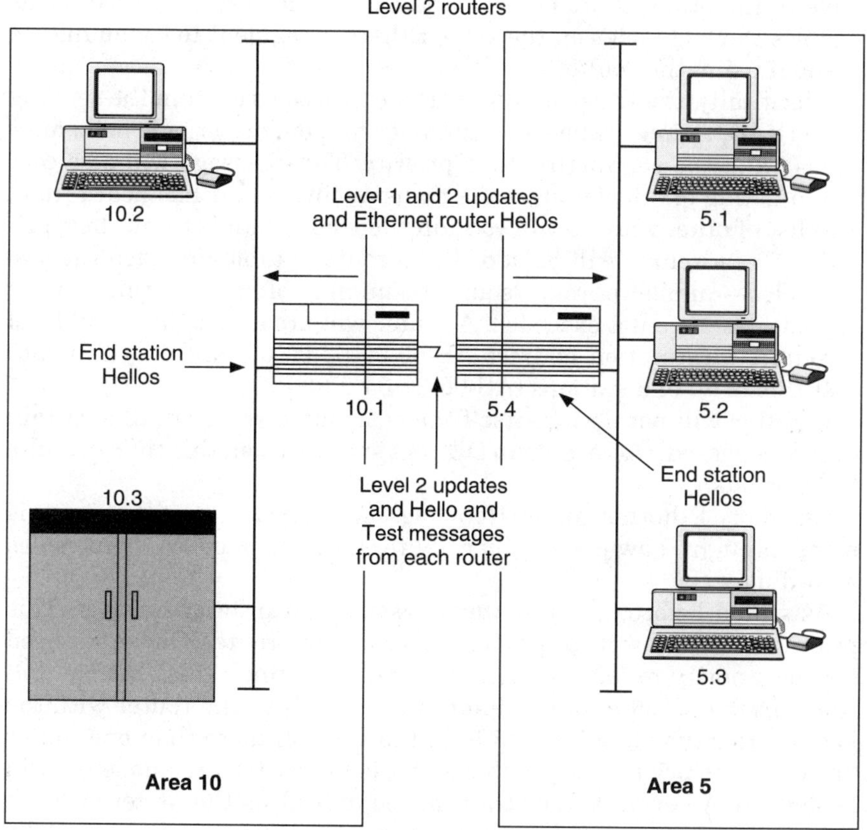

Figure 8.9 *(Continued)*

(DR*) is also selected on that Ethernet circuit. Once the DR is selected, it will remain so until it is taken off-line for whatever reason (other routers must hear from the designated router within a certain time period). One purpose of the DR is to assist end stations in discovering that they are on the same circuit. This is accomplished by setting a special intra-Ethernet bit in a packet that it will forward from one end

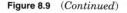

* The designated router is the router to which all end nodes will transmit packets for routing. It is elected by other routers as the router with the highest assigned priority. Its role is discussed later.

node to the other (more on this when end nodes are discussed). This enables the end nodes on the same Ethernet segment to communicate without using the router.

Specifically, the Ethernet router Hello messages contain the sending router's ID, a timer called T3 (the timer for sender periodic hello messages), and the sending router's priority. This message will also contain a listing of other routers the transmitting router has heard from. The list of other routers will contain their node number and their priority. A new router will be added to a router's table provided the two variables—number of routers and the number of broadcasting routing adjacencies—are not exceeded. A router will broadcast this to all level 1 routers (destination address AB-00-00-03-00-00) and it will broadcast this to all end stations (AB-00-00-04-00-00).

A router will not declare itself the designated router until a certain time has passed. (According to DECnet specification, this time defaults to 5 seconds.)

An empty Ethernet router Hello message indicates that the router is being brought down and other routers should modify their tables accordingly.

As stated before, every router is assigned a priority number. This priority could allow it to become the designated router. One other need for the priority number of a router: when routing tables become full (the variable number of maximum routers is hit), the router with the lowest priority will be deleted from the table. If more than one router has the same priority, the router with the lowest ID (area.node ID) will be deleted. An event will be transmitted indicating the router is down.

3. End nodes on an Ethernet circuit use the Ethernet end node Hello message to allow routers to initialize and monitor end nodes on an Ethernet circuit. This packet is transmitted as a multicast packet—"all routers multicast"—and is transmitted by each active end node on an Ethernet circuit to allow all routers to find out about all active end nodes on an Ethernet circuit. The routers will use this to monitor the status of the end nodes on their Ethernet. The routers will make an entry in its table for this end node.

Once a router receives this packet, it should receive Hellos from this adjacency at certain timer periods. If it does not, it will delete this entry from its table and generate an event that the adjacency is down. This period of waiting is set to three times the router's T3 timer (the Hello timer for the router).

4. The Hello and Test message is to test for the operational status of an adjacency. This type of packet is used on "non-Ethernet" (nonbroadcast) circuits and is used when no messages are being transmitted across that line. For example, on a serial line interconnecting two DECnet routers, there may be times when no messages are transmitted on

that line. Periodically, when there are no valid messages to transmit, this message is transmitted so that the opposite end will not think the circuit is down. If this or any other message is not received within a certain time, the routing layer will consider the circuit to be down.

5. An initialization message appears when a router is initializing a "non-Ethernet" circuit. Contained in this message is information on the type of node, the required verification, maximum message size, and the routing version.

6. Finally, a verification message is sent when a node is initializing and a node verification must accompany the initialization.

Updating the routers. Routing messages are propagated through the DECnet internet. Any node on the network can send out a routing message to an adjacent routing node. When this adjacent routing node receives that message, it will compare the routing information in the message to the existing routing database table. If the information in the routing message contains new information (not already in the routing table), the table is updated and a new routing message is generated with the new information by that routing node and sent to all other adjacent routers on the internet. In turn, those routers will update and send it to their adjacent nodes, and so on. This is known as propagating the information. Again, these messages are shown in Fig. 8.9*b*.

If there are multiple areas on an internet (indicating level 2 routers), routers must discard messages that do not pertain to them. For example, when a level 1 router receives an end node or a router Hello message, the first check accomplished is that the incoming message's ID (area.node ID) is the same as the router's ID (the areas should match). If they do not match, the packet is discarded. This means that a level 1 router will not keep a table of any adjacencies for other areas (for Ethernet, it will not keep track of end nodes in other areas). A level 1 router will keep end node tables only for end nodes that have the same area ID as the router's.

Level 2 routers must keep a table of adjacencies to other level 2 routers, besides the adjacencies (level 1 routers and end nodes) in its own (single) area. It will discard any Ethernet end node Hello messages it may receive from areas other than its own or any level 1 routing messages it may receive from other areas. When it does receive a level 2 update message, it will include that router's ID in its update table. The router will also include that ID its next Ethernet router Hello message. A level 2 update will contain an area number and an associated hop and cost number to get to an area. These routing messages will be broadcast using the all-routers broadcast (AA-00-00-03-00-00) in the destination address field of the MAC header.

When a router broadcasts its information to the network, and there is more information in the table than the Ethernet allows for a maximum size packet, multiple packets will be transmitted. This is similar to other routing protocols.

Router operation. As shown in Fig. 8.10, the routing layer is actually split into two sublayers:

1. The routing initialization sublayer performs only the initialization procedures. These procedures include initialization of the data-link layer. This includes setting up the drivers and controlling the Ethernet, X.25, and DDCMP (Digital Data Control Message Protocol). This is the layer that the routing layer of DECnet must talk to.

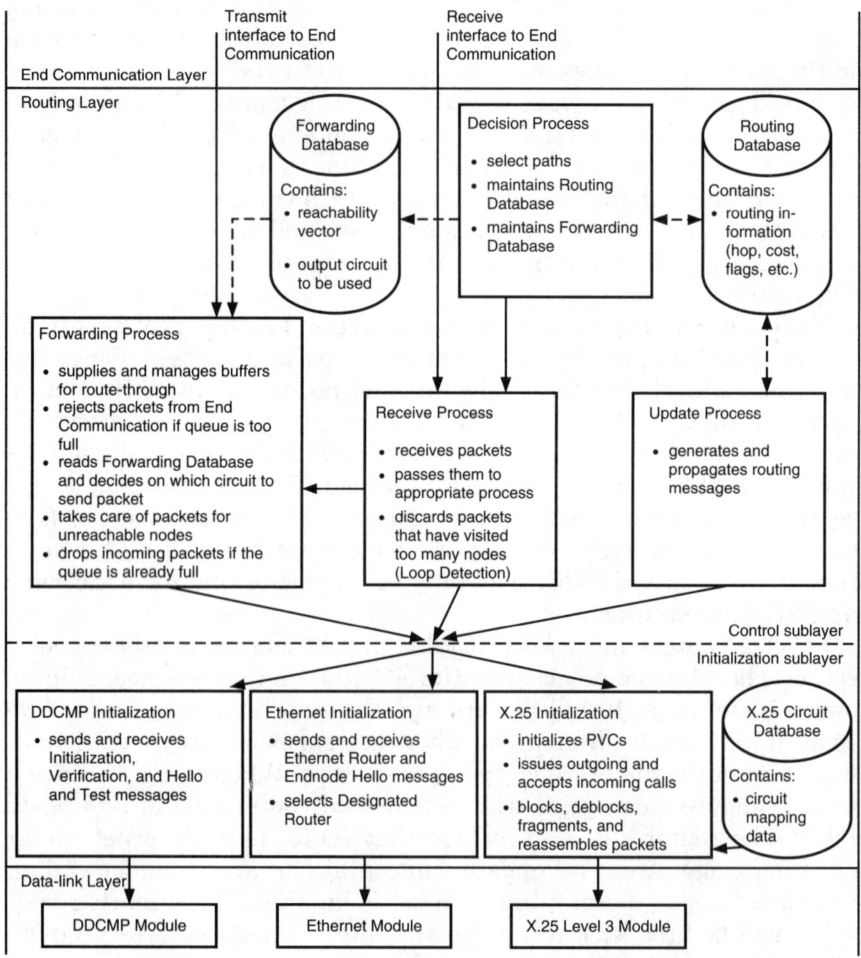

Figure 8.10 Routing layer components and their functions. (*Copyright © 1982 Digital Equipment Corporation.*)

2. The routing control sublayer performs the actual routing, any congestion control, and packet lifetime control. This layer controls five different processes as well as the routing database.

The routing control sublayer is made up of the following five processes:

1. *Decision.* Based on a connectivity algorithm that maintains path lengths and another algorithm that maintains path costs, this process will select a route for a received packet. Those algorithms are executed when the router receives a routing message (not a routable data message). The forwarding database tables will then be updated based on the outcome of the invoked algorithms. The decision process will select the least-cost path to another node (level 1 routing) or the least-cost path to another area router (level 2 routing).

2. *Update.* This process is responsible for building and propagating the routing messages. These routing messages contain the path cost and path length for all destinations. Based on the decision process, it will transmit these messages when required to do so. This process will also monitor the circuits that it knows about by periodically sending routing messages to adjacent nodes. If the router is a level 1 router, it will transmit level 1 messages. However, if it is a level 2 router, it will transmit level 1 and level 2 routing messages.

- Level 1 routing packets are sent to adjacent routers within its home area.
- Level 2 packets are sent to other level 2 routers.
- Level 1 routing packets contain information on all nodes in its home area.
- Level 2 routing packets contain information about all areas.
- Packets containing routing information are event-driven with periodic backup.

3. *Forwarding process.* This process looks in a table to find a circuit (path) to forward a packet onto. If this path cannot be found, it is this process that will return the packet to the sender or will discard the packet (depending on the option bits set in the packet route header, the RQR* bit). This process also manages all the buffers required to support the tables.

4. *Receive process.* This process inspects the packet's route header. Based on the packet type, this process gives the packet to another process for handling. Routing messages are given to the decision process, Hello messages are given to the node listener process, and packets that are not destined for the router are given to the forwarding process.

---

* Request for a return of the packet to the originator if there is an error.

5. *Congestion control.* Uses a function known as transmit management. This process handles the buffers, which are blocks of RAM memory set aside for storing (i.e., queuing) information until it can be sent. It limits the number of packets allowed in the queue. If this number is exceeded, the router is allowed to discard packets to prevent the buffer from overflowing.

Packet lifetime control prevents packets from endlessly looping the network by discarding packets that have "visited" too many routers. This includes the loop detector, the node listener, and the node talker. The loop detector keeps track of how many times a packet has visited the node. It will remove the packet when it has the visited the node a set amount of times. The node listener is the process that keeps track of adjacencies. It determines when a node has been heard from and if the identity of an adjacent node has changed. This is the process that determines whether an adjacency is declared down. In combination with this, the node talker is the process that provides for Hello packets to be transmitted. It places an artificial load on the adjacency so failures can be detected.

Initialization and circuit monitor is the means by which the router will obtain the identity of neighboring nodes. For Ethernet circuits, the Ethernet router Hello and the Ethernet end node Hello message perform these functions.

Forwarding of data in a DECnet environment. As stated before, data starts at the application layer of any network station and flows down through the OSI model towards the physical layer. As the data passes through each of the layers, additional information, known as header information, is added to the beginning to the packet. This information does not change the original information (the data from the application layer) in the packet. It is merely control information so that any node that receives this packet will know whether or not to accept it and how to process it. If the packet is not intended for that node, the header information in the packet will contain information on what to do with the packet.

Simply enough, a router must check its routing table to determine the path for a packet to take to reach the final destination. If the destination is in the local area, the router will send the packet directly to the destination node or to another router in that area to forward the packet to the destination node.

If the packet is for a node in a different area, the router will forward the packet to a level 2 router. That router will send it to another level 2 router in that area. The level 2 router in the other area will forward the packet to the destination node in the same manner as a level 1 router. Remember that level 2 routers act as both level 2 and level 1 routers.

Table 8.2 shows a typical level 1 and 2 routing database table of a level 2 router. This would be router A's (a level 2 router) forwarding routing database. Router A is shown in Fig. 8.11.

From Table 8.2, you should notice that the number of reachable areas from this router is 3, the number of reachable nodes is 4 for area 1 and 2 for area 11, the number of adjacent routes is 2. The table should look a little odd. In the level 1 database is information to two different areas. Level 1 routers are not supposed to keep track of different area node ideas—only the end node IDs for its own area.

This is a multiport router that contains more than just two ports. Therefore, it can assign area and node IDs on a per port basis. Therefore, this node is also a level 1 router for both area 1 and area 11. It must keep track of the nodes in both areas it connects to. In actuality, the router would probably keep two tables—one for each area. It is shown in the same table here for simplicity.

Definitions

Level 1 table descriptions

Forwarding destination of the packet (node and port). This contains the DECnet router address and the port number on the router (assuming the router has multiple ports) for possible packet destinations.

Next hop. The DECnet address (area and node address) that this router must send the packet to for it to be routed to its final destination.

TABLE 8.2 Level 1 and Level 2 Routing Tables

Level 1 Information							
Area 1							
Node	Port	Next hop	Cost	Hops	BlkSize	Priority	Timer
1	1	1.1	3	1	1500	40	—
2	1	1.1	3	1	1500	40	40
15	1	1.1	3	1	1500	50	40
4	2	1.90	3	1	1500	40	30
6	2	1.90	3	1	600	40	40
9.0	2	1.90	3	1	1500	40	—
Area 11							
2	3	11.2	3	1	1500	40	40
30	3	11.2	3	1	1500	40	90
15	3	11.2	3	1	1500		
1	3	11.2	3	1	1500		
Level 2 Information							
Area	Port	Next hop	Cost	Hops	Time		
1	Local	—	—	—	—		
11	3	11.2	3	1	60		
50	3	11.2	6	2	40		

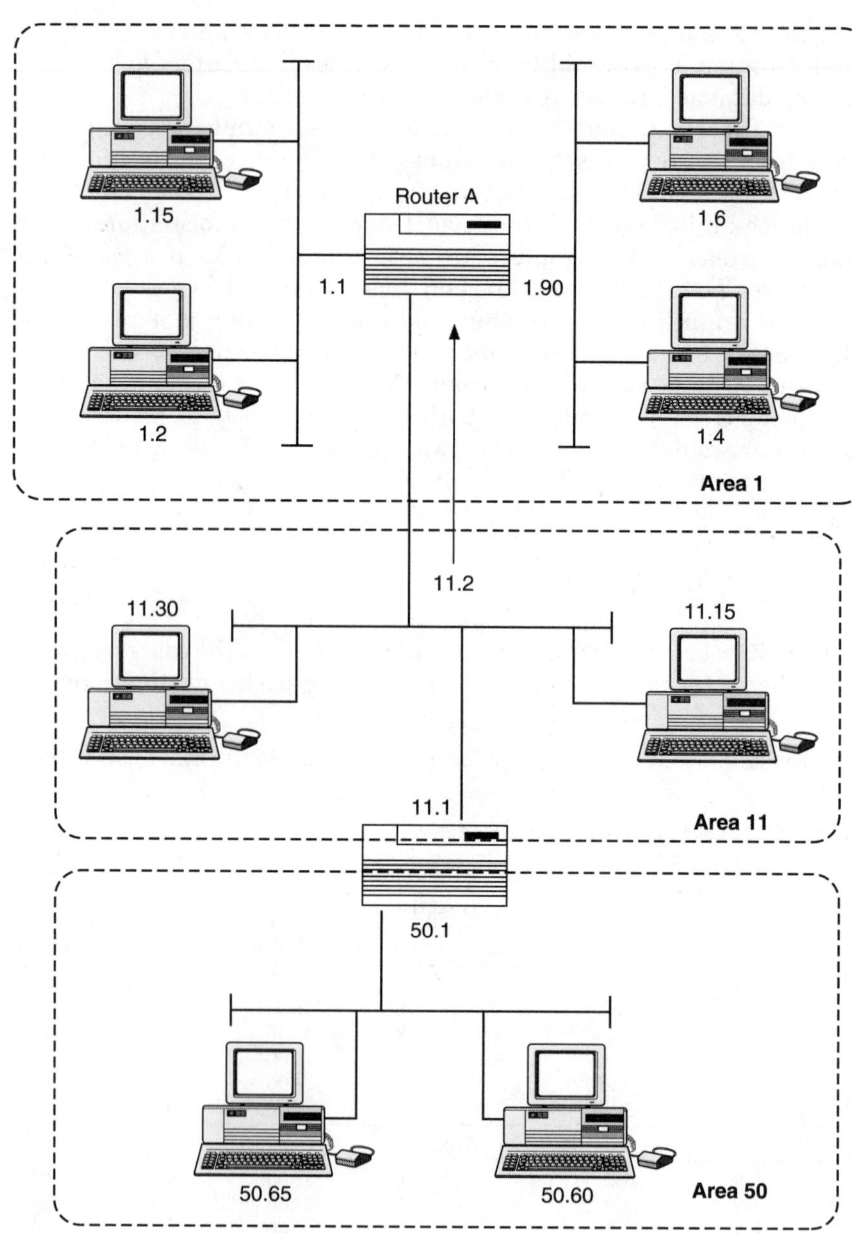

Figure 8.11 Multiple DECnet areas.

Cost. This is a user configurable number that the network administrator will assign to the circuit. Packets are routed based on the path with the lowest cost.

Hops. This is the number of hops (the number of routers) that a packet must traverse before reaching the destination.

BlkSize (block size). This is the maximum size of a packet that can be sent to a destination node.

Priority. The individual priority of that router. This is used to determine a designated router. The priority is also used in the following situation. If the number of the router's parameter is exceeded, then the update of a routing database is as follows:

1. The router with the lowest priority will be deleted from the database unless the new router has a lower priority than any other router in the database.
2. If there are duplicate priority numbers, then the router with the lowest ID (48-bit Ethernet address) will be deleted from the database or the new router will not be added (if its Ethernet address is the lowest). Ethernet addresses are not duplicated. There will not be any decisions after this.

Time. This is a parameter of how long this entry will remain in the table. This parameter is based on the configurable timer known as the Hello time.

Level 2 table descriptions

Destination of the packet (area and port). The DECnet AREA number (not node number) and the port number of the router to direct the packet to.

Next hop. The DECnet address (area and node address) of the router to which a router will send the packet so that it may be routed to its final destination.

Cost. Same as for level 1 table.

Hops. Same as level 1 entry.

Time. Same as level 1 entry.

It is important to note that a router has the possibility of routing a packet through multiple routes. The decision on which route to take is based solely on the cost associated with a path to the final destination.

End node packet delivery. When an end node would like to communicate with another end node on the same Ethernet, it may do so under the following conditions.

If the end node has the destination station's address in its cache table, it may communicate directly with the end node. Otherwise, if the destination station's address is not in the table, it must send the directed packet to the designated router. Refer to Fig. 8.12. The designated router will then perform a lookup to see if the destinated end node is active. If the destination station's address is in the designated router's table, it will forward the packet to the end node with the intra-area bit (in the route header) set to a 1 (to indicate that this packet is destined for the local LAN). The destination station, upon receipt of that packet, will then send some type of response packet back to the originating station (adding that station's address to its local cache). The designated router will not be used for further communication (as indicated by the number 3 in Fig. 8.12).

The originating station, upon receipt of the destination station's response, will add the destination station's address into its cache and then communicate with it directly (no more help from the designated router). The end node cache table may be aged out (the entry is deleted

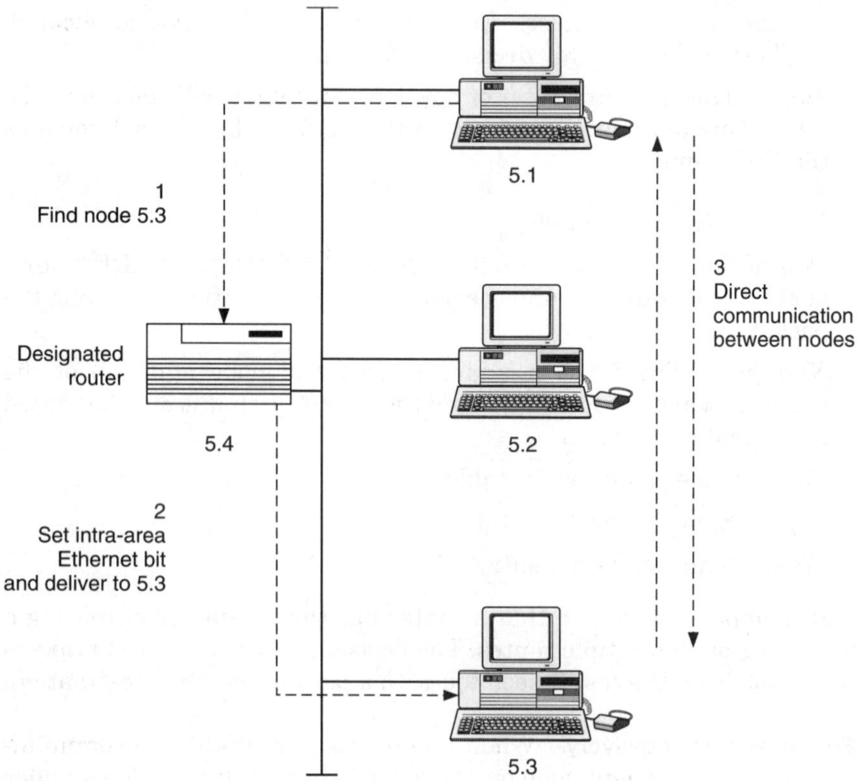

Figure 8.12 End-node communication.

when the station indicated in the cache table has not been heard from for a specified amount of time).

If the end node does not have the address of the designated router (there is not an active router), it will try to send the packet to the destination station anyway.*

A flowchart for DECnet routing is shown in Fig. 8.13.

A few final notes: As shown in Fig. 8.14*a*, there may be more than one area per Ethernet segment. Figure 8.14*a* shows two areas on the same segment: area 5 and area 10. The only stipulation is that there must be two full-function nodes (or routers) on the same segment of Ethernet cable. Each of these routing nodes will have a different area. All of the rules that were stated in the previous paragraphs remain the same (Ethernet router Hellos, level 1 updates, level 2 updates, etc.). Each router controls the nodes in its own area. A single router port may not support two areas.

Figure 8.14*b* shows a typical DECnet internet. It shows level 1 and level 2 routers, designated routers, end stations, and full-function nodes.

End Communication Layer: The DNA Transport Layer

This layer (the transport layer on the OSI model) is used for reliable data transfer between two network stations on the network, no matter where the two reside on the network. This is accomplished by setting up a session, establishing sequence numbers between the source and destination station, and then passing data over the virtual circuit. The DECnet transport-layer protocol that accomplishes this is called the Network Services Protocol (NSP). It provides this as a service to the upper-layer protocols. Figure 8.15 summarizes the functions of the DNA transport layer.

The NSP provides the following functions:

- Creates, maintains, and terminates logical links (virtual circuits)
- Guarantees the delivery of data and control messages in sequence to a specified destination by means of an error control mechanism
- Transfers data into and out of buffers
- Fragments data into segments and automatically puts them back together again at the destination
- Provides flow control
- Provides error control

---

* Not always implemented.

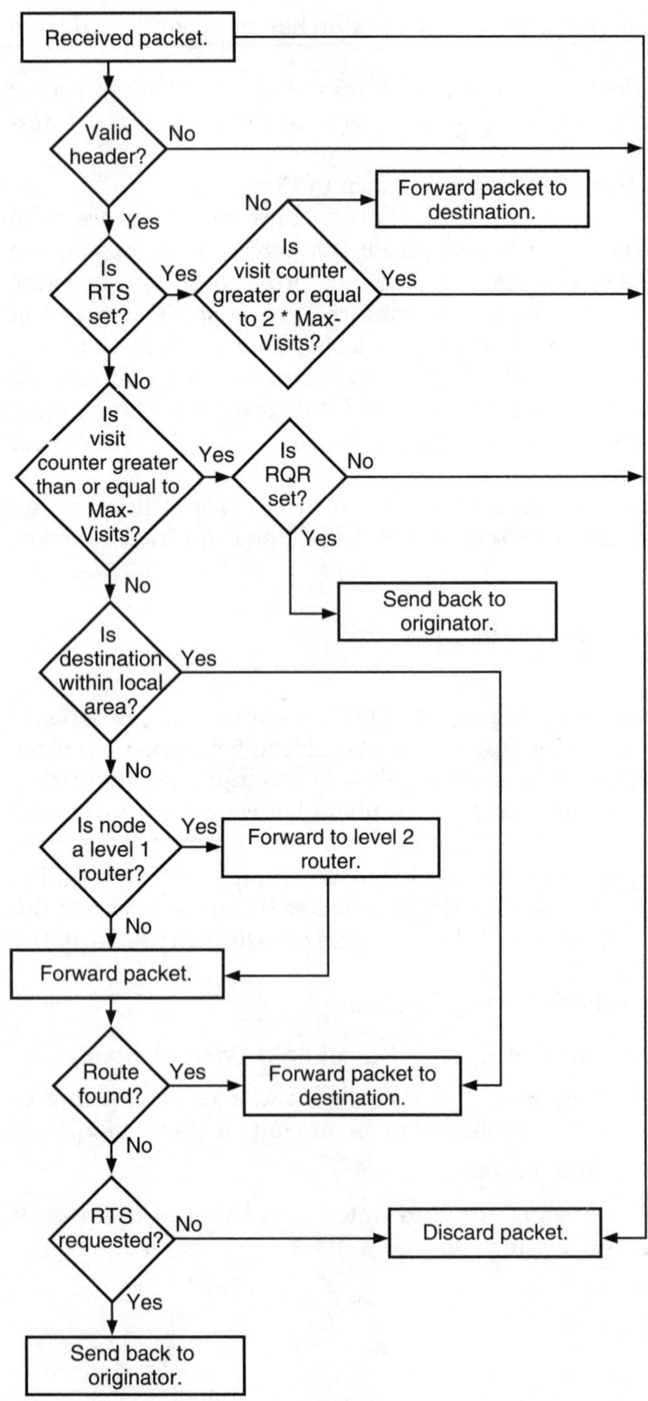

Figure 8.13 DECnet routing. (*Courtesy 3Com Corporation.*)

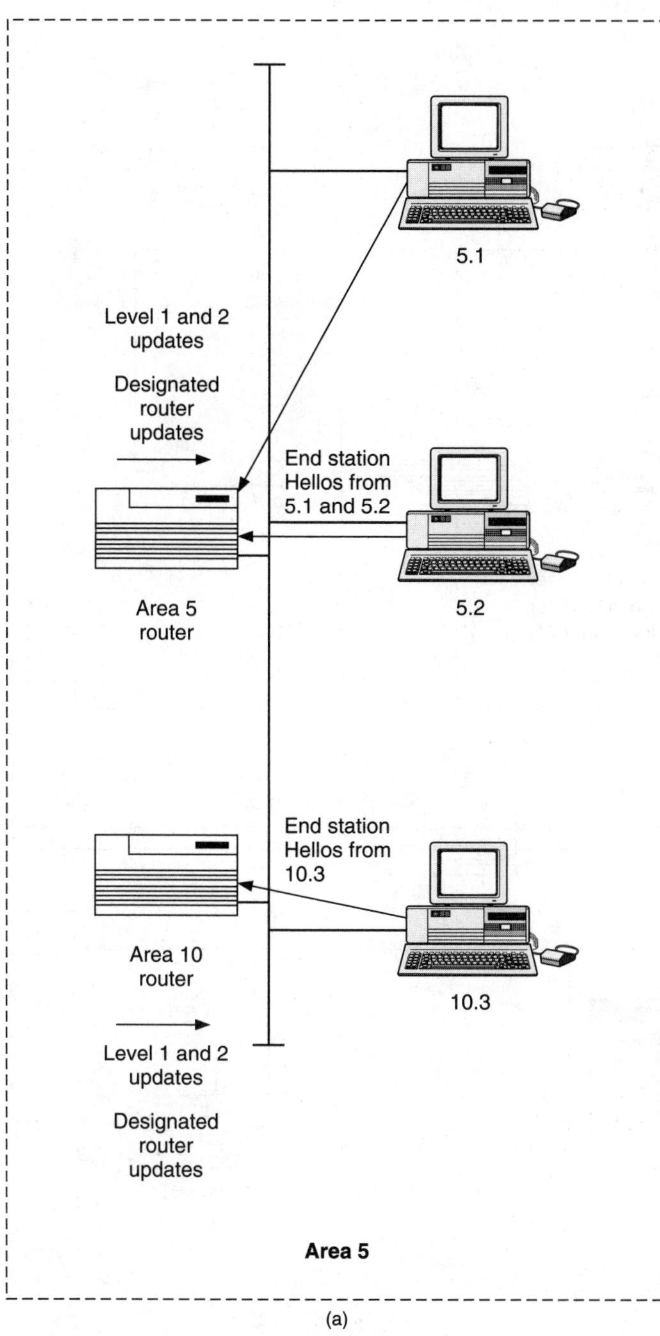

(a)

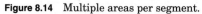

Figure 8.14 Multiple areas per segment.

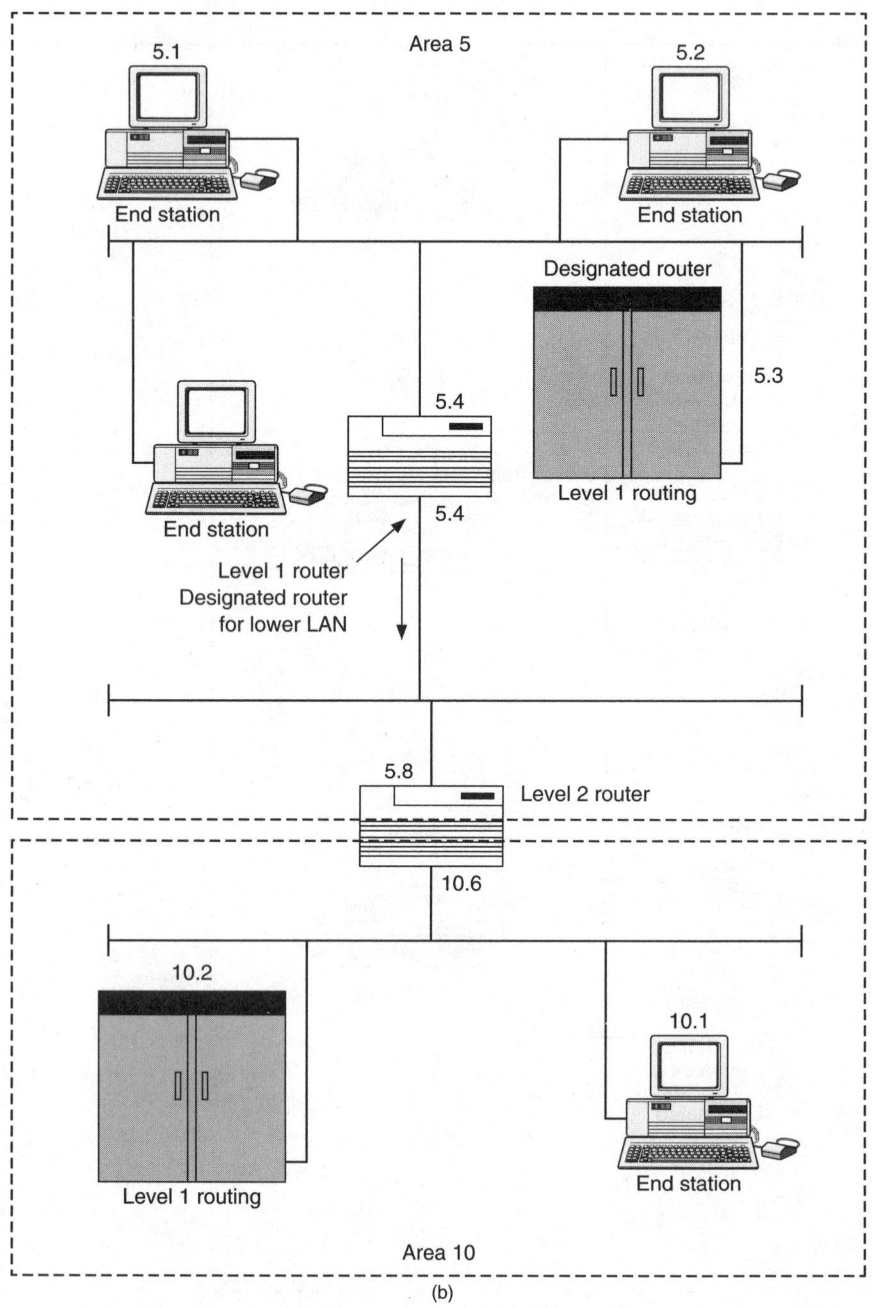

Figure 8.14 Typical DECnet internet.

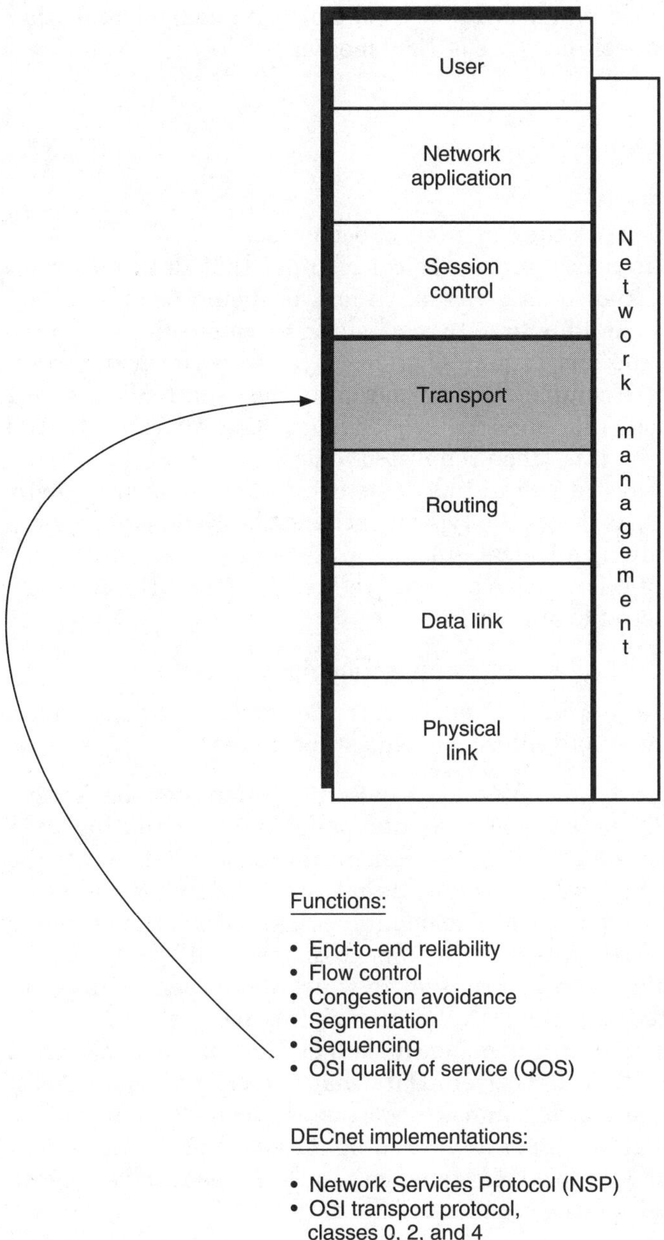

Figure 8.15 Functions of the transport layer. (*Courtesy Uyless Black.*)

To provide for logical link service, flow control, error control, and other functions, there are three types of NSP messages:

1. Data
2. Acknowledgment
3. Control

Table 8.3 expands upon the functions of each type.

A logical link is a full-duplex logical channel that data may pass over. This is also known as a virtual circuit. It should be stated here that the session layer of NSP only requests these connections; it is the responsibility of the end communications layer to perform the work. These processes are completely transparent to the user. NSP sets up a connection, manages it (provides sequencing and error control), and then terminates the link when requested to do so.

There may be several logical links between two stations or to many stations. Figure 8.16 shows the typical exchange between two end stations, A and B, having a logical link.

The exchange of information data between nodes A and B can be carried over two types of channels:

1. *Data channel.* Used to carry application data.
2. *Other data subchannel.* Used to carry interrupt messages, data request messages, and interrupt request messages.

The transport layer also fragments data into a size that the routing layer will carry. There is a maximum number of bytes the routing layer will handle, and it is up to NSP to fragment the data and give it to the routing layer. Each fragment will contain a special number and other control information in the Data Segment message, which the receiving NSP layer will have to interpret in order to understand how to put the data back together again in the order in which it was sent. Only data that is transmitted over the Data Channel is fragmented.

To provide for error control, each end of the virtual link must acknowledge data that it received. Data that is received too far out of sequence will be discarded and a negative acknowledgment will be sent to the originator. Any station sending data will not discard it (it will keep a copy of it in local RAM memory) until it has received a good acknowledgment from the recipient of the data.

Flow control. NSP provides flow control to ensure that memory is not overrun (buffer overflow). Both types of data (normal and interrupt) data can be flow-controlled. When the logical link is first established, both sides of the link tell each other how the flow of data should be handled. This is based on two types.

TABLE 8.3 NSP Messages

Type	Message	Description
Data	Data Segment	Carries a portion of a Session Control message. (This has been passed to Session Control from higher DNA layers and Session Control has added its own control information, if any.)
Data (also called Other Data)	Interrupt	Carries urgent data, originating from higher DNA layers. It also may contain an optional Data Segment acknowledgment.
	Data Request	Carries data flow control information and, optionally, a Data Segment acknowledgment (also called a Link Service message).
	Interrupt Request	Carries interrupt flow control information and optionally a Data Segment acknowledgment (Link Service message).
Acknowledgment	Data Acknowledgment	Acknowledges receipt of either a Connect Confirm message or one or more Data Segment messages and, optionally, an Other Data message.
	Other Data Acknowledgment	Acknowledges receipt of one or more Interrupt, Data Request, or Interrupt Request messages and, optionally, a Data Segment message.
	Connect	Acknowledges receipt of a Connect Initiate message.
Control	Connect Initiate and Retransmitted Connect Initiate	Carries a logical link Connect request from a Session Control module.
	Connect Confirm	Carries logical link Connect acceptance from a Session Control module.
	Disconnect Initiate	Carries logical link Connect rejection or Disconnect request from a Session Control module.
	No Resources	Sent when a Connect Initiate message is received and there are no resources to establish a new logical link (also called a Disconnect Confirm message).
	Disconnect Complete	Acknowledges the receipt of a Disconnect Initiate message (also called a Disconnect Confirm message).
	No Link	Sent when a message is received for a nonexistent logical link (also called Disconnect Confirm message).
	No Operation	Does nothing.

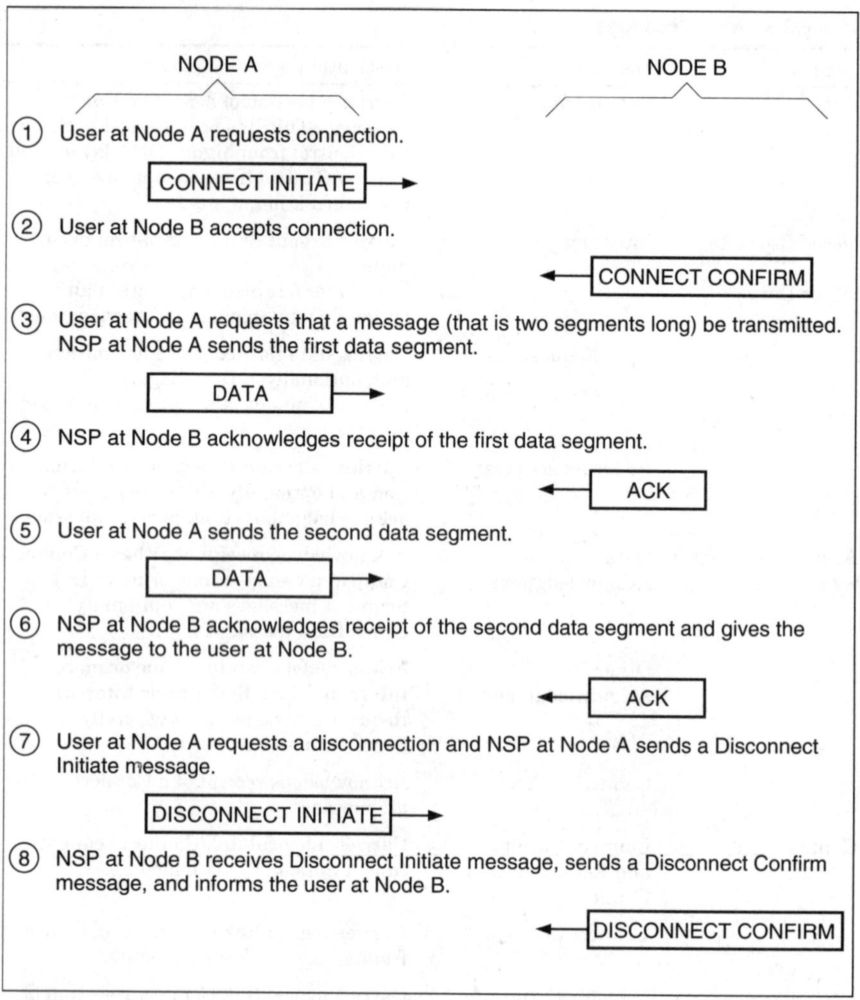

Figure 8.16 Typical message exchange between two implementations of NSP. (*Copyright © 1982 Digital Equipment Corporation.*)

1. No flow control.
2. The receiver will send the transmitter the number of data segments it can accept.

In addition to these rules, each receiving end of the link may at any time tell the opposite side (the transmitter) to stop sending data until further notice.

Figures 8.17 and 8.18 show the flow control and acknowledgment operations.

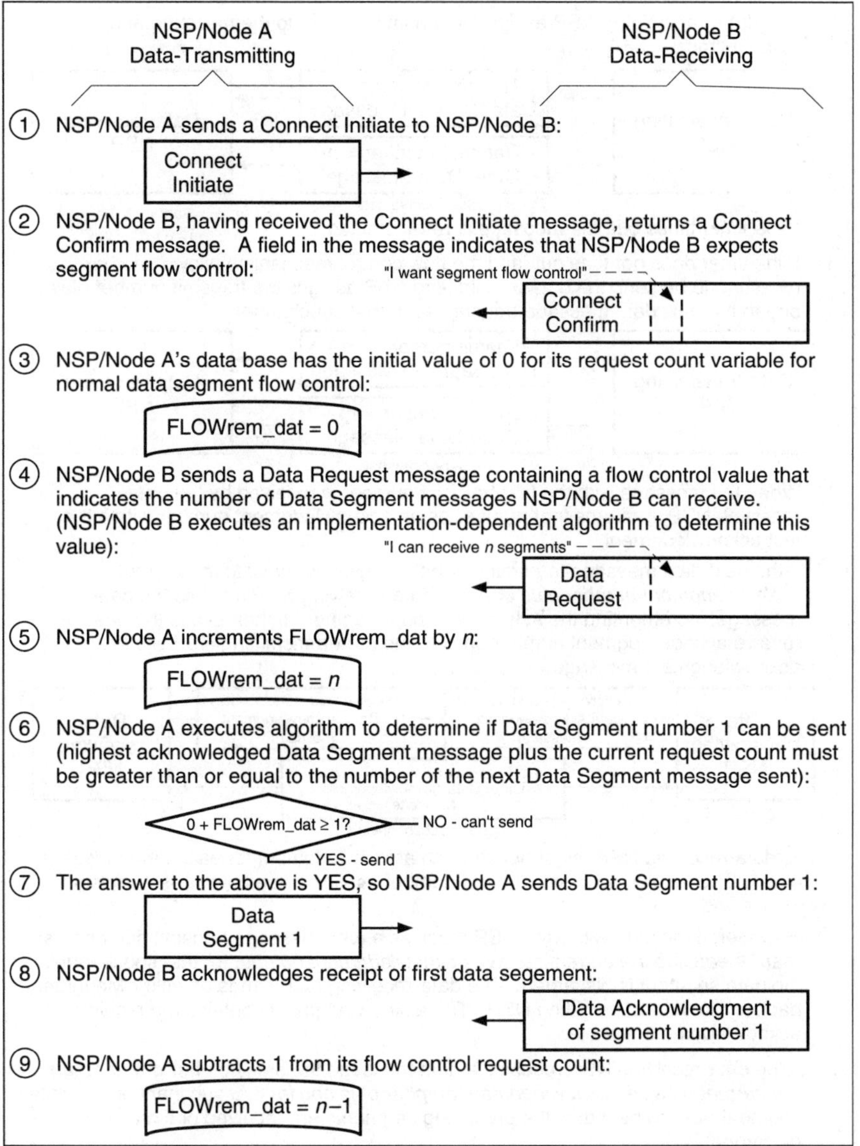

Figure 8.17 Segment flow control shown in one direction on a logical link. (*Copyright © 1982 Digital Equipment Corporation.*)

To provide for efficiency, any data type—whether it is a control data type or an application data segment—may contain the positive acknowledgment being returned for previously received data. This means that there is not necessarily a separate ACK packet for data that is being acknowledged.

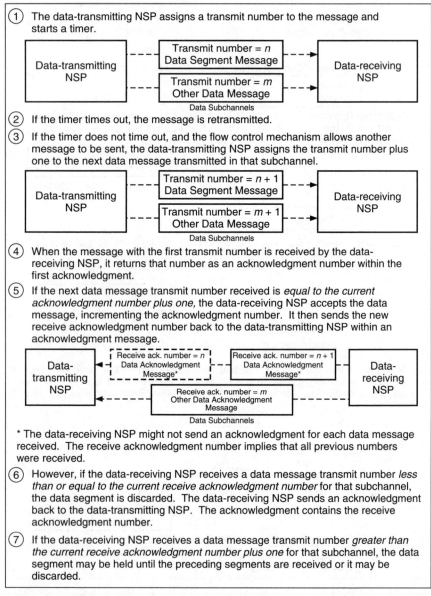

(1) The data-transmitting NSP assigns a transmit number to the message and starts a timer.

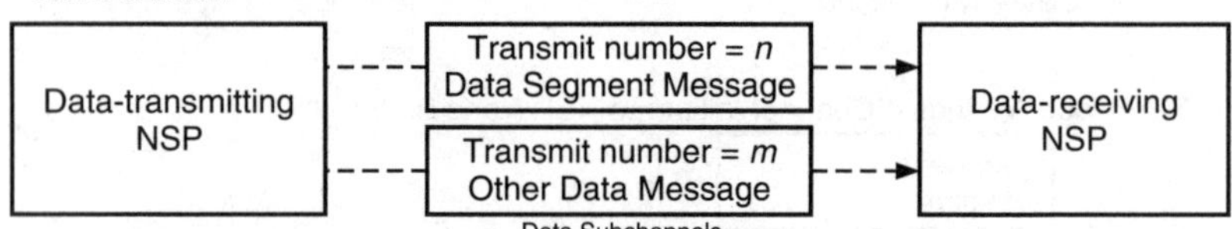

(2) If the timer times out, the message is retransmitted.

(3) If the timer does not time out, and the flow control mechanism allows another message to be sent, the data-transmitting NSP assigns the transmit number plus one to the next data message transmitted in that subchannel.

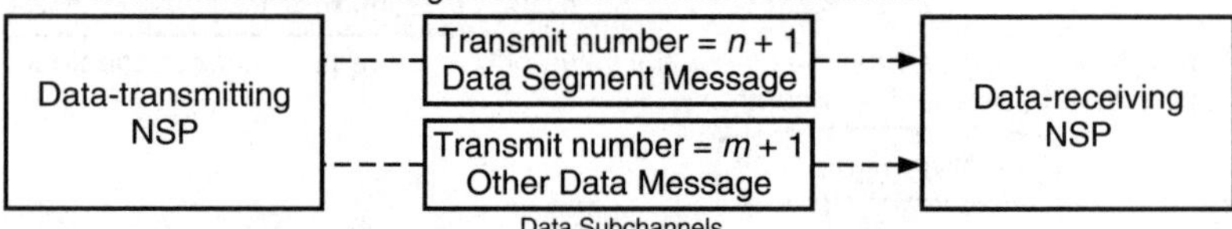

(4) When the message with the first transmit number is received by the data-receiving NSP, it returns that number as an acknowledgment number within the first acknowledgment.

(5) If the next data message transmit number received is *equal to the current acknowledgment number plus one,* the data-receiving NSP accepts the data message, incrementing the acknowledgment number. It then sends the new receive acknowledgment number back to the data-transmitting NSP within an acknowledgment message.

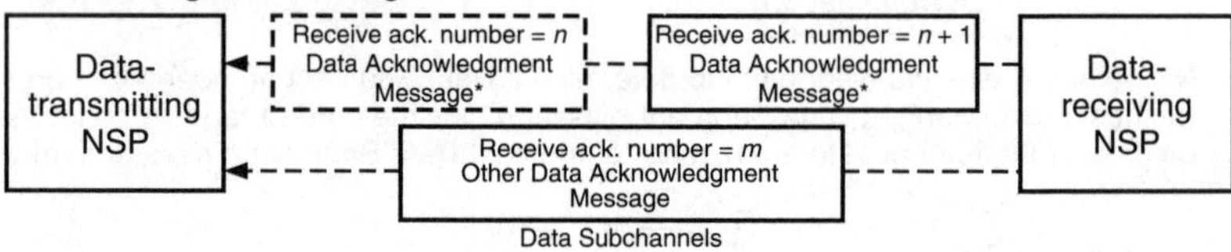

* The data-receiving NSP might not send an acknowledgment for each data message received. The receive acknowledgment number implies that all previous numbers were received.

(6) However, if the data-receiving NSP receives a data message transmit number *less than or equal to the current receive acknowledgment number* for that subchannel, the data segment is discarded. The data-receiving NSP sends an acknowledgment back to the data-transmitting NSP. The acknowledgment contains the receive acknowledgment number.

(7) If the data-receiving NSP receives a data message transmit number *greater than the current receive acknowledgment number plus one* for that subchannel, the data segment may be held until the preceding segments are received or it may be discarded.

Figure 8.18 Acknowledgment operation. (*Copyright © 1982 Digital Equipment Corporation.*)

The Session Control Layer

Refer to Fig. 8.19. This protocol resides at the fifth layer of the OSI model and provides the following functions:

Mapping of node names to node addresses. This maintains a node name mapping table that provides a translation between a node name and a node address or its adjacency. This allows for the session layer to select the destination node address or channel number for outgoing connect requests to the end communication layer. For any incoming connection requests, it allows the session control layer to properly identify the node that is making the connect request.

Identifying end users. This process determines if a process exists as requested by an incoming connection request.

Activating or creating processes. The session control layer may start up a process or activate an existing process to handle an incoming connect request.

Validating incoming connect request. Performs a validation sequence to find out if the incoming connect request should be processed.

These functions are divided into five actions:

1. *Requests a logical link between itself and a remote node.* If the application desires a logical link between itself and a remote node, it will request the session layer for this. It will identify the destination node address or a channel number for the end communication layer by using the node name-mapping table. It will format the data for the end communication layer and issue a connect request to this layer. It will then start an outgoing connection timer. If this timer expires before hearing from the destination (accept or reject), it will cause a disconnect to be reported back to the requesting application layer.
2. *Accepts or rejects a connect from a remote node.* The end communication layer will tell the session control layer of a connection request from a remote (destination) node. The session-control layer will check the incoming packet for source and destination end-user processes (socket or port numbers). With this it will identify, create, or activate the destination end-user process. When the session control layer reads the incoming connection request packet, it will enter a destination address with a destination name in its table. After all this, it will deliver any end-user data to the destination application process. It will also validate any access control information. Refer to Fig. 8.15.
3. *Sends and receives data across a valid logical link.* Basically, it will pass any data between the application layer to the end communication layer to be delivered to the network.

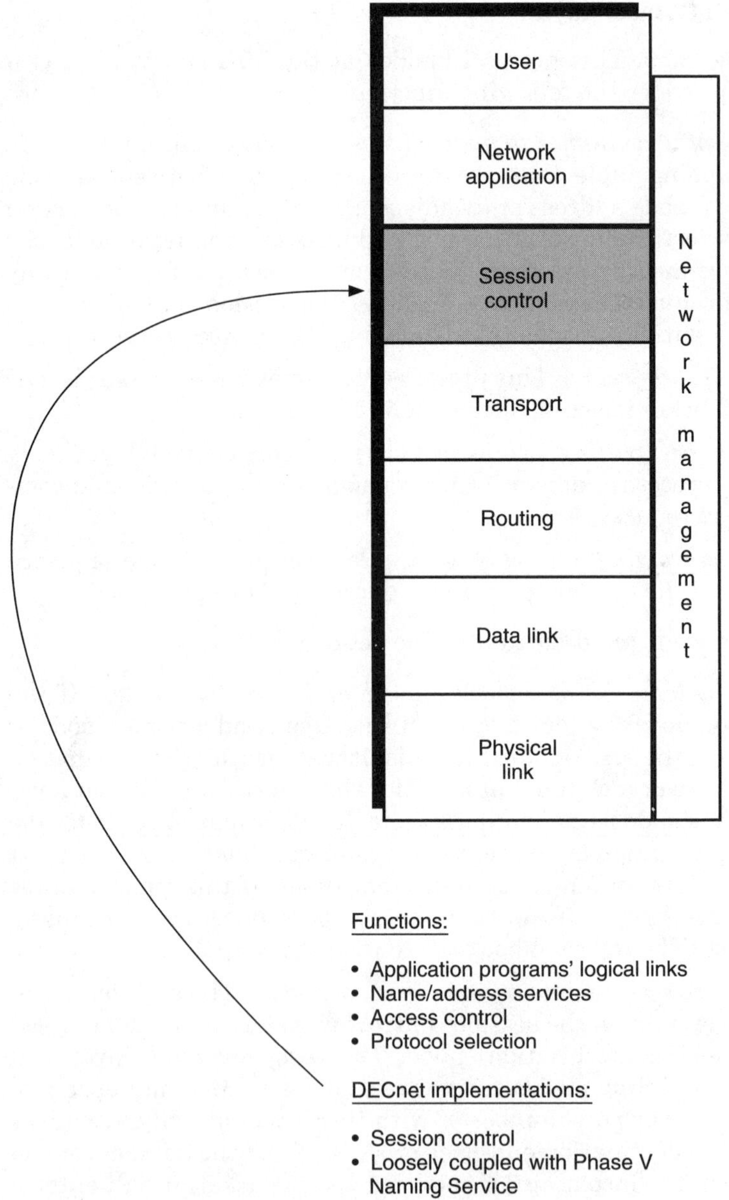

Figure 8.19 The session control layer. (*Courtesy Uyless Black.*)

4. *Disconnects or aborts an existing logical link.* Upon notification from the application process, it will disconnect the session between two communicating nodes. Also, it will accept disconnect requests from the destination node and will deliver this to the application.
5. *Monitors the logical link*

Figure 8.20 shows the relationship between the user processes, the session control and end communication layers.

Network Application Layer

DECnet defines at this layer the following modules, also shown in Fig. 8.21:

1. The Data Access Protocol (DAP) is the remote file access protocol. It enables file transfer between nodes on the DECnet network.
2. The Network Virtual Terminal Protocol (NVT) is the protocol that allows remote terminals to act as if they were local to the processor—the ability to "remote" to another host and act as if that terminal were locally attached.
3. The X.25 Gateway Access Protocol is the protocol that allows DECnet to interoperate over an X.25 link. This protocol is beyond the scope of this book.
4. The SNA Access Protocol allows a DECnet network to interoperate with IBM's SNA. This protocol is beyond the scope of this book.

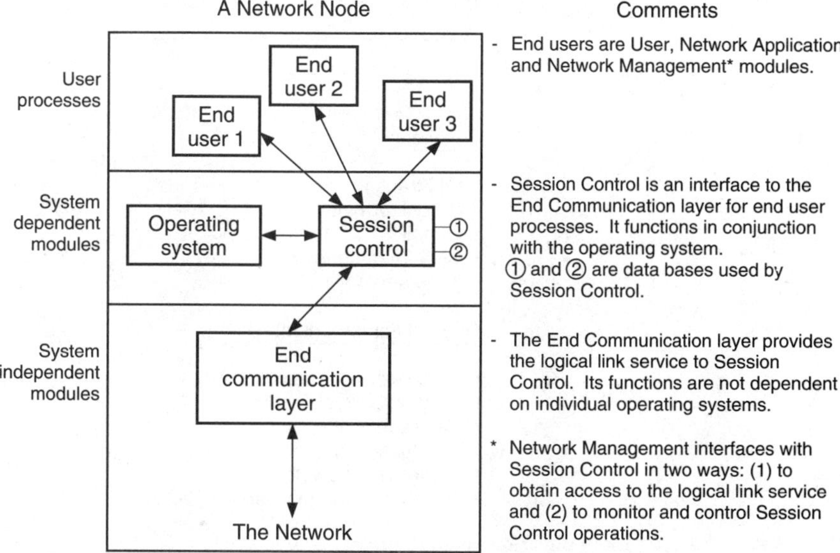

Figure 8.20 Session control model. (*Copyright © 1982 Digital Equipment Corporation.*)

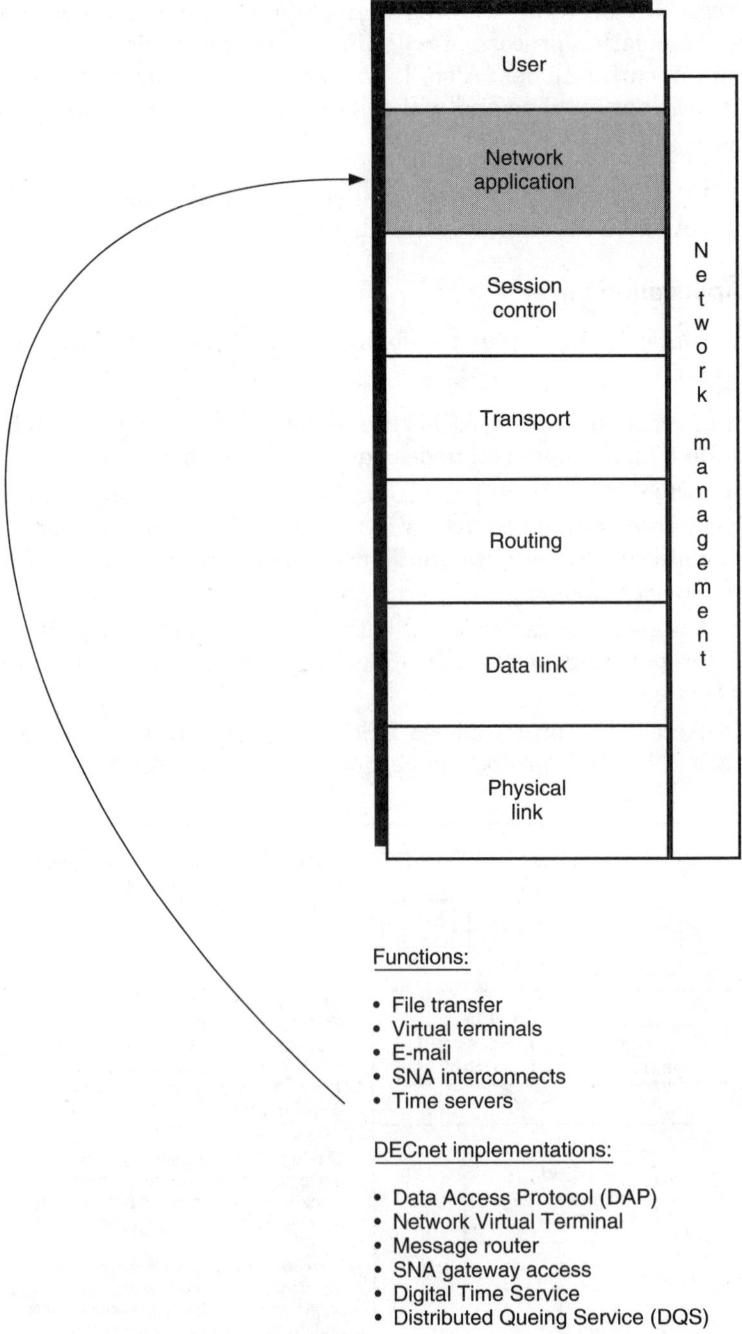

Figure 8.21 The network application layer. (*Courtesy Uyless Black.*)

5. The Loopback Mirror Protocol tests logical links. This protocol is beyond the scope of this book.

Data access protocol (DAP)

The Data Access Protocol is an application-level protocol. DAP permits remote file access within DNA environments.

The following is a listing of the functions of the DAP protocol:

1. Supports heterogeneous file systems
2. Retrieves a file from an input device (a disk file, a card reader, a terminal, etc.)
3. Stores a file on an output device (a magnetic tape, a line printer, a terminal, etc.)
4. Transfers files between nodes
5. Supports deletion and renaming of remote files
6. Lists directories of remote files
7. Recovers from transient errors and reports fatal error to the user
8. Allows multiple data streams to be sent over a logical link
9. Submits and executes remote command files
10. Permits sequential, random, and indexed (ISAM*) access of records
11. Supports sequential, relative, and indexed file organizations
12. Supports wildcard file specification for sequential file retrieval, file deletion, file renaming, and command file execution
13. Permits an optional file checksum to ensure file integrity

DAP operation

The DAP process, by the source and destination communicating station, exchanges a series of messages. The initiation message contains information about operating a file system, buffer size, etc. These are negotiation parameters. Table 8.4 indicates this messages.

Figure 8.22 shows a node-to-node file transfer using DAP and Fig. 8.23 shows a file transfer over a DECnet network.

Network virtual terminal (NVT)

As shown in Fig. 8.24, there are times when a user connected to one host may need a connection to another host on the network. Figure 8.24 shows the overall process for this. The following paragraphs will explain Fig. 8.24.

---

* Indexed Sequential Access Method.

TABLE 8.4 DAP Messages

Message	Function
Configuration	Exchanges system capability and configuration information between DAP-speaking processes. Sent immediately after a logical link is established, this message contains information about the operating system, the file system, protocol version, and buffering capability.
Attributes	Provides information on how data is structured in the file being accessed. The message contains information on file organization, data type, format, record attributes, record length, size, and device characteristics.
Access	Specifies the file name and type of access requested (read, write, etc.).
Control	Sends control information to a file system and establishes data streams.
Continue-Transfer	Allows recovery from errors. Used for retry, skip, and abort after an error is reported.
Acknowledge	Acknowledges access commands and control messages used to establish data streams.
Access Complete	Denotes termination of access.
Data	Transfers file data over the logical link.
Status	Returns status and information on error conditions.
Key Definition Attributes Extension	Specifies key definitions for indexed files.
Allocation Attributes Extension	Specifies the character of the allocation when creating or explicitly extending a file.
Summary Attributes Extension	Returns summary information about a file.
Date and Time Attributes Extension	Specifies time-related information about a file.
Protection Attributes Extension	Specifies file protection codes.
Name	Sends name information when renaming a file or obtaining file directory data.

This protocol allows terminal communications to exist remotely as if the terminal were directly attached to the remote computer.

The main protocol that is used for NVT is called the Terminal Communication Protocol. It is the lower of the two sublayers (the other protocol is the Command Terminal Protocol, discussed later) of the Network Virtual Terminal Service, also known as the foundation layer. Its main goal is to establish and disconnect terminal sessions between applications and terminals. You may think of this as extending the session-control layer to establishing and disconnecting sessions between end points (applications) that are specific to terminals. The end point

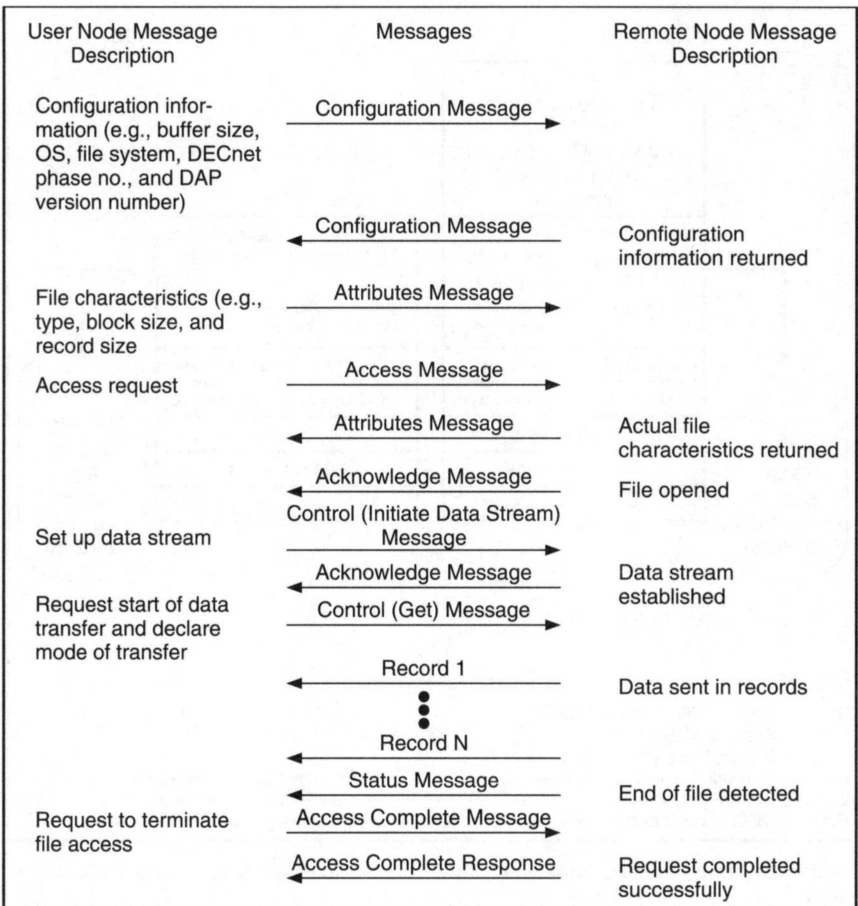

Figure 8.22 DAP message exchange (sequential file retrieval). (*Copyright © 1982 Digital Equipment Corporation.*)

in the host is called the *portal* and the end point in the terminal end is called the *logical terminal.* A portal is a remote terminal identifier in the host, and a connection binds that identifier to an actual terminal. An NVT connection is called a *binding.*

Table 8.5 shows the messages that are used between the terminal and its host using the Terminal Communication Protocol.

The Command Terminal Protocol. The is the second sublayer of NVT. It offers a set of functions mainly oriented toward command-line input. After a connection between a host and network terminal is made, it is this layer that provides control over the network. The control messages that the terminal and host pass between them are shown in Table 8.6.

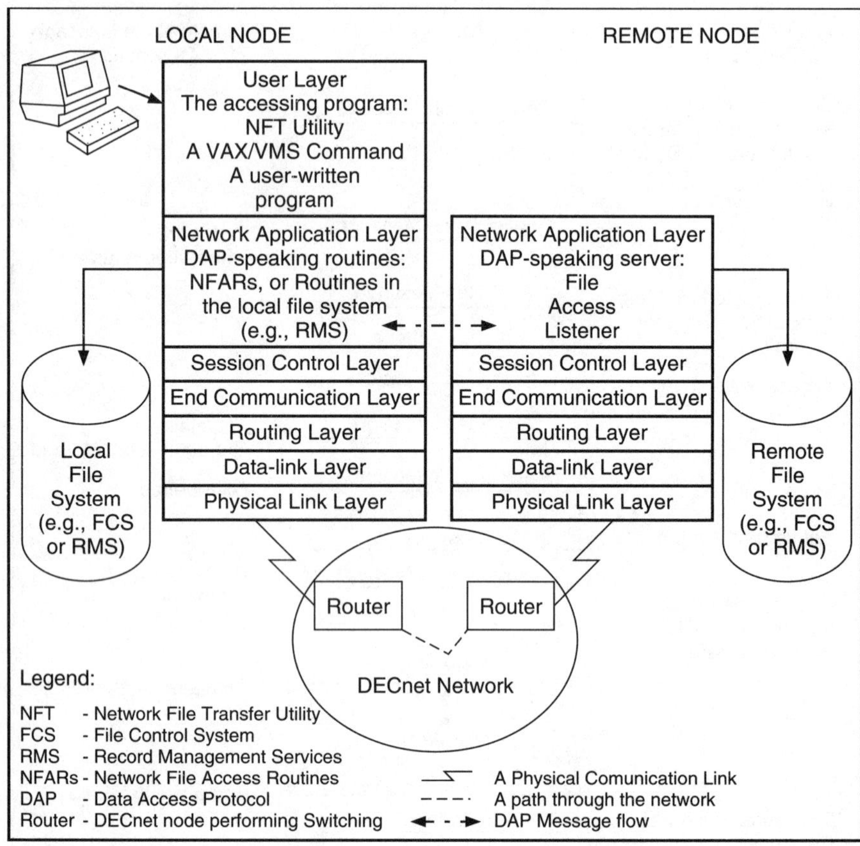

Figure 8.23 File transfer across a network. *(Copyright © 1982 Digital Equipment Corporation.)*

Operation of NVT. With a terminal session between a terminal and a host, the active terminal will request a binding to the destination host. This is shown in Fig. 8.24. The terminal management module in the server system requests a binding to the host system. To accomplish this, it will invoke the services of the terminal communication services function (these actions are listed in Table 8.5). Most DECnet users will know this as the SET HOST <Hostname> command entered at the terminal. The SET HOST will allow a user at one host to connect to another host over the network. That is, a terminal connected to host A may now connect to a remote host B over the network (usually Ethernet).

The terminal communication service tries to connect to the remote system by requesting a logical link from the session control layer. At the destination host, the incoming logical link request is accepted and allocates a portal. This is the beginning of the binding. The host module should accept the logical link. Once the logical link has been established,

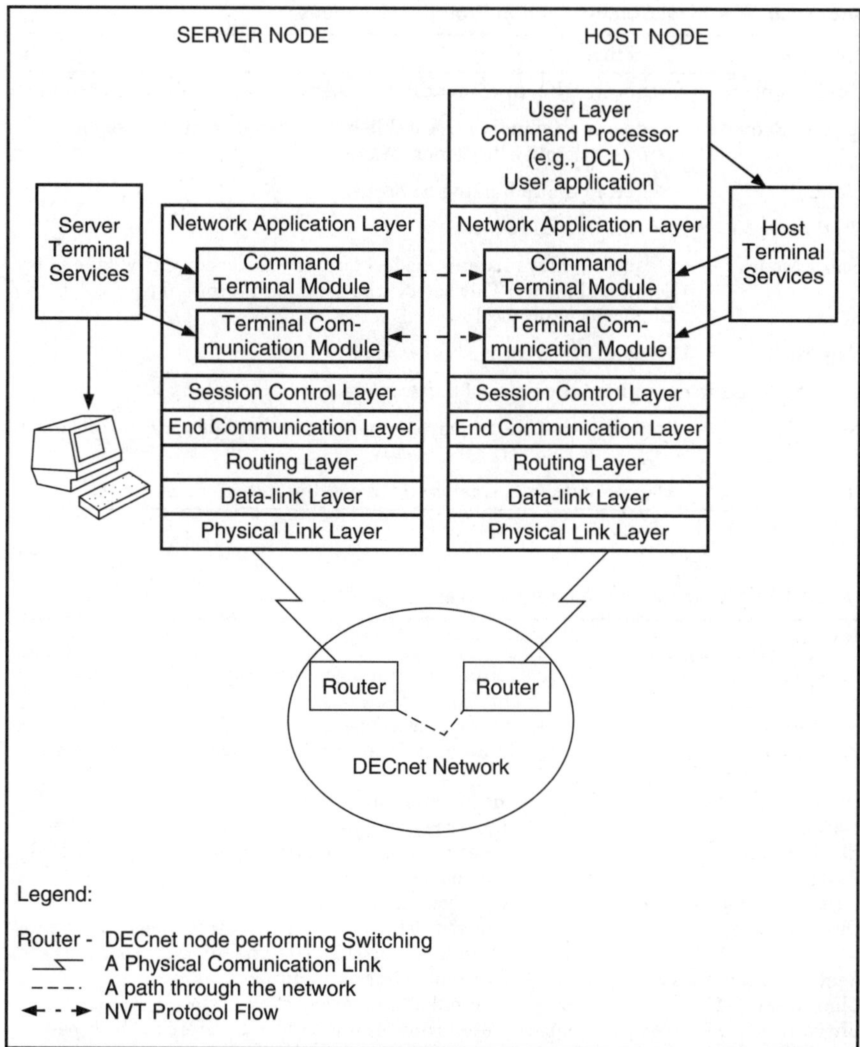

Figure 8.24 Network virtual terminal service. *(Copyright © 1982 Digital Equipment Corporation.)*

the Bind Request is sent and, if accepted, a Bind Accept message will be sent back to the requester. This binding has now been established.

Now that the binding has formed, the host will enter into command mode (the command terminal protocol will now interact on the connection). This action will take place in the first terminal request from the login process. Both ends of the connection will now enter into the command terminal protocol and will remain with this protocol until the end of the connection. Requests and responses will then take place as data is transferred across the link using the command terminal protocol.

TABLE 8.5 Terminal Communication Protocol Messages

Message	Function
Bind Request	Requests a binding; identifies version and type of sending system.
Rebind Request	Requests a rebinding (reestablishes broken communications) for high-availability implementations.
Unbind	Requests that a binding be broken.
Bind Accept	Accepts a bind request.
Enter Mode	Requests entry of a new mode. (The only mode currently defined is command mode.) This selects the command terminal protocol as the higher-level protocol
Exit Mode	Requests that the current mode be exited.
Confirm Mode	Confirms the entry of a new mode.
No Mode	Indicates that the requested mode is not available or confirms an exit mode request.
Data	Carries data (i.e., command terminal protocol information).

TABLE 8.6 Command Terminal Protocol Messages

Message	Function
Initiate	Carries initialization information, as well as protocol and implementation version numbers.
Start Read	Requests that a READ be issued to the terminal.
Read Data	Carries input data from terminal on completion of a read request.
Out-of-band	Carries out-of-band input data.
Unread	Cancels a prior read request.
Clear Input	Requests that the input and type-ahead buffers be cleared.
Write	Requests the output of data to the terminal.
Write Complete	Carries write completion status.
Discard State	Carries a change to the output discard state due to a terminal operator request (via an entered output discard character).
Read Characteristics	Requests terminal characteristics.
Characteristics	Carries terminal characteristics.
Check Input	Requests input count (number of characters in the type-ahead and input buffers combined).
Input Count	Carries input count as requested with Check Input.
Input State	Indicates a change from zero to nonzero and vice versa in the number of characters in the input and type-ahead buffers combined.

The application program in the host system will send terminal service requests to the host operating system terminal services. The host terminal services issue corresponding requests to the host protocol module of a logout of the user from the host. Host terminal services issue corresponding requests to the host protocol module. The server protocol module reproduces those requests remotely and reissues them to the server terminal services.

Termination of this link usually comes from the application program running in the host system. This will happen by a logout by the host application With this, the host terminal communication services will send an Unbind request. The server will respond by releasing the link also. Finally, the host disconnects the logical link.

Figure 8.25 shows NVT message exchanges during this connection.

Figure 8.26 shows the highest layer of the DNA model. This is the user layer. This layer consists of the users or user applications that were written or are being used in a networked environment. This could be specifically written network management, database, or a program that is not part of the DNA model but uses DNA as part of it operation.

Finally, Fig. 8.27 shows the Network Management layer used by DNA. It will not be further explained here, but the figure shows the management functions of DNA.

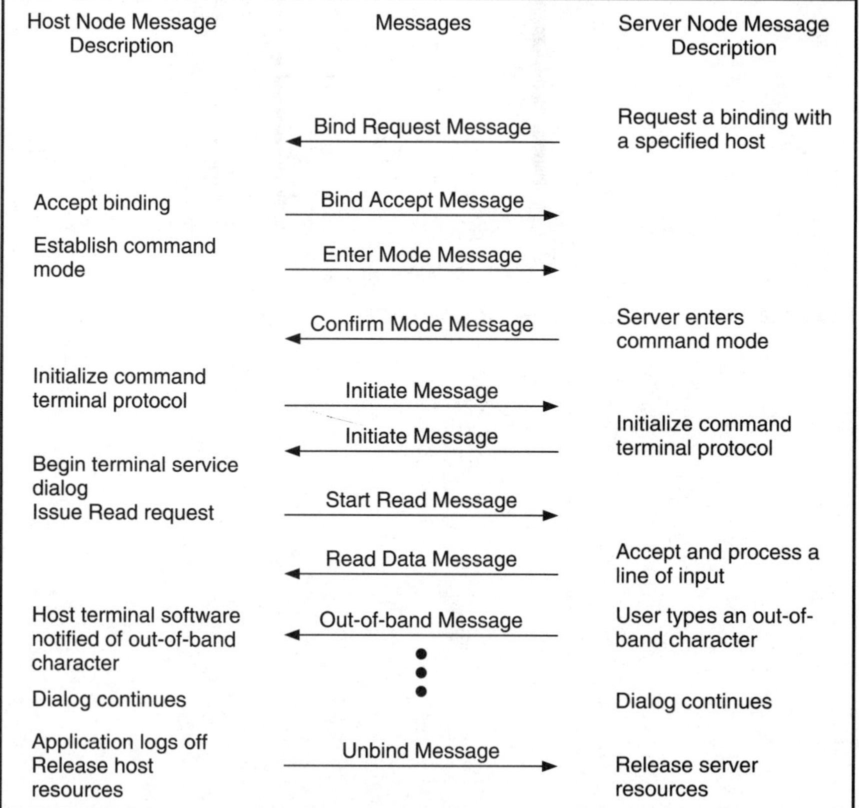

Figure 8.25 Protocol message exchange. (*Copyright © 1982 Digital Equipment Corporation.*)

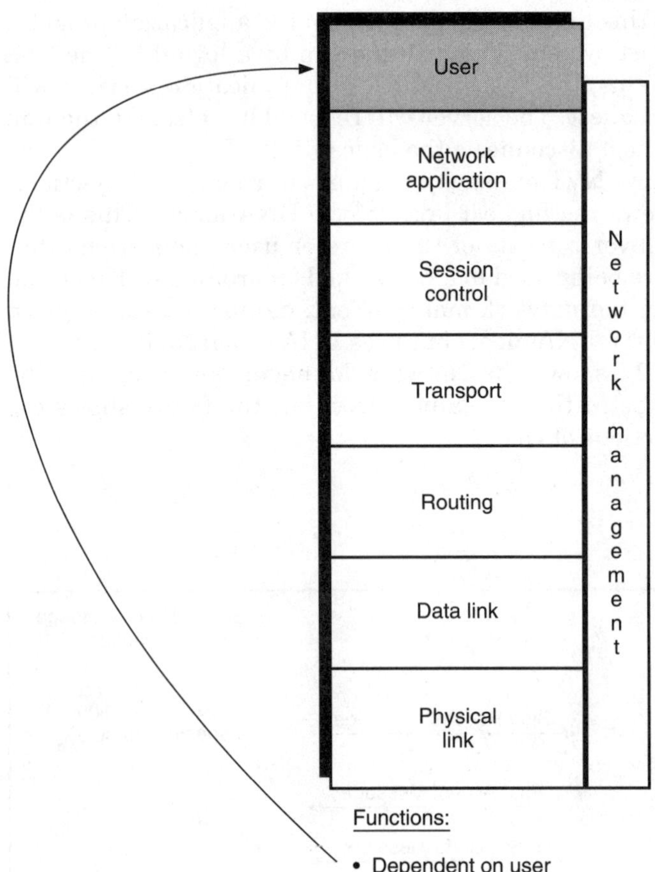

Figure 8.26 The user layer. (*Courtesy Uyless Black.*)

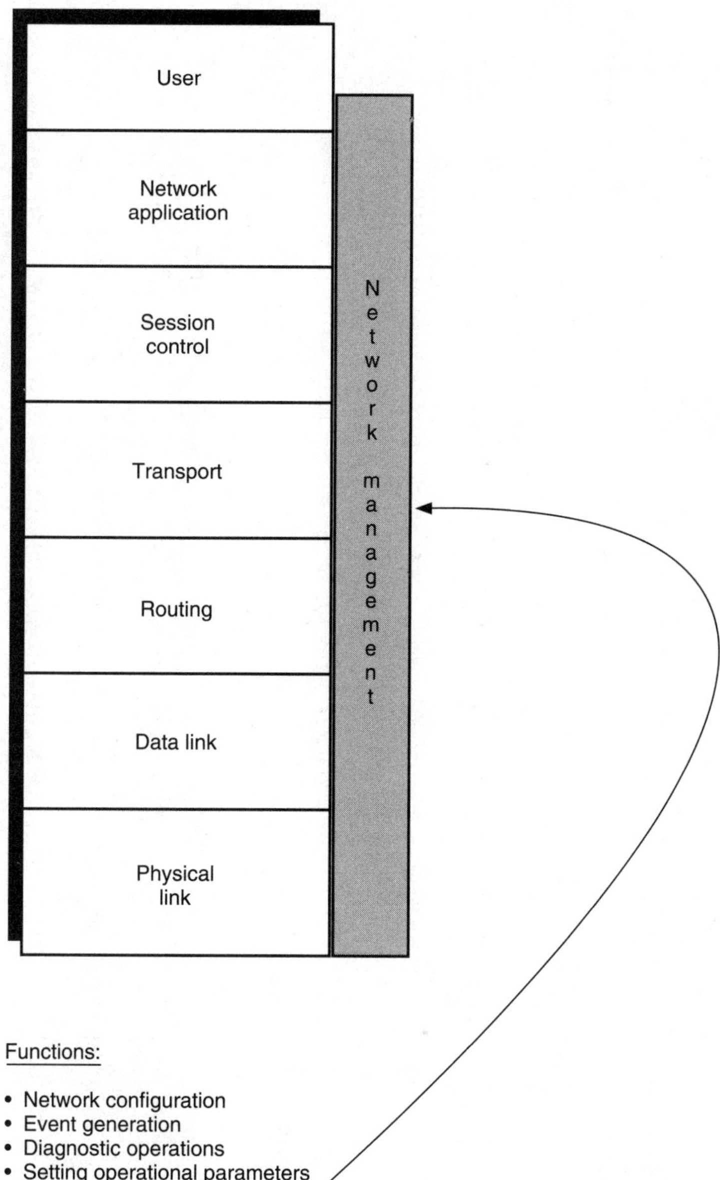

Figure 8.27 Network management. (*Courtesy Uyless Black.*)

Chapter

9

Local Area Transport (LAT)

The Local Area Transport protocol (LAT) is a Digital Equipment Corporation proprietary protocol whose primary function is to allow for the exchange of data between a terminal server service (whether this service is a terminal emulation on a personal computer or a communications server) and its respective application host. These functions have been expanded to include direct host access and direct application access. It is primarily a session layer protocol only and does not have a routing (network) layer involved. The layering of this protocol is shown in Figs. 9.1 and 9.2.

Refer to Fig. 9.1. LAT is sublayered as follows:

1. Service class sublayer
2. Slot sublayer
3. Virtual circuit sublayer

Figure 9.2 defines each of these sublayers. In these figures you should notice that LAT is defined at the OSI session layer. It does not provide network layer services and therefore cannot be routed. It also is allowed to run on top of any data link that IEEE provides. Mainly, it is used on Ethernet/IEEE 802.3 LANs, but is being migrated over to IEEE 802.5 (Token Ring) LANs. The terms that are used in these figures will be discussed in detail after the following explanation on LAT node types. The LAT protocol may be only bridged to another network. It cannot be routed. LAT networks can only be extended by bridges.

Node Types on a LAT LAN

1. *Terminal server.* An asynchronous terminal device that has multiple asynchronous connections on one end and a network connection

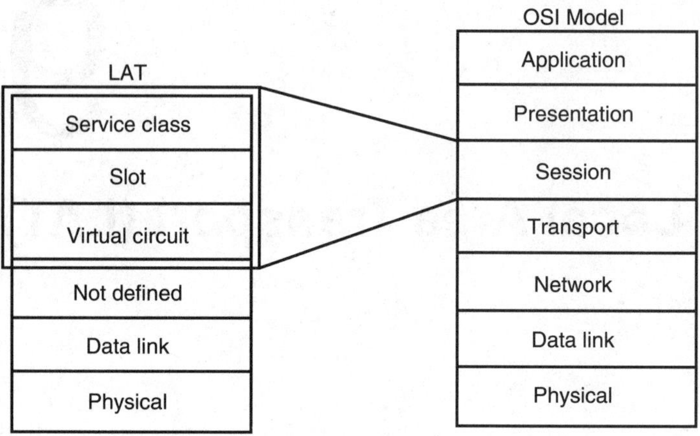

Figure 9.1 LAT and the OSI model. (*Copyright © 1982 Digital Equipment Corporation.*)

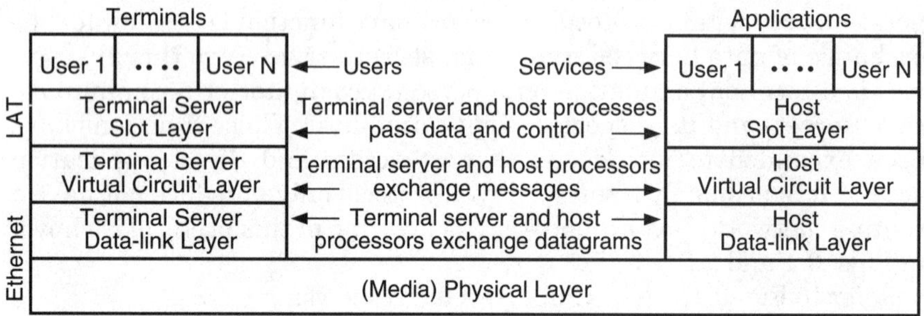

Figure 9.2 LAT layer definitions. (*Copyright © 1982 Digital Equipment Corporation.*)

on the other end. Users can access LAT services on these devices and initiate sessions on these devices.

2. *Load host.* This device is a network station that can download the LAT software to a terminal server. This device is not always needed. Some terminal servers have a local boot device (a local floppy) that can load the LAT software into the terminal server.

The most common environment for the LAT protocol involves a device known as a terminal server. The other name for this device is a communication server. Therefore, in this text, the device will be called a *comm server.*

Comm servers allow any devices that support primarily the asynchronous communications protocol to attach to a network. Refer to Fig. 9.3. This is the anatomy of a comm server. This device has multiple asynchronous connections on one end and one network connection. This device represents one of the older data communications devices in

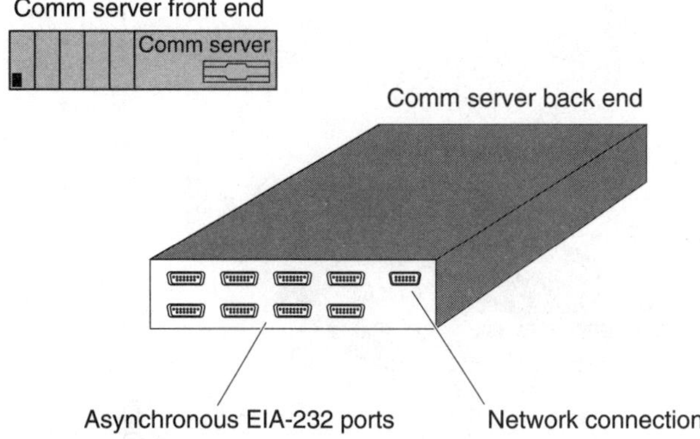

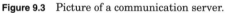

Figure 9.3 Picture of a communication server.

the LAN arena. This device allows asynchronous devices (such as modems, printers, terminals, and even some host ports) connection to a LAN. It is an asynchronous multiplexor.

Communication servers today are still attaching to hosts, terminals, printers, and other serial devices. But with most terminals being replaced by personal computers, and mini and mainframe computers having built-in network controllers, communication servers are providing communications connectivity in a different manner. They are being used in three basic areas, predominately in modem and printer pools. The third is the terminal interface.

Refer to Fig. 9.4. This figure shows the aforementioned devices connected to a comm server. At the bottom of the picture is a modem connection. Modem pools are groups of modems clustered together for use by anyone who has access to the comm server. By connecting modems directly to a communication server, any user with access to the network may have access to one of the modems (provided that no user has already established a connection to that modem port on the comm server). Instead of a company buying one modem for each user on the network, they can buy a few modems, connect them to a comm server and then have the users access the modems through the network. This is extremely efficient, for few modems were used 100 percent of the time. With a connection to the comm server, modems are now accessed by multiple users, thereby increasing the use of the modem. Even if the modem port on the comm server is busy, most networking companies have developed their comm server-to-queue requests to a particular communication server port.

For printers, comm servers can provide remote printing capabilities. For example, a comm server may be connected to the host computer. Another communication server may be placed somewhere on the net-

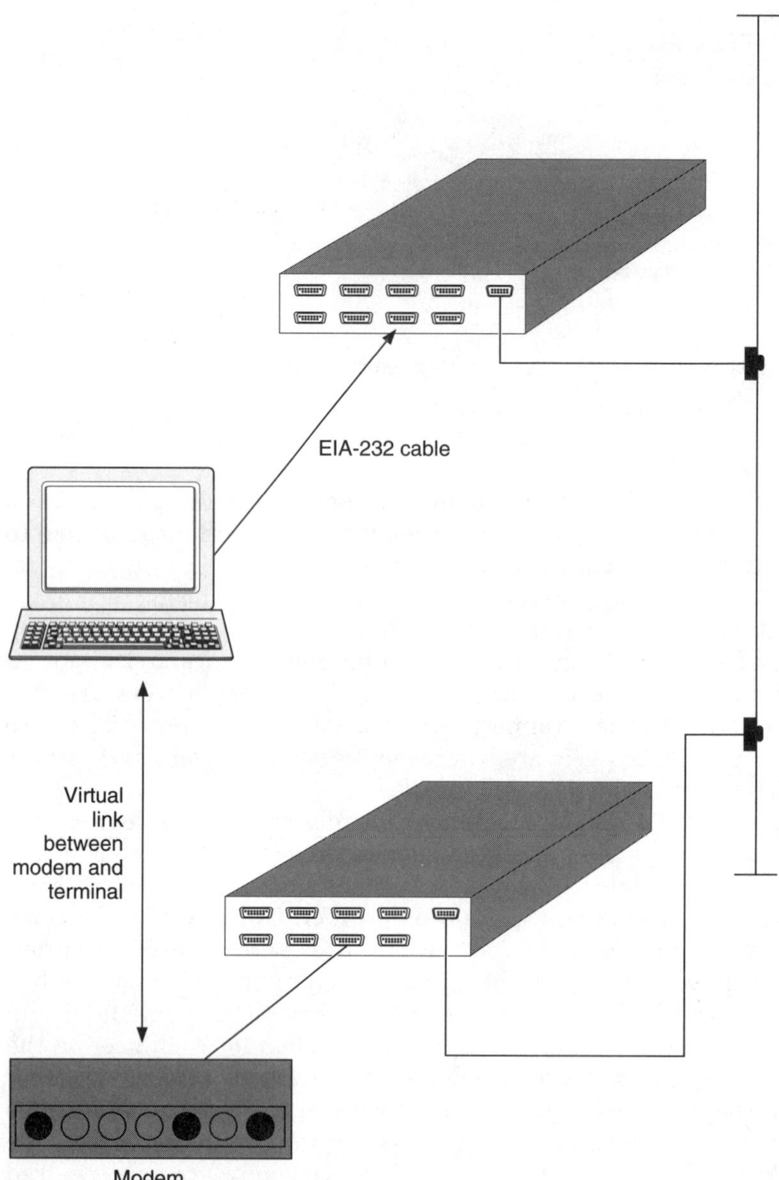

Figure 9.4 Communication server connections.

work. This comm server may have a printer attached to it. A virtual circuit (a session) will be established between the two servers. The print job that is submitted on the host is printed to the comm server and that server will send the data over the network to the comm server with the printer attached.

Devices are connected to the comm server with some type of cable, usually a EIA-232 cable. The comm server is connected to the network. The comm servers provide a virtual connection (a software connection) over the LAN between two devices. Some hosts with an internal network controller (direct attachment to the LAN) have the capability to send the data over the network without the communication server attached to it. A comm server may connect to another comm server or to a directly attached network device.

There are two primary ways to create sessions using comm servers. One is a user-initiated command and the other is an application-initiated command.

With the user-initiated command (connected to a comm sever), the user would attach the device to the comm server. Once the comm server is operational with its internal LAN operating software (in this case, LAT), the user will enter a connect command to the comm server to indicate to the comm server a connection is wanted. This connect command will usually be sent with a name in the form "connect VAX1," where VAX1 is the service name to which the user would like a connection. Refer to Fig. 9.5. This connection is for a service between two comm servers. The virtual link is a software connection that has been established between the comm server and the host computer. The comm server can initiate multiple virtual connections with only one connection on the LAN segment.

Once the connection is made by the two communication servers, the user will never know that they are operating on a comm server. The connection will emulate a direct connection between the terminal and the host.

For a host to connect to a service on the LAN, the setup process is similar, except the host will make the connection with user intervention.

Comm servers may also connect directly to a service that is not another comm server. With this, the remote connection will have a direct connection to the LAN. The comm server may still access this remote service, just as if it were a comm server. The only requirement for all connections is that the LAN software that encapsulates the data to be transferred into a LAN packet must be the same on both sides of the connection.

For the purposes of this chapter, the text will be based on the LAT protocol by Digital Equipment Corporation. LAT is an extremely fast and efficient protocol that allows data to be exchanged between two

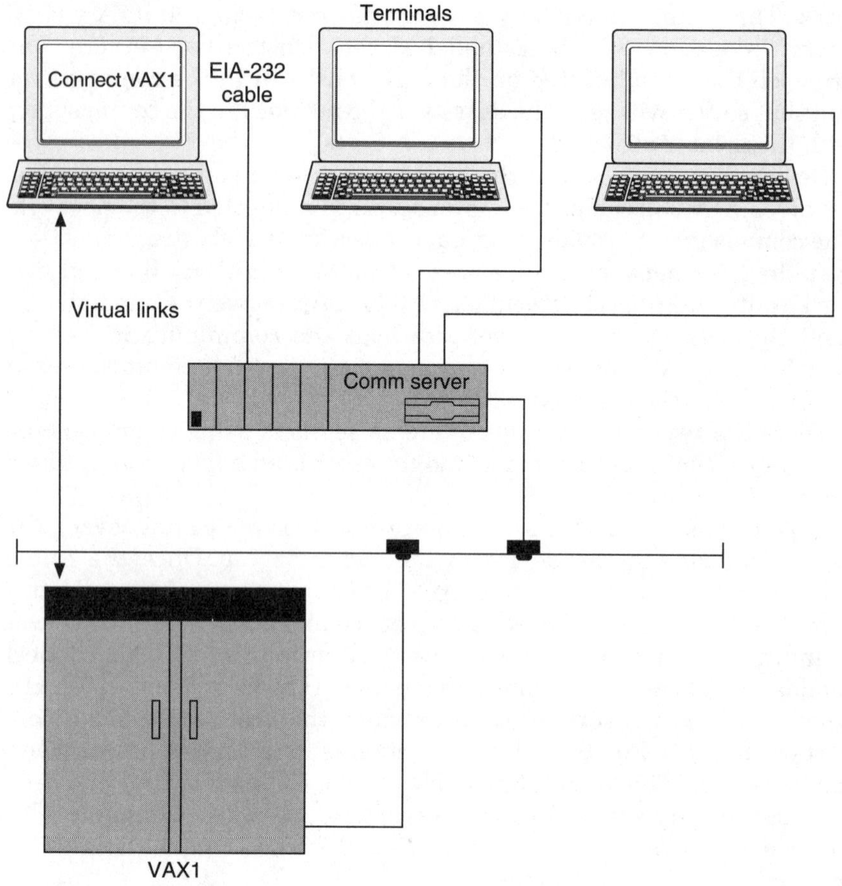

Figure 9.5 Communication server links.

network stations. This protocol is a proprietary protocol written by DEC and was primarily intended to operate their comm servers and give those comm servers connections to services over the LAN. It is meant to operate on a highly reliable, high-bandwidth LAN.

Considering the protocol is proprietary, only the functions of the protocol will be discussed in this text. Packet formats and protocol specifics will not be discussed.

LAT Topology

LAT network stations may communicate on a local LAN or they may be separated by a bridge (Digital documentation refers to this as an *extended network*). Since LAT contains no network layer protocols, it will not operate through a router. It may operate through a router only if that router also supports the transparent bridging protocols. This type of router is known as a *multiprotocol router.* See Chap. 2 on Ethernet and Token Ring for more details on this type of router.

The LAT protocol also assumes that once a connection is established between two network stations, one end or the other (not both) will maintain this connection. Furthermore, the LAT protocol assumes that the bandwidth of the medium (the LAN) is larger than the bandwidth needed for one LAT session. This is needed since the LAT protocol may run over any access method, including serial lines.

This presents a serious consideration of the LAT protocol. It is an extremely fast protocol, and a session may time-out waiting on a response from a remote session. This will not happen when the protocol is operating over a high-speed LAN such as Ethernet. But, when the Ethernet LAN is extended through devices such as a bridge and the remote bridge connection is a slow-speed serial line, the session may time-out. Speeds needed to run LAT over a serial line are usually T1 and above. Speeds at 56 Kbps and below will introduce delays long enough to cause time-outs to occur between two stations separated by a remote bridge. An easy algorithm to remember is to allocate 1 Kb for each user across the WAN link. This means that a 56 Kbps link can support 56 LAT users. Any more users across the link will cause delays.

LAT operates at the session layer of the OSI model. Three sublayers are interpreted at the session layer and are used for the LAT protocol. The other two OSI layers over which LAT may operate are the data-link layer and the physical layer. These last two layers offer the transport of the data over the data link. These two layers were fully discussed in Chap. 2.

LAT uses the Ethernet frame format and the Ethernet type field for LAT is 6004.

LAT was intended to operate over Ethernet and was built to provide the capability for terminals to be clustered into a comm server. The comm server has one connection to the Ethernet, and the other portion of the LAT protocol would operate in the VAX hosts that were directly connected to the Ethernet LAN. The exception to this is that sessions may be established between two comm servers. For that matter, the LAT protocol may operate on any network station. DEC holds the protocol proprietary. If any other company wants to copy it for their machines, they need the licensing from DEC.

Since DEC supports the TCP/IP protocol (from Digital or from the company Wollongong), most companies are not going to do this. The TCP/IP protocol will allow a more robust connection to devices on a LAN, and a lot of companies have reverted to this. This opens up connections to a VAX computer from many different types of computing devices. TCP/IP was designed with this in mind. Refer to Chap. 6 for more information.

In order to operate LAT, there are entities that must exist on the LAN. These entities are:

1. LAT nodes, which are network stations containing the LAT software
2. Network interfaces, which are the controller cards
3. Token Ring (not yet standardized by DEC) or Ethernet LAN, which includes extending devices such as bridges or repeaters

The LAT protocol is defined at the session layer and contains the functions that follow.

Service class layer

This is the highest layer of the LAT architecture. Its functions provide the offering and requesting of LAT network resources on the LAN, service announcements, directory functions, and groups (all will be explained in a moment). This layer uses a single module of protocol known as Service Class 1, which is used for interactive terminals. This type of service class is used by all LAT network stations for all service class functions.

Service Class 1 functions

1. Offers services
2. Assigns service ratings
3. Provides group codes to access services
4. Sends service announcements and builds service and service node directories using information in the announcements
5. Maintains a multicast time on service nodes that determines when service announcement messages are multicast
6. Indicates flow control using the X-ON and X-OFF software flow control settings (for modem ports, it can use the hardware signals of DTR/DSR and RTS/CTS)

At the session layer, flow control is maintained by software X-ON and X-OFF parameters. As a buffer becomes near capacity, it will indicate to the other side of the session to stop sending data by send X-ON character. When it can again begin to accept data, it will transmit an X-ON character. This can be initiated by the user typing the Control-S and Control-Q characters on the keyboard. This would indicate to the service class layer that flow control should be enacted. This would make the slot layer control the flow of data using slot flow control. Figure 9.6 depicts the flow control mechanism.

Basically, there are two types of flow control. One is user-initiated; the other is inherent to the LAT protocol. This is called slot flow control. It is used more for congestion control. Slot flow control will be explained later.

User flow control is initiated by the user. The user can stop or start the flow of data by typing keystrokes into that device which would stop or start the flow of data.

Slot layer

This layer maintains the session between two or more network stations. This layer establishes and maintains the session.

Slot layer functions

1. Establishes and terminates a session
2. Provides for internal flow control for the session
3. Provides for two full-duplex flow-controlled data channels and one nonflow-controlled data channel for each session
4. Ends a session when requested to do so by the service class layer

Definition of the slots

Start slot. This slot will be produced when a session is requested by a terminal server. The corresponding slot layer at the service node

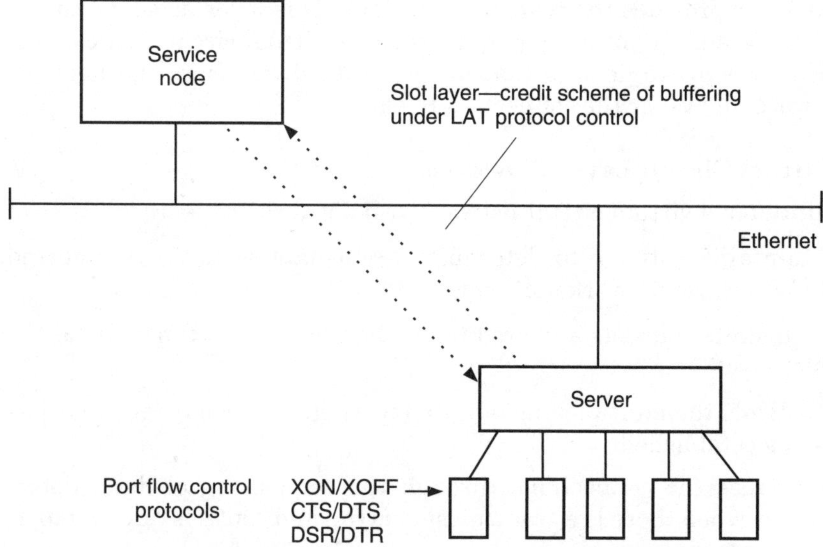

Figure 9.6 Flow control. (*Copyright © 1982 Digital Equipment Corporation.*)

either accepts or rejects this start slot by responding with either a start slot (session accepted) or a reject slot (session rejected).

Reject slot. Transmitted by a service node to reject an incoming connection request.

Data slots. Used after a session has been accepted. While the session is active between the two network stations, data will be transmitted using the data slot. There are three types of data slots:

Data-A slot—Carries user data

Data-B slot—Used to carry port and session characteristics. It is also used to carry break, parity and framing error indicators

Attention Slot—Used to indicate a special condition. Not used in the normal data stream and is called the out-of-band slot. This can be used to indicate the termination of output to a terminal

Stop slot. Used to end the session. This slot will be transmitted when the user disconnects from a service.

Flow control slot. used to control the flow of data during the session. This is to ensure that data will not be lost during the session by making sure that each end of the session has space available to accept data.

This will be covered in more detail later.

Virtual circuit layer

This layer provides the transport for data. This layer acts as either a master or a slave for any virtual circuit. A virtual circuit is a connection between two devices that are not cabled together. The network software allows for the connection to exist.

Virtual Circuit Layer Functions

1. Initiates a virtual circuit between two network stations
2. Maintains a timer to determine when data is to be transferred between two network stations
3. Transmits the slots and credits for the flow control functions of the slot layer
4. Controls the multiplexing of data for when a user has multiple sessions established
5. Manages the connections through the sequencing of data, determines when there is a transmission error, and controls duplicated or data messages

6. Provides a timer for when data has not been sent for a period of time (this is a keep-alive timer to ensure that the virtual circuit is still good even when there is no data to send)
7. Terminates a virtual circuit when the session closes

This is the bottom of the LAT sublayers. The primary function of this layer is to establish and maintain a virtual circuit. This layer does not control a session, but controls a virtual circuit. Refer to Fig. 9.7. A session may be established between two stations. The LAT protocol allows not only for a session to be established, but for multiple sessions to be established at the same time from or to the same network station. Up to 255 virtual circuits may be established between network stations.

These virtual circuits are different for a comm server than they are for a host. A session may be established between two comm servers or between a comm server and a host. (There is LAT software for PCs, but for the purposes of this chapter, it will use examples of comm servers and hosts.) For a session accepted by a host running the LAT software, up to 255 virtual circuits can be connected to it. For a comm server, one terminal port may have up to 255 virtual circuits.

The virtual circuit layer provides an interface for the slot layer for the transmission and reception of data or session-control information. It is this layer that is responsible for transmitting messages between two network stations and for providing for the delivery of error-free data and the sequencing of this data.

Like all the other layers, the virtual circuit (VC) layer also has flow control. With this, a network station may not transmit data until the previous message sent has been acknowledged. If a message sent has not been acknowledged, the VC layer will retransmit the message until it has been acknowledged or until the retransmit limit has been reached.

Each of these protocols will be discussed in detail later in the chapter.

LAT Components

The components that make up the LAT network are:

1. *Master nodes.* Network stations that access services of a resource
2. *Slave nodes.* Network stations that provide services

A LAT network may consist of virtually any number of master and slave nodes but there must be at least one of each. Furthermore, one network station or comm server may be both the master and slave.

LAT communication is the process of exchanging data between the master and the slave. This communication may be either data (user

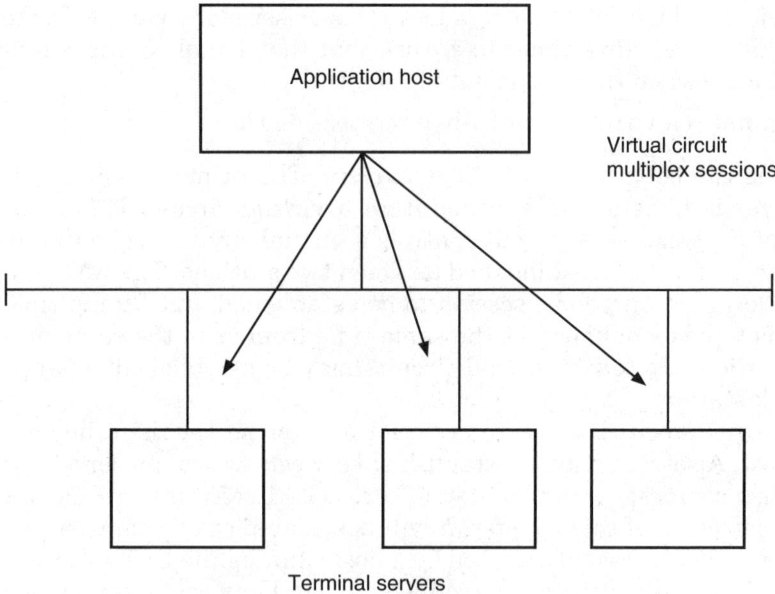

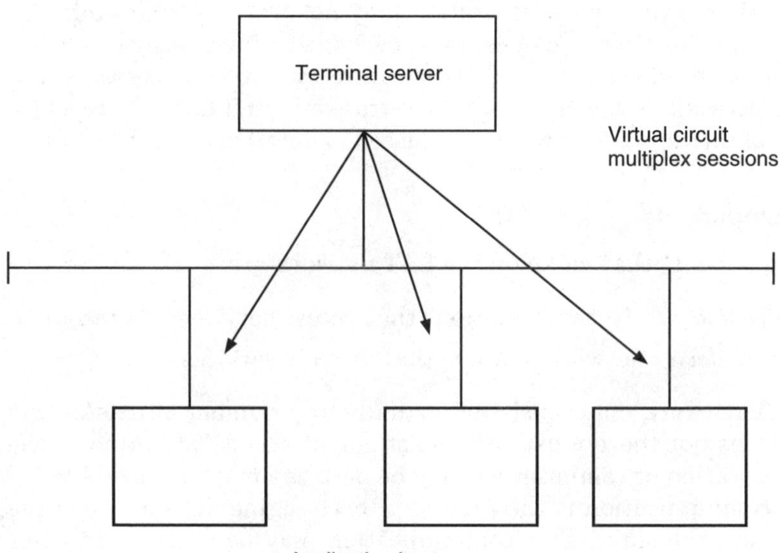

Figure 9.7 LAT service connections.

data) or commands to maintain the session. This process is true peer-to-peer. This means that each network station that supports LAT may be either the master or the slave or it may be both, and any network station may set up a session with another. There is a master and a slave relationship, but any station may connect with another. There is no specification that states only certain network stations will be masters and others will be slaves.

Services

A service is a resource that has made itself available to the LAN (a host, a modem, a non-LAT host, etc.). Any network station that offers a service of LAT is called a *service node*. These resources can include an application program, modems, printers, or any combination of hardware and software.

Each service resource is identified by a unique name. In order to establish data communication between two network stations using LAT, one end must connect to the service by using its name. A unique function of LAT is the capability of providing load balancing between service names. In other words, a service name can be used to identify multiple service nodes providing the same service. This feature does include an automatic failover mechanism in case one service node fails. In addition to this, one service node may provide multiple services.

Any network station that offers a LAT service will broadcast this information to the LAN. This is accomplished using a service-announcement message. Contained in these messages are the available services and identification information, such as the node name that has that service. Any LAT station on the LAN will receive this information and, if their group numbers match, they will build a table of available services.

Before transmission of this message, a service node must calculate the service rating and then it will multicast this message. The calculation of this rating includes the amount of activity on the node, the amount of available memory, and the processor type. This may be a static entry that is entered by the network administrator. For a terminal server, the rating also includes the number of available asynchronous ports and the amount of space available in the connection queue. A service rating is a number from 0 to 255 that describes the availability of the service. Each service in a service node has a rating.

The ending of this process is with the terminal server building service and service node directories.

The Service-Announcement process. With the service information from the message, the terminal server builds two directories in memory:

1. Service directory (contains the following information)
   Service name
   Service identification string (if available
   Node names of service nodes that offer each service
   Current status of the service
   Service rating of the service on each service node
2. Service node directory
   Node name
   Node identifications
   Node address
   Node status

The protocol running in the service node that offers named services will announce its services over the network. This announcement is accomplished with a calculation of its service ratings and then multicasting* the message of the network. The end of this process is the ability of the servers to build service and service-node directories.

Service ratings

For each service in a service node, a rating is calculated and given a rating between 0 and 255. This rating indicates the relative availability of the service compared to other service ratings. This rating is dynamically calculated by a service node for each of the services provided. This rating is comprised of the overall level of activity of the node, the amount of memory, and its processor type. This rating can be a static value provided a network manager. This rating can also provide the number of ports that a server has and the number that are available. Finally, the rating can indicate the amount of space left in a connection queue.

Multicasting service announcement messages

As stated before, a service node will periodically announce its services to all active servers on the network. In the message is information about the node and the services it provides. All services and their associated ratings are in this multicast message. Active servers on the LAN will receive this message and if their group number (group numbers

---

* Multicasting is the ability to send the packet out to the network with a special destination address that all service nodes will be able to pick up and process. Those nodes that do not have this multicast address in their network software will discard the packet.

are explained in a moment) matches any of those in the received message, the information will be copied and stored. If the group number of the received packet does not match its group number(s), it will discard the packet.

These messages are initiated as soon as the LAT software is started. Then they are broadcast at regular intervals as indicated by a multicast timer. This timer is controlled by the network administrator. When a new service is created, a multicast message is transmitted immediately and then only at the timer specification.

Maintaining service and service node directories

Terminal servers that receive service announcement messages will first complete a group match to see if they are allowed to copy the information. If there are one or more common groups, the information is processed.

With this information, the server will build two directories in dynamic memory. For each service, a server's directory contains:

1. The service's name and identification strings
2. The node names of the service nodes that offer a service
3. Its current status
4. The service rating

The service node directory contains:

1. The node name and its identification
2. The address of each known service node
3. Its current status

These directories are used in the process of connection attempts during the session establishment process. Service nodes do not maintain service directories, which is a reason that connection to LAT services is possible only for terminals connected to terminal servers.

In a LAT network, the object is for users to gain access to services that are available on the network. There are instances that security is needed, for not all users need access to all services on the network. Therefore, the group code was implemented to allow terminal servers to select which service on the LAT network they will make available to users.

Service announcements begin as soon as the LAT software is started. There is a timer that provides the interval at which these messages should be multicast. If a new service is created, this service is usually broadcast immediately; otherwise, this timer can be manually set.

Groups

When a LAT entity, such as a terminal server, receives this service announcement message, it will compare the service node group number with its known port group numbers. If there is a match, the terminal service will process the message. If there is not a match, the message will be ignored.

Group numbers range from 0 to 255. They are assigned by the network administrator and are used for security. All incoming messages to the LAT server are compared to a group number. They are assigned to a service, a terminal server, and can even be assigned to an individual port on a terminal server. Each service node and the services it offers can have one or more group codes. These group codes are indicated in the service announcement messages. During the process of reading these service announcement messages, a terminal server will decide whether it should process the data in the announcement or not.

When a terminal server reads the message, it will first do a compare on the group code. If the terminal server finds a match, it will put the information from the announcement message in the appropriate terminal server directories. If there are no matches with any of the group codes, the announcement message is discarded. The terminal server can conserve memory by discarding unneeded messages. Refer to Fig. 9.8. Terminal A can access the service of the modem and the service node (the host). It cannot access the service of the microVAX. Terminal B can access the service of the MicroVAX, but not the modem. It can also access the service node.

Session establishment

A session is an established communications path between two network stations. This path may be between any of the previously mentioned resources.

LAT can offer two functions: the ability to establish a connection and the ability to offer a connection (or service). LAT services are usually held in host machines, but terminal servers can also offer services to the network. Figure 9.9 shows this.

There are two types of connections: user-initiated and host-initiated. With user-initiated, the connection request is from a user trying to establish a connection with a service located somewhere on the LAN.

Host-initiated sessions are application programs on the host that are initiating a connection request to a service on the LAN. This type of service could be an application program establishing a LAT session with a terminal server on the LAN that has a printing service associated with it.

When a user at a terminal server issues a connect request, the terminal server must proceed through a series of steps to establish the connection. The steps are detailed subsequently.

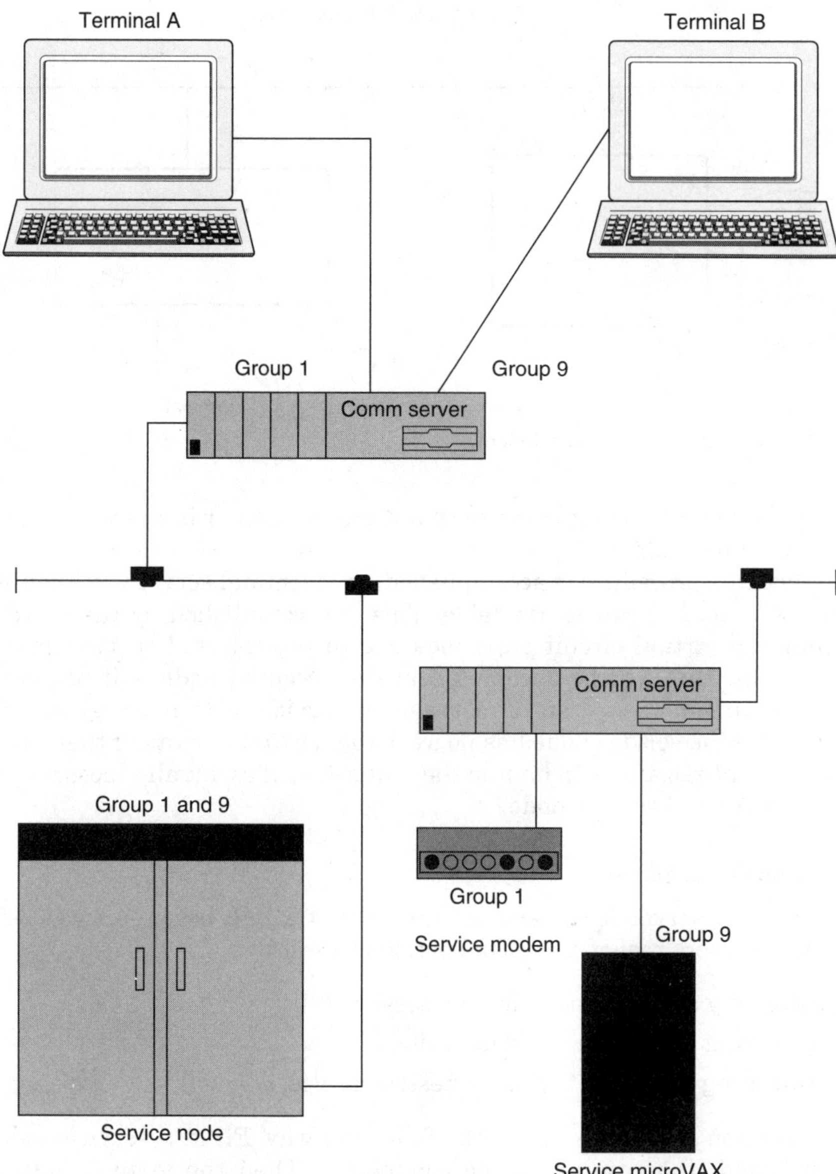

Figure 9.8 LAT group numbers.

If the connection specifies only a service name, it must select a service node before a session is attempted. This is a process of translating the service name into a node name. The server searches its service directory for the service name. If there is none present, the connection attempt is aborted. If there is one present, it will select a service node (more than one service node may provide the same ser-

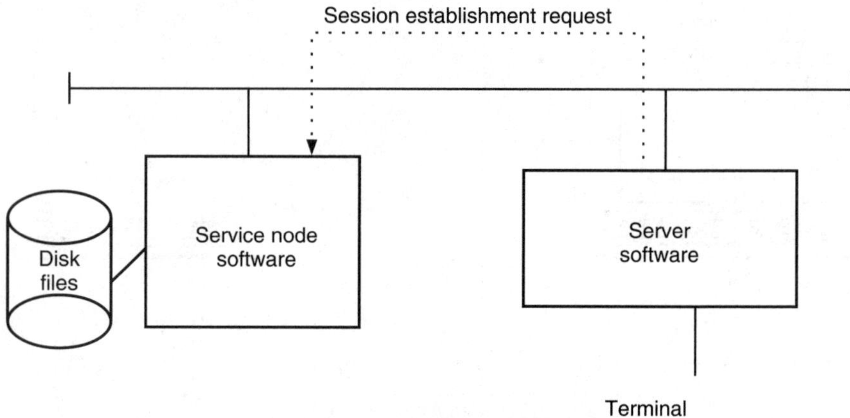

Figure 9.9 LAT session establishment.

vice name) and check to ensure that a group number is shared with it and with its address.

Once this procedure is accomplished, the terminal server will ensure that a virtual circuit is available. This is accomplished by the server sending a virtual circuit start message to the selected service node. Generally, this will be accepted and the accepted node will respond with a virtual circuit start message. A service node may reject the request if the service node has no available virtual circuits, if there are insufficient resources to handle the request, or if an invalid message is received by the service node.

Session establishment

A terminal server is always the initiator of a link between two LAT nodes. Servers respond to a connection request by:

1. Selecting a service node for the session
2. Ensuring a virtual circuit is available
3. Initiating a session to the requested service

A session is established in the following way. First, a service node is selected (the resource to be connected). Then the virtual circuit layer must ensure that a VC exists (only 255 are available) and then a session may be established. Figure 9.10 shows the flowchart of this process.

Sessions may be made to a particular service or to a service node. Remember, there are only two types of session initiation on LAT: a user-initiated request or a host-initiated request. A couple of outcomes can occur:

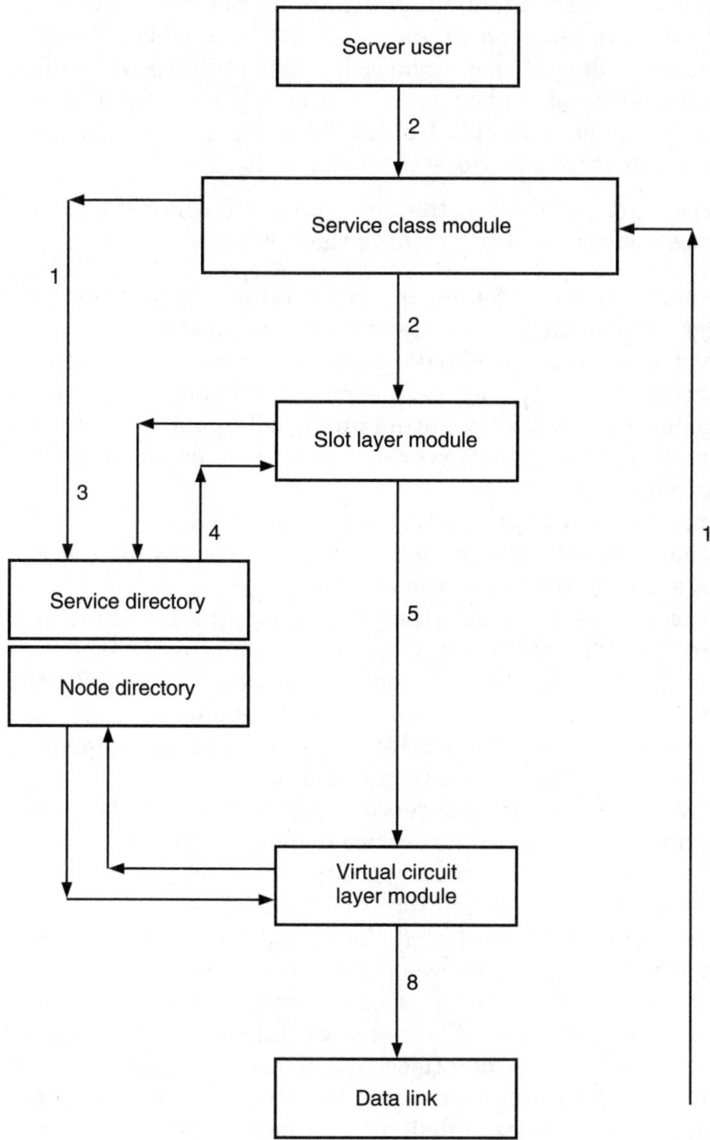

1. Service node multicast received—directory updated
2. User requests service connection
3. Slot layer looks up service name
4. Node offering is found
5. Slot layer requests virtual circuit layer to set up virtual circuit
6. Virtual circuit layer looks up node
7. Node address is found
8. Virtual circuit layer transmits the start message

Figure 9.10 Service updates. (*Copyright © 1982 Digital Equipment Corporation.*)

1. If the service name is not found and the ability to connect automatically to the service (autoconnect is the ability to provide automatic connections regardless of user- or host-initiated requests) is lacking, the connection attempt is aborted. If autoconnect were enabled, the connection would be attempted every 30 seconds until the user attempted to interrupt the process (terminate it).
2. If the service name is present, the terminal server finds the names of the service nodes or nodes providing the service.

Once the service name is found, the terminal server will compare service ratings. If more than one node offers the requested service, the terminal server will provide load balancing. Load balancing is the process of comparing the activity levels of each service node. A high level of activity produces a low service rating and it will not allow new connections. Therefore, a terminal server will select the service node with the highest service rating.

The terminal server will then check the groups codes. The service nodes must share at least one group code with the requesting station. If there is not a match, the request is rejected.

If all the preceding checks out, the requesting station would then obtain the service node's address and session would be established.

For a user-initiated request that specifies a service node with the connection command, the terminal server has to ensure only that the group codes match between the two. If there is at least one group code match, a session is established between the two.

For a host-initiated request, the service node will send a data message to the terminal server with its service node name and its address. The terminal server will then perform a group code check and, if at least one group code is matched between the two, a session is established.

Once a service node has been selected, the virtual circuit layer is tasked with creating a virtual circuit between the two stations. The terminal server will send a VC message to the selected service node. If the service node can accept a connection, it will respond with the same VC message.

However, the service node may reject the request. It may reject the request if there are not enough resources to satisfy the request, if the maximum number of VC is exceeded, or if an improperly formed message is received.

After all this, a session is finally established. Once established, it must be maintained. The process of maintaining a session allows for the passing of data between the two stations, providing flow control, and disconnecting a session.

After a session is established, a virtual circuit enters into the run state at which data is finally transferred over the connection. Data transfer is very carefully controlled over the circuit.

Data transfer

Data is transferred through a system of sublayer VC messages. Before data is transferred between the two, a node must have a credit for every slot. A credit is a marker that allows the node that possesses it to transmit one slot of information to another node. A slot is a segment of data up to 255 bytes long. There is one credit per slot. The slot layer is the layer that handles the establishment and the maintaining of sessions for the service class layer. In turn, the slot layer uses the slot layer to transmit and receive session information over virtual circuits. Information for any session is stored and transmit-ted using one or more slots. A slot is a message segment. This message segment contains information for a single session. The four slot types are:

1. Start
2. Data
3. Reject
4. Stop

The functions of the slot layer include establishing sessions between server ports and service nodes, providing two full-duplex flow-controlled data channels and a nonflow-controlled data channel for each and every session, and the ability to terminate sessions that are requested by the service class layer.

Virtual circuit messages are of three types. They are named for the function that they perform. Data transfer is shown in Fig. 9.11.

1. *Start messages.* These messages are exchanged between a server and a service node to start a virtual circuit. The service node will respond to this request with a start message (sent from its slot layer) or it may send a stop message to reject the connection. Inside the start message is information to start the circuit. This includes the data-link frame size (which, in turn, will determine the size of the virtual circuit messages), the size of the slots, the size of the transmit and receive buffers, and the credits available for the session.

2. *RUN message.* A run message contains session information. This information can be start session requests, credits for slot-layer flow control, user data, port status, or a stop session request. The virtual circuit layer at each network station will exchange run messages with each other until one end or the other sends a stop message. These messages are usually acknowledged by the other end.

Slots are given to the virtual circuit layer by the slot layer to be transmitted in a virtual circuit run message. All sessions on the same virtual circuit share the same run message. The different types of message slots can be intermixed.

The slot layer establishes the first slot on a circuit.

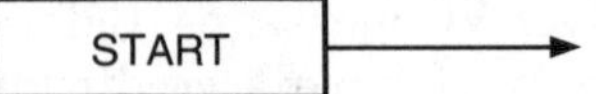

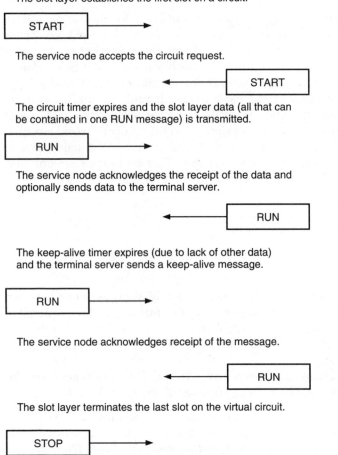

The service node accepts the circuit request.

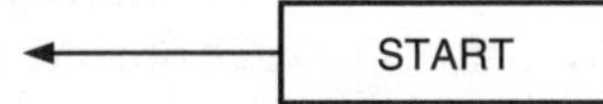

The circuit timer expires and the slot layer data (all that can be contained in one RUN message) is transmitted.

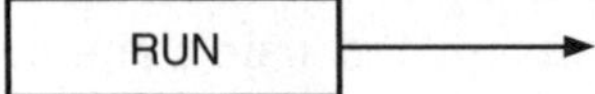

The service node acknowledges the receipt of the data and optionally sends data to the terminal server.

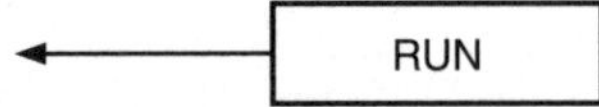

The keep-alive timer expires (due to lack of other data) and the terminal server sends a keep-alive message.

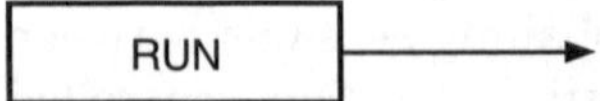

The service node acknowledges receipt of the message.

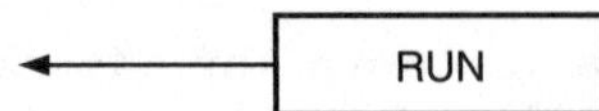

The slot layer terminates the last slot on the virtual circuit.

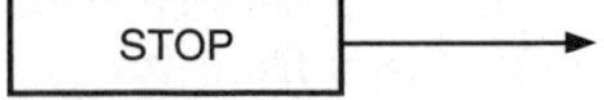

Figure 9.11 LAT communication processes. (*Copyright © 1982 Digital Equipment Corporation.*)

3. *Stop messages.* This message is sent to indicate an end to a virtual circuit. Either end can initiate this message, but usually a server will send this message after the last session on a virtual circuit is disconnected. They are unacknowledged messages.

Upon reception of a frame, the VC layer will hand the data to the slot sublayer. If the service node has anything to send, it will build and transmit the data.

Session flow control

Control of a circuit is simplex. A node may not transmit a run message until the previously transmitted run message has been acknowledged.

The server will continually transmit the message until it is acknowledged or until the retransmit timer expires.

Slot flow control

Unique to the LAT protocol is the idea of congestion control through the use of credits. Credits allow one end or the other to talk, and they indicate how much buffer space is available on the other end of the connection. The slot layer will store information it receives in receive buffers. When the session is active, the receive buffers are filled by the user data and are routinely transmitted to the service node. These buffers may become filled and are not able to be emptied (such as when the session is suspended by the user, i.e., the user switches sessions). In this case, the slot layer will not accept any more data until it can empty its buffers.

Flow of data is based on a credit exchange system between the two entities on a session. During session establishment, the two entities on the session negotiate the number of receive buffers on each end (usually, there are two buffers on each end). For each receive buffer, each end provides the other side of the session with a credit. A credit is simply a marker that allows the node that possesses it to transmit up to one slot (up to 255 bytes) of user data to the other end of the session. When the data is transmitted, the credit is transmitted with the data. Therefore, the credit represents a free receive buffer on the other end of the session. Transmitting a credit ensures that there is room at the other end of the session for the data to be accepted.

Each end of the session maintains a count of credits. When a partner's credit count is greater than 0, the partner can send data. When it runs out of credits, its credit will be 0, and it will not send any more data until the other end of the session sends more credits to it. When one end of the session empties its receive buffer, it will return a credit back to the other end of the session. This operation is shown in Fig. 9.12.

To make the protocol more efficient, data is not transferred in a keystroke-by-keystroke basis. It is transmitted on a timer basis. There is a circuit timer built into LAT that, when expired, will transmit the data in its transmit buffers. There are usually two transmit buffers for every session established. The terminal server will send data only when this timer expires.

If a terminal server has no data to send, it will enter a balanced state. A circuit that has entered this state is known as *inactive*. It is the job of a terminal server to keep up with the state of the service node. With this state, a keep-alive timer is invoked. Each time the terminal server sends out a series of VC messages, it resets the keep-alive timer. There will be a timer for each session.

If the timer should expire, the terminal server will transmit an empty message to the service node and expect a response. The service

The terminal server user requests a service connection. This message includes initial flow control credit(s).

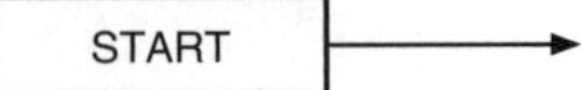

The service node accepts the connection request. The service node also includes initial flow control credit(s).

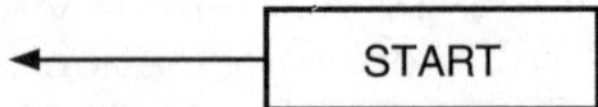

The terminal server user enters one or more characters which are stored in a data slot. If flow control credits are available, the slot is transmitted in a virtual circuit RUN message when the circuit timer expires. The terminal server decrements its flow control credit count for the session.

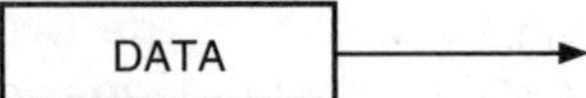

The service node processes the characters and possibly sends a response, usually with new flow control credit(s). The service node decrements its flow control credit count for the session. The terminal server increments its flow control count for the session if the service node sent additional credits.

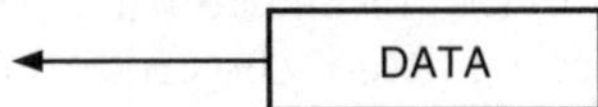

The service node sends some charactors. This step may not be possible if the service node's flow control credit count for the session is zero.

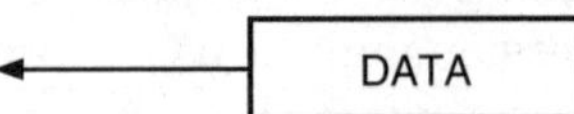

The terminal server processes the characters and optionally sends response data from the user as well as possible flow control credit(s). The server decrements its flow control credit count for the session. The service node increments its flow control if the terminal server sent additional credits.

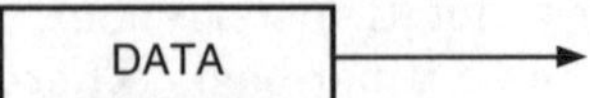

The service node requests disconnection due to the user logging out of the service.

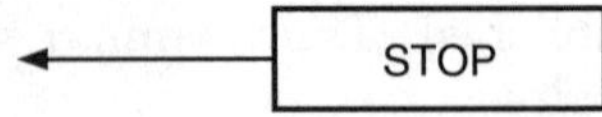

Figure 9.12 Dataflow. (*Copyright © 1982 Digital Equipment Corporation.*)

node will respond with a data message or an empty message just to let the terminal server know the other side of the session is still active. If there was no response to the empty message, the terminal server will retransmit this message until it reaches its retransmit limit. If it reaches its retransmit limit, the terminal may respond with a circuit-down event process. With this, the terminal server considers the service node to be unreachable and will disconnect the session.

LAT can also perform a function known as *automatic failover.* This process is used with VAXclusters. VAXclusters is the physical grouping together of multiple VAX minicomputers on a LAN. By assigning a common service name to two or more cluster members, a user may reestablish communication sessions with the mini in the event that its first session is aborted. With this, the user must re-log in.

Session termination

Finally, there are multiple ways to disconnect a session. First, the user may log out. With this, the user logs out of the service node. The service node will then exchange messages with the terminal server to disconnect the session with the user's terminal server.

Another way to disconnect a session is to type the DISCONNECT command at the terminal server. This disconnects the user from the server.

Other LAT Services

Host-initiated requests

This process occurs when an application program on a general-purpose service node requests an application device. The service node will transmit a multicast request for the address of the server offering the applications device and will then attempt a connection to that server. Servers participate in this type of request by supplying their addresses and by processing host-initiated requests received from service nodes. This is really the reversal of the normal LAT communications, when a server will request a service and attempt the connection to the service node.

There are times when a host needs to initiate the session. This could happen, for example, when the host would like to send data to a terminal server that has a printer connected to it. The host would establish a session to the terminal server port with the printer attached, send the data, and then terminate the connection. This is all accomplished without any user intervention. This is shown in Fig. 9.13. This process involves three steps:

1. The host must translate the service name or the terminal server's name to its 48-bit physical address. With this, a terminal server will receive the message and, if the requested name matches, the terminal

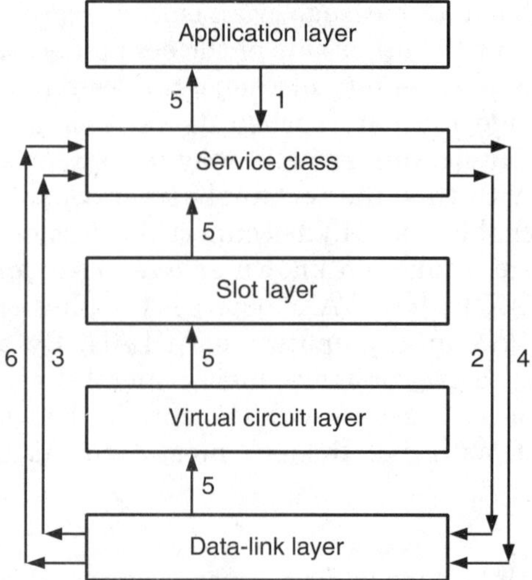

1. An application process on a service node requests a connection to a port or service on a specific server.
2. The Service Class 1 module of the service node multicasts a solicit-information message to get the address of the server.
3. The response-information message received from the server goes directly from the service node's data-link layer to its Service Class 1 module.
4. The Service Class 1 module of the service node sends a command message directly through the data-link layer using the server's Ethernet address. This command message contains the host-initiated request.
5. If the requested port of service is available, the server responds with a virtual-circuit start or run message.
6. If the port of service is unavailable, the server responds with an error status message rejecting the request. An error status message goes directly from the data-link layer of the service node to its Service Class 1 module. If queuing were permitted by the service node, the server might queue a request rather than reject it.

Figure 9.13 Host-initiated request. (*Copyright © 1982 Digital Equipment Corporation.*)

server will respond to the host. In this, the terminal server's Ethernet address will be in the response.

2. Send a message containing the host-initiated request. This is done after the Ethernet address is known. The service node (host) will send a message to that terminal server. The message will contain a request for a particular terminal server port or, if the terminal server supports services, the host may request the service. During the process, group codes are checked. There must be at least one match or the terminal server will reject the request.

3. After this, the terminal server will attempt to allow a session to be established. The terminal server will either accept the host request if a virtual circuit is available, queue the request if the port or the service is busy, or reject the request.

If the terminal server must queue the request, it will place it in a table that may have other connection attempts in it. Queues are maintained by the FIFO method. This means the first entry in is the first one back out (the first connection attempt that was queued will be the next to get the connection).

Session management

Both servers and service nodes will buffer user data, provide flow control between the server and its service node and disconnect that session. When multiple nodes offer a common service, servers can provide automatic failover for sessions to a service is their session is interrupted.

Virtual circuit maintenance

This is the process that is also called a keep alive message. This message is transmitted over a session between a server and its service node when the circuit has been idle for a while (no user activity).

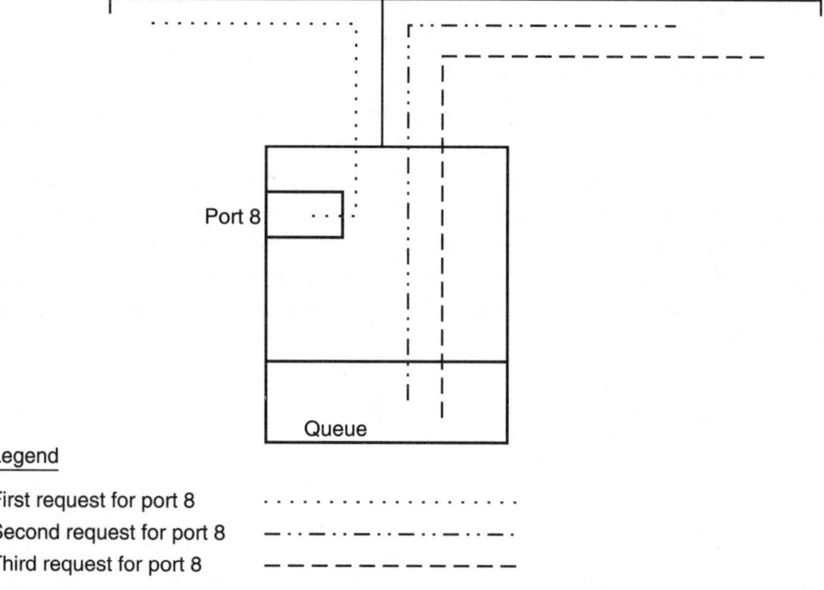

Figure 9.14 Queues. (*Copyright © 1982 Digital Equipment Corporation.*)

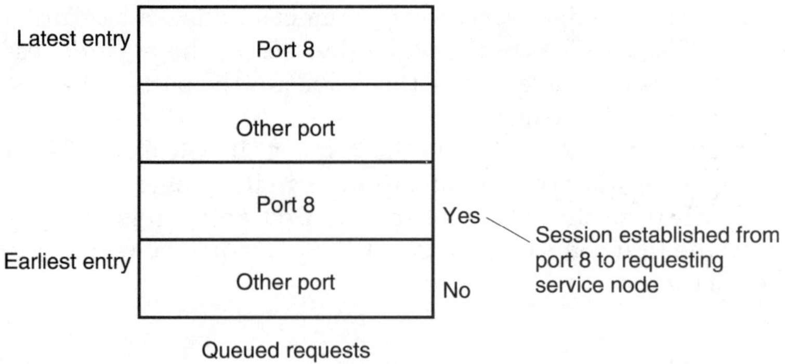

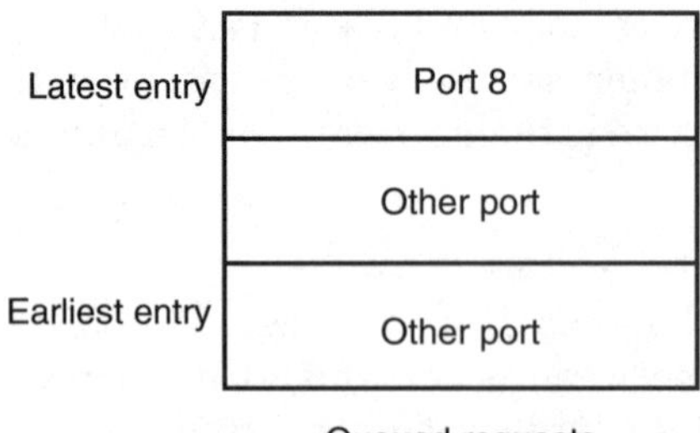

Figure 9.15 Stacked queued entries. (*Copyright © 1982 Digital Equipment Corporation.*)

Connection queue and maintenance

A server will maintain its connection queue by transmitting status messages for each queued request directly to the node that requested the connection. Connections awaiting a connection in the queue can be removed by the manager of that server or by the individual that requested it. Otherwise, when a service becomes avail-able, the connection request is removed from that queue and it will enter the session establishment process. This process is shown in Figs. 9.14 and 9.15.

Chapter

10

Open Systems Integration (OSI) Protocol

The OSI protocol encompasses all seven layers of the OSI model, which encompasses many different protocols. At the data-link layer, the protocol has been established to run over the HDLC, X.25, FDDI, IEEE 802.3, IEEE 802.4, and IEEE 802.5. The OSI architecture differs from other protocols starting at the network layer, which is where this discussion will begin.

This chapter will not give the reader a complete understanding of the OSI protocol suite. This chapter's purpose is merely to introduce the reader to the *basic* concepts and terminology of the OSI protocol suite. It will cover at a simplistic level the routing, transport, and application layers of OSI. For more information on this topic, please refer to the specifications listed in the following pages.

All OSI standards and other international standards are generated by the International Standards Organization (ISO), the Consultative Committee for International Telephone and Telegraph (CCITT), the Institute for Electrical and Electronics Engineers (IEEE), and other various committees.

An ISO International Standards document is prefixed by the letters ISO followed by a code number that indicates it origin (ISOxxxx). The first proposal generated is called a Draft Proposal (DP). Next, the DP will become an Agreed Draft Standard (DIS)—but the code number will always remain the same. As addenda are published, they will have the designations PDAD, DAD, and AD, but the code number will always be the same.

The CCITT is headquartered in Geneva and is a division of the International Telecommunications Union (ITU). The ITU reports to the United Nations Organization. The principal members of the CCITT are the Port, Telegraph, and Telephone authorities (PTTs) of member countries.

The CCITT is responsible for the wide-area aspects of national and international communications, publishing quadrennial recommendations. Each new book publishes recommendations for new facilities and confirms or updates already-existing recommendations. The series prefixed by "X" relate to data network services. The date following the number, for example, X.25 (1980), refers the edition of the recommendation or update.

The following are the important ISO standards and specifications for the OSI protocol.

Physical layer

CCITT X.21	15-pin physical connection specification for circuit-switched networks
CCITT X.21 BIS	25-pin connection similar to EIA RS-232-C

Data-link layer

ISO 4335/7809	High-level data-link control specifications (HDLC)
ISO 8802.2	Local area logical link control (LLC) specifications
ISO 8802.3	(IEEE 802.3) Ethernet standard
ISO 8802.4	(IEEE 802.4) Token Bus standard
ISO 8802.5	(IEEE 802.5) Token Ring standard

Network layer

ISO 8473	Network layer protocol and addressing specification for connectionless network service
ISO 8208	Network layer protocol specification for connection-oriented service based on CCITT X.25 specifications
CCITT X.25	Specifications for connecting data terminal equipment to packet-switched networks
CCITT X.21	Specifications for accessing circuit-switched networks

Transport layer

ISO 8072	OSI transport layer service definitions
ISO 8073	OSI transport layer protocol specifications

Session layer

ISO 8326	OSI session layer service definitions, including transport classes 0, 1, 2, 3, and 4
ISO 8327	OSI session layer protocol specifications

Presentation layer

ISO 8822/23/24	Presentation layer specifications
ISO 8649/8650	Common application and service elements (CASE) specifications and protocols

Application layer

X.400	OSI application layer specification for electronic message handling (electronic mail)
FTAM	OSI application layer specification for file transfer and access method
VTP	OSI application layer specification for virtual terminal protocol, specifying common characteristics for terminals
JTM	Job transfer and manipulation standard—similar to a remote job entry (RJE) function

OSI Routing

There are three major components of the OSI routing architecture:

1. *End System (ES).* An end system is considered to be some type of individual computing device such as a personal computer, a host system, or minicomputer. End systems usually need to know only the destination and the intermediate system to which they can transmit a message in order to have it forwarded to its final destination. These are similar to the end nodes in DECnet.

2. *Intermediate System (IS).* An intermediate system is usually a router. A router is an intelligent device that forwards data through a best path to reach its final destination. A router will submit packets directly to a node (if that is where the destination is) or directly to another router in the path to the final destination.

Intermediate systems differ from the end systems in that they must contain the intelligence to route packets. They also must obtain information about the network on which they reside. This information consists of the various paths that make up the entire network to which they are connected.

3. *Routing Domain (RD).* A group of intermediate systems that operate a particular routing protocol such that the schematic of the overall network is the same for each IS. These domains are represented in two forms: hierarchical or flat.

Hierarchical domain is a domain that has more than one level. IS-IS specifically has two levels. These levels are known as level 1 and level 2. *Flat domains* contain one level. There is now a distinction between IS's in this type of domain.

One other type of domain is called the *administrative domain.* This type of domain is structured so that each domain is a group of IS's that are owned by the same organization and therefore are administered as a single entity. This administration is simplex in that it involves picking a protocol and defining the interfaces between the domains. More times than not, these two domains (routing and administrative) are view as a single entity and the two are commonly known as the domain.

The routing algorithm used with OSI is called a Link State Algorithm (LSA). For those readers familiar with the protocol TCP/IP, there is a similar LSA algorithm known as Open Shortest Path First (OSPF) that uses a Link State Algorithm.

The link state algorithm is vastly different from the more common routing algorithm that is used with most protocols today. This algorithm is known as a Distance Vector Algorithm (DVA) and it is found on TCP/IP, XNS, AppleTalk, IPX (Novell), and other protocols. Link state algorithm offers many benefits in contrast to the distance vector algorithm. Some of these advantages are faster convergence time (reducing the amount of time that loops may form) and lower bandwidth consumption (only bad links are reported and not the whole routing table).

When routers were introduced to the commercial data communications marketplace, they used a static method of updating themselves. This meant that the routing tables (the table a router uses to determine a path to a destination) had to be updated manually. The first protocol that allowed dynamic routing table updates was known as the Routing Information Protocol (RIP), and it is based on a distance vector algorithm.

Distance vector algorithms produce routing tables based on geographical distance (the metric). If a destination is four hops away, the packet to be forwarded must traverse four routers before reaching the destination. This metric is key to the distance vector algorithm structure and operation. The metric could also be based on line bandwidth, line speed, and line delay. It is very simplex and easy to implement. Simply speaking, most router implementations of distance vector algorithm simply allow the network administrator to "turn on" RIP and allow the algorithm to determine the routes on the network. Since distance vector algorithm's routing tables are based on the single distance metric, the algorithm is said to be flat. In other words, it only has one logical peer.

Distance vector algorithms can be placed on a hierarchical level, but this requires manual configuration. Network administrators must manually place "topological" information into the routers—information such as how the routers are connected to one another and the status of each link. Network administrators must think about their network in terms of line speed, etc., in order to place "policy-based routing" into their network routers. This means that certain routers are "trusted" routers and they will update other routers on the network. Still, this is all manual configuration.

When the term RIP is used, the protocol of TCP/IP usually comes to mind. Actually, this protocol was developed by Xerox for their network protocol known as Xerox Network System (XNS). The protocol was placed in the public domain and was also released by the UNIX operating system known as Berkeley UNIX. The wide use of the Berkeley UNIX operating system gave RIP its popularity. This was the first dynamic routing update protocol that allowed network administrators simply to assign metrics (hops) to an interface and let the RIP protocol handle the rest. No longer did network administrators have to statically enter a network number and the number of hops (routers to traverse) distance. RIP would produce this for you.

This had many advantages. Think of a network that involved 50 routers (not uncommon). When one router went down for any reason, all the routers had to mark any paths that used that router as being down. In a static environment, this meant going to each router and manually entering this into the router table. With an update protocol, this path would be automatically marked as being down upon the next routing update.

RIP was a breakthrough, but it also brought on many problems—convergence and scalability being the largest. When a route goes down, it takes a certain amount of time before all the routers can be notified of this. Routing updates are sent from each router, but they are not synchronized. This means that routers send their routing updates and various times depending when their timers expired.

Link state algorithms also use a metric, but it is based on distance and topological data. This algorithm truly represents a hierarchical architecture (those consisting of two or more layers).

Link state algorithms overcome the convergence and scalability problems experienced with distance vector alogrithms. When a router is disabled or a new router is added to the network, having one router as the trusted router will detect a change and it will inform all the other routers of this change. In an link state algorithm internet, only one router will be given this responsibility. In distance vector algorithm internets, all routers are considered "trusted" and therefore all routers will eventually update each other.

Refer to Fig. 10.1. By dividing an internet into areas, loops are avoided, while still allowing for multiple paths and, therefore, redundancy. The area process also helps the routing table updates when a change occurs. With a hierarchical internet, a change will affect only

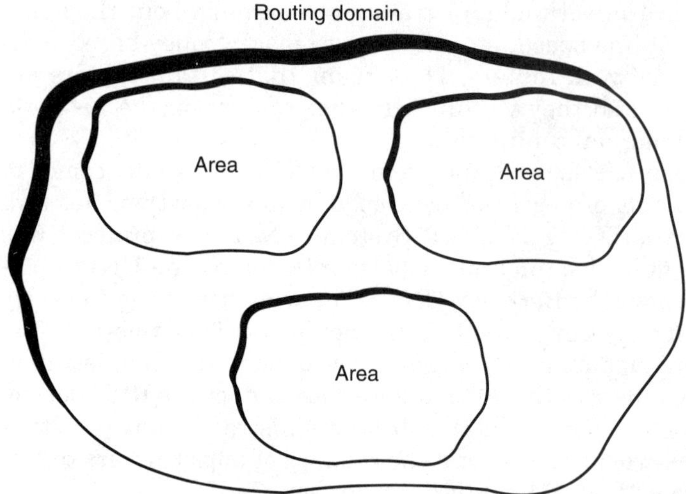

Figure 10.1 Domains and subareas. (*Courtesy Uyless Black.*)

the particular nodes that are in that area. The updates are not passed to those nodes that are not considered to be trusted. That is, those routers that do not need to know about a change will not be updated, and the network will still operate efficiently. With this network, overhead is drastically reduced.

IS-IS protocol. This protocol is the routing algorithm used for OSI, and it is based on the link state algorithm architecture. It supports a two-level hierarchical structure within a domain. Refer to Figs. 10.2 and 10.3.

Routers are divided into level 1 and level 2 routers. Level 1 routers provide routing within an area. This type of routing consists of communication between ES's and level 1 IS's, between level 1 IS's, and between level 1 and level 2 IS's.

Level 2 IS's, as a group, represent the backbone network. The backbone area provides routing between the areas, but within one domain.

As Fig. 10.3 shows, the internet is divided into areas. This has many advantages. First, information about changes in the internet that affect only one nonbackbone area is limited to that area and to the level 2 routers that are connected to the level 1 routers in that area. This information will not be transmitted to any other routers on the internet.

This provides for faster convergence because only the routers that need to know about a change are updated. This provides for fewer

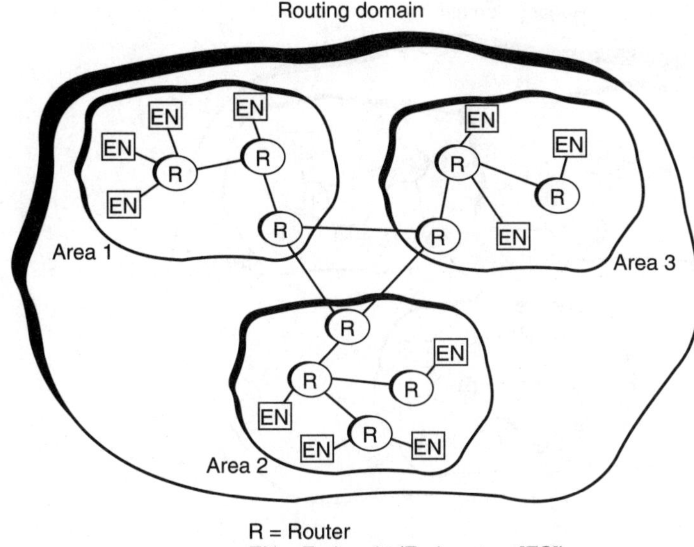

Figure 10.2 Areas, routers, and end nodes. (*Courtesy Uyless Black.*)

lost sessions and better response times. Since link state algorithm-architected internets converge faster, bandwidth is better utilized on the whole internet.

Each IS (on an link state algorithm internet) will contain an image of the whole internet topology. By contrasting this image with other IS's in the area, discrepancies can be resolved quickly. Also, link state algorithm routers usually implement some type of authentication procedure which is designed to ensure that only IS's that have been properly configured and are supposed to be operating on the network are the ones that can gain access to the network.

OSI Addressing

The OSI addressing scheme is one of the most complex addressing schemes when compared to the other protocols in this book. Instead of simply identifying a host with a number, the address can be variable in length and contains many parts. The address scheme was designed for virtually every different type of data communications environment possible. The basic unit of the OSI address is known as the network service access point or the NSAP.

The address scheme is truly global and hierarchical. It is hierarchical in that there are multiple authorities. The highest authority is the

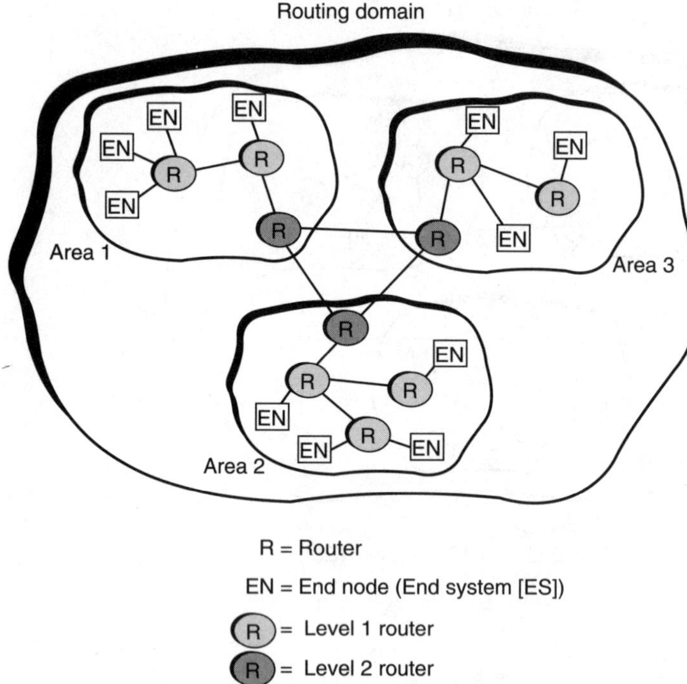

Figure 10.3 Level 1 and level 2 routers. (*Courtesy Uyless Black.*)

standards body known as the International Standards Organization (ISO), which can create up to 90 authorities (such as a phone system). Each of these 90 authorities can create thousands of subauthorities (individual phone companies). These subauthorities may, in turn, create their own subauthorities.

Currently there are seven authorities recognized by ISO:

Local	A local OSI network. A network that is not attached to any other public OSI internetwork.
X.121	An authority that uses the X.25 addressing scheme.
ISO DCC	Consists of subnetworks corresponding to countries or a sponsored country (one not yet participating in ISO).
F.69	TELEX authority.
E.163	Public switched telephone networks.
E.164	ISDN.
ISO 6523-ICD	International Code Designator, a four-digit code according to the ISO 6523 standard.

The OSI addressing scheme consists of four parts:

1. *Initial Domain Part (IDP).* Contains the Authority Format Identifier (AFI) and the Initial Domain Identifier (IDI).

2. *Authority Format Identifier (AFI).* Contains a two-digit value between 0 and 99. This is used to identify a couple of things. First, it is used to describe the IDI format and the syntax of the Domain-Specific Part (DSP); second, to identify the authority responsible for allocating the values of the Initial Domain Identifier. Table 10.1 contains a comparison of OSI addressing and TCP/IP addressing.

3. *Initial Domain Identifier (IDI).* This specifies the addressing domain. Table 10.2 contains a summary of the IDI formats and contents.

4. *Domain-Specific Part (DSP).* This contains the address determined by the network authority. It is an address below the second level of the addressing hierarchy. It can contain addresses of end-user systems on an individual network. The DSP identifies the NSAP to the final subnetwork point of attachment (SNPA). This is the point at which the network forwards the data to the underlying network for delivery to the network node.

Domains. In an OSI internetwork, the network is split into domains. Just as in TCP/IP, a large internet may be split into subnets. In OSI, domains are used to administer the large network address space. Also, in OSI subnetworks are used to identify a physical network. For example, Ethernet and Token Ring are considered subnetworks in the OSI scheme. The domains are areas of a internetwork that are administered by an addressing authority. The addressing authority ensures that all addresses within the domain are unique. A domain is allowed to cover multiple subnetworks.

For example, the U.S. Government uses this addressing format for its implementation of OSI known as Government OSI Profile (GOSIP).

TABLE 10.1 Summary of IDI Formats and Contents

	Address length	Address range	Address format
TCP/IP	32 bits	2**30 nodes	network number.host
OSI	16–160 bits	2**152 nodes	AFI/IDI/DSP

TABLE 10.2 The OSI Address

IDP		DSP			
AFI	IDI	Organization ID	Subnet ID	MAC address	N-Sel
47	0005	0032	1234	53184427	1

The AFI value will be 47 (hex). The IDI value will be 0005. This is the value that is established by the National Institute for Standards and Technology (formerly known as the National Bureau of Standards). The IDI value of 0005 signifies that the address was assigned by the addressing authority of NIST. This is for the entire federal government. The IDI value of 0006 is for the Department of Defense (DoD).

The DSP field will be divided into four subfields. The ORG ID is a value assigned by NIST to signify an individual government organization. The SIBNET ID is used by the organization to identify a subnetwork within the organization's subdomain. The END SYSTEM ID can be used in any way that the subnetwork administrator decides. More than likely, this will be a 48-bit MAC address that is the Ethernet or Token Ring physical address, but it does not have to be. The NSAP SELECTOR (N-Sel) subfield identifies a higher-layer transport entity. For example, a value of 1 in this field identifies the ISO Transport Protocol.

A publication produced by NIST gives the following address as an example:

```
47 00 05 00 32 12 34 53 18 44 27 01
```

which represents:

```
AFI = 47
IDI = 0005
ORG ID = 0032
Subnet ID = 1234
End System ID = 53184427
NSAP Selector = 1
```

This is shown in Table 10.2.

Figures 10.4 and 10.5 show the network layer routing service.

Transport Layer

The OSI transport service is specified in the standard ISO 8073. This is called the Connection-Oriented Transport Protocol Specification.

The main purpose of the transport layer is to provide end-system-to-end-system communication in a reliable fashion. The protocol that accomplishes this enables sequential transfer between two stations. This means that messages should be received in the same order that they were sent. If they are not, an error message should be issued and corrections should be made.

There are five classes of transport layers:

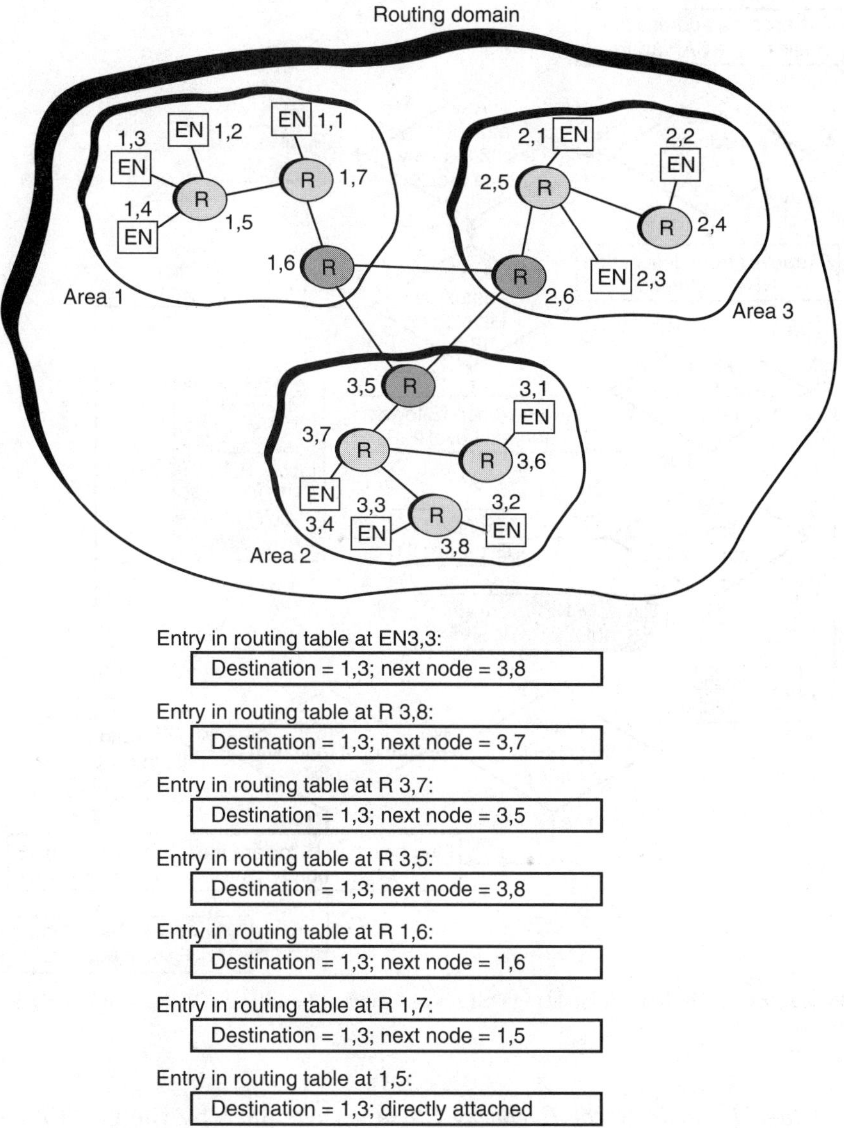

Figure 10.4 Routing operations within and between areas. (*Courtesy Uyless Black.*)

Class 0, Simple Class. This class is primarily used for messaging systems. It is the simplest form of transport protocol and assumes that reliable services are embedded in the network layer. It does require the connection-mode network service (CONS). Most vendors will support this class.

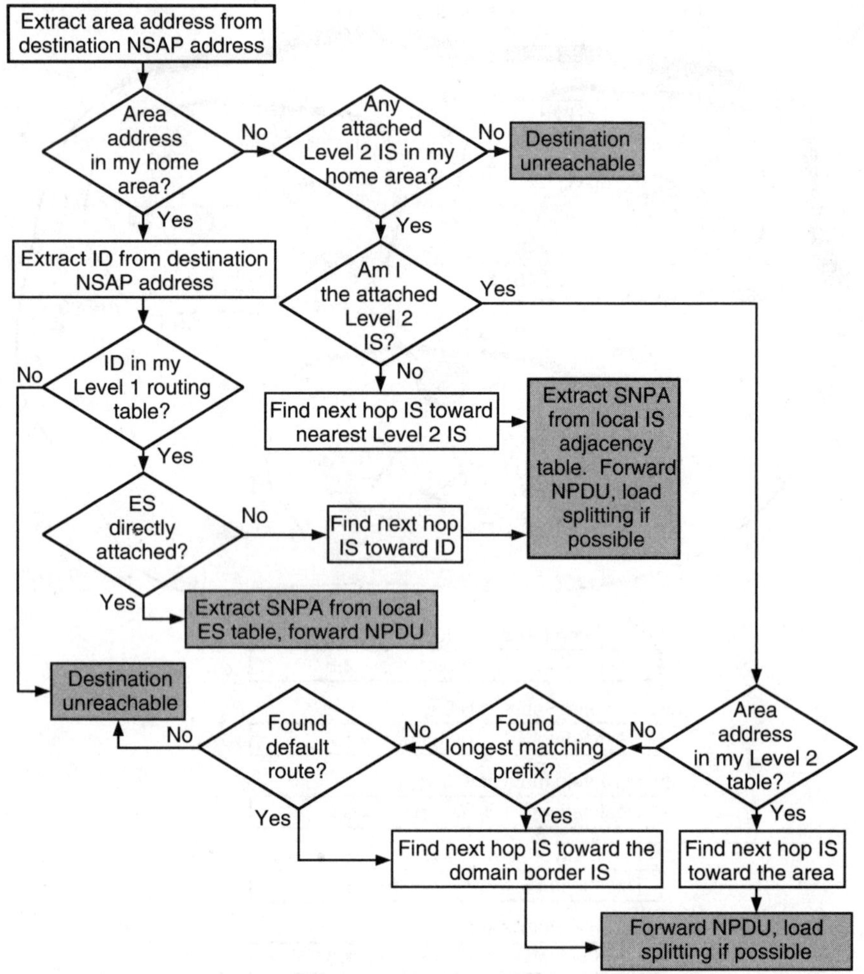

Figure 10.5 Flowchart illustrating OSI router's packet handling. (*Courtesy 3Com Corporation.*)

Class 1, Basic Error Recovery Class. Developed by the CCITT for use with the X.25 protocols for access to packet-switched data networks. Class 1 is similar to class 0, except that class 1 provides sequencing. This class requires the connection-oriented network service (CONS). This class is not very well supported by vendors.

Class 2, Multiplexing Class. This is an advanced version of class 0 in that it provides multiple transport connections to be created using a single network connection. This protocol requires the CONS service.

Class 3, Error Recovery and Multiplexing Class. This class combines the services of class 1 and class 2 and requires the CONS service.

Class 4, Error Detection and Recovery. By far the most widely implemented class, it is also the only class that does not require the CONS service. It can operate over the CLNS* service. It provides the common transport mechanisms that enable reliable data to be transferred between two stations, and it can operate over the CONS service.

Connection mode transport service. When a connection attempt is made at one end of the link and the other end of the link accepts the connection, a session is established. Messages are then sent at one end of this session and should be received at the other end of the session. Messages should be received in the same order they were sent. Any messages that are in error or are sent out of sequence should be resent. If this does not happen, the session will be terminated.

The connection establishment is usually made by the transport layer receiving a request from the session layer. The transport layer will transmit a session request packet to the intended destination. During this phase, the two stations will negotiate parameters, which includes the preferred type of transport class that will be supported and any alternative classes. If the destination accepts this connection packet, it will transmit a connection confirm message to the originator. In this message, the transport class that was selected from the incoming connection attempt packet will be specified.

After this is set up, data may flow across the session. The OSI transport layer supports full duplex communication, which means that each end may send and receive data simultaneously. There are special type of packets that transport data. The actual data transfer is accomplished by the network layer. As stated before, this layer may be connection-oriented network service (CONS) or connectionless network service (CLNS).

During this transfer, data may be expedited. This means that certain small data packets may be transmitted that bypass normal flow control procedures. Classes 2 and 4 support this while class 0 does not.

During the transfer of data, class 2 and class 4 assign send sequence numbers to the packets. This operates like most transport-layer proto-

---

* CONS, or Connection-Oriented Network Service, is a network-layer service that allows a connection to be established before data is transferred on the network layer. CLNS, or Connectionless Network Service, indicates that data may be transmitted by the network layer without setting up a connection.

cols in that the receiver will send an acknowledgment back to the sender which is dependent on the received sequence number. This acknowledgment number indicates exactly how many sequence numbers have been successfully received. Class 0 depends on the network layer to provide this type of reliability. These sequence numbers indicated in which order the transmitter sent the data.

To provide for flow control on the circuit, the OSI transport protocol uses a system called *credits*. The credits determine how many messages the destination is able to accept. A source station can only transmit data up to the amount of the credits. The destination, upon receiving the data, may then return credits to the sender. The sender may then send more data to the destination. If it does not receive any more credits, it cannot send any more data. It must wait. These credits are similar in function to those used in the LAT protocol and very similar to the allocation number used in XNS.

There are many methods that can be used in this scheme. The protocol can be relaxed to state that even if we have only enough room to accept one message, the destination may send more credits back to the source in anticipation that memory will be freed up by the time the next series of messages arrives. Other systems will adhere strictly to the credit scheme in allotting only those credits for which it has room.

Class 4 can use two types of flow control fields. These are the *normal* and the *extended* flow control fields. In the normal flow control, there are 7-bit sequence numbers and 4-bit credit fields. Extended flow control has 31-bit sequence fields and 16-bit credit fields. The reason for this is that, in a high-speed network (FDDI), there lies the possibility that a sequence number may wrap to the starting sequence number before a previous sequence number has left the internet. This would allow two different packets, both with the same sequence number, to be on the network.

One of the unique things placed in the OSI transport layer class 4 is the congestion-avoidance algorithm. This allows a network station to indicate in a transmitted packet that the network station was experiencing network congestion. This works in conjunction with the network layer. It allows the network layer to inform the transport layer of congestion possibilities and allows the transport layer to adjust its flow control window to reduce the amount of packets on the network. When the congestion is deemed to be reduced, the flow control window can be increased.

The transport layer can also reduce its flow control window when it determines that the network layer has lost a packet. With this, the transport layer will reduce its window to 1, allowing only the retransmitted message to be sent. It will then increase the window by 1 each time a packet is acknowledged.

In contrast to other network protocols, the transport layer has the responsibility of fragmenting session layer data. If the transport layer receives a message that is larger than is able to be transmitted, it will fragment the data segment into multiple packets and transmit the multiple packets. The destination transport layer has the responsibility of reassembly of the packets.

As stated before, classes 2 and 4 allow multiple transport connections to one network connection. When a connection is established, the transport layer will assign a 16-bit connection number to the connection. Each side will assign its own connection numbers and inform the remote end of the connection.

When all data has been transmitted and the connection is to be terminated, either side may accomplish this. Normally, the user will decide that a connection is no longer needed and will disconnect the session. This is a relatively simple process, as the side that requests the disconnect transmits a disconnect request to the remote side of the connection. Upon receiving this disconnect request, the remote side will transmit a packet confirming the disconnection.

Session Layer

The session control layer is the layer that resides between the application and the transport service. It is the application interface to the network. It is responsible for organizing communication between two applications. In the process of this, it is also responsible for the management of the communication between the two applications.

Connection control is concerned with session establishment, maintaining the session, and terminating the session. In doing this, it works directly with the transport layer to ask for a connection to be established. The session layer provides many services beyond that of the connection control facilities found in the transport layer. When this layer receives an inbound connection request, it will extract certain information, like access control information, which includes a password and validates it.

It also provides for a proxy entity to be connected, in that a user on one system may access the services of another system without the account control information. This can be seen as a guest account. It will also determine whether the requested application exists on the node. If the application is found, but the application does not respond to the connection request, it will issue an error message back to the originating node.

Data is sent to and from an application using the session layer. The session layer will provide the buffering for this data. The sending of data includes methods for supporting three types of data:

1. *Message interface.* Allows users to send and receive messages of any desired size.
2. *Segment interface.* Allows users to send and receive messages using messages of predetermined size. This size is usually set to the allowable transport data unit size.
3. *Stream interface.* Data is viewed as a stream of bytes with an "end of message" make inserted.

Among the other duties of the session layer is the monitoring of the connection. This entails monitoring of the transport connection and will force a disconnect if it knows that the transport layer has detected a probable network disconnect or when the transport layer does not receive a response to a connection attempt.

To disconnect a session, the application will request the release of a connection at the transport layer. Before this happens, all data will be transmitted, and then the connection will be terminated. The connection can be immediately disconnected if the application layer requests a connection abort and not a connection disconnect.

Session layer address resolution provides for name-to-address resolution. In this, the protocol will maintain cached tables that keep track of objects (i.e., applications, nodes, etc.) which not only reside in the local station, but also reside on the network.

Applications

File transfer, access and management, and X.400

This is the equivalent of the FTP program in the protocol of TCP/IP. It is a file transfer mechanism that promotes a master-slave relationship. The station requesting the connection is called the *initiator* and the station accepting the connection is called the *responder.*

There are five types of documents that may be transferred:

FTAM-1	Unstructured text
FTAM-2	Sequential text
FTAM-3	Unstructured binary
FTAM-4	Sequential binary.
FTAM-5	Simple hierarchical file

Just as with the transport service, there are five classes defined by FTAM:

1. *Transfer class.* This class allows for the transfer of a file, files or parts of a file using a simplex underlying protocol. This allows a user

to copy a file from a remote station to or copy a file to the remote station. It can allow a user to move a file. This allows a user to copy the file, but the original is deleted after the move is successful.

2. *Management class.* This allows files to be manipulated in that they can be renamed, deleted, and their attributes can be read. In some cases, the file attributes may also be manipulated. These fields cannot be transferred across the network.
3. *Transfer and management class.* Combines all the services provided in the previous two classes.
4. *Access class.* Allows a user to read and write to the file.
5. *Unconstrained class.* Allows an OSI designer to choose the functions to be implemented. There are a vast amount of operations that may be performed with an FTAM implementation. Not all of these functions are going to be supported in all the vendor FTAM's implementations. Therefore, FTAM functions are grouped into functional units. These are subsets of all the functions in FTAM.

It is true that FTAM allows for remote file access on a network. The standard mandates the underlying protocol. It defines the semantics of the protocols but, unfortunately, it does not define the programming interface. With this, the user interface to this application may be different from system to system. FTAM will interoperate between different user systems, but the user's interface may be different.

X.400

The last application to be discussed is probably the first OSI application that was commercially available—even before the OSI standard was finalized. X.400 is the messaging system used to exchange messages (mail) between two stations on the network. This is based on a store-and-forward method. This means that a message is created and then sent to a service that will store the message. In proper time, this service will attempt to deliver the message to the proper recipient (forward the message).

There are two entities in this protocol. They are the user agent and the message transfer agent.

User Agent (UA). This is how the users access the X.400 system. It is called the User Agent (UA). The UA collects the information found in the message and it sends it to a Message Transfer Agent (MTA).

Message Transfer Agent (MTA). This systems transmits the messages to the intended recipients indicated on the message header. This system also returns notifications to a message originator.

In order to deliver the message, the user agent must be available. There are times when the UA is not available and the message must be stored for a period of time. X.400 allows for this in the message stores. It is here that a message will be stored until the recipient can accept the message.

The message store acts on behalf of the user agent and the message is simply placed on an X.400 disk drive. This is usually located on the same system as the MTA that is serving that user agent. All messages for that user will be placed in the same location. At certain time intervals, the X.400 system will attempt to deliver the message. If, after a number of times, it cannot deliver the message, it will inform the originator that it could not deliver it.

The messages that a user may send are of simple format—similar to writing a letter. At the top of the message is a header that contains, the user's name, the intended user's name, and miscellaneous items such a carbon copies, etc. The message is addressed using a naming scheme. This is explained as follows: name (proper and surname), group name, and organization name. Based on this, a user's message is completed and will be routed to the destination.

A message will be transferred from message agent to message agent until the final user agent is found. The message will then be delivered to the user agent for delivery to the final user.

The message transfer system can implement two types of receipt notifications. These are *delivery* and *nondelivery.* When a message has been deemed not deliverable, the MTS will generate a nondelivery message back to the originator. On the other hand, a message originator can indicate (when the user creates the message) that a return receipt is requested. Upon the destination receiving the message, a notification will be generated that it was delivered.

Bibliography

ANSI Std.802.2-1985 ISO/DIS 8802/2 Local Area Networks Logical Link Control, 1984 ISBN 0-471-82748-7 Fourth Printing July 1986

Black, Uyless, *Computer Networks Protocols, Standards and Interfaces,* Prentice-Hall, 1987, ISBN 0-13-165754-2 025

Black Uyless, *OSI—A Model for Computer Communications Standards,* Prentice-Hall Inc., 1991, ISBN 0-13-637133-7

Black, Uyless, *TCP/IP and Related Protocols,* McGraw-Hill, Inc., 1992, ISBN 0-07-005553-X.

CCITT X.21-Specifications for accessing circuit-switched networks.

CCITT X.25-Specifications for connecting data terminal equipment to packet-switched networks.

Chappell, Laura, *NetWare LAN Analysis,* Sybex and Novell Press, 1993 ISBN 0-7821-1143-2.

Comer, Douglas, *Internetworking with TCP/IP,* vol. 1, 2d ed., Prentice-Hall, Inc., 1991, ISBN 0-13-468505-9.

Dalal, Yogen K., and Printis, Robert S., *48-bit Absolute Internet and Ethernet Host Numbers,* (available from Xerox Corporation Office Systems Division) 1981.

Digital Equipment Corporation, "Data Access Protocol Functional Specification (DAP) Version 5.6.0," order number -AA-K177A-TK, Oct. 1980.

Digital Equipment Corporation, "DECnet Digital Network Architecture (Phase IV) General Description," order number AA-N149A-TC, May 1982.

Digital Equipment Corporation, "DECnet Digital Network Architecture Phase IV NSP Function Specification," order number AA-X439A-TK, Dec. 1983.

Digital Equipment Corporation, "DECnet Digital Network Architecture Phase IV Routing Layer Function Specification," Version 2.0.0, order number AA-X435A-TK, Dec. 1980.

Digital Equipment Corporation, "DECnet Digital Network Architecture Phase IV Network Management Function Specification," order number AA-X437A-TK December 1983.

Digital Equipment Corporation, "DECnet Digital Network Architecture Phase IV, Session Control Function Specification," Version 1.0.0 Order Number AA-K182A-TK, Nov. 1980.

Digital Equipment Corporation, "Networks—Communications Local Area Transport (LAT)," Network Concepts, order number AA-HY66A-TK, June 1987.

Digital Equipment Corporation, LAT Network Concepts, order number AA-LD848-TK, Oct. 1990.

Digital Intel and Xerox Corporations, *The Ethernet—A Local Area Network,* data-link layer and physical layer specifications, Version 2.0 (also known as the *Blue Book* when ordering from Xerox Corporation) Nov. 1982.

IBM Token Ring Network Architecture Reference, 3d ed., order number SC30-3374-02, Sept. 1989.

IEEE Document Standard 802.1d, May 2, Oct. 1991.

IEEE Document Standard 802.1H, "MAC Layer Bridging of Ethernet in IEEE 802 LANs."

IEEE Document Standard P802.5M-D6, "Unapproved Draft of Media Access Control (MAC) Bridges," P802.1D, 1991.

IEEE Std. 802.5-1989, "Local Area Networks 802.5 Token Ring Access Method," published by The Institute of Electrical and Electronic Engineers, first printing 1989, ISBN 1-55937-012-2.

ISO 8072—OSI Transport Layer service definitions.

ISO 8073—OSI Transport Layer protocol specifications.

ISO 8208—Network Layer protocol specification for connection-oriented service based on CCITT X.25 specifications.

ISO 8326—OSI Session Layer service definitions including transport classes 0, 1, 2, 3, and 4.

ISO 8327—OSI Session Layer protocol specification.

ISO 8473—Network Layer protocol and addressing specification for connectionless network service.

ISO 8649/8650—Common application and service elements (CASE) specifications and protocols.

ISO 8822/23/24—Presentation Layer specifications.

Martin, James, and Leben, Joe, *DECnet Phase V—An OSI Implementation,* Prentice-Hall, 1992, ISBN 1-55558-076-9

Miller, Mark A., *LAN Protocol Handbook,* M&T Books, 1990 ISBN 1-55851-099-0

Miller, Mark A., *Troubleshooting Internetworks,* M&T Books, 1991 ISBN 1-55851-236-5

Naugle, Matthew G., *Local Area Networking,* McGraw-Hill, 1991, ISBN 0-07-046455-3.

Novell NetWare Multiprotocol Router-Basic, v1.0 User Guide, March Novell, Inc., 1992 123-000194-001.

Novell, Inc. NetWare System Interface Technical Overview, Addison Wesley Publishing Company, Inc., 1990 ISBN 0-201-57027-0.

Oppen, Derek C., and Dalal, Yogen K., "The Clearinghouse: A Decentralized Agent for Locating Named Objects in a Distributed Environment," order number OPD-T8103, Oct. 1991.

Request for Comment 768 User Datagram Protocol (UDP).

Request for Comment 791 Internet Protocol.

Request for Comment 792 Internet Control Message Protocol ICMP.

Request for Comment 793 Transmission Control Protocol (TCP).

Request for Comment 1058 Routing Information Protocol (RIP).

Rose, Marshall T., *The Simple Book—An Introduction to Management of TCP/IP-based Internets,* Prentice-Hall, 1991, ISBN 0-13-812611-9

Sidhu, Gursharan S., Andrews, Richard F., and Oppenheimer Alan B., *Inside AppleTalk,* 2d ed., fourth printing, Addison Wesley, January 1993 ISBN 0-201-55021-0

Stallings, William, *Handbook of Computer Communications Standards,* vol. 1, the open systems interconnection (OSI) model and OSI-related standards, 1st ed., fourth printing, Prentice-Hall, 1988, ISBN 0-672-22664-2.

Stevens, Richard W., *UNIX Network Programming,* Prentice-Hall, 1990, ISBN 0-13-949876-1.

Tanenbaum, Andrew S., *Computer Networks,* 2d ed., Prentice-Hall, 1989, ISBN 0-13-162959-X

3Com Corporation Education Services Internet Packet Exchange (IPX) Protocol Student Guide, June 1991.

3Com Corporation, NetBuilder Bridge/Router Operation Guide, manual number 09-0251-000, Apr. 1991.

Turner, Paul, "NetWare Communications Process" (application notes), Novell, Inc., Sept. 1990.

Xerox Corporation, Clearinghouse Protocol, order number XNSS 078404, April 1984.

Xerox Corporation, "Courier: The Remote Procedure Call Protocol," publication number XNSS 038112, Dec. 1981.

Xerox Corporation Internet Transport Protocols, January 1991, XNSS 029101. This book covers the network and transport layers for the XNS protocol.

Xerox Corporation, Sequenced Packet Protocol Connection Parameter Negotiation publication number XNSS 339011, November 1990.

Xerox Corporation, *Xerox Network Systems Architecture General Information Manual,* XNSG 068504, April 1985.

Index

ABOUT THE AUTHOR

Matthew Naugle is employed by Wellfleet Communications as a systems engineer, where he designs and maintains large internetworks for customers. Mr. Naugle has also developed and taught network courses for Northern Virginia Community College. He is the author of *Local Area Networking,* published by McGraw-Hill.